Preaching the New Lectionary

Preaching the New Lectionary

Year B

Dianne Bergant, C.S.A.

with

Richard Fragomeni

A Liturgical Press Book

THE LITURGICAL PRESS
Collegeville, Minnesota

Cover design by David Manahan, O.S.B.

3   4   5   6   7   8

Library of Congress Cataloging-in-Publication Data

Bergant, Dianne.
    Preaching the new lectionary / Dianne Bergant, with Richard Fragomeni.
        p.   cm.
    Includes bibliographical references and index.
    Contents: — [v. 2] Year B.
    ISBN 0-8146-2473-1 (alk. paper)
        1. Lectionary preaching—Catholic Church.   2. Catholic Church. Lectionary for Mass (U.S.).   Sundays and feasts.   3. Bible- -Homiletical use.   I. Fragomeni, Richard N.   II. Title.
    BV4235.L43B47   1999
    251'.6—dc21
                                                              99-16138
                                                                   CIP

Contents

Ordinary Time (Part Two)

Ordinary Time (Part Three)

Ordinary Time (Part Four)

Solemnities of the Lord

Introduction

The Lectionary is a unique genre of ecclesial literature. It is part of the liturgical canon, a collection of books that also includes the Sacramentary, the Ritual Books for Sacraments, the Book of Blessings, the Pontifical, and the Liturgy of the Hours, to name a few. The Constitution on the Sacred Liturgy (no. 24) states that sacred Scripture is the source of the readings and prayers used in the liturgy. The Lectionary, while not identical to the Bible, is drawn from its contents, providing a kind of narrative infrastructure for celebration of the Liturgical Year. The Lectionary is drawn from sacred Scripture by selecting passages from the biblical material (decontextualizing) and then placing these readings within a new literary and liturgical context (recontextualizing), thus creating a new ecclesial genre.

This recontextualization of former biblical material calls for a new way of interpretation, one that takes into consideration the liturgical character and setting of the Lectionary readings. The present commentary is an example of this type of interpretation. It will be fundamentally a literary reading of the texts, but it will also provide historical information whenever something in the text might appear foreign to the contemporary believer.

Features

This commentary is unique in several ways. First and foremost, it employs a literary-liturgical way of interpreting all three readings of each Sunday and major feast of the Liturgical Year. It also interprets the responsorial psalm, which has seldom enjoyed the importance it deserves and has at times even been changed or eliminated. Second, it explicitly situates the interpretation of each day's readings within the theology of its respective liturgical season. This theology is drawn from the specific themes of the readings that make up that particular year rather than from general theological themes otherwise associated with the season. In this way the meaning of the entire season becomes the context for understanding its individual parts. Third, the lections of the season are read in sequential order, from the first Sunday of that season to the last (all of the first readings, all of the second readings, and so on). This kind of reading creates a kind of mini-reading and provides yet another way of understanding the riches of the readings (charts at the beginning of each season demonstrate this).

Limitations

The present commentary does have limitations. Unfortunately, it does not directly engage the other books of the liturgical canon, most importantly the Sacramentary. There are two reasons for this. First, various liturgical books are presently being revised. While the composition of the Lectionary has been determined, the form of the Sacramentary is still in transition. As important as this book is to full liturgical recontextualization, it did not seem appropriate to use the unrevised edition, nor was it deemed wise to delay the commentary until the revision of the Sacramentary appeared.

Second, inclusion of all of the relevant liturgical material would have made the commentary unmanageable. The method employed here is a relatively new one and is offered in a limited fashion. Those who find it helpful are encouraged to use it in other liturgical contexts.

Uses

The commentary is ordered in the following way. Each Lectionary season is first presented by way of a chart showing readings for the entire season. This is followed by the **Initial Reading** of that season, which explains how the lections can be read sequentially across the season from the first Sunday to the last. This procedure is carried out with each of the four readings, so that the theological patterns that are unfolding within the weeks of the seasons can be seen. Because of its length, Ordinary Time has been divided into four sections: Sundays 1–10 (before Lent); Sundays 11–16; Sundays 17–21 (Sundays with the Gospel of John); Sundays 22–34 (the remainder of the year). Each of these sections has a particular thematic focus. After the theological themes of the season are uncovered, a literary reading of the lections of each respective Sunday is provided and the theological themes of that Sunday are brought into dialogue with each other.

Reading the Lectionary in the various ways provided here has great potential for many forms of liturgical ministry. It can quicken the religious imagination of homilists, thus providing fresh new posssibilities for liturgical preaching. It can offer creative insights for those involved in the liturgical preparation for the celebration of feasts and seasons. It can also act as a valuable resource for liturgical catechesis. In so many ways the material in this commentary can contribute toward enhancing the liturgical lives of the faithful.

Development

It is important to acknowledge those upon whose groundbreaking work this approach is built. They are Rev. David N. Power, O.M.I., the inspiration of such an approach, and Bishop Blase Cupich, who wrote his doctoral dissertation under the direction of Professor Power on the topic of the Advent Lectionary.[1] In this work he laid the foundations for the literary-liturgical method employed here.

In the recent past three books have appeared that can act as companions to this commentary. Two of them suggest a way of understanding the Lectionary that corresponds to the one advanced here. In *Scripture and Memory*[2] Fritz West recounts the way Lectionary patterns have been developed and are interpreted by various Christian denominations. He also explains the three-year cycle of readings, which originated within the Roman Catholic tradition but which then spread to the wider Church. In *The Sunday Lectionary*[3] Normand Bonneau provides an overview of the principles that determine the selection of Lectionary readings and an outline of the patterns that shape the seasons of the Liturgical Year.

Very recently a third resource has appeared. In *Preaching Basics*[4] Edward Foley works from many of the same principles noted here as he provides a new way of thinking about preaching. Together these four studies offer a new way of understanding the Lectionary and of opening its riches.

Finally, a debt of gratitude belongs to Richard N. Fragomeni, who introduced me to this approach. He is the one who explained the textual mosaic that introduces each season, and his creative interpretations form the basis of the **Themes of the Day**, which completes the commentary of the Sunday or feast. His contribution to this project has been invaluable.

---

[1] Blase J. Cupich, "Advent in the Roman Tradition: An Examination and Comparison of the Lectionary Readings as Hermeneutical Units in Three Periods" (Ph.D. diss., The Catholic University of America, 1987).

[2] Fritz West, *Scripture and Memory: The Ecumenical Hermeneutic of the Three-Year Lectionaries* (Collegeville: The Liturgical Press [A Pueblo Book], 1997).

[3] Normand Bonneau, *The Sunday Lectionary: Ritual Word, Paschal Shape* (Collegeville: The Liturgical Press, 1998).

[4] Edward Foley, *Preaching Basics* (Chicago: Liturgy Training Publications, 1998).

Advent

First Sunday Isaiah 63:16b-17, 19b; 64:2-7 Rend the heavens and come down	Psalm 80:2-3, 15-16, 18-19 Shepherd-king, make us turn to you	1 Corinthians 1:3-9 We wait for the revelation of our Lord Jesus Christ	Mark 13:33-37 Be watchful
Second Sunday Isaiah 40:1-5, 9-11 Prepare the way of the LORD	Psalm 85:9-14 Let us see your kindness	2 Peter 3:8-14 We await new heavens and earth	Mark 1:1-8 Make straight the paths of the Lord
Third Sunday Isaiah 61:1-2a, 10-11 I rejoice in the Lord	Luke 1:46-50, 53-54 My soul rejoices in my God	1 Thessalonians 5:16-24 Be blameless for the Lord's coming	John 1:6-8, 19-28 There is one among you
Fourth Sunday 2 Sam 7:1-5, 8b-12, 14a, 16 David's kingdom shall endure forever	Psalm 89:2-5, 27, 29 I will sing the goodness of the LORD	Romans 16:25-27 The mystery has been revealed	Luke 1:26-38 Behold, you will conceive

Advent

Initial Reading of the Advent Lectionary

Introduction

This section is an initial reading of the textual mosaic of the Advent Lectionary. It offers us a context for examining the individual lections of the season. It is based on the literary forms of the readings as well as a preliminary interpretation of their content. In a sense, it engages the meaning of the entire season as the context for understanding the individual parts.

First Testament Readings

Reading the First Testament lections in sequential order, from the first to the fourth Sunday, provides an understanding of the season that is slightly different from the usual one. In doing this we see that Advent is not only a season of hope and expectation but also a time of complaint.

The season actually begins with a lamentation. This first reading inaugurates a sort of dialogue, which will continue in the First Testament readings of the remaining Sundays. In the first reading of the second Sunday God responds to the lamentations of the people, speaking words of comfort and encouragement, assuring them of God's presence. The conversation continues on the third Sunday. A prophetic voice responds to God's comforting word. Lamentation is a thing of the past; this reading is exuberant with hope. God seems to have the last word, for on the fourth Sunday God speaks words of assurance. The nation will be reestablished.

Reading this set of lections as a unit, we see Advent as a time of our lamentation and crying out for life, and of God's response. It is a response that awakens in the community a new sense of consolation and hope, a sense that allows the community to go out to proclaim that a new world is possible, a world beyond human oppression and fear. In the enthusiasm for building God's city the final word is God's. God is the one who works, the one who builds the city, not we ourselves. This is the Advent promise in the midst of human misery.

Psalms

The psalm responses of Advent offer us a kind of profile of God. Each one sketches a unique feature that inspires us to trust in God despite the misery described in the first readings, despite the rigor required by the exhortations of the epistles, despite the challenges found in the Gospels. Our trust is well grounded, for as the first Sunday shows us, God is patient and solicitous.

The response of the second Sunday provides the reason for God's solicitude: we are God's own people, in covenant relationship with this almighty, all-loving God. The Magnificat of Mary becomes our own prayer of praise on the third Sunday. With her we acknowledge God's favor toward us and our own lowliness. With her we turn to God in our need, confident that we too will experience God's tender mercy.

Finally, on the last Sunday, we marvel at the steadfastness of God's love, which is not earned but is freely given. Each psalm response acknowledges this wonder. Like those who have gone before us, we have been called and embraced by the love of God. The season of Advent invites us to trust this call and this love and to open ourselves to the mystery that awaits us.

Epistles

We may note a curiosity about these second readings of this Advent cycle. The first reading of this series is the beginning of one epistle and the fourth reading is the closing section of another. The Lectionary has created a kind of mini-epistle, with its own beginning and ending.

The reading for the First Sunday of Advent is an expression of thanks and an exhortation to remain blameless until the coming of the Lord. On the second Sunday the reading reminds us that the Day of the Lord will come, and we are exhorted to live holy and devout lives until the new heavens and earth appear. The epistle chosen for the third Sunday continues in the style of an exhortation and bids the reader to rejoice, to pray, and to render constant thanks. On the last Sunday of Advent, the mini-epistle ends appropriately with a doxology. What began as an expression of thanksgiving and moved into exhortation ends with praise. These readings suggest that Advent is a time in which, by the power of God, direction for living is given to those who are hearers of the word. There is an urgency in the exhortations found here, for Christ is coming.

Gospels

The Gospel readings begin on the first Sunday with a call to stay awake. Something is coming that the believer cannot afford to miss. Both the second and the third Sundays suggest how to live during this time of waiting. On the second Sunday John the Baptist announces that the time is at hand, and he calls for a change of heart. The Gospel for the third Sunday offers this same John as an example of the kind of commitment required of those who expect to see the saving power of God.

It is not until the fourth Sunday that we discover what it is we are waiting for with building urgency. We have been told to stay awake in order to see that God does the impossible and becomes flesh. The annunciation shakes the world with an end-time presence.

Mosaic of Readings

This mosaic of readings shows that Advent is a time centered on the working of God in the midst of human life. Both the misery of human existence and the limits of human power are acknowledged. In the contingencies of life an alternative message is heard: our loving and merciful God acts in the midst of the humbled yet hopeful people and draws possibility out of what is impossible.

Readings

First Sunday of Advent
Isaiah 63:16b-17, 19b; 64:2-7

The reading is a composite of elements of a communal lament (63:16-17, 19) and a prayer that recounts events in the history of the nation (64:2-7). The people feel abandoned even by their ancestors Abraham and Jacob/Israel, and so they cry out to God, whom they call father (v. 16). Because of the mythological implications of physical descent from the gods, the God of Israel is seldom referred to in this way. Here "father" is linked with "redeemer," indicating that it should be understood in the sense of kinship protector, a financial resource in a patriarchal society. The lament reveals that the people are in a desperate situation, unable to help themselves and in need of someone who can rescue them from their plight, and thus they turn to God.

Consistent with the nature of the lament, the people bring a charge against God, actually blaming God for allowing them to stray from the path of righteousness (v. 17). While this may appear to be a shirking of the people's responsibility for their own actions, it is also an acknowledgment of universal divine governance. This latter view insists that whatever happens—whether good or evil—happens because God either wills it or allows it. The people maintain that just as their sinfulness was in some way in God's hands, so now their redemption is dependent on God's good pleasure. God may not have intervened in the past to prevent their transgressions, but the people plead that God will intervene now to reestablish a relationship with them. They pray this trusting that, despite their having acted like those who never heard of God (v. 19), they are still God's special people.

In the prayer, attention shifts from the distress of the people to the mighty works of God (64:3). Those who consider themselves the least deserving of divine kindness hope that God, who worked wonders in the past when their ancestors least expected, will work wonders now on their behalf. They believe that the goodness of God is shown to those who are faithful (vv. 4–5a). They admit they have been unfaithful, and consequently they suffer. Nevertheless, they still insist that they sinned because God hid from them (v. 5b).

Such insistence seems out of place after the kind of recitation of God's goodness that is found here. However, it may be less an accusation against God than an acknowledgment that it is only through the goodness of God that they can be righteous in the first place. Should God remove this favor and cease protecting them from wickedness, the people cannot help but sin.

After admitting their sinfulness the people describe in graphic metaphors the consequences of their evil (vv. 5b–7). They have become unclean, and their uncleanness pollutes everything they touch, just like a menstrual cloth filled with blood that no longer holds the promise of new life. They have lost control of their lives and are buffeted by their own wickedness; they are like dead leaves blown about by the wind. They are lost without God. If God would only turn back to them they would be able to turn back to God.

The reading itself does not contain an explicit message of hope. However, the people have admitted their own culpability and have praised God's past favors. Now they stand confident, waiting for a new manifestation of divine power.

Psalm 80:2-3, 15-16, 18-19

This communal lament contains several images of God: attentive shepherd and imperial ruler (v. 2), military captain and cultivator of vines (vv. 15–16). The shepherd was responsible for the care of the flock, leading it to verdant pastures and protecting it from danger. He had to be patient and solicitous, even when the sheep wandered off and placed themselves in peril. So much time was spent with the flock that a good shepherd learned to recognize the individual bleating sounds of the various sheep. Thus he could be conscious of their whereabouts even when they were out of his sight. God was called the "shepherd of Israel." This explains why the psalmist cries out, "Hearken!" and is confident that God will hear the plea, recognize the voice, and immediately come to the aid of those in need.

The second image is of an imperial ruler, majestically enthroned. Cherubim, composite winged creatures with both human and animal characteristics, stood at the entrance of the temple. Many societies considered the monarchy divine, and so cherubim were also guardians of the royal throne. In Israel the monarchy was human, and cherubim guarded only what belonged to God. They are found in the Garden of Eden (Gen 3:24), on the ark of the covenant (Exod 25:20), and around God's throne (v. 2).

In this psalm the solicitous Shepherd of Israel is also the ruler who sits in majesty, the one to whom the psalmist pleads, "Rouse your power, and come to save us!" The psalm may have originated in the north, since all the names mentioned are of northern tribes; however, here these few tribes represent all the people.

Besides the cherubim, the title "LORD of hosts" is also associated with the ark of the covenant (cf. 1 Sam 4:4). "Hosts" is a military term meaning "divisions of the army." "Hosts of heaven" refers to units of the heavenly defenders, those who fight cosmic battles and who have God as their military leader. Israel believed that whenever necessary God would marshal these forces of heaven and would fight in Israel's defense (cf. Isa 40:26). Israel further believed that this divine fighter was none other than the one who ruled from the heavenly throne, and so the psalmist cries out: "Look down from heaven, and see."

Finally, God is depicted as a keeper of vines. Cultivating a vineyard is demanding and tedious work, and it takes a long time to bring a vine to maturity. Vinedressers must be dedicated, patient people, not unlike the shepherd. Both are dealing with living things that follow their own laws of growth, laws which the ones tending cannot really control. They must be willing to forgo their own comfort in the face of long hours and inclement weather. Picturing God in this way, the psalmist cries: "Take care of this vine!"

What apt images to characterize the relationship between God and the people! Though God is very powerful, like an imperial ruler or a military leader, the care that God provides compares to that of an attentive shepherd or a patient vinedresser. The final plea for help mentions one who sits at God's right hand, traditionally considered the place of honor. This may have originally been a reference to the king, the one who was responsible for the safety and prosperity of the nation. Gradually it was applied to the longed-for royal Messiah.

1 Corinthians 1:3-9

This short passage forms a salutation from Paul to the Corinthian Christians. It begins with customary greetings from both Greek society (grace to you) and

Hebrew tradition (peace). In combination they are more than a simple greeting; they reflect Paul's own faith. Grace suggests unmerited blessing from God, and peace is the fundamental reward of fidelity to the covenant. For Paul, all of this comes from God but through Jesus Christ. Therefore, as Paul greets his companions in faith, he is also expressing a prayer for their spiritual benefit.

The salutation continues with a brief prayer of thanksgiving. Paul expresses gratitude for blessings that were granted in the past to the Corinthians. He states again that these came from God through Christ. In fact, three times Paul states that all the good things the community enjoys have come through the grace of God (vv. 4–6). This may be an indication that the Corinthians have developed a certain smugness about their abilities. Paul, with no envy in his own heart, rejoices in the gifts that others have received from God.

Although it is not clear here which specific gifts Paul has in mind, he refers to two very different kinds. First he mentions rhetorical eloquence and knowledge, abilities that would be held in high esteem by a cultured Greek society. He does not denigrate these "worldly" abilities. Instead, he reminds these Christians that such proficiencies come from God and not merely from human enterprise. He then refers in a general way to spiritual gifts. Without enumerating them he claims that this community is richly endowed with every spiritual gift.

The greeting and petition (v. 3) and the acknowledgment and thanksgiving (vv. 4–6) move to the theological point of the passage, namely, the community's waiting for the revelation of the Lord Jesus Christ. The Corinthian Christians are living in the "time between." Christ already has been born, has died, and has risen from the dead, but they believe that the day of his final revelation is yet to come. In the meantime, they live in anticipation of his return. At issue is the manner of their lifestyle and the character of their commitment in the "time between."

Living in the world, they have to be concerned with the things of the world. Paul is intent on reminding them that the abilities they develop for such living (rhetorical eloquence and knowledge) really come from God through Jesus Christ. Furthermore, all of the spiritual gifts that they enjoy have also come to them from God through Christ. Finally, all these gifts are meant to aid them in living faithfully until the Lord's coming. They are not meant to build up personal self-esteem or as means of competition within the community.

The theme "Day of the Lord" has a long theological history in Jewish tradition. It referred to a time in the future when the reign of God would be definitively established on the earth. This would include reward for the faithful but also judgment for the unrighteous. Paul has this judgment in mind when he assures the Corinthians that the God who has blessed them with so many gifts will provide them with what they need, so that they will be found blameless when the Lord finally returns. Having initially called them in Christ, God will continue to bless them.

Mark 13:33-37

A thrice-repeated command, "Watch!" surrounds a parable that emphasizes the need to be ready at all times, because Christians do not know when the Lord will return. The Greek word that is translated "time" *(kairos)* refers to propitious time, a special time above all other times, rather than mere chronological or sequential time *(chronos)*. *Kairos* is uncommon time, and uncommon events occur within it. Because it does not follow chronological patterns, those to whom the parable was directed had no way of knowing when it would break in upon them, and so they were admonished, "Watch!"

The short parable brings this point home. It shows how, for believers, life between the times is like the situation of servants who remain behind when the owner of the house leaves to travel abroad. Each servant is given a certain authority within the household. They are not to wait idly for the owner's return but are to fulfill their responsibilities conscientiously until that special time arrives. One servant, the gatekeeper, is singled out and told to be on the watch. No reason for the householder's travel is given. In fact, he is really not an important character in the parable. What are significant are the uncertainty that surrounds the time of his return and the vigilance that is required of the servants as they wait.

The first part of the parable is descriptive, reporting what happened to the people in the story. In the second part (vv. 35–37) the verbs used are all in second person plural form, indicating that the injunction to watch is directed toward all those hearing the parable. The story is a metaphor; the point of the story is an imperative: "Watch!"

The four periods of time that are listed—evening, midnight, cockcrow, and dawn—were the four night watches of the Roman military. Like soldiers standing guard, the Christians are exhorted to stand watch and not be caught asleep. Nighttime sleep provides an opportunity for one's enemies to accomplish their villainous purposes. Diligent watchfulness, on the other hand, serves to protect one's property and interests.

The coming of the householder will be sudden and unscheduled, a *kairos* moment. Like the servants of the parable, the Christians are instructed to be prepared at all times. Special care should be paid to those times of greatest vulnerability, the hours of darkness. Although life between the times will go on as usual, it must still be lived with the realization that this is a time of vigilance. Although authority is apportioned to each according to each one's respective work, the servants must realize that their responsibility is delegated and temporary and they will probably have to account for their management upon the return of the owner.

There are three very different yet interrelated dimensions to this short passage. The first (v. 34) is a report of what may well have been a common social occurrence. The second (vv. 35–36) redirects our attention to the early Christians who were living between the times. The final one (v. 37) exhorts Christians of all times to "Watch!" for no one knows the time of the owner's return.

Themes of the Day

The readings of the first Sunday of Advent provide several themes: the faithfulness of those who suffer even as they lament their predicament; the admonition to watch and wait; the expectation of the coming of the Day of the Lord. The placement of this set of readings at the beginning of Advent shapes the context for understanding the entire season. The first Sunday of Advent fixes its gaze on the world of human pain and then moves beyond it to the hope of a brighter future. Lamentation and expectation find fulfillment in the Day of the Lord.

Lamentation in the Midst of Suffering

Lamentation is a prayer of faithful people in the midst of suffering. Although we seldom incorporate such a formal complaint in our public prayer, ancient Israel did. And why not? To whom else, if not to God, can we turn when we are oppressed, overburdened, hopeless? Religious souls lament the absence of God. Tender hearts lament the fate of those who have been marginalized. Broken spirits lament the suffering that touches every life. Through the ages believers have cried out: "Where is God?" or: "How long, O Lord?"

Waiting

Waiting is the prominent theme for this Sunday. Some people wait to be released from suffering, others await the second coming of Christ, still others, the return of the householder. Waiting saps our energies and stifles our enthusiasm. Yet wait we must, and as we wait we wonder: "What should I be doing?"

The readings suggest that we should wait with patient expectation for the day of reconciliation and peace; we should wait in joyful hope that what is to come will come soon. While we wait, we should faithfully fulfill our responsibilities. We believe that we have a future worth waiting for, that there are promises that God will keep. And so we look expectantly to the Day of the Lord, that future day of ultimate fulfillment.

The Coming of the Day of the Lord

Hopeful believers do not wait idly. In the Gospel story the servants are responsible for the work of the household. Paul reminds the Christian community that they have all the gifts and talents they need to live faithfully in this world, awaiting the coming of the Day of the Lord. We too, pregnant with expectation, do everything in preparation for the day of release, the day of return, the day of fulfillment. We must wait for that day in partnership with others who wait. We must be vigilant for justice, faithful to the promises, and compassionate to those who lament. As trustees of the one who is coming, we live in the "in between" time of ambiguity and hope.

Second Sunday of Advent

Isaiah 40:1-5, 9-11

The message of Deutero-Isaiah opens with the exclamation "Give comfort to my people" (40:1a). The plural form of the verb indicates that this imperative is addressed to more than one person, therefore the identity of the prophet is difficult to determine. The passage itself seems to be a kind of prophetic commissioning: God summons a group of people to speak God's own words of comfort. The phrases "my people" and "your God" are covenant language. They suggest that the covenant relationship between God and the people who have suffered still exists.

The verbs "speak" and "proclaim" (v. 2) are also plural, most likely addressed to those who are called to comfort God's people. The Hebrew actually reads "speak to the heart." Since the heart was considered the organ of thought, the phrase means "convince Jerusalem" rather than "be tender toward her." But of what should Jerusalem be convinced? The first two verses suggest that the people of that suffering city had to be assured that they had indeed paid their debt and that their suffering was now over. Perhaps they had to be convinced because there was no recognizable evidence to suggest—and so they did not readily believe—that their release was imminent.

The people are directed to act out their deliverance even before they see evidence of it. Some are told to prepare for the coming of their God by removing any obstacle that might prevent God's approach or obstruct the view of God's glory that onlookers might enjoy (vv. 3–5). The picture sketched here resembles the carefully repaired highway over which victorious kings or generals traveled in triumphant procession on their return home. The people who had suffered so long are here told to prepare such a road, and upon its completion they will behold the glory of their triumphant God. There is an element of universalism here. Not only they but all humankind will see the glory of their God. This wondrous display will be the first proof that they have finally been delivered from their suffering.

A second directive is given, this time to people within Jerusalem itself (vv. 9–11). The city, broken and depleted, is told to announce to the other vanquished cities of Judah the approach of this triumphal procession. The message they are to proclaim is not theirs; it is dictated to them. They are to be heralds of good news. They are to announce that the mighty, victorious God is coming. Though just, God comes with the solicitude of a shepherd. This is the good news of deliverance, and the people are urged to believe that this message is true.

The builders of the highway are told to make God's approach possible; the citizens of Jerusalem are told to announce to others the good news of this approach. The highway builders are to complete their work before they see the glory of the LORD; the people in the city are to herald a procession they themselves have not yet witnessed. In both cases the people are directed to act out their release even before they have tangible evidence of it. What they have is the word of the prophet, whose message employs verb forms that suggest that future events are already accomplished in the present. The people's faith in this word is itself the strongest evidence of their deliverance.

Psalm 85:9-10, 11-12, 13-14

The verses of this passage presume a community waiting for God's word, a prophetic oracle that will announce peace (v. 9). Presumably the people are in distress or they would not be hoping for a word of peace. There is no direct appeal to God here. These verses depict the people awaiting a reply to a plea they must have made elsewhere. Their confidence that God will respond rests in the conviction that they are God's own people. They are faithful people; they trust in God. There is great expectancy here. The people have done what they can to get God's attention. The next move is God's.

These people are not in total despair. They do believe in salvation, and they maintain that the salvation for which they wait is near to them. At least it is near to those who are loyal (v. 10). The salvation described here is associated with prosperity, suggesting that the people's distress has something to do with economic misfortune. The hoped-for prosperity will be bounteous, filling the whole land. It seems these people have suffered a serious setback they cannot remedy by themselves. In faith, they turn to their God for help. After having made their petition, they wait confidently for God's response.

Lovingkindness (*ḥesed*), truth, justice, and peace (v. 11) are characteristics of the covenantal relationship described here. Lovingkindness is covenant loyalty; truth is covenant faithfulness; justice is the covenantal righteousness that comes from God; peace is the wholeness or harmony that results from the covenantal relationship. It is not clear whether it is God who possesses these virtues or the people. In either case they are salvific powers, and their union is a sign of the time of fulfillment. When they meet and embrace, salvation is complete. In order further to characterize the scope of this saving event, the psalmist singles out one partner of each of the two pairs, thus creating another figurative description. Truth springs up from the earth, and justice comes down from heaven. All of creation, from earth to sky, shares in the benefits of the salvation by God.

In the final verses the psalmist returns to the theme of prosperity (vv. 13–14), confident that God will reestablish the wealth of the people and that the land, once barren and forsaken, will yield an abundant harvest. Although the image is of an actual harvest of the fruits of the earth, the reference can stand for any situation that brings forth life and prosperity.

Finally, justice and good fortune join the LORD in triumphal procession, with justice in the lead and good fortune bringing up the rear. The procession is really a theophany, a glorious manifestation of the LORD. The four covenantal virtues described above are really the telltale marks of this manifestation. They are present only because God is there revealing them, making them real in the lives of the people. This revelation of God is in fact the salvation for which the people long, for which they wait in confidence.

2 Peter 3:8-14

The reading from 2 Peter contains three distinct yet connected themes: the delay in the return of the Lord, the apocalyptic dissolution of the world, and the manner of life required of a faithful Christian.

In this passage the author of the letter insists that, despite what seems to many to be a very long delay, the Day of the Lord will indeed come. Paraphrasing a verse from the psalms (Ps 90:4), the author argues that what appears to be interminable to short-lived human beings is as nothing to God, who is from eternity and who lives in eternity. Moreover, God is faithful and keeps promises made to humankind. The promise referred to here probably has something to do with merciful forbearance. The author claims that the Lord delays in coming precisely because of a promise of salvation to all. God's goodness is here providing time for all to come to repentance. Such a notion is found repeatedly in the Scriptures (e.g., Exod 34:6-7; Ps 86:15; Rom 2:4; 9:22).

Though delayed, the end-time will surely come. Its timing, like that of a thief in the night, is unpredictable (cf. Matt 24:43-44; Luke 12:39; 1 Thess 5:2; Rev 3:3; 16:15). Therefore the Christians should not grow weary of waiting, nor should they become careless in their waiting. As God has been patient in the face of their sinfulness, so they must also be patient in the face of God's apparent delay.

The author of the letter next employs apocalyptic imagery to describe how the dissolution of everything, both the heavens and the earth, will take place. Though the idea was common in Greco-Roman thought, this is the only passage in the Second Testament that speaks of a fiery destruction of the world at the end of time. Unlike the Greeks, who saw recurring cycles of destruction, these statements are part of a larger argument that maintains that this destruction has a saving purpose. It is the prelude to the creation of "new heavens and a new earth."

Centuries earlier, someone writing in the tradition of the great prophet Isaiah spoke of "new heavens and a new earth" (Isa 65:17; 66:22). For the Israelite people of the time this was a promise filled with hope. The old and sin-drenched world that dragged them down would be cast aside, and a new and innocent world would be brought to birth in the very midst of the people. For the very same reasons, the message remained a promise of hope for the early Christians. They too were awaiting a time of fulfillment. They too were growing discouraged because of its delay. They too are assured: It is coming!

The third theme, behavior that suits one who stands in anticipation of whatever is to come, is addressed briefly but succinctly. First, apocalyptic judgment will purge the world of sin, and then righteousness will dwell within the new heavens and new earth. The only behavior befitting such a transformation is a life of holiness and godliness, a life without spot or blemish. According to this author, such holiness actually hastens the Day of the Lord's coming. Thus the best reply to any challenge to the Lord's coming is a life of patient devotion.

Mark 1:1-8

Here begins the good news. Just as the first biblical account of God's creative work starts "in the beginning" (Gen 1:1), so Mark's Gospel points to a new beginning of God's manifestation to humankind (v. 1). At the outset (vv. 2–3) the author interweaves the words of the prophets Malachi (3:1, 23) and Isaiah (40:3; cf. Exod 23:20), reinterpreting them to announce the presence of the one who will herald the arrival of Jesus.

Israel's journey to freedom out of bondage in Egypt took them through the desert into a land of promise. This theme became the pattern to speak of other experiences of liberation. Chief among them was the release from Babylonian captivity and the trek back home. This latter was the background for the Isaian reference mentioned above. When the people became disillusioned with their political situation, they began to look for a new liberation and a new religious leader. This was the background for the reference from Malachi. By using these two references to identify John the Baptist, the author is bestowing prophetic authority on one whose austere life and exacting message may have appeared too demanding to be accepted.

Attired like the prophet Elijah (v. 6; cf. 2 Kgs 1:8), John proclaims a baptism of repentance for the forgiveness of sins (v. 4). Unlike the ritual washings of the Essenes at Qumran, another Jewish group that went out to the desert to await the promised one, John's baptism is open to all, not merely to a select group. Everything is astir as the people of the whole Judean countryside and all the inhabitants of Jerusalem go out to him to be baptized (v. 5). The scope and character of the crowds that John attracts signal the spiritual hunger of the people. Some of them may have gone out to see this spectacle of a man, but while there they are seized by his message and they commit themselves to the repentance that he preached. If he is announcing the Day of the Lord, they do not want that day to be one of judgment for them.

John got the attention of the crowds, but he quickly turned it away from himself. He pointed to one mightier than he, one who was coming after him (v. 7). John was a messenger of God, and he knew his role as an agent of God's good news. He was not the long-awaited one; he was the one who prepared the way. Though clearly idiosyncratic, in him there was no spirit of self-aggrandizement. He did not even consider himself worthy of performing a servant's task for this mighty one who was coming. Rather, he taught that his own deeply spiritual baptism of water and repentance would be supplanted by the other's baptism of the Spirit, or effecting of total transformation through the power of God (v. 8).

If John, this voice in the wilderness, was the messenger who would announce the coming of the mighty one of God, the advent of this long awaited one was close at hand. This fact might have been the reason so many people left the villages and towns and cities and went into the wilderness. They were longing for the new heaven and the new earth. They were strengthening themselves for the Day of the Lord, which now must be right on the horizon, or just over the crest of the hill. John's appearance and his message and his baptism all heralded the good news of salvation.

Themes of the Day

The themes of the second Sunday of Advent both enhance and expand those of the first. They include wilderness as the prelude of a new creation, the future made present, and the need for contrite hearts.

Out of the Wilderness

In the wilderness God's salvation comes to a broken people. Such is the paradox of Christian hope, that in the midst of what is seemingly an impossible situation it emerges with vigor. Hope in this context, therefore, is an openness to surprise. It is the surprise that God is in no way limited to the imaginings of human minds and the consequences of human history. Such openness to surprise requires a kind of heart that can see the unexpected. This, in turn, demands a vulnerability, which is always risky. Nevertheless, the risk demanded is founded in hope, the kind of hope that is proclaimed out of the wilderness by John, that is proclaimed out of the future by the coming of the Day of the Lord. It is the kind of hope that trusts that from the impossible, God can work a new creation.

The Future Made Present

There is something of a time warp in Christianity. What is future is made present. The prophetic oracle announces the future as if it is already happening. This sense of the future-present prompts new ways of living. As the future takes root in human lives the present is transformed into a new creation and the Day of the Lord appears.

Too often we live out of the past. Sometimes the remembrance of things past undermines our style of living. Advent suggests that the key to a renewed way of life is the activation and vibrancy of the imagination. To live the future in the present we live in the imagination of things yet to be. We live as if we are saved, and thus we are saved. We live in the promise, and with the human imagination triggered by the comfort of the God who comes from the future, we know the future made present.

The People of Contrite Heart

God's future comes through the wilderness into the broken city and inspires a brokenhearted people. For such is the meaning of "contrite." The contrite heart is a broken heart. It is an emptied-out heart, a hope-filled heart. It is a heart that is unencumbered by the past and that lives currently in the passing of time and the fragility of being alive. The contrite, broken heart can be filled only by what is promised in the future.

In this readiness the contrite heart is transformed into a new creation. Here again is the paradox of Advent. In the middle of the wilderness God works the impossible in those whose hearts are ready for the surprise of hope. God shapes a community of compassion and praise, a community transformed into a future humanity, a community that knows that all good things come from God's future.

Third Sunday of Advent
Isaiah 61:1-2a, 10-11

The individual announcing this prophetic oracle is endowed with the spirit because he has been anointed by the LORD (v. 1). Normally kings and priests are anointed, but this anointing does not appear to have been an actual event. The mission assigned to the prophet does not include royal or cultic responsibilities. The anointing may be a figure of speech, but the duties that accompany it are very real and explicitly social. While there is mention of healing and comforting, the principal function of the prophet is proclamation. He is called to announce liberty, release, and the year of the LORD. It is clear that the afflicted referred to in this passage are victims of a system. The good news to be proclaimed to them promises that they will be the beneficiaries of the year of release, while the oppressive system will have to contend with the vengeance of God.

Mention of the year of the LORD (v. 2) calls to mind the jubilee year (Leviticus 25), the time when debts were forgiven (Deuteronomy 15), when land that had been forfeited was returned to its original owners, and when those imprisoned because of financial adversity were set free. This was a time of great anticipation for the dispossessed and the impoverished. Conversely, it was a time of regret for those who would lose some of their wealth in the forthcoming economic redistribution.

Whether or not such a year of release was ever observed, the idea did become a powerful metaphor for general emancipation and economic restructuring. It symbolized the advent of a new era, a time of deliverance for the disadvantaged. It was considered a year that was instituted through the favor of the LORD, not the goodwill of other people. It was intended to remind the people that once they had been slaves and God delivered them; they had been without land and God allotted them a share in God's own domain; they had been subjugated by stronger nations and God rescued them.

The response to this announcement of good news is an exclamation of praise and thanksgiving (vv. 10–11). The delight of the prophet is seen in the repetition of sentiments, which the parallel construction provides. God's kindness has transformed him; it has altered his appearance. He is clothed in a robe of salvation; wrapped in a mantle of righteousness. He wears salvation and righteousness as garments that cover and protect him. A second poetic parallelism offers another description of his altered appearance. He is adorned like a bridegroom, bedecked like a bride. The wedding couple represents the promise of new life that deliverance brings. The extravagance with which they are attired denotes the good fortune that new life always suggests. Finally, the image of a burgeoning springtime represents the new life of righteousness that God will cause to spring up. It will be a display that all the nations will witness.

The reading begins with a promise of salvation and ends with a prayer of thanksgiving for the salvation granted. It contains several prophetic themes: God cares for the afflicted; God saves through the agency of human beings; God fulfills promises; all things are accomplished through God's grace.

Luke 1:46-48, 49-50, 53-54

This early Christian hymn of praise has strong parallels in the victory hymns of Miriam (Exod 15:1-18), Hannah (1 Sam 2:1-10), and Judith (Jdt 16:1-17). In it, Mary proclaims the greatness of God with her whole being. The terms "soul" *(psychē)* and "spirit" *(pneúma)* should not be understood as different parts of the human person, as is the case in modern psychology. Nor should they be seen as opposed to body *(sóma)* or flesh *(sarx)*. Rather, each term describes the whole person as viewed from a particular perspective. "Soul" refers particularly to the person's vitality, consciousness, intelligence, and will. "Spirit" refers to that aspect of the person that is particularly able to receive the Spirit of God. Here Mary's soul and spirit are praising God for what is being done in her very being.

Like Hannah before her (cf. 1 Sam 1:11), Mary rejoices in the fact that her lowliness is not an obstacle to God's plan. Rather, it is actually evidence that the poor and downtrodden have been visited with salvation. She who is lowly will be called blessed not because of her own piety but because of God's goodness. Her being blessed is not to be seen in God's blessing her with a child (like Leah; Gen 30:13) but in the fact that, with her consent, a child will be born through whom all people will be blessed (cf. Jdt 13:18).

The humility that acknowledged her lowliness does not deny the greatness of the things that will be accomplished through her. On the contrary, the more magnificent the things accomplished, the clearer will God's power and might be seen, for only God could bring about such wonders. Thus, as Mary rejoices in her own blessedness, she is really acclaiming God's goodness and power. This is why she extols the holiness of God's name, which is another way of saying that God is holy. She is praising God for having singled out the lowly and for having reversed their fortunes. This is the way God has acted from age to age, offering mercy to those who are open to it, to those who stand in awe of God's greatness. Mary sees this mercy taking shape in her life in a new and wondrous way, and so she glorifies God for it.

While the first section of the reading describes the great things that God did to Mary, these last verses list some of the past blessings enjoyed by Israel. First is the reversal of fortune that has happened so often in the past: the hungry are filled while the rich are sent away empty (v. 53). The choice of Mary is another example of God's preference for those who do not enjoy abundant prosperity. The reference to the promises made to Abraham places all of God's blessings within the context of the covenant associated with this prominent ancestor (Gen 15:1-21; 17:1-14).

These promises included a pledge that they would be a great nation, that they would be given a land of their own, and that they would live prosperous and peaceful lives secure from outside threats. The history of Israel is an account of the people's infidelity to their responsibilities and God's mercy in the face of their failures. Mary's hymn of praise suggests that the marvels accomplished in her are a final example of God's mercy. The salvation of the people has finally come.

1 Thessalonians 5:16-24

Paul concludes this letter to the Thessalonians with exhortation, encouragement, and blessing. His admonitions are crisp and concrete: rejoice, pray, give thanks. He urges the members of this community to be unceasing in these three practices, assuring them that this is God's will for them. Paul does not overlook the realities of suffering in life, nor does he advocate a false sense of happiness that simply refuses to let in anything painful. The joy he urges is the joy that comes from knowing that in Christ's resurrection even death itself has been overcome. This joy can be manifested in the Christian even in the midst of affliction (cf. 1 Thess 1:6).

Paul admonishes the believers to be thankful in all circumstances. This suggests that there are some situations that do not normally engender gratitude. Still, the realities that will cause Christians to rejoice are the very ones for which they will first be grateful. There is no lengthy description by Paul of how the Thessalonians ought to pray; there is only the close connection here and elsewhere (3:9-10) between prayer and thanksgiving.

The exhortation continues with directives that suggest the presence of charismatic or spirit-filled activity. Paul admonishes the Christians not to quench this spirit (v. 19) and not to despise prophetic utterances (v. 20) but to discern the spirits active within the community (v. 21). The spirit can be manifested in the community in diverse ways (cf. Rom 12:4-8; 1 Cor 12:4-11). This diversity can either enrich the community or be the source of competition or even chaos within it. Paul encourages the Thessalonians to give full rein to the gifts of the spirit while discerning what is genuinely of God and what is not. He singles out one gift in particular, prophecy.

Prophecy is the gift of speaking forth God's word. Tied to covenant responsibilities, it is often a difficult word that calls for conversion. A genuine prophet is usually reluctant to have to speak in this way; likewise a community of believers does not always welcome the challenge that a prophet might pose. Here Paul warns against a too hasty dismissal of the more radical demands of discipleship that might be uttered by those who prophesy. On the other hand, they must be careful not to be swept away by some false prophetic utterance. Paul admonishes the community to test the spirit, to discern what is right and what is not.

Finally, Paul prays that God will bring to completion the holiness of the Thessalonian community in every aspect: spirit, soul, and body. In praying this he is speaking not from a Greek perspective with its dichotomy of soul and body but from a Jewish perspective in which the whole person is regarded in its various aspects. He prays for their holiness because he wants them to be found blameless at the coming of the Lord Jesus Christ. If they are, then the Day of the Lord will be for them a day of rejoicing rather than a day of judgment.

Paul ends on a note of confidence. He assures the Thessalonians of God's faithfulness to the promises of salvation made to them. If they are true to the religious promises they made, God will bring to fulfillment all of the good begun in them.

John 1:6-8, 19-28

"Who are you?" is the hinge question in this reading from the Gospel of John. This is not a simple inquiry about one's name or occupation; it is a very concrete question: Who are you in relation to the Messiah? The first verses of the reading clarify the identity of the Baptist in relation to the eternal Word of God. The second section contains the Baptist's own testimony regarding the relationship between himself and Jesus, the man who was to come after him.

In the first section (vv. 6–8) John is described in terms of his relationship with the light that is to come into the world. He is the divinely chosen witness to this light. He is not the light but is to bear testimony to the light. Some have said that because he was not the light and because the light had not yet entered the world, John was himself in darkness. He was the voice that cried out from the darkness, the voice that proclaimed that the light was soon to come.

In the second section (vv. 19–28) the witness is cross-examined by Jewish religious leaders from Jerusalem. His responses to their questions are all negative: He is not the Messiah; he is not Elijah; he is not the prophet promised long ago. All of these were messianic figures, and John refuses to be identified with any one of them. "Messiah," meaning "anointed one," was a term used of several agents of God anointed for the service or protection of Israel. Kings were anointed (cf. 2 Sam 19:21), as were priests (Exod 30:30) and some prophets (Isa 61:1). In John's day messianic expectations were anything but uniform. The Essene community at Qumran was looking for at least two messiahs, one priestly and one royal. It is possible that some of the followers of John the Baptist believed that he was this anointed one. John's denial dashes these hopes.

Another popular notion held that Elijah, the prophet who had been taken up to heaven in a fiery chariot (2 Kgs 2:11), would return at the end of time. He would purify the priesthood (Mal 3:2-4), restore the tribes of Israel, and mitigate the wrath of God (Sir 48:10). Much later tradition looked to him as the forerunner (2 Esdr 6:26) or companion of the Messiah (*Gen. Rab.* on Gen

49:10). Finally, some people were looking for a prophet sent by God who, in the manner of Moses, would solve the people's legal squabbles (cf. Deut 18:15-18).

After he denies being any of these messianic individuals, John identifies himself: he is "the voice of one crying out in the desert" (cf. Isa 40:3). Taking a familiar text from Isaiah that recounts the leveling out of the wilderness so that the exiles might return home from Babylon, the author transforms it into a description of the Baptist's own ministry. The original clearing in order to make a way for God's people to return to their land now becomes an opening of the way for God to come to the people.

John's role is preparatory; he explains this when the officials question his reasons for baptizing. He further states that the one for whom he prepares is already in the midst of the people but they do not recognize him. This obscure individual will far exceed anything the Baptist might do, because he far exceeds anything the Baptist might be. John is content to be first the witness and then the herald, and nothing more.

Themes of the Day

We are midway into Advent. Traditionally, the third Sunday of Advent is called "Laetare Sunday," the Sunday of Joy. The joy of this Sunday comes both from the message of the readings and from the anticipation that Christmas is nearing. The readings address the question: Who will bring us the good news of God? Three themes address this question: the Messiah is the good news; the Messiah brings the promised gifts; everything must be tested.

The Messiah Is the Good News

The Messiah, as described in the Isaian passage, is the one imbued with the spirit and with the power of the prophet. The Messiah realizes the promises of God's jubilee time, that is, the new era of hope and emancipation. The work of the Messiah will be the work of God, the extraordinary reversal of the ways of power and domination so that justice and praise may spring up among the nations. It becomes obvious in the Gospel that the Messiah is the one proclaimed by the Baptist. John cleared a path for the coming of the anointed one, and from that time on the lives of believers have been the pathway through which the Messiah has entered the world.

The Messiah Brings the Promised Gifts

The Messiah brings justice, glad tidings, healing, liberty, vindication and the beginning of a new era of God's peace. In this, the Messiah radically alters the expectations of those who define reality apart from God's promise. The turn-about that happens when the messianic gifts are offered offends the rich, the proud, and the mighty, as the responsorial canticle declares.

According to Paul, the response of believers should be one of constant re-joicing, praying, and thanks. In other words, the gifts can be received only by hearts open to the promise. The dispositions of joy, prayer, and gratitude cre-ate such openness. Insofar as we have received the gifts, we are changed. No more evil ways, no more despising prophecy, no more false identities. Now everything is made new.

There is a warning, however. Paul admonishes us: Test everything! How do we know that we have received the messianic gifts and are not simply laboring under self or communal deception? Test the spirits!

Test Everything

It is to the victims of the system that the Messiah comes with the gifts of God. The poor, the prisoners, the disenfranchised, the underprivileged, and the lowly are the ones to whom the messianic gifts are offered. These gifts are given to all those who yearn for liberation. Therefore, to the degree that the poor are fed, the naked clothed, and the abused cared for, we know that the messianic age has dawned.

Fourth Sunday of Advent
2 Samuel 7:1-5, 8b-12, 14a, 16

This reading from the history of the royal court is pivotal in understanding the theology that surrounds David and the line of his descendants. It consists of two sections: an account of David's desire to construct a temple suitable for the God of Israel, and a description of the establishment of the Davidic dy-nasty. Although these two episodes in the life of David were mutually inde-pendent, they are bound together here by means of a very clever turn of phrase.

The narrative opens into a situation of good fortune and peace in Jeru-salem. David has been able to amass enough wealth to build a palace for him-self, and he is no longer threatened on any side by enemies (v. 1). The author states very clearly that the peace David enjoys has come to him not through any victory of his own but through the good pleasure of the LORD. He has ad-vanced from being a servant in the court of King Saul to being the undisputed king himself. He has brought his people from their former tribal affiliations to a new political organization, nationhood.

Now David realizes that the progress he and his people have made politically and socially has not carried over to their religious life. The ark of the covenant still dwells in a tent, as if it were the religious standard of a tribal god. David seeks to remedy this. He turns to the prophet Nathan, the religious leader of his time, and tells Nathan that he wishes to build a fitting temple for his God (v. 2). As spokesperson of God, the prophet tells him to proceed with his plans, assuring him that God approves (v. 3). However, the LORD speaks to Nathan that night, expresses disapproval of that plan (vv. 4–5), and offers another.

God's response to David, communicated through Nathan, is quite telling (vv. 8–11). Recounting the history of David's rise to power, God points out that any success that David enjoyed came directly from God. David did not really direct his own fate or the fate of his people, and he will not be in charge of it in the future. God will make him famous; God will give them peace; and God does not need to be ensconced in a royal temple in order to accomplish this.

What follows is the divine legitimation of the Davidic ruling line. There is a play on ideas here rather than a play on words. David sought to build a house (temple) for God, and God promised to establish a house (dynasty) for David. Previously, kings had been directly chosen by God. Both Saul and David were seized by the spirit and anointed by a prophet (1 Sam 10:1, 6; 16:13), signs of divine approval. Now, a divinely founded dynasty gave legitimacy to a ruling family. This legitimation is confirmed when the king is accorded the title "son of God," a technical phrase that characterizes the unique and intimate relationship between God and the monarch.

The reading ends with a promise that the dynasty will endure forever before God. This promise provided stability to the monarchy when it faced difficulties. It was also the foundation of Israel's hope for the future.

Psalm 89:2-3, 4-5, 27, 29

The verses come from a royal psalm that praises God's faithfulness to the promises made to David (cf. 2 Sam 7:16). They contain certain themes that are very important in the Davidic theology. Lovingkindness (*ḥesed*) and faithfulness (*'ĕmûnâ*) are technical terms for covenant fidelity. It should be noted that it is God's love that lasts forever and God's faithfulness that is praised through all the ages. The promises that are a part of this covenant are pure gift from God. Unlike the covenant made with the people through the mediation of Moses (cf. Exodus 19–21), an agreement that required compliance with God's law, this covenant imposes no added responsibilities on David or his descendants.

The psalmist reminds God of some of the content of the pledge that was made to David. One of the first items mentioned is "lovingkindness" (kindness, v. 3a). This is unconditional love, and God promises that such love will endure forever. This love should not be confused with emotional attachment, a sentiment that can fade or even completely disappear. This is a firm and unalterable commitment. God has chosen David, and God will not renege on this choice. Joined to this constant love is covenant faithfulness (v. 3b), a loyalty that will stand as long as the heavens stand. The psalm describes the bond that joins God and David as one that transcends the historical. It is outside of any specific time; it extends throughout all the ages. It also stretches beyond the confines of earth, even into the heavens. It is as if the choice of David were determined by God at the time of creation, and it will last as long as the created world lasts.

The covenant that God makes with David is everlasting, and its consequences unfold in the lives of the descendants of David (vv. 4–5). If the promises of God last forever, than it stands to reason that the family to whom the promises are made will rule forever. The promises also maintain that all other promises made by God to the people of Israel will come to them through the agency of this particular family.

The covenant establishes a unique relationship between God and the Davidic ruler, the relationship of father to son (v. 27). This bond reflects the common ancient Near Eastern belief that the kings were either actual physical descendants of the gods or were adopted as such when they assumed the responsibilities of the throne. It is this tradition that produced the designation "son of god," which was really a royal title that had divine connotations. The theology of Israel did not completely accept this notion of filiation, but it did not totally reject it either. It claimed that the king was *like* a son to God (cf. 2 Sam 7:14) and was initiated into this relationship on the day of his coronation (cf. Ps 2:7).

Besides using the titles "father" and "God," the king refers to God as "rock of salvation," the solid and reliable foundation upon which the king's good fortune is established. The psalm response ends with a restatement of the endurance of the Davidic rule. Several themes are repeated throughout the psalm: God's choice of the Davidic house; the appointment of that house as the ruling family in Israel; the permanence of that appointment; the guarantee of that permanence in the very structures of creation itself.

Romans 16:25-27

In these few verses of praise Paul sums up the central theme of his own teaching, namely, that God's new act of revelation in Christ will bring even the Gentiles to the commitment of faith. Paul calls this "my gospel" not because the content is significantly different from that taught by the other Christian missionaries but because the proclamation to the Gentile world was taken up by him and this new direction in his ministry was later confirmed by the leaders of the Jerusalem community (cf. Gal 2:7-9). The passage itself is a doxology exalting God, who is the real source of revelation.

Paul claims that the revelation of God in Christ was really present in ages past, but as a mystery that was kept secret. Belief that the destinies of the nations was decided at the very creation of the world is a very old idea. These destinies were thought to have been written down, sealed, and hidden, sometimes in the guise of cryptic imagery, to be revealed during a much later period. Sometimes an individual was chosen to break the seal and reveal the destinies (cf. Revelation 5–16), sometimes not.

Another tradition claimed that the revelation of God through Jesus Christ can be found obliquely in the writings of the First Testament. This revelation might have been hidden to the ancient Israelites, but those who have eyes of faith today should be able to read these writings and there discover something of God's plan. Paul insists that God had this plan in mind from the beginning, even though it was very difficult for anyone to comprehend it thoroughly. This understanding of the hidden mysteries would explain the reference Paul makes here to the prophets (v. 26).

The purpose of the revelation of this mystery is universal salvation. All, Gentiles included, are to be brought to the commitment of faith. The faith referred to here is not an intellectual assent to propositions about Christ. It is, instead, a commitment to the person of Christ, a commitment that comes through hearing the word. Finally, as important as the proclamation of this word is, Paul insists that the real work of revelation and salvation is God's. Only to God, the only wise God, through Jesus Christ, does glory belong.

This short doxology sums up not only Paul's teaching but the heart of the Christian message. From ages past God has planned the salvation of all and has revealed this message through the tradition of the past. Now the fullness of this revelation has come in Jesus, and through Jesus the blessings of salvation promised so long ago are given to all nations. Such a message can elicit only unending gratitude and praise.

Luke 1:26-38

The account of the annunciation to Mary is cast in a traditional pattern of angelic birth announcements (cf. to Hagar, Gen 16:7-16; to the mother of Samson, Judg 13:2-7). Such stories alert the reader to the divine significance of future events in the lives of the children to be born. This passage opens with information that places the event described within the broader picture of God's plan of salvation. This event happened within the sixth month of the pregnancy of a couple who can trace their ancestries to two priestly families (1:5). Though it happened to a descendant of the great king David, it happened in an out-of-the-way place in Galilee.

The opening angelic greeting, "Hail, full of grace! The Lord is with you" (v. 28), emphatically states Mary's extraordinary dignity. The common Greek salutation, "Hail!" carries the connotation of "rejoice" and recalls prophecies of restoration, a theme that undergirds the entire account. Typical of angelic appearances, the initial reaction of Mary is fear, but there is another reason to be troubled. In the past, a high price, perhaps even the laying down of life itself, was sometimes exacted of those who had found favor with God (e.g., Noah, Gen 6:8; Moses, Exod 33:12; Gideon, Judg 6:17; Samuel, 1 Sam 2:26). Mary, a woman graced by God, is here invited to be the vehicle of salvation for God's people. This will most likely demand that she endure great hardship.

The angel's response is both reassuring and perplexing. She is first told not to fear, but what she is then told is truly awesome. She, a virgin (v. 27), will bear a son, whose name indicates the role he will play in God's plan. ("Jesus" means "God saves.") He will be a savior; he will be known as the Son of the Most High; and he will be the ultimate descendant of David. Mary's response does not question *that* all of this will happen according to God's plan, but she wonders *how* it will happen, for she is a virgin. Gabriel replies that she will be overshadowed by God's Spirit and power. This figurative language is reminiscent of the cloud that settled upon the tent of meeting, indicating God's presence in the midst of the people (Exod 40:35). The conception within her will be God's doing.

The angel further reassures Mary of the possibility of all of this by giving her a concrete sign. Her relative Elizabeth has also conceived a son, despite what appeared to be insurmountable circumstances (v. 36). The statement that "nothing will be impossible for God" (v. 37) echoes God's words to Abraham in somewhat similar circumstances, assuring him of the future birth of Isaac (Gen 18:14).

The scene concludes with Mary's acceptance. Like other stories of angelic appearances to women in patriarchal worlds, Mary interacts directly with God's messenger without the mediation of her father or intended husband (cf. Gen 16:7-16; Judg 13:2-5). She is not only free of patriarchal restraints, her words suggest that hers is a free response to God as well. Though a servant of the Lord, she is also a model of openness and receptivity, regardless of the apparent impossibility of what is being asked and the prospect of subsequent hardships. The reading shows that the expectations of the past are now being fulfilled; God's plan is being accomplished.

Themes of the Day

The season of Advent shifts direction by the fourth Sunday. On the 17th of December the great O Antiphons of evening prayer have begun to characterize the Messiah in stunning metaphors. A new eucharistic preface is now proclaimed in which the birth of Jesus is announced. It is as if we are already celebrating Christmas. The Lectionary readings carry this changed focus. The time of fulfillment is at hand, and several themes point to this: salvation occurs within history; the mystery hidden is revealed; God works the impossible.

Salvation Occurs Within History

In a significant turn of meaning, the one who wanted to build an edifice for God is told that God will establish a house for him. The house that God will build is a nation. It will not be simply a political dynasty; it will be a people strong in the land, filled with a godly power. This power will come from a covenant that transcends time but is present to history. This covenant travels through time from the throne room of Mount Zion to a backwater Galilean village in the hills.

The world in which we live and the events of which we are a part are the stage upon which the drama of salvation is enacted. God works through real flesh-and-blood people, those who occupy the seats of power and influence as well as those who are unseen and unknown. All carry the promise of salvation in the present and into the future. Such an ennobling vocation! God's future is in our hands. Human history is really the history of salvation.

The Mystery Hidden Is Revealed

For the believer mystery is not mystery because its value cannot be comprehended. Rather, it is mystery because its infinite value and meaning will always extend beyond human comprehension. Increased knowing leads to knowing how much more we do not know of the mystery. We know only in the depth of not knowing. Each turn of God's revealing causes us to wonder at what comes next.

In this tension mystery is revealed. What was hidden is now made known. Jesus, God's salvation in history, establishes a people of covenant promise. Still, the mystery is unknown because it continues to come to us from the future, revealing more and more of itself in the junctures of history.

God Works the Impossible

The waiting of Advent is over. In the face of the impossible God works the possible. Mary is asked to believe this. She is open and accepting. She is to believe something else equally impossible: the old and barren Elizabeth is pregnant, for nothing is impossible for God.

What we have been waiting for all Advent is now revealed. We have been waiting for the realization of the promise made to David. We have been waiting for Mary's yes. According to ancient Christian writers, God waits for Mary's yes; creation waits; Adam and Eve wait; the dead in the underworld wait; the angels wait; and so do we. With Mary's yes, hope is enlivened and history is changed. There is an unimaginable future for all people, a future that comes from God. All nations assemble in justice, compassion, and gratitude. Salvation is created among us, and the fate of history is altered by a godly presence. This salvation resides in the hearts of those who believe in the gift and who stay awake eagerly to know its coming. With David we await it, with the nations we long for it, with Mary we behold it.

The Nativity of the Lord (Christmas)

Mass at Midnight Isaiah 9:1-6 A son is given to us	Psalm 96:1-3, 11-13 Let the heavens be glad	Titus 2:11-14 The grace of God has appeared	Luke 2:1-14 Today a savior has been born
Mass at Dawn Isaiah 62:11-12 Behold, your savior comes	Psalm 97:1, 6, 11-12 A light will shine on us	Titus 3:4-7 Out of mercy, he saved us	Luke 2:15-20 The shepherds came
Mass During the Day Isaiah 52:7-10 Announce the good news	Psalm 98:1-6 All have seen God's salvation	Hebrews 1:1-6 God has spoken through the Son	John 1:1-18 The Word became flesh
The Holy Family of Jesus, Mary, and Joseph (1) Sirach 3:2-6, 12-14 Honor your parents	Psalm 128:1-5 Blessed are those who fear the LORD	Colossians 3:12-21 Over all these, put on love	Luke 2:22-40 The child grew and became strong
The Holy Family of Jesus, Mary, and Joseph (2) Genesis 15:1-6; 21:1-3 Your son will be your heir	Psalm 105:1-4, 6-9 The LORD remembers the covenant	Hebrews 11:8, 11-12, 17-19 The ancestors lived by faith	Luke 2:22-40 The child grew strong

Feast / Date	First Reading	Psalm	Second Reading	Gospel
January 1, **Solemnity of the Blessed Virgin** **Mary, Mother of God**	Numbers 6:22-27 The LORD bless you and keep you	Psalm 67:2-3, 5, 6, 8 May God bless us	Gal 4:4-7 God's Son was born of a woman	Luke 2:16-21 The shepherds came to Bethlehem
Second Sunday After Christmas	Sirach 24:1-2, 8-12 Wisdom lives with God's people	Psalm 147:12-15, 19-20 God's Word became human	Ephesians 1:3-6, 15-18 We are children of God through Christ	John 1:1-18 The Word became flesh
January 6, **The Epiphany of the Lord**	Isaiah 60:1-6 God's glory shines on us	Psalm 72:1-2, 7-8, 10-13 All nations will adore God	Ephesians 3:2-3a, 5-6 Gentiles are coheirs of the promise	Matthew 2:1-12 We saw his star
Sunday After January 6, **The Baptism of the Lord (1)**	Isaiah 42:1-4, 6-7 Behold my servant	Psalm 29:1-4, 3, 9-10 The LORD will bless with peace	Acts 10:34-38 Anointed with the Spirit	Mark 1:7-11 You are my beloved Son
The Baptism of the Lord (2)	Isaiah 55:1-11 Come to the waters	Isaiah 12:2-6 Draw water joyfully	1 John 5:1-9 The Spirit, the water, and the blood are one	Mark 1:7-11 You are my beloved Son

The Nativity of the Lord (Christmas)

Initial Reading of the Christmas Lectionary

Introduction

Employing the same method of reading the Lectionary used in the Advent season, we interpret the constellation of readings that the Christmas season offers. While the Advent season incorporates three cycles of the Lectionary, the Christmas readings—with the exception of the choices for the feast of the Holy Family and the Baptism of the Lord—do not vary. Each group of readings will be examined and interpreted. A presentation of the entire mosaic of readings will follow this exercise.

First Testament Readings

The Midnight Mass at Christmas begins the season. It is a word of emancipation. The people in darkness now see, for the child is born. The close of the season, the feast of the Baptism of the Lord, identifies the child as the servant, the one who brings about this liberation by the word of God that is proclaimed with power. The child-servant heralds a profound reversal. Something cosmic has happened at Christmas: in the midst of the darkness the light that emanates from the child-servant reveals God's intentions to the ends of the earth.

The other First Testament readings in this season unpack the richness of the transformation this birth brings about. The people who were lost are no longer forsaken. The glad tidings of this good news will be sung by the servant, who proclaims liberty to captives and sight to the blind, who gives a name to the nameless and a voice of significance to women and children and those who are forsaken. The transformation touches the very heart of the domestic world of parents and children and calls for an ordering based in love and the promise of the world made new. In this order blessing is found: the blessing of peace, a blessing that is both a hope and a charge. It is a hope for God's peace among the people; at the same time it is a charge to live in such a way as to make the blessing of wisdom real in their lives and in their worlds.

At the end of the Christmas season we are told that God's glory goes forth from the city to the ends of the earth. All nations, races, peoples, tribes, and languages will proclaim the wisdom of God. The mystery of Christmas midnight will gather all people into the promise of God. This is the work of the child-servant. It is a work that is caught up into the reversal of justice and compassion that still whispers in the night.

Psalms

The Lectionary refrains for the Christmas season fall into three categories: declarations of the wonderful work of God among the people; the implications of these works in the lives of those who call upon the Lord; and the universality of these works and the extension of God's glory.

Some of the refrains speak of the reality of the birth of a Savior. They declare that the birth takes place today; it is the present moment that knows the wonder of the Word made flesh. Other psalms are shouts of exultation and praise in face of this wonder. They express the unimaginable joy of those who receive God's gift and find in it their fulfillment.

Toward the end of the season the refrains move us into an understanding of the specific implications of the gift of the child that is born among us. They voice the happiness of those who know the Lord. The blessings of God abound, and this elicits the praises of all the people. The ultimate blessing given is peace.

Epistles

An examination of the epistles of the season shows that they are an extended meditation on salvation. In these Christmas readings we are told that salvation has been given and now has appeared among us. It is offered to all people, and it brings with it the hope and promise of righteousness. Salvation is not our achievement; it comes from God's Spirit.

The implications of this salvation are demonstrated in several epistle readings. Relationships change when salvation is received. First, we are called into forgiveness, patience, and the meekness that allow us to embrace one another in love and mercy. Second, the relationship with God is made intimate, and we are able to call God "Abba." This new way of naming God allows us the inheritance of God, for we find ourselves to be children of God and sisters and brothers in Christ. All of these new relationships take place within the Church, which is not only the place of salvation but, more importantly, the people of salvation. The beauty of God and the wealth of the inheritance are ours in the community of faith.

Salvation is not confined; God's salvation is for all, Jew and Greek alike, and its wealth is to be shared among the nations. Peter preaches the universality of this gift in the name of Jesus, who was anointed by the Spirit. In the power of the same Spirit we are called to the same universality. In our day it takes the form of interreligious dialogue and recognition of the religious value present in other religions of the world.

The epistles offer an ever-widening understanding of salvation, from the first appearance of the gift of Christmas to the preaching of the apostles and to our own appreciation of it.

Gospels

The Gospels for the Christmas season remain somewhat narrative and are punctuated by passages from the Prologue of the Gospel of John, which reveals the theological significance of the Christmas story itself. There are two ways of viewing the Gospels of the season. The first is a simple narrative reading that begins with the birth of Jesus, then moves through the visit of the shepherds to a reading that provides a theological interpretation of the events recounted. The narrative continues with episodes from the life of the young Jesus, followed by a second theological interpretation. It concludes with two accounts of the manifestation of Jesus' true identity, the first to the Magi and the second at his baptism.

The Gospels move from the birth to the baptism. They invite the religious imagination to accept the baby as the gift to the nations, the one whose ministry in the Spirit will make him a servant of both God and humanity. The Christmas season ends with us poised for Jesus' mission and his entry into the place of testing, which will begin the lenten season.

The second way of reading recognizes a kind of chiastic structure:

a) birth
  b) shepherds
    c) theological interpretation
     d) presentation
     d^1) circumcision
    c^1) theological interpretation
  b^1) magi
a^1) baptism

The birth and the baptism are both forms of manifestation; the shepherds and the Magi represent all those to whom the revelation is given, the poor and the prosperous, the Jews and the Gentiles; the theological interpretations can be matched, leaving the presentation and the circumcision as the focal point of the chiasm. In such a structure the accent of importance is placed on the texts at the center. In this case the presentation and the circumcision offer a key insight into the season.

Both accounts show that Jesus was grounded in the practices of his religious tradition. He is willing to be consecrated to God and to be incorporated into God's people. Both accounts also mention Mary's unique role in the drama of the incarnation. At the time of presentation she is told that her child's destiny will pierce her own heart; in the account of the circumcision she is described as reflecting on the mysteries of which she is a part. Jesus is the Lord who comes to his temple; God has visited us in the form of a little child. Mary represents the Church; we rejoice in the birth of the child, but we do so knowing that this child is destined for suffering. The child is born and redeemed, but only so that we can be redeemed and reborn.

Mosaic of Readings

The Christmas cycle is a proclamation of the presence of God in human history. The Lectionary weaves narrative, prophecy, and exhortation together, producing a tapestry of breathtaking beauty. A threefold message is contained in this work of art: (1) something definitive has happened in history and is the work of God; (2) this marvel is a gift that can be received by all people of good will, it is a universal gift extending to all the nations; (3) when received, it forms us into a community that lives by this gift and shows itself to be the place where God has pitched a tent among us. The Church is the community of grace and compassion for the life of the world. Christmas is the promise of Easter in the lives of those who receive the child-servant.

Readings

The Nativity of the Lord (Mass at Midnight)
Isaiah 9:1-6

The reading begins with the announcement of deliverance. Its message of hope and consolation is expressed through the contrast between light and darkness (v. 1). The darkness does not seem to be merely a temporary clouding of the light. Rather, the entire land is in darkness, and the people seem fixed in it. It is to them that a great light comes. This light ushers in a complete reversal of fortune, which the rest of the reading describes. The people did not bring this reversal on themselves; they are the recipients of God's good pleasure (v. 6).

After the initial announcement the prophet speaks directly to God, enumerating examples of God's acts of graciousness toward the people. First, the people embrace the entire experience of salvation with unbounded joy (v. 2). The rejoicing is of the kind that follows either an abundant harvest, when there is enough yield to satisfy the needs of all, or an assessment of the spoils of war after the battles have been won. In each instance, there is a sense of relief that the hardships of the venture are over as well as great satisfaction with the respective fruits that accrued from it.

The prophet next describes how God liberated the people from oppression (vv. 3–4). In the past they were shackled like oxen, forced to do arduous, ignoble tasks. They were subjected to physical abuse at the hands of another. But God intervened and destroyed the instruments of their servitude. The reference to Midian calls to mind the defeat of that nation under the leadership of Gideon (Judg 7:15-25). Not only was that defeat absolute, it was also miraculous, accomplished through divine power. Mention of this battle along with the military title LORD of hosts (cf. First Sunday of Advent, Psalm 80) may also explain the reference to spoils of war. The comparison is clear: God and only God has gained salvation for the people, and that salvation is absolute.

The final verses of the reading sketch a picture that is most astounding. The salvation reported is realized through the agency of a child (vv. 5–6). The responsibility for establishing the peace described here rests on his shoulders. The names ascribed to him signify the feats expected of him. Like every good leader, he will make wise decisions and he will be able to guide others in their judgments. However, he will surpass all others in this regard; he will be Wonder-Counselor! "God-Hero" comes from the Hebrew word *gibbor,* another term with military connotations. This child will be a divine warrior, capable of withstanding all the evil cosmic forces. He will be Father Forever, unfailing in providing for those under his care. He is Prince of Peace, the one who both secures and safeguards it. This peace is more than the absence of war. It means wholeness, completion, harmony. It was a condition in which all things—human beings, animals, and plants—follow their God-given destinies undisturbed.

All of these titles were in some way associated with the Davidic king. He was expected to be a wise ruler, mighty in battle, a father to his people, and the guarantor of peace. However, a more-than-human dimension has been added here. This child may belong to the line of David, but he is an extraordinary descendant. The exercise of his dominion is the saving action of God.

Psalm 96:1-2, 2-3, 11-12, 13

The psalm calls upon the people to praise God for the wonderful acts of salvation that God has performed (vv. 1–3). Three times the psalmist calls them to sing God's praises, each time highlighting a different aspect of the song. First, they are called to sing a new song. This is only appropriate, since their salvation has transformed them into a new people. No longer will laments be acceptable. The only kind of song worthy of the event of the salvation that has unfolded before their very eyes is a hymn of praise.

Next, there is a note of universality to the singing. Not just Israel but all the earth is called upon to sing this song of praise. Finally, along with the call to sing is a summons to bless the name of the LORD. Since a name was thought to contain part of the very essence of the person, a call to bless God's name is really a summons to give praise to some aspect of God's character. The aspect to be praised is the salvation that God has brought about for the sake of Israel. All the earth is called to announce the good news of this salvation and to announce it unceasingly, day after day.

God is here portrayed enthroned as Lord of the entire earth, accomplishing wondrous deeds that all the nations have been able to witness. The final verses (vv. 11–13) show that these deeds include the creation and governance of all the earth as well as the direction and judgment of all nations. Such universal power and dominion could only be wielded by a god who is above all other gods, one who reigns supreme in the heavens but who executes authority on earth as well. God not only performs these marvelous feats but does so with justice and faithfulness. This God is indeed powerful but is also trustworthy. Such is the portrait of the God of Israel that is painted in this psalm.

The reasons for the praise for which the psalmist calls are specifically laid out. God is acclaimed as ruler of the heavens and the earth. It is quite understandable to claim dominion over the earth for God. Even minor gods were thought to exercise some power on earth. However, since heavenly beings were frequently personified as deities in other ancient Near Eastern religions, it is a bit more difficult, though not impossible, to ascribe rule over them to God. It is clear from the early verses of the psalm that here the heavens are merely regarded as elements of natural creation. As such, they join in honoring the Creator. What is interesting is the inclusion of the sea and all of the watercourses over which it has control in this chorus of praise, since the sea was traditionally considered a mythological force of evil. That it is regarded as merely a creature of God is significant.

All of the rejoicing is focused on an upcoming event, the advent of the LORD. The rejoicing itself does not overshadow the reason for the LORD's coming, which is judgment. God will judge the earth. As harsh as the notion of judgment may be, God judges with righteousness and truth (v. 13). Divine judgment is less a question of power than one of harmony and right order. God's rule is one of right order. Salvation itself is a return to this order. Therefore, the judgment of God is really the establishment of harmony, the establishment of peace.

Titus 2:11-14

This short excerpt from one of the Pastoral epistles is a confession of faith in the saving grace of God. The verb "appeared" (v. 11) is testimony to divine revelation. The reading proclaims that God's grace is no longer something for which the people wait with longing. It has arrived; it is an accomplished fact. Furthermore, the universality of this salvation is clearly stated. It is not merely for an elect group, whether Jewish or Christian; it is for all humans *(ánthrōpos)*.

This grace, or good favor, takes the form of salvation, a theological concept with profound Jewish and Hellenistic connotations. In Jewish thought salvation was seen as rescue from the perils of life, and it was accomplished by God. Many narratives of the First Testament recount such salvation. In the Hellenistic mystery religions, which were so prominent at the time of the writing of this letter, the initiates shared in the mythical divine being's victory over death, and they were thereby assured a share in blissful life in the hereafter. In this particular passage the concept of salvation includes aspects of both views. It is because they have been saved from the perils of evil that the Christians have been empowered to live lives of moral integrity in this world; on the other hand, their salvation has come to them through the sacrifice of Christ Jesus, and they still await a future divine manifestation.

The reading also declares that God's saving grace imparts the kind of training that is necessary to combat the forces of a godless world and to live truly Christian lives (v. 12). The author of the epistle does not enumerate what these evil forces might be. (Discerning them may well be even more of a challenge than opposing them.) What *is* confidently stated is the assurance that the power of divine grace will adequately prepare believers to live in moderation, righteousness, and piety, regardless of the opposition within themselves and from others that they may have to face. Such a courageous way of living is evidence that the age of fulfillment has indeed arrived. However, this indication of "realized eschatology" does not erase the expectation of a "future eschatology." Christians live an "already but not yet" existence. Their moral lives are both signs of and expectation of the final fulfillment.

Christ Jesus has achieved this great grace. His sacrifice of himself has redeemed and cleansed those who have accepted him. The moral character of this salvation is apparent in the final verse of the reading. The Christians are redeemed from lawlessness, and they are purified as a people who then perform good works. There is no doubt that this is God's saving grace, but it

comes to the people through Christ Jesus. The Pastoral epistles generally identify God as the savior of all. The Greek in this passage is quite awkward. It
reads, "great God and savior of our Jesus Christ" (v. 13). It is only in translations that Jesus is identified as the Savior. Whatever version is chosen, the intimate relationship between God and Christ is obvious, and that is the point of
the reading.

This passage does not call for hope. As a profession of faith, it affirms a
tenet of belief and holds it out as a truth that calls for commitment. Salvation
has been won by Christ and is offered to all. We decide how we will respond to
it.

Luke 2:1-14

Luke's version of the birth of Jesus is one of the best-known stories of the
Bible. It has inspired both paintings and music down through the ages. Even
small children know about the census, the swaddling clothes and manger, the
shepherds and the angels' song. Our critical examination of the text should
not so demythologize the imagery that we undermine popular religious imagination and overlook the power of the message.

The details of the story serve two very important purposes: they situate
Jesus in first-century history, and they link him with the house of David. The
miraculous incidents that accompany this birth might lead some to conclude
that the event recounted was too otherworldly to be genuinely historical. Such
a position throws into question the very heart of the doctrine of the incarnation. Situating the birth within the world of real Roman rulers underscored
its claim that God was indeed born at this time, in this place, among these
people.

The details also identify Jesus as the Davidic Messiah. Since the Gospel tradition maintains that Jesus was from Nazareth, it was important somehow to
establish him in Bethlehem. The account of the census, regardless of how inaccurate its details may be, explains how his parents happened to be in Bethlehem at the time of his birth. The Davidic link is made again and again. Joseph
was of the house of David, and so he traveled to the town of David to be regis-
tered (v. 4). The first to pay homage to the newborn were Bethlehemite shepherds, simple herders not unlike David himself. Mary and Joseph do not play
the central roles here. Joseph is important because of his Davidic lineage, and
Mary is identified as Joseph's pregnant wife. The entire focus of the story is on
the child.

A second and related theme is God's choice of the most unlikely and frequently overlooked members of society to accomplish God's will. From the
outset this child was treated like an unwelcome stranger, almost an outcast. He
was deprived of the comforts that normally surrounded a birth, born away

from the home of his parents, away from the warmth and love of an extended family. He was not visited by friendly neighbors but by shepherds, a class of people considered unclean because their occupation often required that they deal with both the birth and the death blood of their flocks. The stage is set to tell the story of God's predilection for the poor, the overlooked, and the forgotten. Like his ancestor David, the one who was destined for great things had a humble, even despised, beginning.

Despite the unconscionable affront by human beings, the birth of this extraordinary child was surrounded by celestial grandeur. An angel announced the wondrous event to the lowly shepherds and was then joined by countless other angelic beings who filled the night with their song of praise of God; the glory of God could not be contained, and it burst forth encompassing the shepherds with its brilliance. The disregard of the human community was outstripped by a display of heavenly exaltation.

This simple yet beloved Christmas story contains a complex christology. On the one hand, the author takes great pains to situate Jesus squarely within the human family of David. On the other hand, he identifies Jesus as Savior and Lord and paints a picture of heavenly celebration. Such is the mystery of Christmas.

Themes of the Day

The Church commemorates the birth of Christ with three celebrations of the Eucharist: at midnight; at dawn; and during the day of Christmas. These inaugural celebrations usher in the Christmas cycle with themes that will be revisited several times before the season ends. In the middle of the night the community gathers to meditate on three of these themes: the historical birth of Jesus; the liberating king; and the new age of fulfillment of God's promise inaugurated by this king.

The Birth of Jesus in History

The Gospel clearly situates the birth of Jesus within a historical epoch, that of the Roman rule of Israel in the first century. The proclamation announced on this day places Jesus' birth within the affairs of human life with its struggles and cares. These historical and human details indicate that this birth is not simply an otherworldly event, it happened at a specific time and in a specific place. The incarnation of God happened among us! God comes to us in our time, in our place, in our history.

Once the historical reality is established, the story reveals another dimension of this birth. The ordinary becomes transparent and reveals the extraordinary; the divine is known in the child. Angels appear in order to declare that this is so. Night glows with the radiance of daytime, and the midnight hour is the breakthrough of everlasting light. Only those of humble heart come to know this wonder. The reality of the mystery is offered, but its significance is missed by many. In this case it is not the influential who recognize the gift but those whom society forgets. It is the shepherds, the poor and forsaken subjects of history, who happen upon this birth and who believe. They behold it and they come to embrace it. In fact, it is the nature of this child, born in history, to reverse the orders of power.

The Liberating King

The readings contain strong images of the royalty of the Lord. God is portrayed as a valiant liberator who is worthy of praise and worship. It is God who champions the cause of justice and who brings a liberation that can reverse history and the ways of war, power, and oppression. The coming events will satisfy the needs of all. However, the reversal of the fate of history is made more shocking by the fact that the one who is the mighty warrior and conqueror of the nations is a child, one who rules with peace and integrity.

This child is Jesus. However, the child is the servant who can conquer the alienating forces of history, the one whose life is destined to change the fate of humanity. Furthermore, it is the child as the weak and voiceless one, the one who has neither power nor legal rights, who will shake the empire. God's reversal of the long-standing realities of this world is accomplished through the apparently insignificant, through the gift of this child who is given to us in the middle of the night.

The Age of Fulfillment Has Begun

With the birth of the child something new has happened: the age of God's fulfillment has arrived. This is an age of grace and fresh hope made available to all people of good will. It is an era of redemptive presence, because now all people can walk in the newness of life and grace. This age has come about by the gift of Christ poured out for us. We can see it, touch it, taste it. It is a time when justice and mercy appear, when nations seek the ways of peace, when reconciliation transforms us. And yet, while the age has begun, it is not yet fully realized.

We live in the traces of this hope, believing in its presence and awaiting its fulfillment. In a real sense, although we are celebrating Christmas, we are still an advent people who await the coming of the Lord in the abundance of mercy that is yet to erupt in history. We are a tensive people, not tense with the cares of this age but poised to receive the gift of the ever-deepening promise that was born among us and whose birth continues to astound us at every appearance of hope.

The Nativity of the Lord (Mass at Dawn)
Isaiah 62:11-12

The message of these two short verses is extraordinary in several ways. First, it has been prescribed by the LORD. Second, it concerns the redemption of Israel and is to be proclaimed to the whole world. Third, it deals less with the promise of a future salvation than with the announcement that salvation is already on its way. Fourth, it includes new names for the people and for the city of Jerusalem, names that show that both the people and the city have been radically transformed.

This prophetic notice repeats some of the content of an oracle that appears elsewhere in the book of the prophet Isaiah (40:10). In the earlier oracle it was the LORD God who was coming in might with reward and recompense. Here God is identified with salvation, and it is this salvation that comes with reward and recompense. Salvation has been accomplished. The new names for the people and the city make this clear.

In order to appreciate the significance of the title "the holy people," we must remember that ancient Israel was a nation whose political and social exile was interpreted by the people themselves as punishment for their sins. Now they have a new name, and that name implies that not only are they forgiven, but they enjoy a new identity, as if newly born. The people are also called "the redeemed of the LORD," a title that marks a double relationship with God. The obvious meaning points to a bond between redeemer and redeemed. The former is someone who pays the debt of another and thereby provides deliverance from any kind of servitude; the latter is the one released from the debt. The less obvious relationship implied in the title is one of kinship. Normally it was a close relative who paid the debt. These titles point to the intimate and remarkable attachment that God has for this people.

Zion/Jerusalem is also given new names (cf. 62:2-4), indicating a new identity. The city that was overthrown, depopulated, and plundered will once again attract people to it. It will then be called "Frequented," that is, "not forsaken." The name declares that the desolation of the past is forgotten. Salvation has come to the city.

Psalm 97:1, 6, 11-12

The psalm opens with the traditional enthronement declaration. "The LORD is king!" It is appropriately followed by the exclamation: "Rejoice!" The response suggests that the manner of God's rule calls for celebration, and this celebration extends beyond the confines of Israel to the entire world. Although the LORD reigns over all the earth, the divine king's throne was really established in the heavens after the forces of evil had been conquered and the universe had been put in order. In other words, the divine enthronement follows the creation of the entire cosmos. This explains the universality of God's reign. The LORD is not only king but is first creator, and it is the glory of creation that is seen by all.

Unlike other regimes built merely on brute force or military victory, both of which might fail and result in the dethronement of the former victor, God's rule is constructed in the permanence of creation, in cosmic justice and right order (v. 6). It is not only impregnable, it is also immutable. It stands secure, enabling God to govern undisturbed by any threat and assuring reliable protection to all those under God's jurisdiction. God's rule in human life is as trustworthy as is the order of the universe, for that very order is a sign of God's universal rule. The revelation of God through the glory of creation (vv. 1, 6) is juxtaposed with the reign of God in the lives of the righteous (vv. 11–12). Just as the cosmic forces of good are frequently characterized as light, so the good fortune that flows from upright living is also associated with light. The just do not languish in darkness; they flourish in the light, and in this their hearts are glad.

Both sections of this responsorial psalm report a divine theophany. Likewise, both sections describe a celebrative response to the revelation of God. The first section reports that the earth rejoices, the islands are glad, and the heavens proclaim God's justice. The second section contains exhortation rather than report: be glad, and give thanks. These are fitting responses to the graciousness of God within which the righteous have been blessed.

One might think that only a few are allowed to enjoy these blessings. However, the juxtaposition of these two sections of the psalm indicate that God grants this light and gladness to all on earth. The divine theophany is universal, and so are the blessings that abound because of it.

Titus 3:4-7

The appearance of the saving love of God is the theme of this passage, which was probably part of an early Christian baptismal hymn. The salvation achieved through Jesus Christ completely changed the lives of the newly baptized, drawing a striking contrast between the way they lived before their conversion and the way they live now. As in the reading for the Christmas Mass at Midnight, this passage announces what has already taken place. The love and kindness of God have appeared; it is not a future event for which believers ardently long. Furthermore, it has appeared in time, in history. The coming of Christ coincides with the ultimate manifestation of God's love.

It is clear that this love is a free gift springing from the mercy of God and not simply compensation for righteous living. On the contrary, salvation is bestowed first so that having received it, Christians might then be able to live virtuously. It is this saving grace that justifies them, not any moral effort on their part. Everything is a free gift bestowed out of divine largesse. This includes love, mercy, and justification in this life and the inheritance of eternal life. God's magnanimous giving is celebrated here.

A rudimentary trinitarian formula appears in the reference to baptism. The text explicitly states that it is God's love that appears and it is God who saved us through the washing of baptism. It was God who poured out the Spirit through Jesus Christ. As with the passage from Titus that was read at the Mass at Midnight, there is no clear line drawn here between God as savior and Christ as savior. It may be that such distinctions had not yet been sharply made. What is clear in this reading is that rebirth and renewal come through the Spirit and that divine titles (Savior) and activities (saving) are attributed to Christ.

Although the author uses commonplace Hellenistic religious language such as "rebirth" and imagery such as cleansing through water, the theology of justification is drawn from Jewish thought. There the righteous are those who, though unfaithful, have been acquitted by God. The initiative is always God's, and it is usually exercised in the face of human infidelity. From a human point of view the absurdity of such a situation is unmistakable. Still, accepting the opportunity of freely given justification is not an easy thing to do, and many people do not even believe it is possible. For those who believe it is both possible and desirable, reluctance to avail themselves of salvation is the real absurdity.

This baptismal hymn both proclaims tenets of faith and indirectly exhorts believers to embrace a life of virtue. Since they have been born anew, they can now act in a new way, walking blamelessly in this world in anticipation of the next. Christians are radically changed because God has entered their lives. The appearance of God's love has accomplished this.

Luke 2:15-20

It is because of the Gospel reading that this Mass was formally referred to as the Shepherds' Mass. The passage itself is rich with theological themes: response to divine revelation, theological insight, evangelization, praise of God, contemplative reflection.

One of the reasons that shepherds were considered irreligious by the self-righteous of the time was their failure to participate in regular ritual observance. Their occupation required them to be with the flocks, supervising their grazing and growth and protecting them from harm. This responsibility prevented them from being part of the worshiping community. That they would leave their flocks in the hills and go into Bethlehem in search of a newborn was extraordinary. Should anything happen to the sheep while they were gone, they would suffer a financial setback if the flock was theirs, or they would be liable to the owner if the flock belonged to another. The shepherds were most likely poor, and they would be well aware of the risk they were taking.

This did not deter them. They were responding to divine revelation and had received a heavenly directive. Rather than being irresolute they went in haste, leaving behind what gave them the little security they may have enjoyed. These humble shepherds were the first to respond to a divine invitation to leave all for the sake of this child. While it is true that they did return to their flocks, their willingness to initially leave them has religious significance.

When they saw Mary and Joseph and the baby, they understood what the angel had said. What was it that gave them insight? What enabled them to recognize their Messiah and Lord in this unlikely situation? What is it that enables any of us to see traces of the divine in the very ordinary of life? Might it be the openness to God and the willingness to accept the unexpected that provides eyes of faith that can see beyond appearances?

Themselves convinced of the arrival of the long-anticipated Messiah, they proclaimed this to all they met. Such behavior must have compounded the jeopardy into which they had placed themselves. They had not only abandoned their responsibilities and put their own futures at risk, but they were now making incredible claims. The text does not say that those who heard them were convinced by their words. It says that they were astonished. Evangelization does not itself guarantee success.

The shepherds do not seem to have been influenced one way or another by the reactions of others. They return to their flocks praising God. Their lives may have resumed their normal pattern, but the shepherds themselves could not have been the same. They had had a profound religious experience; they had heard and understood a startling religious truth; they had placed this religious truth above their own personal needs and aspirations. These humble, probably uneducated, people had been transformed into believers, and their final response was praise.

The author inserts one sentence that has little to do with the shepherds. Mary reflected on all of this. She is the believer who has already experienced the power of God, and she stands silently before the mystery of what God has done. She treasures these things in respectful contemplation.

Themes of the Day

Traditionally, the Mass at dawn is called the Shepherd's Mass, because the Gospel text recounts the visit of the shepherds. The readings highlight four themes: God's initiative of universal transformation; the profound gratitude that ensues in face of this gift; the life of baptism that is receptive to God's initiative; and solidarity with outcasts as a sacrament of God's presence.

God's Initiative of Universal Transformation

God has taken the first step in our redemption, and the offer of grace is made to all people who can hear and who will embrace the gift. As a season, Christmas is really a time of universal good will. Widespread change seems to occur at Christmas: human hearts appear to soften, and we greet each other with good wishes and cheer. Because we remember the gift of God's love and receive it anew in our hearts, our interactions are transformed.

Left to our own designs, we tend to set limits and to remain caught in the status quo of our lives and our answers. God disrupts the order of life and by a divine undertaking of grace starts something that can impact the universe. The declaration of Christmas is bold: all of this possibility has already been realized; we can already live by the new name of God's compassion and justice. Transformative love comes alive in our midst, in the city where people dwell. The possibility of a new way of life happens now, and the future will usher it in among us. Receptivity is all that is asked of us.

A Matter of Great Gratitude

In response to God's gracious gift of transformation we are invited to rejoice with grateful hearts. The royal infant whose birth we celebrate is the one who was promised, the one who inaugurates the age of transforming grace. The child is in fact the long-awaited messianic king. He is the source of rejoicing in those who receive him with great gratitude. He is recognized by the angels and by the shepherds but not by the power structures of the city. Only those who are open to God's gift can receive it with thanksgiving. When it is received, however, marvelous things happen. Our identities are changed, all the cosmos joins in the festivity, and righteousness blossoms in history.

The Life of Baptism

For Christian believers the life of baptismal fidelity is the grateful response to the gift of God's initiative. This baptismal life is rooted in the mystery of the triune God, the God in whom believers are baptized. It is a life lived in the rebirth of the spirit of God that animates us to live blamelessly, to live in a way that shows our appreciation of this gift, to live lives that are manifestations of holiness.

It is by living such lives that Christians are able to proclaim that God has truly appeared and to become the place of the ongoing appearance of God's gift of transformation. What becomes clear is that this is not our work; it is the work of God, who has come to dwell with us and in whom we find our cause for celebration. The baptismal life is a life of gratitude for the gift we have received, a gift whose fulfillment will be realized by God in the future.

Solidarity with the Poor

While Christmas morning may be a time for opening gifts and for family celebrations, it is also a time when people of means reach out to those who are less fortunate. Christmas celebrates generosity, first the generosity of God and then our generosity with one another, especially with the poor. Solidarity with the outcasts of society, with those who are barred from the power structures of society, is in keeping with the spirit of Christmas.

The birth of the baby is the source of joy for the poor and those who are scandalously forced to the fringes of Bethlehem. The despised shepherds become the privileged ones to whom the message is announced. God's gift finds a place among the outcasts and continues to dwell at home there. It is indeed a Christmas grace to be able to find God there, to rejoice in the gift, and to respond creatively to it. Thus we become the place where shepherds and kings meet in adoration and where the future of God's justice dawns.

The Nativity of the Lord (Mass During the Day)
Isaiah 52:7-10

The proclamation of good news is dramatically portrayed in this passage in several different ways. It begins with a sketch of a messenger running swiftly over the mountains with the message of peace and salvation (v. 7). The focus here is on the feet of the runner, which highlights his speed and determination. They are beautiful feet because of the message of deliverance they carry. There is an excitement in this scene; the message holds such promise. There is an urgency as well; the people to whom the messenger runs have been desolate for so long, waiting for a ray of hope. The content of the message is peace, good news, and salvation. The messenger announces to Zion that its God is king, the one who rules and controls the circumstances of its existence. By implication, this means that the city will be able to partake in the victory of its God.

The first ones to see the runner are the sentinels who stand watch on the walls of the city (v. 8; cf. 40:9). Since a messenger can bring either good news or bad news, from a distance these sentinels cannot be certain of the content of the message. However, their joyful reaction to the approach indicates that it signals not only a proclamation but the very actualization of the message that will be proclaimed. In a way, the coming of the runner is itself the promise to be proclaimed. The people know what the coming of the messenger means, for what they have longed to see now unfolds before their eyes, and they shout for joy. As is so often the case with the prophetic word, its very proclamation brings about the salvation it announces. Seeing the runner and hearing his words of peace and salvation are themselves the good news. With the announcement of peace and salvation, the LORD has indeed returned to the city.

First the sentinels cry out with joy. Then the very ruins of the city are exhorted to break forth in song (vv. 9–10). No longer need they lie destitute, unable to stand with dignity, without the protection of honor. God comforts and redeems the people dwelling within them. The inhabitants are now a renewed people, and so the city itself is renewed. Peace is no longer a hoped-for dream, nor is salvation only a promise for the future. They are now accomplished facts for which to rejoice.

The prophet sketches yet another dynamic picture. In it we see the arm of God bared, revealing the source of the divine power that effected the deliverance which the city now enjoys. This demonstration of strength serves to remind the people of the might of their protector. It also alerts the other nations to the seriousness with which God acts as protector of this people. It is not enough that Zion is rescued. The other nations of the world must see and acknowledge this power. They must recognize both the scope of God's power and the identity of the people who most benefit from it. Just as the messenger heralds peace and salvation to Zion, so the deliverance of the city heralds the mighty power of God to the ends of the earth.

Psalm 98:1, 2-3, 3-4, 5-6

The psalm belongs to the category of enthronement psalms, praising God as king over all (v. 6). It opens with a summons to sing a new song to God (cf. Psalm 96). The reason for this new song is the marvelous new things God has done. The psalmist follows this summons with an enumeration of some of the acts of God (vv. 1b–3).

God is first depicted as a triumphant warrior whose right hand and outstretched arm have brought victory. The victory sketched in these verses seems to have been historical, one that transpired on the stage of Israel's political experience. However, it is not too difficult for a god to defeat human forces. If God is to be acclaimed as king over all, there must be a more comprehensive victory, one that demonstrates preeminence on a cosmic scale. Behind the image of the triumphant warrior is just such an understanding. The divine warrior is the one who conquers the forces of chaos. This is a cosmic victory. These verses do include mention of a sweeping victory (v. 3). Thus it is correct to say that God's triumph is universal and undisputed.

The focus here is on the particularity of Israel's salvation by God. Two aspects of this victory are mentioned. First, the victory, or demonstration of righteousness, is really vindication meted out in order to rectify a previous injustice. Second, the victory follows God's recall of the covenant promises made to the house of Israel. Lovingkindness *(ḥesed)* and faithfulness *(ʾĕmûnâ)* are closely associate with these promises (v. 3). It is important to remember that this particular psalm praises God as king precisely as a triumphant warrior. This implies that either the righteous character of God's rule or its universal scope was challenged. Thus any victory here is really a reestablishment of right order. In other words, it is vindication.

A second important feature of this reading is its statement about the relationship that exists between God's saving action and the promises that God made. The psalmist claims that it was remembrance of the covenantal lovingkindness *(ḥesed)* that prompted God to save Israel. It was because of the promise made to the ancestors that the divine warrior stepped in and triumphed over Israel's enemies. That triumph, which was revealed to all the nations, is the reason for the psalmist's call to praise God in song.

The final verses elaborate on the musical element of the praise. The instrumental directions are quite specific. They could have originated out of an actual enthronement ceremony. Two instruments are explicitly mentioned, the harp and the trumpet. The first was frequently used as accompaniment for singing; the second might really be a reference to the ram's horn, which, like a clarion, announced days and seasons of ritual celebration. Here, as at the foot of Mount Sinai, it announces the coming of the LORD in glory (Exod 19:16).

Hebrews 1:1-6

This confessional hymn celebrates Christ as the agent of revelation, creation, and salvation. It begins with a comparison of the ways that God communicates with humankind. In the past, God spoke to the ancestors through the prophets; in the present, God speaks a definitive word to the believers through God's own Son. Without in any way disparaging the former way, it is clear that the author of this letter considers divine revelation through Christ far superior to the earlier method. The former method of revelation was fragmentary, incomplete. As a reflection of God's glory and an exact representation of God's being, Christ could be called the perfect revelation of God.

The Father-Son language found in most translations of this passage does not appear in the Greek, with the exception of the references included at the end of the reading (vv. 5–6). It is the sense of the overall passage that suggested the translations. Because of the Father-Son covenantal relationship, the Son of God enjoys a position of unrivaled privilege. This Son is the heir of all things and the agent through which the world was made and through which it continues to be sustained. Besides preeminence, this assertion suggests pre-existence.

The description of this relationship between the Son and God borrows elements from two very different yet related Jewish traditions: the monarchy and wisdom. The first originated in the ancient Near Eastern world, where people believed their kings were either human manifestations of the deity or their actual physical offsprings. "Son of God," a royal title usually conferred on the king at the time of his coronation, was understood literally. Such royal ideology was a serious religious threat to Israel, and many within the nation objected to the establishment of the monarchy (cf. 1 Sam 8:1-22). Political circumstances compelled the people to reconsider, and eventually Israel was able to reconcile having a monarchy within a monotheism (cf. 2 Sam 7:8-17). "Son of God" was demythologized, and the title was understood figuratively rather than literally.

Two of the references at the end of the reading (vv. 5–6) belong to this royal tradition. The first comes from an enthronement psalm (Ps 2:7), the second from the Davidic covenant passage (2 Sam 7:14). When this ideology is applied to Christ a very interesting reinterpretation takes place. The title "Son of God" is remythologized and understood literally once again. This is the meaning intended here.

The author also reinterprets the wisdom tradition. There we find that it was through Wisdom that God created (Prov 8:22-31; Wis 9:9), and Wisdom is the pure emanation of the glory of God (Wis 7:25-26). In this tradition the line between Wisdom as creation of God and wisdom as attribute of God cannot always be clearly detected. This very ambiguity lends itself to christological interpretation.

Since the Son is indeed the "Son of God" as well as the wisdom of God, it stands to reason that he would be superior even to the angels. As the agent of salvation, he sits enthroned in the place of greatest honor, at the right hand of God. The author of this letter has used the royal theology of Israel to illustrate his christological faith. Jesus is indeed the Son of God, the wisdom through whom all things came to be and remain.

John 1:1-18

The Gospel of John begins with one of the most profound statements about Jesus found in the entire Second Testament. Its lofty christology is comparable to that found in the reading from Hebrews. Both characterize Christ as pre-existent; both depict Christ as an agent in the creation of the world. The reading itself falls easily into five parts: a description of the role the Word played in the creation of the world (vv. 1–5); a brief sketch of a witness named John (vv. 6–8); an account of the Word's entrance into the world (vv. 9–14); a second report about John (v. 15); an acknowledgment of our participation in Christ's glory (vv. 16–18).

The opening statement, "In the beginning," recalls a comparable statement in Genesis (1:1). This parallel may be the author's way of implying that the coming of the Word into the world is as momentous as was the first creation. The Word is then described in language reminiscent of the figure of Wisdom personified (Prov 8:30; Wis 7:25). Like Wisdom, the Word was actively involved in creation. Unlike Wisdom, the Word is explicitly identified as divine. In a free-flowing manner the author ascribes life-giving power to the Word, life that gives light. The mention of light enables the author to draw one of his many contrasts. This particular contrast is between light and darkness. At times the light is synonymous with life (v. 5a). At other times it represents truth (v. 5b). At still other times the Word is the light (vv. 7–9).

The witness named John is not further identified. However, it is presumed that it is the Baptist, since the words that appear here are later ascribed to him (v. 15; cf. 1:30). There seems to be a definite need to contrast the Word with John. While the Word is the true light that comes into the world, John is merely the witness who testifies to the authenticity (vv. 7–9) and superiority of this light (v. 15). Though designated by God as a witness to the Word (v. 6), John is neither a peer nor a rival of the Word.

Up to this point, only John is clearly a historical person. The Word resides in some primordial place. Now the Word enters into human history, and the next section describes both the incarnation and the rejection by human beings that the Word faced (vv. 9–14). In a third contrast, the author distinguishes between those who were somehow intimately associated with the Word but did not accept him and those who did accept him and thereby became children of God. "His own" may be a reference to other members of the Jewish community. Here ancestry does not make one a child of God; only faith in the Word made flesh can accomplish this.

Several translations state that the Word "made his dwelling among us" (v. 14). A better reading of the Greek might be "tenting," which calls to mind the tabernacle in the wilderness where God dwelt among the people (Exod 40:34) as well as the tradition about Wisdom establishing her tent in the midst of the people (Sir 24:8). The Word of God, who is also the holiness of God and the wisdom of God, now dwells in the midst of humankind. Women and men have been greatly enriched by this divine presence, transformed by the love that first prompted God's revelation and Christ's incarnation.

Themes of the Day

With this set of readings the Christmas celebration gains a new depth of theological meaning. There is progression of insight from the midnight gathering to the assembly that takes place during the daytime hours. At midnight, the birth in history was proclaimed. At dawn, the initiative of God's gift was declared and the baptized community's joyful gratitude was announced. In this third celebration we meditate on the identity of Christ and on our own new way of life in the Word made flesh. Four themes can be identified: salvation takes place before our eyes; salvation is universal; the child is the reflection of God's glory; and it is with eyes of faith that we recognize the Word of God made flesh.

Salvation in Our Midst

If our eyes are open and alert, we can see marvelous things. We can see that God has won a victory for us. The victory is tangible; it is realized in our midst. What kind of victory is it? It is an overwhelming victory, one that conquers the enemy and conquers permanently. Strong military language accents this victory. The power of God brings about a sweeping triumph that is unparalleled. What is conquered is evil itself, the disruptive powers of sin that choke off life and bring unbearable suffering to weak and strong alike. God has won victory for us, and blessed are those who have eyes to see the messenger and ears to hear the glad tidings of triumph. When the victory is experienced, salvation is ours. We can take it in and make it our own. By this victory God is glorified, the past is made right, and there is righteousness for all.

A Universal Salvation

God's victory has a profound impact upon every place, every time, and every people. The birth of the infant, who is a king in David's line, promises salvation to all who long for it. This salvation is a new vision of wisdom, one that has been realized in Christ, who is God's agent of grace in the world. This means that we humans have another chance at living lives of righteousness. We are now able to be forgiven and to forgive. We have been graced with the presence of one who can make a difference in our lives if only we would be attentive to what is in front of us. It is a new world, one of inclusivity and righteous honor. It is a new age, ushered in by the child who is leading a victory procession.

The Glory of the Child-King

Christ is the source and signal of God's universal salvation. The child-king is the reflection of God's glory, and we are in awe of the wonder made known to us. What we need are eyes of faith to see this marvel of God's wisdom, this reflection of God's glory in the fragility of the child of Bethlehem. The clouds of heaven are opened for just a moment, but it is enough time for us to catch a glimpse of the divine character of this mysterious child. He is the exact representation of God; he sits at God's right hand; he is God's Word made flesh.

The Word of God Made Flesh

Ultimately, the eyes of faith allow us to see the fullness of God's revelation. The glory of the infant king is the very presence of God made flesh. Jesus is the eternal incarnate Word who has pitched his tent among us. Ours is not a distant God. Rather, the incarnate wisdom of God is among us, and we are called to a change of heart that will allow us to see this wonder. But something more happens. In this turn of events the participation in the mystery can be so complete that we can know a deep communion in the reality offered to us in Christ. The marvel is that the child who was born among us can be born again and again in those who believe. The divine Word continues to draw close to those who seek to live lives of sincerity and truth. We, too, can be children of light. Grace becomes incarnate in those who believe, for the salvation of God is made flesh in us. The tent of God is pitched wherever salvation is offered, and the ways of evil and death are overturned. All of this takes place right before our eyes.

The Holy Family of Jesus, Mary, and Joseph
Sirach 3:2-6, 12-14

The book of Sirach (or Ecclesiaticus) belongs to ancient Israel's wisdom tradition. Unlike the prophets, who either call the people back to the religious traditions from which they have strayed or console and encourage them to be faithful in the face of overwhelming suffering, the wisdom tradition is a collection of insights gleaned from the successful living of life. It is instruction that provides a glimpse into a way of living that has brought happiness in the past, but it describes it in order to encourage similar behavior that will bring corresponding happiness in the present or future.

The reading for today is instruction about family life, which describes the kind of living that will result in family harmony. Although the teaching originated from a society that was patriarchal (the father is the head) and a perspective that was androcentric (male-centered), it continues to have value for societies that do not share these biased points of view. The focus is the respect and obedience that children (both male and female) owe their parents (both mother and father). Finally, it is presumed that the children are adults, not young children. The final verses (vv. 12–14) make this clear.

In the face of the patriarchal nature of the original society, the admonition to honor one's mother (v. 2) takes on added importance. The parallel construction within which this reference to the mother is found suggests that respect and obedience are due to both parents and not just the dominant father. We should not overlook the fact that the text states that a mother has authority over her sons, and this authority is confirmed by the LORD (v. 2). In the face of the androcentric bias found in the text, this point is significant.

True to the character of wisdom instruction, Sirach lists the blessings that follow such a way of life. The dutiful child is promised life itself (vv. 1, 6), remission of sins (vv. 3, 14), riches (v. 4), the blessing of children (v. 5a), and the answer to prayer (vv. 5, 6).

The final verses exhort the adult son to care for his father in his declining years. The picture portrayed is moving. The weakness of the elder is contrasted with the strength of the son, who presumably is at the height of his own powers (v. 13b). This son is told not to use his strength against his frail, elderly father but rather to use it for the older man's benefit. This should be the case whether the father's infirmity is physical or mental. There is no mention of caring for his mother in the same way. This may be because in patriarchal societies it was presumed that women would be cared for by their fathers or brothers, then by their husbands, and finally by their sons. The head of the family was normally not so vulnerable as to be in need of care. At issue is not a question about which parent needs care but an admonition to give it where needed.

Finally, the entire teaching about respect for parents, from the commandment (cf. Exod 20:12; Deut 5:16) to this admonition in Sirach, takes on a completely different perspective when we remember that this is addressed to an adult child and the responsibilities of respect and obedience are those of offspring who are mature.

Psalm 128:1-2, 3, 4-5

This psalm is classified as a wisdom psalm. It is clearly descriptive instruction that teaches, rather than an address directed to God in praise or thanksgiving. The psalm contains some of the themes and vocabulary associated with the wisdom tradition, examples of which include reward and punishment; happy, or blessed; ways, or path. It begins with a macarism (v. 1), which is a formal statement that designates a person or group as happy (or blessed). This statement includes mention of the characteristic that is the basis of the happiness and then describes the blessings that flow from that characteristic. In this psalm those called happy are the ones who fear the LORD, who walk in God's ways (vv. 1, 4), and the blessing that flows from this attitude of mind and heart is a life of prosperity (vv. 2–3).

In the wisdom tradition fear of the LORD is the distinguishing characteristic of the righteous person. It denotes profound awe and amazement before the tremendous marvels of God. While this may include some degree of terror, it is the kind of fear that accompanies wonder at something amazing rather than dread in the face of mistreatment. The one who fears the LORD is one who acknowledges God's sovereignty and power and who lives in accord with the order established by God. If anyone is to be happy and enjoy the blessings of life, it is the one who fears the LORD.

The blessings promised here are both material good fortune and a large and extended family. Large families, like vast fields, were signs of fertility and prosperity. They not only provided companionship through life and partnership in labor, they were also assurances of protection in a hostile world. The promise of future generations guaranteed perpetuity for the family; its bloodline and its name would survive death and would endure into the next generation. Although the androcentric bias in the psalm is seen in its reference to the fruitful wife and numerous children (the Hebrew reads "sons"), the concern is really with the family as a cohesive and abiding unit.

The last verses of the psalm redirect the focus from the good fortune of the individual to the blessings enjoyed by the nation. Mention of Zion, Jerusalem, and Israel are indications of this. The blessings come from God, but God resides at the heart of the nation in Jerusalem, the city of Zion (v. 5). The good fortune of the individual is really a share in the good fortune of the nation.

And all of these blessings are the result of right relationship with God. The psalm begins and ends on the same note: Blessed are those who fear the LORD.

Colossians 3:12-21

An exhortation to virtuous living is introduced by the reasons for such a manner of life. Because the Christians are God's chosen ones, holy and beloved, they should act accordingly. This moving characterization is followed by a very demanding program of behavior. The notion of clothing oneself with virtue does not suggest that such behavior is superficial or merely outward show. It refers to the practice of wearing a uniform of some kind that readily identifies the role one plays in society. Christians are to be recognized on sight by their manner of living.

The virtues themselves (vv. 12–15) are all relational. They are directed toward others, requiring unselfish sensitivity. They may demand great sacrifice. This is especially true about bearing with the annoying, even repugnant behavior of others and forgiving them when they have been offensive. The motivation for such self-sacrifice is the forgiveness that the Christians have received from God. The list continues with an admonition to love, the highest of all virtues. The peace of Christ, which is placed before them, should not be confused with mere tolerance or control imposed from some outside force. It is an inner peace that comes from a right relationship with God and, therefore, from true harmony with others.

The author seems to provide directives for some kind of communal practice. The Christians are urged to open themselves to the transforming power of the word of Christ, to instruct and advise each other, to join in praising God through psalms and other religious songs. All of this might take place during some kind of liturgical event, or it could be a part of everyday life. Whichever the case, the virtues that are fostered and the manner of living that is encouraged are all communal.

The final directives (vv. 18–21) reflect the household codes that were prevalent in the Greco-Roman world of the time (cf. Eph 5:22-29). This was a patriarchal world where the men who headed the families exercised total control over their wives, their children, and their slaves. There certainly must have been mutual concern within the families themselves, but it was not mandated by law. The heads of households held the lives of the members in their hands, to do with them what they deemed fit. In such a social context, the admonitions found in this passage are quite revolutionary.

While the author still insists that wives must be subject to their husbands, he instructs the husbands to act toward them with love and thoughtfulness. Children are still told to obey their parents, but fathers are advised to be moderate in the training of their children lest discipline become oppressive. The Christian virtues listed at the beginning of the reading, when practiced within the context of the family, appear to have transformed the patriarchal social customs of the day. What is emphasized in this Christian household code is not patriarchal privilege but male responsibility in the familial relationships. This means that in Christ, the relationships between man and woman and child have been radically altered.

Luke 2:22-40

This account of the presentation of Jesus in the temple is a celebration of piety, that of Mary and Joseph, of Simeon, and of Anna. It is clear that Jesus was raised in an observant family. Five times the author declares that the parents of Jesus conformed to the ritual prescriptions of the law (vv. 22, 23, 24, 27, 39). Just as they had complied with the imperial decree to be enrolled in the census (2:1-5), so now they observe the religious requirements of purification (cf. Lev 12:1-8) and redemption of the firstborn (cf. Exod 13:2, 12).

The first ritual requirement sprang from the belief that the life-power within blood was sacred and belonged to God. Because of the mysterious nature of its power, it was to be kept separate from the secular activities of life.

When separation was not possible, the people and the objects that came in contact with the blood had to be purified. It is obvious why birth and death were surrounded with many purification regulations. The second ritual requirement was a way of reclaiming the firstborn male child, who, they believed, really belonged to God. Buying back the child was a way of acknowledging God's initial claim.

Simeon, like the prophets of ancient Israel, had the Spirit upon him (cf. Isa 61:1). Three times the author states that it was the Holy Spirit that directed him (vv. 25, 26, 27). The consolation of Israel for which he waited was probably the time of messianic fulfillment. Seeing the child, he recognized him as the object of his longing, the one who was both the glory of Israel and the light to the rest of the world. He also predicted the opposition that Jesus would inspire. Some would accept him and others would not.

This latter scene must have taken place in an outer court of the temple where women were allowed, for Simeon then explicitly addressed Mary. This was very unusual behavior, for typically men did not speak to women with whom they were unfamiliar, especially in public. His words are somewhat enigmatic. It is clear why the rejection of her son would be like a sword in Mary's heart, but what this might have to do with the thoughts of others is not as obvious.

Another woman joins the group, Anna the prophetess. She is old and a widow, constantly in the temple praying and fasting. Like Simeon's, her entire life has been an advent awaiting the fulfillment of messianic promises. She probably witnessed the meeting with Simeon, hearing what he said, for she is convinced of the identity of the child and she proclaims this to all those who have cherished messianic hopes.

Though neither Simeon nor Anna belong to the ranks of formal temple personnel, they are the ones who recognize the divine child, while the others do not. This should not be seen as an anti-Judaic bias. It points to the fact that religious insight comes from fidelity and genuine devotion rather than official status or privileged role. God and the ways of God are revealed to those who have open minds and open hearts. The piety of this man (v. 25) and this woman (v. 37) dispose them to the unexpected revelation of God.

The family returns to Nazareth to resume its unpretentious life, but it is not the same. Even though the child grows up like other children, he is merely waiting for his time to come.

Themes of the Day

In an era when so much talk is devoted to the discussion of family values, the readings for this feast contribute several insights to the conversation. Three themes are particularly evident: the newness of relationships that comes about in Christ; the respect that adult children owe their parents; the need to honor the wisdom of the elderly within the community.

In Christ All Relationships Are Made New

Parallels can be drawn between cultural codes of behavior and the kinds of relationships that are to be fostered within the Church, the household of God. In fact, the cultural mores can be reinterpreted through the lens of Christian teaching. Relationships in both the family and the Church are made new because of the experience of Christ. Those who believe in Christ, while still adhering to certain cultural codes of conduct, are asked to consider new and ever more balanced ways of relating in view of their lives as Christians. This is true for all relationships: parent and child, husband and wife, brother and sister. In Christ all must be embraced as equal members of the household of God.

Adult Children and Their Parents

The importance of family loyalty is announced and celebrated. The internal cohesion of the family, though largely spoken of in terms of the patriarchal bias and structures of the times, is seen as nourishing all the members and the family system itself. While it is important that children of all ages honor their parents, this is an exhortation to adult children to respect and honor their aging parents. Such a caring relationship is vital in an age of mobility, nursing homes, and the lack of extended families to broker the needs of their aging members. No easy solution is available; however, the point is clear. From God's perspective, loving care of aged members is non-negotiable. It is a family virtue that is to be kept sacred.

The Wisdom of the Elderly

Wisdom comes with time and experience. It is religious fidelity to God and to the ways of the covenant. Such wisdom is a source of blessing for the community. It provides insight and a perspective that allows the community to know the mystery and the presence of God. When the wisdom of the elderly is respected, the young are enriched by the stories of the past. The wisdom figures can point the community to places where God is working and where the divine can be found. It is their respect for tradition that allows the elderly to speak prophetic words that can change the course of the future and inspire noble deeds of courage in the face of great pain. In reverencing the elderly and their wisdom, the community of believers receive Christ.

Optional Readings for the Holy Family of Jesus, Mary, and Joseph
Genesis 15:1-6; 21:1-3

The reading consists of two short episodes. The first recounts the promise of an heir; the second reports the fulfillment of that promise. In the first episode God makes a promise to which Abram protests. God then responds to the protest with a second promise, and Abram accepts God's words. The second episode has no specific structure, but there are words that link it to the first.

The opening phrase of this reading, "the word of the LORD came to Abram," is a technical expression for prophetic revelation. That the message was conveyed during a night vision strengthens the revelatory importance of the message. Any kind of supernatural experience can be terrifying, and so the first words of the revelation are words of reassurance: "Fear not" (cf. Gen 26:24; Isa 40:9; Jer 30:10). This reassurance is further expressed in God's initial twofold promise of protection and reward.

Although the Hebrew of verse 2 makes translation difficult, the meaning of the verse is clear. Regardless of the nature and measure of the rewards that God might bestow upon Abram, they will be of little value, since Abram is childless. What is deplorable for Abram is his lack of an heir, someone who will carry on his name and ensure that after his death his land and other assets will be kept within his family. This does not mean that Abram does not value children as blessings in themselves. It means that without an heir the future of his family is in jeopardy. In the face of this, Abram is prepared to adopt one of his servants (Eliezar, whose name means "God is my help").

God dispels Abram's consternation with a second prophetic pronouncement: Abram will have an heir of his own, and not only one but as many as there are stars in the night sky. However, despite the wonderful promises made by God, namely, protection, reward, and now posterity, in this reading Abram receives no assurance that these promises will be fulfilled. It is no wonder he has questions!

The second episode in this reading indicates that the reason for Abram's initial questioning is his advanced age. In this reading there are no mighty signs; there is only God's word and the star-studded sky. Yet in the face of what he perceives as a natural obstacle, he believes, and his faith is credited to him as righteousness. Since faith and righteousness both refer to one's relationship with God, it is clear that Abram is in right relationship with God.

The second episode is linked with the first by vocabulary: said and promised (21:1). What God said came about; what God promised was fulfilled. Abraham had been faithful to God; God was now faithful to Abraham (this new name means "father of many" cf. 17:5). Several features highlight the exceptional nature of this birth. First, it was announced through divine revelation during a night vision (15:1, 4). Second, it occurred despite Abraham's advanced age (21:2) and initial incredulity (15:2). Finally, the child was named Isaac, which means "he laughed." Who laughed? Was it the incredulous Abram (cf. 17:17)? Or was it the God who makes incredible promises and then fulfills them?

Psalm 105:1-2, 3-4, 6-7, 8-9

The responsorial psalm is a call to thanksgiving and praise. In the first six verses the verbs are all in the imperative form. The very first verse contains the three most important themes of this entire section: give thanks; invoke; make known. It is the wondrous deeds of the LORD that prompt such response. Believers are summoned to give thanks for them and to proclaim them to all people. They are to call on the name of the LORD, not in petition but in praise. The summons to sing (v. 2) indicates the liturgical dimension of this praise. The psalmist is calling the entire community publicly to praise and thank God for God's goodness toward them, and to spread the word of this goodness to others.

Two very significant themes are found in the second stanza: God's holy name and God's face. In the ancient world a name was not only a way of distinguishing one person from another, it often described part of the very essence of the person. Names had great power, depending upon the power possessed by the bearer of the name. Because God is holy, God's name is holy. Therefore to praise and give glory to God's name is to praise and give glory to God. One's face or countenance is frequently regarded as a reflection of one's interior. For this reason, the phrase becomes a reference to the entire person. Thus to seek the face of God is to seek God's presence.

The mention of Abraham, Isaac, and Jacob calls to mind the promises made concerning offspring (Gen 15:4-5; 26:23; 35:12). The wonderful deeds for which the believers are to give thanks and praise and witness are the fulfillment of these promises. The descendants of Abraham, Isaac, and Jacob to whom the psalmist speaks are themselves the proof of God's faithfulness to the ancestors. They are the ones who are being called to seek God's presence and to be faithful. The LORD is not only the God of the ancestors but their own God as well. In fact, God's judgments *(mishpāt)*, or governance, extends throughout the earth. The word also means "justice," and so it not only states God's universal authority but it also describes the preeminent quality of righteousness with which God's authority is exercised over all.

God cut a covenant with Abram (Gen 15:17) and thereby assumed certain obligations, the fulfillment of certain promises. These included the promise of descendants, the promise of land, and the promise to be the patron-god of the people. Eventually the notion of covenant evolved into an understanding of mutual obligations, but here it seems to be a free gift from God, a gift that God will never forget, that will be binding generation after generation.

We can now see more clearly the reasons to be thankful. God's magnanimous generosity gives us a glimpse into God's holiness, and we can better appreciate the call to praise God's holy name. We can understand why we should seek God's face, God's presence, so that we too can live securely under God's governance. Today we are the beneficiaries of God's promises, we are the descendants of Abraham and Isaac and Jacob, who have been invited into covenant with this gracious God.

Hebrews 11:8, 11-12, 17-19

Although the reading extols three of Israel's earliest ancestors, namely, Abraham, Sarah, and Isaac, the principal focus of attention is on the faith of Abraham. Three different incidents from his story are retold in such a way as to highlight this faith.

The first incident retells the account that begins the ancient Abraham tradition (cf. Gen 12:1). Abraham was called by God to leave the home of his father and to go to a land that God would show him, a land he would receive as one receives an inheritance. This land would be Abraham's by right, but only because of the generosity of the one who really possesses the land, not because Abraham had in any way earned it. The original story says nothing about faith or obedience, while this version is riveted on these two themes and declares that it was precisely because of his faith that Abraham obeyed. Here faith has less to do with the content of religious belief than with the trusting attitude toward God that enables belief. Abraham left the familiarity of one land for the uncertainty of another because of his faith in God.

At the time of the conception of Isaac, Abraham's faith became apparent a second time. Both he and Sarah were beyond their childbearing years, yet he believed that the impossible was possible with God, that Abraham would have not only one heir, but heirs beyond counting (cf. Gen 15:5; 22:17). God had promised that this man, whose generative powers were "as good as dead," would produce numerous descendants. Abraham's faith is rooted not so much in God's power as in the promise God had made, and because of this faith he received generative powers.

Finally, and definitively, Abraham's faith is manifested in his willingness to respond to God's further testing of his utter trust in God and to sacrifice his only son, Isaac. The foreseeable consequences of his conformity to this testing (*peirázō*, v. 17) are shattering. Isaac is the child through whom descendants will continue. To sacrifice him is to nullify God's initial promise and to forfeit his (Abraham's) future and the future of his household. Just as his faith led him to leave the blessings of his past (v. 8), so his faith leads him to relinquish the possibilities of his future.

The word "offered" *(prosphérō)* appears twice in one verse (v. 17). The first verb is in the perfect tense, denoting a completed action; the second is imperfect, indicating that the sacrifice was never really made. Even though Isaac was not actually sacrificed, the text says that Abraham did indeed offer up his son. Once again, his faith is based on God's ability to bring life where there is no life. Could not a God who brought life through a man who was as good as dead raise someone who was really dead? Believing that God could bring about the first marvel enabled Abraham to believe that God could also accomplish the second. The author states that Abraham's receiving Isaac back is a symbol. But a symbol of what? Does this refer to the eventual resurrection of all? This may well be the reference, but the text is not clear.

Luke 2:22-40

This account of the presentation of Jesus in the temple is a celebration of piety, that of Mary and Joseph, of Simeon, and of Anna. It is clear that Jesus was raised in an observant family. Five times the author declares that the parents of Jesus conformed to the ritual prescriptions of the law (vv. 22, 23, 24, 27, 39). Just as they had complied with the imperial decree to be enrolled in the census (2:1-5), so now they observe the religious requirements of purification (cf. Lev 12:1-8) and redemption of the firstborn (cf. Exod 13:2, 12).

The first ritual requirement sprang from the belief that the life-power within blood was sacred and belonged to God. Because of the mysterious nature of its power, it was to be kept separate from the secular activities of life. When separation was not possible, the people and the objects that came in contact with the blood had to be purified. It is obvious why birth and death were surrounded with many purification regulations. The second ritual requirement was a way of reclaiming the firstborn male child, who, they believed, really belonged to God. Buying back the child was a way of acknowledging God's prior claim.

Simeon, like the prophets of ancient Israel, had the Spirit upon him (cf. Isa 61:1). Three times the author states that it was the Holy Spirit that directed him (vv. 25, 26, 27). The consolation of Israel for which he waited was probably the time of messianic fulfillment. Seeing the child, he recognized him as the object of his longing, the one who was both the glory of Israel and the light to the rest of the world. He also predicted the opposition that Jesus would inspire. Some would accept him and others would not.

This latter scene must have taken place in an outer court of the temple where women were allowed, for Simeon then explicitly addressed Mary. This was very unusual behavior, for typically men did not speak to women with whom they were unfamiliar, especially in public. His words are somewhat enigmatic. It is clear why the rejection of her son would be like a sword in Mary's heart, but what this might have to do with the thoughts of others is not as obvious.

Another woman joins the group, Anna the prophetess. She is old and a widow, constantly in the temple praying and fasting. Like Simeon's, her entire life has been an advent awaiting the fulfillment of messianic promises. She probably witnessed the meeting with Simeon, hearing what he said, for she is convinced of the identity of the child and she proclaims this to all those who have cherished messianic hopes.

Though neither Simeon nor Anna belong to the ranks of formal temple personnel, they are the ones who recognize the divine child while the others do not. This should not be seen as an anti-Judaic bias. It points to the fact that religious insight comes from fidelity and genuine devotion rather than official status or privileged role. God and the ways of God are revealed to those who have open minds and open hearts. The piety of this man (v. 25) and this woman (v. 37) dispose them to the unexpected revelation of God.

The family returns to Nazareth to resume its unpretentious life, but it is not the same. Even though the child grows up like other children, he is merely waiting for his time to come.

Themes of the Day

Once again the feast and the readings focus our attention on true family values. Three are particularly evident in these readings: God's impossible promises; trust in God, and true family values.

God's Impossible Promises

God promises an heir to a couple that cannot produce a child, and when the promise is fulfilled and the child is born, God asks for the life of that child. The future of the family rests on the shoulders of this heir. Neither the name of the family nor its inheritance will survive without someone to carry them into the future. The impossibility of God's demands is overwhelming. The hopes that were kindled by the promise and that blazed brilliantly with the child's birth now lie like ashes on a heap. Is God reneging on the promise of a descendant? Is God playing with people's dreams and aspirations? Or could it be that God is preparing them for yet another marvel? If once before God could bring life out of what could not bear life, might God be planning something marvelous once again? Is the God of surprises ready to reveal a new surprise?

Trust in God

The couple had placed their trust in God's initial promise, and it was fulfilled. Now Abraham, as the representative of the entire family, is asked to hope against hope, to relinquish the one in whom all the hopes of the future rest. Trust operates on different levels. The first is the level on which the promises are made. There one looks for the realization of what has been pledged. On a second and deeper level one trusts not so much in the promise as in the one who makes the promise. Here the impossibility of what has been pledged can be overlooked because of the reliability of the promise-maker.

Our God is a God of surprises, of the paradoxical, of the preposterous. This is a God who opens closed wombs, who rescinds death sentences, who takes an obscure child and makes him the light to the nations. Trust in such a God requires that we sacrifice our own presuppositions so that in expecting nothing from God we are open to everything. If our faith in God is to stay alive, the vision of the promise will always elude us. It has to be greater than our grasp, because once we think we have it, it ceases to be alive and dynamic.

True Family Values

Children are both the guardians of the past and the promise of the future. To them we entrust our traditions, our family customs, the obligations of our faith. Through them the dreams that we dream take forms that we never envisioned.

The wisdom of the elderly can see what is incredible. The years they have lived have taught them that miracles do happen. Their weathered faith enables them to recognize the face of God even in the unexpected. Living in the presence of God, they can open themselves to receive God's gifts. They have learned to allow the promise to overtake them.

In the face of all this mystery the human heart can only sing with gratitude. We live in the presence of God, and this sustains us through whatever seems impossible. Thanksgiving opens us to receive God's promise and God's gifts.

January 1, Solemnity of the Blessed Virgin Mary, Mother of God
Numbers 6:22-27

The blessing found in this reading may be one of the oldest pieces of poetry in the Bible. It is introduced by a statement that gives the content of the blessing both Mosaic and divine legitimation. Although it is the priests who ultimately bless the people, it is Moses who receives the blessing from God and who delivers it to Aaron and his sons (vv. 22–23). These are examples of mediatorial roles, one played by Moses and another by Aaron and the priests.

YHWH, the personal name of God, is repeated three times in the blessing (vv. 24–26). There is some question about the actual use of this blessing, since there is a tradition standing to this day that forbids the use of the personal name of God. People believed that a name possessed some of the very identity of the person named. To know someone's name was to possess intimate knowledge of and to enjoy some form of control over that person. To know and use God's name presumes this kind of intimacy and control. In order to guard against such presumption, some other word or title was pronounced in place of God's name. According to the *Mishnah,* an ancient collection of Jewish law that dates back to about the third century of the common era, God's personal name was pronounced only when the blessing was used in the temple. Whatever the case may be, the power of the personal name of God cannot be denied.

The blessing itself is crisp and direct. It is addressed to "you," a singular pronoun that can refer to an individual or to the entire nation understood as one. Each line invokes a personal action from God: to bless with good fortune and to keep from harm; to look favorably toward and to be gracious; to look upon and to grant peace. Actually there is very little difference in the petitions. They all ask for the same reality, that is, the blessings that make life worth living. This could mean different things to different people at different times, but basically they are asking for peace. Peace is the fundamental characteristic of Jewish blessing, the condition of absolute well being.

The reading opens with God giving directions to Moses. It closes with a final word from God. The priests are told to invoke God's name on the Israelites. The Hebrew would be better read, "put my name" on them. This evokes the image of placing one's name on property in order to certify ownership. The priests are instructed to put God's name on the Israelites, indicating that they belong to God and that God will certainly bless them.

Psalm 67:2-3, 5, 6, 8

The verb forms in this psalm make it difficult to categorize. Some commentators believe the verbs are in past tense, and they classify the psalm as a prayer of thanksgiving for blessings already received. Others consider them a form of wish or bidding prayer, a moderate request for blessings not yet enjoyed. However the verbs are read, it is safe to consider the psalm as a prayer of blessing.

The psalm begins with a slight adaptation of the first words of the blessing used by Aaron and the priests who descended from him (v. 2; cf. Num 6:24-26).

This use of this Aaronic blessing in a congregational prayer suggests that the favors once promised to that particular priestly family are now sought for the entire people. The metaphor of God's shining face refers to the favorable disposition that a smiling countenance reflects. The psalmist asks that God look favorably upon the people, that God be benevolent toward them.

God's goodness toward this people will redound to God's reputation among other nations. They will see the people's good fortune and will interpret it as the fruit of God's saving power on their behalf and God's continued rule over them. These other nations will conclude that only a mighty and magnanimous God would be able to secure such good fortune. Here prosperity is not used as leverage against others. Quite the contrary, it benefits even those who may not be enjoying it. It does this because it is perceived as coming from God and not merely as the product of human exploits or ingenuity.

The psalm moves from an acknowledgment of divine rule over one people (v. 3) to an announcement of universal divine governance (v. 5). All nations will not only rejoice over God's goodness, they will also be guided by that same God, and ultimately they will praise that God (v. 6, 8). In other words, the good fortune of one nation is testimony to salvific activity of God. This in turn becomes the occasion of salvation for all the earth. One nation is the source of blessing for all. This is the fulfillment of a promise made to Abraham (cf. Gen 12:2-3).

The psalm ends with a prayer for continued universal blessing. It is the past tense of the verb in this verse that has led some commentators to conclude that all of the blessings referred to earlier were also bestowed and enjoyed in the past. They maintain that the plea here is that God continue to bless the people so that all nations will continue to revere God. Whether past or future, the psalmist believes that all good fortune comes from God. Others see this and praise God, and in this way God is made known to all the earth.

Galatians 4:4-7

The mission of Christ to the world is the major focus of Paul's teaching in the verses that make up this reading. The designated time refers to that time in history when God brought the messianic expectations to fulfillment by sending his Son into the world. The word for "send" *(apostéllō)* carries the idea of authorization, as in the case of an envoy. The primary stress of this verb is less on the actual sending than on the commission, especially when it is God who sends. This passage, then, is concerned with the mission entrusted to Christ by God. Referring to Christ as God's Son establishes his divine nature; acknowledging that he was born of a woman establishes his human nature. The christology in this passage is rich and complex.

According to Paul, the goal of Christ's mission was to transform the Galatians from being slaves under the law to being adopted sons of God. Normally, in patriarchal societies only male offspring can inherit. Since legal status is the primary focus of this passage, the androcentric bias here becomes obvious. In a more egalitarian society the fundamental message of change of status, while inclusive, would remain basically the same.

Paul is here setting up the contrast between servitude under the law and freedom in Christ. In order to do this he uses a social custom of his day. If an heir was too young to claim inheritance, a legal guardian was appointed until the heir came of age. Paul compares the believers to underage minors, who, until the designated time had come, could not claim what might be rightfully theirs. The law acted as legal guardian. All of this changes with the coming of Christ. Christians are no longer minors bound to the tutelage of the law. They are legal heirs, adopted children because Christ is the only true Son. Does anyone need proof of this? The very fact that they are filled with the Spirit of Christ and dare to call God by the intimate term "Abba" should be evidence enough.

Paul's attitude toward the law is not as negative as it appears to be elsewhere (cf. Rom 7:7-24). Here it is a necessary guardian that carefully watches over minors until they are mature enough to take care of themselves. It is binding in order to teach; it restricts in order to instruct. Though it is inferior to the Spirit of Christ, it is faithful and trustworthy. However, once the Spirit takes hold of the believer, dependence on the law ends and freedom in the Spirit, the rightful inheritance of the children of God, begins.

The reading ends as it began, declaring that all of this is God's doing according to God's plan. God sent the Son to make sons and daughters of the rest of us. This is accomplished by means of the indwelling of the Spirit, which empowers us to call God "Abba," tender Father.

Luke 2:16-21

This reading for the feast of the Solemnity of Mary is essentially the same as that of the Christmas Mass at Dawn. However, these verses include mention of the circumcision and naming of Jesus. Although this is a slight difference, the addition shifts the focus of the passage away from the shepherds to the child and his parents. First, the sight of this lowly family opened the eyes of the shepherds so they could understand the meaning of the message announced by the angels. Then, Mary took all these mysterious events into her heart and there pondered their meaning. Finally, Mary and Joseph arranged for the child to be circumcised and named.

Circumcision was the ritual that initiated the males into the community of Israel. It was enjoined by God on Abraham and all his descendants, and from that time forward it was considered a sign of the covenant (Gen 17:9-11). As observant Jews, Mary and Joseph fulfilled all the prescriptions of the law, seeing that the child was circumcised as custom dictated.

In addition to being circumcised, the child was named. When the angel appeared to Mary and announced that she had been chosen to be the mother of the long awaited one, the angel also told her that the child would be named Jesus (1:31), which means "savior" (cf. Matt 1:21). Now almost everything that the angel had announced has come to pass. Mary will have to wait to see how he will acquire the throne of his father David and rule the house of Jacob forever (cf. 1:32f.).

Themes of the Day

Liturgically, the Octave of Christmas commemorates several celebrations: the Solemnity of the Mother of God; the day designated for prayers for global peace; the beginning of the new year. The Lectionary contains a variety of themes that resonate with these celebrations. The major themes are, first, the person of Mary as the example of faith and contemplation and, second, the blessing of peace for the new year.

Mary

The Gospel story, with the addition of the mention of the circumcision and naming of Jesus, is the same passage that was read for the celebration of the Christmas Mass During the Day. Placed within the context of the Solemnity of the Mother of God, however, the reading has a different emphasis. Here Mary is the focus, not the child. Although the shepherds are depicted as gaining insight into the presence of God by seeing this holy family, it is Mary who is described as holding all these things in her heart. She is the one who ponders the significance of these events.

By her willingness to hold all things in her heart, Mary becomes to Christians an inspiration of contemplation and reflection. She inspires us to consider deeply the significance of events rather than to go blandly through life without meaning or direction. She inspires us to constant reflection on the truths of the faith that continue to be made real in life's experiences. She inspires us to fidelity to the practices of our faith, practices which are the disciplines of souls that lead the community to a clearer focus on God's presence in human affairs.

Blessings and Prayers for Peace in the New Year

The theme of peace appears on many levels; its meaning, "fullness of life," bursts forth in every reading for today. The ancient prayer/blessing of peace is an appropriate start for the new year. In personal affairs and family concerns, in community and world organizations, peace is at a premium. We long for it, we pray for it. When God blesses us with peace, hearts are stilled and souls are at rest. This blessing of peace resonates well with the angels' wish for people of good will. The beginning of a new year is a good time to reach out to others and to pray for God's blessing of peace for each dimension of human encounter.

Peace is also our inheritance in Christ. As adopted children of God, we have been given the freedom to live in a godly manner, calling God our Abba. If we are resolved to live this new identity, we will be granted the freedom of heart that shows itself in works of peace and justice. Right relationships in the covenant activity of God are the pathways of peace. Our commitment to respond to God's initiatives in Christ and our willingness to be a new creation are solid new year's resolutions for all who are interested in peace on earth.

Second Sunday After Christmas
Sirach 24:1-2, 8-12

In many ways this reading from Sirach resembles a poem found in the book of Proverbs (8:22-31). The characterization is quite interesting. First, Wisdom is personified as a woman. This is quite significant when we remember the high regard within which wisdom was held. Second, she is not dependent on another to pay her homage. She sings her own praises, and she does this publicly, both before her own people and in the midst of the very court of God. From the outset it is clear that this Woman Wisdom is no ordinary being. She is revered both on earth and in the heavens.

As a creature of God, Wisdom's glory is really derived from the excellence of her creation. It is this that she praises, and she does so among her people and within the divine court. It is unusual that a woman, even Woman Wisdom, should be granted admission to the court of God and be allowed to speak about anything, much less herself, before the high God and the hosts or courtiers of God. The origin and identity of this mysterious woman has challenged commentators from the beginning. The image has been interpreted in various ways. Some believe she was originally an ancient Israelite goddess. However, as Israel developed a monotheistic faith, she lost her divine prerogatives.

Other commentators consider Woman Wisdom a personification of a divine attribute. In this view she is not an independent deity but a characteristic of God. Although she is a creature of God, she enjoys extraordinary privileges. She exists before anything else has been created, and she does not seem to face death or destruction. The ambiguity of the text does not provide a definite explanation of this mysterious figure.

This reading from Sirach adds an element not found in earlier portraits of Woman Wisdom. It states that although she was free to roam throughout the universe, she was in search of a dwelling place for herself, a place where she would be able to rest. Her role in creation seems to have provided her some measure of universal influence, and so she could have decided on almost any place. However, it was the Creator-God who determined where she would abide, and God decided that it would be in Israel that she would dwell (vv. 8–12).

Deciding the proper place for Woman Wisdom to settle was not a divine afterthought. It seems to have been part of primordial creation itself. One can conclude from this that the establishment of cosmic Wisdom in the midst of Israel, decreed as it was at the primordial event, is here seen as part of the very structure of the created cosmos. Wisdom was there from the beginning, ministering to God but waiting to be revealed in a special way to the children of Israel. Once she was revealed to this people, she is exalted and admired, she is praised and blessed.

Psalm 147:12-13, 14-15, 19-20

The passage is from the final stanza of a hymn of praise of God. It highlights God's protection of and solicitude toward the people of Israel. Both Jerusalem, the capital of the nation, and Zion, the mount upon which the city was built, came to represent the people. They are called upon directly to praise God (v. 12). This summons is followed by a listing of some of the many wonderful works of God that elicit such praise. All of them point to the uniqueness of the bond that holds God and this people together.

God protects the people by fortifying the city. The ancient practice of building walls around cities provided them with a defense against possible attack and gave them a vantage point from which to observe the activity outside the walls (v. 13a). As strong as these walls might have been, the gates of the city put it in jeopardy, for they had to provide entrance for the normal traffic of the city, for travelers and traders, for those who farmed outside the walls. The city was somewhat vulnerable at its gates. The psalmist calls the people to praise God, who has strengthened them precisely at this their most vulnerable spot (v. 13).

Walls also act as borders. They define the limits of personal property and they determine the sweep of the city. Protected as they are, the people of Jerusalem/Zion are truly blessed. They can go about their daily lives with a sense of security, for the fortification provided by God has assured them of peace (v. 14).

Furthermore, this peace has enabled them to prosper, since they do not have to invest time or resources in defense measures.

Prosperity is symbolized by the wheat, which is abundant and is of the finest quality. Both of these characteristics represent the blessing bestowed by God. The abundance suggests either expansive fields that were never ravaged by wild animals or invading enemies, or else an extraordinary yield from a smaller plot of land. In either case the people would consider themselves singularly blessed by God. The exceptional quality of the wheat demonstrates the fertility of the land. Again, this is land that has been spared the despoiling that usually accompanies war. This is a land that has known peace.

The psalmist paints a dynamic picture of the powerful word of God. It is like an emissary who runs swiftly throughout the earth, both proclaiming and bringing about what has been proclaimed. God speaks, and it is accomplished. God promises to protect and to provide for the people, and it is done.

This same powerful word is spoken to Israel, but with a different emphasis and with different consequences (vv. 19–20). It is God's special word, God's law, the law of life that will ensure God's continued protection and care. Just as Jerusalem/Zion (the people) is singled out for special consideration, here Jacob/Israel (the nation) is chosen for a unique relationship. No other nation has been so blessed. No other nation has been given God's law of life. This is the people of God. This privilege is the reason to praise God.

Ephesians 1:3-6, 15-18

The reading opens with a benediction (vv. 3–6), a common way to open letters as well as prayers (cf. 1 Kgs 5:7; 2 Cor 1:3-11). It also serves as a solemn, courtly form of congratulation (Ruth 4:14). This benediction blesses God who has blessed us with "every spiritual blessing." As is always the case in Christian theology, the blessing of God comes to us through the agency of Christ. This agency is important enough to be mentioned in every verse of the benediction.

The blessings themselves are distinctively of a spiritual, even cosmic nature. First is election in Christ. The theme of election has its origins in the Jewish tradition (Exod 19:5-6; Deut 14:2). What is unique here is the idea of primordial predestination. Predestination refers to that act whereby God's love, from all eternity, determines salvation in Christ. Although the author is writing to specific individuals, there is no sense here that some are predestined for salvation and others are not. The point is that salvation in Christ is not an afterthought; it was in God's plan from the beginning.

The believers were not chosen *because* they were holy and blameless but *that they might be* holy and blameless. Once again it is clear that salvation is the cause and not the consequence of righteousness. The reading goes on to say that believers were chosen for adoption into the family of God. It is through Christ, the only real Son of God, that others can become God's adopted children. Although it is not explicitly stated here, the implicit baptismal theme is in the background of this passage. The benediction ends as it began, with a reference to praising God.

The second part of the reading is a twofold prayer: first, of thanksgiving that the baptismal grace referred to in the benediction has taken effect in the lives of the believers, and second, of petition that the believers will grow more and more into the kind of people they were predestined to become.

The author acknowledges the faith and the love of the members of the community. Although there is warmth in this greeting, one does not get the sense that the author knew this community intimately. He has heard about them, commends them for their devotion by thanking God for it, and includes them in his own prayers.

The prayer itself is for wisdom, one of the primary baptismal gifts. The tradition of praying for wisdom can be traced as far back as Solomon (cf. 1 Kgs 3:5-9). Unlike this royal prayer, which asks for the ability to govern well, the goal, wisdom, for which the author prays is spiritual: to know God, to understand the hope within the great call of election, to appreciate the excellence of the inheritance that comes with adoption as children of God.

John 1:1-18

The Gospel of John begins with one of the most profound statements about Jesus found in the entire Second Testament. Its lofty christology is comparable to that found in the reading from Hebrews. Both characterize Christ as preexistent; both depict Christ as an agent in the creation of the world. The reading itself falls easily into five parts: a description of the role the Word played in the creation of the world (vv. 1–5); a brief sketch of a witness named John (vv. 6–8); an account of the Word's entrance into the world (vv. 9–14); a second report about John (v. 15); and an acknowledgment of our participation in Christ's glory (vv. 16–18).

The opening statement, "In the beginning," recalls a comparable statement in Genesis (1:1). This parallel may be the author's way of implying that the coming of the Word into the world is as momentous as was the first creation. The Word is then described in language reminiscent of the figure of Wisdom personified (Prov 8:30; Wis 7:25). Like Wisdom, the Word was actively involved in creation. Unlike Wisdom, the Word is explicitly identified as divine. In a free-flowing manner the author ascribes life-giving power to the Word, life that gives light. The mention of light enables the author to draw one of his many contrasts. This particular contrast is between light and darkness. At times the light is synonymous with life (v. 5a). At other times it represents truth (v. 5b). At still other times, the Word is the light (vv. 7–9).

The witness named John is not further identified. However, it is presumed that it is the Baptist, since the words that appear here are later ascribed to him (v. 15; cf. 1:30). There seems to be a definite need to contrast the Word with John. While the Word is the true light that comes into the world, John is merely the witness who testifies to the authenticity (vv. 7–9) and superiority of this light (v. 15). Though designated by God as a witness to the Word (v. 6), John is neither a peer nor a rival of the Word.

Up to this point only John is clearly a historical person. The Word resides in some primordial place. Now the Word enters into human history, and the next section describes both the incarnation and the rejection by human beings that the Word faced (vv. 9–14). In a third contrast, the author distinguishes between those who were somehow intimately associated with the Word but did not accept him and those who did accept him and thereby became children of God. "His own" may be a reference to other members of the Jewish community. Here ancestry does not make one a child of God; only faith in the Word made flesh can accomplish this.

Several translations state that the Word "made his dwelling among us" (v. 14). A better reading of the Greek might refer to "tenting," which calls to mind the tabernacle in the wilderness where God dwelt among the people (Exod 40:34) as well as the tradition about Wisdom establishing her tent in the midst of the people (Sir 24:8). The Word of God, who is also the holiness of God and the wisdom of God, now dwells in the midst of humankind. Women and men have been greatly enriched by this divine presence, transformed by the love that first prompted God's revelation and Christ's incarnation.

Themes of the Day

This Sunday could be called Wisdom Sunday. It celebrates Christ, God's incarnated gift, who comes to dwell in our midst. The divine Word, who has pitched a tent among us, is associated with the fulfillment of Wisdom and with our participation in her power. Several themes emerge from this association: Wisdom was present from the beginning of time as a cosmic force; Wisdom lives in the midst of the people; Christ is the fulfillment of Wisdom and the agent of our salvation.

Wisdom as a Cosmic Force

Wisdom is part of creation from the beginning and holds sway over cosmic affairs. She inspires the praise of all creation. Told by God to live among the people, she is in their midst as a source of inspiration and encouragement for them. When joined with the Prologue of the Gospel of John, Wisdom is seen as incarnate in Jesus. In Jesus, Wisdom is the Divine Word that dwells among us. In this Word all creation has come to be and is sustained in life and destiny.

Wisdom Lives Among the People

Wisdom dwells in Zion, in the holy city of Jerusalem, in the midst of the city of God. When Wisdom dwells at the heart of the community, three changes occur. First, protection is offered to the people. There is no fear, no threat; all are secure in Wisdom's abiding presence. Second, with Wisdom comes a sense of God's sustaining mercy and love. Third, the protection and blessing that Wisdom brings draw forth the praises of God. The people, all of the city, are inspired to give praise and thanks to God for Wisdom's wondrous gifts.

Christ, the Agent of Salvation

God is praised and blessed for the wonders of the divine gifts offered to us. Within this blessing there is the profound awareness that it is Christ who makes all good things possible. Christ is the agent of our salvation. In fact, the promise of salvation is proclaimed from the beginning of creation. Just as Wisdom was told by God to pitch her tent among the people, so the divine Word, bringing the gift of salvation, has pitched a tent amidst the people. This gracious act of God is an assurance that salvation is offered to all who are willing to receive it. Thus Christ, divine Wisdom and God among us, is the promise that all creation can be regenerated. This new life is the way of peace, the way of gratitude. It is the way of praise and thanks for the protection and blessing of God.

January 6, The Epiphany of the Lord
Isaiah 60:1-6

The reading opens with a twofold summons: Arise! Shine! The feminine form of the verbs suggests that the city of Jerusalem is being addressed. Although it had been downtrodden and enshrouded in darkness, it is now called out of this desperate state. The illumination into which it emerges is not merely the light of a new day, a new era of peace and prosperity. It is the very light of God, the glory of the LORD. This expression usually refers to some kind of theophany, some kind of manifestation of divine majesty. The oracle that follows the summons suggests that the divine majesty that is revealed is the restoration of Zion/Jerusalem.

The assertion that Jerusalem enjoys the light of divine glory while every-one else is wrapped in a darkness that covers the entire earth (v. 2) is reminis-cent of one of the plagues that befell Egypt when the pharaoh refused to release God's people from their confinement in that land (Exod 10:21-23). Certainly the allusion was not lost on those for whom this prophetic an-nouncement was intended. The privilege that Israel enjoyed in that first in-stance and the benefits that this privilege afforded them serve here as incentive for relying on God's continued care of Israel.

This prophet states again and again that other nations will witness the glory of the LORD as it is revealed through the salvation of Israel (cf. 40:5; 52:10; 61:11; 62:11). Here the prophet makes the same claim (v. 3). The light that Jerusalem provides for others is really the radiance of God's glory, and that glory is in fact the manifestation of its deliverance. Thus Jerusalem's re-demption enables others to behold and to walk in God's light. It is now the messenger of good news for others. This is why Jerusalem is summoned, "Rise up in splendor!"

Jerusalem is not only delivered by God from its misfortune, it is reestab-lished as a thriving city. Its dispersed inhabitants return, its destroyed reputa-tion is restored, and its despoiled prosperity is reconstituted (vv. 4–5). This is not a promise to be fulfilled in the future; Jerusalem's salvation is an accom-plished fact. It is happening before its very eyes. The major centers of wealth and wisdom once again send their wares to Jerusalem. The wealth from land and sea pours into the city. Such good fortune is evidence of God's favor. This is another reason why the city is summoned, "Rise up in splendor!"

Psalm 72:1-2, 7-8, 10-11, 12-13

In this royal hymn the psalmist is asking God to bless the king so that the king in turn can bless the people. Ancient monarchs exercised incredible control over the lives of their subjects. Despite the scope and depth of this influence, the authority described here is not unregulated. Rather, it is under the juris-diction of God.

The psalmist begins with a prayer, asking God that the king be given a share in God's own justice (vv. 1–2). This is the same justice with which God governs the world and all of the people in it. It is the justice that gives birth to harmony and to the peace (v. 7) that embodies complete well being, and it will enable the king to govern in a way that will provide the people with the peace and well being God wills for them.

These people are explicitly identified as belonging to God; presumably they are the people of the covenant. Thus this is no ordinary king; he is one who has been placed over the covenanted people to rule them as God would, in justice and righteousness. The test of the character of the royal rule is the care given to the most vulnerable of the society, the poor. The psalmist asks God to grant righteousness to the king so he can protect the defenseless and guarantee for them a share in the prosperity of the nation.

The psalmist turns to the rule of the king itself (v. 7). He prays first for its steadfastness: may it last forever, until the moon be no more. Actually, it is not the reign itself that is the object of the psalmist's prayer but the righteousness of the reign. Since it is really God's righteousness, he prays that it will take root and flourish throughout the rule of this particular king and that it will even outlast him, enduring along with peace until the end of time.

The psalmist next prays that this rule of justice be extended to include the entire world and all of the nations within it (vv. 8, 10–11). Since the sea frequently symbolized chaos (cf. Ps 89:9-10), the expression "from sea to sea" (v. 8a) delineates the inhabitable land that lies securely and thrives peacefully within the boundaries of chaotic waters. "The River" (v. 8b) suggests a specific waterway that marks a land stretching to the end of the earth. Both of these sweeping images sketch a reign that encompasses all the world.

The kingdoms listed provide a specific profile of this universal rule (vv. 10–11). Tarshish is thought to have been a Phoenician commercial center in southern Spain; Sheba was in southern Arabia; Seba was a royal Ethiopian city in southern Egypt. If "the River" refers to the Euphrates, these sites trace the outline of the ancient Near Eastern world. The cities not only provide the borders of the reign of righteousness, they also signify its good fortune. They are all well-established, flourishing, internationally respected centers of commerce and trade. If they are the outposts of this remarkable kingdom, how successful its center must be!

The reading ends with a picture of righteousness in action (vv. 12–13). If the test of justice is the solicitude shown the needy, the prayer of the psalmist has been answered. The kingdom is rooted in the righteousness of God, and the most vulnerable in the society have an advocate in the king.

Ephesians 3:2-3a, 5-6

The preaching of the gospel is the major focus of this reading. However, there are four very significant themes connected with it and interwoven in the passage: ministry or commission; revelation; mystery; co-heir.

Oikonomía (ministry) comes from two Greek words: *oíkos,* meaning "house," and *nomós,* meaning "law." It means the "law of the house." The word itself might be better translated "administration" or "management." This is because ministry has too often been understood as works rather than as deputized responsibility for some aspect of the household, which is the meaning here. In this reading the *oikonomía* was assigned directly by God, thus making the writer of the letter both responsible for the believers and accountable to God.

The gospel message that the author preached, specifically that in Christ the Gentiles are co-heirs, co-members and co-partners with the Jews (v. 6), had been revealed to him by God. This is a very important point, for within the early Church the gospel message was usually handed down from one member to another (cf. 1 Cor 11:23). It may be that new insights into God's plan were considered new revelations, and it might have been necessary to regard them in this way in order that they be deemed genuine.

According to the author, the status of the Gentiles had to be revealed because it had been secret until now (cf. Col 1:25-26). The apostles and prophets, to whom the Spirit revealed this message, constitute the foundation of the Church (cf. Eph 2:20). In other words, it is through this appointed messenger that the Spirit has revealed a new revelation to the established Church. The message of this new revelation is this: in Christ the Gentiles are co-heirs, co-members, and co-partners with the Jews.

Since what qualifies one as an heir is life in the Spirit of Christ and not natural generation into a particular national group, there is no obstacle in the path of Gentile incorporation. The body to which all belong is the body of Christ, not the bloodline of Abraham. The promise at the heart of gospel preaching is the promise of universal salvation through Christ, not of descendants and prosperity in a particular land. This is a radical insight for a Church with Jewish roots and traditions.

The early Church may have cherished the hope and conviction of universality, but it seems that it had to rethink what this might mean. The message of this passage claims that the Gentiles are co-heirs precisely as Gentiles and not as initiates who have come to Christ through the faith of Israel. This new revelation does not demean the importance of the Jewish faith for Jewish Christians. It respects it but does not insist upon it as a prerequisite for admission into the Church. The one thing necessary is to be "in Christ."

Matthew 2:1-12

As we near the end of the Christmas season, we read another popular Christmas story: the Three Kings, or Three Wise Men. Actually, they were astrologers, men who studied the heavenly bodies and there discovered the meaning of human life on earth. The account is a kind of *haggadah,* a Jewish story fashioned from diverse biblical material intended to make a theological point. This does not mean that the story is not true. It means that the truth of it is more in the total story and its meaning than in any or all of its details.

The story itself has developed a *haggadah* through which we now understand it. For example, the text says that there were three gifts, not three men. It identifies the three gifts, but does not relate gold with kingship, frankincense with divinity, or myrrh with suffering. It does not name them (Caspar,

Balthasar, and Melchior), nor does it say that one was black. All of this is hag-gadic addition.

Modern astrologers tell us that there actually was an unusual astral phe-nomenon around this time. It is likely that the author of this account provided a theological explanation for it. This story itself is dependent on elements from several earlier biblical traditions: the fourth oracle of Balaam the Moabite speaking of a star rising out of Jacob (Num 24:17); a reference to the kings of Tarshish, Sheba, and Seba, who render tribute and bring gifts (Ps 72:10-11); and the promise that gold and frankincense will be brought on camels from Midian and Ephah and Sheba to Jerusalem (Isa 60:6).

Lest the astrological details lead us to believe that this is a myth, the author situates the events squarely in time and place: the reign of Herod, Bethlehem, and Jerusalem. Since they believed that astral marvels frequently accompanied the birth of great kings, it is understandable that the astrologers would go straight to the Judean king. The entire royal establishment ("all Jerusalem") was frightened by news of this birth, for the child would be a potential rival. The learned of the court ("the chief priests and the scribes") knew where to find the child. They relied on the prophetic message to tell them where to look, but they rejected its identification of the child as a legitimate ruler. Knowing the tradition is no guarantee of loyalty to it.

The report of the astrologers' veneration of the child is brief yet stirring. The star actually led them to where he was. Finding him, they prostrated themselves before him and paid him homage. The text does not say that they honored Herod in this way, so this should not be seen as tribute for a king. This is probably the kind of veneration they reserved for a god. The as-trologers were well adept at discerning truth. They read the astral signs; they recognized the true identity of the child; and they understood a message in a dream that told them to return home another way.

These anonymous men come out of obscurity and they return to obscu-rity. All we know is that they were not Israelite, and this is the whole point of the story. It illustrates that people of good will, regardless of their ethnic or re-ligious background, are responsive to the revelation of God. Their openness brought the astrologers to the child, and they did not go away disappointed. This child draws Jew and Gentile alike.

Themes of the Day

The Christmas season reaches an apex on the Solemnity of the Epiphany. Tra-ditionally known in many parts of the world as Little Christmas, it is a com-memoration of the manifestation of God to all the nations. In some liturgical traditions this feast is the central celebration of Christmas. It commemorates not only the birth of Christ and the visit of the Magi but also his baptism in the Jordan and the manifestation of his glory at the wedding feast of Cana. In the Roman Catholic tradition the focus is on the first of these commemorations: the visit of the Magi and the implications of that visit for the glorious manifestation of God to all the peoples of the world. The readings for this solemnity develop the importance of this manifestation. Three themes dominate: Jerusalem is the source of light for the nations; Christ is the revelation of God to all the nations; new relationships are established in Christ between Jew and Gentile.

Jerusalem Is the Source of Light

There is a wonderful summons to alertness and presence of mind and heart, a call for all the nations to witness the marvelous works of God that shine as light in the midst of the surrounding darkness. This is no ordinary light. It is a light that has God's holy city Jerusalem as its source. The people of Israel have enjoyed the radiance of God's glory and are now set as a beacon for the nations. All the ends of the earth can witness the wonder of God's light in the midst of the city, its people, its rulers, and its way of life.

The light of God is known in the ways in which the most vulnerable in the city are cared for and acknowledged. In just action and righteousness the city becomes the beacon of God, and all the nations are attracted by this light. The quality of the light leads the way through the darkness and sustains the world in goodness and peace.

Christ as the Light to the Nations

Led by a star, the astrologers come in search of the infant king. They have been attentive to the marvels of the universe, and there they have read signs in the heavens. They represent all who search for truth in the wonders of creation and in the wisdom of their own cultures of origin. Because they searched with eyes of faith they were able to recognize the gift of God when they found him, even though he did not conform to their initial perception of a royal heir.

They came from the far corners of the earth, Gentiles who followed the light and who found the new king whose reign would bring justice and righteousness into human affairs. They returned home, enlightened by their visit to God's place of revelation. Their encounter shows that in Christ the light of God is given to all people of good will, Jew and non-Jew alike.

The New Relationships Between Jew and Gentile

The manifestation of God among us changes the ways in which we perceive one another. Christ's birth provides us with the light by which we see a new criterion for relating. The Magi who come in faith to worship the child represent the multi-ethnic and cultural diversity in civic and parish situations as well as the many religions of the world. To us, who are related no longer merely by blood affiliation or national origin, Christ offers the spirit of holiness as the ground for our relationships. This new universal belonging will be manifest in the community of believers, who live no longer in the darkness or in exclusivity and sin but by a new dispensation of grace. All people, regardless of race or ethnic origin, can be co-heirs with Christ.

Sunday After January 6, The Baptism of the Lord
Isaiah 42:1-4, 6-7

This is the first of four passages (49:1-6; 50:4-9; 52:13–53:12) traditionally known as the Servant Songs. They are a unique set of poems that identify a mysterious figure who acts as a pious agent of God's compassionate care. Presumably it is God who speaks, and it is God who singles out this servant and gives him a special function to perform within the community. The uniqueness of this person can be seen in the title bestowed on him by God: "my servant." Very few people were so called by God: Abraham (Gen 26:24); Moses (Num 12:7); Caleb (Num 14:24); Job (Job 1:8). The one most frequently referred to in this way was David (2 Sam 3:8). The parallel construction in this first verse further identifies the servant as someone chosen by God and one with whom God is pleased.

Most significant in this description of the servant is his having been endowed with God's own spirit. Earlier Israelite leaders were thought to have been seized by the spirit: judges (Judg 6:34; 11:29, 32; 14:19); kings (1 Sam 16:13); prophets (Mic 3:8; Ezek 11:5). Those who received the spirit were thus empowered to act within the community in some unique fashion. The particular needs of the community determined the character of this action. God's saving power was brought to the community through the agency of various individuals. The servant in this song has received the spirit of the LORD in order to bring forth justice to the nations.

The manner in which this justice is executed is quite extraordinary (vv. 2–4). It is not harsh and exacting, making a public pronouncement of God's judgment of Israel. Instead, it is gentle and understanding, willing to wait for the establishment of God's universal rule. This justice will not compound the distress of an already suffering people. Rather, it will be a source of consolation.

God speaks again, this time directly to the servant (vv. 6–7), indicating the role the servant is to play in the life of the community. The verbs used all reveal the deliberateness of God's choice: I called you; I grasped you; I formed you and set you. The mission of the servant is clearly determined by God, not by the servant himself. The parallelism between "covenant of the people" and "light for the nations" suggests that covenant is to be understood in a general sense, underscoring the universalism referred to elsewhere (vv.1, 4), rather than in the exclusive sense usually associated with biblical covenant.

The responsibilities that flow from the servant's election are all aspects of the commission to bring forth justice (vv. 1, 6). Although these tasks single out specific situations of human suffering, they probably stand for any form of darkness and confinement. Several themes converge here. The servant is called to bring forth justice to the nations and to be a light to the nations. This light will open the eyes of those relegated to the darkness of confinement. Most likely the reference here is not to the release of Israelites but of those outside the believing community. The passage describes the deliverance of the whole world, not the rescue of Israel from its particular bondage. The universalism here cannot be denied.

Psalm 29:1-2, 3-4, 3, 9-10

This hymn of praise describes the LORD as sovereign over the heavens and the earth. It begins with a call to praise (vv. 1–2). Unlike most psalms of this kind, here the call is addressed to heavenly, not human beings. The scene is the celestial court where the divine council (the Hebrew reads "sons of God") assembles (cf. Job 1:6; 2:1). They are there in attendance, and they are called on to render honor to God. The imperative verb form used here indicates that this is not an invitation; it is a command. These heavenly beings are charged to sing praise to God's glory and might.

The glory of God usually refers to some kind of divine manifestation. The psalmist declares that this glory is revealed in God's name. Traditional people believe that there is power in a person's name, since the name embodies part of that person's very essence. How much more is this the case with the name of God! The great respect in which God's name was held explains why the people of Israel were forbidden to pronounce it. The psalm reports that this wondrous name was revered in heaven as well as on earth. The entire council is enjoined to pay homage to God, who is revealed as sovereign.

God's sovereignty is further manifested in the power God exercises over the forces of nature (vv. 3–4, 9–10). The voice of the LORD thunders over the waters (v. 3). This is a description of the mighty storm-god whose voice is the thunder itself, who in the beginning conquered the forces of chaos, characterized as ruthless, destructive water. Although the characterization within the psalm suggests that God acts here as a mighty warrior, the imagery paints a slightly different picture. According to this psalm, God did not need a heavenly army to quell the chaotic waters. God's commanding voice was powerful enough. As in the first account of creation (Gen 1:1–2:4a), God's voice is itself creative power and divine splendor (v. 4).

God thunders. While this may appear to be a demonstration of the devastating power of God's voice, the context of the psalm reminds us that its focus is God's superiority over the forces of destruction. Therefore, this verse is a reminder that the power of God's word can be felt both in heaven and on earth. In calling the heavenly beings to praise God, the psalmist is calling them to acknowledge all of these marvels.

The last scene brings us back to the divine council, to the heavenly temple and the throne of God (vv. 9c–10). All who are present there praise God with the joyous acclamation: "Glory!" There God sits triumphant above the flood waters. (The only other place in the Bible where the word "flood" is found is in the Genesis account, 7:17.) The scene is majestic. God's thunderous voice has silenced the forces of chaos, and now God reigns supreme forever as king of heaven and earth.

Acts 10:34-38

The scene is the house of Cornelius, a newly converted Roman centurion. Normally, an observant Jew like Peter would not enter the home of a Gentile. The first words of his discourse ("In truth, I see") indicate that he was not always open to association with Gentiles as he is now. It was a newly gained insight about God that changed his view of those who did not have Jewish ancestry. He realized that "God shows no partiality" (vv. 34–35; cf. Deut 10:17; 2 Chr 19:7) and, therefore, neither should he. All are acceptable to God, Jew and Gentile.

According to Peter, God's message of peace was given initially to Israel, but this does not cancel the fact that it is meant for all. Inclusivity is the centerpiece of this reading. God shows no partiality, and Christ is Lord of all. Not even Peter, who knew the historical Jesus intimately and should have understood the implications of the message he preached and the example he gave, originally understood the radical nature of this gospel. But now he can testify that it is truly good news of peace.

Peter presumed that although they were Gentiles, because they were living in Judea his audience would have heard something about the life and ministry of Jesus, if only in the form of gossip. As a Roman centurion stationed in this small country, Cornelius certainly must have known something, for his station would have required that he be informed of anything that might threaten the Roman Peace. Mention of Jesus' baptism by John (v. 37) would have called to mind another disturber of the peace. Even though he was an irritant to the Jewish leadership, the unrest he caused would have been known to the Roman officials.

Although each of these incidents had a political side, this does not seem to have been the motivation for citing them. It seems, instead, that Peter was recalling incidents that manifested the power that was evident in the ministry of Jesus and the universal scope of that ministry.

The power of Jesus' ministry flowed from his having been anointed by God with the Holy Spirit. This reference to anointing is probably an allusion to his baptism, when the heavens opened and the Spirit descended upon him (Luke 3:21-22; 4:14, 18; cf. Isa 61:1). It was in and through this power that he had performed such miracles as releasing those who were in the grip of the devil. Peter makes a point of this last particular miracle, probably because those possessed by demons were considered the most unclean of the unclean. Despite this, Jesus did not relegate them to the margins of society, as the self-righteous purists might have done. He touched them; he healed them. Like Jesus, Peter was now moving in circumstances (contact with Gentiles) that were considered by some to be unclean. Like Jesus, he disregarded such a judgment, and he refused to conform to such a manner of estrangement. Peter was convinced that with God there is no partiality.

Mark 1:7-11

The reading consists of two parts: an identification of the central message of John's preaching, and a description of the baptism of Jesus by John. It is the gist of John's preaching that has prompted commentators to label him a precursor. He not only comes before Jesus, but he prepares the people for Jesus. He does this by contrasting himself and the baptism he performs with Jesus and the baptism he will bring. John does not hesitate emphasizing his own inferiority in comparison with Jesus.

In the first place, he states that Jesus is more powerful than he is. Though no explanation of this power is given, the sense of the text suggests that John is talking about the power of Jesus' authority, or simply the greater power of his being. Jesus is so far superior to him that John is not even worthy to perform a menial task like loosening the strap of his sandal, a task usually performed by household slaves. John is not demeaning himself here. Rather, he is glorifying Jesus.

John next contrasts their respective baptisms. His is with water. Many ancient religions practiced ritual cleansing. Such action had symbolic inner value because of the cleansing properties of water. Jesus' baptism will be in the Holy Spirit. This could be a reference to the eschatological time of fulfillment, when God promised to "sprinkle clean water upon you to cleanse you from all your impurities" and to "give you a new heart and place a new spirit within you" (Ezek 36:25-26).

No explanation is given as to why Jesus would submit himself to a baptism of repentance. It may have been simply an expression of piety. According to this account it seems to have been a very uneventful occasion. Only Jesus saw that the sky was rent in two; only he saw the dove descend; and the voice spoke directly to him. There is no indication that anyone else saw or heard anything. This appears to have been a private affirmation of his messianic importance.

Several different traditions converge to make this an extraordinary account. The theological meaning is both rich and complex. First, the Spirit descends upon Jesus as it had descended upon the prophets centuries earlier (cf. Isa 61:1). Thus one can say that there is a prophetic dimension to the messianic vocation of Jesus. Second, while the address "You are my beloved Son" has definite royal connotations (Ps 2:7), since kings were believed to be related to the deity, there is also a divine aspect here. In addition to this, the address is reminiscent of the description of the servant of the LORD (Isa 42:1b). To the prophetic character of the vocation are added a royal dimension, an aspect of divinity, and one of servanthood. Finally, the designation "beloved Son" recalls another beloved son, Isaac, the one who faced the knife as his father was put to the test (Gen 22:2). In the background of the messianic vocation lurks the specter of suffering and even death.

The baptism by John did not accomplish in Jesus what it might have accomplished in others, namely repentance for sin. But it did provide him with what was far more meaningful. It occasioned a divine affirmation of his messianic identity.

Themes of the Day

With this feast the Christmas cycle comes to a close. The celebration expands the universality of God's presence that was proclaimed on the Epiphany and locates it in the messianic mission of Jesus established at his baptism. This feast might be seen as the summary of the entire liturgical cycle: the one who is born among us is the servant of God who brings to all the nations a universal promise of justice and the fulfillment of hope. Three themes emerge: the servant of God is the hope and light of all the nations; the mission of the servant is universal and evokes the response of the entire cosmos; the baptism of Jesus declares him the universal servant, whose divine affirmation makes him the beloved child of God.

The Servant of God Is the Light and Hope of the Nations

The servant of God is the one who is anointed with the Spirit and given a mission by God. The mission is a universal charge to proclaim and establish justice for all the nations. The servant is both the light that guides those in darkness and a source of clarity for judgment and understanding. He is also the one through whom God's saving action is accomplished. This servant is given to the nations as the promise of liberation and as the hope of the age to come. Jesus is this servant, and his mission is directed to all peoples. In God's work there is room for everyone. There is no partiality when it comes to the offer of light and the work of justice.

The Cosmic Response to the Work of the Servant

The servant's work among the nations is so influential that it evokes the response of all creation. In the face of such a universal gift, the heavens and earth erupt in praise and wonder of the mystery revealed by God's servant. God's voice is creative; it speaks over creation and over the head of Jesus as he emerges out of the waters of the Jordan. The work of God includes the regeneration of nature; the work of Jesus begins in the waters that rejoice at his presence.

Jesus Is the Universal Servant, Baptized by John

Anointed by the Spirit, Jesus is commissioned to begin his prophetic work and ministry, a work of inclusivity and the relinquishment of bondage and fear. As the heavens open Jesus is identified as the beloved one of God. By God's good favor the community of believers is identified with Jesus the servant of God. Through baptism Christians share in the prophetic and divine ministry of Christ. They too receive an imperative with baptism, an imperative of committed service to the poor and to the cause of compassion. The feast of the Baptism of the Lord is a reminder of the call to Christian service.

The season of Christmas ends with the community poised for the lenten journey of baptismal renewal.

Optional Readings for the Baptism of the Lord
Isaiah 55:1-11

This powerful prophetic oracle contains some of the most moving sentiments placed in the mouth of God: "come," "receive," "eat," "drink." God's invitation is extended both to those who are able to pay for food and drink (v. 2) and to those who are not (v. 1). All are invited to come to the LORD in order to be refreshed and nourished. The reference is certainly to something more than ordinary food and drink, since those called are also told to listen. The word of God is itself a source of rejuvenation.

The specific object of the invitation is the reestablished covenant as announced by God (v. 3). The reference is to the royal covenant, the one made with David and his house. Although it was instituted as an everlasting covenant, the people broke the bond by their sins. God is now eager to restore this bond. The oracle states that just as David's success proclaimed God's majesty to the nations, so the people called here will be a witness to God's mercy and love. Just as David was the source of blessing, peace, and fullness of life for his own nation, the people called here will be a comparable source of blessing for nations they do not even know.

After this bold promise is made, the people are told to turn to the LORD; sinners are exhorted to reform their lives and to seek forgiveness from God. These are not suggestions; they are imperatives. The people are summoned to repentance. Then God's plans will take effect, just as the rain accomplishes what it is intended to accomplish. God's way is compassion and re-creation, and this renewal will last forever.

Isaiah 12:2-3, 4bcd, 5-6

This hymn of thanksgiving anticipates favors that will be granted and enjoyed in the future. Therefore one might consider it a hymn of confidence as well. God is declared "savior," and bolstered by this characterization, the writer is unafraid and takes courage. The theme of water appears here as it did in the preceding reading. Though the imagery differs slightly, in both cases the water is transformative. Earlier it represented new creation; here it is water of salvation.

The theme of witness reappears here as well (vv. 4–5). The writer calls on the community to praise the glorious name of God, the name that represents the very character of God. They are to extol the marvels that God has accomplished and proclaim them to the nations. The most celebrated of these wondrous works is the transformation of the people themselves. In other words, the transformed lives of God's people will announce to the nations the marvels that God has accomplished.

The third and final theme found in this response highlights the importance of Jerusalem. This city was both the royal capital of the Davidic dynasty and the site where the temple was built. It is the second aspect that is the focus here. The city itself is called upon to rejoice. The reason for this exaltation is the presence of God in its midst. Although the temple was the concrete representation of this divine presence, it is the presence of God and not the temple building that is fundamental (cf. Jer 7:3-4). The theology of the passage has come full circle. The presence of God in the midst of the people is the source of the writer's confidence of future deliverance.

1 John 5:1-9

The reading is a testimony to trinitarian faith. It describes God as the one who begets (the Father); it identifies Jesus as the Son of God; and it credits the Spirit as the one who testifies to the triumph of Jesus' death and resurrection. It also sketches the way believers participate in this trinitarian reality.

The very first verse begins with a simply stated yet foundational christological declaration: Jesus is the Christ. The word "Christ," meaning "anointed one," has a long history in Jewish thought. In ancient Israel kings (2 Sam 2:4) and priests (Exod 30:30) were anointed. Gradually these customs developed into messianic ideas (Isa 9:5-6; 61:1), which after the resurrection were attributed by Christians to Jesus. Here the messiahship of Jesus is coupled with his divine sonship (v. 5).

This verse states a second theological theme: faith in this Jesus makes believers children of God. A form of the verb "to beget" is used three times: those who believe are "begotten by God"; God (the Father) is the one who begets; those "begotten by God" are to be the object of the love of others. Here faith and love *(agápē)* are intimately linked. While it is faith in Jesus, Messiah and Son of God, that brings one into the family of God, once incorporated, one is expected to love God and all those others who have also been begotten by God through faith in Jesus.

The reading moves from faith and love to obedience. It does not identify the commandments to be observed but states that they are not burdensome. It may be the author wanted to insist that faith and love are not merely interior dispositions but must be manifested in some external way. The direction taken by love, as stated earlier (v. 1), is here reversed. Before, the focus was on love for God, which presumes love for others. Here it is on love for God's children, which reveals itself in love for God and observance of God's commandments. It seems that these two loves are so connected that it makes little difference which comes first. One form of love always results in the other.

Faith also reveals itself in its victory over the world (vv. 4–5). The world *(kósmos)* can be understood in three ways: the totality of natural creation, the inhabited world generally, and the inhabited world subject to sin. The context of this passage suggests that the third meaning is intended. Faith in Jesus the Messiah and Son of God triumphs over evil. It challenges anything that questions the exalted nature of Jesus and the power that flows from it. Jesus inaugurated the reign of God and has ushered in the new age of fulfillment. He accomplished this not merely at the time of his baptism (through water), when he received his messianic commission, but at the time of his death and resurrection (through blood), when he conquered death.

Just as the Spirit testifies *(martyréō)* to the meaning of the water and the blood, so the water and the blood (the baptism and the death of Jesus) testify to the truth of Jesus' exalted state (Messiah and Son of God). According to law and custom, there are now three witnesses. The author ends by insisting that if human testimony is accepted in accord with human custom (cf. Deut 19:15), how much more should the testimony of God be accepted. The trinitarian focus of this reading is clear.

Mark 1:7-11

The reading consists of two parts: an identification of the central message of John's preaching and a description of the baptism of Jesus by John. It is the gist of John's preaching that has prompted commentators to label him a precursor. He not only comes before Jesus, he prepares the people for Jesus. He does this by contrasting himself and the baptism he performs with Jesus and the baptism he will bring. John does not hesitate emphasizing his own inferiority in comparison with Jesus.

First, he states that Jesus is more powerful than he is. Though no explanation of this power is given, the sense of the text suggests that John is talking about the power of Jesus' authority, or simply the greater power of his being. Jesus is so far superior to him that John is not even worthy to perform a menial task like loosening the strap of Jesus' sandal, a task usually performed by household slaves. John is not demeaning himself here. Rather, he is glorifying Jesus.

John next contrasts their respective baptisms. His is with water. Many ancient religions practiced ritual cleansing. Such action had symbolic value because of the cleansing properties of water. Jesus' baptism will be in the Holy Spirit. This could be a reference to the eschatological time of fulfillment, when God promised to "sprinkle clean water upon you to cleanse you from all your impurities" and to "give you a new heart and place a new spirit within you" (Ezek 36:25-26).

No explanation is given as to why Jesus would submit himself to a baptism of repentance. It may have been simply an expression of piety. According to this account it seems to have been a very uneventful occasion. Only Jesus saw that the sky was rent in two; only he saw the dove descend; and the voice spoke directly to him. There is no indication that anyone else saw or heard anything. This appears to have been a private affirmation of his messianic importance.

Several different traditions converge to make this an extraordinary account. The theological meaning of this event is both rich and complex. First, the Spirit descends upon Jesus as it had descended upon the prophets centuries earlier (cf. Isa 61:1). Thus one can say that there is a prophetic dimension to the messianic vocation of Jesus. Second, while the address "You are my beloved Son" has definite royal connotations (Ps 2:7), since kings were believed to be related to the deity, there is also a divine aspect here. In addition to this, the address is reminiscent of the description of the servant of the LORD (Isa 42:1b). To the prophetic character of the vocation are added a royal dimension, an aspect of divinity, and one of servanthood. Finally, the designation "beloved Son" recalls another beloved son, Isaac, the one who faced the knife as his father was put to the test (Gen 22:2). In the background of the messianic vocation lurks the specter of suffering and even of death.

The baptism by John did not symbolize in Jesus what it might have symbolized in others, namely repentance for sin. But it did provide him with what was far more meaningful. It occasioned a divine affirmation of his messianic identity.

Themes of the Day

With this feast the Christmas cycle comes to a close. The celebration expands the universality of God's presence proclaimed on the Epiphany and locates it in the messianic mission of Jesus established at his baptism. This feast might be seen as the summary of the entire liturgical cycle: the one who is born among us is the servant of God bringing to all the nations a promise of justice and the fulfillment of hope. Two major themes emerge: water as a symbol of the messianic age, and the testimony of God.

Symbol of the Messianic Age

Water is a rich symbol with multi-dimensional meanings. Essential for life, water represents fertility and bounteous prosperity. It possesses the mysterious ability to transform the barren desert into a luxurious carpet of blossoms. It refreshes and nourishes; it is the source of life; it is life itself.

Water is also a symbol of the spiritual life. It issues from some hidden well-head in God, and it gushes forth as a fountain of refreshment and regeneration. The messianic age, a time of well being and complete fulfillment, is envisioned as a time of feasting on the fruits of a fertile and productive land, a land that resembles a well-watered garden. It is a time when the thirst for God will be slaked and what is dried up will be rejuvenated.

Finally, water can also represent the enemy. It can overwhelm the familiar and the secure and wash away any hope of rescue. It can swallow life up and become its unforgiving grave. Because of the threat posed by unruly or chaotic waters, it is also a symbol of death. However, those who are able to pass through these malevolent waters emerge transformed, reborn, a new creation. The waters have been sanctified by Jesus. When he entered them to be baptized, he calmed their fury for all time. At the completion of this symbolic act they released their grip on him, and he emerged to be identified as the beloved Son of the all-holy God. Water is now the secret hiding place of God.

The Testimony of God

Some truths are self-evident; they can be recognized by all, and they do not need to be substantiated. Other truths are so amazing that they need the verification of reliable witnesses. The life-giving quality of water belongs to the first type; the divine origin of Jesus belongs to the second.

The baptism of Jesus was an event that marked him as the Son of God, but how could this be confirmed? Who but God could authenticate such a claim? And God did authenticate it! The heavens were torn apart; the Spirit descended upon Jesus; the voice of God acclaimed him Son. The testimony of God—Father, Son, and Spirit—cannot be denied.

A similar testimony confirms Jesus' divine sonship—the Spirit, the water, and the blood. Water and blood flowed from Jesus dead body, but through his conquest of death the water and the blood are no longer signs of death. They now witness to his victory over death and the glory of his resurrected life. By faith we too enter his victory; with him we pass through water and blood; and the testimony of God authenticates our own resurrection life.

Lent

First Sunday			
Genesis 9:8-15 I establish my covenant	**Psalm 25:4-9** Your ways are love and truth	**1 Peter 3:18-22** The Flood prefigured baptism	**Mark 1:12-15** Jesus is tempted
Second Sunday			
Genesis 22:1-2, 9a, 10-13, 15-18 The sacrifice of Abraham	**Psalm 116:10, 15-19** I will walk before the LORD	**Romans 8:31b-34** God did not spare Jesus	**Mark 9:2-10** This is my beloved son
Third Sunday			
Exodus 20:1-17 The law given through Moses	**Psalm 19:8-11** Words of everlasting life	**1 Corinthians 1:22-25** Christ, stumbling block/wisdom	**John 2:13-25** Destroy this temple
Fourth Sunday			
2 Chronicles 36:14-16, 19-23 The wrath and mercy of God	**Psalm 137:1-6** I will never forget you	**Ephesians 2:4-10** By grace you have been saved	**John 3:14-21** The world is saved through Jesus
Fifth Sunday			
Jeremiah 31:31-34 A new covenant	**Psalm 51:3-4, 12-15** Create a clean heart	**Hebrews 5:7-9** Christ learned obedience	**John 12:20-33** The grain dies and produces fruit
Palm Sunday of the Lord's Passion			
Isaiah 50:4-7 I will not hide my face	**Psalm 22:8-9, 17-20, 23-24** Why have you abandoned me?	**Philippians 2:6-11** Christ humbled himself	**Mark 14:1–15:47** Passion

Lent

Initial Reading of the Lent Lectionary

Introduction

The lenten readings can be interpreted as a theological matrix that is the source for an understanding of the readings of the individual Sundays of Lent and a key for an appreciation of the lenten season itself. The matrix that is presented is based on the patterns of meanings offered in the literary forms and the content of the readings themselves. Read in columns, beginning with the first Sunday of Lent and concluding with Palm Sunday, the lections provide an overview of the meaning of the entire lenten season.

First Testament Readings

The First Testament readings celebrate the covenantal relationship of God and the people. They are an extended meditation on the ways of delivery and of reception of the various covenants. God's covenants are marked by a rainbow, a test of faith, inscription on stone tablets, the policy of a pagan king, receptive hearts, and finally by a servant who speaks a word that rouses the weary. The relentless desire of God to be in relationship with the people clearly comes forward in this set of readings.

Approaching the readings in this way, we can say that Lent is a season of covenant making. In each case it is God who initiates the action; in each case it is the people who can do nothing but receive the gift that God offers and allow the covenant relationship to take root in their hearts and in their lives. Furthermore, God does not give up when people turn away. In fact, the extent to which God goes to ensure the permanence of this relationship is incredible; God becomes a servant who will suffer for the sake of the covenant.

Psalms

The lenten responsorial psalms create a collage of human responses to the overwhelming invitations to an intimate relationship with God. They range from lamentation to praise. The responsorial psalm for the first Sunday sets the tone of our reply to God's covenant-making activity. Those who keep the covenant follow God's ways of love and truth. In other words, God's initiative sets our lives aright. This is put more clearly on the second Sunday: to walk in the presence of the LORD is to walk in the midst of life, among the living.

The sense of life and love in God's covenant becomes an act of thanks and praise on the third Sunday, where the covenant is celebrated as perfect and refreshing the soul, as sweet to those who walk in love and truth. For those who are not faithful to the covenant, on the fourth Sunday there is a sense of regret and lamentation, even exile. On the fifth Sunday we acknowledge our guilt and pray that God will create clean hearts in us so that we might live by a renewed sense of the covenant, which is written on our hearts. The lamentation returns on Palm Sunday, where we maintain that even if we feel forsaken we will still sing the praises of the LORD.

Epistles

The epistle readings focus on the identity of Christ and on our identity in Christ. As Noah was saved from the waters of chaos, Christ our exalted Lord saves humanity by his death and leads us into the waters of regeneration. This same Lord is seated at the right hand of God and from there makes constant intercession for us. In the presence of Christ we come to know God and to know that God does everything on our behalf. If God is for us, who can be against us? Christ is also characterized as the wisdom and the power of God, the crucified one upon whom we rest.

Christ's death reveals the lengths to which God's love will go; Christ's resurrection is the sign of the richness of God's tender mercy. Mercy and grace are ours, not through our own works but because of the works of Christ. In this same Christ we have become the handiwork of God. Finally, we are called to obey Christ, who was obedient even unto death. We are invited to have the same self-emptying love in us that was in Christ.

Gospels

The passages taken from the Gospels of Mark and John offer a narrative of salvation. The season opens with an announcement of good news and a call to transformation. The remaining Gospel passages constitute an unfolding of the meanings of Jesus' initial words. We get a glimpse of the fulfillment of his proclamation in his own transfiguration. Speaking with Moses and Elijah, he is declared God's beloved Son. We are told to listen to him, for in his words we find the power of God.

This godly power cleanses the temple and raises up the new temple of Jesus' own body. In dying like the grain of wheat, he will bring forth a yield that is abundant. He is the one who will be lifted up, and in him all who believe will have eternal life. Jesus and his message is the light for our world. His death is proclaimed in the certain hope of the resurrection. The lenten Gospel readings reveal many facets of Christ.

Mosaic of Readings

The lenten season offers us a rich mosaic of meanings. Reading the passages in columns shows that the season is a time of fulfillment. God is the covenant maker, and in Christ this covenant is fully realized. It is a covenant of salvation, aligned with the past and now open to the future that will be ushered in by the resurrection of Jesus. Lent is a time when God fashions an intimate relationship with us, the repentant ones, those who believe in the good news.

Readings

First Sunday of Lent

Genesis 9:8-15

The reading is an account of the covenant that God entered into after the Flood. It was made with Noah, with his descendants, with all the living creatures that were in the ark, and with the earth itself. The covenant was promissory, God pledging that never again would unruly waters destroy the world and its inhabitants. In the ancient Near Eastern world turbulent water was the symbol of ultimate, even mythological chaos. A vast and terrorizing flood was viewed as a return to the primordial chaos out of which the world had been created in the first place (cf. Gen 1:2). For this reason, the promise in this tradition carried more than meteorological implications. It had something to do with control over primordial chaos.

The ancient stories of creation frequently included some kind of cosmic battle between chaos and a youthful warrior god. The bow in this particular narrative may well have been a reference to the weapon of the divine warrior, who was victorious over the forces of primordial chaos. This interpretation of the bow is supported by several Mesopotamian artifacts depicting a creator-god with arrows in a quiver. Hanging the bow in the sky would be a sign that the primordial war was over and that all of creation could rest secure. Like the divine rest after creation (cf. Gen 2:2-3), the act of hanging up the bow heralded the establishment of order in the universe.

Many ancient Near Eastern civilizations preserved a story of a major flood that completely enveloped the entire world. The tradition may have originated out of the memory of an actual deluge that was soon regarded as the primordial flood, and the individuals saved from this disaster were considered the few survivors from whom the human race began anew.

In addition to being a beautifully colored arc that appears in the heavens proclaiming the end of a violent storm and the return of calm, the meteorological bow came to be seen as the divine archer's weapon, a weapon that was now unnecessary. An eternal sign of a cosmic covenant, the bow would be a reminder of the pact made with all creation. God was the fearsome warrior who fought and shackled the forces of chaos. Since only God could so lash out, the bow served to control divine power. It was intended to act as a reminder to God, not to humankind.

Several other aspects of this covenant should be noted. First, it was made with all creation. If the character of the sign identifies the type of covenant, then a visible bow in the sky marks the covenant as one made with all creation. Second, it is multi-generational. It is made not only with those present but with those who will come in the future as well. This unfolding of generation after generation is yet another characteristic of natural creation. Finally, the biblical flood narrative is not merely a story of the return of primordial chaos: it is a story of deliverance. God directed Noah, the only one who found favor with the LORD, to build an ark so that he and his family and some of the animals might escape the punishing waters of the flood. Creation is also redemptive.

Psalm 25:4-5, 6-7, 8-9

The psalm response opens with a prayer for divine guidance. The word "ways" has very close association with the wisdom tradition and refers to a manner of living, specifically the way of righteousness or the way of evil. The term often designates movement or direction on a road rather than the road itself. Here it could refer to a style of life. "Paths" appears in parallel construction with "ways" and also refers to a style of life. When this expression is used in reference to God, it can mean either God's own ways of acting or the ways that God teaches humankind to go. This psalm seems to allow for both meanings.

Understanding the words from the perspective of God's ways of acting makes us attentive to the salvation accomplished by God (v. 5), to God's covenantal commitment (v. 6), and to God's own uprightness (v. 8). Regarding the first theme, the psalm gives no indication as to the character of the salvation wrought by God. Was the psalmist in physical danger? Was the deliverance from personal misfortune? Coupled with the reading from Genesis, the threat could have been cosmic annihilation. Whatever the case may have been, the psalmist asks for insight into God's saving ways, presumably in order to sing God's praises and to offer thanks for God's goodness.

Covenant language is very strong in the second stanza (vv. 6–7). "Compassion" comes from the word *ráḥam* (womb), and might be translated "womb-love." It refers to a deep and loving attachment, usually between two people who share some kind of natural bond. "Kindness" (or lovingkindness, *ḥesed*) denotes loyalty to covenant obligations. Following the Hebrew, some translations contrast God calling to mind covenant commitment and the psalmist's former sins. This plea that God remember may be the psalmist's way of asking for God's forgiveness.

The final stanza comments on the righteousness of God (vv. 8–9), which is attentive to both the sinners and the *ʿănāwîm* (humble). Both groups are taught the way of the LORD, the way God acts toward people's infidelity and their loyalty. Presumably the first group will be taught that wickedness will be punished, while the second will be assured that their righteousness has not gone unnoticed.

Way of the LORD can also refer to the manner of living God expects of humankind. In this case, it is probably a reference to the law, for it is there that the will of God is to be found. The psalmist would then be asking for guidance to discern God's will in order to live in accord with it. This interpretation does not negate the preceding explanation; it simply gives it a slightly different perspective.

God's saving action calls for a response. Having been saved, what responsibilities do we now have? How should we live so as not to fall back into the situation from which we were saved? If God has established a covenant with us, what are our covenant obligations? What have we taken upon ourselves as we entered into this relationship? Finally, if God is just, what kind of lives should we be living? The psalmist prays: Teach me your ways. Show me how you have acted; show me how I should behave.

1 Peter 3:18-22

The author of 1 Peter speaks of the efficacy of Christ's death. The reading does not so much develop theological themes as join them together, one leading to the next. In this way he treats Christ's sacrifice as a sin offering; the saving acts of Christ that took place after his death; the flood waters as a prefiguration of the waters of baptism; and Christ's ultimate exaltation in heaven.

The efficacy of Christ's suffering and death is the principal theme from which all other themes in this reading derive their meaning. Christ's suffering was a sin offering, like the sacrifices of expiation that were offered daily in the temple, with the blood of the victim being sprinkled on the altar. Unlike the sin offerings that were made repeatedly and expiated only individual guilt, Christ's sacrifice was effective for all time and for all people. Christ's suffering was vicarious; it was endured for others. Like the servant in Isaiah (Isa 53:4-6), this was an innocent man who bore the guilt of the unrighteous. Finally, Christ did all of this so that we might be brought to God and have access to God's saving grace.

Physical death did not put an end to Christ's saving work. Alive in the Spirit, Christ went to preach salvation to the dead. This reference is an allusion to an apocalyptic eschatological tradition. A composite of several different biblical strands, it stems from a narrative found in 1 Enoch, an intertestamental book that was very popular in early Christian times. In it, Enoch, sent by God to rebellious angels, announces that they would be confined to prison. Since their rebellion is clearly linked with the flood (Genesis 7–9), these angels were thought to be the "sons of heaven" who took the daughters of men as wives (cf. Gen 6:1-6).

1 Peter reinterprets this tradition, replacing Noah with the risen Christ and changing the condemnation of the defiant angels to the preaching to the spirits. The explicit reason for Christ's preaching in the realm of the dead and the identity of the spirits that were there are not clear and consequently have spawned a variety of interpretations. However the details are understood, the gist of the tradition is clear: Christ's salvific power extends to all, even beyond the confines of this life.

The author sees Noah and the flood as a type of Christ and baptism. Just as Noah saved others from the devastating waters of the flood, so Christ saved others from the ultimate destruction of separation from God. Just as those in the ark had to endure the flood in order to come into a new creation, so Christians must pass through the waters of baptism in order to take on a new conscience. The author of 1 Peter insists that baptism is not merely a simple cleansing. Rather, it is a transformative experience, just as the resurrection was a transformative experience for Christ.

Finally, Christ's descent into the realm of the dead is followed by an ascension into heaven. Here Christ occupies the place of honor at the right hand of God. The innocent Christ has been both vindicated and exalted. Once again the angels are mentioned. However, there is no thought of rebellion here. These heavenly beings are all subject to the glorious Savior.

Mark 1:12-15

The account of the temptation (vv. 12–13), though succinct, is charged with theological meaning. Each word carries a wealth of tradition. For ancient Israel, the Spirit was a manifestation of the mighty power of God. It was the

Spirit that propelled the judges into the action that saved Israel from its enemies (cf. Judg 3:10). It was the Spirit that provided the kings with what they
needed to consolidate the tribes into a cohesive nation (cf. 1 Sam 16:13). It was
the Spirit that took obscure individuals and made them prophets of God (cf.
Isa 61:1). This was the Spirit that drove Jesus into the wilderness.

The wilderness was not a romantic place. It was rife with danger. Inhabited
by wild animals, it was also the refuge of bandits and the discarded of society.
More significantly, it had been the place of Israel's testing (cf. Num 10:11–
21:34). Bereft there of all of the supports that an established society had to offer,
the people were thrown on the providence of God. The wilderness had a long
tradition of being the place of trial. Again and again the people failed the test.

Forty days held special meaning for the two men who represented, respectively, Israel's law and prophets. Moses fasted for forty days and forty nights as
he wrote the Ten Commandments on tablets of stone (Exod 34:28). Elijah
fasted for the same length of time as he walked to Horeb (1 Kgs 19:8). It was in
this same tradition that Jesus fasted.

Originally Satan was seen as a kind of juridical adversary, the one who accused someone of wrongdoing. Only later did accusation develop into instiga-
tion of the evil and temptation to acquiesce to it. Gradually several unconnected
characterizations of evil beings from either the heavens or the underworld
began to merge into this concept, until it resulted in the picture found in this
reading. Now Satan, the personification of evil, roams the world in an attempt
to turn human beings away from God.

Jesus was driven into the place of testing, as were some of the major figures
of ancient Israel. There he was prepared for the ministry that lay ahead of him.
The announcement of this ministry (vv. 14–15) is a summary of the content
of his preaching. Though short, it contains several of the major points of his
message. First, he announced that the time *(kairós)* had arrived. This is not ordinary chronological time but a decisive moment. In eschatological thought, it
is the time of fulfillment.

Following the announcement is an explication of the character of this special time; it is the advent of the reign of God. Israel had long awaited the reign
of God. Being constantly at the mercy of more powerful nations, or being
ruled by kings who did not hold God's will in the forefront of their administration, the people longed for a time when they would be free from foreign influence and able to pursue their religious destiny. Jesus taught that this would
only happen if the people were to repent, undergo a change of heart *(metánoia),*
and accept the good news that he preached. While this message sounds simple,
its implications are unsettling. Jesus' interpretation of God's will did not correspond to the predominant understanding of his day, and a change of mind
and heart is a lifelong task. His announcement of such a ministry was fraught
with danger.

Themes of the Day

For too long we have thought that Lent is a time for us to sacrifice our wants and our desires, to give up things in order to devote ourselves to God. The readings for today and for all of the Sundays of Lent show us that, in a sense, the opposite is true. This is not a time for us to deny ourselves of something, but a time for us to receive. We are not the ones who are meant to accomplish great things for God. Rather, it is God who acts; it is God who makes the sacrifice; it is God who accomplishes great things for us.

The readings for this Sunday provide us with a kind of synopsis of the entire lenten season. They acknowledge that we are living in the midst of conflict; they sketch God as initiating a relationship with us even in the midst of this conflict; they end with a proclamation of the good news of salvation.

We Live in the Midst of Conflict

With the exception the responsorial psalm, each of the readings describes a different kind of conflict within which we might find ourselves. The first is a world-wrenching upheaval such as happens during social discord, war, or natural disaster. We become victims of forces beyond our control, and we have no place to hide. We are completely vulnerable and can only cling to the hope that somehow God is with us. The second kind of conflict is spiritual, the struggle between right and wrong, between fidelity and disobedience. The author of 1 Peter suggests that we are in the throes of this struggle and only the graciousness of God can deliver us. Finally, the Gospel passage depicts Jesus struggling, as we all do, with temptation. These readings have not fabricated a fictional view of life. Rather, they have accurately reported what we have all experienced at one time or another.

God Initiates a Relationship

In the midst of the conflicts of life God initiates a covenantal relationship. God saves the world from the chaos into which it was thrown, makes a covenant with all living things and with the earth, and sets a bow in the heavens as a perpetual reminder of the covenant. Christ dies for sinners and offers them a baptismal bath that will save them from the chaos of their lives. The Spirit drives Jesus into the desert, there to be tested but to emerge triumphant. His victory is not for him alone but for all those who will heed his words and follow his example. In each instance it is God who initiates a remarkable act that saves: the covenant, the baptismal bath, and the proclamation of the reign of God.

The Good News of Salvation

The bow in the sky is a sign of the good news of the covenant; baptism is both the good news of salvation for us and our pledge of fidelity to God; Jesus' proclamation is that the reign of God is at hand. His message is not like John's, which was merely one of repentance. The good news is a positive message that the reign of God is in our midst. It has been inaugurated by God, as all good things have their origin in God. It was the Spirit that drove Jesus into the desert only to reappear among us as God with us. Baptism is our entrance into this glorious reign. With the psalmist we celebrate God's graciousness in inviting us into this covenant relationship. The season of Lent is a time for us to reflect on God's goodness and to decide upon an appropriate response to it.

Second Sunday of Lent

Genesis 22:1-2, 9a, 10-13, 15-18

For at least two major reasons the story that is frequently called The Sacrifice of Isaac would be better named The Testing of Abraham. First, the text itself states that "God put Abraham to the test." Second, Isaac is never really sacrificed. The opening verses (vv. 1–2) set the contours of the drama that is about to unfold. The very name Abraham, which means "father of a multitude" (cf. Gen 7:15), designates the destiny of this man. It also marks the significance that progeny has for him. He will not be able to fulfill his own destiny if he does not have descendants. It is also important for the story that we remember that this is a test, an occasion to prove the quality of the man through some form of adversity (cf. Job). The readers know this, but no one in the story does. In other words, the fundamental identity of the man is being put to the test.

There is a word in the Hebrew text that, unfortunately, is not always translated. It is *ná'* ("Take *now* your son . . ."). This particle of entreaty or exhortation indicates that the speaker regards the words spoken as logically called for given the situation. This is not a request but a directive that the speaker believes is appropriate in this particular context. God knows the significance of this son. This is not some anonymous offspring; it is Isaac, Abraham's only son, the one he loves. Whether or not Abraham had other sons, this was the only son upon whom his hopes were pinned. This was the one on whom his future rested. This was the child of his destiny. *Na'* suggests that it is precisely for this reason that Isaac must face the knife. The significance of this son underscores the importance of the test. Is Abraham willing to jeopardize his own personal meaning and to relinquish hope for a future?

From a human point of view Abraham's response is terrifying. His initial answer upon being called by God shows his total availability: "Here I am." His actions demonstrate his unquestioned obedience. In the face of such horror the economy of words and the absence of emotion are startling. But the point of the story is not the death of Isaac. Thus the author moves quickly past the description of the preparation for the killing which, both author and reader know, will not take place. This is a test, and Abraham has passed it. His devotion (fear of God) is beyond reproach. The alacrity with which he obediently responds is coupled with piety that is demonstrated in his decision to offer a ram as sacrifice in place of his son.

Pictures that erroneously depict the angel staying Abraham's hand misunderstand the manner through which God communicates in this story. Abraham is responsive to what he *hears* either from God (v. 1) or from the angel, who is in heaven (vv. 11, 15). The verses that recount his future blessing make this clear. It was because he acted as he had, withholding nothing from God (v. 16), because he obeyed the voice of God and the messenger of God (v. 18), that ultimately he will be blessed. Abraham has relinquished his natural claim on the child of promise, and now he is blessed with a promise of more children than he can count (cf. 12:2-3; 13:16; 15:5; 26:4, 24). God will not be outdone in generosity.

Psalm 116:10, 15, 16-17, 18-19

The first verse of this excerpt from a hymn of thanksgiving is variously translated. Although most English renditions state that the faith of the psalmist remained constant even when he announced that he was in great distress, the Hebrew suggests that it was precisely the constancy of his faith that enabled him to speak of his ordeal. This verse is linked with an acknowledgment of God's concern for the fate of the righteous *(ḥāsîdîm)*. Despite how others may interpret their plight, their death is precious, that is, of inestimable value. Both verses suggest a situation that conflicts with a traditional understanding of retribution: the faithful should not be afflicted; the righteous should not have to face a wretched death.

It seems that before the psalmist could open his heart in thanksgiving he had to deal with the apparent contradiction that suffering often presents. Is it really a sign of God's displeasure? Must it always be seen as a consequence of sinful behavior? In the first verse the psalmist clearly asserts that such is not necessarily the case; misfortune and culpability are not to be equated. Having asserted this, he then proclaims a kind of gratitude that arises out of a sobered yet realistic perception of life. A deeply faithful person must be grateful despite and perhaps even in the midst of suffering, not merely in its absence.

The relationship between the psalmist and God is strikingly characterized in the metaphor "servant" and its parallel "son of your handmaid." Although the first image has taken on a profound theological connotation (servant of God), the second clearly identifies both images as classifications within a structured household. A slave born into a household had neither a justified claim to, nor any guaranteed likelihood of, emancipation. By using these legal metaphors to characterize his relationship with God, the psalmist is dramatizing his own situation. Like a slave that has no hope of release, he was bound to a life of great difficulty. However, God looked kindly upon him and loosed him from his servitude.

The rest of the psalm draws the outlines of a ritual of thanksgiving. Included in such a ritual is a confession of praise, a call on God, and the taking of vows. All of this takes place within the setting of a liturgical assembly (vv. 17–19). Each of these elements is a testimony to the religious sentiments of the psalmist. The actual thanksgiving *(tôdâ)* is a public acclamation of God's saving action. The name of God, which is a manifestation of the very essence of God, is called on in the song of thanksgiving, thereby proclaiming before all the people God's salvific presence. Vows that are made in time of distress are later fulfilled during the *tôdâ*. Finally, it is in the holy city of Jerusalem within the courts of the temple that all this takes place, underscoring the sacredness of the ceremony.

The psalm moves from faithfulness in the face of distress, through release from servitude by God, to public celebration of thanksgiving for this deliverance. The elements of lament are accompanied by confidence in God's compassion and gratitude for God's goodness.

Romans 8:31b-34

The language of this excerpt from the letter to the Romans resembles that of the law courts. One characteristic of the courts is that there are two sides to every case; one is in favor of it, and one is against it. A second example of juridical influence is the content of Paul's questioning. He wonders who will bring a charge against God's chosen ones, who will condemn them, who will justify them. He identifies God as a judge. The first question asked is an *a fortiori* argument, moving from the greater to the lesser: "If God is for us, who can be against us?" ("If these things are done when the wood is green what will happen when it is dry?" [Luke 23:31]). His manner of argumentation is rhetorical questioning. These are not queries seeking information; rather, they are questions that have obvious answers. This shows that Paul, the great preacher, was quite adept at the judicial conventions of his day.

This technical language and the juridical approach serve Paul's own theological argument. He is emphasizing the immeasurable love of God. In a world that was fearful of capricious gods, deities that cared little for human beings, the claim that God is for us is a bold statement. But such was the belief of the Hebrew people, and Christians inherited that conviction. Using the *a fortiori* technique, Paul argues that if the sovereign God is on our side, then regardless of what can be mustered against us, it is nothing in comparison to God's power.

Paul's second question, an *a fortiori* statement, yields another unusual perspective but one that is reminiscent of a narrative in the Israelite tradition. Like Abraham (cf. Gen 22:16), God is willing to sacrifice a beloved son. However, unlike Abraham's son Isaac, God's son Jesus is not spared at the last moment. He suffers vicariously "for us all." Paul asks: If God was willing to make the supreme sacrifice of handing over this beloved Son for our sake, is it possible that God would deny us whatever other trivial things we might need? Both of these questions highlight God's prodigality toward us.

The form of the questioning changes. The beneficiaries of God's good graces change as well. Sometimes it is God's chosen ones who are blessed, and other times it is "us." Paul now employs simple questions and provides each with an answer: Who would dare bring a charge against God's chosen ones? Paul answers his own question with another: Might it be God the judge? That, of course, is the only one who could bring charges. But after all that God has done for them and given to them, would God condemn them? The apparent response is, it seems unlikely. The final question asks: Who will condemn them? Again Paul responds with a question: Might it be Christ Jesus? This too seems unlikely. According to Paul, after Jesus has willingly died for us he would certainly not turn around and condemn us. Besides, he is now interceding for us.

Although Paul first mentions the death of Jesus, he moves immediately to his resurrection and exaltation at the right hand of God. The right hand is the favored hand, and to sit at one's right hand is to occupy the seat of honor. Having sacrificed himself for the sake of others, Jesus deserved that distinction. It is this same Jesus who now pleads on our behalf. Who or what can be against us if God and Christ are so much for us?

Mark 9:2-10

The account of the transfiguration of Jesus knits together traditions of Israel's past, insights into Jesus' own identity, and a glimpse into the future of eschatological fulfillment. The word for transfiguration *(metamorphóō)* literally means "to change form." Many religious traditions believe that gods can easily change into different forms. Various schools of mysticism maintain that human beings and certain animals as well can change their forms. In Jewish apocalyptic hope the righteous will take on a glorious new heavenly form. Although this account emphasizes the new brilliance of Jesus' clothing, it is he who was transfigured. The question then is not can it happen, but what does it mean?

Peter, James, and John, privileged to witness this transfiguration, seem to form an inner circle. Their presence makes this a historical event, not a celestial one. Although only Jesus was transformed and only he spoke with the apparitions, the disciples were caught up into the experience as well. They beheld the transfigured Jesus, along with Moses and Elijah. They were overshadowed by the cloud, and the voice spoke directly to them.

The account contains many details associated with Moses and Elijah. Both are associated with mountains (Sinai, Exodus 19; Horeb, 1 Kings 19); both underwent a kind of transformation (Moses' face was made radiant, Exod 34:29-35; Elijah was transported in a fiery chariot, 2 Kgs 2:11). Finally, these men are associated with two very important traditions. First, together they represent the basis of Israel's tradition, the law and the prophets respectively. Second, they both prefigure the prophetic dimension of the messianic era (cf. Deut 18:15, 18-19; Mal 3:1, 23).

Peter's plea for permission to set up three tents recalls the feast of Tabernacles, when the Jews remembered the temporary dwellings in which they lived during their sojourn in the wilderness. By the time of Jesus the feast had taken on messianic undertones (cf. Zech 14:16-19). If Peter's request springs from a desire to enjoy messianic blessings, Jesus' final directive to tell no one until after the resurrection reminds him that Jesus' debasement must precede his glorification. The transfiguration is, then, a prefigurement of that fulfillment.

The words from the cloud are both clear and cryptic. Jesus is identified as the beloved Son, reminiscent of Isaac, who was also a beloved son (cf. Gen 22:2). The voice directs the three disciples to listen to Jesus. This could be understood in a very general sense, but the words of Jesus on the way down the mountain suggest something more specific. It is clear that the disciples did not understand what he meant by "rising from the dead." The connection with Isaac and Jesus' final charge suggest that the voice is referring to Jesus' teaching about his death. It may be that the transfiguration was intended to prepare the inner circle of disciples for the unthinkable suffering and death in order to strengthen them in advance.

Themes of the Day

Last Sunday we reflected upon the gifts that God has graciously bestowed upon us. Today we continue that meditation and we deepen it as we focus our gaze, not on the gifts, but on the one giving them. It is God who is in our midst, God who did not spare the beloved Son. This same God now makes some demands on us. In order to enjoy the incredible blessings that God has in store for us, we must be willing to relinquish our own dreams for the future.

Relinquish Your Future

We all have dreams for the future, dreams about improvement and fulfillment, about success and well being. Our dreams are not necessarily selfish; we all want peace and a better world for our children and grandchildren. Our traditions, whether religious or cultural, set before us aspirations that call for some form of personal transformation. Such aspirations are admirable, even profoundly spiritual. Yet it sometimes happens, when we are following the inspiration of our most devout aspirations, that obstacles are thrown in our path preventing us from following our dreams. In fact, it seems that we are being asked to give up what we were sure was God's will for us. Illness or disability prevent us from being of service to others; accidents alter the circumstances of our lives; we may discover that we have been misled by another. In all of this we are forced to relinquish our cherished dreams for the future.

Accept My Future

God does not call us out of our dreams into a vacuum. If we are asked to relinquish a possible future, it is only to be offered another possible future, God's future. Our aspirations may be noble, but the possibilities that God offers will outstrip them in excellence. Abraham was promised an heir; he relinquished his hold on his heir, and he was granted heirs beyond counting. Jesus came as a rabbi; he allowed himself to be handed over to death, and he was revealed as the beloved Son who sits at God's right hand.

Are we able to relinquish our hold on what we believe will be our future in order to receive a future that is not ours to control, a future beyond our imagination? Do we really believe it is God's plan that we be caught up into the transfigured glory of Christ? And even if we answer yes, who has not wondered, with Peter and James and John, what rising from the dead might mean?

Those preparing for baptism will soon be asked to do just this. They will be required to relinquish the dreams they previously held in order to embrace the future God has in store for them, a future with Christ as the basis and model of all they will do and be. Those of us who are already joined to Christ will be asked to recommit ourselves to this transformative experience. How deep will our commitment go?

Our Future Is Christ

The question is, where do we place our trust? Is it in our own dreams and plans for the future, or have we placed it in the hands of Christ, who died for us and who intercedes for us in heaven? Do we need a glimpse of Christ's transfiguration in order to believe in his resurrection? Do we have to see and touch Jesus, or are we able to believe because we have heard the message he proclaimed? God's future in Christ is open to us, but we must accept it in faith even when we do not fully understand what it means.

Third Sunday of Lent

Exodus 20:1-17

The Ten Commandments (in Hebrew, "the ten words") are considered the foundation of Israelite law. They include the basic conditions for covenant membership. They begin with a self-proclamation by the God who has already acted on behalf of the people (v. 2). This proclamation is less interested in an identification of God for its own sake than it is a declaration of the authority that is the basis for the covenant, an authority that was established through past experience. The history of deliverance by God, which is part of this self-proclamation, is the basis of the allegiance that is sought here. It is important to note that Israel's obedience is intended to be a response to God's goodness, not the condition for it. Deliverance has already taken place; the initiative has been God's.

The stipulations are apodictic in form (You shall . . . you shall not . . .). They were meant to be absolute and applicable in any situation; sanctions for violation of them were severe. Acknowledgment of the LORD's deliverance of the people from bondage to the gods of Egypt is the basis of conformity to these stipulations. This is why Israelites were forbidden to revere other gods (v. 3); why they were told that they may not carve images for themselves (v. 4). Perhaps Israel's religion was aniconic (without image) because it was so easy to move from reverence for an image to veneration of an idol. A breach of the statutes in this list would bring severe punishment down on the heads of the transgressors, even to the fourth generation (vv. 5–6).

Since Israel believed that one's name contained something of one's own identity, disregard for the name was an insult to the person. Thus the vain use of the name of God was comparable to the profanation of God's divine being (v. 7). This is especially true in situations of false promising, insincere swearing, or magical rituals. Observance of the Sabbath was rooted in the creation of the world (vv. 8-11; cf. Gen 2:2-3). This gave primordial legitimation to the cornerstone of Israel's liturgical practice. Furthermore, Sabbath rest was guaranteed to children, slaves, work animals, and foreigners—all dependents in a patriarchal society. (Perhaps women were not mentioned because Sabbath rest had been enjoined on them at the time of creation.) In these commandments Israel was first forbidden to worship other gods and then told how to worship its own.

It is clear that these commandments were directed toward adults. This is also true about the command to honor one's parents (v. 12). Too often this injunction has been relegated to younger children, and adult responsibility has thus been minimized. Murder, adultery, stealing, lying, and coveting (vv. 13–17) all threaten the social fabric of the group. Each crime begins with disrespect of and ends in violation of a companion covenant member. This explains why they are serious.

The prohibition against coveting a neighbor's wife but not one's husband (v. 17) betrays the gender bias of the writer (speaking only to men) or of the society (presuming that women have no legitimate sexual desire). This bias notwithstanding, there are no other social distinctions here. These commandments were really meant to be observed by all. Basically they provided a sketch of the God with whom the people were in covenant, and they outlined how these covenanted people were to revere their God and live with one another.

Psalm 19:8, 9, 10, 11

Six different synonyms are used to extol the glories of the law. Although the general theme of the psalm is praise, its tone is didactic and exhortative. It describes the blessings that acceptance of the law can impart. It does this not merely to describe the law but also to persuade the people to embrace it as the will of God and to live in accord with it. Each one of the statements in this psalm identifies the law as belonging to the LORD. This is not just any religious law; it is uniquely Israel's, because in a very specific way it represents the will of the God of Israel.

When most people today talk about law, they normally mean legal enactments that have some degree of binding force. While this is certainly one dimension of the meaning of the Hebrew word, *tôrâ* might be better translated "instruction" or "teaching." As found in the Bible, the law consisted of directives for living a full and god-fearing life. Teaching the law was the special task of both the wisdom school and the priesthood. The former group collected and safeguarded the insights gleaned from various life experiences. The latter group functioned, in a society that believed that ultimate wisdom was revealed by the deity, as mediators between God and the people.

If the law is understood as the will of God for human beings, then the qualities enshrined in that law could legitimately be considered reflections of divine attributes. If the law is thought to be that point where an encounter with God takes place, then those who are shaped by the law will be godlike. The qualities associated with the law that are found in this psalm are some of the most highly prized attributes in any tradition. The law is perfect or complete; it is trustworthy, upright, and clean; it is pure and true. Fidelity to the law should lead one to the godliness that is enshrined within it.

The effects of the law enumerated here are all relational, enhancing human life itself. The psalmist maintains that the law imbues the soul with new vitality; it gives wisdom to those who would not ordinarily have it. It delights the heart; it enables the eyes to see dimensions of truth otherwise obscured. It establishes an enduring attitude of awe; it is a path to righteousness. This description of the law shows clearly that the psalmist found it life-giving and not restrictive, ennobling and not demeaning. Reverence for the law seems to promise the best that life has to offer.

The law is said to be more valuable than gold and sweeter than honey. Gold is precious not only for its own sake but also for the use to which it can be put. In like manner, as the word of God, the law has its own intrinsic value. However, as the psalm demonstrates, its worth is also found in its ability to accomplish the effects listed here. In its purest state, the sweetness of honey delights the palate. As a sweetening agent it can completely change the taste of food. In like manner, as the word of God the law is to be savored for its own sake, but it also provides a particular flavor to everything within its influence. The law of the LORD is something greatly to be desired.

1 Corinthians 1:22-25

In these few verses, which are filled with contrasts and paradoxes, Paul accomplishes several things. He dismantles the evaluative criteria that formerly divided two cultures and replaces it with a religious standard; he redefines wisdom and folly; and he contrasts God's ways with human ways. He does all of this as he argues for the prominence of the crucifixion of Christ in the lives of believers.

In the tradition of Israel the saving works of God were often accompanied by marvelous signs that demonstrated God's presence and power. These signs were thought to be visible expressions of the nature of the saving act. They were either understandable in themselves or they were explained to the people by some agent of God who possessed insight into their meaning. From God's point of view they could be considered traces of divine manifestation. From a human point of view they came to be considered evidence or proof of God's presence or power. To demand these signs was to require visible, identifiable acts or events in which God's claims could be validated.

The Greeks, on the other hand, cherished rationalism and appealed to reason rather than faith. Philosophy, the love of wisdom, became the ideal. Although this philosophy took many different forms, at the heart of each school of thought was an appreciation of every kind of learning. Chief among these accomplishments were the practical knowledge gleaned from the mastery of life and its various situations and the ethical standards necessary to live in harmony with this knowledge.

Paul criticizes the Jews for their demand for signs and the Greeks for their preference for knowledge, because in clinging to what they could understand they had set themselves up as authorities for identifying God's ways. He insists that the crucified Christ is the standard against which everything is judged. The customary wisdom of these two cultures would reject a crucified Christ. He did not conform to the prominent messianic expectations of Israel; a suffering Messiah was too much to accept. His disgrace made him a laughing-stock in the eyes of the Greeks; a truly prudent wise man would not have acted with the abandon that Jesus exhibited.

However, God's ways frequently reverse human standards. Paul argues that the vulnerable and debased Christ is in fact the power of God; the ridiculous and despised Christ is really the wisdom of God. In this light it becomes clear that what the Jews and the Greeks rejected as foolishness was actually authentic wisdom, and what they cherished as wisdom was really misguided and folly. However, it takes faith to see this. Those who are called and who are open to this call will be able to recognize it. They will understand that what passes as human wisdom is empty in comparison to faith.

It would seem that within the Corinthian community the cultural differences that formerly may have separated the ethnic groups do not hold the importance they once did. The determining factor is no longer the origin and character of wisdom; it is now faith. There are those who believe in the power of the crucifixion and those who don't. The former are the wise; the latter are the foolish.

John 2:13-25

The reading revolves around the theme of temple. Jesus' actions there are acted-out prophecy and his words are prophetic forthtelling. The entire episode is framed by reference to the observance in the city of Jerusalem of the Jewish feast of Passover, the feast of Israel's salvation (vv.13, 23).

At first glance it seems that Jesus' intensity was aroused by the erosion of temple decorum and the diminishment of religious fervor this represented.

Roman coins, the currency of the day, were stamped with the head of Caesar and sometimes with the image of pagan gods. This made them unfit for temple use, so money changing became indispensable. The Jews, who came from around the world for major feasts, probably did not bring along animals for sacrifice. Thus the sellers provided a necessary service. All of this took place in the temple precincts, a vast area that included the outer court and the court of the Gentiles but not the sanctuary, or temple proper.

Two words for temple are used in this passage. Only *hierón* appears when the entire temple area is intended (vv. 14, 15), and Jesus uses *naós* when he is referring to his body (vv. 19, 21). The Jewish authorities mistakenly use *naós* in a general sense, though Jesus uses it here very specifically.

Why was Jesus so irate? He accused the merchants of making the temple a marketplace. But a part of it really was a marketplace. The transactions were legitimate, they were conducted in the appropriate temple area, and they were essential supports of the temple service. The explanation of his behavior is found both in an allusion to a passage from the prophet Zechariah (14:21), who said that at the end-time there would be no need for merchants in the house of the LORD, and in a psalm text remembered by the disciples. This latter passage states that zeal for the house of God makes the psalmist vulnerable to the scorn and abuse of others (Ps 69:9).

With his action and his words Jesus makes a double claim. First, by driving the merchants out of the temple precincts, he announces that the time of fulfillment has come. Second, identifying God as his Father affirms his right to make such a claim and to act in accord with it.

The Jews, most likely the temple authorities, demand that Jesus give further justification for his actions. Using *naós,* the word for temple proper or sanctuary, in referring to his body, he predicts his death and resurrection. This corresponds to the earlier allusion to Zechariah and the replacement of the temple sacrifice by his own suffering. His challengers take his words literally and believe he is speaking about the temple within which they stand and which is still under construction. This encounter ends with a second statement about the disciples remembering. It would require their experience of the risen Lord for them to be able to gain insight into this last saying.

The reading ends with a play on the word for "believe." The disciples believed the Scripture (v. 22); many believed when they saw the signs Jesus worked (v. 23); yet Jesus did not believe enough in them to trust them. With the knowledge that belongs to God, he knew the fickleness of the human heart.

Themes of the Day

We ended last week's meditation with a reflection on our belief that Christ is our future. For the remaining Sundays we will reflect on the significance of this Christ for our lives and on the gift of this Christ for the lenten season. These are the three Sundays for the scrutinies that the catechumens must undergo. They too will consider the role that Christ will play in their lives as Christians. For all of us Christ is the new temple, the wisdom of God, and the power of God.

The New Temple

The temple of Jerusalem was not only the place where believers went to offer sacrifice to God; it was also the place where God dwelt in the midst of the people. It was built over the navel of the universe, the *axis mundi,* that spot where the world above and the world below come into conjunction with the world of history, thus enabling the three worlds to communicate. The temple was a sacred place because of where it was located and because of what took place within it.

When Jesus identified himself as the new temple, he was claiming to be the center of the universe, the spot where three-way cosmic communication occurred, the presence of God in the midst of the community. When we accept him in faith, we are acceding to his claims. We are agreeing that he is the center of our universe, the medium of our communication with God, the presence of God in our midst. We may profess this belief, but do our lives reflect it?

The Wisdom of God

Although the law is considered by some to be a rigid set of precepts, it is really more a collection of directives that have grown out of the experience of life. The Hebrew word *tôrâ* might best be understood as "instruction" or "teaching." Thus the law is really a kind of codified wisdom. It is accorded the highest praise because it points to God. For this reason alone it should be cherished more than gold. It reflects the order that God intended for the world, and thus it is worthy of our respect.

We believe that Jesus is the wisdom of God. This means not only that in him God's wisdom is made known but also that he is the way that points to God. While laws often embody distinctive cultural values or customs, as wisdom of God Jesus crosses cultural boundaries and breaks down cultural distinctions. As the wisdom of God Jesus fulfills the expectations of any and all codes of law.

The Power of God

Two marvelous religious institutions, the law and the temple, witness to the power of God in the lives of believers. The first has endured down through the centuries to our own day; the second survives in the various religious hopes of both Jews and Christians. As significant as these institutions have been and continue to be, they pale in the light of Jesus, who is identified as the power of God. God's power is not revealed in lofty precepts or in magnificent stones but rather in the broken and pierced body of Jesus Christ. This Sunday we are given the opportunity to discover whether we consider these claims empty foolishness, stumbling blocks, or the ground of our faith.

Fourth Sunday of Lent
2 Chronicles 36:14-16, 19-23

The reading can be divided into three parts: a brief summary of the sinfulness of the nation (vv. 14–16); a description of the punishment that befell the people because of their wickedness (vv. 17, 19–21); and an account of the decree directing them to return to Jerusalem and rebuild the temple (vv. 22–23).

The first verses constitute a statement about the religious history of Judah. They acknowledge the infidelity of the political and religious leaders and of the people themselves. The identification of the three distinct groups is significant. It suggests that the religious well being of the people was the responsibility of both the monarchy and the priesthood. It states that the populace too had "added infidelity to infidelity," engaging in behavior unworthy of the people of God. While "abominations of the nations" may refer to more than idolatrous practices, pollution of the temple is certainly a cultic violation.

The account is quite poignant, as it describes how, despite the sinfulness of the people, God was moved to compassion. Again and again reforming prophets (messengers) were sent to this corrupt nation but to no avail. Not only did they ignore the prophets, they actively derided them. According to this account, it was this callous contempt that unleashed the avenging anger of God. The demise of the monarchy, the collapse of the temple system of worship, and the deportation of the people were the inevitable consequences of this hardhearted obstinacy.

The punishment was brutal and sweeping. What had been desecrated through the wickedness of the people was now purified through the inexorable fury of God's wrath. What was not destroyed was appropriated by the conquerors. Because the people had failed to observe the Sabbath, the entire land would now be deserted in a Sabbath rest of seventy years (cf. Jer 25:11). Here again, the punishment exacted fit the crime.

The reading ends on a note of hope. Just as Jeremiah had prophesied the demise of Judah, so he foretold the collapse of its conqueror and captor (Jer

25:12). There is a note of universalism here; a foreign king is inspired by the God of Israel (v. 22). The king was not an unsuspecting pawn in the hands of God. He was well aware of the salvific role he was playing on the international stage. He did not deny the scope of his influence or the power he wielded, but he credited the God of Israel as the source of it all. Although reasons were given for the destruction of the temple and the deportation of the people, no reasons are given for its rebuilding or their return. It is simply because of the graciousness of God.

Whether or not this report is historically accurate is not an issue. What is important is the character of its message. First, it underscores the universality of God's jurisdiction. It is not limited to the confines of Israel; God can issue a command even in a foreign land and even to a non-Israelite. Second, God can deliver Israel through the agency of a non-Israelite. Third, the final words of this reading, of the entire biblical book, and of the Jewish canon (this is the last book) exhort the people to go to Jerusalem and rebuild the temple. The political implications of this directive continue to be profound.

Psalm 137:1-2, 3, 4-5, 6

The psalm response is rich in religious sentiment. It describes inconsolable despondency (vv. 1–2), fierce resentment (vv. 3–4), and heartfelt commitment (vv. 5–6). The background of these sentiments is clearly identified: the people had been snatched from their beloved Zion, and they were then held captive somewhere in Babylon. To compound the despair that engulfed them as a consequence of this disaster, they were taunted by their captors. The verb forms of the first verses (vv. 1–4) suggest the psalmist is describing a situation that took place in the past. The form of the self-imprecation (vv. 5–6) indicates an attitude that prevails in the present.

There are several reasons why the exiled people cannot sing their religious songs in a foreign land. First, it would be incongruous to extol God's mighty deeds while the nation sat in defeat. This would be especially true when their defeat was considered by some as evidence of God's inability to save them. Second, at this time in history people normally believed that the rule of a god was territorial, and it was appropriate to pay homage to the god within whose territory they resided. Third, the Israelites considered Babylon an unclean land. Therefore, it was unseemly to pray to the holy God of Israel in such a profane place. For any one or for all of these reasons the Israelites refused to sing their religious songs, and so they put their accompanying instruments aside as well.

The appeal for song made by the captors was a cruel taunt. They asked for mirth from those who had been dispossessed and exiled and who were now in despair. They asked for songs that celebrated God's triumph and magnanimity (cf. Pss 46; 48; 76) and extolled the glories of Jerusalem and of the temple (cf. Pss 84; 87; 122) when the people were bereft of comfort and the city and sanctuary they loved so well were in ruins. How could they sing in such a place and under such circumstances?

Then the psalmist cries out in both anguish and passion: How could I forget Jerusalem? It is unthinkable that such a thing should happen. But if it should. . . . The psalmist then calls down a curse. If the unthinkable happens, if I forget Jerusalem, let my right hand become useless. If I pick up my harp to play one of the joyous songs that belong to my devastated city, let the hand that would pluck out the melody wither. If I try to sing, let my tongue cleave to the roof of my mouth and render me speechless. Loyalty to Jerusalem, even as it lies ravaged and desolate, must be placed above any personal consolation the psalmist may seek. This loyalty will take the form of silence and also of remembering. Jerusalem and the temple will continue to exist in the religious memories of this humiliated, despoiled, disheartened, yet dedicated people.

Ephesians 2:4-10

The image of God sketched in the first verses of this reading is dynamic. God is rich in mercy; has great love for us; and has brought us to life, raised us up, and seated us with Christ in glory. This portrait is followed by a glimpse into the meaning of our salvation. Unable to save ourselves, we receive this salvation as a pure gift from God. We are God's handiwork, created in Christ Jesus. There is no question about the magnanimity of God. We have earned nothing; everything has been given.

The contrast between the graciousness of God and our human inadequacy is drawn in bold strokes. When we were dead in sin, God made us alive in Christ. Why? Not because we deserved it but because God is rich in mercy, because God loves us. Mercy (the Greek *èleos*) corresponds to covenant lovingkindness *(ḥesed)*. It denotes trust and loyalty. The love of God that invokes this mercy is *agápē,* the self-giving love that forgives and transforms. God has freely chosen to be bound to us in covenant regardless of our failures and our inadequacies. The lengths to which God will go to show mercy are incomprehensible. God's love is unfathomable.

The character of our union with Christ is seen in the author's choice of verbs. "Brought us to life," "raised us up," and "seated us" are all prefixed with the Greek preposition *sýn.* This preposition has the basic meaning of "being with" in a very personal sense. It denotes acting together, having a common destiny. These verbs signify that believers share in Christ's quickening, Christ's resurrection, and Christ's exaltation. The tense of the verbs indicates that this has already happened; it is not some promised eschatological future. Although it is not explicitly mentioned, the imagery suggests that there is an allusion here to baptism, for it is then that we enter into these Christ-events. The reference to coming ages is plural, not singular, as is the case when the final age is meant. This suggests that God's mercy is not a once-for-all gift but will unfold again and again, enriching both the individual and the Church as a whole.

All these marvels are accomplished in Christ. This theme is really the heart of Paul's theology. Salvation is a grace that we receive "in Christ," because of Christ. Grace and faith are essential components of salvation: God bestows the grace and we accept it in faith. Good works are important but only as a result of having been saved, not as a condition for it. Realizing that we have not earned our salvation and we do not really deserve it prevents us from boasting in our accomplishments. This saving grace was given to us when we were dead in our transgressions, our willful acts of disobedience. For some reason beyond our comprehension, God looked upon us and loved us.

While it is true that as creatures we are God's handiwork, it is consistent with this passage, which speaks of rebirth in Christ, to think of salvific re-creation. We are made anew, and we are called to a new way of living determined for us by God at the very time our salvation was decided. Both the salvation and the way of life have been given by God in love and must be accepted by us in faith.

John 3:14-21

The themes in this reading move like the waves of the sea. Each grows in strength, swells, and then disappears into the next. Image folds into image until the entire story of salvation has been told: lifting up, Son of Humanity/Son of God, world, believe/judgment, light/darkness.

Just as healing came to those who looked upon the bronze serpent that Moses raised up before them in the wilderness (Num 21:8-9), so life eternal comes to those who believe in the Son of Humanity (the Greek has *ánthrōpos* —"humankind"), who is raised up in both ignominy and exaltation. The image of something raised up suggests that Jesus was tied to a pole, as was the effigy of the serpent. However, the verb used means "to be raised in exaltation." Choosing this verb with its various meanings, the evangelist is saying that it was precisely in his humiliation that Jesus was glorified. This thought calls to mind the suffering servant in Isaiah, who also suffered for others and who, in his affliction, was "raised high and greatly exalted" (Isa 52:13).

"Son of Man" is a Semitic idiom that refers to a symbolic figure who will inaugurate the last days (cf. Dan 7:13-14). The way the thought is developed here, one is led to conclude that this Son of Humanity is also the only-begotten Son of God (vv. 14–16). The juxtaposition of these two titles brings together the diverse and rich theologies that each represents. As different as these representations may be, here is one characteristic they share in common: both the Son of Humanity and the Son of God are agents of eternal life for all.

The author maintains that God's love for the world is so deep and so magnanimous that nothing is spared for its salvation, not even God's only Son. God gave/sent this Son first in the incarnation and again in his saving death. Though it was not God's intent, the plan of salvation became judgment for some. The word for "judgment" means "to make a judicial decision," but it is generally used to mean a negative ruling. Decisions are made on the basis of certain criteria. In this passage faith in the Son of God is the deciding factor. Those who believe are saved; those who do not believe call down judgment upon themselves.

A second theme expresses the same idea, the theme of light. The richness of this symbol can be seen in these few verses. First, it is a characterization of the Son who came into the world (v. 19). It also corresponds to the truthfulness that accompanies living a righteous life (vv. 20–21). These themes are actually dimensions of the same reality: Christ is the true light, and those who choose Christ live in that light, that is, in the truth; those who do not believe are in darkness.

Finally, this reading speaks about the world. Although it was created as good, it often stands in opposition to God and, consequently, is in need of being saved. This is the situation that is presumed here, otherwise there would be no need for salvation. This is the world that God loved (v. 16); this is the world into which the Son was sent (v. 17); this is the world into which the light came (v. 19).

Themes of the Day

Continuing our consideration of the significance of Christ for our lives, we see that he is the one who is lifted up and through whom we gain eternal life. The primary theme of today's readings is the mercy of God, which can be considered from three aspects: God is rich in mercy; God's mercy lifts us up; the blessings of God flow from being lifted up by the mercy of God.

God Is Rich in Mercy

Each of the readings provides us with an example of how God is rich in mercy. God's use of Cyrus as an instrument of the deliverance of the Israelites from exile, even though he was not a believer and even when he was not aware of being used by God, shows the extent of God's mercy. Every circumstance and any person can be an opportunity for demonstrating its scope. In fact, it is often the situation or the individual we least expect that has been chosen to manifest God's mercy to us. This same mercy is shown in God's desire to bring us to life with Christ even when we were dead in sin. We are able to enjoy such favor because God first looked with merciful favor on Jesus, who is the source of eternal life for others.

God's Mercy Lifts Us Up

"Mercy" means that strict justice is set aside in favor of compassion. A dispossessed people is raised out of defeat and given another chance at self-determination, success, and prosperity. Sinners who are justly condemned to severe punishment are raised out of despair and offered a reprieve. The whole world is raised up out of darkness when God's own Son is sent into that world as Savior rather than judge. God's mercy raises us out of loss and hopelessness, out of darkness and sin, so that we might enjoy the blessings of life.

The Blessings of God Flow from God's Mercy

The mercy of God flowers in various and significant ways. People who had been exiled are allowed to return home; people who were dispossessed once again embrace what they so tenderly cherish. Their cries of lamentation are replaced by shouts of joy. Sinners are given another chance; any trace of their transgression is washed away in the blood of Christ. This miracle of divine mercy fills them with gratitude and praise. The whole world is offered the opportunity of new life in Christ. Those who accept the offer stand in silence before the manifestation of God's incomparable mercy.

God raised the eyes of the people in the wilderness so they might be healed, raised the nation from exile so it might be restored, raised Jesus from the dead so he might be Savior to us all. We too have been raised up so we might live in truth and become the visible sign of God's mercy in the world. We have been made a new people, free from the restraints of the past. Joined with Christ we become God's handiwork, creations that bear the seal of the great Creator. We are the very sacrament of God's mercy. The forgiveness we have experienced and the new life within us shine forth as witness to the mercy of God.

Fifth Sunday of Lent
Jeremiah 31:31-34

This short oracle of salvation contains a message that is both inspiring and challenging. At the heart of its eschatological vision is the promise of a new covenant for a people who, because of their infidelities, had been chastened for a time but who would ultimately be restored. This oracle carries a message of hope, forgiveness, and transformation.

Although Jeremiah was a southern prophet who prophesied long after the collapse of the northern kingdom, his message was full of promise for both the house of Judah and the house of Israel. He announced that in the future time of eschatological fulfillment both kingdoms would be united once again and God would relate to the people as an undivided community. These people would be united as they had been when they were first founded as a people. They all claimed the same ancestors, and now they would all enjoy the same future.

While certain aspects of this new covenant might resemble features of the past, others would be radically different. The text clearly states this difference. Whereas the old covenant included laws inscribed on stone tablets and was entrusted to the community as a whole, the law of the new covenant will be written on the hearts of the individual members. Where the former covenant required external conformity, the new one will call for interior commitment and transformation. The new covenantal relationship will be entered into freely. Each individual will be directed from within. This will require total openness to God and the ability to discern God's will amidst a myriad of possibilities. The challenge required of the relationship will be greater than that required of the first covenant.

One of the most notable characteristics of this reading is the fact that the promise of a new covenant is made to a sinful people (vv. 32, 34). There is no mention here of any prior repentance and reform on the part of the people. It speaks only of the generosity of God. Furthermore, the Hebrew reads "cut a covenant" (v. 31), denoting a ritual action, a ceremony consisting of an animal being cut in two and the covenant partners passing between the two parts. This rite signified the penalty under which they placed themselves should they violate the agreement being "cut." If unfaithful, they would be willing to face the same fate. God was serious about this covenant and expected that Israel would be serious as well.

The reading includes a technical covenant formula: "I will be their God, and they shall be my people." The words of the formula mark the specificity and exclusivity of this relationship: "I and no other will be their God," and "among all the nations of the world, they will be my people." Because these are the words of God, they possess performative force. In other words, the very proclamation of the words effects what they describe. When God says this, it actually comes to be. The very words of God established the covenant. The hope envisioned for the future begins to take shape in the present. It is actually the magnanimous compassion of God that forgives the sins of the people and through this interior covenant creates them anew as a transformed community.

Psalm 51:3-4, 12-13, 14-15

This penitential psalm consists of a plea for mercy in the face of guilt (vv. 3–4), a prayer for inner renewal (v. 12), and a vow made in thanksgiving (vv. 13–15). It provides a glimpse into the inner soul of the psalmist as well as a sense of how the psalmist perceives God. As with most biblical laments it begins with sentiments of distress and helplessness, moves through expressions of trust and confidence, and ends with declarations of thanksgiving for having been heard.

The invocation is replete with theological concepts. Although it begins with a plea that God might be gracious in view of the psalmist's transgressions, its primary focus is on God's goodness. The psalmist invokes God's covenant loyalty *(ḥesed)* and womb-love *(raḥămîm)*. Of the three words used for sin, "offense" *(peshaᶜ)* is the word that implies a breach in relationship. The term itself is a collective, denoting the sum of misdeeds and a fractured relationship. Such violations cannot be overlooked; it will end in one of two ways. God either will severely punish the offenders or will renew the relationship. All of this is evidence of the solemn bond that already exists between the psalmist and God and of the psalmist's reliance on God's regard for this bond.

"Guilt" *(ᶜāwōn)* denotes twisted behavior or perversion. It too has a collective connotation, meaning that this is not merely one infraction but a manner of behavior. The third term *(hattāʾâ)* is the most commonly used word for sin. Although it means "miss the mark," the failure involved is usually deliberate, not accidental. The psalmist uses three very dynamic verbs when asking for forgiveness: "wipe out," "wash," and "cleanse." The first suggests vigorous erasing; the second implies the treading or pounding that was part of washing clothes; the third indicates a deep cleansing of dross from metal or disease from the body. The very language shows that the admission of guilt and the plea for forgiveness are profound and comprehensive.

In using *bārāʾ*, the technical creation word (cf. Gen 1:1), when asking for a heart that is ritually clean and a spirit that will not falter (v. 12), the psalmist is acknowledging the radical nature of the transformation sought and the fact that only God can effect it. Where there is divine creation, there is a new order of existence. It is this for which the psalmist prays.

The prayer is cast in negative terms as well: do not cast me from your presence; do not take your Spirit from me. Instead, restore the joy of salvation that I forfeited, and instill in me a spirit that will freely accept the responsibilities of this new relationship. Having previously rebelled and violated the covenant bond, the psalmist now begs for an intimate connection with God.

The passage ends with a pledge. Having been created anew, the psalmist promises to teach other transgressors about God's ways. This can mean either the way God works or the way God wants us to behave. Both meanings can hold here. With regard to the first meaning, the very one who rebelled against covenant responsibilities is now a witness to God's lovingkindness and merciful love. With regard to the second, the repentant, re-created psalmist will now promote fidelity to covenant obligations.

Hebrews 5:7-9

This short reading is confessional in nature. Each of its three verses offers a slightly different view of biblical christology. The first refers to the depth of Jesus' suffering, the second to a major lesson he learned through suffering, and the third to the mediatorial role he gained by that suffering.

Although some of the elements in the first verse are straightforward and easy to understand, others are ambiguous and therefore difficult to interpret. It is obvious that "in the flesh" is an allusion to Jesus' humanity. In the biblical sense of the term, the flesh *(sárx)* is not evil, but it is fraught with limitations and weaknesses. Because it is subject to deterioration and death, it came to signify many things that were associated with human frailty, such as vulnerability and fear. For Jesus to have taken on the flesh was to have taken on these limitations and weaknesses as well. This means that he was vulnerable to everything to which everyone else was vulnerable.

The reference to his anguished prayer immediately calls to mind his agony in Gethsemane (Matt 26:36-46; Mark 14:32-42; Luke 22:40-46). In the Synoptic tradition, before Jesus acquiesces to the will of God he pleads that the chalice of suffering be taken from him. If this is the allusion intended, there seems to be an inconsistency, for we know that ultimately he did endure the death that caused him such dread. Most likely, the reference here is to the traditional Jewish image of a righteous person's impassioned prayer. Its sentiments are reminiscent of those found in the psalms that describe agony, terror, and depression (cf. Psalms 22, 31, 38). The emotion that is suggested demonstrates how thoroughly Jesus embraced his human nature. He offered these prayers as a priest offers sacrifice, and he was heard because of his reverence, or godly fear.

The second verse is no less ambiguous. Though Son of God, Jesus learned what every human has to learn, namely, acceptance of God's will in the circumstances of life. The surest way to learn this lesson, though perhaps the hardest, is through suffering. This notion is not meant to cast doubt on the character of Jesus' divine sonship. Rather, it points once again to his willingness to assume every aspect of human nature, even those most difficult to bear.

All of this becomes comprehensible when we examine Jesus' role as mediator of salvation. He has endured torment of body and anguish of soul. He has known agony, terror, and depression. His experience of being human is now complete. He can fully understand human distress and the desire to escape it. He can speak to those in affliction as one who himself has been ravaged by human sorrow but who despite it has clung fast to God's will. From a human point of view, he is one with the human condition. From God's point of view, he is the one who can now show others how to accept with docility the circumstances of life over which they have no control. Just as he learned to accept God's designs in his life, so now he can teach others to do the same.

Jesus offered prayers and supplications, and he was heard. Might it be that, like a mediator-priest, he offered these prayers for others? Was the answer to his prayer perhaps the conferral upon him of the role of source of salvation of others?

John 12:20-33

The reading begins with a report of the approach of the Greeks. The identity of these people is uncertain. Since they came to the city to worship at the feast, they may have been Greek-speaking Jews. It is not clear from the original text whether they themselves came up to worship or merely accompanied those who did. If it was the latter case, they might have been proselytes or simply enterprising businesspeople who knew that the crowds who gathered for the feast would be prospective customers of some sort.

It is important to note that the text does not suggest missionary activity. Neither Jesus himself nor any of the disciples went out to these Greeks. They came on their own initiative. Mention of Philip, Andrew, and Bethsaida all indicate the Greek influence of the time. Though Jews, both men have Greek names; though Bethsaida is a Semitic name, the city itself is just over the border in Gentile territory. This mention of Greeks suggests the inclusion of the Gentile world in the salvation brought by Jesus. Jesus replies to Philip and Andrew's information about the Greeks with an announcement: His hour has come!

This "hour" is the time of Jesus' glorification (v. 23), but it is also the hour that he dreads (v. 27). It is the time of both his anguish and his exaltation. Actually, the relationship between his anguish and his exaltation is demonstrated through the imagery he uses to describe his fate (v. 24). Only through the willingness to relinquish one form of life can there be hope for another. This is true for the grain of wheat and for human existence itself. The Semitic idiom "Son of Man" refers to a symbolic figure who will inaugurate the last days (cf. Dan 7:13-14). Its inclusion here indicates that the glorification of Jesus inaugurates the final age.

These references to death and subsequent fruition apply not only to Jesus' situation but also to that of his followers. They too must be willing to die in order to live. The words "love" and "hate" indicate that there is a choice here.

Though strong words for contemporary Westerners, they merely express contrasting attitudes and thus imply preference. Disciples, those who serve Jesus, must choose. If they follow Jesus in his death, they will share in his exaltation.

The interior struggle Jesus endured is revealed in his prayer. Should he ask to be preserved from this hour of anguish/exaltation? But it was for this hour that he came into the world in the first place. Therefore he accepts it. He prays that God's name, the essence of God's being, might be glorified. It seems that the glorification of God's name will be accomplished through Jesus' own death and exaltation.

God's answer is directed to Jesus (v. 28), but meant for the crowd (v. 30). The paradox is evident. The people hear something, but they are not even sure what it is they hear. Some believe it is thunder; others think an angel has spoken to Jesus. No one realizes that it is the voice of God, nor do they seem to have grasped the meaning of the words spoken. They do believe that Jesus' prayer was answered from heaven, even though they did not understand the specifics of that answer.

Themes of the Day

In previous Sundays we have been offered several images of Christ for our meditation. He has been presented to us as the new temple, the wisdom of God, and the power of God. Like the serpent in the wilderness, he was lifted up and became the source of life to all who look upon him in faith. Today we see him as the grain of wheat that dies in order to bring forth much fruit.

All of the readings together offer us three other themes for our consideration: the tension of time, the fruits of this hour, and the judgment that follows refusal to live in the hour of fulfillment.

The Tension of Time

The moment of eschatological fulfillment gathers together the sense of the past ("the days when Christ was in the flesh"), the future ("the days are coming"), and the present ("the hour has come"). We live in the time when the past and the future are made present; we live in the already-but-not-yet time of anticipation/fulfillment. This is a moment of great ambiguity—of fear and trepidation but of electric excitement. It is a moment of decision. We hover at the edge of dawn, weighing whether to step forward into the new day or to return to the darkness of night.

It is always difficult to leave behind what we know so well, even when we are trapped in the grip of some demon. We say that we want a new life, and we probably mean this, but taking the first step into that life is both frightening and demanding. So much is being asked of us.

The Fruits of This Hour

What does this hour bring? A new covenant, a deep interior relationship with God that is not based on law but that overflows from a commitment of the heart. It brings an abundant harvest that springs from a simple grain of wheat. It brings a promise from God's own Son that those who serve him will be honored by God and those who obey him will enjoy eternal life. Who would not want such favors? Who would not run to accept them from the willing hands of a gracious God?

Although the hour brings all of these blessings, it does not do so without a price. The new covenant could only be written on new hearts; the abundant harvest sprang from the dying grain of wheat; eternal salvation was won at the price of Christ's blood. The moment of eschatological fulfillment is also a moment of decision. Will we step into the new day, or will we return to the darkness of night?

Judgment

The refusal to live in this eschatological hour means that we choose to live in unredeemed time, in an unredeemed world, a world that belongs to the prince of darkness. It means that we are satisfied to sit amidst the ruins of our broken covenants, to remain covered with the guilt of our sins, to continue to be enslaved by the addictions that cripple us. As challenging as the message of these readings may be, the last note is one of hope. Jesus has driven out the prince of darkness and has drawn everyone to himself. The strength to step into the new life is offered to us. It can overcome the demons that control us, because it is the power of the almighty God.

Palm Sunday of the Lord's Passion
At the Procession

Mark 11:1-10 (A)

The account of Jesus' entry into Jerusalem can be divided into two parts: a description of the directions for getting the colt on which Jesus will ride into the city (vv. 1–7) and the acclamation of the crowd that accompanies his entry (vv. 8–10). His actions in this account have symbolic meaning, and they reinterpret several royal messianic traditions. This is particularly true about the details surrounding the acquisition of the colt. Jesus does not enter the holy city on foot like a pilgrim would. Instead, he rides in on a colt like a messianic king (cf. Zech 9:9). "Colt" could refer to the young of any number of animals.

What is important is not the specific species but the fact that no one has yet ridden on this animal. In a sense, it has not yet been profaned.

Two other features of the account contain royal allusions. First, kings had the right to impress privately owned animals into their service whenever necessity seemed to dictate such action. (Even today, in an emergency officials can similarly appropriate what they need.) This practice could explain both Jesus' directive and the subsequent compliance of those who initially questioned the disciples' behavior. Second, the explanation given, "The Master *(kýrios)* has need of it," suggests that some kind of prerogative on Jesus' part is in the background. Jesus is in complete control of this incident. He knows in advance what is available, what can be done, and what should be said. He gives his disciples directions to follow, and they find that in each instance he had preknowledge and authority.

The narrative identifies both Bethany and Bethphage, two villages that are east of Jerusalem. Though Bethphage is closer to the Holy City, either village could have been the site of this episode. The point of the narrative is the dramatic scene of Jesus coming over the crest of the eastern hill at the Mount of Olives, a place long associated with the appearance of the Messiah (cf. Zech 14:4).

The people around spread their cloaks on the ground before Jesus as their ancestors had formerly done in deference to a king (2 Kgs 9:13), and they praise him with an acclamation taken from one of the psalms (Ps 118:25-26). "Hosanna" is really a cry for help. It means, "Save us, we pray!" However, the likely use of the psalm at annual temple festivals resulted in a change in its function if not in its meaning. Coupled with the blessing that follows in the next verse of the psalm, it became part of the liturgical greeting that met pilgrims as they entered the temple. In this narrative the bystanders direct the acclamation to Jesus, thus making it a cry of homage and not merely one of greeting.

There is a kind of chiastic structure to the entire exclamation: Hosanna . . . Blessed . . . Blessed . . . Hosanna. The structure itself suggests that the one who comes in the Lord's name and the kingdom of David that is to come are somehow intimately related. It leads one to conclude that the kingdom will be inaugurated by the one who comes in the Lord's name. All of this points to Jesus' fulfillment of the Davidic messianic expectations. This is reason to exalt "in the highest!"

John 12:12-16 (B)

This account of Jesus' entry into Jerusalem is quite straightforward. Although very few details are given, they are all rich in theological meaning. The context of the occasion is the feast of Passover, the commemoration of Israel's liberation from bondage and new birth as an independent nation. This celebration explains the presence of crowds that either participated in the event or witnessed it. In this Gospel version these crowds go out to meet Jesus rather than accompany him on his approach to the city. Only in this version do the people carry palms, a symbol of victory. (Palms were waved during the celebration of the recapture of Jerusalem [1 Macc 13:51]; they were offered in homage to kings [1 Macc 13:37; 2 Macc 14:4]; they are held by the elect as they stand before the victorious Lamb [Rev 7:9]).

The words the crowd uses in their cry of exclamation indicate the kind of victor they think Jesus is. They praise him with the acclamation that is a cry for help: "Hosanna" ("Save us, we pray!"). The blessings that follow in this passage identify Jesus in two ways: he is the one who comes in the name of the Lord, and he is the king of Israel. The messianic implications are obvious. The one who comes in the name of the Lord does so in order to inaugurate the time of fulfillment, the reign of God. Although there were many traditions identifying this mysterious individual, the most common of Jesus' day seems to have been the Davidic tradition. The people believed that a descendant of David would reestablish the monarchy.

The jubilant waving of palms and the joyous singing of the psalm verses suggest the kind of nationalistic enthusiasm that frequently surfaced in Jerusalem during major festivals. Jesus counters any possibility of such enthusiasm with a symbolic act of his own. Rather than reinforce the misconceptions of the people by riding into the city triumphantly seated on a horse, he mounts a donkey. The author of the Gospel makes explicit the meaning of this action by citing an abbreviated passage from Zechariah. The prophet describes the coming of the messianic king, who will be righteous and will bring salvation but who will also be meek and riding on a donkey (9:9).

The reading ends with a declaration of the disciples' initial lack of understanding. The crowds had been wrong in what they seemed to have anticipated, namely a triumphant conqueror. The disciples too misunderstood the meaning of the events they witnessed. Exactly how they originally perceived this event is not reported in the account. It would take the death and exaltation of Jesus for them to understand its meaning and to grasp just what kind of a Messiah Jesus was and what kind of messianic reign he had inaugurated.

At the Mass

Isaiah 50:4-7

The dynamics of hearing and speaking focus prominently in this passage. The claim is made that God has both appointed the speaker to a particular ministry and provided him with what is essential if the ministry is to be effective, namely, ears to hear God's word and a well-trained tongue to speak that word to others. This word is alive and fresh each day, for God opens the speaker's ears morning after morning. This means that he must be always attentive to hear the word that is given. Although the speaker is identified as a disciple (one who is well trained), the description is precisely that of the prophet, one who hears God's word and proclaims it.

The ability to speak and the words that are spoken all come from God. They are given to the speaker, but they are for the sake of the weary. Although the text does not indicate who these weary might be or the character of the words themselves, it does seem to presume that these people are in some way downtrodden and that the words are words of comfort.

A heavy price is exacted of the speaker. He suffers both physical attack and personal insult. He is beaten; his beard is plucked; he is spit upon. Despite all this he does not recoil from his call. More than this, he does not even seem to ward off the blows that come his way. He willingly accepts what appears to be the consequence of his prophetic ministry to the weary. No explanation is given as to why this activity should precipitate such a violent response from others or even who these persecutors might be. All we know is that the ministry generates such a response and the speaker does not abandon it or take himself out of harm's way. The suffering endured is willingly accepted.

In the face of all the affliction the speaker maintains that God is his strength. This is quite an unusual statement, for such maltreatment would have normally been interpreted as evidence that God was on the side of his persecutors. Although he has been assaulted, the speaker declares that he is not disgraced and he will not be put to shame. There are no grounds for the speaker to make these claims other than utter confidence in God, certainty of the authenticity of his call, and a conviction of the truth of the words he communicates.

Much of the content of this passage resonates with that found in many of the laments. However, there is really no complaint here, just a description of the sufferings that accrue from faithfully carrying out the mission assigned by God. If anything, this passage resembles a declaration of confidence in God's sustaining presence.

Psalm 22:8-9, 17-18, 19-20, 23-24

The psalm is a combination of a lament (vv. 8–9; 17–20) and a thanksgiving song (vv. 23–24). The imagery used is both vivid and forceful. In some places it is so realistic that one cannot distinguish with certainty factual description from poetic metaphor. While the psalm may have grown out of the struggle of one person, mention of the assembly *(qāhāl)* adds a communal liturgical dimension to its final form.

The opening verses describe the derision that the psalmist must endure from onlookers. These spectators are not explicitly identified as enemies. They are merely people who look upon the affliction of the psalmist and revile him rather than comfort him. The actual taunt is graphically described. Those who mock him part their lips to sneer at him, perhaps to hiss. They wag their heads in ridicule. The most cutting derision may be the words they hurl at him. He is reviled not only because he suffers but primarily because in his suffering he clings to God in confidence. It appears that the onlookers are mocking what they consider to be the psalmist's misplaced trust. Their taunt throws into question whether there is any point to such trust. Does God really care what happens to this pitiful man?

The metaphors used to describe the bystanders are trenchant. They are characterized as encircling dogs or some other type of predatory pack ready to tear him limb from limb. They are bloodthirsty assailants assaulting his body. They are rapacious thieves stripping the very clothes from his back. Nothing is safe from their savagery, neither the psalmist's person nor his possessions. In the end he lies humiliated, stripped, and wounded. His integrity has been challenged, and his trust in God ridiculed.

Neither the mockery nor the brutality of these onlookers can undermine the devotion of the psalmist. In the face of all this suffering, he clings to hope. Turning to God, he prays for a sense of God's presence and for deliverance from his misery. He does not seek reprisals; he seeks relief. These verses do not tell us whether or not the psalmist perceives his suffering as punishment for some offense, but they do indicate that the psalmist does not believe his unfortunate predicament should keep him separated from God. Suffering and devotion are not incompatible.

The reading ends with an exclamation associated with thanksgiving. This implies either that the psalmist's entreaties have been heard and he has been granted relief from his suffering or that he is convinced it will happen and he rejoices in anticipation. Since one's name holds part of one's essence, to proclaim the name of God is to recognize and praise the greatness—in this case the graciousness—of God. The text suggests that this acclamation will take place within a liturgical assembly. The psalmist will make a public declaration of gratitude and praise. Although the identification of the assembly as a gathering of brothers (v. 23) reveals a clear gender bias, the further mention of the descendants of Jacob (the Hebrew has "seed"; v. 24) indicates the intended inclusivity. The psalmist will proclaim his praise and thanksgiving before all the people so that all the people can join him in praising God.

Philippians 2:6-11

This christological reflection on the nature and mission of Jesus can be divided into two parts. In the first (vv. 6–8) Jesus is the subject of the action; in the second (vv. 9–11) God is. The first part describes Jesus' humiliation; the second part recounts his exaltation by God.

The first verse sets the tone for the actions of Christ Jesus. He did not cling to the dignity that was rightfully his. Two phrases identify this dignity: he is in the form of God; he is equal to God. Since the form of something is its basic appearance from which its essential character can be known, if Christ is in the form of God, he enjoys a godlike manner of being. The parallel phrase restates this in a slightly different way: he is equal to God. The verb reports that Christ did not cling to this prerogative; he did not use his exalted status for his own ends. Christ freely gave up the right to homage that was his.

Once again the verb plays an important role in this recital. Not only did Christ relinquish his godlike state, he emptied himself of it. The contrasts drawn here are noteworthy. Though in the form of God, he chose the form of a servant or slave. Without losing his godlike being, he took on the likeness of human beings. This does not mean that he only resembled a human being but really was not one. Christ did take on human form, but the qualification suggested by "likeness" points to the fact that he was human like no one else was human. Although the word "Lord" (*kýrios*, a word that is also applied to God) is not found in these early verses, the contrast between Lord and slave stands conspicuously behind it.

Christ emptied himself and took on the human condition. The final verb states that he then humbled himself and became obedient. Having taken on the form of a slave, he made himself vulnerable to all the particulars of that station in life. For a slave obedience is the determining factor. The extent of his obedience is striking. Compliance with God's will in a world alienated from God requires that one be open to the possibility of death. In a sense, Christ's crucifixion was inevitable. It was a common punishment for slaves, the nadir of human abasement. Such ignominy was a likely consequence of emptying himself and taking on human form.

The exaltation of Christ is as glorious as his humiliation was debasing. It is important to note that while Christ was the subject of his self-emptying, his super-exaltation is attributed directly to God. Once again there is a play on words and ideas. Just as "form" and "appearance" denote being, so "name" contains part of the essence of the individual. In exalting Jesus, God accords his human name a dignity that raises it above every other name. It now elicits the same reverence that the title "Lord" (*kýrios*) does. Every knee shall do him homage and every tongue shall proclaim his sovereignty.

The extent to which Christ is to be revered is total. The entire created universe is brought under his lordship. This includes the spiritual beings in heaven, all living beings on earth, and even the dead under the earth. Distinctions such as spiritual or physical, living or dead, are meaningless here. All will praise Christ, whose exaltation gives glory to God.

Mark 14:1–15:47

This passion account is a continuous narrative with coherent chronological sequence. Each scene within it, though a discrete story in itself, is connected with what precedes it and moves the drama resolutely forward. The episodes include a plot to put Jesus to death (14:1-12); the preparation for the Passover and the events of the supper (vv. 12–26); Peter's denial foretold (vv. 27–31); the agony at Gethsemane (vv. 32–42); Judas' denial and Jesus' arrest (vv. 43–52); the trial before the high priest (vv. 53–65); Peter's denial (vv. 66–72); the interrogation before Pilate (15:1-15); the mockery of the soldiers (15:16-20); the crucifixion and death of Jesus (15:21-41); the burial (15:42-47).

The major events recounted seem to be following some prearranged plan. The first episode (14:1-14) foreshadows the conclusion of the entire passion narrative: the woman who anoints the head of Jesus does so in anticipation of his burial. Other examples can be seen in the predictions of the betrayal of Judas and of Peter's denial and their later occurrences. Jesus describes in advance the circumstances surrounding the acquisition of the room for the supper. During the meal he alludes to the shedding of his blood and his future eschatological celebration. He also foretells his resurrection (14:28).

Several themes run throughout the account. The feast of Passover becomes the reason for the enemies' initial caution, the context for the betrayal by Judas and the celebration of the Lord's Supper, and the release of Barabbas instead of Jesus. Such attentiveness to the feast points up the observance of Jesus and his band and the hypocrisy of his enemies.

Jesus' relationships with various people is consistent throughout. He may respect the authority of the religious and political leaders who seek to put him to death, but he does not cooperate with them. He is identified as the Son of Man (14:21, 41, 62), the Son of God (15:39), the Christ, Son of the Blessed One (14:61); yet he associates with or is thrown in with those relegated to the margins of society. He dines at the home of a leper (presumably cured); he defends the extravagance of a woman who intrudes on a dinner; he is in prison with thieves and murderers; he is mocked by ordinary soldiers; he is crucified along with common criminals.

The entire narrative lays bare the contradiction of Jesus' life and the paradox of God's reign. The initial fear of the religious leaders shows that Jesus had a following among the people, but it was the people who cried for the release of Barabbas and the death of Jesus. Among his intimate followers only the women remained faithful: one anointed him, others kept watch at his crucifixion and took note of where he was buried. Of the men who knew him well, one betrayed him, another denied him, and the rest fled for safety. It was a foreigner, a centurion, who publicly acclaimed his divinity.

The eschatological preeminence of Jesus is illustrated in several places: he announces that he will rejoice in the new reign of God (14:25), he will be raised up (14:28), and he will be exalted with God (14:62); at his death the veil of the temple curtain was split (15:38), and at the moment of his greatest agony he was recognized as the Son of God.

Themes of the Day

In this final lenten Sunday, as we prepare to enter the sacred time of Holy Week, we look again at the significance of Christ in our lives. We recognize him as our Savior, but we look more closely in order to discover just what kind of savior he is. We find that he has taken the form of a slave; he has been glorified with a name above all other names; he continues to suffer with us.

A Self-Emptying Savior

We have not been saved through military power but through the kenotic humility of Jesus. Though he was really in the form of God, Jesus came in the form of a slave. We have a Savior who was crushed for our iniquities, nailed to a cross as a convicted felon, and there endured the sense of abandonment. Why has God stooped so low? Why did Christ empty himself so completely? We could say that all of this happened because Jesus was obedient to God's will in his life, regardless of where this led him. This may be true, but it does not answer the fundamental question: why does God love us with such abandon?

A Highly Exalted Savior

We have a Savior who was lifted up and exalted precisely because he emptied himself of his divine prerogatives. He became one of us in order to show us how we are to live. Unlike conquerors who triumph by putting down their opponents, Jesus was raised up because he himself was first willing to be put down. The passion recounts the extent to which he willingly offered himself. Because of this, he has been exalted above everyone and everything else. His glorification was won at a great price, but it is now his by victory and not by mere bestowal. His name commands the homage that no other name can claim, and it does so because he first handed himself over to us.

An Example for Us

We have a Savior who first offered himself *for* us and then continues to offer himself *to* us as an example to follow. As he was willing to empty himself for our sake, so we are told to empty ourselves for the sake of others. The best way to enter Holy Week with him is in the company of those with whom he has identified himself: the poor and the broken; the humiliated and the marginalized; those who suffer the abuse of others; those who never use rank to force their will. If we are to be saved we must go where salvation takes place: in our streets and in our homes where violence rages; in the dark corners of life where despair seems to hold sway; wherever the innocent are abused or the needy are neglected; wherever there is misunderstanding or fear or jealousy. We must go wherever Christ empties himself for our sake.

Triduum

Holy Thursday Exodus 12:1-8, 11-14 Passover meal	Psalm 116:12-13, 15-18 Our blessing cup is a communion	1 Corinthians 11:23-26 Proclaim the death of the Lord	John 13:1-15 He loved them to the end
Good Friday Isaiah 52:13–53:12 He was wounded for us	Psalm 31:2, 6, 12-13, 15-17, 25 Into your hands	Hebrews 4:14-16; 5:7-9 Jesus learned obedience	John 18:1–19:42 Passion
Holy Saturday vigil readings	Romans 6:3-11 Christ will die no more	Psalm 118:1-2, 16-17, 22-23 Give thanks to the LORD	Mark 16:1-7 The crucified is raised

Triduum

Initial Reading of the Triduum

Introduction

The readings for the Triduum offer us a very different kind of mosaic. This is because of the unique character of the readings of the Easter Vigil. While the epistle and Gospel passages of all three days can be read in columns, the readings from the First Testament and the psalm responses for the vigil make up a unit in itself. Despite this slightly different configuration the patterns can be traced, and the meanings that emerge can provide a theological matrix for the Triduum.

First Testament Readings

The readings for Holy Thursday and Good Friday offer us two examples of vicarious sacrifice. The paschal lamb was slain as a substitute for the lives of the people. The Suffering Servant was also sacrificed so that others might live. Both were innocent victims; both were led silently to slaughter. While these images might point implicitly to Jesus, the First Testament readings of the vigil service take us in another direction. They recapitulate the story of salvation that leads us to the waters of baptism.

Our reflection begins in the darkness of chaos out of which God calls light. Human beings are created and history begins. A hint of the intensity of God's desire to provide a future that far exceeds anything we might imagine can be seen in the story of Abraham and Isaac. That God does not really want the children of promise to perish is clear from the account of their crossing through the sea into freedom. God's love has the passion of a spouse. Even if the covenant relationship is threatened, this love will remain steadfast. God will provide for these people in all their needs, quenching their thirst with waters of life. They have but to walk in God's ways and they will find peace. Even if they turn away and are unfaithful, God will pour clean water over them and give them new hearts.

Psalms

The psalm responses are variously songs of thanksgiving for the amazing care and protection we have received from God, hymns of praise of the graciousness of God that has saved us and led us into a place of peace and prosperity, cries for help when we face insurmountable challenges or adversities, promises of fidelity to God and to the ways of God, and prayers that spring from hearts that long to rest in God. They are all brought to a conclusion with a psalm that rejoices in the victory of the one who was rejected but has been exalted at the right hand of God.

Epistles

The mini-epistle that is created when the three readings are placed end to end develops the theological meaning of the sacrifice of Jesus. It begins with the official Christian proclamation of the eucharistic meal as the reenactment of the death of the Lord. This is followed by a priestly interpretation of the meaning of his death. It concludes with an explanation of our participation through baptism in Jesus' death and resurrection. We begin with a report of events that transformed a festive meal, and we end with a reminder of how we are transformed by the saving action of God that comes to us through these events.

Gospels

The Gospel passages trace the theme of Jesus' selfless sacrifice of love. It begins with an account of his self-emptying service of others. Though he has the power of God at his disposal, he strips himself, gets on his knees before his disciples, and renders a service that only the humblest servants perform. The passion narrative details the extent to which Jesus was willing to humble himself. He endured rejection, ridicule, and abuse, and he did it with the dignity of a king and the beloved Son of God. Having been lifted up on the cross, he was also lifted up from the dead. The one who was cast down has now been raised up.

Mosaic of Readings

These three days have traditionally been set aside for our reflection on the most sacred mysteries of our faith, namely the suffering, death, and resurrection of Jesus. However, the readings offer us a slightly different picture to consider. Just as contemplation of his suffering and death always includes some mention of his resurrection, so the readings that report the events of his life, all include mention of our participation in these mysteries. We do not sit on the sidelines as uninvolved spectators. This is our story, and we are part of it whether we accept the love that is offered to us or not. We are the ones who are cared for and nourished by God; we are the ones God lifts out of darkness and leads through the struggles of life. Even in his resurrection Christ beckons us to join him.

Readings

Holy Thursday, Evening Mass of the Lord's Supper
Exodus 12:1-8, 11-14

The reading sets forth the ritual prescriptions for the annual celebration of the feast of Passover. The very first verse states that the establishment of the memorial, the determination of its date, and the details of the rite itself were all decreed by God. Since the event of the Exodus marked Israel's beginning as a people, it is only fitting that the feast that commemorates this beginning be positioned at the head of their year.

The very first words of the passage assert that the power of God is effective even in the land of Egypt. This is a profound theological claim for several reasons: (1) it means that rule of the God of Israel is not limited to the boundaries of the land of Israel; (2) it describes Israel's God as superior to the gods of Egypt, ruling where these other gods do not; (3) it implies that Israel's God exercises authority over the lives of the Egyptians themselves, striking down their firstborn.

The celebration takes the form of a meal, at the center of which is a lamb. Because of the significance of this ceremony, the selection, slaughter, and consumption of this lamb are carefully determined by ritual ordinance. The lamb must be male, because the people cannot afford to lose the reproductive potential of the females of the flock. It must be a year old so that it has enough maturity to embody the salvific significance that will be placed upon it, yet not be so old as to have lost its fundamental vitality. Like everything that is set aside for consecration to God, it must be free of all blemish.

The Passover lambs must be slaughtered in the presence of the entire community and then eaten in the respective households. Presumably this is an evening meal, since the lambs are to be slaughtered at twilight. The entire household must join together for this feast, men and women, children and servants. The lambs must be eaten in their entirety; nothing of the sacrifice can be left over lest it be thrown out like refuse. For this reason small households should join together to ensure total consumption of the animal. Even the manner of dress is prescribed. They must be clad like those in flight.

The ritual itself may have originated from an ancient nomadic ceremony. Herders frequently moved during the night from winter pasturage to places of spring grazing. Before their move one of the choicest members of the flock was sacrificed in order to ensure the safety of the rest of the flock. Its blood was then somehow sprinkled around the camp. This was done because of blood's apotropaic value; that is, it could ward off any threatening evil.

Elements of this ritual can be seen in the Passover ceremony. The night travel, the slaughter, and the marking with blood have all now taken on historical meaning. What was initially a sacrifice for pacification of an evil deity is now a memorial of God's protection and deliverance. The blood of the lamb, which originally warded off night demons, was now a sign of salvation for all those whose doorposts were marked with it. The night journey in search of new pasturage became the flight for safety into the wilderness. This ritual was to be a perpetual memorial of the time when the LORD passed over the Israelites.

Psalm 116:12-13, 15-16bc, 17-18

This psalm is an example of a temple service of thanksgiving. In it someone who made an appeal to God and promised to perform some act of devotion when the request was granted now comes to the temple and, before God and the assembly of believers, gives thanks for the favor granted and fulfills the vow that was made. Most vows were promises to offer some form of sacrifice (cf. Ps 56:13); holocaust (cf. Ps 66:13; Lev 22:18-20); peace offerings (cf. Ps 50:14; Lev 7:16; 22:21-22); cereal offerings and libations (cf. Num 15:3, 8).

The psalm response opens with an acknowledgment that there is nothing the psalmist can do and no gift that can be offered that will even begin to compare with the favors that have been received from God. Inadequate as it is, the psalmist still renders what can be offered, expressing devotion by offering a cup of salvation. It is not clear exactly what the cup of salvation is. It might be a libation offered in thanksgiving. Or it could be a festive drink, the wine that was shared at a sacred meal, a symbol of the joy that God's graciousness has produced. Whatever its identity, it serves as a cup of joy for having been saved.

Along with the offering of this wine is the proclamation of the name of God. Since God's name holds part of the divine essence, to proclaim that name is to recognize and praise God's greatness, in this case the graciousness of God's saving action. The cup is taken up and God's name is proclaimed.

The psalmist insists that, contrary to any appearances, God is concerned with the fate of the righteous. The psalmist's own situation is an example of this. The psalmist may have suffered, but ultimately God did intervene. Mention of the righteous *(hāsîdîm)* indirectly identifies the psalmist as one of this group. The psalmist could be making another point here: virtue and misfortune are not incompatible; good people do in fact suffer. Still, the point of this psalm is not the sufferings the psalmist had to endure but the deliverance that came from God and the psalmist's response to divine graciousness.

The relationship between the psalmist and God is strikingly characterized in the metaphor "servant" and its parallel metaphor, "son of your handmaid." Although the first image has taken on a profound theological connotation (servant of God), the second clearly identifies both images as classifications within a structured household. A slave born into a household had neither a justified claim to, nor any guaranteed likelihood of, emancipation. By using these legal metaphors to characterize his relationship with God, the psalmist is dramatizing his own situation. Like a slave that has no hope of release, he was bound to a life of great difficulty. However, God looked kindly upon him and loosed him from his servitude.

The last verses (vv. 17–18) clearly identify the ceremony that will take place as a public ritual. A sacrifice of thanksgiving will be offered (cf. Lev 7:11-18), the name of the LORD will be proclaimed, and vows will be paid in the presence of the people of God. The psalmist who once faced the prospect of death now stands in the midst of the assembly, humbled and grateful to God.

1 Corinthians 11:23-26

This account of the institution of the Lord's Supper draws on the "Jesus tradition." The language used is technical and formulaic; what Paul received he now hands down (cf. 1 Cor 15:3). This does not mean that he received this tradition in direct revelation from the Lord but that he received it by word of mouth, the usual way a religious heritage is transmitted. This manner of expression establishes the ecclesial authority of the teaching. It also demonstrates Paul's own conviction that the risen Christ transmits the tradition through the agency of the members of the body of Christ, the Church. Since such transmission of tradition was a custom in both the Greek schools and the Jewish synagogue, the audience would understand what Paul was doing regardless of their ethnic or religious background.

That the account comes specifically from the Jesus tradition and not from the early Christian tradition generally is evident in the recital of the words of Jesus. They actually give instruction for the continual celebration of the liturgical reenactment. The fact that they are the words of Jesus gives divine legitimation to the *anámnēsis* (ritual of remembering) enjoined upon the community of believers. The words themselves are found within a succinct account of Jesus' Last Supper, wherein he draws lines of continuity between the old and new covenants and makes clear their differences.

Jesus' attention is on the bread and the wine. Faithful to Jewish table etiquette, as either the head of the household or the host he gives thanks and breaks the bread (v. 24). He identifies the bread as his body, about to be given vicariously on behalf of those present. The fact that Jesus was actually with them when he said this makes the meaning of his words quite enigmatic. Was this really his body? Or did it represent his body? Believers have interpreted this in various ways down through the centuries. One thing is clear; they were charged to repeat among themselves what he had just done.

When the supper was over Jesus took the cup and pronounced words over it as well (v. 25). This cup is identified with the new covenant (cf. Jer 31:31-34) and with the blood of the Lord, which, like sacrificial blood, ratifies the covenant. This statement shows how the Jesus tradition has taken the new covenant theme from Jeremiah and blood ratification from the Jewish sacrificial system, incorporated them, and reinterpreted them. This verse ends as did the previous verse, with a charge to repeat the memorial.

Jesus' sharing of the bread and the cup was a prophetic symbolic action that anticipated his death. The ritual reenactment of this supper would be a participation in his death and a sharing in the benefits that would accrue from it. In it the risen, exalted Lord continually gives what the dying Jesus gave once for all. In the memorial celebration the past, the present, and the future are brought together: the past is the commemoration of his death; the present is the ritual of remembrance itself; the future is his *parousía,* his coming again.

The reason for repeating Jesus' actions and words is that they signify his salvific death. Believers live an essentially eschatological existence, anticipating the future as they reenact the past.

John 13:1-15

The actual account of the washing of the feet is introduced by a few references. They include identification of the time of year as that of the feast of Passover, a note about Jesus' relationship with God and his foreknowledge of his own death, a statement about his love for those called "his own," and a report about Judas' complicity with the devil. All of this information sets the context for the narrative that follows.

The actual washing of feet was unusual for several reasons. Although it was a common practice of Eastern hospitality, it should have been done upon arrival at the house and not when everyone had already reclined at table. It was normally done by people of negligible social station: by slaves in a class-conscious household or, in a patriarchal society, by women. Here it was done by the one who could boast divine origin and who was both Lord and teacher of those at table. While foot-washing was a common social practice, as a symbolic action it here had theological significance and was intended as an example to be followed by all those present.

What looks like self-abasement by Jesus is really an expression of his love. By washing their feet, Jesus showed the extent of the love he had for his disciples. Because of his love, he was willing to empty himself of all divine prerogatives and to assume the role of the menial household slave. Because of his love, he was willing to empty himself of his very life in order to win salvation for all. The love he had for his disciples is the model of the love they were to have for each other. In other words, they were to be willing to empty themselves for the sake of each other.

This symbolic action of foot-washing was misunderstood by Peter. He saw the humiliation in such behavior, but he did not perceive its real meaning. He would not allow Jesus, his Lord, to abase himself in this way. But Jesus would not allow Peter to refuse the gesture without dire consequences. To reject the symbolic action was to reject its profound theological significance. If Peter would not participate in Jesus' self-emptying, he could not enjoy the blessings it would guarantee.

In trying to explain the meaning of his action, Jesus played on the ideas of clean and unclean. Customary washing of feet could make the disciples physically clean, but this foot-washing could make them clean in a spiritual way, that is, all of them but Judas. Jesus knew that Judas had turned traitor and so was not clean. On one level Peter understood this explanation; on another level he did not. He seems to have thought that the more he washed the more he would be spiritually cleansed. Since their being washed symbolized their participation in Jesus' self-emptying, limited washing was adequate. Jesus assured Peter that he would understand later, presumably after Jesus' resurrection.

Never did Jesus deny the dignity that was his as God, but he did not use it to safeguard his own comfort or well being. Instead, it became the measure of his own self-giving and the example of the extent of self-giving his disciples should be willing to offer to others. During his Last Supper Jesus gave himself completely to those present and charged them to give themselves completely as well.

Themes of the Day

This is the first day of the solemn Triduum, the most sacred moment of the Liturgical Year. On each of the three days we meditate on some aspect of the same question: what is the meaning of Passover? Holy Thursday opens this meditation by considering God's initiative in these wondrous events. Three themes are prominent: the Passover, which is the saving action of God; our response to God's Passover; and the wonder of God's love.

God's Passover

Here at the beginning of our meditation on the Passover, we see that it is God who passes over, saving us, nourishing us, serving us. The initiative is God's; the magnanimity is God's; the self-emptying is God's. We have nothing to contribute to these amazing happenings. We have only to open ourselves to receive the wondrous gifts that have been won for us.

God passes over us as a protective angel, preserving us from harm, leading us out of bondage into freedom. All we have to do is accept the salvation that is offered to us through this spectacular act of love. God also passes through mere human companionship and becomes the covenantal meal that sustains us. Along with this heavenly bread comes the guarantee of eternal life. It is ours only if we will accept it. Finally, Jesus passes beyond being Lord and master and kneels before us as our humble servant. If we are to belong to him, we must allow him to wash our feet. In each instance, the saving action is God's. For no other reason but love, God offers us salvation, nourishment, and service.

Our Response

"How shall I make a return to the LORD?" On this day of Eucharist, our only response is thanksgiving. When we give thanks we are merely opening ourselves to the graciousness of God. We are giving God the opportunity of overwhelming us with blessings. We participate in God's many passovers by accepting God's magnanimity. Our sacrifice of thanksgiving is really our openness to receive the sacrifice of God—the sacrifice of the lamb, whose blood on the doorpost liberated our future; the sacrifice of Christ's body and blood, which became our food and drink; the sacrifice of Jesus' self-emptying service, which stands as a model for our own service of others.

The Wonder of It All

Who could have imagined that any of this would happen? A motley group of runaway laborers escapes from the clutches of their superpower overlords; bread and wine is changed into the body and blood of a man who is being hunted down; the Son who was sent by God into the world washes the feet of his disciples. This is all incredible; it is no wonder that Peter initially resisted. It is so difficult for self-possessed, self-directed human beings to relinquish control of their lives and to stand ready to receive the gift of God. We do not question whether God *can* do such marvels, but we stand in awe that God *would*. God's love for us is beyond comprehension.

Finally, on the first night of this holy Triduum, we are left with the directive, "As I have done for you, you should also do." The graciousness of God toward us prompts us to pass over from being served to serving others. Our thanksgiving is expressed in our own self-emptying service of others. Having received the gifts of God, we give them away; they flow from God through us to others.

Good Friday of the Lord's Passion
Isaiah 52:13–53:12

An account of the afflictions of a righteous man (53:1-11b) is here framed by two utterances of God (52:13-15; 53:11b-12). This portrait of innocent suffering challenges the traditionally held conviction that evil brings on its own penalty and, therefore, misfortune is evidence of sinfulness. In place of this view of retribution is a picture of one who not only suffered at the hands of others but did so for the very people who had unjustly afflicted him. The framework of God's words serves to legitimize this unconventional theological position.

It is clear that God is speaking in the closing verses, because only God would be able to bless the servant in the manner described (53:12). Since the servant is similarly identified in both of the framing parts, it is safe to conclude that it is God who speaks in the introduction as well. The overriding theme in both parts is the relationship between the humiliation of the servant and his exaltation.

The opening verses do not suggest that the servant's exaltation is reward for his humiliation. Rather, it is precisely *in* his humiliation that he is exalted. He is raised up even as the bystanders are aghast at his appearance (52:13-15). The closing words explain how this can be the case. The will of God is accomplished in his willingness to bear his afflictions at the hands of and for the sake of others (53:11b-12).

The actual account of the servant's suffering is narrated from the perspective of those who have been granted salvation through his tribulations. It begins with an exclamation of total amazement. Who would have ever thought that the power of God (the arm of the LORD) would be revealed in weakness and humiliation? The details of this humiliation are then sketched (53:2-9). Unlike many righteous individuals whose lives contain episodes of misfortune, this servant lived a life marked by tribulation from beginning to end. Added to his physical distress was rejection by a community that held him in no regard.

The account is interrupted by a confession of the narrator's personal guilt and an acknowledgment of the servant's innocence. The narrator first states the traditional way of understanding the servant's plight: "We thought of him

. . . as one smitten by God" (53:4). Then the new and astonishing insight is proclaimed: "He was pierced for our offenses" (v. 5). This startling insight contains two important points: innocent people do in fact suffer for reasons that have nothing to do with their own behavior; and the suffering of one can be the source of redemption for another.

The account of the servant's sufferings continues (vv. 7–9). Here his non-violent attitude is clearly defined. He did not retaliate; he did not even defend himself. In fact, he willingly handed himself over to those who afflicted him. The image of a lamb led to slaughter suggests that the servant knew that he too would die at the hands of his persecutors. Still, he chose to be defenseless. Even in death he was shamed, buried with the wicked. There was nothing in this appalling life or death that served as a clue to the significance of this suffering or its redemptive value or the source of exaltation it would become. God's ways are astounding.

Psalm 31:2, 6, 12-13, 15-16, 17, 25

The theme of trust permeates this psalm response (vv. 2, 15). Although it contains elements of complaint or lament and of petition, it opens with a testimony to the psalmist's conviction that there is refuge in God (v. 2). The image suggests that he (identified as a male servant, v. 17) is fleeing some kind of peril and turns to God as a sanctuary in this flight. Further in the psalm (v. 16) he pleads to be rescued from his enemies and persecutors. Thus, threatened by such dangers, the psalmist seeks protection in God, and he is certain he will find it there.

The covenant relationship between God and the psalmist is apparent in several places. First he appeals to God's justice, or righteousness, a characteristic of the covenant. This appeal also suggests the innocence of the psalmist. He would hardly call upon God's justice if he were in any way guilty. Evidence of the relationship can also be seen in the way the psalmist identifies both God and himself: You are my God (v. 15); I am your servant (v. 17). Finally, the psalmist appeals to God's lovingkindness *(ḥesed)*, a technical term describing covenant loyalty. It is clear that this relationship is the reason for his confidence. It is why he flees to God.

Complete confidence in God does not prevent the psalmist from pleading with God. His first concern is shame. This is not an inner attitude or state of mind. It is public disgrace. In many Eastern societies it is referred to even today as "losing face." It is the opposite of possessing honor, an attribute more important than riches. A man without honor is an outcast in society, and for many people death is preferred to such disgrace.

The psalm does not clearly explain the initial cause of the psalmist's loss of honor. In a society that believed suffering was the consequence of wickedness, it could have been almost any kind of misfortune. Whatever it was, the psalmist was regarded as someone who was not only dead but who was then forgotten (v. 13). Since in this culture at this time the only way an individual could survive after death was in the memory of the living, to be forgotten was doubly deplorable. The psalmist was also treated like a broken dish, not only shattered but also discarded. Whatever the misfortune was, it was regarded as shameful.

The description of his shame is a collage of metaphors that characterize his disgrace. He is an object of reproach, a laughingstock, a dread. He is shamed before everyone—enemies, neighbors, even friends. He has already lost his honor. What will reinstate it is vindication, and only God can accomplish this. Only God can show that the psalmist was innocent in the first place.

The psalmist prays that God's face might shine upon him. Since the face identifies the person and reflects the attitudes and sentiments of that person, seeing the face of God would be a kind of divine manifestation. The psalmist is probably not asking for such a revelation but rather for the light that comes from God's face. In other words, he is asking for God's good pleasure. His last words are an exhortation to others to trust in God as he has. To the end, his confidence will not be swallowed up by any disgrace he might have to endure.

Hebrews 4:14-16; 5:7-9

The reading consists of two distinct yet related parts. The first (4:14-16) contains a double exhortation: hold fast to faith; approach the throne of grace with confidence. It develops the theme of Jesus the high priest who intercedes for us. This is a high priest who was tempted in all things and therefore can sympathize with our struggle.

The basis of constancy in the confession of the community is the identity of Jesus. He is Son of God as well as the great high priest. Just as the high priest passed through the curtain into the presence of God in the holy of holies, there to sprinkled sacrificial blood on the mercy seat (Heb 9:7), so Christ, exalted after shedding his own blood, passed through the heavens into the presence of God. Being the Son of God, his sacrifice far exceeds anything that the ritual performed by the high priest might have hoped to accomplish.

His exalted state has not distanced him from us. On the contrary, he knows our limitations. He was tried to the limit but did not succumb. Furthermore, it is precisely his exalted state that gives us access to the throne of God. Unlike former high priests who approached the mercy seat alone and only on the Day of Atonement, Christ enables each one of us to approach God and to do so continually. This first section of the reading ends with the second exhortation. The confidence we have in our relationship with Christ should empower us to approach the throne of God boldly, there to receive the grace we need to be faithful.

The second section (5:7-9) is confessional in character. Each of the three verses offers a slightly different view of biblical christology. The first refers to the depth of Jesus' suffering, the second to a major lesson he learned through suffering, the third to the mediatorial role he gained by that suffering.

"Days when Christ was in the flesh" is an allusion to Jesus' humanity. In the biblical sense of the term flesh *(sárx)* is not evil, but it is fraught with limitations and weaknesses. Because it is subject to deterioration and death, it came to signify many things associated with human frailty, such as vulnerability and fear. For Jesus to have taken on flesh was to have taken on these limitations and weaknesses as well.

The reference to his anguished prayer calls to mind his agony in Gethsemane (Matt 26:36-46; Mark 14:32-42; Luke 22:40-46). The reference here is probably to a traditional Jewish image of the righteous person's impassioned prayer. Its sentiments are reminiscent of those found in the psalms that describe agony, terror, and depression (cf. Psalms 22, 31, 38). Jesus offered these prayers as a priest offers sacrifice, and he was heard because of his reverence, or godly fear.

Though Son of God, Jesus learned what every human has to learn, namely, acceptance of God's will in the circumstances of life. The surest way to learn this lesson, though perhaps the hardest, is through suffering. This notion points once again to Jesus' willingness to assume every aspect of human nature. As mediator of salvation Jesus endured torment of body and anguish of soul. He knew agony, terror, and depression. He could fully understand human distress and the desire to escape it. He was truly one with the human condition.

John 18:1–19:42

This passion narrative can be divided into three parts: the arrest of Jesus and his examination by the high priest (18:1-27); the trial before Pilate (18:28–19:16a); and the crucifixion, death, and burial (19:16b-42). Throughout this account Jesus is portrayed as serenely in control of the events that eventually culminate in his death. Again and again his kingship makes itself evident, until he is finally lifted up in exaltation on the cross. Unbelief is exposed as resistance to God, and those who condemn him condemn themselves by this fact. Blame is placed more on the Jewish authorities than on the Romans, not out of any deep-seated anti-Semitism but because the Christian community at the time of the writing of the Gospel was in desperate need of Roman approval in order to survive.

The undisputed sovereignty of Jesus is seen from the very first to the last episode. A cohort of Roman soldiers, a group of about six hundred, along with representatives of the religious leaders of Israel, come to arrest Jesus. Not until he provides a display of his divine power does he allow them to take him. Later he stands with authority before Annas the high priest, insisting that he has been arrested without cause. He acknowledges his authority to Pilate, pointing out that his rule is not of this world. He further announces that while authority is his by right, Pilate's is merely by appointment. Finally, only when all things have been accomplished does he hand over his spirit. From beginning to end Jesus is in complete control.

The divine identity of Jesus is the fundamental reason for both his authority and the calm he exhibits. This identity is established at the outset. In the garden, three times (18:5, 6, 8) he responds to those who have come out after him with a simple self-identification: *Egó eimi.* "I AM [he]." This is not lost on his accusers, who argue with Pilate that to claim to be Son of God makes Jesus liable to death. This claim strikes fear in Pilate's heart, and instead of releasing Jesus, he hands him over to be crucified.

The title of king is an explicit point of much controversy. It is the center of the discussion with Pilate, who questions Jesus about it and then retreats somewhat when Jesus openly admits his royal status. Jesus' claim to kingship becomes the occasion for the mockery of the soldiers, the rejection by the religious leaders, and the crowd's choice of Caesar rather than Jesus. This possible conflict with imperial sovereignty influences Pilate to capitulate to the people's angry demands and to hand Jesus over to be crucified, but not without asserting this kingship by means of the inscription on the cross. The kingship of Jesus plays a pivotal role in this drama.

There is no misunderstanding in the accusations made against Jesus nor in the execution of the plan to put him to death. Those responsible know what they are doing. Judas, an intimate companion, betrays him; the same Roman soldiers, who had been thrown back by his power, arrest him; the religious authorities condemn him for the very messianic posture that they should have recognized in him; Pilate hands him over to the Jewish authorities even though he finds no fault in him. In this account unbelief is exposed as resistance to God. Despite this, God's plan of salvation moves inexorably forward.

Themes of the Day

We continue our meditation on the meaning of Passover. On Good Friday we discover that Jesus is our Passover. Three different faces of Jesus our Passover are offered for our reflection: the prophetic suffering servant; the great high priest; and the triumphant king. Today's meditation ends with reflection on the power of the cross.

The Prophetic Suffering Servant

Silent like the paschal lamb that was sacrificed on behalf of the people, the suffering servant of the LORD allowed himself to be handed over to the slaughter. Though innocent, he took upon himself the guilt of the very ones who were victimizing him. We marvel at the willingness of those who place themselves at risk in order to save anyone who is vulnerable or anyone whom they love. But to do so for one's torturers is beyond human comprehension. Yet that is what Christ our Passover has done. He is the true Suffering Servant; he is the one who has allowed himself to be taken, to be afflicted, to be offered as the sacrifice for others. It is his blood that spares us; it is his life that is offered. Through his suffering this servant justifies many. He is our true Passover.

The Great High Priest

Jesus is not only the innocent victim, he is also the high priest who offers the Passover sacrifice. Because he is one of us, he carries many of our own weaknesses. But it is because he is without moral blemish that, in him, we all stand before God. On this solemn day we behold his battered body, but we also look beyond it to the dignity that is his as high priest. Garbed as he is in wounds that rival the ornate garments of liturgical celebration, he offers himself on the altar of the cross. He is our true Passover.

Triumphant King

"King of the Jews" was the crime for which Jesus was tried and sentenced and executed. It was the title that was inscribed above his bloody throne. To those passing by he appeared to be a criminal, but he was indeed a king. His crucifixion was his enthronement. Lifted up on the cross, he was lifted up in triumph and exaltation. Furthermore, he was not a conquered king; he was a conquering king. He willingly faced death and stared it down. As he delivered over his spirit, death lay vanquished at the foot of the cross. Within a few days this would begin to become clear to others. He is our true Passover.

The Power of the Cross

On Good Friday the cross gathers together all three images of Christ. It is in the light of this cross that we see clearly how all three must be accepted at once, for we never contemplate one image without contemplating the others. In the midst of the passion we see the victory; when we celebrate Easter, we do not forget the cross. As we venerate this cross, we gather together the memory of all of the living and the dead. With our petitions we bring to the cross all the needs of the world. In this way the cross becomes the true *axis mundi,* the center of the universe, and Christ is revealed as the true Passover.

Easter Vigil
Genesis 1:1–2:2 (First Reading)

This first creation account is remarkable in several ways. It is replete with measured literary patterns. Each act of creation begins with the phrase, "Then God said," and ends with the temporal designation "evening . . . morning . . . the first day . . . the second day . . ." and so on. First the universe is fashioned, and then it is appointed with all of the heavenly luminaries. Next the sea and the sky and the earth are prepared as resourceful habitat for various animals. The appearance of these living things is described with another pattern: "Then God said . . . and God made . . . God blessed" (vv. 20–22, 24–28). The very structure of the narrative bespeaks order and rhythm, interdependence and care. Again and again an evaluation is pronounced: "God saw how good it was."

According to this account, order is brought forth from chaos; light is summoned from the darkness. God's creative activity is effortless. It is all accomplished by divine word. God speaks and creation appears; the word is the deed. The universe moves according to unwritten yet well-known laws. One word from God sets it all in motion. The potential for life seems to be in the waters of the sea and in the earth itself. All it needs is a word from God and it will burst forth.

The most extraordinary creature is humankind. The woman and the man are the only creatures made after the image and likeness of God and given the responsibility to manage (subdue and have dominion) the rest of creation as caretakers. Only when all was completed and deemed "very good" did God rest.

Psalm 104:1-2, 5-6, 10, 12, 13-14, 24, 35 (A)

The nature hymn, from which the psalm response is taken, recalls the Genesis story of creation and is certainly one of the most beautiful psalms in the entire Psalter. It begins with a self-summons to sing the praises of God. It is clear that the psalmist is overwhelmed by the splendor of the universe and is brimming with praise for the creator of such grandeur. In fact, this awesome experience of creation is itself a revelation of God. The brilliance of nature is God's glorious robe. To behold creation is to encounter God.

Of all the creation motifs present in the psalm, the most prominent here is water. The earth itself was established amidst cosmic water and then covered with protective ocean water as with a garment. Hearty spring waters refresh the earth and the animals that find their home both on the land and in the sky. Water brings vegetation to life on the earth, making it a steady source of food. Although it was initially chaotic and threatening, through God's gracious act of creation water has become the indispensable source of life for all living creatures.

The creation narrative and this psalm response both underscore the fact of God's activity. None of this happens haphazardly, nor is there any struggle between God and the forces of nature. All of nature serves the designs of God. In fact, in the psalm it is God who acts through nature; God sends the springs and raises the grass. God has created these marvels and then works through them for the benefit of all. No wonder the psalmist is inspired by creation to sing the praises of the Creator.

Psalm 33:4-5, 6-7, 12-13, 20-22 (B)

The verses of this psalm response contain a collection of various themes. The passage opens with a statement that reflects the fundamental basis of ancient Israel's faith in God. This faith is rooted in the truth of God's word, in the faithfulness of God's works, in the justice of God's covenant, and in the steadfastness of God's love. Everything else flows from these convictions.

The psalm picks up the theme of God's word and carries us with it back to the creation account of Genesis, where this word establishes the heavens and separates the waters of the deep. The stability of natural creation is evidence of God's power and faithfulness. God's creation provides a welcoming and sustaining home for all living beings. Creation is so vast that the psalmist's gaze cannot even begin to encompass all of the reasons for praising the great Creator-God.

The psalmist moves from creation in its universality to history in its particularity. One people has been chosen by this Creator-God to be a special people, to be God's own inheritance. The macarism "Happy the nation" (here, "Blessed the nation") denotes election, returning us to the themes with which this response opened. The placement of these themes is significant. Creation imagery is bracketed by covenant language. This literary arrangement can make two quite startling theological statements. First, it implies that the covenant that God made with this special people is as firm and reliable as is creation. Second, it suggests that from the very beginning creation actually serves the goals of the covenant.

Genesis 22:1-18 (Second Reading)

This passage is an account of the testing of Abraham. However, here the son takes center stage. This is not some anonymous offspring; it is Isaac, Abraham's only son, the one he loves. Abraham may have had another son (Ishmael), but Isaac was the only son upon whom his dreams were pinned. He was the hope of the future, not only of his father but of the entire people who would eventually trace their ancestry back to Abraham. Isaac was the child of destiny, both of his father and of the entire race.

Just as Abraham appears to be willing to sacrifice his beloved son, so Isaac seems to be willing to allow this to happen. There is no mention of struggle on his part. Though he inquires about the sacrifice, the answer given him by his father seems to satisfy him. Isaac is the innocent victim, the one who carries the wood of the sacrifice on his back up to the mountain where his life will be offered.

The fact that in this story Isaac is spared does not mitigate the horror of the scene depicted, nor does it alter the portrait of a brutal deity. God requires the innocent blood of the beloved son, and the father is willing to comply.

Abraham relinquishes his natural claim on the child of promise, and at the end of the account he is blessed with a promise of more children than he can count (cf. 12:2-3; 13:16; 15:5; 26:4, 24). We may not understand God's plan, but we cannot deny that though God may at first appear to demand the impossible of us, in the end God will not be outdone in generosity.

Psalm 16:5, 8, 9-10, 11

The psalm verses speak of covenant relationship with God and the confidence that abounds from it. Two images express this relationship. The allotted portion of land is the inheritance that each tribe was given and which was handed down within the tribe generation after generation. This land provided the people identity and membership, sustenance and prosperity. Without land they had no future, and they would not last long in the present. Here the psalmist is claiming that God has replaced the land in the religious consciousness of the people; the blessings and promises customarily associated with land are now associated with the LORD.

The second image is the cup. This might be the communal cup passed around from which all drank. Such an action solidified the union of those who drank from the common cup. When this action took place at a cultic meal, those participating in the feast were joined not only to each other but to the deity as well. The psalmist declares that this unifying cup is really the LORD. In other words, the psalmist is joined so closely with God as almost to defy separation. God is there, at the psalmist's right hand, standing as an advocate or a refuge.

Such protection is reason for profound rejoicing. Regardless of the terrifying, even life-threatening ordeals the psalmist must endure, God is steadfast. In the face of things, this kind of confidence in God may appear to be foolhardy, but the psalmist's trust is unshakable. Ultimately the fullness of joys will abound in the presence of God.

Exodus 14:15–15:1 (Third Reading)

We have come to that point in the story of liberation where God takes complete control of the situation. This divine leadership is exercised under several different forms: the words of God, the angel of the LORD, and the pillar of cloud. First, God gives specific directions to Moses. Next, the angel leads the people to the sea and then moves behind them as they pass through the parted waters. Finally, the column of cloud, which originally led the people, moves to the rear of the company. There, along with the angel, it serves as a buffer between the fleeing Israelites and the pursuing Egyptians. The escape from Egypt has been accomplished through the power of God.

While this narrative may appear to be an account of the struggle between the people of Israel and the Egyptian pharaoh, it is really a battle between divine forces. The pharaoh, thought by his people to be a god, is in mortal combat with the God of Israel, and it is the God of Israel who emerges triumphant. Not only is the LORD able to protect the Israelites and secure their release, but this is accomplished in the pharaoh's own land and against his own armies. The religious establishment of Egypt is no match for the God of Israel.

The waters of the sea represent the waters of chaos. God parts them just as the great Creator parted the carcass of the monster of the deep at the time of creation. The jubilation that follows this defeat is not so much because of the death of the Egyptians as because of the victory of God over the forces of chaos, be they political or cosmic.

Exodus 15:1-2, 3-4, 5-6, 17-18

This is a hymn of thanksgiving for deliverance and guidance. It recounts the miracle at the sea, the event that demonstrated God's mighty power and put an end to Israel's bondage in Egypt, and it reports Israel's entrance into and establishment in the land of promise. Recalling these marvelous feats, the poet praises God's glorious triumph.

As comments on the preceding reading stated, this is less a description of violence and the destruction of enemies than of deliverance of a favored people. The characterizations of God underscore this; they all represent some kind of relationship with the people. God is a savior; a patron God who guided and protected the ancestors; a warrior who conquered cosmic evil; a divine ruler who reigns forever and ever.

There is an explicit cultic dimension to this hymn. It contains a threefold mention of the sanctuary: the mountain of God's inheritance; the place of

God's throne; the sanctuary itself (vv. 17–18). This sacred place was important because it was the spot where the people offered sacrifice to God. More than this, it was the privileged place on earth where God dwelt in the midst of the people. It was usually erected on that site believed to be the center of the universe, the place where heaven, earth, and the underworld met. The poet is here thanking God for deliverance, but also for God's perpetual presence among the people. This presence is important because it will ensure God's continued protection.

Isaiah 54:5-14 (Fourth Reading)

Metaphors taken from familial relationships in a patriarchal household are used to characterize the covenant bond that exists between God and the people. Both God's love and God's wrath are portrayed in terms of a marriage bond that was established, then violated, and finally reestablished. Although the reading does not say that Israel has been unfaithful, the implication is there. God is a loyal but dishonored husband and Israel is an unfaithful wife. The male bias here is obvious.

Looking past these narrow and offensive gender stereotypes, we can still appreciate the underlying description of God's love. It is intimate, like a marriage bond (v. 5); it is forgiving and tender (vv. 7–9); it is everlasting (vv. 8, 10). Just as God originally created a covenant bond, so now God lovingly re-creates it. The reference to Noah and the new creation after the flood suggests this (v. 9), as does the description of the reestablishment of the people in a city decked out in precious jewels (vv. 11–12).

Covenant language is very strong in this reading. The reconciliation promised is called a "covenant of peace" (v. 10). Lovingkindness (*ḥesed*, vv. 8, 10) denotes loyalty to covenant obligations. "Compassion" (vv. 7, 10) comes from the word *rāḥam* (womb) and might be translated "womb-love." It refers to a deep and loving attachment, usually between two people who share some kind of natural bond. It only appears as a characteristic of God's love after the human covenant partner has sinned. Hence there is an aspect of forgiveness in the very use of the word.

Psalm 30:2, 4, 5-6, 11-12, 13

This is a psalm of thanksgiving for deliverance from the peril of death, the netherworld, the pit (v. 4). The reference to death can be to illness, to depression, or to any serious misfortune that can threaten life itself. Whatever it might have been, the danger is now past; God intervened and saved the petitioner. In addition to the actual calamity, the psalmist is also concerned with enemies who would take delight in the misfortune. The prayer asks to be preserved from this insult as well. Following the initial plea is an acknowledgment of deliverance. God has heard the petition and has granted the request.

The psalmist next turns to the congregation of believers and calls on them to praise God. As with the preceding reading, the psalm does not explicitly state that the suffering endured was the deserved penalty for some wrongdoing. However, since that was the customary explanation of misfortune, such a conclusion could be drawn. Still, retribution is not the point of the prayer. Rather, the psalm compares the vast difference between God's wrath and God's graciousness. The former is short-lived; the latter is everlasting.

The psalmist turns again in prayer to God, pleading for pity. There is no suggestion that God has turned a deaf ear to earlier cries. Quite the contrary. The psalmist announces that grief and mourning have been turned into relief and rejoicing. This is the reason for the thanksgiving in the first place. Regardless of the nature of or reason for the misfortune, God can be trusted to come to the aid of one who cries for help.

Isaiah 55:1-11 (Fifth Reading)

This powerful prophetic oracle contains some of the most moving sentiments placed in the mouth of God. First, God's invitation is extended both to those who are able to pay for food and drink (v. 2) and to those who are not (v. 1). All are invited to come to the LORD in order to be refreshed and nourished. The reference is probably to something more than ordinary food and drink, since those called are also told to listen. The word of God is itself a source of rejuvenation.

The real object of the invitation is God's announcement of the reestablishment of a covenant bond (v. 3). The reference is to the royal covenant, the one made with David and his house. Although it was instituted as an everlasting covenant, the people broke the bond by their sins. God is now eager to restore this bond. The oracle states that just as David's success proclaimed God's majesty to the nations, so the people called here will be a witness of God's mercy and love. Just as David was the source of blessing, peace, and fullness of life for his own nation, the people called here will be a comparable source of blessing for nations they do not even know.

After this bold promise is made, the people are told to turn to the LORD; sinners are exhorted to reform their lives and to seek forgiveness from God. These are not suggestions, they are imperatives! The people are summoned to repentance. Then God's plans will take effect, just as the rain accomplishes what it is intended to accomplish. Unlike human beings who work for justice and reparation, God's way is compassion and re-creation, and this renewal will last forever.

Isaiah 12:2-3, 4, 5-6

This hymn of thanksgiving anticipates favors that will be granted and enjoyed in the future. Therefore, one might consider it a hymn of confidence as well. God is declared "savior," and it is because of this characterization that the writer is unafraid and takes courage. The theme of water appears here, as it did in the preceding reading. Though the imagery is slightly different, in both cases the water is transformative. Earlier it represented new creation; here it is water of salvation.

The theme of witness reappears here as well (vv. 4–5). The writer calls on the community to praise the glorious name of God, the name that represents the very character of God. They are to extol the marvels that God has accomplished and proclaim them to the nations. The most celebrated of these wondrous works is the transformation of the people themselves. In other words, the transformed lives of God's people will announce to the nations the marvels that God has accomplished.

The third and final theme found in this response highlights the importance of Jerusalem. This city was both the royal capital of the Davidic dynasty and the site where the temple was built. It is the second aspect that is the focus here. The city itself is called upon to rejoice. The reason for this exaltation is the presence of God in its midst. Although the temple was the concrete representation of this divine presence, it is the presence of God and not the temple building that is fundamental (cf. Jer 7:3-4). The theology of the passage has come full circle. The presence of God in the midst of the people is the source of the writer's confidence in future deliverance.

Baruch 3:9-15, 32–4:4 (Sixth Reading)

This passage, taken from a book attributed to the secretary of Jeremiah (cf. Jer 36:4), is considered one of the Bible's hymns in praise of wisdom (cf. Proverbs 8; 9; Sir 24:1-22; Wis 7:22–8:21). It begins with the characteristic summons: "Hear, O Israel" (v. 9; cf. Deut 6:4) and continues with an explanation of the reasons for the nation's exile in the land of its foes. Basically it was because the people had turned from the law, the fountain of wisdom (vv. 10–13).

The mysterious female figure that appears in these verses is more than a wise woman; she is Wisdom itself. This representation of wisdom should not be considered a figure of speech. While many passages maintain that one of the chief characteristics of God is divine wisdom, the image found here suggests more. Wisdom Woman appears to enjoy an existence intimately associated with yet clearly distinct from God.

The description of Wisdom is reminiscent of images found elsewhere in the Wisdom literature. First, the question is posed: Where can Wisdom be found? (cf. Job 28:12, 20). In answer, the poet sketches an account of primordial creation. Wisdom was there with the Creator (vv. 32–35; cf. Prov 8:22-31; Wis 8:1), and only the Creator knows the way to her (v. 31).

Although she is inaccessible to all but God, she is given by God to Israel (3:36; cf. Sir 24:8-12). Because Wisdom is the way of God (3:13), she is also identified with the law (v. 4:1; cf. Sir 24:23). Ultimately, the way of Wisdom is conformity to the law; conformity to the law is the way to life; those who follow this way will be happy.

Psalm 19:8, 9, 10, 11

Six different synonyms are used to extol the glories of the law (*tôrâ*, meaning "instruction" or "teaching"). The psalm describes the blessings that acceptance of the law can impart, but it does so not merely to describe the law but also to persuade the people to embrace it as the will of God and to live in accord with it. What is described here is not just any religious law; it is uniquely Israel's, because in a very specific way it represents the will of the God of Israel.

In a very unique way, the law is that point where an encounter with God takes place. It consisted of directives for living a full and god-fearing life. The qualities associated with fulfillment of the law are some of the most highly prized attributes found in any religious tradition. The law is perfect or complete; it is trustworthy, upright, and clean; it is pure and true. Fidelity to the law should lead one to the godliness that is enshrined within it.

The effects of the law are all relational, enhancing human life itself. The law imbues the soul with new vitality; it gives wisdom; it delights the heart; it enables the eyes to recognize truth; it generates awe; it is a path to righteousness; it is more valuable than gold; it is sweeter than honey. The law of the LORD is something greatly to be desired. This description of the law shows clearly that the psalmist found it life-giving and not restrictive, ennobling and not demeaning. Reverence for the law seems to promise the best things that life has to offer.

Ezekiel 36:16-17a, 18-28 (Seventh Reading)

The prophet claims that the Israelites brought on their own downfall through lives of violence and idolatry. Their sinfulness polluted the land, and so they were expelled. What is more despicable, according to this prophet, is the fact that their shameful behavior and the punishment they had to endure because of it doubly dishonored the holy name of God. It was for this reason that God relented and gave them another chance.

The renown of God's holy name among the nations is an important theme in this reading. The spectacular events of Israel's initial election and the prosperity with which the nation was subsequently blessed should have been a witness to the surrounding nations of the unbounded generosity of God. Because the people failed in this, God decided to re-create the nation and to do it in a way that the name of the God of Israel would be synonymous with mercy and compassion.

The regeneration of the nation is accomplished in several steps. The first is a ritual of cleansing. The people have polluted themselves, and so God washes them with clean water. This symbolic action represents the inner cleansing that takes place. Next, God takes away their hard hearts and gives them tender hearts, and gives them a new spirit which is God's own spirit. This new heart and new spirit will transform the inner being of the people, enabling them to live lives of integrity. Although the verbs are in a perfect or future form, it is a special prophetic perfect, implying that this future transformation has already been accomplished. God's regeneration of the people has already taken place.

Psalm 42:3, 5; 43:3, 4 (A: When baptism is celebrated)

These two psalms really constitute one song, so they are often linked together. The first is a lament, expressing the longing for God that the psalmist experiences. This is a profoundly spiritual thirst, probably a desire for some form of worship in the temple. The liturgical imagery is obvious: procession to the house of God, keeping festival. It seems that the psalmist even exercised some form of leadership within the worshiping community, leading the procession. The context of this lament could be exile, making this a fitting response to the preceding reading. Despite the suffering that is evident, there is no despair there. The psalmist does seem to anticipate ultimately standing in God's presence, beholding God's face.

The lament of the first psalm is replaced in the second by the petitions addressed to God. Whatever the suffering may be, the psalmist experiences it as darkness and, consequently, pleads with God to send light that will lead the psalmist to God's presence (another reference to the temple?). There is confidence here; God's fidelity is invoked. Where earlier the psalmist nostalgically remembered the house of God, here return to that house seems to be a future possibility.

The last verses of the psalm response resemble a prophetic announcement. It is cast in the future form, but it is less a hesitant hope than a confident expectation. The grief and lament of the opening verses have given way to gladness and rejoicing. God has heard and answered the prayer of the psalmist.

Isaiah 12:2-3, 4bcd, 5-6
(B: When baptism is not celebrated)

This hymn of thanksgiving anticipates favors that will be granted and enjoyed in the future. Therefore, one might consider it a hymn of confidence as well. God is declared savior, and it is because of this characterization that the writer is unafraid and takes courage. The theme of water appears here, as it did in the preceding reading. Though the imagery is slightly different, in both cases the water is transformative. Earlier it represented new creation; here it is water of salvation.

The theme of witness reappears here as well (vv. 4–5). The writer calls on the community to praise the glorious name of God, the name that represents the very character of God. They are to extol the marvels that God has accomplished and to proclaim them to the nations. The most celebrated of these wondrous works is the transformation of the people themselves. In other words, the transformed lives of God's people will announce to the nations the marvels that God has accomplished.

The third and final theme found in this response highlights the importance of Jerusalem. This city was both the royal capital of the Davidic dynasty and the site where the temple was built. It is the second aspect that is the focus here. The city itself is called upon to rejoice. The reason for this exaltation is the presence of God in its midst. Although the temple was the concrete representation of this divine presence, it is the presence of God and not the temple building that is fundamental (cf. Jer 7:3-4). The theology of the passage has come full circle. The presence of God in the midst of the people is the source of the writer's confidence of future deliverance.

Psalm 51:12-13, 14-15, 18-19
(C: When baptism is not celebrated)

This may be the best known of the Penitential Psalms (cf. Psalms 6, 32, 38, 51, 102, 130, 143). Although it is considered a lament, it also contains elements of a confession of sin and a prayer for forgiveness. This passage opens with a plea for restoration. The clean heart and new spirit spoken of here correspond to the same themes in the prophetic reading for which this psalm is a response. Such a prayer could be considered a veiled confession of sin, for it is a request for inner transformation. This is reinforced by the plea that God not cast the psalmist out but rather grant again the joy of salvation.

The psalmist next promises to announce to other sinners the salvation of God. Gratitude for having been forgiven becomes active service to others. The new life that results from the clean heart and steadfast spirit becomes an outward proclamation of God's gracious mercy. Others will see it and will themselves be converted and return to God.

The interior nature of this transformation can also be seen in the character of worship that flows from it. External performance, regardless of how faithfully it is done, is not enough. The psalmist goes so far as to say that God is not even pleased with practices of worship. This may sound exaggerated, but it is in keeping with the theme of inner transformation so prominent in the prophetic reading and psalm response. Once again heart and spirit are the focus of the psalmist's attention. The clean heart is now also a humble heart; the steadfast spirit is now also contrite. The inner renewal effected by God is now complete.

Romans 6:3-11

Paul here explains how baptism has enabled the Christians to participate in the death and resurrection of Jesus. As they were engulfed in the water, they were buried with him in death; as they emerged from the water, they rose with him into new life. Paul's real intent in drawing these lines of comparison between the death and resurrection of Jesus and the baptism and new life of the Christians is ethical exhortation. He seeks to encourage them to set aside their old manner of living and to take on the new life of holiness.

While the descent into baptismal waters can symbolize Christ's descent into death, there is another dimension of the water imagery that strengthens Paul's argument. There is a long tradition that cosmic waters were chaotic, therefore, death-dealing (cf. Genesis 6–9; Job 22:11; Ps 73:13-14; Isa 27:1). To be engulfed by water is to be swallowed by chaos and death. Christ is plunged into the chaos of death; the Christians were plunged into the death of chaos. By the power of God Christ rose to a new life of glory; by the power of God the Christians are raised to the glory of a new life.

Paul characterizes their former lives as slavery to sin. This old enslaved self has to be crucified. Just as death had no power over the resurrected Christ, so sin would have no power over the baptized Christian. Crucifixion is a fitting image for Christian conversion not only because of the role it played in Christ's death but also because the torment it entails exemplifies the suffering that a change of life will exact of the Christians. However, the cross is the only way to new life.

Psalm 118:1-2, 16-17, 22-23

The refrain ("His mercy endures forever") indicates that this thanksgiving psalm was intended for congregational singing. The psalm itself is a song in praise of God's power and victory. God is depicted as a mighty warrior whose strong hand prevails over forces that can threaten the life of the psalmist. God's goodness and mercy toward the house of Israel are seen in this victory. The communal character of these sentiments suggests that the threat from which the people have been saved is some kind of national enemy. Having been spared, the psalmist extols God's good favor, actually becoming a witness to the grandeur of the saving works of the LORD. The gift of salvation by God engenders witness to others of the graciousness of this saving God.

The final image is the metaphor of reversal of fortunes found so often in religious literature. The situation is always the same. A righteous person is rejected, sometimes even persecuted, by other members of the community. When the patron steps in to correct this unjust situation, the righteous one is not only vindicated but is also elevated to a position of great importance. Here, the stone that was rejected becomes the very foundation of the entire building. Applying this metaphor to the psalmist, one is led to conclude that the suffering endured was unwarranted. The stability of the entire community is dependent on the innocent one who was originally rejected. This individual was first a witness to salvation by God and is now the agent of salvation for others.

Mark 16:1-7

Several important themes are interwoven in this short episode from the tradition of the empty tomb. First, the actions of the women followers of Jesus demonstrate an absence of faith in his resurrection. They went to anoint his dead body, not to witness to his glorious new life. He died the day before the Sabbath; it is now the day after. Therefore, the anointing was probably not an embalming, which, as a procedure intended to preserve the body, would have taken place as soon after death as possible. Most likely this anointing was meant to stave off the stench of decomposition.

However we understand the nature of the anointing, the visitors to the tomb seem to have believed that Jesus was dead and that his body would be undisturbed. Further evidence of this is seen in their concern about the stone at the entrance of the tomb. They expected the tomb to be sealed and inaccessible to them. They were surprised when they discovered that the stone had been rolled back and they were able to enter the tomb.

Second, the account describes a supernatural experience and a divine communication. The surprise of the women turned to amazement when they entered the tomb and, instead of the dead Jesus, they found a young man, presumably an angel, clothed in white. He responded to their amazement in the way heavenly messengers traditionally respond to human beings who are overwhelmed by a supernatural experience. He first addressed their apprehension and only then delivered his heavenly message (cf. Gen 15:1; Isa 7:4; Luke 1:13, 30).

Third, the women who came to attend to the dead are now the first witnesses to God's power over death, and they become the first heralds of the resurrection. These women are named; they are known to the community (cf. Mark 15:40, 47). The words of the heavenly messenger are both a proclamation and a commission. First, he attests to the death and the resurrection of Jesus. Lest anyone doubt the force of the events of the past days, he states that Jesus truly died. Then he announces the resurrection. The power of God has raised Jesus from the dead (the verb is aorist passive). The proclamation given the women is also a commission. They are to announce the resurrection to the disciples and Peter and to direct them to go to Galilee. There the witness of the women will be confirmed by an appearance of the risen Jesus.

The reading leaves us with several unanswered questions. Why is Peter singled out from among the other disciples? Is it because of his leadership position within the group? Or is this a way of reassuring the one who had denied Jesus that he has been forgiven? And why are they to leave Jerusalem and go to Galilee? Is the political situation in the city still too dangerous for them? Or is the ministry of Jesus directed back to the place where it began, there to be brought to completion?

This story points to two very different resurrection traditions: the empty tomb and the appearances of the risen Lord. While it belongs to the first category, it refers to the second. Each tradition addresses different aspects of this great act of God, which cannot be adequately described or comprehended. Each tradition requires faith of those who actually had the experience and of those who are told of it.

Themes of the Day

During the Easter Vigil on Holy Saturday evening, we complete our reflections on the meaning of Passover. On Holy Thursday we saw that God is the one who passes over; on Good Friday we recognized that Jesus is our Passover. Today we ourselves are drawn into the mystery as we contemplate our own passing over. Holy Saturday is a time of liminality. We are no longer in one place, but we have not yet arrived at the other. We are in the crossing. We are moving from darkness into light, and we do this by passing through water.

The Passage Through Water

The vigil readings recount our journey from darkness into light, from the chaotic waters of creation to the saving waters of baptism. We begin at the dawn of creation, when God separated the waters and called light out of the darkness, ordered the world and made it pulsing with life. The unfathomable nature of the trust that is exacted of us as we embark on and remain faithful to this journey is seen in the test to which Abraham is put. In order to embrace the new life that God has planned for us, we must be willing to relinquish all that we hold dear in this life. This includes all our hopes and dreams and even that upon which we have based our future. God must be our hope and our dream; God must be the foundation of our future.

In the dark of the night we must be willing to follow God into the unknown. If we can do this, if we can risk all and leave behind the life to which we have grown accustomed, we will be able to survive in this period of liminality. All we need to sustain us at this time is the confidence of knowing that God, who is our redeemer, loves us with indescribable passion. Secure in this love, we will be able to turn to God for all that we need. Embraced by God's everlasting covenant, we believe that we are being led to a land that is abundantly fertile and secure from all that might harm us. It is in this liminal stage that we can accept God's commandments of life and promise to live according to God's plan for us.

The vigil readings end with a promise of regeneration. The waters that at first threatened us now cleanse us. We are given new hearts that will enable us to live the life of faith to which we will soon again commit ourselves. We now stand at the threshold of a new creation. The period of liminality is over. Our next step is into the waters of baptism, there to be re-created, to be born anew, to die and to rise in Christ. Then our passing over will be complete, and we will be embraced by Christ our true Passover.

Easter

Easter Sunday Acts 10:34a, 37-43 We ate and drank with him	**Psalm 118:1-2, 16-17, 22-23** The day the LORD has made	**Colossians 3:1-4** Seek what is above **(or)** **1 Corinthians 5:6b- 8** Clear out the old yeast	**John 20:1-9** He is risen
Second Sunday Acts 4:32-35 One heart and mind	**Psalm 118:2-4, 13-15, 22-24** Give thanks to the LORD	**1 John 5:1-6** He conquered the world	**John 20:19-31** Jesus stood in their midst
Third Sunday Acts 3:13-15, 17-19 You put him to death	**Psalm 4:2, 4, 7-9** Let your face shine on us	**1 John 2:1-5a** Jesus is the expiation	**Luke 24:35-48** Thus it was written
Fourth Sunday Acts 4:8-12 Salvation through no one else	**Psalm 118:1, 8-9, 21-23, 26, 28, 29** The rejected stone is the cornerstone	**1 John 3:1-2** We shall see God	**John 10:11-18** The good Shepherd
Fifth Sunday Acts 9:26-31 Saul saw the Lord	**Psalm 22:26-28, 30-32** I will praise you	**1 John 3:18-24** This is his commandment	**John 15:1-8** The vine and the branches

Sixth Sunday **Acts 10:25-26, 34-35, 44-48** The Spirit given to Gentiles	**Psalm 98:1-4** The LORD revealed to the nations	**1 John 4:7-10** God is love	**John 15:9-17** There is no greater love
Ascension **Acts 1:1-11** Jesus was lifted up	**Psalm 47:2-3, 6-9** All you people, clap your hands	**Ephesians 1:17-23** (or) **Ephesians 4:1-13** Jesus is seated in heaven	**Mark 16:15-20** Jesus is taken up to heaven
Seventh Sunday **Acts 1:15-17, 20a, 20c-26** Witnesses to resurrection	**Psalm 103:1-2, 11-12, 19-20** The LORD is enthroned	**1 John 4:11-16** God is love	**John 17:11b-19** That they may be one
Pentecost **Acts 2:1-11** Filled with the Holy Spirit	**Psalm 104:1, 24, 29-31, 34** Send out your Spirit	**1 Corinthians 12:3b-7, 12-13** Baptized in the Spirit (or) **Galatians 5:16-25** Fruits of the Spirit	**John 20:19-23** Receive the Holy Spirit (or) **John 15:26-27; 16:12-15** The Spirit will guide you

Easter

Initial Reading of the Easter Lectionary

Introduction

The entire Easter season celebrates the membership of the newly initiated people. Within the context of the liturgy the texts read during this time constitute a mystagogical catechesis, or formative instructions for neophytes. One of the distinctive features of this season is the absence of First Testament readings. Selections from the Acts of the Apostles replace them.

First Readings

The first readings create a kind of Easter proclamation. On Easter itself Peter traces the drama of redemption from Jesus' ministry in Galilee to his resurrection. During the following Sundays the transformation that took place with the community of believers is offered to the neophytes as an example. The unity within the community is described, and the forgiveness offered to those who did not recognize Christ is noted. Next the wonders wrought by the Spirit are proclaimed: the sick are healed; zealous persecutors become devout followers; Gentiles are converted. After Jesus had ascended to heaven the community reconstituted itself so it would be ready for the coming of the Spirit. The neophytes must realize that they themselves are the harvest of Pentecost.

Psalms

Most of the psalm responses are taken from thanksgiving songs. This is a fitting prayer for those who have gone down into death with Christ and have risen to new life. Gratitude is the prayer of the believing heart. For a brief moment during this season, when we recall our former blindness, we beg for God's mercy. Otherwise the prayers are hymns that celebrate Jesus' victory over death and his enthronement at the right hand of God in glory. The season ends on a note of praise.

Epistles

The epistles contain instruction for Christian living. Having been born anew through baptism, we are exhorted to seek the things that are above, to live as faithful children of God by obeying the commandments, especially the commandment of love. Empowered by the Spirit of God, we are charged to share the individual gifts we have received for the good of the entire body.

Gospels

The various Gospel passages are woven into a tapestry depicting the risen Lord's final days on earth. There are scenes of encounters with Jesus at the tomb and of his visits with the disciples, who were locked away for fear of the authorities. There is a picture of him as the good shepherd, and another as the true vine. There is one of his ascension, and one of him breathing the Holy Spirit on the disciples. The extraordinary dynamic love underlying all these events is God's love for Jesus, and for us.

Mosaic of Readings

The presence of the risen Lord is the central theme of the Easter season. He resides at the heart of the community of believers; he is revealed to them in the breaking of the bread. He not only lives with us, he also lives through us. We make him present to the world as often as we live lives that mirror his, lives that are truly Spirit-driven. Easter is a time of new beginnings and new hope. It is the time of fulfillment. The entire world cries out: Hallelujah!

Readings

Easter Sunday

Acts 10:34a, 37-43

Peter's discourse is really an announcement of the scope of the spread of the gospel. The story of Jesus from his baptism, through his ministry, to his death and resurrection has been reported all over the land. The power of Jesus' ministry flowed from his having been anointed by God with the Holy Spirit. The reference to anointing is probably an allusion to his baptism, when the heavens opened and the Spirit descended upon him (Luke 3:21-22; 4:14, 18; cf. Isa

61:1). It was in and through this power that Jesus performed good works and healings. Peter lists himself as a witness to all of these wonders.

The text suggests that Peter is speaking to a Gentile audience. Judea is referred to as the "country of the Jews," and the rejection that Jesus experienced at the hands of his own people is mentioned. All of this indicates that the Jews were a group other than those being addressed. The allusion to the message of the prophets implies that the hearers would have known to whom Peter refers. However, this does not mean that they were Jews, since there were many Gentiles in Judea at this time who were interested in Jewish tradition and practice and who would have been acquainted with the important prophetic teaching.

Although Jesus' ministry had a beginning, namely his baptism by John, it does not seem really to have had an ending. It continues through those who were commissioned to preach the gospel and to bear witness to it. This is precisely what Peter is doing in this reading, bearing witness to the resurrection of Jesus (v. 40) and proclaiming the universality of its effects (v. 42).

Peter's teaching regarding the resurrection includes several important aspects. First, it is clearly a work of God. Second, it is a genuine resurrection from the dead and not merely a resuscitation. That it occurred three days after Jesus' death is evidence of this. Third, Jesus was seen by some and then ate and drank with several of his followers, Peter among them. This demonstrates that the appearances of the risen Christ were genuine physical experiences and not some kind of hallucinations.

Finally, the fruits of the resurrection are both transformative and all-encompassing. Peter claims that Jesus, appointed by God, is the one who fulfills the role of the eschatological arbiter, judging the living and the dead (v. 42; cf. Dan 7:1). He further asserts that this judgment scene was the wondrous event to which the prophets testified. Peter is here explaining the mystery of Jesus in terms of prophetic expectation and thus is at once both reinterpreting earlier prophetic tradition and developing new theological insight. With just a few words Peter has placed Jesus at the heart of both the prophetic and the apocalyptic traditions of Israel.

The judgment that Jesus brings is one of forgiveness of sin. He judges not to condemn but to save and to transform. Furthermore, though born from the people of Israel and rooted within that tradition, he was raised up by God to bring forgiveness to all. The power of the resurrection is not circumscribed by ethnic or religious origin. It is open to all who believe in Jesus. This is truly good news to the Gentiles.

Psalm 118:1-2, 16-17, 22-23

The responsorial psalm is a song in praise of God's power and victory. The refrain ("His mercy endures forever") indicates that this thanksgiving psalm was intended for congregational singing. The communal character of these sentiments, seen in the reference to the house of Israel, suggests that the threat from which the people have been saved is some kind of national enemy. God's goodness and mercy toward the house of Israel are made manifest in this victory. The Hebrew word for mercy *(ḥesed)* is a technical theological term denoting God's steadfast love for God's covenant partners, the chosen people of the house of Israel. Having been spared, the psalmist extols God's good favor, actually becoming a witness to the grandeur of the saving works of the LORD.

God is depicted as a mighty warrior whose strong hand prevails over forces that can threaten the security of the people and the very life of the psalmist. The bias for right-handedness is obvious. The right side of a person was considered the stronger side, the honorable side. All good things were on that side. Conversely, the left side was weak, untrustworthy, sinister. The image of God's right hand connotes strength and triumph. It suggests that God's victory was won in a righteous manner.

This divine achievement in itself made God deserving of praise and thanksgiving. However, there seems to be a personal element in this victory. In the wake of God's triumph the psalmist is preserved from death. As a result of this magnanimous deed, the psalmist will publish abroad the mighty works of the LORD. Here again, the individual and communal aspects of this thanksgiving psalm are intertwined.

The final image is the metaphor of reversal of fortunes, found so often in religious literature. The situation is always the same. A righteous person is rejected, sometimes even persecuted, by other members of the community. When the divine patron of the sufferer steps in to correct this unjust situation, the righteous one is not only vindicated but is also elevated to a position of great importance. In this psalm the stone that was rejected becomes the very foundation of the entire building. The Hebrew identifies this stone as "the head of the corner." Although some interpret it as the capstone that completes the building, the reference is probably to the cornerstone that links two walls at right angles, thus holding up a significant part of the building's weight.

It is not clear to whom this metaphor of the cornerstone refers. However, as the verses of this psalm are arranged for our liturgical use, it seems that the speaker who survived the threat of death is the referent. This salvation was brought about by God, and it is recognized as a marvel for which to give praise and thanks.

Colossians 3:1-4 (A)

The passage, short as it is, contains the fundamental teaching about the resurrection and the way the death and resurrection of Christ transform the lives of

Christians. It is set against the backdrop of ancient cosmology. The verbs used are quite telling. Besides the imperatives, which address the present and remain open to all future presents, there are also verbs in the perfect tense, denoting the finality of some actions.

Two different realms are delineated: the world above and the world below. In a three-tiered cosmology this delineation has two possible meanings. On the one hand, it could refer to the earth and the netherworld; on the other, to the heavenly realm and the earth. Although early Christian theology spoke of Christ descending to the netherworld after his death, there to release the souls of the righteous awaiting resurrection, the reference in this passage to God's right hand indicates that the second interpretation is the one intended. The earth is the world below, and the heavenly realm is the world above.

Christ rose from the dead and is now in the realm of heaven. Two images characterize the relationship between the risen Christ and God. First, Christ is seated at God's right hand. This suggests a heavenly imperial throne room where God reigns supreme and Christ sits next to God in the place of honor. The bias for right-handedness is clear. As explained above, the right side was considered the strong side, the side of goodness and favor. Enthroned there, Christ both enjoys God's favor and, as God's "right hand," bestows blessings on others and administers God's righteousness. The second image states that Christ is "in God." This means that having gone through the death of human life, Christ has been raised to a new life. In a new and total way Christ's being is rooted in God.

The admonition to the Christians flows out of belief in this reality. As believers, they are joined to Christ. Consequently they have died with Christ and they have risen with Christ. Therefore, they should turn their attention away from the things of this world and commit themselves to the things of heaven. They are called to a life that reflects this new reality. The specifics of such a life are outlined elsewhere, but one can presume that being joined to Christ would result in behavior like that of Christ.

While the admonitions are explicit imperatives, the statements about dying with Christ and being raised with Christ are in perfect tense. This is not a dimension of Christians' future expectation, but it is an accomplished fact. They are indeed joined with Christ, and joined, they are already with Christ in God. They have not left this world, but they are summoned to be attentive to the things of another world. In fact, they live in two worlds or, to use eschatological language, they have already entered "the age to come."

The passage ends with mention of Christ's ultimate appearance and a promise that those joined with Christ will also appear in glory. Here is an example of a complex eschatological view: "already, but not yet." Joined to Christ, Christians are living in the final age already, but this age of fulfillment is not yet complete.

1 Corinthians 5:6b-8 (B)

The reference in this reading to yeast calls to mind the Jewish feast of the Unleavened Bread (cf. Exod 12:3-10; Deut 16:3-4), which marked the beginning of the barley harvest. Though originally an agricultural celebration, it was eventually joined to the herding feast of Passover, and together they became a commemoration of God's deliverance of the people from the bondage of Egypt. The reference to "our paschal lamb, Christ" marks this combining of festivals.

During the first seven days of the feast only bread made from the flour of the new grain was to be eaten. It was prepared without leaven, the dough that was left over from the previous baking. Because leaven ferments and also causes ingredients around it to break down, it was considered both corrupt in itself and an evil influence. Nothing from the old year and certainly nothing corrupt was to be brought into the fruits of the new harvest.

Paul uses this abstention from leaven, which marked the transition from one year to the next, as a metaphor for the Christians' conversion from life before Christ to life with Christ, from the old age to the age of fulfillment. He exhorts them to rid themselves of their former way of life, for even the slightest trace of corruption can undermine the good that they might do. "A rotten apple spoils the whole barrel."

Continuing with imagery taken from these combined Jewish festivals, Paul emphatically states: "For our paschal lamb, Christ, has been sacrificed." The allusion is to the death of Jesus, which, like the sacrifice of the Passover lamb, saved the people by vicariously assuming the guilt of the community. In order fittingly to celebrate this Passover, the Christians must now purge themselves of all leaven of the past. They must put aside works of corruption and wickedness and commit themselves to lives of sincerity and truth.

John 20:1-9

The resurrection stories begin with a report of Mary Magdalene's visit to the tomb. It is the first day of the week while it is still dark. Reference to darkness rather than the dawn of a new day, which would be traditional, may be the author's way of incorporating the light/darkness symbolism. In other words, lack of faith is a life in darkness. Identifying the day as the first of the week will take on significance in subsequent Christian theology. It will be likened to the dawning of a new creation, or to the eschatological time of fulfillment.

No explanation is given for Mary's visit. The text does not say that she came to weep or to anoint the body. It simply says that she came to the tomb. Seeing that the stone had been moved, she presumed that the body of Jesus had been taken away. She seems to have entertained no thought of his resurrection, only the removal of his body. She ran off to tell Peter and "the other disciple." The text is rather cryptic. For some reason Mary speaks in the plural: "We don't know where . . . ," and the disciple who was with Peter is not named.

The reading contains a definite bias in favor of this other disciple. He is referred to as the one whom Jesus loved (an allusion to John?), and he is the only one in the account who is said to have believed. He is beloved, and he is faith-filled. The text also hints at Peter's privileged status within the community. He is the one to whom Mary runs, and when the two men hurry to the tomb, the other disciple waits until Peter enters before he himself goes in.

The details about the burial wrappings are significant. They are still in the tomb, though the body is not. If the body had been merely transported to another tomb, burial wrappings would still have been needed, and presumably they would have been taken along. However, if the body had been carried away in order to desecrate it, the cloths would probably have been discarded. No explanation is given for why the head cloth was rolled up separately. The interpretation of these details seems to have been left to the character in the narrative. We are not told what Peter thought about them, but the beloved disciple noted these things and believed. It is unusual that resurrection faith would spring forth from an experience of the empty tomb rather than from an appearance of the risen Lord, but it is the case here.

The reading ends on a curious note. The reason for the general lack of faith of the disciples is given: they did not understand the Scripture concerning the resurrection of Jesus. Regardless of how Jesus might have instructed his followers while he was still with them, they were ill equipped to comprehend his suffering and death, to say nothing of his rising from the dead. They would need both a resurrection experience and the opening of their minds to the meaning of the Scripture.

The choice of this reading for Easter Sunday highlights the incomprehensibility of the event. The fact that neither Mary, probably Jesus' closest female disciple, nor Peter, the leader of the Christian community, was prepared spontaneously to embrace the truth of the resurrection should caution us lest we too glibly presume to grasp it. There is much in the reality of the resurrection that continues to challenge as well as sustain us.

Themes of the Day

Easter is the season of mystagogical catechesis, the instruction that unpacks the hidden mystery of the experience of the sacraments of initiation received or renewed on Easter. The readings of each Sunday concentrate on some aspect of this mystery. The central theme of this Sunday is newness of life in Christ. This newness is not without its historical context. It burst forth first in the resurrection of Christ, and then through the preaching of the first Christians. Yet history is broken open by this newness in unimaginable ways.

Newness in Christ

In the Northern Hemisphere the world is coming alive. You can see it in the trees; you can smell it in the air. There is a freshness about to burst forth. It seems to be standing on tiptoes, eager to reveal itself, ready to be born. The life that was hidden in the darkness of winter is impatient to appear in all its glory. Nature itself seems poised to reenact the drama of death and resurrection.

On Easter Sunday the changes in nature all point to the transformation par excellence, the death and resurrection of Christ, and the transformation that takes place in us as we participate in that resurrection presence. The readings testify that if we die with Christ, we will appear with him in glory; if we cast out the old yeast, we will be fresh dough. And when this wondrous transformation takes place, everything is new; everything is fresh.

To what newness are we called? To what must we die in order to rise transformed? What old yeast of corruption must be cast out in order that we might be fresh dough? On Easter we renew our baptismal vows. What is it that we really renounce? Ours is a world of violence, of prejudice, of indifference. Too often we harbor feelings of anger and resentment, of selfishness and disdain. Easter proclaims that Christ has died and has risen; with him we die to all the wickedness in our lives and in our world, and we set our hearts on higher things—on sincerity and on truth.

History Is Broken Open

Though we know well the Easter story, we never fully grasp its meaning. The stone has been rolled back and the tomb is empty; resurrected life cannot be contained. Like the first believers, we so often continue to live with our dashed hopes and our misunderstanding of God's mysterious power. Like the first believers, we come to the tomb and expect to find death, but instead we find signs of a new life that we cannot even begin to comprehend. Like the first believers, we do not realize that history has been broken open and is now filled with the resurrected presence of Christ.

History no longer makes sense. The one who was maliciously singled out and shamefully hung on a tree was really the one set apart by God to judge the living and the dead. Who can comprehend such a paradox? But then, who goes to a tomb expecting to find life? History has been broken open, and now we really do not know what to expect!

This same resurrection power works in our own lives. "This is the day the LORD has made . . . it is wonderful in *our* eyes!" We too hear the Easter proclamation. By it, we too are brought into the power of the resurrection.

Second Sunday of Easter
Acts 4:32-35

This short passage is one of the best-known descriptions of the early Christian community (cf. Acts 2:42-47). Although it depicts values and relationships that were highly prized by the early Christians, the picture sketched is probably more theologically idealized than it is historically accurate. The principal values that characterize this community are unity in mind and heart (v. 32a); sharing of possessions (v. 32b); and apostolic witness (v. 33). While sharing possessions was a response to an ancient Jewish directive (cf. Deut 15:4), being of one mind and heart characterizes the Greek concept of friendship. Thus this picture of communal harmony espouses values from both cultures.

The primary focus here is on sharing of possessions, not communal ownership. Most likely this practice was adopted so that the needs of all members would be met. This calls to mind ancient Israel's image of the ideal end-time, when the people would finally be faithful to the law and there would be no poverty in the land. Since the early Christians regarded themselves as the people of God living in the time of fulfillment, it is easy to understand why they would believe they were to structure the patterns of their society according to this ideal.

One of the practices employed in order to accomplish this ideal is described in the reading. Property and houses were sold and the proceeds were laid at the feet of the apostles for distribution. The iterative Greek verb forms suggest that the practice was voluntary and repeated by various individuals. It could not have been universally practiced. Some members had to retain their property, or where would anyone have lived? Other biblical narratives demonstrate the selectivity of this practice.

The role played in the early Christian community by the apostles is quite clear. First and foremost, they were witnesses to the resurrection of Jesus. This made them prominent within the community and was probably the source of their exercise of authority. During his lifetime they had been commissioned by Jesus as apostles. Now they functioned within the community as his representatives, exercising authority in his place. The proceeds of the sale of goods were laid at their feet as a sign of the obedience and submission. They were the ones who decided upon the distribution of goods among the needy.

The ideals of this community were noble. They held out a way of life that may appear to be an ideal yet, through the grace of the resurrection, is attainable.

Psalm 118:2-4, 13-15, 22-24

The responsorial psalm consists of excerpts from a song of thanksgiving that seems to be part of a liturgical celebration. The psalm contains both individual and communal features: the language in the first and third sections (vv. 2–4, 22–24) is plural, while the speaker in the middle section (vv. 13–15) is clearly an individual. The refrain ("His mercy endures forever") establishes the psalm's congregational liturgical character.

The psalm itself begins with a call to give testimony to the goodness of God. This call is threefold in structure and inclusive in nature. The "house of Israel" designates the people of the covenant; the "house of Aaron" refers to the priesthood; "those who fear the LORD" is probably a reference to "god-fearers," or proselytes of non-Israelite origin (cf. Ps 115:9-11). The Hebrew word for mercy *(ḥesed)* is a technical theological term denoting God's steadfast love for those in covenant with God. Presumably the leader of the liturgical assembly calls out to the members of each respective group, and they in turn declare God's faithfulness.

The voice is singular in the second section of the responsorial (vv. 13–15). It testifies to a time when the psalmist was under great duress, suffering at the hands of others and being overpowered. In the face of this oppression God stepped in and saved the psalmist from ultimate defeat. The acknowledgment of deliverance is followed by an individual song of praise (v. 14), which uses the language of one of Israel's oldest hymns of victory (Exod 15:2a). The song, long associated with God's deliverance of the people from Egyptian bondage, acclaims the faithfulness of God: "My strength and my courage is the LORD."

The rescue of the individual is linked to the salvation of the entire community. They are the righteous who live in tents (v. 15). This reference to tents could be another allusion to the Exodus experience and the sojourn in the wilderness, or to the feast of Tabernacles, when the people remembered and celebrated this emancipation and sojourn. Whichever the case may be, the shout of victory proclaims God's deliverance of the people.

In the third section (vv. 22–24) the congregation speaks again, announcing the reversal of fortune that has taken place. The one who had been rejected and hard pressed by enemies has now been saved and exalted by God. Throughout this account of suffering and salvation, it is very clear that deliverance and exaltation are the works of God and not the accomplishments of human beings. This saving act may have happened to an individual, but the entire congregation has witnessed it and marvels at it.

In genuine liturgical fashion the responsorial psalm brings us to the present moment. Although the salvation described occurred in the past, the psalmist insists that *today* is the day that the LORD has made, *today* is the day that we rejoice in God's saving work. This liturgical perspective enables believers of any generation to identify their own time as the day of salvation and to rejoice in it.

1 John 5:1-6

The reading is a testimony to trinitarian faith. It describes God as the one who begets (the Father); it identifies Jesus as the Son of God; and it credits the Spirit as the one who testifies to the triumph of Jesus' death and resurrection. It also sketches the way believers participate in this trinitarian reality.

The very first verse is rich in theological meaning. It begins with a simply stated yet sophisticated christological declaration: Jesus is the Christ. The word "Christ," meaning "anointed one," has a long history in Jewish thought. In ancient Israel kings (2 Sam 2:4) and priests (Exod 30:30) were anointed. Gradually these customs developed into messianic ideas (Isa 9:5-6; 61:1), which after the resurrection were attributed by Christians to Jesus. Finally, the messiahship of Jesus was coupled with his divine sonship (v. 5).

This first verse states a second theological theme: It is faith in this Jesus that makes believers children of God. A form of the verb "to beget" is used three times in this verse: those who believe are "begotten by God"; God (the Father) is the one who begets; the begotten of God are to be the object of the love of others. Here faith and love *(agápē)* are intimately linked. While it is faith in Jesus, Messiah and Son of God, that brings one into the family of God, once there, one is expected to love God and all those others who have also been begotten by God through faith in the same Jesus.

The reading moves from faith and love to obedience. It does not identify the commandments to be observed, but it does state that they are not burdensome. It may be that the author wanted to insist that faith and love are not merely interior dispositions but must be manifested in some external way. The direction taken by love, as stated earlier, is here reversed. First the focus was on love for God, which presumes love for others. Here it is on love for God's children, which reveals itself in love for God and observance of God's commandments. It would seem that these two loves are so connected that it makes little difference which comes first. One form of love always results in the other.

A second way that faith reveals itself is in its victory over the world. This is stated three times (vv. 4–5). The "world" *(kósmos)* can be understood in three ways: the totality of natural creation, the inhabited world generally, and the inhabited world subject to sin. The context of this passage suggests that the third meaning is intended here. It is faith in Jesus as Messiah and Son of God that triumphs over evil.

Such faith challenges anything that questions the exalted nature of Jesus and the power that flows from it. Jesus alone is the Messiah who has inaugurated the reign of God and has ushered in the new age of fulfillment. He accomplished this not merely at the time of his baptism (through water), when he received his messianic commission, but at the time of his death and resurrection, (through blood), when he conquered death. The Spirit of truth testifies to this. Jesus alone shares in God's own nature and, thereby, can refashion women and men into children of God. It is through faith in him that believers can conquer the evils that threaten them.

John 20:19-31

Two resurrection appearances form a kind of diptych. The hinge that connects them is the person of Thomas. Absent for the first event, he is the central character of the second. His absence is curious, since on both occasions the doors of the room where the disciples were gathered were securely locked, "for fear of the Jews" (v. 19). Why had Thomas not gathered with the rest of the disciples? Was he not afraid? Or was he too afraid to be associated with them? The reason for his absence is never given. However, it does provide an occasion for another encounter with the risen Lord and the demonstration of faith that ensues.

The two resurrection appearances have several details in common: both occur on the first day of the week; despite the closed doors Jesus appears in their midst; he addresses them with a greeting of peace; he calls their attention to his wounds. Each of these details is laden with theological meaning.

The first day of the week is the actual day of the resurrection (v. 19) or the day that will eventually commemorate it (v. 26). The entire reckoning of time has been altered. Where previously the conclusion of the week had religious meaning, now the focus was on the beginning, on the future. The closed doors not only secured the disciples from those who would be hostile toward them, but they also underscore the mysterious character of Jesus' risen body, which is not impeded by material obstacles. The wish of peace, the common greeting of the day, was also a prayer for the eschatological blessings of health, prosperity, and all good things. Finally, by calling attention to the wounds in his hands and side, Jesus showed the disciples that he was really the crucified one now risen.

According to this account, it is on the evening of the resurrection itself that the Holy Spirit is bestowed on the disciples. They are commissioned to go forth, to declare salvation and judgment. Though this charge comes from Jesus, it is a continuation of the commission he received from God. The trinitarian testimony is clear. The image of breathing life into another is reminiscent of the creation of Adam (cf. Gen 2:7) and the restoration of Israel (cf. Ezek 37:9). This very act by the risen Lord casts him in a creative/re-creative role.

Thomas represents the second generation of Christians, those who are called to believe on the testimony of others. The faith required of him is, in a way, more demanding than that required of those who actually encountered the risen Lord. Viewed in this way, his doubt is understandable. While we may judge him harshly for it, Jesus does not. Instead, he invites Thomas to touch him, an invitation not extended earlier to the other disciples. The story does not say that Thomas actually touched the wounds, only that he cried out in faith: "My Lord and my God!" The other disciples recognized that the one in their midst was their Lord. Thomas declared that the risen Lord was God, a profession of faith that outstrips the others.

According to Jesus, as profound as was Thomas' ultimate faith, it does not compare with the faith of those who do not enjoy the kind of experience of the Lord described here. Thomas should be remembered not because he was absent or because he doubted but because, like us, he was called to believe on the word of others. And like Thomas, we know how difficult that is.

Themes of the Day

Our catechetical reflections brings us to reflect on the presence of the risen Lord. Where is he to be found? Each of the readings offers an answer to this question. The risen Christ is to be found in the community of believers, in the preaching of the disciples, in the forgiveness of sin, and in the physical manifestation of Christ's own wounds.

In the Community

Filled with faith in the risen Lord, believers attended to the needs of one another and in that way effectively brought forth the end-time. This end-time living was a tangible reality. Even non-believers recognized that there was something marvelously different about the community, and they exclaimed in awe: these Christians, see how they love one another. Faith in Jesus, the Messiah and Son of God, transforms ordinary people into children of God. Along with their new distinction comes a new way of living. Children of God live lives that are pleasing to God, lives that make faith and love tangible in the world.

In the Preaching of the Disciples

Thomas is the patron of those who must accept the truth of the resurrection on the word of others. Down through the ages, this is how it has been. There is no physical proof to which we can point, only the witness of others. Even the empty tomb is only an empty tomb. Evidence of the truth of the resurrection-claims is the change in life it effects, and we can all attest to this change. Time and again we have been touched by the power of the word of God; time and again it has brought our lives out of darkness into light, from the stranglehold of death to the birth of new life. The preaching of the disciples has been not only instructive, it has also been transformative.

Like Thomas, we might tend to doubt when the claims of the preacher seem too amazing, the demands too extreme. Those who preach may be no more credible than was Thomas. Yet these are the ones to whom the message has been given. It is the power of the tangible word of God, passed on and proclaimed by weak and limited human beings, that makes the risen Lord mystically present in the midst of the world.

In the Forgiveness of Sin

On that first Easter evening, Jesus came to the frightened disciples in order to make them ministers of divine forgiveness. His presence to them was the first instance of reconciliation. Today this same power in the Spirit given by the risen Christ reconciles sinners with God and, thereby, with the rest of the believing community. The words of forgiveness are the tangible agents of the mystical presence of the risen Christ.

In the Wounds of Christ

Jesus offered his wounds to be touched. He does this yet in our day. Believing that the community is the body of Christ, when we touch the wounds of the community we are putting our hands into the wounds of the risen Lord. These wounds in Christ, as shocking as they may appear to be, are really glorious wounds because the risen Lord has identified with them, has made them his own. However, as with every other example offered to us in the readings of today, we need faith to recognize the tangible presence of Christ in our midst.

Third Sunday of Easter
Acts 3:13-15, 17-19

This reading is part of a speech that Peter gave to a Jewish audience. Initially he identifies with his hearers, calling them brothers and referring to the "God of our fathers." (The gender bias here is obvious.) However, he dissociates himself from them and from their leaders when he accuses them of putting

Jesus to death. He himself stands on the side of Jesus as a witness to the resurrection. Peter's attitude toward the Jews of his time is not a case of anti-Judaism. He is opposed to those who refuse to accept Jesus as Messiah, not to the religion as a whole.

Peter's christology is rooted in the prophetic tradition of ancient Israel. He calls Jesus God's servant and then describes him as the righteous one who was handed over to persecutors. He does this by employing language that is reminiscent of the suffering servant tradition found in the teaching of the prophet Isaiah (cf. Isa 53:11-12). Furthermore, he makes a clear connection between this suffering servant and the Messiah, something that the tradition of Israel had never explicitly done. As he weaves various thematic threads together he reinterprets the earlier traditions and develops his own Christian theology.

The divine titles "the God of Abraham, the God of Isaac, and the God of Jacob, the God of our fathers," appear in the account of the burning bush (cf. Exod 3:6, 13, 15), where it identifies the God that was revealed to Moses with the God of the ancestors. By using this rich, ancient title, Peter is saying that the God who first revealed the promise of descendants and land to the ancestors and who then chose Moses to lead the people to freedom has now, by means of the resurrection, glorified the crucified Jesus.

There is a constant play here between the themes of life and death. Jesus is called the author of life, and yet he was put to death. He endures an ignominious and agonizing death, yet he is glorified (raised to new life). Pilate, a foreigner, holds the fate of the author of life in his hands. At first he is ready to spare Jesus' life, but then he hands him over to death, releasing instead someone who had taken the life of another. It is clear that regardless of the strength of the powers of death that are unleashed, the forces of life are ultimately triumphant.

While Peter places blame for the death of Jesus on his hearers, he also acquits them of some of the guilt that accompanies the deed, ascribing their offense to ignorance. He seems to be implying that had they known better they would have acted better (cf. Luke 23:34). This is a very interesting pastoral strategy. As a result of his witnessing to the resurrection and his preaching of the good news, they now do know better, and so they should reform their lives. Now they have no excuse.

Responsibility for the death of Jesus as presented here is a complicated matter. From a human point of view the ignorance of those involved is a mitigating circumstance. From God's point of view Jesus' suffering and death bring to fulfillment some of the messianic expectations found in the prophetic tradition. The point of the passage is the power of God to bring life out of death, not the assignment of blame for the death. It should be noted that the same power that raised Jesus can erase the sin of the offenders, thereby raising them to new life as well.

Psalm 4:2, 4, 7-8, 9

Two different but related sentiments are expressed in this responsorial psalm. One is lament, the other confidence. The verses open with the psalmist in great distress, turning to God and pleading for relief (v. 2). The innocence of the petitioner is implied when God is described as being just, since justice requires that innocence be recognized. A relationship seems to have been already established, for there is a reference to past instances of God's deliverance. Relying on the blessings of that past, the psalmist entreats God to act again in the same protective manner, to intervene on the psalmist's behalf.

For a moment, attention turns to those standing nearby (v. 4). In their presence the psalmist now testifies to the same faith and confidence that formed the initial prayer. This faith and confidence is based both on personal innocence and on divine trustworthiness. The psalmist claims to be numbered among the faithful ones *(ḥāsîd)*, to be one who has been loyal to the covenant relationship. It is such loyalty that guarantees God's favor. This conviction is based on the theory of retribution, which holds that the good will be rewarded while the evil will be punished. If this principle holds true, the psalmist will certainly be heard, for one can be sure that God will answer the prayers of a *ḥāsîd.*

The psalmist turns again to God. This time the supplication includes others as well. The appeal for God's favor is taken from the ancient blessing of the high priest Aaron (cf. Num 6:25f.). The image suggests that God's face lights up with pleasure at the sight of the righteous. To look favorably on someone is to bestow blessing. The psalmist prays for this blessing for all.

"Heart" is one of the richest biblical terms. Although on occasion it does denote the physical organ, it usually refers either to the totality of one's inner nature or to one of the three traditional personality functions—emotion, thought, or will. Virtually every immaterial act is attributed to the heart. The declaration "You put gladness into my heart" is an affirmation of the fullness of joy the psalmist experiences as a result of the relationship with God. This joy is accompanied by the assurance of security. The psalmist can lie down in peace *(šālôm)* and sleep, confident in God's ever-present watchful care (v. 9).

There is no indication here that the distress of the psalmist has been diminished. Instead, the verses highlight the psalmist's change in mind and heart. Based on the psalmist's own fidelity, this change results in confidence in God's faithfulness to the covenant. Confidence fills one with gladness and calms one's fears and anxieties so that sleep is possible. In fact, it is only in God that the psalmist rests secure. Neither people nor prosperity can fill this petitioner with the deep peace or full joy that comes from being in a covenant relationship with God.

1 John 2:1-5a

The address "My children," with which the reading opens, has traditionally been considered evidence of the author's affection for those to whom he writes. While such an interpretation may capture some of the meaning of the expression, by itself it overlooks the traditional wisdom character of the address. In certain educational situations teachers frequently spoke to their students in this way (cf. Prov 4:1; 5:7). The message contained in this passage suggests that it should be understood within the context of the wisdom tradition.

Although knowledge of God is a very important theme here, this is not an example of Gnosticism, a theory that claims that knowledge itself is salvific. On the contrary, the passage may actually be a denunciation of a Gnostic point of view, for it insists that the knowledge it champions leads one to observance of God's commandments (v. 3). It further states that anyone who claims knowledge but does not keep the commandments does not possess the truth (v. 4). This teaching is in accord with the wisdom tradition, which promotes righteous living.

The major portion of the reading goes beyond promotion of righteous living. It offers encouragement for the believers for those times when they stray from righteousness and do in fact sin. In these times, Jesus will be an advocate (*paráklētos*) for them before God. Jesus does not here assume the role of comforter, a role traditionally assigned to the Spirit. Rather, he is described as an intercessor, the one who atones for the sins of the world.

Several themes are brought together in these verses, contributing to a profile of the exalted Christ. First, Jesus is in the presence of God, having been raised gloriously from the dead. Second, he is described as righteous, despite the fact that he was condemned to death as a criminal. Third, the shedding of his blood was, at the time of his death and throughout all time, the sacrificial offering (*hilasmós*) that atones for sins. In light of this, believers should take heart. If they do sin, they have a worthy advocate who is in a position to intercede before God on their behalf. The universality of this intercession is clearly stated. The atonement is for the whole world, the entire inhabited world that is subject to sin.

The knowledge of God that is discussed here is experiential knowledge, a knowledge that results in a relationship with God. To know God is to keep the commandments; to keep God's word is to live in God's love. Therefore one can say; to know God is to love God, and both knowledge and love of God manifest themselves in obedience to God's commandments.

Although there is some ambiguity regarding the meaning of "the love of God is truly perfected in him," the context suggests that it refers to the believers' love for God rather than God's love for the believers. There is an eschatological character to this love. While the instruction clearly urges obedience to God's commandments in the present time, because human frailty enters in there is always the call to a more perfect obedience in the future. This means that the believers' love of God is being made more and more perfect as they become more and more obedient. Love is constantly being brought to fulfillment.

Luke 24:35-48

The brief introductory mention of the Emmaus event (24:13-32) sets the context for reading the passage that follows. It identifies the two major themes found in most post-resurrection appearance accounts: the experience of the risen Lord, and the ritual meal of the community. It very succinctly states that they recognized the risen Lord in the breaking of the bread. Though the details are different, the movement of the following episode is similar.

The text does not clearly identify who is present for this experience of the risen Lord, but it is presumed to be a relatively large group of women and men alike (cf. 24:33). Jesus addresses them with the customary Jewish greeting: "Peace be with you." Their response is telling; they are terrified, for they think they are seeing a ghost. Why would they think this? Could it be that they recognized him, yet they did not know what to make of his appearance, for they knew that he had been killed? This is not like the Emmaus event, where the two disciples walked with the Lord, listened as he explained the Scriptures, yet did not recognize him until the breaking of the bread.

Jesus rebukes them for having doubts. He then attempts to dispel two of these doubts by showing that it is really he and that he has a real body. He calls their attention to the marks of the nails in his hands and feet. Yes, it is really the same person whom they had known before, the one who was crucified and who died on the cross. He next invites them to touch him in order to realize his corporeal nature. He is not a ghost; his body is real. They still do not believe, but now they are overwhelmed with joy and wonder rather than fear and terror.

The final demonstration of his corporeal reality is his eating of a piece of cooked fish. Although this is not the official ritual meal of the community, it may have eucharistic overtones (cf. 9:16). The point of the meal is not the menu but the fact of Jesus' eating. The text does not say that those present shared in the meal, simply that he ate in order to convince them of his bodily presence. If they would be so convinced, they could then become witnesses of the resurrection.

Having assured the disciples of his bodily resurrection, Jesus proceeds to explain his suffering and death by turning to the Scriptures. Once again he asserts that he is the same Jesus who was their companion before the crucifixion.

He does this by reminding them of what he told them before. He maintains that all three of the major parts of the Bible, namely the Law (Moses), the Prophets, and the Writings (psalms), contain traditions that he fulfills. Their eyes have beheld the risen Lord. Now their minds are opened to the profound meaning of their religious tradition. Jesus shows them how his own story fulfills the story found in the Scriptures.

Although no specific citations are given, Jesus turns to the Scriptures to show that they specifically refer to the suffering, death, and resurrection of the Messiah; the role he plays in repentance and remission of sin; the universality of this message of salvation; and the privilege Jerusalem enjoys as the place from which this salvific preaching will be launched. Jesus then announces that those present will be witnesses to these marvels.

Themes of the Day

This is the season of mystagogical catechesis, the ecclesial instruction that unpacks the hidden mystery of experiencing the sacraments of initiation received or renewed on Easter. The first sentence of the Gospel reading sets the context for the themes of today: they recognized him "in the breaking of the bread." Like the first disciples, we too recognize him in the breaking of the bread. But who is it that we recognize? And what does this recognition require of us?

Who Is He?

Jesus is situated at the heart of Israel's most cherished traditions. He is the servant of the God of the early ancestors, the long-awaited Messiah, the innocent sufferer portrayed in the prophetic tradition. He is a real person, rooted in the religious history of a real people. He is the fulfillment of their deepest aspirations. When the disciples, who themselves were rooted in these traditions, recognized the risen Lord in the breaking of the bread, their eyes were opened to the meaning of this heritage. For them the sacramental meal was an occasion of mystagogical catechesis.

When we gather around the table for the same sacramental meal, we too encounter the risen Lord. There the sacred traditions of our religious heritage are opened for us and we too are enabled to recognize him in the traditions and in the breaking of the bread.

What Is Required?

In order to encounter the risen Lord in the breaking of the break and in the breaking open of the word, we need docile hearts ready to embrace the deepest meaning of our religious heritage. We need hearts that have been purified in the love of God; hearts that have been totally transformed. If we profess faith but are not truly faithful, we are liars. What does it mean to be faithful today? What does the commandment of love require of us? Jesus did not turn away from those who were closest to him yet who did not understand him. Instead, he invited them to an even more intimate communion. The commandment of love requires nothing less from us. We must love those who are distant and those who are close, those who might reject us and those who misunderstand us. We must love totally, as God loves.

Having recognized the risen Lord, we, like the people described in the first reading, must live reformed lives. Having recognized the risen Lord, we, like the people addressed in the second reading, must be obedient to God's commandment of love. Having recognized the risen Lord, we, like the disciples portrayed in the Gospel, must preach the good news of God's forgiveness to all nations. Easter faith assures us that all of this is possible. The prayer of the psalm has been answered. God has looked favorably upon us. The Easter mystery now unfolds in our midst.

Fourth Sunday of Easter

Acts 4:8-12

The first reading for this Sunday is a response by Peter to the leaders of the Jewish community in Jerusalem. It seems that he and his Christian companions were challenged to justify the healing of a man who was crippled. In his reply Peter draws a distinction between these leaders, along with those who have not accepted Jesus as the source of salvation, and himself and other Christian believers. The factor that distinguishes these two groups is faith in the power of the name of Jesus. Peter claims that it was in the power of this name that the man was healed (v. 9) and it will be in the power of this same name that all will be saved.

The story follows a familiar pattern found in many biblical stories: someone in the story faces a challenge; at first the challenge is not met; a miraculous event calls the protagonist back to the challenge; a second chance is given. In the Gospel narrative the entire life of Jesus and the claims his life made constitute the trial. Here the rejection is at the hands of the leaders of the people. The wonder is the healing of the crippled man. Finally, although rejection calls down judgment, God's judgment never precludes ultimate salvation.

Once again Peter speaks out against the leaders of the people, not because they are Jewish but because they rejected Jesus. He employs an image taken from the world of builders and construction. According to Peter these leaders are like the builders who reject a particular stone as unsuitable. In the pattern of reversal so prominent in Gospel stories, this repudiated stone becomes the cornerstone, the most important stone in the building (cf. Ps 118:22). Both the courage to confront the leaders and the wisdom to know what to say to them come from the Holy Spirit.

In one way this passage is an explanation of the power that God intended for the leaders; in another way it is a kerygmatic proclamation directed toward them. At the heart of Peter's message is the fundamental gospel formula: "whom you crucified, whom God raised from the dead." This is not a static announcement; it is a dynamic pronouncement with powerful salvific implications. Jesus was not raised from the dead merely for his own benefit. Rather, his resurrection became the fountain from which springs salvation of every kind. For the crippled man, salvation took the form of healing; for others, it can take the form of spiritual transformation.

The urgency of the gospel message is clear. Jesus is the cornerstone of the building, the foundation upon which the entire community rests. The name of Jesus is the one and only source of salvation, hence no one can afford to reject it.

Psalm 118:1, 8-9, 21-23, 26, 28, 29

The song that serves as the responsorial psalm begins and ends with the same summons to give thanks to God. This forms a kind of *inclusio.* The call by the psalmist appears to be directed to others, probably to a community of believers. The reason for giving thanks is God's trustworthiness, which is demonstrated in two ways. First, the expression contains the technical covenant term for mercy or steadfast love *(ḥesed).* Second, it maintains that such love will last forever. The use of this covenant language is further evidence of the identity of the community. The psalmist addresses a group of believers, reminding them of God's faithfulness. This faithfulness is reason enough to give thanks.

What follows is wisdom instruction (vv. 8–9). Two proverbs in the comparative "better . . . than" form insist that trust in God far exceeds trust in mere human beings, even powerful princes. In keeping with the wisdom tradition, this is unambiguous instruction, not an imperative. Wisdom simply states what has been observed or learned from experience. The presumption is that the wise will freely decide on this course of action in order to live in harmony with the established orders in life.

The next verse is a kind of refrain that appears twice (v. 21). It is different from the rest of the responsorial in that it is a personal prayer of thanksgiving addressed directly to God rather than a testimony of God's goodness addressed to the community. In it God's attentiveness and saving intervention are acknowledged. The psalmist knows from experience that God is indeed faithful to covenant promises made. Based on this past, gratitude is appropriate and trust in God is well founded.

A new image is introduced that draws a clear distinction between God's judgment and human judgment. The stone rejected becomes the stone preferred (v. 22). The Hebrew identifies this stone as "the head of the corner." Although some interpret it as the capstone that completes the building, the reference is probably to the cornerstone that links two walls at right angles, thus holding up a significant part of the building's weight. Once again, the community is witness to this wondrous reversal of fortune. These verses do not indicate to whom the psalmist refers. However, as a response to the first reading, the reference to Jesus as the rejected but now preferred cornerstone is clear. Here the point of the metaphor is the unreliability of human judgment. It is far better to trust in God.

A second wisdom form appears (v. 26a). Called a "macarism" from the Greek word for "bless," it points out the religious significance of something that, because it may not conform to social customs, might otherwise elude our attention. Like the Beatitudes, which are somewhat counter-cultural, they give us God's point of view, not that of human beings. The one who comes in the name of the Lord is blessed or happy, regardless of what the surrounding society may think. Once again, this is God's judgment, not human judgment.

There appears to be a liturgical aspect here, for the community blesses God from the "house of the Lord." The responsorial psalm ends with the thanksgiving refrain (cf. v. 21) and the summons to give thanks that forms the *inclusio.* The goodness of God has been profiled. Gratitude is the only fitting response.

1 John 3:1-2

These two short verses are brimming with theological meaning. The first and more important point is the love that God has for believers. The second theme is eschatological fulfillment. Although the latter is dependent upon the former, it is also a direct result of it.

The love *(agápē)* of which the author speaks is generative; it is transforming; it makes believers children of God. Everything that happens in the lives of believers is a consequence of their having been re-created as God's children. This introduces a related theme. As children of God they are a new reality; hence they are not accepted by the world, the old reality. Certain similarities between Jesus and the believers are drawn. The world, the entire inhabited world that is subject to sin, recognizes only its own. It did not recognize the only begotten Son of God and it does not recognize these new children of God. The implications are clear. Believers should not be surprised if they encounter the same kind of rejection, even persecution and death, that befell Jesus.

The reading does not identify what it is about Jesus and the believers that is so difficult for the world to comprehend. However, it is probably the manner of living that flows from their relationship with God, a manner of behavior that contradicts the lifestyle promoted by the sinful world and that results in the world's rejection of what it cannot claim.

The "now but not yet" of Christian eschatology is clearly stated. As a consequence of God's love, believers have already been reborn as children of God. However, their transformation has not yet been completed, nor has it been fully made know to them. All of this is dependent upon a future manifestation. It is not clear from the text whether this will be a manifestation of Christ or of God. Although the Greek construction is ambiguous, the theological intent is not. Actually, any manifestation of the risen Christ is a manifestation of God, and in like manner, the ultimate manifestation of God is found in the risen Christ.

Having been made children of God, the community of believers is promised an even fuller identification with God. They will see God as God is, for they will be like God. The Hellenist influence here is obvious. Widespread in the ancient world was the notion that a reality can be understood only by another reality similar to it. The basis of this hope is the ultimate vision of God, a vision that is denied believers "now" but which is promised for "later."

John 10:11-18

This description of Jesus as shepherd falls into two distinct yet related sections, each introduced by the self-proclamation "I am the good shepherd" (vv. 11, 14). In the first Jesus sketches the external behavior of a good shepherd; in the second he explains the reason for his unselfish attitude. The introductory words, "I am" *(egō eimi),* suggest that this discourse is a form of divine revelation (cf. Exod 3:14). This becomes quite clear in the second section. The images of shepherd and sheep may sound strange, even offensive, to contemporary ears, since sheep are seen as animals who thoughtlessly follow the command of their leaders. In the ancient world, where the majority of people were relatively defenseless, the metaphor not only tempered the power that leaders exerted but also reinterpreted the relationship between leader and those led.

The word "good" means noble rather than skilled. As shepherd, Jesus is committed to the well being of the sheep. He is not like those shepherds who were condemned by the prophets (cf. Ezekiel 34). They not only failed in their responsibilities, they actually took advantage of their charges. Jesus, on the other hand, is willing to lay down his life for those under his care. Contrasting himself with a hireling suggests that there is some kind of deep relationship between him and the sheep. This relationship is described in the second section.

The first section depicts Jesus in very human terms. He is a conscientious shepherd who is willing to protect his flock even to the point of risking his own life for them. The second section places this image within the context of a much higher christology. This shepherd is intimately related to God. Although the Greek setting of the Gospel cannot be denied, the Jewish roots of the Christian faith throw light on this saying. In the Hebrew mind-set, to know another is more than being acquainted with that person. It implies sharing an intimate relationship. Jesus states that he has a mutual, intimate relationship with his sheep. He goes on to say that this relationship is based on the mutual, intimate relationship that he has with God.

The universality of Jesus' shepherding is clearly stated. He is willing to care for and die for other sheep who, though they are not yet included in his flock, are nonetheless his. Sheep, even when they are mixed within another flock, can recognize the voice or sound of their own shepherd. Jesus is saying that these other sheep will recognize him and will then be brought into his flock. In the end there will be one flock and one shepherd.

The death of Jesus looms large in this reading (vv. 11, 15, 17, 18). It is a vicarious death; he voluntarily lays down his life for others. Here the metaphor of the shepherd is an apt image of the life and death of Jesus. However, the reading does not leave us with his death but with his resurrection. It states that God loves Jesus for his willingness to lay down his life and to take it up again. The high christology can be seen in the apparent control that Jesus has, not only over his death but also over his resurrection. He has the power to take up his life again. The final verse states that he received this power from God. The universally salvific death of Jesus is the work of the Father through the Son.

Themes of the Day

On this Sunday, traditionally known as Good Shepherd Sunday, the readings offer us a magnificent meditation on salvation. Two major themes emerge: the one who saves, and the power of salvation.

The One Who Saves

The images are striking! The one who saves is not a mighty warrior who comes in military array. There are no weapons; there is no show of force. The one who saves is the one who was rejected. It is the one who was hunted down, humiliated, tortured, and hung naked on a tree, there to die in shame. The one who saves is the cornerstone of the building, holding it together, forming a firm foundation so that the structure will not collapse. The one who saves is a lowly shepherd, entrusted with sheep, not with affairs of state. The one who saves is an unlikely Savior. Nonetheless, it is in his name that the man is restored to health. It is in his name that people take refuge and ultimately rejoice. He has the power over life and death, his own and that of his sheep.

This characterization of the one who saves should give us pause. Perhaps we look in the wrong places for a savior. Perhaps we have appropriated the mind-set of our day and believe that evil can only be corrected through force. Perhaps we think it is necessary to be in the public eye and accepted according to popular standards in order to accomplish something worthwhile. Perhaps we have chosen the wrong stone to hold our edifice together, the wrong leader to ward off threats to our peace and security. Perhaps we need the insight that comes from Easter faith to see things as they really are.

The Power of Salvation

What looks like a healing is more than a mere cure. The man who was crippled now walks in the power of the name of Jesus, a name that itself means "savior" (cf. Matt 1:21). The cure is merely an outward sign of a much deeper inner reality. The saving power in this name is for all people, even for those sheep who do not yet belong to this fold. Furthermore, it is for all time; God's mercy endures forever.

This saving power, this mercy, is nothing less than steadfast covenant love. It is the kind of love that broke open the world in the death and resurrection of Jesus and overflows as healing grace; it is the kind of love that compels the shepherd to put himself at risk for the sake of the sheep. It is a love that re-creates us as children of God. This love has already taken hold of us. Through baptism we are God's children now; Easter celebrates this reality. What we will eventually become has not yet been revealed.

When salvation is brought to its fulfillment, there will be a great illumination and we will recognize the marvelous dignity that is ours. We will see that we have been made like God, and we can now act as God acts. We can bring the saving grace of God to a world in desperate need of healing. We can do this in our families, in our local communities, in the workplace, in so many situations of our lives. Is it any wonder that we would cry out: Give thanks to the LORD . . . God's mercy endures forever?

Fifth Sunday of Easter

Acts 9:26-31

Several narrative themes are woven together in this account of Saul's encounter with the early Christian community in Jerusalem. The most prominent theme is the witness to the marvelous transformation that the grace of God can effect; even a persecutor can become a disciple. Coupled with this is the role played by other members of the Christian community. Underlying the entire account is a familiar narrative pattern: preaching, persecution, vindication. Finally, the reading ends with a summary that both generalizes and idealizes the growth of the Christian movement.

The Jewish context of the events recounted in the narrative is obvious. The setting is Jerusalem; the apostle Paul is still known as Saul, his Jewish name; the concluding summary outlines the progress of the missionary activity of the church in Jerusalem. It seems to be very important that Saul be somehow established as a member of this founding community. This will not only reconcile him with some of the very people of the community that he once opposed (cf. Acts 8:1), but the reconciliation will later serve as credential of authenticity when he moves away from Jerusalem and begins his own unique ministry.

Saul, the formidable persecutor, has now become a disciple of the risen Lord. Initially he meets resistance, not to his message but to his claim of conversion. It takes another member of the community, Barnabas (son of consolation, cf. Acts 4:36), to intercede for him, to speak on his behalf, to witness to the salvific grace of God that transformed him into a believer. If God can raise Jesus from the dead, surely God can re-create Saul. In fact, Saul's rebirth as a disciple is a sign of the grace that has been unleashed by the resurrection. It was the risen Jesus that Saul encountered (cf. Acts 9:5; 22:8; 26:15), and it is that same risen Jesus that he now proclaims. The power of God is unfathomable.

Saul's attempt to persuade Greek-speaking Jews of the power of the name of Jesus and their deadly reaction is reminiscent of Stephen's debate with the so-called Synagogue of Freedmen (cf. Acts 6:8–7:60). He preaches; he is persecuted by them; he is ultimately vindicated by God. While Saul's apostolic fervor may not have convinced the Greek-speaking Jews of God's choice of Jesus, it certainly convinced members of the Jerusalem community of the genuineness of his conversion.

The placement of the final summary that reports the condition of the church is interesting. It suggests that there is a relationship between the peace the church enjoyed and the sense of security it must have felt knowing it no longer had to fear the passionate opposition of one of its chief persecutors. This summary follows a pattern found elsewhere in Acts: the church faces a great crisis; it is rescued in a way that leaves no doubt that it is the Lord who rescues them; confident of the Lord's protection, the church finds peace and continues to flourish (cf. Acts 5:17-42).

Psalm 22:26-27, 28, 30, 31-32

These verses constitute an individual's hymn of thanksgiving. Though individual, the one giving thanks does so within the setting of a believing community.

Evidence of this is found in the first verse of the psalm: a vow is fulfilled (v. 26). A vow was a verbal promise to perform some act of service of God, to make an offering, or to abstain from something as a response to a blessing received from God. It is a kind of thanksgiving offering. Here the psalmist fulfills this vow in the midst of believers. This may be a reference to some liturgical gathering.

The assembly consists of those who fear God. While such fear may imply terror before the awesomeness of divine power, in the wisdom tradition it denotes piety and reverential obedience. The context of worship suggests that the latter meaning is intended here. It is in the company of devout believers that the psalmist performs the religious deed promised earlier. The nature of this deed is not revealed, but the next verse suggests that it has something to do with a meal to which the poor are invited. This could be simply a charitable feeding of the hungry. However, the psalm with its response indicates that the reference is to a ritual meal at which the poor or lowly eat their fill.

The psalm itself may be an individual hymn of thanksgiving for God's blessing, but this blessing is not limited to the psalmist, and the praise it engenders will come from all who seek the Lord. This circle of devotees moves out from the assembly of believers (v. 26) to all the ends of the earth and to all the families of nations (v. 28). The boundlessness of God's blessing is clearly seen. There is no ethnocentrism or religious chauvinism here. Rather, the universal reign of the one God is sketched.

The scope of God's reign even stretches beyond life into the realm of the dead. Initially God was considered the patron deity of the chosen people. As the monotheistic faith developed, the people envisioned God's reign as encompassing all of the living. Such a perspective is seen in this psalm. However, the realm of the dead was still not included (cf. Pss 6:6; 115:17). God was the God of the living. A different understanding is present in this psalm. It claims that the dead do indeed pay homage to the Lord. Furthermore, they pay homage to the Lord alone. Both the living and the dead have known the providential care of God, and they all acknowledge this in the praise and the reverence that they show.

The scope of praise extends even further. The members of the assembly of believers and the families of the nations represent those in the present who pay homage to God; the dead represent those from the past. In this psalm the circle of believers also includes future generations, descendants yet to be born (vv. 31-32). Thus past, present, and future are all included in the realm of God, all enjoy God's blessings, and all offer praise and give thanks.

The psalm ends with an exhortation to hand down from generation to generation the tradition of the righteousness of God, a righteousness that shows itself in providential care and blessing.

1 John 3:18-24

In this reading the believers are addressed in two different ways. The first, "Children" *(tekníon),* is used by the author as both a term of endearment and an expression of authority over the addressees. The second, "Beloved" *(agapētoí),* makes a connection between the love God has for them and the love they should have for one another. In this reading the author both instructs and exhorts, two functions exercised by wise teachers. This reading, which is trinitarian in character, also links in a very significant way three important theological themes: Christian love, confident belief, and faithful obedience.

The first exhortation is to active love. It is not enough to proclaim love for God; its authenticity must be demonstrated through concrete action. There seems to have been a sense of guilt somewhere in the community. Perhaps members were not faithful to their initial commitment; perhaps their love for God or for one another had waned and they were fearful of divine judgment. The writer assures them that the love God has for them far exceeds any guilt they may experience. They are called to believe this, thus making their faith one that is rooted in confidence regarding divine love.

The confidence that is encouraged will also be manifested in the way the believers turn to God in prayer. Their petitions should spring from the certainty that they will receive from God whatever they ask. A further reason for confidence is the past faithfulness of the community. The author assures them that just as they have been fundamentally faithful in fulfilling their covenant obligations and in doing what is pleasing before God despite occasional lapses, so God will faithfully uphold the promises of loving forgiveness and constant divine presence that were made to them.

Although only one commandment is placed before them here, its focus is twofold. They are to believe in the name of God's Son Jesus Christ and to love one another. This exhortation calls for a statement of faith in Jesus' divine nature (somehow captured in his name), the basis of authentic Christian faith, and commitment to a way of life that demonstrates loving behavior, the basis of genuine Christian living. The mutual abiding character of the union that joins believers and God is clearly stated: faithful believers abide in God and God abides in them. This mutual indwelling is accomplished by the Spirit, which was given to the believers by God.

This last comment completes the sketch of trinitarian theology found in the reading. Viewing it from the perspective of trinitarian relationships, we see that Jesus is called the Son of God and the Spirit is identified as the gift of God that was bestowed upon the faithful. Viewing it from the perspective of trinitarian involvement in the lives of the faithful, we see that the ground of Christian confidence is the great love of God; the focus of Christian faith is commitment to the name (identity) of Jesus Christ, the Son of God; the assurance of divine indwelling is the gift of the Spirit.

John 15:1-8

The allegory of the vine calls to mind the song of the vineyard found in Isaiah (cf. Isa 5:1-7). There the prophet condemns the house of Israel and the people of Judah for their infidelity. He proclaims that this vine will not be pruned or hoed but will be allowed to fall into ruin. In contrast, Jesus claims to be the true vine, the one that faithfully brings forth good fruit.

We must be careful about how we understand the descriptive adjective "true" lest we perpetuate any unacceptable anti-Judaic sentiments. While it is clear that in this passage lines are drawn between those who accept Jesus and those who do not, these lines do not distinguish one nation or religious group from another. In the first place, the metaphor itself does not contrast Christian faithfulness with Jewish infidelity. In both cases the vines have to be pruned of unproductive branches, indicating that neither community is completely faithful. We must also remember that the vines in the earlier metaphor were described as "choicest." Israel was a favored nation.

Despite the fact that it was favored, the first vine produced wild grapes. Though the claim is not explicitly made, the implication is that Jesus, the true vine, will bring forth a good crop. If this is not an anti-Judaic statement, on what grounds can it be made? It is made on the grounds of divine self-revelation ("I am"; *egō eimi;* cf. Exod 3:14). Jesus makes a divine claim. Some accept his word and some do not. Having made this claim, Jesus then describes himself as the unique mediator of God's grace. Jesus is the vine, but it is God's vineyard. It is God who prunes and trims, and it is God who is glorified in the abundant yield.

The metaphor of vine and branches characterizes the intimate nature of the relationship between Jesus and his followers. In fact, a vine is made up of its branches. The life of the vine is the life of the branches. Jesus lives in his branches, and his branches live in his life. The vine bears fruit through its branches, and the branches bear the fruit of the vine. This is an apt metaphor for describing the intimacy of such union. The vine is not totally dependent on any one branch or group of branches. Therefore it can endure pruning without withering and dying. However, there is no vine if there are no branches at all. In such a case there is only a trunk, and that is not the metaphor Jesus uses here.

The basis of this union is acceptance of and fidelity to the words of Jesus (vv. 3, 7), not ethnic or national identity. The importance of allegiance to these words, this teaching, cannot be overemphasized. It is this message that shapes the religious identity of the disciples. The bond that is the source of union is faith. It joins one to the vine and to the other branches. It also entitles one to access to the blessings of God (v. 7), since the prayers of the branches can be seen as the prayers of the vine, and God is attentive to the vine.

The vitality expressed by this image is unmistakable. The vine and the branches are alive with the life of God. This union is offered to all who would listen to the words of Jesus, accept his divine claim, and live in union with him and his other disciples.

Themes of the Day

The Easter drama continues to unfold. On the first Sunday we were dazzled by the wonder of the resurrection. Next we paused to discover the presence of the risen One. On the third Sunday we recognized ways in which the Easter proclamation was heard and known. Last Sunday we saw that the fruit of the proclamation is salvation. Today we see that salvation brings an ecclesial community into being. This community is joined to Jesus as branches are part of the vine; it is a multifaceted community; it is devoted to good works and to prayer.

The Vine and the Branches

Jesus announces, I am the vine; you are the branches. This is a daring image. It claims that the community lives and acts only with the life of Jesus. It is also an intimate characterization of the community of believers, who share the same divine life. The Church, the extension of Christ in the world, is truly a mystery. It thrives on Christ's resurrected life, which surges through all its members. We live in Christ as Christ lives in us.

A Multifaceted Community

The early Church was a multi-ethnic community. It included inhabitants from Jerusalem, from all of Judea, Galilee, and Samaria, even Damascus. Some of these people were firmly rooted in Jewish customs, others were more Greek in their culture. The community included disciples who had been followers of Jesus from the beginning of his public ministry as well as persecutors like Saul, who had been converted. This community is the fulfillment of the promises made so often in the past, that the saving power of God would reach the whole world.

Our own ecclesial community of believers is also multi-ethnic. Where formerly parishes or liturgical assemblies might have been more homogeneous in ethnic background and economic status, today there is much greater diversity and rapid change of character. Like the early Christians, we too are often suspicious of newcomers. They may come from groups with whom we have known conflict. They may speak a language that is foreign to our ears, or they may have religious customs that leave us uncomfortable. In the face of all of this variety, the Church can still be at peace, it can make progress, it can enjoy the consolations of the Holy Spirit. It is for us to open our hearts to the various manifestations of God's power and to fashion a community that in its diversity gives glory to God.

Devotion to Good Works and to Prayer

All of the readings underscore the good works in which the believers are engaged. Saul commits himself wholeheartedly to the proclamation of the gospel, preaching to the very people he once persecuted. The piety of the psalmist testifies to God's goodness before the company of devout believers, the families of the nations, and the coming generations. The author of the letter of John insists that it is not enough to talk about love. Believers must demonstrate their love for God and for each other in deeds. Joined to Christ as branches are a part of the vine, we too are enlivened and thereby bear fruit in abundance.

Sixth Sunday of Easter
Acts 10: 25-26, 34-35, 44-48

The scene is the house of Cornelius, a newly converted Roman centurion. Cornelius' deference to Peter shows that he recognizes Peter as a messenger of God. Peter's response is an acknowledgment that he is indeed only a messenger, not a god. Normally, an observant Jew like Peter would not enter the home of a Gentile. The first words of his discourse ("In truth, I see") indicate that he was not always open to association with Gentiles as he is now. It was a newly gained insight about God that changed his view of those who did not have Jewish ancestry. He realized that "God shows no partiality" (vv. 34–35; cf. Deut 10:17; 2 Chr 19:7), and therefore, neither should he. All are acceptable to God, Jew and Gentile, man and woman.

The real power of the narrative is seen not in the disposition of Peter but in the action of the Holy Spirit. In fact, Peter's courageous preaching is interrupted by the action of God. The righteous, God-fearing Gentiles gathered in the house of Cornelius receive the Holy Spirit and speak in tongues without the agency of Peter or his Jewish-Christian companions, even without having been baptized. This is a kind of Gentile Pentecost scene. As with that earlier event, the prophecy of Joel is fulfilled: the Spirit is poured out (cf. Acts 2:17-21; Joel 3:1-5), and there is a miracle of speech (cf. Acts 2:5-12).

In this account, speaking in tongues is less important as a supernatural gift in itself than as a manifestation of the presence of the Spirit. There would have been no way of knowing that the Gentiles had received the Spirit had there been no objective external sign. And what better way of demonstrating the extraordinary character of this outpouring than by means of an amazing display of speech in tongues!

While Peter's companions are surprised that the Spirit is given to those who have not been circumcised, Peter intervenes on behalf of the Gentiles. He has just insisted that God shows no partiality. Now all in the house have witnessed the truth of this gospel message. Peter recognizes that the Gentiles have received the Spirit "even as we have." He concludes: it is clear that God has accepted the Gentiles; the Church can do no less. Here the ritual of baptism is a sign of the Church's acceptance of God's action, not the agency of that action. Those who received the Spirit at the first Pentecost and those who have received it at this second Pentecost are joined by a special bond, the shared outpouring of the Spirit.

God's unmediated action usually indicates a new direction for the believing community. Total acceptance of Gentiles, the new direction reported here, is demonstrated in three ways: the outpouring of the Spirit, the recognition of this phenomenon by the Church, and Peter's extended stay with the new Christians. Although the reading does not describe how this time was spent, one can presume that whatever the case, prolonged association with Gentiles would be frowned upon by more conservative Jewish Christians in Jerusalem. After all, Peter was the leader of the Church, and his acceptance of the Gentiles had great significance.

Psalm 98:1, 2-3, 3-4

The responsorial psalm opens and closes with a summons to sing praise to the LORD. The first verse explicitly calls the people to sing a new song to God (cf. Psalm 96). The reason for this new song is the marvelous new activity of God. The psalmist follows this summons with an enumeration of some of the wonderful acts of God (vv. 1b–3).

God is first depicted as a triumphant warrior whose right hand and outstretched arm have brought victory. The victory sketched in these verses seems to have been historical, one that transpired on the stage of Israel's political experience. However, it is not too difficult for a deity to defeat human forces. If God is to be acclaimed as king over all, there must be a more comprehensive victory, one that demonstrates preeminence on a cosmic scale. Behind the image of the triumphant warrior is just such an understanding. The divine warrior is the one who conquers the forces of chaos. This is a cosmic victory. These verses speak of a sweeping victory (v. 3). Thus it is correct to say that God's triumph is universal and undisputed.

The focus here is on the particularity of Israel's salvation by God. Two aspects of this victory are mentioned. First, the victory, or demonstration of righteousness, is really vindication meted out in order to rectify a previous injustice. Second, the victory follows God's recall of the covenant promises made to the house of Israel. Lovingkindness *(ḥesed)* and faithfulness *(ʾĕmûnâ)* are closely associated with these promises (v. 3). It is important to remember that this particular psalm praises God precisely as a triumphant warrior. This implies that something about God was challenged. Thus any victory here is really a vindication of God.

A second important feature of this psalm response is its statement about the relationship that exists between God's saving action and the promises God made. The psalmist claims that it was remembrance of the covenantal love that prompted God to save Israel. It was because of the promises made to the ancestors that the divine warrior stepped in and triumphed over Israel's enemies. That victory, which was revealed to all the nations, is the reason for the psalmist's call to praise God in song.

The final verses elaborate on the universal scope of the praise that is given to God. "All the ends of the earth have seen the salvation by our God" and, in response to this, are called to praise. Because the earlier part of the psalm speaks of God's vindication before the nations, it is not clear whether these other nations are witnessing the blessings that God bestows only on Israel or are themselves recipients of God's good favor. There is actually very little difference between these two interpretations.

Simply witnessing to the salvation of Israel realized by God can be a blessing for the nations, a blessing for which they give praise. By it they will know that God is faithful to the covenant promises and that God can indeed reverse the misfortune endured by the house of Israel. In seeing this they can be led to an acknowledgment of God's indisputable might, an acknowledgment that makes them believers in the God of Israel.

1 John 4:7-10

In these few verses we find some of the most profound theological, christological, soteriological, and communitarian tenets of the Christian faith. The heart of the message is the teaching about love. Several dimensions of this reality are examined: Love is of God; it begets others of God; it is revealed in the salvation realized through the sacrifice of the Son of God. The most startling statement about love is: God is love! This divine love is *the* fundamental theological reality.

Although his proper name is not mentioned here, Jesus is identified as the Son of God, who originated outside of the world of history but who was sent into that world. He became the expiation *(hilasmón)* for the sins of others, winning for them a second chance at life. Although the author addresses the hearers as "Beloved" *(agapētoí)*, the communitarian exhortation that follows, "let us love one another," is as applicable to the author as it is to the audience. As a member of the community, the author is also begotten of God through love and summoned to love others in return.

The love described here is not merely an expression of the best that the human spirit has to offer. It is neither exemplary piety nor altruistic concern for others. Actually, there is nothing human about it. It is divine in its origin, and only those who have been begotten by God can have a share in it.

God initiates this love, and it is best exemplified in Christ's own selfless offering of himself for others. When Christians are called to live in this self-giving love, more than an imitation of Christ is being required of them. Rather, it is because they have been begotten by God and somehow share in the very nature of God that they can be exhorted to live out this divine love as God does and as Christ did.

The knowledge of God that accompanies being begotten by God is not merely knowledge "about" God. Even unbelievers can acquire this. Rather, it is experiential knowledge, knowledge that comes from touching and being touched deeply in one's own divinized nature. Those who have no love have not been begotten by God, and consequently, they lack this inner knowledge; those who do not enjoy such knowledge have never been begotten by God and, therefore, do not live in such love.

In the event that anyone should question this teaching, the writer provides evidence of the truth of what is claimed. God's love was manifested in this way: The only Son of God was sent into the world—that entire inhabited world that is subject to sin—in order to suffer and to die in expiation for its sins. The only Son of God endured death that the world might have life through him. This is the extent of God's love for the world. Although earlier in the reading the writer called believers to replicate this love in their own lives, here the focus is on the unbelievable character of God's love. Nothing can compare with it; it is, in fact, almost impossible to comprehend. Nonetheless, this is the love that is presented to believers for their contemplation and for their ultimate imitation.

John 15:9-17

This passage is one of the best-known discourses on love. The Greek word used is neither ʿerōs, the passion that seeks some form of possession of the person or object loved, nor *philía,* which denotes the love of kin or those very closely related. The word used is *agápē,* a word that in itself is very similar to *philía* but which in John's Gospel has special theological meaning. It is the only word used to describe the love for God, and it carries this connotation when applied to love for neighbor. The word appears nine times in this reading, weaving together the love that God has for Jesus, the love that Jesus has for his friends, and the love the friends have for one another.

The source of this love is divine love itself: "As the Father loves me, so I also love you" (v. 9); "Love one another as I love you" (v. 12). The disciples are invited to live in this love (vv. 9, 10), to abide there. The verb *(ménō)* means "to stay in a place." It suggests a permanence associated with God. The union that is offered is not intended to be a passing occasion; it is to be a lasting state of being. It will be accomplished through obedience. In this, Jesus is both the model and the mediator. As he was obedient to the commandments of God, so the disciples must be obedient to his commandments. In fact, it is through their obedience to him that they will be obedient to God.

Jesus promises the disciples that if they abide in his love and obey his commandments they will abide in his joy as well. Although the passage does not describe the character of this joy, we can presume that it flows from union with God. Furthermore, it is a joy that is not diminished by sacrifice, even the sacrifice of laying down one's life for another (v. 13).

The profile of friendship is clearly sketched. A friend is someone so close to you that you are willing to lay down your life for that person. While we might assume that the love for this friend *(phílos)* is *philía,* we see that Jesus is talking about *agápē,* the love that he has for his friends, the love that is like God's love. The disciples are the friends of whom Jesus speaks. They are not slaves who obey blindly. Chosen by Jesus, they have heard and accepted God's will as spoken by him. They have responded freely, like friends would respond. Thus he calls them friends, and because of his love for them he is willing to lay down his life for them. They, in turn, must similarly love one another and, presumably, be willing to lay down their lives for one another.

The love described here is active love, reaching out to others—God to Jesus, Jesus to his disciples, the disciples to one another. But it must not stop there. This active love must move out beyond the confines of the group of chosen ones into the broader world. Those who have been chosen for love have also been elected to mission. They must go forth, and their love and obedience must bear fruit in the lives of others. This fruit will endure (the Greek has a form of the verb "to abide"). The circle will be completed when God grants the requests made by the disciples in the name of Jesus.

The reading ends with the injunction that sums up the entire proclamation: "Love one another."

Themes of the Day

Our mystagogical catechesis continues with a consideration of the boundless love of God, which brought the Church into being in the first place and which has continued to sustain and strengthen it down through the ages. This is a love that cannot be circumscribed by human boundaries but is universal in its scope. It is a love that can completely transforms us.

The Boundless Love of God

The boundlessness of God's love is seen in the fact that God loved us even before we were deserving of God's love. In fact, it was God's love that made us able both to receive and to give love in return. Love is of God; love is God. How easily we can think this thought or speak these words; yet how difficult, even impossible, it is to comprehend what they mean. Even the most sublime human love has boundaries beyond which it cannot pass, limits beyond which it will not go. It can wax and wane, ebb and flow; it can flare up and die out. Without diminishing our love in any way we can be distracted from it; without doubting its presence we can question its reliability. Not so the love of God. It has no boundaries, no limits. It is constant and trustworthy. God is love, and so all the attributes we assign to God can be assigned to love.

The Boundless Love Breaks Boundaries

Talk of love can either be so abstract as to be removed from human experience or so embellished as to be empty of meaning. We can only really recognize love in its many concrete manifestations. Love is patient, kind, and forbearing; it believes, it hopes, it endures. The love of God is also universal; having no boundaries, it includes all. It breaks down the barriers between Gentile and Jew, between slave and free, between the poor and the prosperous, between women and men, between the healthy and the ailing, between young and old. God's love is boundless, without perimeters; distinctions are not divisions.

God's Love Transforms Us

Embraced by such love, we are gradually transformed. We begin to recognize God's love in places where we never suspected it would be found. We discover that what we once judged unclean may merely be an unfamiliar openness to God's truth. We discover that our own insistence on legitimate religious practice may really be spiritual elitism. Our eyes are opened to ways we have tried to confine God's love to the conventional boundaries that we ourselves have set. As we are drawn into God's love, we can eagerly embrace the command-ments that help us to live righteous lives.

As the Church of the risen Lord, we are to give witness to God's love wher-ever we find it. We acknowledge that this boundless love extends to all nations and all peoples. We realize that the power of our Easter experience brings with it a certain universality of grace and gift. The Christian community bears wit-ness to this by its own loving inclusivity. God is love, and to the extent that we can love as universally as God does, we will know that we live in God and that God lives in us.

The Ascension of the Lord
Acts 1:1-11

The very first verse of this reading can be considered a kind of literary pro-logue, perhaps written to a patron named Theophilus ("Lover of God"). It states that this is the second of a two-volume work (cf. Luke 1:3). The author tells us that the first volume dealt with the life and ministry of Jesus until the time of his ascension. This reading is at the beginning of the second volume and can be divided into two distinct parts. The first part (vv. 1–5) mentions briefly the ministry of Jesus and some of his post-resurrection activity. The second part (vv. 6–11) recounts one particular event, Jesus' ascension into heaven.

The author of Acts points out the importance of the ascension. From a lit-erary point of view, it is the last episode of one volume and the first of the second, thus linking the two volumes. From a theological point of view, it brought a kind of closure to the earthly activity of Jesus while at the same time launching the apostles on their own ministry. The ascension was a turning point in the life of the Church. Although the followers of Jesus had not yet re-ceived the Holy Spirit, they had known the Spirit through the presence of, and their instruction by, Jesus.

A point is made that the apostles were instructed by Jesus both during his lifetime and after his resurrection. It seems that the focus of the latter instruc-tion was to convince them that he was really alive. If he had indeed been raised from the dead, then what he taught before as well as after his resurrection should be heeded. As the author of this passage tells the story, it sounds like everything was a form of preparation of the apostles for the task before them.

Two encounters with Jesus are then described. The first (vv. 4–5) reports the instructions he gave the apostles in preparation for Pentecost. The great upcoming event will be the time of fulfillment of God's promise. They will be baptized with the Holy Spirit. He reminds them of what he taught them in the past. This baptism will be significantly different than the baptism of John, with which they were already familiar (cf. Matt 3:11; Mark 1:8; Luke 3:16; John 1:33). They will come to know the Spirit as Jesus had during his lifetime.

The second encounter is the ascension itself (vv. 6–11). The question posed by the disciples does not suggest lack of faith. Quite the contrary. Since the restoration of the rule of Israel was considered a sign of the end-time, their question shows they believed that the end-time had come. They are correct, but they misunderstand the nature of the end-time and the character of its signs. These matters are within God's control. As for them, they will be empowered by the Spirit. Jesus last words assure them of their transformation and inform them of their mission. He will leave them but the Spirit will come, and then they will experience him through the presence of that Spirit.

The actual account of the ascension is brief. Jesus is lifted up and concealed by a cloud. Attention shifts to the men who now appear (angels?). They rebuke the disciples (once again the male bias is clear), and assure them that Jesus will return on the clouds just as he left. The Church is now in a liminal state. Jesus has left, but the Spirit has not yet come.

Psalm 47:2-3, 6-7, 8-9

A ritual of enthronement clearly unfolds in the verses of this psalm. It begins with a call to praise God with both a ringing cry and with clapping of hands. The cry *(rinnâ)* is a shout of jubilation connected with a divinely appointed sacrifice. Clapping hands is also a common ritual action. One of the derivatives of the Hebrew word for clap *(tāqaᶜ)* is "trumpet." Perhaps the liturgical clapping of hands is a substitute for the blowing of the trumpet. These two words clearly situate the psalm in a cultic setting.

The occasion for the liturgical celebration is the enthronement of God. Two very significant divine titles are used in this passage: Lord and Most High. Lord (YHWH) is the personal name of the God of Israel; Most High *(ᶜelyôn)* is an ancient Semitic title that first appears in the Abraham/ Melchizedek narrative (Gen 14:18-22). In that narrative it is the name of the god of Salem, a shortened form of Jerusalem. When the city became the center of Israelite worship, the title was applied to Israel's God. It now signifies the superiority of YHWH.

The enthronement itself appears to establish YHWH's sovereign reign. The Lord rules over all the earth (vv. 3, 8), over all nations (v. 9). In a world that believed each nation had its own divine patron, this was either a claim of the preeminence of YHWH over all other gods or an assertion of monotheistic faith. In either case, all people are called to acclaim the kingship of God (v. 8).

The notion of the kingship of the Lord has cosmic and mythological underpinnings. The ancients believed that before creation the forces of good were in mortal combat with the forces of evil. A great cosmic battle ensued from which good emerged triumphant. The divine leader of this victorious company assumed the role of creator and reordered the cosmos. When this was completed, a heavenly palace was constructed for this great god, who then ascended the throne, there to rule over the entire universe maintaining the order that had been established. In Babylon, the enthronement of their god was repeated each year during the New Year festival.

While there is no explicit mention of cosmic victory in this psalm, there are reasons why this understanding lies close to the surface of interpretation. The most obvious is the title "Most High." In the earlier tradition, this was the name given to "the creator of heaven and earth" (Gen 14:19). When this title was applied to the God of Israel, all of the attributes associated with that name were appropriated as well. Therefore, if and when the kingship of God was commemorated, even though the primary focus of attention was God's national or political significance, this cosmic dimension would be in the consciousness of the people. In their minds, their God was not only king over all the earth and the peoples that dwelt there but was also king over all the powers of heaven.

Ephesians 1:17-23 (A)

This reading, though addressed to believers, is a series of intercessions. While the gifts for which the petitioner prays flow from faith in "our Lord Jesus Christ," the relevance of the wisdom tradition is clear. The prayer is for a spirit of wisdom and revelation, those gifts that are necessary for insight and understanding. While this may sound a bit like Gnosticism, the belief that special God-given knowledge *(gnōsis)* set some people apart from the rest, it is clear that union with Christ is what sets Christians apart. The revelation referred to here is really necessary enlightenment to understand the mysteries that have already occurred. The verb forms used indicate that the action has been completed and the results of the action are effected in the present.

The prayer is for a threefold spiritual enlightenment (enlightenment of their inner eyes). The petitioner asks that the believers may know the hope of the calling they have received from God, the riches of the glory of God's inheritance in the holy ones, and the surpassing greatness of God's power to those who believe. These marvels have already taken place; it is for the believers to recognize them.

The power referred to throughout the reading belongs to God. It was God's power that raised Christ from the dead and seated Christ in the place of honor in heaven; it was God's power that made all things subject to Christ and exalted Christ as head of the Church. It is this same power that is now called upon.

The view of Christ contained in this passage is quite exalted. Having been raised from the dead, Christ now sits at God's right hand, high above all of the other heavenly creatures. Most likely principality, power, virtue, and dominion are references to celestial beings once thought to be divine but now considered merely classifications of angels. However they are understood, they were certainly considered superior to human creatures. Here, a human creature has been exalted above them. Mention of names given in this age or in the age to come ensures that nothing is beyond Christ's rule (cf. Ps 110:1). It is universal in scope and duration.

The body metaphor, characterizing the Church, is introduced at the end of the reading. Exalted by God, Christ is made the head of the Church, which is the body of Christ. As members of this exalted body, believers share in Christ's fullness, in Christ's exaltation. Seated in the heavens above all other creatures, Christ's glory fills the universe. This reading is a prayer that the believers be granted the wisdom and insight to grasp these mysteries and to live lives informed by them.

Ephesians 4:1-13 (B)

The unity within the Church is the overarching theme in this reading. It begins with a catalogue of social virtues that characterize the Christian and is followed by a list of seven elements that bind Christians in faith. The diversity within the Church is then described as having come from Christ and as contributing to the Church's proper functioning, not as a threat to its unity.

There is an ironic tone to the ethical exhortation in this letter. From prison Paul is admonishing the Christians to lead the kind of life that in fact has resulted in his own captivity. Still he insists that only such a life is worthy of the call they have received from God. The initiative is from God; their virtuous living is the appropriate response to God's choice of them. The Greek verb *(peripateō)* means to walk on a certain path, a theme that is prominent in the wisdom tradition (cf. Prov 4:11; Mark 1:3). It suggests that a righteous life is more than conformity to a collection of regulations. It is a commitment to set oneself on a particular path and to hold fast to that path even in the face of difficulty.

All the virtues cited are relational attitudes that foster community harmony. Humility and gentleness are in many ways similar. The first keeps one from seeking to gain prominence over others; the second is consideration of others. Patience, which literally means long-tempered as opposed to short-tempered, and forbearance, constitute a single thought. They enable one to deal courteously with people who are difficult, and to do so out of love. Such conduct engenders peace within the community and enables the members to preserve the unity that comes from the Spirit.

This unity is grounded in their belonging to the one body of Christ, their being filled with and fashioned by the one Spirit of God, and their being moved by the one hope of their call to salvation. Their life is trinitarian; they have all been called by God to salvation in Christ through the Spirit. This is the basis of their unity, which is expressed in their allegiance to one Lord, their commitment to one faith, and their practice of one baptism. The final unifying element is their belief in the one God of Jewish monotheism, who is both transcendent ("over all") and immanent ("in all") and actively at work in all of creation ("through all").

Finally, the diversity within the community (v. 11) need not threaten this unity, for it is attributed to Christ (v. 7). In order to explain this, the author reinterprets an earlier Israelite tradition (Ps 68:18). There, the victorious God ascends Mount Zion along with enemies, who are now captives, and there receives tokens of homage. Here, the victorious Christ ascends to God, taking with him all whom he has saved though his death. The author states that Christ had ascended because he had first descended into the lower regions of the earth, presumably the land of the dead. Having descended so low, he could now ascend through all seven levels of heaven to its very heights.

It is Christ's exaltation that frees him from all limitations and enables him to bring everything to fulfillment, bestowing grace on all without altering their diversity. The body with its many, diverse, and interdependent members is an apt image of this living Church. A church united in its members is an apt manifestation of Christ, who in his exaltation has matured to his full stature.

Mark 16:15-20

This account of the ascension of Jesus ties together many themes found elsewhere in the Gospel. It begins with a resurrection experience. Jesus appears to the remaining apostles. This will be the last time he shows himself to them. It marks a turning point in his relationship with his closest followers. From now on, the rest of the Church will turn to them for guidance and instruction.

Jesus commissions the apostles to preach the gospel to all. It is intended for all people, women and men, Gentile and Jew. The last directive Jesus gives to his followers before he is taken from their sight is for the evangelization of the entire world. The text says "every creature"; what follows indicates that the gospel is to be preached to all people.

Although we are not told here the content of the gospel, its salvific nature is clear. Those who believe will be saved; those who do not believe will be condemned. Faith in the message of the gospel is crowned by baptism into the death and resurrection of Jesus. This faith is not some form of Gnosticism, unique information that grants one membership in a privileged world of knowing. It is religious insight that leads one to identification with the risen Lord. With this identification come extraordinary powers: the ability to cast out demons, to speak in tongues, to handle dangers of all kinds. These miraculous powers are signs of the presence of the Lord. Just as Jesus performed wonders during his lifetime, in the power of his name his followers will do likewise.

After having commissioned them, Jesus was taken from their sight. The reading clearly states that he is taken up by another power, just as he was raised from the dead. This reflects the early Church's concern to show that it is the power of God that is active in Jesus, not some other kind of miraculous force. Jesus is then referred to as the Lord Jesus, a title that denotes the distinction he now enjoys as exalted sovereign. He takes his place at the right hand of God. Because of the bias in favor of the right hand, anything on that side was considered privileged. The place to one's immediate right was the place of honor at a banquet or any other formal gathering. As exalted Lord, Jesus takes his rightful place of privilege next to God.

The concluding verse succinctly summarizes the entire apostolic age: the apostles went into the entire world and preached the gospel; the Lord was with them, confirming their ministry through wondrous signs. Although the apostles are engaged in evangelizing, they do not do it alone. The Lord is with them, providing the inspiration and the grace they need to be successful. At the time of his ascension Jesus promised accompanying wondrous signs. During this early period of the Church the promise was fulfilled.

Themes of the Day

The feast of the Ascension is really a kind of liminal moment in the Easter season. It is a time between times; a moment when we have left one place in our journey but have not yet arrived at a second. While the narratives that describe the ascension fit well into the unfolding story of redemption, the feast itself celebrates one aspect of the resurrection itself, namely, the exaltation of Jesus. The readings help us through this paradox. They allow us to focus on this theological point while we commemorate a turning point in the life of the Church. We do this by considering the enthronement of Christ in the heavens and the new body of Christ on earth.

The Enthronement of Christ

Many of the Easter accounts have directed our attention to the appearances of Jesus, which were intended to strengthen the Christians' belief in his bodily resurrection. The emphasis was frequently on certain physical characteristics: he ate food; he invited Thomas to touch him. In many of these accounts Jesus seems to have been saying: "I am the same one who walked with you before. This is the body that you have always known." Today we stand awestruck watching Jesus ascend into the clouds of heaven, there to be enthroned at the right hand of God. Today is a day to be overwhelmed by the reality of the divinity of the one whom we have known in his humanity.

Amidst shouts of joy and exaltation, Christ is enthroned in heaven in both his divinity and his glorified humanity. Like the conquering creator-god, he has overcome his enemy (death) and now reigns over his new creation (the Church). For our part, we live between the time of his departure and the time of his return. Today we rejoice in one aspect of this mystery, his triumphant ascension; soon we will celebrate the second, the coming of his Spirit. Even though he has left us physically, we do not live without him as we wait. He is present with us in a new way, in a new body, in the Church.

The New Body of Christ

Christ, who ascended into heaven in his body, carries on what he began on earth through his new body, the community of believers. He teaches through its apostles and evangelists. He ministers through its prophets and pastors. In and through the Church, Jesus continues to heal and to comfort, to forgive and to include. We have not been left alone; we have his power, the same power with which he performed marvels when he walked the earth. We have not been left alone; we have each other. Together we make up the new body of Christ. Together we await the fullness of this body. It is this new body that stands between the times, secure in what we have, confident of what we will be given.

Seventh Sunday of Easter
Acts 1:15-17, 20a, 20c-26

This passage shows Peter assuming leadership in the community. With the betrayal of Judas the circle of twelve apostles had been broken, and it had to be restored. As there had been twelve tribes in Israel, so it was necessary that the new Israel be built on the foundation of twelve apostles. Despite the fact that women were also in the assembly (cf. Acts 1:14), only men are mentioned and addressed, exposing the gender bias of the writer, the patriarchal structure of the community, or both. One hundred twenty was the number required to set up a local Sanhedrin (m. Sanh. 1:6). The author was careful to show that the governing body of the early community was constituted according to Pharisaic standards.

Twice in his instruction to the community Peter points out what he believes is necessary. First it was necessary that the Scriptures be fulfilled (v. 16). Then it is necessary to choose someone who had been with the company of disciples during Jesus' ministry from the time of his baptism by John to his ascension (v. 21). The Scripture passage to be fulfilled is somewhat oblique. "Let their habitation be desolate; and let none dwell in their tents" (Ps 69:26). It is employed to describe the miserable fate of Judas.

The choice of this reference illustrates a very common early interpretation technique. Frequently when the community was faced with circumstances it could not adequately explain, it turned to the Scriptures for enlightenment. Passages that in their original context had little or no connection with the present crisis were chosen to provide encouragement or explanation. In this way the biblical tradition was kept alive and enhanced. In this case, the treachery of Judas probably seemed inexplicable to the followers of Jesus. However, though they must have considered it contemptible, if they were able to see that it somehow fulfilled an inspired Scripture they might be able to deal with it more easily.

The need to replace Judas is also linked to a biblical citation: "May another take his office" (Ps 109:3). The choice of his successor was a major responsibility of the community. Peter declared that to be eligible a person had to have been among the company of disciples from the time of Jesus' baptism to his ascension as well as a witness to his resurrection. It appears that the apostles were considered primarily witnesses. Two men were nominated. Although more information is given about Joseph, called Barsabbas (son of the Sabbath), also known as Justus, the lot fell to Matthias. The personal qualifications of the man appear to have been less important than his part in the fulfillment of the number twelve.

The process described was one of selection, not election. Casting lots might appear to some to be a process of chance. However, it was an ancient Israelite method of determining God's will (cf. Lev 16:7-10). The prayer that preceded the casting of lots illustrates the faith of the assembly. They knew that only God can read the sentiments of the human heart; only God knew which of the two men should be selected. They were confident that God would determine the outcome. Judas had forfeited his share in the ministry, and now it would go to Matthias.

Psalm 103:1-2, 11-12, 19-20

The responsorial psalm begins and ends with a summons to bless the LORD. Although the word "bless" is often used as a benediction, a prayer for God's presence or grace for the future, in this case it is a call to praise or to thank God for blessings already received.

The call to "bless the LORD" is normally addressed to someone other than the psalmist. This song of praise begins with a self-address (vv. 1–2). The Hebrew word that is translated "soul" *(nepesh)* comes from the word for "breath." It yields over twenty different meanings; chief among them are life-breath (or soul), life, living person. The reference here is probably to that center within the psalmist from which all life forces flow. This is not merely a spiritual or immaterial reality; it encompasses every aspect of the person. This understanding is corroborated by the phrase "all my being."

In the biblical world a person's name was an expression of that person's unique identity. In many ways names held more significance for people then than they do today. One could exercise power over another simply by somehow controlling the other's name. There were times during Israel's history when, in their attempt to show great reverence for God, the people paid homage to God's name rather than directly to God (cf. Deut 12:11, 21; 14:23f.; 16:2, 6, 11). Even when they did this, they were very careful to avoid using the divine name itself. Still today, we show the same respect when we merely use the consonants YHWH or the substitute LORD (small uppercase letters) rather than the name itself.

The reason for praising or thanking God, the benefits to which the psalmist refers, is God's disposition of lovingkindness and merciful forgiveness (vv. 11–12). Two images that denote immeasurable distance are used to describe the breadth of God's devotion. They are the distance between the heavens and the earth, and the area between east and west. Human eyes can only envision a fraction of the expanse of the heavens or the stretch that lies between the horizons. What is perceived is only infinitesimal; the reality is beyond comprehension.

These images describe the scope of God's love and forgiveness. The first characterizes God's covenant commitment, or lovingkindness *(hesed),* to those who "fear God," an expression that connotes the righteous. The second indicates the extent of God's willingness to forgive. Out of covenant love God puts our transgression so far from us that the distance cannot even be imagined. All of this is reason to praise and bless the LORD.

Finally, God's universal and cosmic dominion is sketched. As victorious conqueror (see Psalm 47, The Ascension of the Lord) God is enthroned in heaven, from there to rule over both heaven and earth. Therefore it is fitting that the inhabitants of heaven be summoned to bless the LORD. The Hebrew has "hosts" rather than angels. These would be the heavenly armies, who might previously have been thought to be semi-divine celestial bodies but who are now understood as part of God's heavenly court. As inferior beings, they do God's bidding.

1 John 4:11-16

Once again the author addresses the audience as "Beloved" *(agapētoí)*. What follows is an exhortation to replicate in the Christian community the love that God has for believers. The love that believers must have for one another is the same love that God has shown for them. Just as God's love was manifested in the unselfish and salvific sacrifice of Jesus, so Christians must love others with an unselfish and forgiving love. Such love cannot be seen itself. However, it does manifest itself as works of love. It is the fruit of such love, namely love for others, that can and must be made visible.

The reading develops the idea of the mutual abiding of God in believers and believers in God. This presence manifests itself in two ways. First, the uncompromising love of God is both cause and effect of this mutual indwelling. God cannot be seen, but the fruits of the love of God can be. The Spirit of God, the same Spirit that inspires unselfish love, is evidence of the abiding presence of God and the love of God. Second, believers' acknowledgment of Jesus as the Son of God who was sent by God to be the Savior of the world is also evidence of God's abiding presence. This knowledge should not be confused with some kind of Gnostic insight that by itself guarantees a form of mystical union. This passage clearly insists on active love of others as manifestation of the authentic love of God.

The reading ends with the remarkable statement of God's identity: God is love! From this flows the mutual indwelling that so marvelously characterizes Christian life.

John 17:11b-19

Jesus' concern for his disciples is plainly stated in this prayer, which contains several fundamental theological themes. They include the union between Jesus and God, which Jesus shares with his followers; the relationship between holiness and truth; and the antagonism of "the world." Prayed shortly before his death, the prayer takes on profound significance.

In the Gospels Jesus routinely refers to God as Father, a designation that addresses origin. Since his society was patriarchal (father-headed) in structure and androcentric (male-centered) in perspective, the image of father as applied to God would be more common than that of mother. Although the metaphor of father as applied to God is found in the prophets (Isa 64:16; Jer 3:4), it does not seem to have been commonly used in early Israel. When it does appear, it characterizes the compassionate relationship between God and the whole people, not merely an individual. Furthermore, there is no suggestion there that the people shared in the divine nature. God was a father to them because God created them and protected them.

Especially in the Gospel of John, Jesus appears to have used the term in a more intimate manner. Though he invited the disciples to call God "Father" (cf. Luke 11:2), he did not equate their relationship to God with his own. He always spoke of "my Father" (John 14:2; 15:1) or "the Father" (John 10:15; 16:3), but never "our Father." His relationship was unique; he was *of* God (John 1:1), sent *by* God (John 17:18), and about to return *to* God (vv. 11, 13). On the other hand, it was not by nature but through union with Jesus that the disciples would participate in this unique relationship with God. Through this union they would be kept within the protection of God's name (a dimension of God's very being).

This union is characterized by the word "holy" *(hágios)*. The Father is holy (v. 11); Jesus prays that his followers will be consecrated (same Greek root, v. 17); he consecrates himself that they may be consecrated in truth (v. 19). It is God's word that is truth, and it is in acceptance of God's word through Jesus that the disciples share in this holiness.

Having sketched the contours of union with God, Jesus acknowledges the resistance that God's word encounters from the world. Because of this word, Jesus himself was hated by the world; and now, because of the same word, his followers will suffer the same fate. While he was with them, he was able to protect them—except for one, presumably Judas. The reference here is not to the natural world but to that dimension of human society that is antagonistic toward God.

A very interesting dynamic is described in this passage. The world is antagonistic toward God's word, toward Jesus, and toward his followers. This is a world to which neither Jesus nor they belong, yet both he and they are sent into it. Jesus does not pray that they be taken from the world but that they be protected from the evils of it. We must not forget that this is the world that, despite its sinfulness, God loves (John 3:16). The disciples have been invited into the union of Jesus and his Father. Now that Jesus is about to return to the Father, they are sent into the world in his stead to continue the mission that he began.

Themes of the Day

We are still in the liminal time in between, a time of change and transition. The readings describe the apostles in that kind of time trying to cling to what they have known while realizing that things are no longer what they were before. For them the in-between time is very frightening. It demands that they rethink their priorities, reorder their lives, and reconstitute their community. If they are to further the teachings of Jesus and continue his ministry they will have to learn how to deal with this period of transition. They will have to negotiate two major issues: acceptance of the in-between time and fidelity to the religious tradition.

In-Between Times

We all go through major transitions during our lifetime. Some of these are quite common, like marriage and childbirth, illness and diminishment, or separation through death. Other changes are startlingly thrust upon us, like displacement because of war, sudden unemployment, or loss through natural disasters. Such times force us to look anew at circumstances in order to discover how we will rebuild our lives.

Religious transitions can also be very traumatic. When the theological grounding of our beliefs is questioned, or the practices that have nourished our spirits seem to be empty of meaning, we might feel like we are adrift in a sea of chaos with no compass to guide us and no port in sight. We might be tempted to abandon the entire religious enterprise and to allow superficial realities to dictate our actions. We might see only the ruptures in our lives and not the points of continuity. In-between times like these challenge us to re-examine the religious tradition itself.

Fidelity to the Religious Tradition

When we are in the midst of religious turmoil, it is important to retain some form of continuity. The apostles did just that. They realized that the bodily absence of the Lord did not mean the end of the community of believers. They had already endured the denial of Peter, the betrayal of Judas, and the scattering of a large number of followers. Rather than give up, they reconstituted themselves as the Twelve after the pattern of their immediate past as well as their tribal past.

They furnished us with a model for our own reinterpretation of tradition. Not willing to relinquish their religious reality, they interpreted it in new yet faithful ways. They clung to the fundamental message of Jesus, remembering that he had prayed for them. If on the threshold of his passion he had been their advocate before God, how much more would this be the case now that he was exalted! Jesus did not abandoned them, he entrusted them to one another.

Rather than surrender to despair, the early Christians opened themselves to the great love out of which they had been fashioned and into which they were now formed. This love of God and of others enabled them and will enable us to be confident in the throes of anxiety and to be faithful in the midst of confusion. We too will be able to cling to the traditions that continue to bind us to God and to one another.

Pentecost Sunday

Acts 2:1-11

The Jewish feast of Pentecost was one of the three major pilgrim festivals of Israel. Originally an agricultural feast marking the end of the grain harvest, it was also called the feast of Weeks because it was celebrated seven weeks or fifty days after the feast of the Unleavened Bread. As with the other two pilgrim festivals it eventually took on historical importance, commemorating the giving of the law at Sinai. The fact that it was a pilgrim feast explains why devout Jews from every nation were in Jerusalem at this time. Although only devout men are mentioned (v. 5), we know that women and children also made the pilgrimage. This is an example of the author's gender bias.

The reading from Acts does not tell us precisely who was in the room when the Spirit descended. Was it the one hundred twenty who had gathered earlier (cf. Acts 1:15)? Was it only the twelve apostles (cf. 2:14)? Contrary to some translations, the Greek does not use gender-specific language, so we cannot say that it was a gathering made up exclusively of men. (The later reference to the Joel passage would suggest that it was not; cf. 2:17-18.)

The external manifestations that accompanied the outpouring of the Spirit were all phenomena associated with a theophany, an experience of God. For example, thunder accompanied God's revelation at Sinai (cf. Exod 19:16); God spoke to Job from the whirlwind (Job 38:1) and to Moses from the burning bush (Exod 3:2). The text reports that these phenomena were audible and visible while the actual outpouring of the Spirit was not. However, as those in the room were filled with the Spirit, they began to speak in other languages, a feat that could only have some supernatural origin.

The same Greek word *(glōssa)* is used for the tongues of fire that appeared above each one and for the foreign tongues that were subsequently spoken. There is a question whether the reference here is to communicative speech (foreign tongues) or ecstatic speech called "glossolalia." Since the people who came to see what had happened did understand the bold proclamations of these Spirit-filled preachers, the meaning here seems to be communicative rather than ecstatic speech (vv. 6–11).

The crowd that gathered because of the loud noise was confused, astonished, and amazed. They knew that those speaking were Galileans, presumably because of some feature of their speech. Yet the hearers were able to understand the message in their own dialect. Because the Galileans spoke in tongues and those in the crowd heard in their own speech, some commentators have suggested that there was a miracle in hearing as well as in speaking.

The exact nature of this marvel is less significant than is its meaning. It was clearly a manifestation of the universal presence and power of the Spirit. Some commentators believe that it demonstrated the reversal of the fragmentation of peoples that occurred when languages were confused after the people attempted to construct the tower of Babel (cf. Gen 11:1-9). The outpouring of the Spirit and the preaching of the gospel to all nations are seen by some as the reuniting of the human race and the gathering of all into the reign of God.

Psalm 104:1, 24, 29-30, 31, 34

This hymn is remarkable in its depiction of God as the creator and sustainer of all life. It begins, as do other hymns of its kind, with a summons to praise. The call to "bless the LORD" is normally addressed to someone other than the psalmist. Twice a self-address is used (vv. 1, 35). This forms a kind of *inclusio* that divides the responsorial psalm into two parts. The first treats God as the wondrous creator; the second describes God's providential care.

The Hebrew word that is translated "soul" *(nepesh)* comes from the word for breath. It yields over twenty different meanings; chief among them are life-breath (or soul), life, living person. The reference here is probably to that center within the psalmist from which flow all life forces. This is not merely a spiritual or immaterial reality; it encompasses every aspect of the person. Every aspect of the psalmist's being is called upon to give praise to God.

God is described as robed in majesty and glory, wrapped around with radiant light. This is the way the commanding gods of the ancient Near East were depicted. The psalmist does not claim that God is visible but that God's garments are discernible. In other words, the splendor the psalmist beholds is an indication of God's presence. God is perceived through the glories of creation.

The natural world is not only marvelous in its appearance, it is diverse in its manifestations as well. The variety and complexity of its forms are astounding. This splendor is attributed to the wisdom of the Creator. In the biblical tradition there is an intrinsic link between creation and wisdom (cf. Prov 8:22-31; Wis 9:9). Wisdom was understood as insight into, harmony with, or power over the orders of reality. These orders were established by God at the time of creation, and they are sustained by the same creative power.

In the second part of the psalm God is extolled as the one who cares for all living things. All creatures look to God for sustenance. From a human point of view creation is not a static act, completed once for all in the distant past. We experience creation as an ongoing event. The act of creation and power of the Creator are perceived in the constant renewal of life that unfolds before our eyes. In a very real sense creation is more than a primordial event, it is a personal experience.

The psalm then shows that the life forces of the natural world do not operate in a manner independent of the divine will. God sustains life by providing food, but God can also bring on death by taking back the breath of life. When this happens, the creature returns to the dust from which it was initially taken (cf. Gen 2:7; Job 12:10). God is both the original Creator and the one who continues to control the forces of nature.

Finally, God not only creates but re-creates. The ongoing forces of nature are re-creative. Life is sustained and perpetuated. The word for spirit *(rûah)* is the same as that found in the story of creation, where a mighty wind swept over the waters (Gen 1:2). That was the first creation. The psalm claims that the spirit of the LORD can bring about a new creation. This is reason enough to bless the LORD.

1 Corinthians 12:3b-7, 12-13 (A)

This reading consists of three different yet related themes: an acclamation of the lordship of Jesus, a defense of diversity within the community, and the body metaphor that characterizes that diversity.

The acclamation "Jesus is Lord" is rich in both Jewish and early Christian meaning. Lord *(kýrios)* was the official title of the Roman emperor. To proclaim Jesus as Lord was to set up a rivalry between the followers of Jesus and the ruling political authority. Since most if not all of the emperors claimed to be somehow divine, this rivalry was both political and religious. Furthermore, because the Roman government was involved in the death of Jesus, such a challenging claim would place those who made it at great risk for their lives.

The word "Lord" is also used in the Septuagint, the Greek version of the First Testament, as a substitute for God's personal name. To use this title for Jesus is to ascribe to him the attributes of God. This use may not have set up a political rivalry between Jesus and God, as was the case with the Roman emperor, but it certainly did make serious religious claims. It is important to note that the acclamation uses the name of the man Jesus, not his religious title, Christ. It is this man who is placed on the same level as the God of ancient Israel. No one would make such a claim were it not for the promptings of the Holy Spirit. This is a cry of faith, a testimony to the divine character of this man from Galilee.

Paul next launches into a discourse on the varieties of functions within the Christian community. In sketching this diversity he uses two triads: gifts, ministries, and works; Spirit, Lord, and God. Although the latter triad suggests a trinitarian perspective that associates one set of functions with each of the divine persons, it is clear from the text that all of the activities are manifestations of the Spirit (v. 7).

Gifts *(chárisma)* refers to those operations of the Spirit, notably speaking in tongues and prophesying, that were usually operative during worship. Ministry *(diakonía)* was service within the community. It included duties that were often considered menial, like serving at table or collecting money. Paul may have included this reference in order to show that within the community of believers, no task is ignoble. Works *(enérgēma)* were feats of great energy or divine power. Since all of these gifts or ministries or works were manifestations of the Spirit, no one was to be considered superior to another. Further, they were not given for the self-aggrandizement of the one who received them. All were given for the benefit of the entire community.

The diversity found within the community is compared to the complexity of the human body. Each part has its own unique function, but all parts work for the good of the whole. This metaphor characterizes several aspects of the community. First, it portrays unity in diversity, a unity that is far from uniformity. Second, it underscores the lack of competition among members, one activity elevating itself above the others. Lowly service is no less important than charismatic gifts. Third, it points up the interdependence that exists within the community.

In this community there are no more stratifications, whether religious (Jew or Greek) or social (slave or free).

Galatians 5:16-25 (B)

Paul instructs the Galatians out of the context of the wisdom tradition. Though translated "live," the verb *(peripateō)* really means "walk," suggesting a path or a way (cf. Prov 4:11; Mark 1:3). In this tradition there are only two ways, the right one and the wrong one. There is no middle ground; one must make a fundamental choice. The content of Paul's exhortation fits perfectly into this manner of thinking. The Christians must decide between following the desires of the flesh and following those of the spirit.

"Flesh" *(sárx),* which means "body," includes everything that pertains to physical existence or life in this world. It soon came to refer to the weakness of physical existence. The law seeks to control the behavior that results from this weakness. When the law is unsuccessful in its attempt to control, the works of the flesh produce sexual depravity (immorality, impurity, lust), religious infidelity (idolatry, sorcery), social discord (hatreds, rivalry, jealousy, fury, selfishness, dissensions, factions, envy), and disorderly behavior (drunkenness, orgies). Those who follow this way forfeit their right to inherit the kingdom of God.

"Spirit" *(pneúma)* means wind, breath, spirit, and thus it connotes the principle of life. It soon came to refer to the noble aspects of human life. It is used to speak of the spirit of living things (specifically humans) as well as the Spirit of God. When Paul contrasts the spirit and the flesh, he seems to be referring to the spiritual dimension of the individual, which is an intrinsic aspect of the person (vv. 16–17). When he contrasts the Spirit and the law, he seems to be speaking of the Spirit of God (v. 18).

However we understand the reference to spirit, Paul's exhortation is the same, for he believes that the natural spiritual dimension of the person is energized by the Spirit of God. For him, a spiritual life is a life lived in the Spirit of God, and the fruits of such a life are the fruits of the Spirit (vv. 2–23). One who follows this way is guided by the Spirit rather than by the directives of the law (vv. 18, 23). Paul is not here criticizing the law. Rather, he is identifying its function. It is a reliable guide for those who have no other guide. Before the coming of Jesus it performed its function well, but now those who are guided by the Spirit have no need of the law's directions (v. 18).

Paul not only contrasts the way of the flesh and the way of the spirit, he also describes the conflict that exists between them. They appear to be opposing inclinations within human beings, not forces external to them. Because they are within us we constantly experience the conflict of their opposition, and we frequently suffer the consequences of this conflict. We may not act in ways that we intend (v. 17; cf. Rom 7:15-20). Paul recognizes that choosing the way of the spirit over the way of the flesh is a lifelong process.

The reading ends with a play on meanings. Just as Jesus' flesh (physical body) was crucified, so those who belong to Christ crucify their flesh (human weaknesses). Doing this, they have chosen the way of the spirit over the way of the flesh. Paul exhorts the Galatians to follow this Spirit.

John 20:19-23 (A)

This appearance account treats the resurrection and the bestowal of the Spirit upon the disciples of Jesus as having occurred on the same day, for the event described took place "on the evening of that first day of the week" (v. 19). The account contains several salient details. First, the incident takes place on the first day of the week. Second, it occurs despite the doors being closed. Third, Jesus appears in the midst of the disciples. Fourth, he addresses those present with a greeting of peace. Fifth, he calls their attention to his wounds. Sixth, he confers the Spirit on them and entrusts them with the power of binding or loosing. Each of these details is laden with theological meaning.

This first day of the week is the actual day of the resurrection (v. 19). It is clear that the entire reckoning of time has been altered by the event that occurred early in the morning. Where previously religious meaning was given to the Sabbath, the conclusion of the week, now the focus is on the beginning, on the future. The locked doors secured the disciples from those who had had some part in the arrest, trial, and crucifixion of Jesus. His followers had reason to fear that these people might be hostile toward them as well. The closed doors also underscore the mysterious character of Jesus' risen body. It is not impeded by material obstacles; it can move as it wishes and where it will.

The wish of peace, which was the common Jewish greeting of the day, was also a prayer for the eschatological blessings of health, prosperity, and all good things. When Jesus wishes peace for his disciples, he is proclaiming the arrival of this time of fulfillment. By calling attention to the wounds in his hands and side, Jesus shows the disciples that he is not a figment of their imaginations or some kind of ghost from the netherworld. He is the same man who was crucified, but now he is risen. Apparently the disciples recognized the Lord, because they rejoiced at the sight of him.

The bestowal of the Holy Spirit is introduced by a second salutation of peace. The image of breathing life into another is reminiscent of the creation of Adam (cf. Gen 2:7) and the restoration of Israel after the Exile (cf. Ezek 37:9). By breathing in this way, the risen Lord portrays himself as one who can create or re-create. One of the Hebrew words for breath *(rûah)* is also translated "spirit," and so there is a long tradition of linking spirit and breath. The spirit of God is also the breath of God.

The disciples are commissioned to go forth, to declare salvation and judgment. The language describes the activity of a judge, who decides whether the defendant is bound to the consequences of the charges or loosed from them. Most likely the authority that is here given to the disciples is much broader than this. The phrase "bind and loose" (or forgive) is similar to "flesh and blood" or "left and right." Each expression names the opposite poles, but together they are meant to include everything that is between them as well. These are ways of describing totality: "flesh and blood" refers to the whole body; "left and right" includes the entire horizon; "bind and loose" suggests complete authority. With the bestowal of the Spirit the disciples are authorized to continue the mission of Jesus.

John 15:26-27; 16:12-15 (B)

It is only in the Fourth Gospel that the Holy Spirit is called the Advocate (Paraclete). Although the title comes from the Greek word for comfort *(paráklēsis)*, the meaning here is "helper" or "advocate." It is not clear who is being helped, Jesus or the disciples. Actually it does not make much difference, since one who helps Jesus continue the work he began is certainly helping those who are the recipients of Jesus' work. Two very important features of the Advocate are stressed in this reading: the relationships between Jesus, the Spirit, and the Father; and the role played by the Advocate in the search for truth.

The beginnings, and only the beginnings, of a trinitarian understanding of God are discernible in this reading. Twice it states that the Advocate will proceed from the Father (v. 26). This explicitly identifies the Father as the divine fountainhead within the Trinity. The relationship between the Advocate and

Jesus is quite different. Although the Father is the source from whom the Advocate proceeds, it is Jesus who does the sending. Upon being sent, the Advocate will then, along with the disciples, bear witness to Jesus. Furthermore, the Advocate, also called the Spirit of Truth, will glorify Jesus and will illuminate for the disciples what has been revealed to them through him (16:13-14).

Finally, Jesus' relationship with the Father is also unique. First, in order to send the Spirit from the Father, Jesus must be intimately associated with and present with the Father. Furthermore, Jesus claims that what belongs to the Father is also his. This suggests that what the Spirit of Truth reveals belongs to the Father and to Jesus. The basic outlines of trinitarian theology have been drawn: the Father is the divine source; the Son shares in what the Father has; and the Spirit reveals the mysteries of the Father and the Son.

The second important theme of the reading is the role played by the Advocate in the search for truth. The role is threefold: to bear witness, to glorify, and to instruct. To what do the Advocate and the disciples bear witness? Most likely to the claims that Jesus made about himself and about the things to come. The disciples can be considered reliable witnesses because they were with Jesus from the beginning of his ministry. The Advocate comes from God and for this reason can also be considered reliable. The emphasis on trustworthy witnesses indicates how important the notion of solidly established truth is in this reading.

It seems that the disciples have failed to comprehend much of what Jesus has revealed to them. In addition to this, there is much more that he would reveal, but they are not yet ready for it. It will be the role of the Spirit of Truth to glorify Jesus and to lead the disciples to ever deeper understanding of and further insight into Jesus' revelation. The Spirit will not proclaim new or obscure truths but rather the meaning of the life and teaching of Jesus. When Jesus leaves the disciples and returns to the Father, he will send the Spirit of Truth to continue what he has begun. He will depart, but the Spirit will remain with them.

Themes of the Day

The community has been living in the in-between time since the ascension of the Lord. Today it celebrates the dramatic inbreaking of the time of fulfillment. The feast celebrates the fullness of the Spirit and the great gathering together of nations. The feast also brings the Easter season to its conclusion. Like the finale of a majestic symphony, the readings for today recapitulate many of the themes that appeared throughout the Easter season: christology, trinitarian theology, reign of God, repentance, salvation, mission, universality. All are brought together as we are brought together into the body of Christ.

In the Fullness of the Spirit

At last the plan of salvation has been brought to its conclusion. The risen Lord has been exalted to his rightful place next to God, and he has sent his Spirit to fill the earth with God's power. The world is charged with divine energy; it needs but a spark to ignite it with life and with excitement. This vitality explodes into the extraordinary: tongues are loosed and speech overflows its linguistic constraints; charismatic gifts flood the valleys of human habitation; barred doors are burst open and frightened hearts are calmed. The Spirit of the Lord fills the whole world.

The Great Gathering

Once again we gather together for one reason, only to discover that God has gathered us for another. Strangers assemble to fulfill personal obligations, and they experience a phenomenon that bonds them together for life. Individual religious devotion is swept up into communal divine revelation. Through the Spirit of God, we are reconciled to each other and then together we spend ourselves for the common good. Through the Spirit of God the world is renewed, the community is revitalized, and we come to know the mysterious yet all-pervasive peace of Christ.

If this has all really happened, why does our world look the same? Why is there so much religious and ethnic rivalry? Why do we continue to make distinctions between Jew and Gentile, slave and free, woman and man, distinctions that favor one at the expense of the other? Why is there so little peace, or comfort, or solace? Why do we refuse to forgive or to be reconciled? Is Pentecost merely a feast that we celebrate in red vestments? Has the face of the earth really been renewed?

The answer is yes! Resoundingly, yes! The Spirit has been poured forth and works wonders wherever human hearts are open to its promptings. The earth is renewed each time rivalries are resolved, distinctions are recognized as merely expressions of diversity, peace is restored, comfort and solace are offered, and forgiveness is granted. We are immersed in the vigor of the Spirit of God; all we have to do is open ourselves to it and the reign of God will be born in our midst.

Ordinary Time (Part One)

First Sunday (Baptism of the Lord)			
Second Sunday 1 Samuel 3:3b-10, 19 Speak, your servant is listening	Psalm 40:2, 4, 7-10 Here I am, LORD	1 Corinthians 6:13c-15a, 17-20 Glorify God in your body	John 1:35-42 They stayed with him
Third Sunday Jonah 3:1-5, 10 Turn from your evil ways	Psalm 25:4-9 Teach me your ways	1 Corinthians 7:29-31 The world is passing away	Mark 1:14-20 Repent and believe
Fourth Sunday Deuteronomy 18:15-20 A prophet like me	Psalm 95:1-2, 6-9 Harden not your heart	1 Corinthians 7:32-35 Be free of anxieties	Mark 1:21-28 He taught with authority
Fifth Sunday Job 7:1-4, 6-7 Restless upon dawn	Psalm 147:1-6 Praise the LORD	1 Corinthians 9:16-19, 22-23 I must preach the gospel	Mark 1:29-39 Jesus cured many
Sixth Sunday Leviticus 13:1-2, 44-46 Lepers outside the camp	Psalm 32:1-2, 5, 11 I turn to you, LORD	1 Corinthians 10:31–11:1 Be imitators of me	Mark 1:40-45 He was made clean

Seventh Sunday Isaiah 43:18-19, 21-22, 24b-25 I wipe out your offenses	Psalm 41:2-5, 13-14 Heal my soul	2 Corinthians 1:18-22 Jesus is God's yes	Mark 2:1-12 The Son of Man has authority
Eighth Sunday Hosea 2:16b, 17b, 21-22 I espouse you forever	Psalm 103:1-4, 8, 10, 12-13 The LORD is kind and merciful	2 Corinthians 3:1b-6 You are a letter of Christ	Mark 2:18-22 The bridegroom is with them
Ninth Sunday Deuteronomy 5:12-15 You were once slaves	Psalm 81:3-8, 10-11 Sing with joy	2 Corinthians 4:6-11 Jesus' life in your body	Mark 2:23-28 Lord of the Sabbath
Tenth Sunday Genesis 3:9-15 Enmity between offspring	Psalm 130:1-8 With the LORD is mercy	2 Corinthians 4:13–5:1 We believe and speak	Mark 3:20-35 The end of Satan

Ordinary Time (Part One)

Initial Reading of the Ordinary Lectionary (Part One)

Introduction

This period of Ordinary Time is really an interlude between seasons. Christmas is behind us, and in a few weeks we will be entering the season of Lent. Although time and again we might catch a glimpse of the future, a hint of what lies ahead for Jesus and for those who are his disciples, during this interim period our readings invite us to reflect on various aspects of our discipleship.

First Testament Readings

Although the first readings were probably chosen because in some way they reflect or support the theology found in the Gospel selection for the day, read in a column they offer a theological pattern with its own unique meaning. Read consecutively, they paint an interesting picture. The first three readings deal with the prophetic call. Two of them depict ways of responding to it: open acceptance, or rejection of the call followed by resentment. In the third reading the people are promised a prophet who will proclaim to them the word of God.

Four readings turn our attention to life itself. We first consider its harshness and then the way that the merciful love of God can and does transform it. The last two readings leave us hanging. One is an exhortation to observe the Sabbath; the other recounts the announcement of the ongoing enmity between humankind and the forces of evil. In its own way, this set of readings outlines the history of salvation. Despite our vulnerability and our failures, the goodness of God follows us.

Psalms

The psalm responses reflect various devotional attitudes. There is praise for the marvels that God has accomplished; there are expressions of gratitude for God's goodness, and repentance for our failure to remain faithful. There is instruction for righteous living, and there is prophetic proclamation. Just as the set of first readings ends on a note of apprehension, so this set of responses concludes with a penitential psalm.

Epistles

The continuous readings from the first and second letters to the Corinthians provide us with instruction for daily living. We are admonished to revere our bodies as temples of God, to live uprightly and without anxiety because our time here is short. Paul declares his commitment to the gospel and then offers himself in this as an example for others to follow. We are encouraged to be secure in the constancy of Jesus and to acknowledge that any success we might enjoy comes from the goodness of God, for we are merely earthen vessels through whom the glory of God shines. This set of readings ends on a note of hope. We are told that if we live in the spirit of faith we will ultimately dwell with God in the heavens.

Gospels

After the Johannine account of the call to discipleship, the Gospels simply follow the Markan version of the good news. Jesus announces the coming of the reign of God and then demonstrates its power by driving an unclean spirit out of a troubled man. He continues this form of ministry throughout all of Galilee. He challenges the purity code by curing a leprous man so that he can be brought back into the embrace of the community, and he assumes divine authority by forgiving sin. When his disciples are criticized for not fasting or for plucking grain on the Sabbath, he defends them with his own authority. He concludes by warning those who misconstrue the origin of his power that theirs is a very serious sin.

Mosaic of Readings

The major theological focus of this set of readings is discipleship. The call to discipleship accompanies baptismal commitment and is extended to all. Ordinary people in ordinary walks of life are invited to proclaim the gospel through their very lives. When they accept this remarkable call, they are becoming radically transformed and are given the power to remain faithful regardless of the difficulties they must face. In fact, their very suffering becomes an occasion for evangelizing. It is very clear that discipleship begins and ends in Christ and in the power of God, which is able to transform ordinary people into faithful followers.

Readings

First Sunday in Ordinary Time
The Baptism of the Lord

Second Sunday in Ordinary Time
1 Samuel 3:3b-10, 19

This vivid and dynamic account is both a call narrative and a theophany (a manifestation of God). Samuel slept in the chamber of the temple where the ark of God was kept. It is quite unusual that someone other than the high priest would have access to this most sacred place. This should not be seen as a kind of sacristy responsibility given to the youngest of the team. The author may be indicating that Samuel is a person who is destined for great things. There are at least two reasons why he might spend the night in the temple. He may have been there in order to tend the lamp that was kept burning before the ark. Or this could have been a cultic incubation meant to prepare an individual to receive some communication from God. The first reason is probably the case here, since the text itself mentions the lamp and since he is genuinely surprised at hearing the voice.

Most likely the events described took place at the approach of morning, for the lamp was almost empty of oil. There is disarming innocence in Samuel's mistaking the voice of God for that of Eli. The text explains why such a misunderstanding could have occurred: Samuel had not yet had any direct communication with the LORD. It is curious that Eli misunderstood, not once but twice. Since the ark was a sign of God's presence in the midst of the people, he should have expected an occasional communication from God. It is further curious that God called the inexperienced Samuel rather than the seasoned priest Eli. It may mean that something new was happening, that a new period in the history of the people was opening, that a new day was on the horizon.

When he finally realized that it was God who was calling Samuel, Eli directed him to ask God to speak and to assure God that he was listening with open ears and an attentive heart. Samuel did as he was directed. The Hebrew says that the LORD came, and stood, and called Samuel a fourth time. This last experience was more than a call. It included another kind of physical presence.

There is a clear difference between Samuel's relationship with God before this experience and his relationship after it. Though pious, the young Samuel did not know God well; he had received no revelation (v. 7). This encounter was transformative; a bond had been forged between himself and God. His responsiveness opened him further, enabling him to receive the word of God and, presumably, to speak it to others. Samuel's influence is attributed to God's direction in his life. It was God who made Samuel's words effective; they did not fall to the ground (translated from the Hebrew). The image comes from agriculture. Noble words, like fertile seeds, bring forth good fruit in abundance. By contrast, idle words fall to the ground and produce nothing worthwhile. Samuel heard God's word, and then he spoke it.

Psalm 40:2, 4, 7-8, 8-9, 10

The psalm response contains three principal themes: thanksgiving for release from some difficulty; dedication to God who is the savior; and personal witness in the midst of the community. It begins with a report of the psalmist's past deliverance by God (v. 2). Though in distress, the psalmist waited in expectant hope and with patient trust. Hearing the cry for help, God first stooped down and drew the suffering believer out of the troubling situation, and then put a new song into the psalmist's mouth. The former lament or cry for help had been heard and was now replaced by a grateful song of praise (v. 4).

The psalmist claims that in this situation God does not want the customary sacrificial rituals that form the basis of the cultic tradition. (The rituals include a sacrifice or communal meal that was part of the festival of thanksgiving; a gift offering presented as an act of homage to God; a holocaust or burnt offering of an entire animal; and a sin offering, which was a sacrifice of expiation.)

This apparent dismissal of the ritual should not be seen as a repudiation of the sacrificial system. Instead, it indicates that a deeper commitment is required here. Public worship, as important as it is, can become mere external ceremony. What God wants is an ear that is open to obedience (v. 7) and a willingness to delight in God's law (v. 9), an interior commitment that will result in a life of righteousness and faithful worship.

The responsorial verses end with the psalmist standing before the worshiping assembly *(qahal)* and publicly proclaiming the wondrous acts of salvation that God has accomplished. It is through this kind of testimony rather than in the conventional cultic manner that the psalmist shows gratitude for having been delivered from distress. Such witnessing not only proclaims the goodness of God, but it can also inspire others within the community to turn to God with the same kind of expectant hope and patient trust so that they too may enjoy deliverance by God. It can encourage them to open their ears in obedience and to delight in God's law.

The subject of the psalmist's public proclamation is the justice or righteousness of God. This characteristic is fundamental to God's very nature. It means that because of God all things are in order, in right relationship. It signifies God's faithfulness to all promises made to women and men. God's rewards and punishment flow from this sense of right order and fidelity. The psalmist's proclamation contends that commitment to God and reliance on God's adherence to covenantal promises will assure blessing.

Having been delivered, the psalmist is now at the disposal of God; has now an ear open to obedience and a tongue loosed for proclamation; is now a herald of the righteousness of God.

1 Corinthians 6:13c-15a, 17-20

Paul furnishes the Corinthian community with instruction on the sanctity of the human body *(sṓma)*. He is talking about the physical, corporeal dimension of the human being, not some kind of ethereal or spiritualized body. Paul does indeed highly regard both the human spirit *(pneúma)* and the human soul *(psyché)*, but he does not agree with the view of those who stress the spirit to the denigration of the body. According to him, since it is through one's body that union with Christ is possible, this same body is to be revered.

He contrasts the sanctity of the human body with sexual immorality *(porneía)*. Since the word comes from the verb "to sell" *(pérnēmi)* it literally means "sex for sale." The term covers a wide range of sexual improprieties such as prostitution, fornication, adultery, licentiousness, even incest, sodomy, and unlawful marriage. Such behavior has no place in the kingdom of God, not only because it is a violation of the integrity of the perpetrator (v. 18) and of another human being but because it defiles the intimate bond that exists between Christ and every Christian. The body is for the Lord and the Lord is for the body. This is a bold statement in a world where sexual promiscuity was widely tolerated and rampant. However, God highly values the human body, as evident in the bodily resurrection, first of Christ and then of others.

It is through our bodies that we are members of Christ, and so joined, we become one spirit with Christ. The image used here is one of intimate union, oneness of body and spirit. It is not a sexual image; it does not suggest that our bodies are joined to the body of Christ. It is a metaphor that signifies incorporation; our bodies are members of Christ. Because of this incorporation, any form of sexual impropriety is unthinkable.

Paul goes on to assert that our bodies are temples of the Spirit, the same Spirit with whom we are one through our union with Christ. Temples were not only designated sites for sacrifice and prayer. They were also the sacred places on earth where the deity dwelt. If our bodies are temples, that means that God dwells within us. Paul's teaching about the indwelling of the Spirit of God is very clear here. He believes that because the Spirit claims our bodies as its abode, we no longer have absolute rights over them. In fact, they have been purchased for God at the price of Christ's blood, and God exerts authority in their regard. As temples, our bodies should be kept sacred, free from whatever might defile or debase them.

Paul's final admonition is brief but quite revealing. He calls upon the Corinthians to glorify God in their bodies. The fundamental point of the reading is moral sexual behavior, hence he is probably urging them to live lives of sexual uprightness. The statement also presumes that God can be glorified in and through our bodies. They are not vile, they are remarkable. They are not worthless, they are precious. They are the means by which we touch the mysteries of God.

John 1:35-42

The account of the first disciples reports the witness of John the Baptist rather than any direct call by Jesus. It is an example of how John was ready to decrease so that Jesus could increase (cf. John 3:30). Not jealous of his own importance as a preacher and religious leader, John directs two of his disciples to Jesus. He identifies Jesus as the Lamb of God (cf. 1:29), a title that reveals something of John's own religious insight. The designation may be based on an interpretation of the description of the suffering servant found in the prophet Isaiah (cf. Isa 53:7). There the servant, though innocent of transgression, gives his life as an offering for the sins of others. It is uncertain whether or not the Baptist understood Jesus in this way, but the author of the Gospel certainly did.

Two other titles are used to describe Jesus: Rabbi (v. 38) and Messiah (v. 41). The meanings of both words are given, suggesting that the readers might not be familiar with Hebrew. "Rabbi" is the usual way of addressing a religious teacher. As the story unfolds, we see that this is precisely how the two disciples relate to Jesus. Since students usually gathered somewhere for instruction from the teacher, the disciples ask where this gathering would take place so that they too might join the group. Jesus invites them to follow him, which they do. This can be understood on two levels: they went behind him to the place where he was staying, or they listened to his words and became his followers.

The second title, Messiah, is really an act of faith on the part of Andrew. Whatever Jesus told him convinced him that Jesus was the long awaited one.

At this time in Israel's history there were several different messianic under-standings. Since royalty, priests, and prophets were all anointed in some way, a messianic expectation emerged from each tradition. The royal tradition ex-pected the Messiah to reestablish the Davidic monarchy. The priestly tradition looked for a cultic leader, while the prophetic tradition awaited a revolution-ary reformer. Earlier reference to the suffering servant suggests that this latter designation is the kind of Messiah implied here.

The final point to be considered is the manner in which individuals came to be disciples of Jesus. Although God is always the one who initiates a rela-tionship, it does not always occur through a direct communication with God. There are times when intermediaries play important roles. This is one such case. Initially it is John the Baptist who points to Jesus. When Jesus does invite John's disciples to follow him, it is after they have first approached him. The same is true in the episode with Peter. Andrew is the one who recognizes something in Jesus, and Jesus interacts with Peter only after Andrew has brought his brother to him. In both instances the faith of an associate begins one's own journey to discipleship.

Themes of the Day

Ordinary Time is ushered in with a meditation on the call to discipleship. This call is not reserved for a select few. It accompanies our baptismal commitment and is issued to all Christians. The readings outline the various stages of this call and provide a sketch of some of the characteristics of each stage. We should not be surprised to see that disciples are very ordinary people. Yet in their ordinariness they frequently act in extraordinary ways. The basic stages of the call to discipleship are the invitation, the discerning process, and the re-sulting transformation.

Invitation

Discipleship is not something we take upon ourselves. It is an invitation from God. It might come to us in the form of an inner call, a kind of a dream or in-spiration. Or our interest might be captured by a person or an event that first attracts us and then beckon us to investigate further. It can come in the inno-cence and naivete of childhood, in the vigor of young adulthood, or in the wisdom of years. It comes when God calls. We could be called during some re-ligious event, while we are in the embrace of our family, or when we are out with our friends. The ordinariness of the occasion can sometimes deceive us into misjudging the significance of the event. But if we are attentive to the promptings of our heart we will be given the insight needed to recognize what is really happening; we are being called by God.

The Discerning Process

The second stage of the call to discipleship involves some kind of discernment that seeks to discover whether the experience is a genuine invitation or an illusion. Most of us need help recognizing moments of religious importance. Because these are moments when the Spirit of God breaks through, we need spiritual people to help us interpret the action of God. We turn to the community, since the call itself comes from the Spirit of God that resides within and directs this community. It is there that we find women and men who are practiced in the ways of God, who can help us test the spirit. They might be recognized religious leaders or prophetic guides, or they could be friends or loved ones who know us well and who are attuned to the workings of God in their own lives. When we are called to be disciples, we are caught up into something much larger than ourselves alone, and so we should involve other people who have been touched by God.

The Resulting Transformation

The call to discipleship is a call to radical transformation. We hear the call and we stand open to whatever God will ask of us: "Speak, I am listening." We follow Christ's invitation and we launch out into a new way of life: "Where do you live? Come and see." We no longer belong solely to ourselves; as disciples, we belong to the body of Christ. We belong to the reign of God; we are now part of the mission of Christ. As disciples, we are called to proclaim to the world the justice of God. What a glorious honor this is! There will be time during the liturgical year to reflect on the price this will exact of us. Today, we rejoice in the fact of having been called to a radical transformation through a series of conversions.

Third Sunday in Ordinary Time
Jonah 3:1-5, 10

This episode in the story of Jonah begins with a report of the coming of the word of the LORD to Jonah. This is a technical phrase identifying him as a prophet sent by God. However, the recipient of God's word is not Israel, as is usually the case, but Nineveh, Israel's mortal enemy. On the east bank of the Tigris River, this city was the capital of Assyria during the latter years of its glory. Although many of the historical and geographic details about the city found in the book of Jonah are inaccurate, the city was known throughout the ancient Near East as one of the most brutal of its day. For this reason it became the symbol for wickedness in the ancient world. It is to this despised city that the prophet is sent with a pronouncement of judgment and punishment.

The action that takes place within the narrative is rapid. The paucity of words in describing what happens adds to the speed of the movement. This underscores Jonah's desire to complete his task as soon as possible, as well as the immediate and surprising response of the people of the city. The uncommon size of Nineveh emphasizes the extent of its arrogance and wickedness and the scope of repentance that is needed if it is to be saved. For reasons not stated, Jonah does not go into the heart of the city. He enters only a third of the way and there proclaims the message he has received from God.

Forty signifies a significant biblical period of time. It is the length of the Flood (Gen 7:4, 12, 17) and of Moses' conversation with God on Mount Sinai (Exod 24:18; 34:28); it is the length of time it took Elijah to travel to Mount Horeb years later (1 Kgs 19:8). A period of forty days is given to the Ninevites so that the entire population can be notified of the impending punishment. In a sense, forty days is a favorite length of time determined by God.

The people of Nineveh heed the message of the prophet, believe in God, and proclaim a fast. The incongruities of the story are striking. First and most important, God is concerned with the salvation of a nation other than Israel, in fact, a nation that has been brutal toward the chosen people. This demonstrates the universality of divine compassion and willingness to forgive. Second, the city renowned for its wickedness repents of its sins as soon as it hears the proclamation of a prophet from one of the backwater nations it has oppressed. This unpretentious prophet from an insignificant nation is heeded without delay. Third, the comprehensiveness of the spirit of repentance that sweeps through the city is exceeded only by its geographic breadth. All people, great and small, put on the garments of penance.

The reading ends with a description of reversals. The people of Nineveh turn from the evil they are doing, and so God turns from the evil that threatens them. The sudden conversion of this contemptible city speaks loudly of the graciousness of God and the transformative power of God's word. Even the worst sinners can repent and be made new.

Psalm 25:4-5, 6-7, 8-9

The psalm response opens with a prayer for divine guidance. The word "way" is closely associated with the wisdom tradition and refers to a manner of living, specifically the way of righteousness or the way of evil. The term often designates movement or direction on a road rather than the road itself. Here it could refer to a style of life. "Paths" appears in parallel construction with "ways" and also refers to a style of life. When this expression is used in reference to God it can mean either God's own ways of acting or the ways that God teaches humankind to go. This psalm seems to allow for both meanings.

Understanding the words from the perspective of God's ways of acting makes us attentive to the salvation accomplished by God (v. 5), to God's covenantal commitment (v. 6), and to God's own uprightness (v. 8). Regarding the first theme, the psalm gives no indication as to the character of the salvation wrought by God. Was the psalmist in physical danger? Was the deliverance from personal misfortune? The threat could have been cosmic annihilation. Whatever the case may have been, the psalmist asks for insight into God's saving ways, presumably in order to sing God's praises and to offer thanks for God's goodness.

Covenant language is very strong in the second stanza (vv. 6–7). "Compassion" comes from the word *rāham* (womb), and might be translated "womb-love." It refers to a deep and loving attachment, usually between two people who share some kind of natural bond. "Lovingkindness" *(hesed)* denotes loyalty to covenant obligations. The Hebrew suggests that the psalm is speaking of God's remembrance of covenant commitment and not of the psalmist's former sins. This plea that God remember may be the psalmist's way of asking for God's forgiveness.

The final stanza comments on the righteousness of God (vv. 8–9), which is attentive to both the sinners and the *anawim* (humble). Both groups are taught the way of the LORD, the way that God acts toward people's loyalty and infidelity. Presumably the first group will be taught that wickedness will be punished, while the second will be assured that their righteousness has not gone unnoticed.

The phrase "Your ways, O LORD" can also refer to the manner of living that God expects of humankind. In this case, it is probably a reference to the law, for it is there that the will of God is to be found. The psalmist would then be asking for guidance to discern God's will in order to live in accord with it. This interpretation does not negate the preceding explanation; it simply gives it a slightly different perspective. God's saving action calls for a response. Having been saved, what responsibilities do we now have? How should we live so as not to fall back into the situation from which we were saved? If God has established a covenant with us, what are our covenant obligations? What have we taken upon ourselves in entering into this relationship? Finally, if God is just, what kind of lives should we be living? The psalmist prays: Teach me your ways. Show me how you have acted; show me how I should behave.

1 Corinthians 7:29-31

Paul is teaching about the end-time. Unlike the regular measure or unfolding of time *(chrónos)*, this is a different notion of time *(kairós)*, a time of greatest theological significance. It refers to decisive moments, those that are ordained by God, those that mark the inbreaking of God's action. It is frequently the time of fulfillment, of divine revelation. It denotes critical moments in the life of Jesus: his inauguration of the reign of God, his passion and death, his return at the end-time.

Because in many ways *kairós* is "time out of time," it calls for a manner of living and acting that in ordinary circumstances might appear eccentric. The normal priorities of life, priorities necessary for personal survival and the continuation of the race, give way to very different behavior. Instead, fasting is called for rather than eating, continence rather than procreation. It is not that the customary demands of life are to be scorned. This unusual manner of living is a way of responding to the singular character of *kairós*.

It is from this point of view that Paul exhorts the Corinthians as he does in this passage. What he says suggests that the *kairós* is fast approaching but has not yet arrived. However, he advises the Christians to live in the present age as though it had already come. The exclusively male reference (act as not having wives), may reflect an earlier belief that the man was the active partner in procreation. Here the men are exhorted to refrain from sexual activity, not unlike the restraint imposed upon them during periods of military service. This *kairós* time is not unlike such a period, when customary living must be set aside for another pressing responsibility.

Weeping and rejoicing are normal reactions to the events of life. Because the values and aspirations of the age to come differ from those of this age, our reactions will be different as well. What ordinarily makes us cry may not elicit the same response in the *kairós* future; what normally brings us pleasure may cease to have that effect. The insecurity of material possessions will become so evident that we will recognize the futility of acquiring more. We will indeed deal with this world as though not dealing with it. Paul admonishes his hearers to assume this way of living even before the *kairós* moment is fully upon them. Time is running out and the world as they know it is passing away. Paul wants them to be ready for Christ's return.

Mark 1:14-20

The public ministry of Jesus begins after the arrest of John the Baptist. The temporal relationship between these two ministries is not explained in this passage. The focus here is on the activity of Jesus. However, mention of John's arrest may have been the author's way of alerting us to the danger that accompanied any behavior or teaching that could be seen as prophetic. Jesus' way of life may have been rather conventional. He came to the villages and towns of Galilee rather than to the wilderness of Judea. However, his message was startling. It was the gospel, or good news, of the kingdom of God.

This phrase, "kingdom of God," is rich in theological meaning. In the earliest traditions it was identified with the people of Israel, and it had very definite political meaning. However, even during the time of Israel's monarchy, God was considered the real ruler of the people, and the monarch was the one who administered in the place of God. The failure of the monarchy prompted the people to look to the future, to a time when another king, one who was totally faithful to God, would establish a kingdom that would truly be the kingdom of God. This would be a time when all would be steadfast in their commitment to God. Down through the ages the prophets looked forward to this future time. They encouraged the people to turn away from their lives of sin and to dedicate themselves anew to the reign of God.

Jesus inaugurates his ministry with this bold declaration: "The kingdom of God is at hand." This is an extraordinary time *(kairós)*, the time of fulfillment of all expectations. After the initial announcement Jesus calls for repentance. Just like the prophets of old, he calls for a *metanoia*—a change of heart, a return to God. He also calls for belief in the truth of the proclamation that the kingdom of God is indeed at hand.

The announcement of the good news is followed by an account of the call of the fishermen Simon, Andrew, James, and John. Playing with the image of casting nets, Jesus summons them to follow him, to cast their nets and together gather up other followers. Several aspects of this scene are significant. First, unlike the disciples of other famous rabbis and Greek teachers, these followers are called to work with Jesus, not merely to learn what he has to teach. Second, while this reading says nothing about the family responsibilities of the brothers Simon and Andrew, it does indicate that James and John have family ties. In a patriarchal society the abandoning of one's father violated a fundamental kinship relationship.

The abruptness with which these men leave their familiar lives and all of the relationships and obligations associated with them is a final indication of the radical nature of life in the kingdom of God. This is truly a new way of living in the world.

Themes of the Day

This period of Ordinary Time is really an interlude between seasons. Christmas is behind us, and in a few weeks we will be entering the season of Lent. Although time and again we might catch a glimpse of the future, a hint of what lies ahead for Jesus and for those who are his disciples, during this interim period our readings invite us to reflect on various aspects of discipleship. Having considered the call to discipleship last week, today we reflect on the first and most important responsibility of this call, namely, evangelization, the goal of which is the proclamation of the reign of God. The character of God's reign is not revealed this Sunday, but the urgency of our acceptance of it certainly is.

Evangelization

God seems to choose the most unlikely people to preach to others. Apparently it does not matter who *brings* the good news but who *receives* it. Jonah was a prophet who was sent to outsiders, people who were considered enemies of God's own people. The first disciples were fishermen who spoke to the women and men of their own country. God's salvation is intended for all, and it seems to make little difference who brings this good news.

There is some similarity in the messages; it is a call for repentance. The grace of God requires a new way of living, a turning to God in faith and commitment. In addition, the good news proclaimed first by Jesus and then by his disciples announces the advent of the reign of God. Those who hear this message are invited into the age of fulfillment. This salvific reign is a reign of truth, compassion, and kindness. It is a way of life that leads to justice, that teaches the ways of a humble God. It is a way of life lived in the holiness of the call itself. Repentance is necessary because we have not been living in this way.

Urgency in Acceptance

There is an urgency in these readings. Unless we embrace the gospel now and live it fully, we may run out of time. The world in its present form is passing away, and God's call demands a total response. Like the disciples, we must leave our nets, the familiarity of our former ways of living, and follow the call we have heard in the depths of our hearts. We may be called from a life we enjoyed, as the Corinthians were, or we may be called like Jonah to a life from which we try to escape. In either case God's call to discipleship is persistent, even unrelenting. As demanding as it may seem, we should be grateful that God does not give up.

As disciples we are called not only to enter the reign of God but to promote it and to spread it. We are ambassadors of God; we bring the good news of salvation, and we do this wherever we are and in whatever we do. Having been called by God, we now begin to live our lives in a totally different way, guided by the values of the reign of God rather than those of the world that is passing away.

Fourth Sunday in Ordinary Time
Deuteronomy 18:15-20

Prophecy is a form of divine communication. Throughout the ages people have devised various ways of establishing some form of communication with divine beings. The laws of Israel condemned all such forms of divination, maintaining that only God could initiate the communication. While Israel did believe that some form of revelation often occurred in dreams and visions, they considered prophecy to be the primary means of divine communication.

Moses is not normally thought of as a prophet, but this text clearly states that he is. In fact, he is considered the prophet par excellence. He received the word of the LORD in the form of the Law, and he acted as God's spokesperson promulgating this Law to the community. In this passage Moses promises that God will not leave the people without a mediator. Rather, just as he had been chosen by God to be a prophet (Exod 4:12), so another would be raised up. In fact, this promise of a prophet is in response to a request that the people themselves made at the foot of Horeb (v. 16; cf. Deut 5:23-26). There, in fear, they realized that they could not approach God directly but would need a mediator.

This text underscores several important characteristics of the prophetic individual. First, the true prophet will not independently assume the role of spokesperson but will be raised up by God (vv. 15, 18). Second, this prophet will not be an outsider but will be called forth from among the people (v. 15). Third, the LORD will put the words in the mouth of the prophet, so that the message proclaimed will not be the message of the prophet but will be the message of God (v. 18). Finally, because this prophet speaks God's words, in God's name, with God's authority, anyone who disregards the message or who speaks in the name of any other God is liable to divine punishment.

This promise of a future prophet developed within the religion of Israel, leading people down through the centuries to wonder whether or not particular individuals may in fact be this promised prophet. Ultimately it became an important dimension of Israel's eschatological expectation, often combined with the figure of the mysterious Elijah, who would inaugurate the messianic age (cf. Mal 2:23 [4:5]). The early Christians understood this as a reference to Jesus (cf. John 1:21; 6:14).

This explicit description of the prophet notwithstanding, it has always been difficult to distinguish between the true prophet and the false prophet. Both make claims and call for a following. The only real gauge for judging one from the other is the ultimate unfolding of history. Whose message was reliable? However, this passage does give some clues for discernment. The true prophet is like Moses, steeped in the religious tradition and faithful to its requirements, humbly reliant on God for direction and courage, committed to the well being of the community even when the community rebels, willing to step aside when it appears that the work of God is being handed over to another.

Psalm 95:1-2, 6-7, 7-9

The responsorial psalm combines an invitation to praise, a plea for openness, and a word from God. The invitation is given three times: "Come, let us sing joyfully" (v. 1); "Let us come into his presence" (v. 2); "Come, let us bow down" (v. 6). Together they seem to be a reenactment of liturgical movement. There is the initial summons to praise followed by an invitation to enter the presence of God (presumably the temple), there to bow before God in worship. God then addresses the reverent community.

The relationship that exists between God and the people is characterized by means of several metaphors. God is the rock of their salvation (v. 1). A rock is solid and secure. It affords grounding for whatever relies on it. Rocks also provide refuge and shelter from inclement weather and from various dangers. It is an apt image to refer to God as the protector of the people. God is also clearly identified as creator (v. 6). This can be a reference to God as the creator of the universe and everything within it, or it can be a more personal reference to the fashioning of a disparate group of individuals into a coherent community. The image that follows suggests the latter interpretation.

The psalmist identifies the community as the flock and God as the shepherd (v. 6). In a pastoral community such a relationship was quite intimate. Shepherds took total responsibility for their sheep, caring for them and protecting them even at the risk of their own lives. For reasons such as this, shepherd became a fitting metaphor to describe the monarch, who was expected to act in this same way on behalf of the people of the realm. In this psalm the images of rock and shepherd illustrate the people's perception of God as protector.

Having depicted God as a caring and devoted protector, the psalmist turns again to the people and issues a serious plea to be open to the voice of God. This plea suggests that "today" the people who have been gathered together will hear God's voice. Since this gathering is clearly liturgical in character (v. 6), it is safe to conclude that the word from God will be a part of the actual liturgical celebration. The people have come to worship God and to receive some word from God that will comfort them or set a direction for their lives.

The word that follows is an appeal by God to respond positively to God, not in the spirit of rebellion that governed their ancestors while they were in the wilderness (cf. Exod 17:1-7; Deut 6:16). During that earlier time the people had demanded signs that would prove the presence and power of God acting on their behalf, despite the fact that they had witnessed God's gracious deliverance of them from Egyptian bondage. God desires hearts that are open, not hearts that have been hardened by selfishness or a lack of faith. "Today" the descendants of those rebellious wanderers are called upon to respond with open faith and willing obedience.

1 Corinthians 7:32-35

The teaching of Paul contained in this passage has led some interpreters to conclude that, while not outrightly opposing marriage, Paul believes that the unmarried state is to be preferred. While such an interpretation is quite accurate, it is important to understand Paul's bias. It is true that he contrasts the commitments of the two states of life, but he does so because he firmly believes that the end is near.

Although he says he would like the Corinthian Christians to be free from anxieties, he really means that he wants them to be anxious about the right things. He contrasts anxiety about the things of the Lord with anxiety about the things of the world. The first are to be preferred over the second. The real contrast he draws is between commitment to the Lord and involvement in the things of this world. Paul knew, as we know, that those involved in the things of the world can be very committed to the Lord, and those committed to the Lord can possess a very shallow spirituality. He is more concerned with the quality of commitment than with the particular state of life.

One cannot deny that those who are married have responsibilities that the unmarried do not have. Pledged to another, they are somehow accountable to and for that other person. In the most immediate way they have assumed responsibility for the survival of the race, and they must be concerned with the things of this world so that the next generation can enjoy a prosperous future. While those who are not married also have obligations to the next generation, they are not as immediate and intimate as are those of women and men who are married.

Paul is concerned here about the demands the world makes upon those who are involved in it, and this means everyone. However, he knows that those whose primary responsibilities are grounded in the world can have divided loyalties and can really be torn by this. This is especially true when the form of this world is said to be passing away (cf. 1 Cor 7:31, Third Sunday in Ordinary Time). According to Paul, in this latter situation it is better to be free of the responsibilities of marriage and to be totally dedicated to the things of the Lord.

This admonition reveals something of Paul's understanding of the mutuality of marriage. His descriptions are not exclusively or even primarily of men. In fact, the women and men in each of the states of life are characterized in the same way. The unmarried individuals desire lives of devotion to God without the same kind of reliance on another person. Likewise, the married man wants to please his wife as much as the married woman wants to please her husband. They appear to be unselfishly committed to each other, not one subservient to the other.

Finally, Paul is careful to admit that he is giving an opinion and not an injunction that would impose restraints upon his hearers. This is non-binding counsel. However, Paul is convinced of the benefit of this counsel, especially in light of the impending return of Christ. This last point colors everything he says here.

Mark 1:21-28

The major portion of this narrative is an account of an exorcism that Jesus performs in the Galilean village of Capernaum. However, the story actually begins and ends with statements about the teaching of Jesus. In fact, the exorcism itself is identified as "a new teaching with authority." Therefore is it clear that the underlying theme of the reading is the authenticity of the teaching of Jesus.

Following the custom of the time, Jesus, an adult male member of the community, took his turn at teaching those gathered in the synagogue. The people were accustomed to the manner of teaching of the scribes. These official teachers or interpreters were students of the law who relied for their authority on the precedents already set by the teaching of others. Jesus, on the other hand, taught as one having authority in his own right. The people in the synagogue recognized this and marveled at it. The exorcism that Jesus performed may have been primarily an outward manifestation of this unusual authority.

There was a man in the synagogue who had an unclean spirit that caused him severe physical suffering. The people of the time believed that evil spirits who roamed the world caused havoc whenever and wherever they could. What appeared to be contrary to a set pattern was believed to have been caused by such spirits and was considered unclean. If such an afflicted person was found in a holy place like the synagogue, he certainly would have to be removed. Jesus does not have the man leave; instead, he casts out the evil spirit. Thus he establishes the reign of God in a previously disordered situation. In a sense, this account describes a confrontation between the power of good and the power of evil.

The evil spirit called Jesus by name, thereby presuming to have some power over him. The names used are noteworthy. "Jesus of Nazareth" might identify him by his place of origin, or it might associate him with the Nazirites, or consecrated ones (cf. Num 6:2-21). "Holy One of God" is a rare title and probably refers to Jesus' distinctive relationship with God. However we understand the names, they are certainly references to Jesus' unique status. The evil spirit's acknowledgment of Jesus' superiority is confirmed by the question posed: Have you come to destroy us (the spirit speaks in the name of a multitude of spirits)? The spirit clearly knows that this is a confrontational encounter and that Jesus has the edge.

As he confounds the evil spirit, Jesus demands that it not speak. Does he not want others to know who he is? Within the context of a narrative that makes a point of authoritative teaching and power over evil spirits, this order seems rather strange. However, one must remember that the primary focus of the story is the authority of Jesus, not his identity. That will have to be revealed later. Just as the people were astonished by the teaching of Jesus, so they are amazed at his power over the evil spirit. Jesus may have been able to silence the spirit, but his fame as a teacher and an exorcist spread throughout Galilee.

Themes of the Day

Continuing our reflection on the theme of discipleship, this week we address three pressing questions: Why would we be willing to accept the demands of discipleship and change our way of living? Where do we turn for direction in this radical transformation? How does this transformation change us?

Why Are We Willing to Change?

The answer to this question is apparent to anyone who has ever seriously reflected on life. We want to change because in so many ways we are being strangled to death by demons. We are caught in dysfunction and sin, and try as we may, we do not seem able to rid ourselves of their shackles. We live in the midst of the battle between good and evil, the struggle of human finitude and failure. We may begin with good intentions, but we are so often sidetracked or derailed along the way. We are plunged into the throes of human suffering and pain, and there seems to be no escape from it. And what is perhaps the most difficult to accept is that evil appears to have the upper hand in this conflict.

The demonic seduces us in more ways than we can count, and we are often caught in its web before we recognize what has happened. It is only when we are in its grip that we realize that the pleasures it holds out to us cannot really satisfy the desires of the human heart. It is only then that we reach out for salvation, that we heed the invitation of the reign of God.

To Whom Do We Turn?

There have always been many and varied voices that claim to have the remedy for our ills. Preachers and politicians have stirred up crowds and ignited their emotions. Promises have been made and predictions advanced, yet the conflict goes on; the demons continue to hold sway. And then a voice is heard in the midst of the chaos of our lives. This voice rings with authority: "Be quiet! Come out!"

The demons recognize the authority in the voice of Jesus. They know who he is, but the people around him do not. They acknowledge his power over them, but again and again Jesus finds himself in conflict with the crowds and with their leaders over the question of his authority. How can this be, since he has the credentials of the true prophet as described by Moses? In fact, he exercises the very authority of God. Failure to comprehend Jesus' true identity probably stems from mistaken expectations. We may be able to admit that we want and need a savior, but we may not always grasp the implications of this desire. Little by little light will be thrown on the person of Jesus during the coming weeks.

How Will We Be Changed?

When we are released by Jesus from the demons that possess us, we are freed from the stranglehold of evil and liberated to live far less encumbered and divided lives. We will then see that we can be so liberated in any lifestyle, within any commitment. No earthly reality will possess us, neither relationships nor obligations nor even religious practices. Rather, we will be possessed by Christ, who liberates us for the reign of God. Therefore, whether married or unmarried, whether in the midst of the community or at its margins, we will be able to heed the voice of God in our hearts and to recognized Jesus in our midst.

Fifth Sunday in Ordinary Time
Job 7:1-4, 6-7

Crushed by the torment of his own situation, Job bemoans the harshness of life itself. He uses three images to characterize it. It is like hard military service, which makes terrible demands on an individual and jeopardizes one's very life. It is like the quandary of a hireling, who is always beholden to another and who has little or nothing to say about the conditions of work. Finally, it is like the predicament of a slave, who has nothing to say about anything and is totally dependent upon the slaveholder. These metaphors not only describe the tribulations of life, but they also express the helplessness that is experienced in it. So many circumstances are beyond human control, and women and men often feel helpless in the face of them all.

After characterizing life in general, Job turns to the misery of his own life. His days are charged with hardship and his nights are fraught with sorrow. Rather than providing him with the respite he so desperately needs, the nights fill him with restlessness. There is nowhere for him to turn. Life seems to be armed against him, and there is neither defense nor escape. It is no wonder that he cries out.

The transitoriness of life is also troubling to Job. His days come and go as swiftly as the fingers of a deft weaver operating a shuttle. One would think that this breathtaking passage of time would give him some comfort. It might mean that his days of suffering were soon to come to an end. On the other hand, it might suggest that there was no opportunity for his sorry fate to be reversed, and consequently, there was no hope for him. A second image illustrates both the ephemeral nature of Job's life and its emptiness. It is like a wind that has no substance. It comes and goes, cannot be directed, and leaves nothing of value behind it.

Job sees no value in the life that has been thrust upon him. It is filled with affliction and empty of meaning. The whole tenor of his complaint suggests that Job believes he is being treated in a way that ill befits him. Nowhere does he acknowledge that he has brought such hardship upon himself. And nowhere does he express compliant acceptance of his lot.

This last point is a very important one for believers to remember. Religious devotion does not require that we refrain from complaining. In fact the biblical tradition contains many examples of righteous people lamenting the circumstances of life and complaining to God. There are many laments among the psalms (e.g., Psalms 51; 60). The book of Lamentations is an entire book of complaints. Perhaps the book of Job is the classic example of the righteous complainer. Complaints can actually be statements of faith, for the plea that God alleviate suffering is both an acknowledgment of God's power and an act of confidence that God will intervene. Job's complaints spring from such sentiments.

Psalm 147:1-2, 3-4, 5-6

The responsorial psalm opens with the a summons to praise the LORD (*Hallelujah* in Hebrew). Such hymns of praise have a very definite pattern. The summons itself *(hallelu)* appears in a plural verb form, suggesting a communal setting. It also contains an abbreviation of the divine name *(jah)*. At times it is addressed to the righteous of the land, at other times to the earth or to the heavenly bodies. The reasons for praising God are then given. Despite the fact that the response for today consists of only a few verses, this basis structure is quite evident. There is first a clear summons to praise; then several reasons for praising God are given.

The summons to praise God also states that God is good and gracious. Examples of God's goodness are then given. God gathers the people after they have been dispersed and rebuilds the city of Jerusalem, which had been destroyed. This has always been regarded as more than merely a political restoration. It was a second chance at being God's chosen people, almost a new creation. It was linked with the promises of a "new covenant" (Jer 31:31), a "new heart and . . . a new spirit" (Ezek 36:26). God has also comforted them and sustained them. The extent of God's graciousness is seen here, for it was shown to a sinful people, not one who had remained faithful.

It is not enough that God reestablishes the nation and rebuilds Jerusalem, the center of the people's religious, political, and social life. God also comforts them in their suffering, caring for them with tenderness. Throughout the tradition, God is described as being particularly attentive to the needs of those in distress. God is here depicted as personally involved in nursing those who are wounded. In the context of this psalm the wounds from which they suffer may well be the consequences of the punishment meted out for their sins. Having afflicted them, God now cares for them.

The reference to the numbering and naming of the stars may at first seem out of place. However, a closer look will reveal the role this reference plays in describing God. Many people believe that their destiny is determined by the positions of the heavenly bodies. By stating that God is the one who numbers the stars and names them, the psalmist is making a claim of God's creative power over these heavenly bodies. Therefore one can conclude that the destiny of individuals or of entire nations is totally under God's control. Furthermore, while God is just, God is also compassionate.

The final reasons for praising God are God's power, wisdom, and justice (vv. 5–6). Though not mentioned, these characteristics have already been described. God's mighty power was demonstrated in the reestablishment of the people and in the power over the heavenly bodies. It is particularly in the wonders of creation that divine wisdom is manifested. Finally, God's justice is seen in the punishment meted out to the guilty and in the tender care given to those who suffer. All of this is reason to praise the LORD.

1 Corinthians 9:16-19, 22-23

Preaching was the very reason Paul had been called to follow Christ (cf. Acts 9:15; 22:10; 26:16). In his eyes, he deserved no special credit for this, and therefore, he had no grounds for boasting. He had not been called because of his righteousness, nor because of his great proficiency in the various forms of rhetoric. He had been called because God so ordained it. In fact, because of the circumstances out of which he had been summoned (while persecuting the infant Church), it should be clear that Paul's vocation was determined by God, was directed by God, and was successful because of God.

The issue was not *if* Paul preached, but *how* he preached. Did he do so willingly and with enthusiasm or was it done grudgingly, with resentment? Paul realized that it was his destiny that he preach; he had no option but to preach. Because it was his destiny, it would be woe to him if he did not preach. Misfortune would fall upon him, not because God would step in and punish him. It would fall upon him because, being unfaithful to God's will for him, he would be unfaithful to himself and would experience the sense of unfulfillment that always accompanies such faithlessness. On the other hand, if he discharged his commission faithfully he could expect to receive the wages that were due to one who worked conscientiously. What this recompense might be, Paul does not say.

Whether he was faithful or not, Paul had been entrusted with a certain charge *(oikonomía)*. He was responsible for the rule *(nómos)* of the house *(oíkos)*. He had been given stewardship with regard to the most precious treasures of the household of God, the people for whom the word of God was intended. Accepting his charge, he could expect to be paid for his services, but a fair wage was all he had a right to expect. It seems that there were times when he waived his right to financial support and preached free of charge. Perhaps the earlier reference to boasting springs from a situation where Paul preached without pay, and he wished to point out that this was no cause to boast. He seems to have preferred preaching at no cost, for then he would be beholden to no one and would be able to preach the gospel without being concerned about offending his audience. Still, whether he received wages or not, he was just doing his duty.

There is a very thin line between being free of the constraints placed upon him by others and being willing to accommodate himself to their needs. Paul is willing to conform himself to others without compromising the gospel. He avoided those things that might scandalize others; he refrained from imposing regulations that might be meaningless or even offensive but only if they did not seem to be essential to the gospel message. His adaptability and versatility were sometimes criticized by those who rigidly insisted on conformity to practices that, though valuable in their time, had ceased to have meaning in a new context. Though he himself was committed to the religious traditions of the past, Paul's primary commitment was to the new reality ushered in by Jesus.

Mark 1:29-39

This reading draws together three distinct yet connected episodes and a summary statement. It opens with a healing account that describes Jesus and his followers leaving the synagogue, suggesting that it is the Sabbath. They entered Simon's home and Jesus was brought to his ailing mother-in-law. Without speaking a word, he raised her up *(egeíro)*. She was healed and she began to minister to them *(diakonéo)*.

Though a straightforward story, it is charged with theological meaning. First, Jesus excuses himself from certain Sabbath regulations and heals on the Sabbath. A similar act will later be considered an infraction of religious observance (cf. Mark 3:2). Second, the verb translated "helped her up" is frequently used in resurrection accounts. In the ancient world, those who were ill were thought somehow to be in the grips of the powers of death. Finally, while the story suggests that after her healing the woman "waited on them," the verb signifies more than traditional woman's domestic work. In other narratives it connotes ministry or service within the community. This story is an account of Jesus exercising unique authority over the powers of death. The one released from this power then goes about ministering to others.

The second episode is also a healing account. In it the townsfolk bring their ill and demon-possessed family members and friends to be cured. The sun has gone down, so they are not guilty of carrying burdens on the Sabbath. The report of Jesus' marvelous deeds is given without detail. He heals and he casts out demons who are then forbidden to reveal his true identity.

The contradictions in this episode are striking. Jesus' fame has so spread that he is compelled to flee to a solitary place to pray. The imperfect form of the verbs indicates that a prolonged period of time was intended. Simon and the others think that Jesus should exploit his celebrity. In their eyes his behavior is filled with contradiction. He performs spectacular feats and then runs away. Jesus realizes that the crowds are coming because they want miracles. He, on the other hand, wants crowds to come to hear the gospel he will preach, yet he still performs miracles. The demons seem to know who he is and what he is about, while his followers and the crowds he attracts misunderstand him and his mission. Everything in this episode is complicated.

The reading ends with a statement that condenses the entire ministry of Jesus into preaching and driving out demons. These two works are actually very closely connected. The principal message of Jesus' preaching is the long-awaited establishment of the reign of God (cf. Mark 1:15; Third Sunday in Ordinary Time). However, before God's reign can take firm root and thrive the reign of evil must be dislodged and cast out. Driving out demons was really a confrontation between the power of God in Jesus and the power of evil (cf. Mark 1:21-28; Fourth Sunday in Ordinary Time). The exorcisms acted as external proof of the authority of Jesus and of the trustworthiness of the gospel he preached. Therefore, it is appropriate to condense the works of Jesus in this way.

Themes of the Day

Today the readings offer us snapshots from the photo album of life. We see three related dimensions of human existence: the harshness of life, Jesus relieving us of this harshness, and the disciple preaching Jesus' message of salvation. In their own way the readings continue the theme of discipleship and also add to the portrait of Jesus that is being painted.

The Harshness of Life

Disappointment and suffering come to everyone. For some people sorrow seems to be the very essence of life. It can take such hold of us that the happiness of the past is swallowed up, the beauty of better days is forgotten, and the hope of a brighter future is imperiled. Life ceases to be an adventure and takes on the guise of drudgery. At such times we no longer view suffering as an ordeal that must be endured for a time but will eventually pass. Rather, suffering appears to be our permanent fate, and life seems too short for suffering to run its course. When it takes hold of us in this way, we become identified with our distress; we are the tormented.

Jesus Relieves Us

Jesus knows the harshness of life, because he is one of us. More than this, he sees it in the lives of people he loves, and he is touched by their torment. He has come to release people from the demons that possess them, from the illness that undermines their lives. He has come to bring the reign of God, the reign of peace and fulfillment. He has come to heal the brokenhearted, to bind up their wounds. His liberating and healing power goes out to all those who approach him. If we invite him in, he will sustain us.

The Disciple Preaches the Message

Paul identifies himself as a messenger of this gospel of salvation and fulfillment. The issue is not *if* he preached, but *how* he preached. Did he do so willingly and with enthusiasm, or did he do it grudgingly? He insists that he had no option but to preach, because it was his destiny. Still, he does it wholeheartedly, with fervor and the commitment of one who himself has been released from the clutches of his demons. He is so committed to his mission that he empathizes with all those who will hear his preaching. He identifies with the slaves, the weak, the brokenhearted, all those who know well the harshness of life. He does this so that the message he preaches does not appear to be disassociated from the realities of life.

Just as we so easily identify with Job in his suffering, so should we identify with Paul in his commitment to evangelization. By the power of God, Jesus addressed the needs of his day; by the power of the same God, Paul addressed the needs of his. Now it is our turn. We are the disciples who must bring the good news to the brokenhearted, to those who are enslaved, to those who are weak. We are the ones who will then share in the blessings of this good news.

Sixth Sunday in Ordinary Time
Leviticus 13:1-2, 44-46

Leprosy is a general term that covered a wide variety of chronic skin diseases. In a Mediterranean climate like that of Israel/Palestine, such diseases if untreated can be quite distressful. However, the real tragedy of such an affliction was less the physical discomfort the person had to endure than the social estrangement and the religious or ritual alienation that was imposed because of it. The physical condition caused the skin to be broken and bodily fluids to exude. The issue here is bodily boundaries, not hygiene. Bodily fluids belonged within the body. Therefore emissions other than the normal functions of elimination were clearly out of place.

All cultures determine their own meaning and organize their own structures, but each one does it in a distinctive way. More specifically, a culture's definitions identify what fits within a particular classification and what does not. When something either fits uneasily within one category or straddles two of them, it is considered an anomaly. The anomaly can be given an enhanced significance or one that is diminished, depending upon the culture. (In some cultures a person with epilepsy is thought to be specially touched by God and is treated as a holy person; in other cultures such a person is ridiculed or even shunned.)

This text states that those with skin ailments were deemed unclean, were banished from the community, and were required to keep their distance from others. In fact, should someone unknowingly approach them, they were to warn them by crying out, "Unclean, unclean!" (v. 44). In fact, it was their very state of being unclean, not merely the physical condition itself, that was thought to be contagious. Anyone who had direct contact with someone or something that was unclean was considered unclean.

Clean and unclean were religious designations, and so the priest was involved in making such determinations. When the conditions that made a person unclean no longer held, it was necessary for the person to undergo some rite of purification before being readmitted into the community. This too was regulated by the priest.

Finally, probably because such social and religious alienation was so severe, it was believed the condition was brought on by some kind of sin (Num 12:9-10). This made the one with leprosy not only physically loathsome and socially dangerous but morally reprehensible as well.

Psalm 32:1-2, 5, 11

The psalm response comes from one of the seven psalms known in Christian devotion as the Penitential Psalms. Though cast in the form of a thanksgiving, it might be more accurately considered a wisdom psalm. It opens with a double macarism ("blessed," or "happy"), a literary form identified with the wisdom tradition. In a unique way this form highlights something of the value system of Israel (or of Christianity; cf. Matt 5:3-12; Luke 6:20-22). It states the *real* basis of happiness as opposed to what might be conventionally considered desirable. More frequently than not, the macarisms are quite counter-cultural, challenging the merit of customary aspirations. The macarisms in this psalm response exemplify this.

The double statement of blessedness introduces a wisdom teaching about the benefits of God's merciful pardon, something that is valued more highly than prosperity or reputation. In it the psalmist gives a triple description of sin and of the forgiveness that God grants if there is repentance. "Fault" *(pesha²)* is really rebellion, a rejection of God's authority. Through the mercy of God, this rebellion has been lifted up *(nāśā²)*; the burden has been taken from the shoulders of the sinner. "Sin" *(hătā²â)* means failure, or missing the mark. This failure to measure up is covered up *(kāsâ)* by God. "Guilt" *(ʿāwōn)* also means iniquity or perversion. God does not judge *(hāshab)* that one is iniquitous or perverse.

The psalmist declares that anyone who is so treated by God is truly blessed. However, this is not an example of cheap grace. This blessing of forgiveness is not given indiscriminately. Rather, it is given to those who have honestly sought forgiveness, who have admitted their sinfulness and have repented of it. It is clear that the psalmist is such a person (v. 5). Using some of the very vocabulary found in the macarisms, the psalmist acknowledges "sin," does not try to "cover" any "guilt," and admits "fault." Accordingly, God "took away" the "guilt" of the psalmist's "sin." It appears that the objective description of the "blessed" is really a personal testimony of the psalmist's own experience of sin, repentance, and forgiveness.

The response ends with an exhortation to rejoice. Just as it began with the theme of happiness, so it closes with exultation. As with the discussion about divine mercy, so with this call to rejoice: it only applies to those who are righteous, or upright in heart. If one is just, then rejoicing is not only encouraged, it is probably a spontaneous response to God's magnanimous mercy.

Wisdom teaching consists of the insights into life that have been gained by reflection on experience, insights that may have come from personal experience but that can be applicable for many. The teaching in this psalm response certainly fits this category. The psalmist's experience of personal contrition and divine clemency is offered as an example for others to follow.

1 Corinthians 10:31–11:1

Paul has been talking about the delicate balance that existed between the freedom he enjoyed because of his faith in Christ and the need he had to accommodate himself to those to whom he was preaching. He feared that they would be repelled by something that was not intrinsic to the gospel (cf. 1 Cor 9:22-23, Fifth Sunday in Ordinary Time). In this passage he is directing his hearers to do the same. The gospel is demanding enough. People do not need to be burdened with obligations that are extraneous to its message.

The reference to eating and drinking is a case in point. Many religious traditions have food customs that govern what the members should eat or drink, when they should eat or drink it and with whom, and what is considered taboo in this regard. Judaism and many of the religious sects of the Greco-Roman world had such regulations. Without insisting that new converts to Christianity observe any such customs, and without dismissing them as irrelevant, Paul maintained that the glory of God must be the measure by which every custom should be judged. Whatever practices the Corinthians retained or assumed, their religious value was no longer found in their former importance but in their accommodation to faith in Christ. Furthermore, the context within which they were practiced played a significant role in determining this.

Paul insisted that neither food laws nor the assertion of one's freedom should be the governing principle in the lives of Christians. The glory of God and sensitivity to the consciences of others should be the driving force. The complexity of the makeup of the early Christian communities complicated adherence to this principle. The communities consisted of Jews who had a very detailed dietary system that was integral to their sense of identity as the chosen people of God. To expect them to relinquish this was asking a great deal. However, to require that others take it on themselves was no less a demand.

The Greeks too had regulations regarding food, regulations steeped in religious meaning. Expecting that they could set them aside without difficulty was also unrealistic. Conflict occurred whenever the attitudes that operated within one religious system were transferred to another. For example, those within the community who considered the worship of idols to be nothing but empty ritual might be able to eat food that was originally offered to these idols without feeling guilty. Recent converts from idol worship might experience serious inner turmoil over any such association with their idolatrous past. On the other hand, some Gentiles within the community would not feel obliged to abstain from the flesh of certain animals, since the obligation arose from a tradition that was not at all part of their own religious past. When Christians with such different religious backgrounds sat down to share a meal, these issues frequently surfaced. The policy to follow at such times was to avoid giving offense.

The passage ends with a final admonition: "Be imitators of me, as I am of Christ." Paul has indeed adapted himself to the needs of others, and he has done this after the example of Christ. The Corinthians are exhorted to do the same.

Mark 1:40-45

This short account of the healing of a man with leprosy is yet another example of how Jesus performed some work that demonstrated his miraculous power, yet he demanded that word of this amazing event not be publicized abroad (Fourth and Fifth Sundays in Ordinary Time). Several explanations of this curious feature have been advanced. However, it is best to explain it within the particular context of the specific narrative, as will be done here.

The man in this story was suffering from the kind of skin ailment referred to in the first reading. Though socially alienated and ritually unclean, the man did not adhere to the laws governing those afflicted as he was. Instead, he boldly approached Jesus and begged to be made clean. It was probably no accident that he came to Jesus, for he knew that Jesus had miraculous power. It is interesting that he asked to be made clean, not to be cured. Social and religious acceptability seem to be more important to him than physical healing.

Jesus was moved with pity (the verb *splanchnízomai* suggests deep inner groanings). However, were he to touch an unclean man he would become ritually unclean as well, since this state was considered contagious. If the Gospels tell us anything about Jesus, it is that he regarded human need as more important than ritual regulation. Besides, the touch that others expected would render Jesus unclean actually healed the man and restored him to the state of ritual purity. Since cleanness was a ritual designation, it had to be verified by a priest (Lev 14:1-32). Jesus instructed the man to observe this requirement, for he would need approval from the priest to reenter the community and to participate in its religious life.

Although Jesus sent him off to the priest, there is no report that he went there to fulfill the prescriptions of the law. We are told that, contrary to the stern command of Jesus, the man publicized the event far and wide. However, the fact that he broadcast the news of his cure indicates that he went about among people. The fact that Jesus was engulfed by crowds of people indicates that they believed that the man had been cured. Either he had been certified or the effects of the cure were obvious to all.

Once again the news of his marvelous power seems to have prevented Jesus from going about his mission as he would have desired. He wanted to announce the good news of salvation, but the people were captivated by the wonders he could perform and they sought him out in order to witness these exploits for themselves and, perhaps, benefit from them. Consequently, Jesus chose the seclusion of solitary places rather than the press of the crowd and their misunderstanding of his mission.

Themes of the Day

Our reflection on the harshness of life begun last Sunday continues this week, as we consider the toll that suffering exacts of us. Although the disease of leprosy itself may be foreign to the experience of most people today, the fear it engendered and the anguish it caused those afflicted illustrate some of the personal and communal consequences of human suffering. The themes of today's readings include: the price of human suffering, the inclusivity of the reign of God, and the one who suffered evangelizes.

The Price of Suffering

Sometime in life everyone will have to endure physical, mental, emotional, or spiritual suffering. We know this is the case, so we try to prepare ourselves for the inevitable. Yet when it comes, as prepared as we try to be, it can overtake us with such fury that we fall back defenseless. We look to others for support and assistance, and if we are fortunate, we find it. However, even in the most supportive of communities suffering may exact a price we may not be prepared to pay. It tends to alienate us from those who are healthy and secure.

Leprosy may be an extreme example, but it reveals several aspects of suffering. First, there are the circumstances of the misfortune itself. These might include pain, anxiety, diminishment, and ultimately death. In addition, suffering can sap our energy, jeopardize everything we have achieved, and leave us unproductive and feeling worthless. There are also social consequences. Suffering reminds us of our own finitude and the contingent nature of all of life. It threatens people's sense of order, and they often tend to dissociate themselves from those in pain. Finally, the one suffering and unable to get beyond the distress may seem to be quite annoying. Others may want to distance themselves from such a bothersome person.

God's Reign Includes All

Jesus is not deterred by human suffering. He welcomes all who approach him; he touches what might repel others. His healing touch reincorporates those who have been ostracized; his loving embrace reassociates those who have been alienated. In the reign of God there are no outsiders. All belong to Jesus, and, therefore, all belong to each other. Those who have been shunned because of some physical condition or social status have been brought back into the circle of the community, and the community is made whole again. The one afflicted belongs to the community, and the community is now an authentic manifestation of the inclusive reign of God.

The One Who Suffers Evangelizes

Too often we merely endure suffering and miss the opportunity to reap the benefits it can yield. In suffering we witness to human vulnerability and our desperate need of each other and of God. There, at the edge of life and on the fringes of the community, we may experience the tenderness and compassion of God, the loving touch of Christ that can heal our souls if not our bodies. It is there that we may most authentically participate in the cross of Christ. Joined to him we are anything but unproductive or worthless. If we turn to the Lord in time of trouble, we will begin to experience the joy of salvation, and our lives will proclaim it to others.

Seventh Sunday in Ordinary Time
Isaiah 43:18-19, 21-22, 24b-25

The reading is part of a proclamation of salvation. Speaking through the prophet, God describes the uniqueness of the regeneration that God's own saving power will effect. There is a familiarity about the imagery employed, and at the same time, there is a startling claim of newness.

Israel's faith was based on the liberating events of the past. Snatched from the bondage of Egypt, protected and sustained while in the wilderness, and finally led into a land overflowing with milk and honey, its self-identity was rooted in the memory of its history, and its liturgical celebrations reenacted aspects of it. Israel was a people of memory. Therefore, to be told by God's spokesperson to "remember not . . . consider not" must have been unsettling. What could the prophet mean? Especially Second-Isaiah, who perhaps more than others relied on the earlier traditions in his prophecies.

Most likely the prophet was calling the people away from inordinate dependence on the past, a dependence that prevented them from seeing the astonishing new thing that God was accomplishing before their very eyes. Faithful reverence for tradition is one thing, but insistent absorption in it is quite another. When the former is the case, older traditions can serve to fashion the understanding of new events and insights. When the latter is the case, openness to the newness of God is very hard to achieve. God is doing something new here, and the people must put aside the past in order to receive God's new graciousness.

Just as in the past God led the people through the wilderness, so in this time God will make a way through the desert so the people can pass in safety. As God provided for them during the wilderness sojourn, so God will provide for them now. Remembrance of God's past tenderness always acted as assurance of continued tenderness in the present. In this way, remembering the past strengthened them for the present. However, resting in the security of past favors and in the assurance of being God's chosen people led to complacency and transgression. The people no longer felt the need to call on the LORD. They strayed from God's protection, piling up sin after sin. The past had always challenged or comforted them. Now they had betrayed this past.

The new thing that God desires to accomplish is a new creation, a new reality so overwhelming that the people of Israel could never have imagined it
by themselves. While the new way that stretches out before them is truly astounding, most amazing of all is the transformation that takes place in the
people. Though they have been sinners, the merciful God will wipe out their
guilt; and they will stand before others as forgiven, re-created by God. They
will not only praise God for this gracious rebirth, they will also witness it to
the rest of the world.

Psalm 41:2-3, 4-5, 13-14

The responsorial psalm begins with a macarism (vv. 2–3) in the style of a wisdom psalm (cf. Ps 32:1-2, 5, 11; Sixth Sunday in Ordinary Time). However, the
subject matter is more closely related to the lament that describes the
psalmist's distress and deliverance by God.

The macarism declares blessed the one who is solicitous for the needy, for
when that person is thrown into distress, God will act as deliverer. Those who
care for the less fortunate will not be forsaken by God in the day of their own
misfortune. In keeping with the wisdom tradition of instruction, this is an important lesson to learn. As is often the case with the macarism, it states as
blessed a circumstance that appears to challenge the customary standards of
the day. Society does not normally attend to the very vulnerable. That is precisely why they are vulnerable. This teaching claims that caring for such
people will actually ensure care for ourselves when we are in need.

Deliverance by God takes two forms. The first mentioned is protection
against enemies (v. 3). This is not so much release from the trouble as protection against falling into it in the first place. The claim is that God will keep and
preserve the psalmist (v. 3).

The second form of deliverance is restoration to health after illness (vv.
4–5). As is often the case in prayer of this kind, illness is associated with sinfulness. It is a form of disorder in the physical world caused by some kind of
disorder in the moral world. Since the Israelites believed that these two
spheres were intimately connected, they concluded that one brought about
the other. Therefore, the one who was ill was thought to be in some way responsible for the illness. In the past the psalmist had prayed that God would
be gracious and would forgive. It is clear from the rest of the psalm that this
prayer had been heard. The psalmist had been forgiven, and this forgiveness
was both a form of divine healing and is here used as a witness to others of the
mercy of God.

The psalmist made a confession of sin. This is the second sign of moral integrity, the first being concern for the lowly (v. 2). It is this integrity that encourages the psalmist to make a bold request of God: "Let me stand before you

forever." To stand before God is analogous to being forgiven, to being healed. It is the reward for integrity.

The last verse of the responsorial psalm is a doxology, a praise of God. Although this declaration of praise seems to begin in the same way as does a macarism, the introductory Hebrew word means "bless" or "praise" *(bārûk)* not "blessed" or "happy" *('ashrê)*. The hope is that this praise will stretch from eternity past to eternity future. The prayer ends with a congregational affirmation of approval. "Amen. Amen" means surely, surely! Decidedly yes!

2 Corinthians 1:18-22

It appears that Paul was forced to defend the merit of his apostolic ministry. In doing so he bases his defense on the trustworthiness of God. This is a bold tactic, but then the ministry itself and the message on which it is grounded are bold as well.

The question seems to have been one of consistency. Too often people say one thing and then do another, or they are of two minds on the matter, saying yes one moment and no the next. If in the normal affairs of life this kind of inconsistency leads to mistrust, how much more in matters of faith. Paul is well aware of this, and that is why he argues strenuously that his ministry to the Corinthians has never demonstrated such inconsistency. Quite the contrary, it has been as constant as God has been faithful.

Paul continues his argument by providing three different examples of God's faithfulness. It can be seen first and foremost in the person of Jesus Christ, the Son of God, who has been the center of the preaching of Paul and his two companions, Silvanus and Titus. There was not even a hint of inconsistency in Jesus. Playing with the phrase "yes and no," Paul shifts the focus from inconsistency to obedience. In Jesus there is only yes, only complete acceptance of God's will, and only total faithfulness. Just as Jesus says "yes" to God, so Paul and the Corinthians say "Amen," a form of affirmation and agreement. Those who concur in this way are thereby associated with Jesus' acquiescence to God. Both the "yes" of Jesus and the "Amen" of the believers redound to the glory of God. Finally, both words connote truth and thus contribute to Paul's argument in support of his own credibility.

The second example of God's trustworthiness is found in the fulfillment of the promises made throughout the ages, all of which are brought to completion in Jesus. The people may have had to wait a long time for these promises to be realized, but realized they were, and in a manner so astonishing as to confound them. Just as "yes" was a sign of Jesus' obedience, here the same word marks him as the realization of God's graciousness to the people.

The gift of the Spirit is the third example of God's trustworthiness. Paul argues that God redeemed the Christians through Christ, anointed them, and then sealed them with the Spirit. He uses a commercial image to characterize the role played by the Spirit in the lives of the believers. The seals that are affixed to merchandise signify ownership. (This is a very popular trend today with designer clothing.) The seal of the Spirit functions in the same way. It marks the Christians as belonging to God. The seal also acts as a pledge of deposit *(arrabōn)*, a guarantee of future blessings. This reference to the Spirit reveals the trinitarian dimension of Paul's faith. God redeems us through Christ and marks us with the Spirit.

As significant as this theology may be in itself, here it serves as an argument in defense of Paul's ministry. Paul has identified the word of his preaching and that of his companions Silvanus and Titus with the very words of God. He has also linked his own anointing and that of the Corinthians with Christ, the anointed one. Finally, all have been sealed with the Spirit. With this argument Paul has grounded his defense in trinitarian theology.

Mark 2:1-12

The reading is a composite of a miracle story and a conflict story that includes a pronouncement statement about Jesus. Most likely, the miracle (vv. 1–5a, 11–12) acts as the framework for the conflict (vv. 5b–9), which generates the pronouncement (v. 10). The people have heard that Jesus has returned to Capernaum, and they crowd around him. He is intent on preaching the good news (v. 2), while they appear to be interested in his healing power (v. 3).

The details of the miracle story are dramatically recounted. The ingenuity and persistence of the friends of the paralyzed man are remarkable. Even Jesus is impressed. It is their faith in Jesus that moves him to act. However, operating out of the notion that illness is somehow associated with sin, he speaks words of forgiveness rather than healing. It is these words that set up the conflict between Jesus and the scribes who are present in the crowd. They criticize him, not aloud but within themselves. They realize that the issue here is the authority by which Jesus makes the claim of being able to forgive sin. While they are correct in believing that only God can forgive, they are blind in not recognizing the power of divine forgiveness active in the person of Jesus.

Forgiving sins is more difficult that curing sickness. However, forgiveness cannot be easily verified, as can a cure. Therefore, it is both easy and presumptuous to claim to be able to forgive, and such an audacious claim is blasphemous. Actually, Jesus does not say, "*I* forgive you." He states, "Your sins are forgiven." (Using the passive form was a common way of circumventing the use of the divine name.) Knowing what the incredulous scribes are thinking, Jesus challenges their silent condemnation of him. He points out that in forgiving the man he has already performed the more difficult feat, and so to heal him is merely to make external the internal transformation that has taken place.

Although they make no public protest, the scribes are outraged by Jesus' appropriation of divine authority. For his part, Jesus speaks directly to this challenge: "The Son of Man has authority to forgive sins on earth." In the Synoptic tradition "Son of Man" is the title Jesus most frequently uses to identify himself. It is a Hebraic expression that simply means "human being." However, it is used in the book of Daniel in reference to that supernatural being who will come in the clouds at the end of time (cf. Dan 7:13). There is great debate among scholars as to the meaning of the phrase. Since it has overtones of both humanity and deity, it is probably best to allow it to retain its ambiguity. Actually, its use in the Gospel usually emphasizes the destiny of Jesus more than his identity. Here he is the unusual being through whom the power and authority of God are exercised.

The story ends with the man being sent home and the crowds being astounded by what they have seen. Like the friends (and the man?) who have exhibited faith, the crowds give glory to God for what they have witnessed. Only the scribes are unbelieving.

Themes of the Day

This Sunday we continue the theme of last week: the one who suffers becomes the one who evangelizes. Perhaps an even more important theme found in the readings is the content of the evangelization. While there are many dimensions to this content, its ultimate message is the newness of life that comes from God.

The One Who Suffers Evangelizes

The man who suffered from paralysis was an evangelizer both while he was afflicted and after he had been cured. Before the healing, he witnessed to his faith in Jesus by the mere fact of allowing himself to be brought to the healer. After he had been cured, his very presence announced to the world the healing power of God. Both witnesses were genuine; both messages must be proclaimed.

The Message That Is Proclaimed

Those who are suffering have much to teach us. They can be living examples of patience in the midst of pain, human dignity in the presence of poverty or diminishment, thoughtfulness toward others even when one is in great need. People who have learned to accept the hardships they cannot change often radiate a quality of peace that is astonishing. Realizing the fragility of life, they live what they have with the relish and enthusiasm of a child. They have much to teach us about what matters and who counts, what should be cherished and what we can relinquish.

Perhaps the greatest lesson that they can teach is our total dependence on God. Whether they are delivered from their afflictions or not, those who suffer can herald a message of hope—certainly hope they can be cured, but more than that, hope that life can be worth living under any and all circumstances. This is not a false hope. Rather, it is a hope that allows us to say yes to life even in the midst of hardship.

Newness of Life

Whether or not we are relieved of our misfortunes, the fundamental message of the reign of God is newness of life. It is the radical shifting of human existence—those whose lives were a wasteland see them flowing with refreshing waters; those who are searching for meaning have the word of God preached to them; those who are paralyzed are able to stand up and walk; the promises that God made are fulfilled. Most important, those who have sinned are forgiven. The redemptive power of God is set loose in the world. We can prepare for it. We can remove the roof and lower the mat, but the radical newness comes from God. This is the good news. This is what causes people to be awestruck and to give praise to God.

Eighth Sunday in Ordinary Time

Hosea 2:16b, 17b, 21-22

The prophet Hosea appears to be talking about his wife Gomer. However, it is clear that their marriage relationship has become an analogy for the covenant relationship between God and Israel. The desert, which in some biblical passages symbolizes deprivation and rebellion, is here a place of commitment. The reference calls to mind Israel's original encounter with God and the mutual agreement entered into out of graciousness and love. Hosea was not hankering after the nomadic life. Rather, he was appealing to an earlier time when Israel was like a chaste virgin, innocent and willing to commit itself to God. To lead Israel back to the desert is to return to that untarnished period of engagement and to recommit to the covenant relationship. This romantic image depicts the passion that God feels for Israel.

The move toward recommitment was initiated by God, but the prophet maintains that Israel will respond, and the response will be exactly what God had desired. Called back to the place of its initial espousal, Israel will return to a state of innocence and will enter into a covenantal partnership. Previously the people had experienced God's graciousness in the events of their liberation from Egyptian oppression. Now God's compassion is just as obvious as it had been that first time, perhaps even more so. The need to return and start anew suggests that something had gone wrong. However, this did not deter God, who was willing to initiate a commitment once again.

A slight shift takes place in the reading. In the first verses (vv. 16b, 17b) God is speaking *about* Israel. Here (vv. 21–22) God's words are directed *to* the people. The marital image appears again, with God as the initiator. The words used underscore three characteristics of the espousal: (1) it will be forever; (2) it will include a bride-price or fortune brought to the marriage by the groom, which becomes part of the legacy enjoyed also by the bride (cf. 2 Sam 3:14); and (3) it will have a purpose. Unlike the former relationship, which was shattered by the sins of the people, this one will be everlasting. This word does not mean that it will be indestructible but that it will be perpetual.

The bride price with which God will establish the marriage includes technical covenant characteristics: righteousness *(sedeq)*, which is the moral standard that describes the nature of God; justice *(mishpāt)*, which refers to the just claims that God can and does make; lovingkindness *(ḥesed)*, the bond of steadfastness that is at the heart of divine covenant love; mercy or compassion *(raḥămîm)*, God's love, which resembles the love of a woman for the child of her womb. These are the riches that God brings to the covenant commitment.

The goal of the covenant is: "know the LORD" *(yādaᶜ)*. Such knowledge is personal, experiential, intimate. The verb also refers to sexual intercourse (cf. Gen 4:1). Here it furthers the marital metaphor. As in marriage, the purpose of this commitment is intimate knowledge of the covenant partner.

Psalm 103:1-2, 3-4, 8, 10, 12-13

The responsorial psalm begins with a summons to bless the LORD. Although the word "bless" is often used as a benediction, a prayer for God's presence or grace for the future, in this case it is a call to praise or to thank God for blessings already received. The call to "bless the LORD" is normally addressed to someone other than the psalmist. Here it is a self-address (vv. 1–2). The Hebrew word that is translated "soul" *(nepesh)* comes from the word for breath. It yields over twenty different meanings, chief among them are life-breath (or soul), life, living person. The reference here is probably to that center within the person from which all life forces flow. This is not merely a spiritual or immaterial reality; it encompasses every aspect of the person. This understanding is corroborated by the phrase "all my being."

In the biblical world a person's name was an expression of that person's unique identity. In many ways names held more significance for people then than they do today. One could exercise power over another simply by some-how controlling the other's name. There were times during Israel's history when, in their attempt to show great reverence for God, the people paid homage to God's name rather than directly to God (cf. Deut 12:11, 21; 14:23f.; 16:2, 6, 11). Even when they did this, they were very careful to avoid using the divine name itself. Still today, we show the same respect when we merely use the consonants YHWH or the substitute LORD (small uppercase letters) rather than the name itself.

The reason for praising or thanking God, the benefits to which the psalm-ist refers, is God's willingness to pardon, to heal, and to redeem or save, acts that flow from God's lovingkindness *(ḥesed)* and compassion *(raḥămîm,* vv. 3–4). These two attributes are not only closely associated with covenantal commitment but, as is seen in the Exodus tradition, are integral aspects of God's own name and identity (v. 8; cf. Exod 34:6). It is out of this mercy that God acts, not requiring the harsh punishment that the sins of the people war-rant.

The extent of God's mercy is further sketched by means of the figure of speech "east to west," which denotes immeasurable distance. Human eyes can only envision a fraction of the stretch that lies between the horizons. What is perceived is only infinitesimal; the reality is beyond comprehension. So is the compassion of God. Out of covenant love, God puts our transgression so far from us that the distance cannot even be imagined. This is reason to praise and bless the LORD.

Finally, the psalmist uses a familial image to characterize God's compas-sion. Although the reference is to the compassion of a father for his children, the word itself comes from the word for womb *(reḥem)*. Here compassion is much more intimate than empathy felt for those who suffer. It is womb-love. In other words, the love that God has for us is the love that a mother has for the children of her womb. This explains God's commitment to us, and it is certainly reason to bless the LORD.

2 Corinthians 3:1b-6

When unknown apostles or itinerant preachers went from city to city or church to church, they carried letters of recommendation that would both in-troduce them to the new group and authenticate their ministry (cf. Acts 9:2; 22:5). This reading begins with Paul questioning whether he and his compan-ions really need such letters. They did not present letters of recommendation upon their arrival at Corinth, nor will they request letters from Corinth to be submitted to the community that they will visit next.

One wonders why letters of recommendation are so important here. Were these men unknown, or were they suspect? Did Paul have to prove himself because he was not one of the original apostles? Did his behavior make people question his authenticity? Or did they doubt the orthodoxy of his message? The passage provides no information in this regard.

Using various metaphors, Paul weaves together several themes from early Israelite theology. He first declares that the Corinthians themselves are the recommendation, written on the hearts of Paul and his companions. The heart metaphor recalls two prophetic pronouncements. The first declares that when the new covenant is established God's law will be written on the hearts of the people (cf. Jer 31:33). By identifying the missionaries as ministers of this new covenant (v. 6), Paul is implying that this prophecy is fulfilled. In the second prophetic passage, God promises to remove the people's stony hearts and to replace them with hearts of flesh (cf. Ezek 11:19; 36:26).

The heart metaphor in this passage does not carry all of the nuances that are part of the prophetic references that contrast stone tablets and living hearts. However, these nuances are probably in the background. Here the contrast is between letter, upon which a recommendation is written in ink, and heart, upon which the recommendation is written by the Spirit of God.

The final verse of the passage (v. 6) gives a slightly different overtone to the letter metaphor. The authentication appears not in customary writing but in the unmistakable traces of the Spirit. The Corinthians themselves are the letter of recommendation. Their acceptance of the preaching of the missionaries and the quality of their Christian way of living can be read by all. It is a witness to the authenticity of Paul's ministry.

Letters of recommendation are intended to confirm the qualifications of the one for whom the letter is written. Paul humbly acknowledges that the missionaries are in fact qualified, but it is because of what God had done in and through them and not because of anything that they are or have done. Paul's trinitarian theology is evident here: the qualification of the missionaries comes from God; Christ is the author of the letter of recommendation and the agent of their confidence; the letter is written by the Spirit, who is also the source of life.

Mark 2:18-22

This Gospel story is an example of how Jesus was constantly being put to the test. The conflict here is between the behavior of the disciples of Jesus and the behavior of the disciples of John the Baptist and the Pharisees. The latter carry on the custom of occasional fasting, while the former did not seem to fast at all. Although Jesus was not directly criticized, presumably he was responsible for the religious behavior of his followers. If he himself had valued the religious custom, he would certainly have made sure that his followers did as well. Their failure reflects on the standards he had set for himself and for them.

Jesus responds to this challenge by means of a parable. This is a wisdom technique that draws from the experience of life and uses comparison or analogy to convey the truth or moral lesson that is learned from that experience. Fasting has its place. It is appropriate as a manifestation of repentance for sin (cf. 2 Sam 12:16-17); as a means to avert disaster (cf. Ezra 8:21-22); or simply as a form of personal devotion (Ps 69:10). However, the coming of the reign of God is a time of rejoicing and celebration. In such a situation of jubilation, fasting is inappropriate.

In order to demonstrate this, Jesus employs the image of a wedding feast and the rejoicing that envelops the bridegroom. When the bridegroom is present, feasting is in order. There will be opportunity to return to practices of devotion when the wedding celebration is over.

In the patriarchal setting of Jesus' time, the presence of the bridegroom and the behavior of the male guests would be of more interest than that of the bride and the women who celebrated with her. The point of the parable is not gender preference but the role played by circumstances in determining the timeliness of religious practices.

Jesus likens the establishment of the reign of God to the wedding feast. Furthermore, reference to the bridegroom's being taken away rather than just leaving at the end of the festivities suggests that Jesus is identifying with this bridegroom and indirectly predicting his future passion and death. Although the parabolic image is the feast itself and behavior that is suitable for it, the focal point of the argument is the presence of Jesus the bridegroom and behavior that is fitting for his followers, both while he is with them and when he is absent.

Two other parables reinforce the incompatibility of feasting and fasting. Rejoicing in the reign of God is analogous to unshrunken cloth and potent, new wine. The old cloak is not strong enough to withstand the tension that will occur when the new material is washed and shrinks. It will pull apart and both the old and the new cloth will be useless. Likewise, old wineskins do not have the durability needed to hold the vitality of new wine. They will burst and everything will be lost. We must be careful not to rush to pit the religion of Christianity against that of Israel. Here Jesus is merely explaining why his disciples do not fast. This is the time of the inauguration of the reign of God. Rejoicing is in order.

Themes of the Day

During this segment of Ordinary Time we have been looking at various aspects of discipleship. The readings invite us to look again and again at many of the same themes, though each time in a slightly different way. Last Sunday our attention was trained on the content of our evangelization. This Sunday we look again at the character of the disciples themselves. The major themes for our consideration today are: the radical change of character that occurs when one becomes a disciple; the relationship with God that is the essence of this change; and the witness of life that ensues.

Radical Change of Character

Commitment to Jesus and the acceptance of discipleship that follows this commitment result in a radical change in the shape and quality of our lives. We become new people who are not only filled with new wine but who have taken on new wineskins. Discipleship is not something that we add to our lives like a patch of unshrunken cloth. It does not consist merely in our assuming new religious practices or offering a bit of service. Discipleship calls for a total transformation of life. We probably continue to do much that we have always done; we live and work with the same people, we enjoy many of the same things, but as disciples all is completely new. It is like a marriage commitment that colors our entire lives. A fundamental change takes place when we marry; we are the same people, and yet we are radically different.

Relationship with God

The change occurs because we have entered into a new and radical relationship with God, a new covenant initiated by God. This is a covenant of the Spirit, not of external law. Discipleship stems from our baptismal call from God. We respond to it, but we do not initiate it. We are led by God into a kind of courtship; God inviting us into a deeper and deeper love. This relationship is intimate; it touches the very core of our beings. Just as in marriage a woman and a man become a couple, we literally become new people. When people are married, their lives flow from that relationship; their perspective is enriched; their work is energized; even their demeanor is changed. So it is when we become disciples of Christ; we enter into a relationship no less intimate and all-consuming than marriage.

Witness of Life

Disciples live in the spirit of the one they are following. John the Baptist preached repentance, and so his disciples performed the practices of repentance. Jesus heralds the reign of God, and as his disciples we are called to live lives that are faithful to that new age. We are to rejoice at times of rejoicing, to weep in times of sorrow, and in between, during the ordinary times, to pursue the tasks of life in the spirit of Jesus. We are to love with the abandon of God, to forgive as God forgives, to be compassionate as God is compassionate. Our lives are to be letters of recommendation witnessing to the world that the reign of God has indeed come, that the Spirit of God does transform lives, that the Lord is kind and merciful.

Ninth Sunday in Ordinary Time
Deuteronomy 5:12-15

The Decalogue, or Ten Commandments, summarizes the most important religious, familial, and social dimensions of Israel's life. Within this collection the commandment to observe the Sabbath acts as a bridge connecting obligations toward God and responsibilities for others. It is the only commandment that includes the rationale for its observance, a rationale situated at the heart of Israel's identity.

Sabbath comes from the Hebrew word for rest *(shābat)*. Its very name states the principal manner of observance. The Sabbath is the LORD's day, a day set apart from other days. It is a period of sacred time or "time out of time," when normal activity ceases and attention to the things of God becomes primary. While some form of worship is normally the way "time out of time" is marked as sacred, the commandment states that rest from work is the primary way the sacredness of the day should be observed. Rest from the activity that is required if one is to survive and prosper is a way of acknowledging total dependence on God. This act of acknowledgment is itself a form of worship.

The injunction begins with a positive imperative, "Take care," or "Watch carefully" *(shāmar)*. Although it is essentially synonymous with "Remember" *(zākar,* v. 15; cf. Exod 20:8), it includes the idea of diligent observance.

In this version of the Decalogue, rest on the Sabbath is connected with Israel's deliverance from Egyptian oppression. By refraining from labor, the people will be commemorating God's freeing them from the hard labor of bondage. Remembering their own state of servitude and the graciousness of God in their deliverance from it, it is only right that they should observe this day by granting the same freedom from labor to their own servants. In this way they will be reenacting God's saving action. Sabbath thus becomes the memorial day of liberation.

The Sabbath rest is to be observed by the entire household. Even the resident alien is included in this commemoration, a procedure reminding the people of the time when they were aliens in a foreign land. It might sound strange that even the animals were granted rest, except that work animals were often considered extensions of their owners. Besides, they would not be engaged in work if the workers were not.

The religious observance of the Sabbath is one of the marks of the people of God. In fact, it came to be regarded as *the* sign of the covenant (Exod 31:13, 17). Sabbath rest is not only an indication of humanitarian sensitivity providing the people with well-needed rest and relaxation, it is also a mark of social consciousness, attending to the needs of their servants and of those among them who did not enjoy all the privileges the law granted to full covenant members. Along with the acknowledgment of God's redemptive intervention and provident care, this Sabbath principle of rest permeates the religious character of Israelite law.

Psalm 81:3-4, 5-6, 6-8, 10-11

The congregation is summoned to the celebration of the fall festival variously called Tabernacles, Booths, or the feast of Ingathering. Of the three pilgrimage feasts (Passover and Pentecost are the other two), this was probably the most important and the best attended (cf. Lev 23:33-43; Num 29:12-39; Deut 16:13-17). It was a week-long harvest festival marking the culmination of the agricultural year, a time for giving thanks to God for the abundance the earth had provided. During this time the people lived in temporary huts. This custom may have originated as an actual practice, the huts providing shelter during the harvesting. Later, when the festival was celebrated in Jerusalem after the harvest, this custom was retained but took on new meaning. It was then a way of remembering the time of their sojourn after being liberated from bondage in Egypt, when temporary huts were the only dwellings available to them.

All of the ancient agricultural festivals were gradually linked with the Exodus experience (v. 6). They took on great historical significance, each emphasizing some aspect of this foundational event. By the time of the people's return from exile in Babylon, the public reading of the law had became an important feature of the celebration of this feast (vv. 10–11; cf. Neh 8:1-18). This reading of the law underscores the importance of listening to God. It points to the responsibilities that are theirs as God's special people.

The structure of this psalm response recalls elements of the ritual enacted during the celebration of this festival. The trumpet is sounded, calling the people to the feast (vv. 3–4). There they listen to the words of God (vv. 6–11). The Hebrew is unclear. Did the psalmist hear an unfamiliar voice, or was it the message of the revelation that was strange? Most likely it was the former, for what follows (vv. 7–8) appears to be a reference to liberation from Egypt. As is quite common in cultic celebrations, after God's gracious deeds are recounted the obligations of the people are recited (cf. Exod 20:2ff.; Deut 5:6ff.). Since God has so favored them, they in turn are obligated to God.

This psalm should not be viewed as merely a short form of recitation of the law. Rather, it contains elements of a covenant renewal ceremony. Although the communal gathering is not explicitly identified as the feast of Ingathering, it is clearly a specific liturgical celebration, at the heart of which is a reflection of the mutual exchange between God and the people. The law that is given to the people is really a set of directives that indicate how they should respond to the magnanimous providence of God shown to them in the past. God's mighty acts on their behalf reveal God's true identity in their regard. Obedience to the law reveals their true identity as the people of this magnanimous God. The feast of Ingathering is a time set apart when the people can remember this and recommit themselves to the God who has always been committed to them.

2 Corinthians 4:6-11

Although Paul speaks about the life and ministry he shares with his missionary companions, he is really talking about the power of God in Jesus Christ that is manifested through them. He plays on the image of light, linking its creation by God (v. 6; cf. Gen 1:3) to his own ministry of evangelization. God, who brought light into existence, is the very light that enlightened the missionaries to go into the world and preach a message of enlightenment. Paul uses the image in a slightly different way when he claims that it is this same God whose glory shines forth as brilliant light from the face of Jesus Christ. The countenance of Moses, made resplendent by his encounter with God, comes immediately to mind (cf. Exod 34:29-30). In both cases it is the glory of God that shines forth.

Without denying the brilliance of this light and the illumination that brings about enlightenment to everything in its range, Paul turns his attention to the negligible character played by the evangelizers themselves. One might think that such a dazzling light would be held by a vessel of comparable worth. On the contrary, the vessel is relatively worthless. According to Paul, this is so that the power to enlighten will be recognized as coming from God and will not be mistaken as belonging to the lamp from which it emanates. It is the light that is important, not the container that holds it.

The human vessel through which the wondrous power and glory of God shine forth is subject to every sort of human affliction, yet it is not destroyed by it. Paul gives a few examples of the adversity that the missionaries face, and then he relates the suffering to the dying of Jesus. He is not here referring to the death of Jesus into which believers are plunged at baptism. Rather, he is talking about dying, the ongoing process of pain and diminishment that we face because we are mortal.

Paul describes missionary suffering in this way in order to emphasize the lifelong participation in the sufferings of Jesus that it demands. Returning to the notion of shining forth, he maintains that it is precisely through this bodily identification with the physical dying of Jesus that the resplendent life of Jesus will be revealed. As a brilliant light can shine forth from a paltry lamp, so the resplendence of the life of Jesus can radiate from a frail mortal person.

The reading ends on a note of paradox. Those who live are constantly given up to death. However, this death is the way to life. Identified with the sufferings of Jesus, the living persons witness to his life. Jesus lives through them just as the light shines forth from the lamp.

Mark 2:23-28–3:6 (B)

The reading consists of two conflict stories, one dealing with the behavior of the disciples, the other with a healing by Jesus. Both occurred on the Sabbath, and that is the point of contention. The Jews treasured the Sabbath as a gift from God. It linked the people with the creation of the universe (Exod 20:8-11) as well as with their own deliverance from bondage in Egypt (Deut 5:12-15). Refraining from work was a way of acknowledging that they prevailed because of the goodness of God and not because they had been able to provide for themselves.

The behavior of the disciples is not censured because they helped themselves to the heads of grain from someone else's crop. The law of the land was very sensitive to the physical needs of travelers. It allowed them to snack as they passed the fields (Deut 23:25). The Pharisees charged that this was reaping and threshing, an occupation that was forbidden on the Sabbath (Exod 34:21).

In challenging the behavior of the disciples, the Pharisees are really questioning the religious devotion of Jesus, who was with them at the time and, as their leader, was responsible for their conduct. In many societies even today such a personal challenge seriously threatens the social standing of the individual. It constitutes public shaming. The only way to save face is to counter the challenge with another one. Jesus did just that. He answered the question with a second question, employing an argument from Scripture.

Citing an incident from the Davidic tradition (1 Sam 21:1-6), he showed that at times human need superseded even religious law. (The fact that Ahimelech was high priest at that time and not his son Abiathar does not cancel the force of the argument.) David, long considered the model of piety, did not transgress a Sabbath regulation, but he did lay aside an injunction of the law

(Lev 24:5-9). If he could act in this way, certainly the lord of the Sabbath could do the same.

The conflict continues in the synagogue. In a daring action Jesus heals a man with an impairment. From the perspective of the Pharisees he has violated the Sabbath. However, once again Jesus has put human need above the law. More than this, the Jews believed that on the Sabbath God rested from everything except creating new life and executing judgment through death. Healing is a form of creating life. When Jesus healed, he was acting in a way that only God should act on the Sabbath. This very behavior made a bold claim.

Jesus identified himself as the lord of the Sabbath. Claiming no authority but his own, he challenged the Pharisees' custom of "putting a hedge around the law" to ensure that it would not be violated. By the time of Jesus, this oral law had expanded to 613 individual precepts. Under such circumstances it had become for the people more a burden to carry than a gift from God to be cherished and enjoyed. This is what Jesus challenged, not the law itself. He was an observant Jew, but he interpreted the law in a way that was different from that of some of the leaders of his day. The fundamental question remains: By what authority does he do such things?

Themes of the Day

As we move toward the end of this cluster of Sundays, we adjust our focus once again. Although we still consider the theme of discipleship, we see it today through the lens of christology. We reflect on the radicalness of the person of Jesus in order to understand the radicalness of our discipleship. Only then will we consider the character of discipleship and the measure of suffering it may entail.

By What Authority?

By what authority does Jesus make the claims that he does? Through what power does he accomplish the deeds that he performs? He moves through our lives with such gentleness and calm, yet so often he upsets the status quo, the comfortable patterns we have established for ourselves. He lives by a principle that we all accept but frequently misunderstand: people in need come first! Laws and regulations are necessary if peace and harmony are to reign in society, but people in need come first. Religious practices and customs demonstrate the depth of our commitment to God, but people in need come first.

Jesus does not challenge the law, but he does challenge the way we interpret it. He is the Lord of the Sabbath, and of the law, and of our doctrine. He points out what is essential and what can be changed. He teaches us to interpret our cherished traditions through the lens of human need, not rigid compliance. He is the Son of Man, the one on whose face shines the glory of God. This is the authority by which he makes his claims.

Earthen Vessels

As disciples, we are earthen vessels that contain the glory of God. Through us the life of Jesus is revealed, a life that is faithful to traditions yet bold in its fidelity. When we put people in need first, we could find ourselves in opposition to the status quo, to a "me first" attitude or a consumerist mentality. We may have to forgo convenience so that others have necessities. As difficult as this may be, as weak in these matters as we find ourselves, the power of God takes hold of us and the glory of God shines forth from us, and we can accomplish great things in Christ's name.

The Dying of Jesus

The radicalness of Jesus put him in conflict with forces in his world. The radicalness of our discipleship does the same to us. We may be afflicted in various ways, crushed by others, full of doubts ourselves. Yet in the face of this we cling to him. We may be persecuted, even struck down. Yet in the face of this we cling to him. God knows that we are merely earthen vessels; God knows that we are subject to criticism and misunderstanding. In the midst of all of this God shines in our hearts, keeping us from despair, from being abandoned, from being destroyed. Joined to Jesus we are one with him, and it is out of this union that we live and serve. We do not merely imitate Christ, we are incorporated into him, and as such we carry in our bodies the dying of Jesus.

Tenth Sunday in Ordinary Time
Genesis 3:9-15

This reading is part of one of the best-known stories of the Bible. However, as often happens familiarity does not always guarantee accuracy. It has traditionally been referred to as the Fall, suggesting that the couple originally enjoyed some kind of supernatural status from which they were reduced. Actually, the extraordinariness of many of their features and of everything that surrounds them should be attributed to the mythic character of the narrative and not to any preternatural gifts that were lost. A second way this story has been understood is as a fall from grace. This is not accurate either, since it is not until the Christian era that grace is understood as a state of being from which one can fall. It is best to think of this simply as a story about sin. This part of the narrative recounts some of the consequences brought on by the violation of a prohibition set down by God.

The nakedness of the couple has also been variously interpreted. They had been naked before they sinned, and it had not caused shame. What had changed? Although it has often been associated with sex, a look at the vocabulary would indicate otherwise. Two different though related words are used for "naked." The one that describes them immediately after their creation by God is the most frequently used and simply means being uncovered (*ʿârôm*). However, the one used to describe them after their sin indicates that they are exposed (*ʿêrōm*), fully aware of their inability to hide their guilt before God. This second word appears in the Bible only ten times (also Ezek 16:7, 22, 39; 18:7, 16; 23:29; Deut 28:48), and it always connotes some kind of spiritual deprivation.

After the sin the woman and man are not only naked (spiritually exposed), they are also unwilling to take responsibility for their fault. Each blames another. The woman admits that she was tricked. The serpent (not to be understood as the devil) had not really lied to her. Their eyes were indeed opened and they now knew right from wrong. As is usually the case with temptation, she allowed herself to be misled.

Initially described as cunning (*ʿārûm*, Gen 3:1), the serpent is now cursed (*ʿârur*). While several Hebrew verbs are translated "curse," this one means to bind with some kind of a spell, to hem in with obstacles, to render powerless to resist. This cunning creature is now banned from other animals and brought low, forced to eat dust, the very symbol of death and decay. The limits of its power are sketched in the final condition of its punishment. There will be constant hostility between the serpent and the woman, between the various manifestations of temptation and the children that she will bear. Contrary to the Marian interpretation captured in the pictures of the Immaculate Conception, it is the offspring who will have his heel on the serpent's head, not the woman. This final declaration states that throughout their lives human beings will always have to battle temptation.

Psalm 130:1-2, 3-4, 5-6, 7-8

The psalm response comes from one of the seven psalms known in Christian devotion as the Penitential Psalms. It opens with a cry for relief (vv. 1–2), which is followed by an acknowledgment of the helplessness of sinful human beings in the presence of the righteous God (vv. 3–4), a confession of faith (vv. 5–6), and an acknowledgment of God's covenant love (vv. 7–8).

The psalmist has been cast into the very depths of misery. Depths refers to deep waters, the place of ultimate chaos, the place where death reigns and life has no power. This misery could be a form of physical affliction, an interior torment, or some kind of hardship brought on by another. The psalm itself is not specific. Whatever the case may be, the psalmist knows where to look for help. God is prevailed upon to turn an open ear to this fervent supplication. This in itself is an act of faith and trust. Faith that God *can* come to the psalmist's aid and trust that God indeed *will*. There is no direct correlation made here between the psalmist's misfortune and possible sin, but what follows suggests that there is some kind of connection.

The psalmist contrasts two ways of understanding God's manner of dealing with sinners. The first focuses on strict retributive justice. If God ever meted out the exact punishments that human sin deserves, no one would be able to endure it. This admission asserts not only the character of human culpability but also its scope. Rebellion against God is a serious matter, and all women and men are guilty of it. Even those who are fundamentally upright deviate at times from the path of righteousness.

The psalmist insists that God acts toward sinners in a very different way. Moved by compassion, God shows mercy to those who have sinned and grants them forgiveness. There is no way that human beings can earn this forgiveness. It is a free gift from God, granted so that God may be revered or feared (*yārēʾ*). While this expression includes the notion of dread and terror, its principal connotation is reverence and awe in the face of God's majesty and power. Here it is God's willingness to forgive that evokes such awe.

The proper attitude of one who fears God is trust (the verb is also translated "wait for"). Trust requires that we bide our own time until God's designated time. Willingness to wait is frequently the measure of one's trust. The psalmist is willing to wait, but not without eager anticipation. In fact, the psalmist waits for God to put an end to the terrors that accompany misery and the afflictions that characterize life; more than a sentinel waits for the dawn to extinguish the darkness and terror of night and bring to conclusion the arduous time of watching.

The psalmist maintains that God will surely act in the future because God is committed to Israel with covenant love (*ḥesed*). This love is the basis of God's mercy and forgiveness, of God's willingness to redeem Israel from all its sins. It is also the basis of the psalmist's own trust in God's graciousness.

2 Corinthians 4:13–5:1

Paul begins his discourse with a reference to a claim made by a psalmist who kept faith in God even in the midst of affliction (cf. Ps 116:10). Like the ancient poet, Paul is struggling with issues of life and death. In this instruction he uses several different metaphors to illustrate the contrast that exists between them. While his concern is for the people who will hear the gospel message he preaches, the primary focus of his preaching is the resurrection of Jesus and its results in the lives of those who believe. All of the imagery used flows from this fundamental tenet of Christian faith or further characterizes it.

Paul's confidence is in God, who raised Jesus from the dead and who will also raise all those who believe in Jesus. He maintains that both he and the Corinthians belong to that latter group. In fact, he declares that the more people hear of God's goodness to him and to the Corinthians, the more they will join their ranks in glorifying God.

Not even the sufferings that are part of the Christian life can discourage Paul. Without minimizing their severity, he contrasts them with the rewards of a life of faith. He contraposes the outer self with the inner self, the unseen with the seen, the transitory with the eternal, the earthly with the heavenly. In each of the first members of the pair, death holds sway; in each of the second members, resurrection triumphs. Paul is actually contrasting the present age with the age to come, the time when all believers will be raised with Jesus and will stand in God's presence (v. 14). The word "therefore" (v. 16) suggests that Paul's unshakable confidence rests on this resurrection faith.

It is because they live in the "now but not yet" that Christians experience both the diminishment of this age and the glory of the age to come. They often experience both at the same time. Their outer selves waste away, but their inner selves are renewed. In fact, the glory that is produced in them is the product of the affliction they willingly endure. According to Paul, measure for measure there is really no comparison, even though the sufferings can be seen and the glory is imperceptible. Contrasting this age and the age to come, he contends that the former is temporary, as is everything that is part of it, but the latter is eternal, as is everything associated with it.

Using more concrete imagery, Paul insists that while we remain in this age our dwellings are temporary, susceptible to ruin and collapse. Like everything else in this age, they are ephemeral. However, there are dwelling places for us in the age to come, heavenly dwelling places made of durable material that lasts forever. Paul is here probably talking generally about a state of being rather than specifically about our bodies. However, this is the final contrast of the two ages, and as such it can be seen as bringing his instruction back to the theme of resurrection with which it began.

Mark 3:20-35

This reading contains an example of intercalation, a distinctive characteristic of Mark's Gospel where one narrative is sandwiched within another. Here, a report of a hostile encounter with scribes from Jerusalem (vv. 22–30) is found within one about the arrival and concern of members of Jesus' family (vv. 20–21, 31–35). Though very distinct stories, when placed together as they are here, they interpret each other.

The narrative states that Jesus came home, probably not to Nazareth, the place he originally called home, but to Capernaum, the place he has now made his home. His relatives (later identified as his mother and his brothers, v. 31), have come to seize him, to take charge of him with strength if need be. They believe that he is beside himself, out of his mind. Why they think this is not stated. Most likely they have heard of the claims he has been making and of the wonders he has performed, and they might fear for his safety. Their concern betrays their lack of faith in the authenticity of these claims and in the origin of the wonders.

The scribes also misunderstand Jesus, but it is not out of concern for him. They acknowledge that he has extraordinary power to cast out demons, but they ascribe this power to the prince of demons. They speak of Beelzebul (Baal-zebul, or "Lord of the temple"), while Jesus speaks of Satan. Both are references to the same spirit of evil.

Once again the challenge of the scribes is an attempt to shame Jesus (cf. Mark 2:23-28, Ninth Sunday in Ordinary Time). It calls for a response that will demonstrate that he has retained his honor. He counters their accusation with not one but two parables. He first points out the absurdity of their allegation, maintaining that neither a house nor a kingdom would be able to endure if either were divided against itself. Both would collapse from within. In order for either the house or the kingdom to stand firm it would need internal coherence and stability. With a second image Jesus alludes to the ruin of a house when one stronger than the householder attacks and plunders the property. Before this pillage can be accomplished the attacker has to incapacitate the householder, thereby preventing any kind of resistance. This parable suggests that Jesus is indeed incapacitating the evil one and is bringing the house of evil to ruin.

Jesus ends his riposte with a pronouncement that is dire in its consequences. To impute the power of the Holy Spirit that is at work in Jesus to the spirit of evil is an unforgivable blasphemy.

Attention turns again to the family of Jesus, who are outside, while Jesus is inside in the midst of a gathered crowd. They have already demonstrated their misunderstanding of Jesus' mission. Jesus now makes a daring statement about family ties. In a society where familial bonds and obligations supersede all other responsibilities, Jesus claims that real kinship is determined by acceptance of the will of God, not by blood or marriage. Acceptance of God's will and God's marvelous deeds is the fundamental challenge in both of these stories.

Themes of the Day

We conclude our meditation on discipleship with a final consideration of the power of God. We have seen that it is this power that transforms ordinary women and men into faithful followers of Jesus. It is the same power that makes them fearless in danger and steadfast in the face of opposition. In today's readings this power is pitted against the forces of evil. We see that this conflict is resolved in two ways: God's power can be misconstrued, or it can bring forth a new family of faithful believers.

The Power of God Versus the Forces of Evil

We do not have to live long before we realize that we are participants in a constant struggle between good and evil. We see it in the world at large. Good people war with one another, unjust economic systems that were set up to help people now exploit the vulnerable. Groups committed to various goals demean those who disagree with them. In our families we may encounter infidelity, abuse, and alienation. We find in ourselves strains of addiction, resentment, despair. We who are the offspring of the woman in the garden are in constant enmity with the offspring of the serpent. However, the exorcisms performed by Jesus and his disciples show that God's power is supreme and can cast out the demons themselves.

God's Power Misconstrued

Those who do not want to accept goodness that does not conform to their standards for or models of it frequently dismiss it by claiming that this goodness is actually evil. People who refuse to obey corrupt or outdated laws are often prosecuted; some people who work in solidarity with the oppressed to change unjust social structures are labeled anarchists. They follow in the footsteps of Jesus, who was accused of operating with the power of the prince of demons. Such attitudes may spring from ignorance or misunderstanding, but when they are the product of hardness of heart, they are nothing less than blasphemy, the sin against the Holy Spirit.

There is a very stern warning here. Even those who were the closest to Jesus, the members of his own family or kingroup, misunderstood the origin of his power. We who claim kinship with him but who rely on our own power and insight are no more preserved from error than were they. It is only in the power of God that we can stand secure. We are told to take heart in this matter and to fix our gaze on the things of God.

New Kinship Bonds

It is the power of God that re-creates us. Acceptance of Jesus as the one who wields the power of God makes us brothers and sisters of Jesus and, like Mary who bore him to the world, mothers of him as well. In this same power we can be victorious in our struggle with the offspring of the serpent; we too can cast out the demons that have taken possession of us and of others. We too can gather with those who sit around Jesus, listening to his words and being transformed by them. By the power of God we are made a new people with a new identity and a new destiny. By the power of God we will enjoy the fullness of redemption.

Ordinary Time (Part Two)

Eleventh Sunday Ezekiel 17:22-24 I have exalted the small tree	Psalm 92:2-3, 13-16 Give thanks to the LORD	2 Corinthians 5:6-10 Please the Lord	Mark 4:26-34 Like a mustard seed
Twelfth Sunday Job 38:1, 8-11 God stills the waters	Psalm 107:23-26, 28-31 Give thanks to the LORD	2 Corinthians 5:14-17 New things have come	Mark 4:35-41 The wind and sea obey him
Thirteenth Sunday Wisdom 1:13-15; 2:23-24 Through the devil, death came	Psalm 30:2, 4, 5-6, 11-13 I will praise you, LORD	2 Corinthians 8:7, 9, 13-15 Supply the needs of the poor	Mark 5:21-43 I say to you, arise
Fourteenth Sunday Ezekiel 2:2-5 A prophet in a rebellious house	Psalm 123:1-4 Pleading for God's mercy	2 Corinthians 12:7-10 When I am weak, I am strong	Mark 6:1-6 A prophet without honor
Fifteenth Sunday Amos 7:12-15 Prophesy to my people	Psalm 85:9-14 Let me see your kindness	Ephesians 1:3-14 God chose Christ	Mark 6:7-13 He sent them out
Sixteenth Sunday Jeremiah 23:1-6 God is the shepherd	Psalm 23:1-6 The LORD is my shepherd	Ephesians 2:13-18 Christ is our peace	Mark 6:30-34 Sheep without a shepherd

Ordinary Time (Part Two)

Initial Reading of the Ordinary Lectionary (Part Two)

Introduction

Ordinary Time is just that, ordinary. The readings for this segment treat aspects of life that meet us day in and day out. They offer us a perspective for discovering that ordinary does not mean empty or dull. Ordinary is really the norm, and so we are treated to insights that can deepen our appreciation of the norm.

First Testament Readings

Once again the first readings are in some way linked with the Gospel. However, they create their own narrative when read consecutively. They all depict God contending with conflict or opposition. God reverses the status of certain trees in order to demonstrate God's own sovereign rule, as if it has been challenged. God responds to Job's demand for an explanation by showing that Job would not be able to understand God's reasons even if he were told them. The enmity between God and the devil is illustrated in God's commitment to life and the devil's desire for death. The messengers of God must also face opposition: Amos is told to go home, and Ezekiel has to deal with a rebellious people. Finally, even those who had been charged to care for the flock proved to be unfaithful. Taken together, the readings show that God's patience is sorely tried.

Psalms

The responsorial psalms paint a very interesting picture of human response to divine activity. There are hymns that praise God for the power and might that is shown in these conflicts. There are also pleas for mercy and forgiveness when the believers realize they are no better than the people who stood in opposition to God. The last psalm portrays the tender care God provides for those who allow themselves to be cared for by the gentle divine shepherd.

Epistles

The continuous readings from two different epistles give us a glimpse of issues that faced these early communities and the theology that governed the way they were told to handle them. With the Corinthians we learn that all of our actions, whatever they may be, should be motivated by the love of Christ. When we faithfully act in this way, we are indeed a new creation, fashioned after the pattern of Christ. We will then treat each other with the same love we have received from Christ, and we will be willing to accept the limitations of our lives, realizing that God's grace is enough. With the Ephesians we hear this same idea of living our lives "in Christ." It is in Christ that all enmity will be overcome; he is our peace.

Gospels

The Gospel readings are all clustered around the theme of christology. Each one offers a picture of a particular facet of Christ. Before we examine any of these striking pictures, we pause for a moment to consider the meaning of metaphorical language. This helps us to probe the deep meaning of the characterizations of Jesus that present him as one who wields the power of the Creator, who has authority over death, who wears the heavy prophetic mantle, and who is so confident of the authenticity of his mission that he authorizes others to share in it with him and to continue it in his absence.

Mosaic of Readings

These readings create a mosaic depicting various aspects of human resistance to God and of God's willingness to forgive this rebellion and to offer women and men of all ages an even greater share of divine grace. It is as if God's love will not be thwarted, it will not allow itself to be conquered by sin. Although the readings provide us with guidelines for faithful living, they really invite us to step back and stand in awe of the loving God that is ours.

Readings

Eleventh Sunday in Ordinary Time
Ezekiel 17:22-24

With this fable about a cedar tree, Ezekiel pronounces an oracle of salvation. The metaphor of the tender shoot calls to mind a similar reference to the house of David, where that dynasty is described as a branch or twig (cf. Isa 11:1). In both instances the favored sprout is cultivated by God until it grows into an exceptional plant able to care for itself and to yield blessings for others. The connection between these two metaphors is applicable, since the tender shoot in this passage is destined to be planted on the heights of Israel, the very place from which the Davidic dynasty ruled. There is a further, though subtle, connection between these two images. The topmost branches of a tree are often referred to as the crown. The tender shoot spoken of here could be regarded as a sprig of that crown. The branch or twig in the Isaian passage grows out of the trunk of Jesse, the family of David. In both cases a mere sprig contains great promise for the future.

The words spoken here come from the LORD. They describe a reversal that will be performed by God. What was once insignificant and vulnerable will be exalted. The shoot taken from the crown of the tree will be planted on a high and lofty mountain, a site that is traditionally regarded as the place where God dwells. There it will flourish, produce branches, yield fruit, and provide shelter for every kind of winged animal. All of this will evoke the admiration of those who gaze upon it. This tree, which will be specially cultivated by God, is unlike the trees of the open field, which are wild. It will be a chosen tree, a majestic cedar, known for its strength and its precious wood.

There is a messianic flavor to the image in this passage. Whether it is an allusion to the initial lowliness of the Davidic house and its rise to prominence or to the initial insignificance of the entire people and their ultimate achievement, the image itself describes one of the most basic tenets of Israel's faith: God chooses the weak of the world to confound the strong. The dramatic exaltation of this noble tree will bear testimony to this reversal before all of the other trees. Its splendor will declare that the LORD is the one who overturns the fortunes of the lofty and of the lowly, of the vigorous and of the withered.

The divine force of these prophetic words is underscored in the very last verse: The LORD has spoken it, and it is done. This is an example of performative language, the kind of speech that brought light out of darkness, that separated the primordial waters and caused the dry land to appear (cf. Gen 1:3-31). The transformation of the tender shoot is but another wonder performed by the sovereign LORD.

Psalm 92:2-3, 13-14, 15-16

The psalm begins with a declaration of the appropriateness of thanking God. One's name was really an integral part of one's very being. Therefore, to praise the name of the Most High is to praise the LORD. Singing praises is a way of thanking God. Hymns of thanksgiving normally include reasons for gratitude. Although these verses do not mention specific examples of God's beneficence for which the psalmist is grateful, there is an allusion to the goodness that God has shown and that should elicit thankfulness. Lovingkindness *(ḥesed)* and faithfulness *(ʾĕmûnâ)* are part of the vocabulary of covenant. Nothing is more worthy of our gratitude than the inestimable privilege of covenant relationship with a kind and faithful God.

The cultic dimension of this prayer can be seen in the psalmist's declaration that it is good to praise God throughout the night, even until dawn. This suggests some kind of vigil, the kind that was normally part of the devotional life that unfolded at shrines. Individuals often held prayerful vigils in petition for some favor from God or in thanksgiving for a blessing received. As is frequently the case with religious people, thankfulness overflows and cannot be adequately voiced in a simple statement. Here the psalmist says that it is good to spend a night of prayer giving thanks to God.

The rewards of righteousness are graphically sketched, using imagery from the natural world of the Near East. The fertility of the familiar palm tree and the longevity of the neighboring cedar of Lebanon are apt metaphors for the blessings that will flow from fidelity to one's covenant responsibilities. The statement about the house of the LORD and the courts of God (v. 14) suggests the temple and is a second allusion to worship. To be "planted in the house of the LORD" is probably a reference to temple devotion, which could be part of the life of any Israelite, rather than to temple service, which was reserved for just a few men. Just as trees were planted near water, their source of life, so the righteous are planted in the presence of God, their source of life.

The fruitfulness of the righteous is further described. It will endure even into old age, a time when living things normally cease to be productive. The vicissitudes of life that too frequently wear people down will not undermine their fruitfulness, because they are planted in the presence of God, the source of all life. As long as they are faithful in their covenant commitment, they will be able to draw on the strength and life-giving forces of this presence.

Finally, these remarkable lives will bear witness to the uprightness of God. Once again, the covenant relationship is the basis of this hymn of thanksgiving. The righteous are blessed because they have been faithful. However, the fruitfulness of their lives is a sign that God too has been faithful to the covenant promises that were made.

2 Corinthians 5:6-10

Here Paul instructs the Corinthians on how to live in this time, a time when, though committed to the Lord, they do not see the Lord face-to-face. While there is explicit direction for the believers to be confident and, based on this confidence, to live courageously (vv. 6, 8), this is really a sermon that draws a clear distinction between this life and the next. It emphasizes the need to live by faith in this life, because we cannot live by sight alone.

Paul uses spatial metaphors to drawn a clear distinction between the state of being in this life and that of being in a life to come. The contrast is between being at home *(endēméō)* and being abroad *(ekdēméō)*. It is a question of fully belonging. During this life believers are at home in the body but away from the Lord. In the next life it will be just the opposite; they will be away from the body and at home with the Lord.

Paul is not here denigrating the body. Rather, he is using a very concrete metaphor to characterize a state of being. Nor is he suggesting that believers do not really belong to this life but that their real home is in heaven. Instead, he is saying that their home is with the Lord, and in this life they are not fully with the Lord. Finally, Paul does not disdain this life. Instead, he prefers being with the Lord, and because he cannot enjoy the presence of the Lord fully in this life, he prefers the next life, where union with the Lord will be full.

Verse 7 holds the key to Paul's instruction: while in the body, believers walk by faith and not by sight. Though not completely at home with the Lord, they are not really totally separated from the Lord either. They live by faith in the Lord, committed to those things that are unseen. Trusting that full union is in the future, they live in the present while following the example of the Lord, desiring to please him whether at home or abroad.

Paul ends his exhortation with a sobering thought. At the end of this life all will stand before Christ to be judged according to whether or not they did in fact live lives of faith after his example. Carrying his argument to its final conclusion, Paul maintains that those who did not live such lives will not be able to be fully at home with the Lord. This judgment carries a universal dimension: all will be called to appear (v. 10) before God. However, it also has a personal dimension: each will be individually accountable. While salvation is a gratuitous gift from God, it requires personal acceptance and faithful response.

Mark 4:26-34

In his teaching Jesus frequently used parables, a form that is associated with the wisdom tradition. In many ways parables are brainteasers. They engage two very different realities and use one to throw light on the deeper meaning of the other. They are used by sages precisely because they force the hearers to stretch their imaginations and to make connections they ordinarily would not make. Jesus used this literary form to teach about the reign of God, that mysterious reality that seems to belong to another world yet is within our grasp here.

Although the word "parable" is not used, the first saying (vv. 26–29) is certainly parabolic, describing how the reign of God works. It is like seed that has been planted by an individual but then takes root and grows and produces in some secret place within the earth. The seed itself may be quite inconsequential, but deep within itself it possesses great potential. Furthermore, although this potential unfolds before the eyes of human beings, the secrets of its growth are really beyond human comprehension. Human beings plant the seed, watch it grow, and harvest its yield, but the seed works in its own mysterious ways.

So does the reign of God. It takes root and grows and produces in secret places within human reality. In fact, it is usually found in places where one would least expect to find it—among the poor and despised, in the hearts of those who suffer, in the lives of the persecuted. The potential of the reign of God is often contained in what appears to be inconsequential. Yet it thrives in its own mysterious ways.

The amazing qualities of a seed are the focus of the second metaphor (vv. 30–32), which is actually identified as a parable. Contrary to the claim within the saying, the mustard seed is not really the smallest seed among the plants. Nor does it actually produce the largest plant. Parables are figures of speech, and they often contain figurative language, language meant to make a point, not to describe things accurately. Here the exaggeration emphasizes the paradox of this negligible seed producing the largest plant. The parable points to the phenomenal growth of the reign of God. It also suggests its universality. Just as the branches of the plant become so spacious that the birds of the heavens can roost there, so the reign of God will grow so vast as to provide shelter for all.

The passage ends with a summary statement about Jesus' teaching in parables. It is a curious statement, for it suggests that the crowds understood the meaning of the parables, but Jesus had to explain them to his disciples. It may really mean that the parables themselves could be comprehended on several different levels, and while the crowds might grasp the obvious meaning, Jesus revealed their deeper meaning in private to his disciples. The parables of Jesus forced his hearers to stretch their imaginations and to make connections they might not ordinarily make. The presumption was that those who followed Jesus were always willing or able to do this.

Themes of the Day

The period after Easter is called Ordinary Time, not because it is banal or un-eventful but because there are no significant liturgical seasons or major feasts of the Lord within it. In a sense it is like most of life, average and somewhat routine. However, this does not mean that it is devoid of theological significance or religious possibility. The readings for today demonstrate this. Like much of life, they all deal with common themes: a tree, personal maturity, human life, a modest seed. Also like much of life, these simple, everyday realities abound with religious relevance. The readings today remind us that poetic imagery is an apt way of describing the mysterious presence of God in our midst; that this mystery unfolds by degrees like the gradual process of growth; that we need faith to understand the parabolic.

The Exaggerated Presence of God

Metaphors are not merely clever literary devices that delight the mind and tweak the imagination. Sometimes they are the only avenue we have to describe or illustrate something that cannot be captured by precise definition. Parabolic, symbolic, or poetic language carries us into a world of meaning that is closed to strict rationality. It takes us beyond the confines of structure, language, and ordinary experience, there to leap into mystery. It enables us to see beyond the surface of things. It even allows us to consider the possibility of what is incredible.

Although God is present in all things, sustaining them and allowing them to follow their natural courses, God really transcends all things. Therefore metaphorical language may be the best means for speaking about God and the things of God. It enables us to live in the tension created by the metaphor, a tension that both reveals something about God and conceals God's real nature. It allows us to deal with the mystery of God without profaning it. We know that the reign of God cannot be contained in a mustard seed, yet we also know that it is a wonderful image of it, for it helps us to realize that the smallest may well be the greatest.

The Mystery Unfolds Gradually

Today's readings employ images that illustrate gradual growth. The cedar began as a seedling. It took years to grow into the magnificent tree that it is. The same is true of the mustard tree. It is not an overnight phenomenon. It requires time to develop the trunk and branches that make up this remarkable plant. The development of moral integrity in a human being is just as gradual.

Rooted in God, it flourishes in God's presence and produces fruit even into old age. So it is with the reign of God. It begins in very ordinary circumstances, and it matures gradually until it has spread itself far and wide.

We See with Eyes of Faith

Although the mystery of the reign of God unfolds within human history, we need eyes of faith to recognize it. Like the cedar and the mustard seed, it grows within the concreteness of human experience. Just as the life force that thrusts the branches farther and farther out cannot itself be seen, so the reign of God is mysterious, even incomprehensible. Still, it is there, inviting us, urging us to move forward, transforming our world.

Twelfth Sunday in Ordinary Time
Job 38:1, 8-11

The reading from Job reports a theophany, a self-revelation of God. Job hears the voice of God from within a storm wind. Using questions, a pedagogical technique associated with the wisdom tradition, God leads Job into a deeper appreciation of certain aspects of God's own self. These questions also enable Job to look beyond the natural world he knows and to consider the forces of nature in a new way.

The questions themselves are more rhetorical than they are requests for answers. God asks questions about the primordial events of creation and the order within the universe that resulted from these events. Throughout this interrogation, there is one fundamental question: Who did it, or who is the creator? There is no doubt in anyone's mind that the creator of this well-working universe is the very one who is posing the questions.

The entire portrayal is mythological in character. In many ancient myths a great battle between the forces of good and the forces of evil preceded creation. Creation itself was actually the ordering of the elements of the universe after this battle had been won. The only one who had the competence initially to bring about this order and continually to preserve it was the creator-god. This section from God's speech to Job addresses God's power over the primordial waters, a common symbol for chaos. The God who shut in the sea, setting limits beyond which it could not go, was the very one who was speaking to Job. The principal insight about God revealed to Job through this questioning was that God was the creator of the world.

The imagery is commanding. The unruly sea was born as from a womb and was then confined behind closed doors. The clouds and darkness that often accompany the stormy sea are merely coverings that were made by God. This proud primordial force is characterized as an infant in swaddling clothes. Clearly, the sea is no match for God.

Job may not have been present at God's cosmological victory, but he is certainly able to appreciate the order that was born of it. He would have known violent storms and the clouds and darkness that were part of it. If he never realized it before, this theophanic questioning by God should have helped him realize that regardless of the fury of the storm and the danger it might pose for women and men, God still had control over the elements of the universe. The forces of nature are not themselves divine but only function within the limits set for them by God. Specifically, the sea, the principal symbol for chaos, is like a vulnerable infant, needing to be cared for and trained. Such insights should have filled Job with both confidence in God and courage in the face of threats to his safety.

Psalm 107:23-24, 25-26, 28-29, 30-31

The responsorial psalm is part of a communal prayer of thanksgiving. In it God is praised for having saved seafarers, those who have risked their lives by traversing dangerous waters (vv. 23–24). Sea *(yām)* is the name of one of the Canaanite gods who threaten the order of the world. In many ancient Near Eastern myths the sea is defeated in the primordial battle by a warrior deity. It is bound but never completely destroyed, and so it remains a constant threat until the end of time, when it will finally be defeated (cf. Rev 21:1). Until that time only one with the power of the primordial warrior is able to keep the monster leashed. In this psalm those who sail the sea have witnessed the power of the Lord in re-harnessing this threatening force.

The Sea of Galilee is noted for the sudden violent storms that rise without warning. On the waters a boat can easily be caught unaware and tossed to and fro. Menacing waves can force it up to the height of their crest and dash it just as far down to the depths, casting those in the boat into a panic, afraid for their lives. The psalmist uses this well-known experience as a metaphor to describe the plight of those who find themselves overwhelmed by circumstances of life. They are like those who are cast about in the sea.

The faith of the people can be seen in the fact of their crying out to the Lord. They knew where to turn in their distress. There was no question about their vulnerability and need for rescue. They were not so self-sufficient as to think they could ride out the storm, withstand its rage through their own resources, and come out of the experience stronger and more self-reliant. These people believed they were facing an adversary with cosmic force, and they knew they were helpless before it.

The description of the rescue is as dramatic as is the depiction of the storm. With no effort at all the LORD quells the fury as one would hush a restless babe in swaddling bands (cf. Job 38:9). By the power of God the savage gale is reduced to a gentle breeze. The mythical monster of the deep is no match for God. In the final scene those who have been delivered from the danger of the sea are filled with joy and gratitude and brought safely to harbor. Once again the LORD has demonstrated the kindness *(ḥesed)* that flows from the covenant bond. Committed to these people, God has not left them in distress. Just as they were led through the waters of the sea in Egypt, here they have been brought out of the waters of the sea. This is certainly reason for praising God and giving thanks.

2 Corinthians 5:14-17

In this passage Paul uses plural language, but it is clear that he is really talking about himself. He insists that the love of Christ leaves him no choice. He is compelled both to accept the significance and implications of faith in Jesus' death and resurrection and to preach this message to others. Christ's love is no sentimental emotion. It is dauntless, even fearsome, expressed in Christ's sacrificial death on behalf of others. It is clear that Paul's own steadfast faith is based on this christological understanding.

In these few verses Paul draws several contrasts. The first and most obvious is between life and death. He further distinguishes between judging things from a human point of view ("according to the flesh") and judging in another, unspecified, way. Finally, he separates what is new from what is old. He does all of this in order to emphasize the unprecedented nature of what has been accomplished through the death and resurrection of Jesus.

In this reading the claim that Jesus died for all is less a statement about the vicarious quality of his death than one about its representational character. In other words, Jesus not only *stands in* for others, he actually *stands for* them. The reference to the new creation calls Adam to mind. Just as Adam stood for all humanity and his sin was the sin of all, so Christ represents the entire race and his death is the death of all. If this is the case and Christ is truly the representative of all, then all are also raised to new life through the power of his resurrection. Paul plays with the idea "to live." He maintains that those who live an ordinary human life live it now in an extraordinary way, no longer for themselves but for Christ, who now lives a resurrected life. Christ died for all, now all live for him.

This insight into the mystery of the resurrection has completely transformed the way Paul perceives both Christ and those who are joined to Christ. In the past he may have judged them from a very human point of view (according to the flesh), but no longer. Previously, Paul (Saul) had regarded Jesus as a renegade, one who led people away from the true worship of God. His conversion gave him new eyes, a new way to see the reality beneath the surface. He now understands Jesus from a more than human point of view, from the point of view of faith.

It is because of his new perception of Jesus—as the one who died and has been raised and who represents all others—that Paul perceives these others in a new way. They are a new creation, transformed by the death and resurrection of Jesus. Once again Paul alludes to the eschatological distinction between this age, when all creation is bound to the present world, and the age to come, when all things will be brought to fulfillment and the reign of God will be established completely and forever. Those who have died and been raised with Christ are the first fruits of this new creation.

Mark 4:35-41

Most of the miracles of Jesus are either healings or exorcisms. This one is clearly a nature miracle, though it does contain a feature that resembles an exorcism. Jesus rebukes the powers of the storm as one would rebuke a demon (cf. 1:25). After a long day with the crowds Jesus and his disciples are on the shore of the lake. From there they enter a boat to go over to the other side. The stage is set for the miracle.

It is not by accident that the powers of chaotic water are harnessed in this nature miracle. In several ancient Near Eastern myths (e.g., *Enuma Elish*) the powers of chaos are portrayed as personified monsters of the deep. A careful look at the first creation account in Genesis reveals vestiges of this kind of thinking. There we see that it was out of the watery abyss that God drew order (Gen 1:2). Chaotic waters also play an important role in the Exodus tradition. In that foundational story of deliverance, God split the waters of the sea in order that the people might cross over to safety (Exodus 14–15). Traces of God's victory over chaotic waters are also found in other places in the Bible (cf. Pss 74:13-14; 89:9-10; 104:6-7).

All these traditions depict the life-and-death conflict between the forces of righteousness and the forces of evil. This is the cosmic and eschatological battle between creation and destruction, and throughout these traditions it is the mighty Creator-God who triumphs and creates anew. The author of this Gospel narrative portrays Jesus as the one who alone can triumph over chaotic water. The disciples certainly recognized this, if only faintly. They asked a question, the answer of which they should have known: Who is this who has power over the sea? Their religious tradition would have told them: This is the Creator-God!

The disciples themselves act toward Jesus in several different ways in this short passage. At the outset they are concerned with his well being. They whisk him away from the crowds and allow him to sleep in the stern of the boat as they try to maneuver it across the sea. When the boat begins to fill with water, they turn to him for help, believing that he is able to save them from harm. However, their words indicate that they are not confident that he will. This is the lack of faith that Jesus challenges. Finally, after they witness his remarkable authority, they are in awe of him, wondering what manner of man he might be.

The question with which the episode ends captures the gist of the account. Who is this man? By what authority does he act? This is not an idle query. It is really the fundamental question raised by the ministry of Jesus. The force of his teaching and the miraculous character of his deeds were not denied. What was questioned was the origin of the power that he exercised. This was doubly an issue, because Jesus did not invoke the power of God before he spoke or acted; he simply spoke or acted and left to those around him to decide about him for themselves.

Themes of the Day

The ordinariness of life can often numb us to the throbbing possibilities of God's power or blind us to the reign of God that takes shape in our midst. Once again the readings help us to peel away what obstructs our sight and to sensitize ourselves to what pulsates within life. We begin by looking again at the way the love of Christ works in us.

The Love of Christ Impels Us

Paul insists that this love completely transforms us, mind and heart. No longer do we judge anything or anyone according to human standards. No longer do we meet injury with assault, insult with retaliation. No longer do we relegate people to the margins of society or hoard the goods that others need to survive. We no longer live for ourselves; we no longer look at life as we did before. Everything is changed in this new worldview. We understand ourselves differently. We perceive ourselves neither as superhuman individuals who are far superior to the rest of humankind nor as wretched human beings who do not deserve to be treated well. Instead, we recognize that, like Job, we sometimes think we are more capable than we really are. Yet God lovingly takes us by the hand and leads us to new insight. Or like the apostles, we are often terrified by what we must face in life, yet Jesus calms our fears and protects us from what might overwhelm us. Most important, we perceive God differently.

We See God Differently

Impelled by the love of Christ and transformed by its power, we begin to perceive God differently. Like Job, we move from viewing God as a deity who is so distant from us that the circumstances of our lives appear to be irrelevant, to realizing that everything is ultimately in God's hands and everything follows the course on which God has set it. For our part, all we can or need do is entrust ourselves to this loving God who cares if even a sparrow falls to the ground. Like the disciples, we begin to realize that this man who shares in all of our human vulnerability is able to direct the power of the Creator.

Impelled by the love of Christ, we come to see that God is sincerely interested in our fears and misfortunes; God is with us in the midst of the storms of life and ultimately is in control of the chaos that threatens us, whether we recognize this or not.

We See with Eyes of Faith

As we saw last week, we need eyes of faith to recognize the power of God at work in the events of our lives. The vision that God provided for Job was of the universe he knew so well but had failed to understand. The insights to which Job came enlightened his understanding of creation, of the Creator, and of himself, a finite creature. Several of the disciples were seasoned fishermen. They knew that sea quite well; they should have been prepared for its fury. They also knew Jesus; they had lived closely with him for some time. Now they saw him in a different light. In both cases faith opened their eyes.

Thirteenth Sunday in Ordinary Time
Wisdom 1:13-15; 2:23-24

In these few short verses we get a glimpse of the author's understanding of the human person (anthropology) and perspectives on death and life after death (eschatology). Appropriating the Hellenistic concepts of soul, imperishability, and immortality, he has reread the Genesis accounts of creation and sin.

The first verse (1:13) states that God did not make death. This claim calls to mind the second story of creation, where God placed the man and the woman in a garden that contained all that was needed to satisfy their physical needs. However, not content with what God had provided, they violated God's command and thereby brought death upon themselves. Such a reading of the account does not take into consideration the part of the narrative that describes the man as having been made out of the dust of the ground, the perishable substance that symbolizes death.

The first verse further states that God does not delight in the destruction of life but made all things that they might endure. It claims that there is good in everything that has been made (v. 14). This reflects Israel's deep appreciation for the natural world, human beings included. Such an appreciation is in direct opposition to any view that perceives the natural world as evil or fallen or inferior to some kind of spiritual reality. Israel believed that all came from the hand of God and nothing was to be disdained.

The teaching about immortality *(athanasía)* found here is remarkable. Although he is influenced by both the Jewish tradition of covenantal retribution and the Greek psychology of the immortal soul, Pseudo-Solomon's view of immortality is unique. Inheriting the Jewish belief in the relationship between righteousness and life and borrowing the Greek notion of immortality, he claims that "justice is undying [immortal]" (v. 15). His argument develops in the following way: Israel believes that righteousness characterizes the relationship of human beings with the immortal God; therefore, righteousness too is immortal.

The final verses (2:23-24) demonstrate how the author reinterpreted a second concept. The Epicureans believed that incorruption or imperishability *(aphtharsía)* was a divine quality that rendered the gods invulnerable to disintegration. Jewish tradition held that humankind was made in the "image of God" (Gen 1:26-28). The author argued that, though mortal by nature, as images of God human beings were meant to be imperishable. He elaborates on the Genesis account of sin, linking the wily serpent (Gen 3:1) with the devil, who in much later traditions instigates the evil. This is how he arrives at the conclusion that the physical decline and decay to which women and men are subject is caused by the envy of the devil. Although there is no biblical tradition about the envy of the devil, it is found in *The Life of Adam and Eve,* an apocryphal book that appeared at about the same time as the Wisdom of Solomon.

Psalm 30:2, 4, 5-6, 11, 12, 13

This is a psalm of thanksgiving for deliverance from the peril of death, the netherworld, the pit (v. 4). The reference to death may be as well to illness, to depression, or to any serious misfortune that can threaten life itself. Whatever it might have been, the danger is now past; God intervened and saved the petitioner. In addition to the actual calamity the psalmist is also concerned with enemies who would take delight in the misfortune. The prayer asks to be preserved from this insult as well. Following the initial plea is an acknowledgment of deliverance. God has heard the petition and has granted the request.

The psalmist next turns to the congregation of believers and calls on them to praise God. As with the preceding reading, the psalm does not explicitly state that the suffering endured was the deserved penalty for some wrong-doing. However, since that was the customary explanation of misfortune, such a conclusion could be drawn. Still, retribution is not the point of the prayer. Rather, the psalm compares the vast difference between God's wrath and God's graciousness. The former is short-lived; the latter is everlasting.

The psalmist turns again in prayer to God, pleading for pity. There is no suggestion that God has turned a deaf ear to earlier cries. Quite the contrary. The psalmist announces that grief and mourning have been turned into relief and rejoicing. This is the reason for the thanksgiving in the first place. Regardless of the nature of or reason for the misfortune, God can be trusted to come to the aid of one who cries for help.

2 Corinthians 8:7, 9, 13-15

Paul appeals to the generosity of the Corinthians, who are apparently economically secure. Believers in other Christian communities are suffering severe financial need, and Paul pleads with the Christians in Corinth to come to their assistance. He does not argue here from a purely humanitarian perspective but from one that is steeped in theological principles.

He begins by flattering the Corinthians, pointing out to them the charismatic gifts they have already acquired (cf. 1 Cor 12:4-11). He maintains that they have not only demonstrated these praiseworthy abilities, they have actually excelled in them. The Corinthians prized the faith that enabled them to work wonders, their facility with words that manifested itself in prophecy and preaching and glossolalia, and the depth of their understanding of God and the ways of God. Their openness to the preaching of Paul revealed them to be an earnest people devoted to the things of God. Paul appeals to these characteristics as he pleads with them to embrace this new venture with the same enthusiasm they have shown in other areas of Christian living. He ends his plea with a reminder of the love he has shown them. The implication here is that they should show this same kind of unselfish love to others.

Paul then turns to the example of Jesus, who willingly relinquished life itself for the sake of the Corinthians. Paul's rhetorical skill can be seen in the way he plays with the concepts of rich and poor. He declares that Jesus, who as God was rich beyond measure, for the sake of the Corinthians renounced all his divine privilege and became human with all the limitations that are part of the human condition. More than this, Jesus became the poorest of the poor, offering himself for their benefit. Through this incomprehensible generosity on his part, the Christians have become rich with divine grace. This example of Jesus' generous giving is placed before the Corinthians as a motivation for their own generosity to other followers of Jesus.

Paul does not want them to divest themselves of all their resources. If they did this they would most likely suffer the same need they are being asked to alleviate, and then someone else would have to come to their aid. He does not want their generosity to be an undue burden for them. He is merely asking that they give out of their abundance, for this is the basis of Christian sharing. There should not be excess in one segment of the community when there is need in another. Instead, there should be sharing of what they have individually received from God. Paul assures the Corinthians that those with whom they are generous have riches to share as well. These may not be material treasures, but they are resources of which the Corinthians have need.

The passage ends with a citation from the book of Exodus (16:18), which recounts how the people in the wilderness were given manna by God according to their need. No one had too much and no one had too little; all were satisfied.

Mark 5:21-43

Two miracle narratives are intercalated, joined together so they can interpret each other. Both stories include the subject of faith, the issue of ritual purity, the question of life and death, the span of twelve years, and the power of God in Jesus. There are contrasts between women and men, the prominent and the marginal, public and private, faith and incredulity.

The distraught father, a very prominent man, is an official of the synagogue, and his proper name is given. He comes to Jesus openly, as a man in a patriarchal society would, but his approach is not one of social cordiality. He throws himself at the feet of Jesus and pleads with him. The unidentified afflicted women, on the other hand, has been the victim of both her ailment and those who attempted to heal her. Her funds have been depleted, and because of her hemorrhage she is ritually unclean. She does not presume to approach Jesus directly, nor does she plead. Instead, she boldly violates both social and religious prohibitions. She is a woman and she is ritually unclean, but she deliberately touches him. This is the only miracle story where Jesus does not initiate the cure. The one afflicted reaches out of her own accord and snatches the power of God, and it is a marginalized woman who does so.

Although the contrasts between the woman and the man are striking, in the most important issues they are the same. Both the woman and the man act out of faith. They believe that Jesus has the power to heal, and Jesus grants their wishes.

Several factors link the woman of one story and the girl in the other. Both are unnamed and referred to as daughter, suggesting that what happens to them is more important than their identities. Still, they are in relationship with the community and not outcasts. Both are ritually unclean and in a sense outside the circle of total acceptability. Twelve years is the duration of the woman's ailment and the span of the girl's entire lifetime. Both were prevented from contributing to the future of the community; the woman's reproductive potential was impaired and the girl's was halted.

The faith of the woman and the man are in contrast to the incredulity of those gathered at the home of Jairus. Initially they may have believed that Jesus could bring the official's daughter back to health, but now they ridicule him for suggesting that he can bring her back to life. Jesus disregards the same purity regulation that the afflicted woman had. He does not accept the finality of the girl's death, and he touches her lifeless body. In both cases, the touch that would have rendered another unclean is actually the means through which Jesus transfers the power of God.

The healing of the woman, though performed in public, because of the crowd was really a private affair. The raising to life of the girl, though accomplished in private, was in danger of becoming widely known. At the heart of each of these stories is the question of faith in Jesus and his power over sickness and death.

Themes of the Day

The readings for this Sunday provide us with yet another christological meditation. Last week we stood in awe of Jesus, who wields the power of the Creator. Today we see that he also has authority over the forces of death. He stands before us not only as one who inspires awe but also as a model of generosity after whom we can pattern our lives.

Authority over the Forces of Death

This ordinary man is able to reach deep into the world beyond life and rescue a young girl from the jaws of death. This is the same man who earlier, while being jostled by the crowd, felt healing power leave him in order to restore an afflicted woman. Repeating the words of the disciples in the boat, we wonder, Who is this man? Is this someone with whom we want to become involved? On the other hand, can we afford not to get involved with him? This is a man who can lead us to life even in the midst of death. He is someone who is interested in the well being of everyone, even those who may not be highly valued by society—women and children, the chronically ill, those who carry the seeds of death within them. He opposes death because he is committed to life. He willingly enters into battle with it, emerging victorious and celebrating his victory by restoring others.

A Model of Generosity

God's graciousness toward us should prompt us to be generous toward others. What we receive as life-enhancing gifts we must share with those in need, those in the throes of death-dealing poverty or illness, those to whom life has not been kind. As we have been favored by the healing touch of God, so we must extend that same loving touch to others. The love of Christ impels us to be openhanded as we approach those in need. Following Jesus' lead, we must not only give to them, we must also allow them to take from us. At times this will require that we share material resources; at other times it might mean that our energy will be drained in our service of them. In all of this, Jesus has set the example for us to follow.

Fourteenth Sunday in Ordinary Time

Ezekiel 2:2-5

The call and the commission of the prophet Ezekiel are recounted in this brief passage. The essence of the message can be divided into three parts. (1) There is the acknowledgment of the fundamental action of God ("I am sending you"). (2) This is followed by a delineation of the responsibility of the prophet ("you shall say to them") and (3) a description of the response of those to whom the prophet is sent ("they shall know").

Ezekiel is called "son of man" *(ben-ʾādām)*, an epithet that merely means human being. This is not the mysterious son of man *(bar-ʾĕnôsh)* who is described in another tradition as coming on the clouds (cf. Dan 7:13). Here Ezekiel is reminded that even though he is a spokesperson of the mighty God, he is still only a human being. His human weakness is set over against the strength of a spirit that puts the prophet on his feet. There is question about whether this spirit belongs to the prophet himself or is a spirit from God. Since what the prophet is expected to do would call for exceptional courage and energy, the reference is probably to a spirit from God.

Ezekiel does not assume the role of prophet to himself. It is God who says to him, "I am sending you" (vv. 3–4). His is an official mission with all the authority this entails. He will be the representative or envoy of God, the details of his ministry decided by God. It is God who sends him to the people that God selects with the message that God determines. God has chosen a mere human (son of man) to accomplish God's designs.

The fundamental charge of his ministry is straightforward: "You shall say to them" (v. 4). The prophet is sent by God to deliver a message from God. The content of the message is not given here, but the authoritative proclamation that announces it as a divine oracle is stated: "Thus says the Lord GOD." The authentication of a claim to speak in the name of God is always a serious matter. Whoever makes such a claim takes on a weighty burden, for to speak falsely in God's name or to speak without the authority to do so usually incurs grave penalties.

The voice assured Ezekiel that "they shall know that a prophet has been among them" (v. 5). There is no guarantee that the people will heed the message of the prophet. In fact, the voice seems to imply they will not. This experience of God is not a reassuring one for Ezekiel. He is told that the Israelites, to whom he is being sent, are a rebellious people, hard of face and obstinate of heart. Furthermore, they have always been rebellious, from the time of their ancestors to the prophet's own day, so there is little reason to think they will acquiesce to a message from God now. Still, whether they resist the prophet or heed him, they will know that he is a prophet of God. Since the only sure way of knowing that a message is truly prophetic is whether or not what it predicts comes to pass, this sounds very much like a portent. The people will know that there has been a prophet among them because the dire consequences of their rebelliousness have fallen upon them.

Psalm 123:1-2, 2, 3-4

This psalm is a fine example of piety expressed in prayer. Although it is short, it can still be divided into three parts. The first is an expression of total trust in God (vv. 1–2); the second is a petition for God's help (v. 3); the third is a description of the distress from which the psalmist hopes to be delivered (v. 4). The psalm moves from being the prayer of an individual to a communal request.

The sentiments of the psalmist are clearly stated at the outset. Lifting up one's eyes is a gesture of humble longing. The majesty of God is depicted in the simple reference to celestial enthronement. Not only does God dwell in the heavens, but God reigns from there as a king governs from the throne. A depiction of royal enthronement is the most notable symbol of sovereignty. The metaphor sets the stage for the substance of the psalm.

The attention that the psalmist gives to God is now compared to the diligence with which servants in a household attend to the hands of their masters and mistresses. This could imply a kind of cringing attentiveness that stems from fear of chastisement. However, the whole tenor of the psalm suggests that the hands of God will dispense blessing rather than punishment, and so the demeanor of the rulers of the household should be understood in the same way. The servants look to the householders for favors. Furthermore, the word translated as "pity" (*ḥānan*) denotes a heartfelt desire to give to someone in need. It expresses the action of a superior to an inferior. It is an appropriate word to indicate concern that will result in beneficial action.

Finally, the plight of the community is recounted. The people who have turned to God for help are overwhelmed by the disdain within which they are held. Details of their predicament are not given, but they appear to be victims of the pride and arrogance of others. They are in an inferior position not only in regard to God but also in their relationship with others. Regardless of the desperate nature of their situation ("more than sated"), they have turned to God with confidence, trusting that this sovereign God who reigns over all will snatch them from their predicament and be openhanded in bestowing the favors that they need.

2 Corinthians 12:7-10

Once again the exceptional oratorical skill of Paul takes center stage. In the four short verses this reading comprises we see Paul break open the meaning of his own apostleship by situating it squarely within the paradox of the cross of Jesus. He does this by trading in paradoxes. He turns the contrasts exalted/ humbled and power/weakness upside down, stripping them of their customary guise and clothing them with startling new meaning.

Paul has had extraordinary revelations (v. 7). He does not deny this, but he knows it is foolish to allow himself to be overly elated or lifted up because of any spiritual favors he has received. In fact, he realizes that such self-aggrandizement could easily develop into a personality cult. If this occurred, there is the possibility that he might become the center of attention to the detriment of the gospel he had been sent to preach. So this would not happen, he is stricken with a thorn in the flesh, a messenger of Satan. Just what this affliction might have been is not clear. As a thorn of the flesh it is indubitably something obvious, something concrete, something that can be perceived. Many commentators believe it was a physical ailment. Others think it refers to some kind of disorder in one of his churches. Whatever its nature, it was an affliction that humbled him just at the time when he might have been exalted.

Paul was not complacent in his suffering. He did not unquestioningly accept this hardship. He prayed to be relieved of it, not once, or twice, but three times. All his correspondence shows that his ministry, not his personal advantage, was always uppermost in his mind. Therefore we can presume that he was reluctant to accept this thorn in the flesh not because he did not want to suffer but because he saw it as an impediment to his ministry.

The response he received from God posed another paradox: "Power is made perfect in weakness." Paul came to know that real power is to be found in vulnerability, for stripped of power one is more likely to turn to God. The more powerless one is, the more open one can be to God's power. Conversely, the more capable one may be, the less one is prone to look to God for help. Humbled as he is by his affliction, Paul feels most powerful, for he knows it is the power of God that is working through him. Furthermore, because of the public character of his affliction, others will recognize that anything that Paul accomplishes is really the effect of God working through him.

These paradoxes would sound like foolishness were they not grounded in the mystery of Christ's death and resurrection. It was when he was the weakest that he was the strongest. Now, when Paul is the weakest, enduring insults, hardships, persecutions, and constraints, he is strong with the power of Christ. It is a bold boast that Paul makes, but he is making it to believers, who have accepted the bold claims of Christian faith.

Mark 6:1-6

This narrative that describes conflict and rejection has also perplexed its interpreters down through the centuries. First, Jesus returns to his hometown (literally father's house, *patriá*), and he is identified as the son of his mother. It is precisely because he originated from these people that he is rejected by them. There is a long-standing tradition that Mary remained a virgin, yet the story speaks of brothers and sisters.

The presence of his disciples suggests that the visit is more official than casual. Jesus comes as a teacher. Adult men took their turns explaining the Scriptures in the synagogue. Thus the fact that Jesus did so was not extraordinary. What upset the crowd was the content of his message. Theirs was not the kind of astonishment that gave birth to faith. It was the kind that grew out of skepticism and developed into rejection.

These people were not ignorant of Jesus' teaching and the marvelous works he had accomplished. They did not question these things. What they challenged was the source of these wonders. Their questions did not spring from awe but from resentment. Who did he think he was? Without realizing it they were asking the right question but for the wrong reason. Had they really wanted to know, it might have been revealed to them.

Jesus is identified as the son of Mary rather than the son of Joseph, as would have been the custom of the day. Some read this to mean that Joseph was really not the father of Jesus. Two very different conclusions have been drawn from this interpretation. First, that Mary was a virgin, a long-standing tradition in the Christian community. Second, that Jesus was illegitimate, a position that has been occasionally advanced. There is no indication anywhere in the Gospels that the people of the village questioned the fatherhood of Joseph. Had they thought that Jesus was illegitimate, they would most likely have marginalized both Mary and Jesus. Had they thought that Mary was a virgin, they would have realized Jesus' uniqueness and not have been surprised by his power. The designation probably means that Joseph was already dead.

Does the reference to the brothers and sisters of Jesus challenge belief in the virginity of Mary? For some, the virginity of Mary is not an important issue, and they interpret the Greek words in a narrow sense, maintaining that Mary and Joseph had other children. Those who believe in Mary's virginity interpret the Greek to include cousins as well as siblings, an understanding of kinship that is acceptable in many cultures. One's interpretation really depends on theological beliefs that are beyond the evidence in this passage.

The point of the story is the rejection by those who knew Jesus the best but apparently understood him the least—a situation not uncommon for those who have been drawn by God from out of the group to speak God's word to that group. The people in this story lacked the faith required for the power of God to be effective in their midst. Though astonished by Jesus (v. 2) they were scandalized (v. 3), and he was amazed at this (v. 6).

Themes of the Day

Our meditation on Jesus continues. This week he wears the heavy mantle of the prophet. The readings sketch the broad outlines of this messenger of God. They also describe the kind of rejection the prophet must face. Finally, the epistle speaks of strength in weakness.

The Prophet

One would think that Jesus' extraordinary abilities and liberating teaching would have been readily accepted by the people who were anxiously awaiting some revelation of God. Such was not the case. In fact, many people struggled with the prophetic dimension of Jesus and ultimately rejected him because of it. It is not easy to recognize a true prophet. Just because someone makes claims in the name of God there is no guarantee those claims are authentic. There may be signs that can help us recognize the true prophet, but even they are not always clear-cut. It is not uncommon that we heed the voices that sound very much like our own.

Without Honor

Frequently those with prophetic insight are treated without honor. The people to whom Ezekiel was sent were hard of face and obstinate of heart, a rebellious house. What an indictment! Yet these are words that could well be addressed to some of us today. People who should know better, who have not been faithful to God or to each other, compound their offense by rejecting the very one sent to them by God to bring them back to the covenant relationship.

The Galileans who heard Jesus' words were no better. They questioned his authenticity because they felt that they knew him so well. They thought that he was no better than they were and, therefore, that he had no right to act superior. We so often resent people who can do what we cannot. This resentment can be magnified when the person is someone with whom we have grown up, a member of the family or of the community. Why do we so often reject the insightful ones among us?

Strength in Weakness

True believers recognize and admit their human frailty. They also know that genuine weakness does not impede the saving action of God. In fact, God seems to prefer to act where pride and self-satisfaction do not prevail. These are obstacles to personal transformation. They are also obstacles to effective ministry. When we open ourselves in humility and honest piety, the power of God can flood our minds and hearts and shine forth from us to all those around us. There will be no doubt in any mind as to the origin of this wondrous reality. It will be very clear that though it comes *through* us, it comes *from* God. The receptivity of Paul in this matter is in sharp contrast to the rebellion of the people at the time of Ezékiel and the resistance of those who thought they knew Jesus so well.

Fifteenth Sunday in Ordinary Time
Amos 7:12-15

The dialogue between the prophet Amos and Amaziah, the priest of the shrine at Bethel, demonstrates the different perspectives that accompanied the two charges and the tension that often resulted when they were in conflict. Amos had been called by God and sent to prophesy to the people of Israel (v. 15). Amaziah, on the other hand, was an official employee of the crown (v. 13) and was responsible for the cultic activities at Bethel, the royal shrine.

Amaziah calls Amos a seer *(hōzeh)* rather than a prophet *(nābîʾ)*. There was probably no slight intended here, since the two designations were often used interchangeably. The seer was one set apart from the rest of the community, primarily by special personal gifts. Frequently the prophet was attached to the court or to a shrine and served there by prophesying prosperity for the king and the people and disaster for the enemies of the nation. At times these two abilities were found in the same person. Most likely Amaziah recognized Amos' special gifts; he just did not want him to use them at the shrine over which he exercised jurisdiction.

Bethel was an important shrine in the northern kingdom of Israel. In this reading the priest directs the prophet to go to Judah, the southern kingdom, and there to earn his bread. This suggests that various religious leaders were either employed by the shrine itself or else supported themselves by the donations they could secure from the people who frequented the shrine. There is no suggestion of fraud or freeloading here. Amos' economic needs were not the issue; his welcome there was.

This passage does not explicitly tell us why Amos was not wanted. It does say that Bethel was the royal sanctuary. This may imply that all prophesying that went on there had to abide by the good will of the king. Having no loyalties to this court, Amos could not be depended upon to conform to its wishes. He might even be setting himself up against royal authority. Perhaps that is why Amaziah tells him to flee, to leave quickly, lest harm come to him. However, wanted or not, he had been sent by God and he was determined to stay.

The prophet defends his call from God and, in doing so, his right and responsibility to prophesy in Israel. He had not chosen to be a prophet, he had been chosen. He was not the kind of prophet who enjoyed royal patronage and was connected with the court or a particular shrine, nor had he belonged to any prophetic guild. He was a prophet of God, independent of any institution. He had been a herder and a dresser of trees. From these simple occupations he had been summoned by God to be a prophet and then sent to the people of the northern kingdom. His coming to Bethel was due entirely to the command he had received from God.

Psalm 85:9-10, 11-12, 13-14

The verses of this passage presume a community waiting for God's word, a prophetic oracle that will announce peace (v. 9). Presumably the people are in distress or they would not be hoping for a word of peace. There is no direct appeal to God here. These verses depict the people awaiting a reply to a plea they must have made elsewhere. Their confidence that God will respond rests in the conviction that they are God's own people, they are faithful people, they trust in God. There is great expectancy here. The people have done what they can to get God's attention. The next move is God's.

These people are not in total despair. They do believe in salvation, and they maintain that the salvation for which they wait is near to them. At least it is near to those who are loyal (v. 10). The salvation described here is associated with prosperity, suggesting that the people's distress has something to do with economic misfortune. The hoped-for prosperity will be bounteous, filling the whole land. It seems that these people have suffered a serious setback they cannot remedy by themselves. In faith, they turn to their God for help. After having made their petition, they wait confidently for God's response.

Lovingkindness (*hesed*), truth, justice, and peace (v. 11) are characteristics of the covenantal relationship described here. Lovingkindness is covenant loyalty; truth is covenant faithfulness; justice is the covenantal righteousness that comes from God; peace is the wholeness or harmony that results from the covenant relationship. It is not clear whether it is God who possesses these virtues or the people. In either case, they are salvific powers, and their union is a sign of the time of fulfillment. When they meet and embrace, salvation is complete. In order to further characterize the scope of this saving event, the psalmist singles out a partner of each of the two pairs, thus creating another figurative description. Truth springs up from the earth, and justice comes down from heaven. All of creation, from earth to sky, shares in the benefits of the salvation by God.

In the final verses, the psalmist returns to the theme of prosperity (vv. 13–14), confident that God will reestablish the wealth of the people and that the land once barren and forsaken will yield an abundant harvest. Although the image is of an actual harvest of the fruits of the earth, the reference can stand for any situation that brings forth life and prosperity.

Finally, justice and good fortune join the LORD in triumphal procession, with justice in the lead and good fortune bringing up the rear. The procession is really a theophany, a glorious manifestation of the LORD. The four covenantal virtues are really the telltale marks of this manifestation. They are present only because God is there revealing them, making them real in the lives of the people. This revelation of God is the salvation for which the people long, for which they wait in confidence.

Ephesians 1:3-14

The reading opens with a benediction (vv. 3–6), a common way to open letters as well as prayers (cf. 1 Kgs 5:7; 2 Cor 1:3-11). It also serves as a solemn courtly form of congratulation (Ruth 4:14). This benediction blesses God who has blessed us with "every spiritual blessing." As is always the case in Christian theology, the blessing of God comes to us through the agency of Christ. This agency is important enough to be mentioned in every verse of the benediction.

The blessings themselves are distinctively of a spiritual, even cosmic, nature. First is election in Christ. The theme of election has its origins in the Jewish tradition (Exod 19:5-6; Deut 14:2). What is unique here is the idea of primordial predestination, that act whereby God's love from all eternity determines salvation in Christ. Although the author is writing to specific individuals, there is no sense here that some are predestined for salvation and others are not. The point is that salvation in Christ is not an afterthought; it was in God's plan from the beginning.

The believers were not chosen *because* they were holy and blameless but *that they might be* holy and blameless. Once again it is clear that salvation is the cause and not the consequence of righteousness. The reading goes on to say that believers are chosen for adoption into the family of God. It is through Christ, the only real Son of God, that others can become God's adopted children. All of this is grace, received through Jesus, who is God's beloved; and all of this grace is the reason for our praise of God. Although not explicitly stated here, a baptismal theme is implicit in the background of these verses.

The agency of the Lord Jesus Christ is addressed in another way. As we were destined for adoption through Christ, so we have been redeemed by his blood. Our redemption exacted a ransom, for we were being redeemed from sin. The ransom was the blood of Christ, which he willingly paid out of the riches of his grace. The author insists that all of this was done so that God's plan would finally be brought to fulfillment, the plan to bring all things together in Christ. The reference to heaven and earth (v. 10) picks up the cosmic dimension that was mentioned at the beginning of this passage (v. 4). Adoption, redemption, forgiveness of sin, and the gifts of wisdom and insight are all pure grace, gifts from God, bestowed on us through Christ.

In the last section (vv. 11–14) Paul seems to make a distinction between "we" and "you." The first group knew Christ before the second group did. The identity of these first believers is not clear. However, Paul places himself in that group. Still, those who came afterwards were no less a part of the unity accomplished by Christ. They heard the gospel and were sealed by the Spirit, probably at baptism. The group to which Paul belonged was chosen for the praise of God's glory (v. 12). The others seem to have been the first fruits *(arrabōn)* of the inheritance of the earlier group. Perhaps they were second-generation Christians. Whoever they were, they too were called for the praise of God's glory.

The reading begins and ends with praise of God. Regardless of when believers have been called, they have been called to praise God's glory. Adoption, redemption, and forgiveness of sin are the primary reasons for praising God's glory.

Mark 6:7-13

This is an account of the first missionary venture of the Twelve. In it they are given some explicit directions on what to take with them on their journey and how to act. Although they are given the power to drive out unclean spirits, it is quite clear that they can only do this through the authority of Jesus. In other words, they are now commissioned to participate in the ministry of Jesus with the very power of Jesus.

They are allowed to take sandals and a stick with them, presumably to ward off wild animals and to protect themselves from snakes. However, they are not to take other provisions along, such as extra clothing or food or even money. They are not to carry a bag within which they might take anything away with them. They must not give the impression that they hope in any way to benefit from their ministry to others. Finally, they must accept the hospitality that is offered to them. They are to stay in the first house that receives them lest they appear to be, or actually are, trying to take advantage of the generosity of others. The Twelve are being initiated into the mission of Jesus, and they must participate in it in a truly self-sacrificing manner.

Jesus here prepares the Twelve for possible rejection and failure. There is no guarantee that they will be received or that the message they bring will be heeded (v. 11). If and when this happens, they should rid themselves of any trace of the obstinate people. To shake the dust of a place from their sandals was the symbolic act that Israelites performed when returning from a foreign land. It was a precaution that no unclean substance should profane the Holy Land or Jerusalem, the sacred city. If the Twelve performed this action, those Jews who had not welcomed them would understand the seriousness of the judgment being passed on their behavior.

With these instructions the Twelve set out. The ministry they were to perform was a combination of words and deeds: preaching repentance, driving out demons, healing the sick. This was in accord with the very first words proclaimed by Jesus: "The kingdom of God is at hand. Repent, and believe in the gospel" (Mark 1:15, Third Sunday in Ordinary Time). Since the presence of demons and the diminishment caused by illness were considered concrete evidence of the power of evil in the world, people believed that exorcisms and healings were victories of God's power, which broke the bonds of evil. Through them, the reign of God was established in place of the reign of evil. The message of salvation that accompanied these wonders was testimony to this salvific power of God.

It is clear that the kingdom is God's, but it is inaugurated through the ministry of Jesus. Here Jesus brings the Twelve into God's saving work. They are not invited, they are commissioned. They are sent out as one in authority sends out delegates or envoys. The authority is not theirs, nor is the message. They are merely sent in place of the other. However, it is through their agency that the wonders are performed.

Themes of the Day

Several themes that were considered last week appear in today's readings. We see again the nature of the prophetic ministry and the kind of people who are called to it. Today we are told very clearly that we are the ones who are to continue this ministry in our time.

The Prophet and Prophetic Ministry

These readings show once again that God chooses ordinary people and confers on them an extraordinary responsibility. Amos was a shepherd and a dresser of sycamores. Most of the apostles were fishermen. Paul was a tentmaker. Christians today are mechanics and clerks, teachers and engineers, doctors and housekeepers. These are all people following ordinary trades or professions, but what they do in them is truly remarkable. They touch minds and hearts and souls, and they heal them. They instruct and comfort people, and they help to drive out the demons that possess them. They participate in very ordinary ways in the extraordinary establishment of the reign of God.

Last week we saw that the most unlikely were chosen to further the reign of God. Ezekiel faced a resistant people, and Paul suffered from some ailment. This week we see that Amos was probably too rustic and that the apostles appear to be inexperienced. Not any one of them was particularly distinctive according to the standards of the world; they were not celebrities. Yet one of them called for a total reevaluation of the social structure of his people, another helped an entire nation come to grips with its exile, and the rest set out to convert the entire world. These ordinary people were truly extraordinary.

In Him We Have Been Chosen

Jesus inaugurated the reign of God on earth. He chose disciples and sent them out to continue the work he had begun, to preach his gospel, and through healings and exorcisms to conquer the forces of evil that threatened that reign. And now we have been called; in him we have been chosen in all of our brokenness and vulnerability. The task to which we have been called is awe-inspiring; and every spiritual blessing in the heavens has been bestowed upon us so that we will be able to accomplish it. If we allow Christ's saving power to take possession of us, we too will further his prophetic ministry. We will bring the saving grace of God to the world that is terrified and that writhes in pain; we will bring it to those places where healing is needed and where demons still hold sway. We will bring all things under the headship of Christ.

Sixteenth Sunday in Ordinary Time

Jeremiah 23:1-6

The reading begins with an indictment of the monarchy and an oracle of judgment; it ends with an oracle of salvation that promises a renewal of the royal house of David. Jeremiah contrasts the notions of scattering and gathering in his development of the shepherd theme, a familiar theme that highlighted the responsibility the leaders had for guiding and safeguarding the people.

The indictment of the leaders of the people is terse and decisive. They have not only neglected the people of God, they have actually misled them, and just as wild animals would, they have caused them to be scattered, probably a reference to the Exile. God had put them in charge of the people, and so it is God who will remedy the situation. This will be done by means of reversals. Because the shepherds had not cared (exercised oversight) for the flock, God would care (exercise oversight) for the punishment of these derelict leaders. They had scattered the sheep; God would gather them up again. They had been false shepherds; God would be the true shepherd. The responsibility for the exile of the nation is here clearly placed on the shoulders of the monarchy.

At first God will work directly with the people, gathering them together, bringing them back to their home. There they will once again live in peace and will be able to increase and multiply, just as the family of Noah was able to do after the Flood, the first great catastrophe of the human race (cf. Gen 9:1). God then promises to raise up a new royal shepherd, a righteous leader who will govern the nation wisely and justly. It is important to note that the new human shepherd will be chosen after the nation has been reassembled, not before. It is clear that the reorganization of the people will be the work of God, not of any human leader, not even a divinely appointed one.

The oracle of salvation (vv. 5–6) opens with the conventional eschatological look to the future time of fulfillment ("the days are coming"). By itself the dynasty does not seem to have been able to produce a worthy king. It was necessary for God to step in and provide them with one. The promise of a righteous ruler who will spring from the stump of the hewn tree of David calls to mind earlier prophetic promises (cf. Isa 11:1). This king will not be like the shepherds who failed both God and the people. He will be righteous, and he will do what is righteous. In fact, his very name, "The LORD our justice," will attest to his righteousness.

There is a clever play on the meaning of the names here. Zedekiah was the throne name of the king who reigned in Judah at the time of the Babylonian Exile. His name means "righteous is the LORD." The history of Israel shows that he never lived up to that name. Here, God is giving both the nation and the monarchy a second chance. The coming king will be everything the former king was not. He will reestablish both Israel and Judah, and he will do it in the righteousness that comes from God.

Psalm 23:1-3, 3-4, 5, 6

This responsorial psalm is one of the most familiar and best-loved psalms of the entire Psalter. It paints vivid pictures of a carefree existence, peaceful rest, and abundant fruitfulness. Although "shepherd" suggests a flock rather than merely one sheep, here the focus is on the individual. In addition to this image, God is characterized as a host, one who supervises a banquet and within whose house the psalmist ultimately dwells.

The psalm opens with a metaphor that sets the tone of the entire song. It is the responsibility of the shepherd to find pastures that will provide enough grazing and abundant water for the entire flock, to lead them there without allowing any of the sheep to stray and be lost, to guard them from predators or dangers of any kind, and to attend to their every need. To characterize the LORD as a shepherd is to trust that God will discharge all these responsibilities. The personal dimension of the psalm shifts the care given to the entire flock to concern for one individual, making God's care a very intimate matter. Not only are the physical needs of the psalmist satisfied, but the soul, the very life force *(nepesh)* of the person, is renewed.

The guidance of the shepherd is more than provident, it is moral as well. The psalmist is led in the paths of righteousness (v. 3), and this is done for the sake of the LORD's name. Since one's name is a part of the very essence of the person, this indicates that the way of the LORD is the way of righteousness. Following this, we can say that the magnanimous care shown by the shepherd flows from enduring righteousness rather than from some passing sentiment of the heart. This is confirmed by the reference to the covenant kindness *(ḥesed)* that surrounds the psalmist (v. 6). In other words, the divine shepherd's tender commitment to the flock, and to each individual within it, is as lasting as is God's covenant commitment.

The psalmist is confident of the Lord's protection, as demonstrated in his mention of the shepherd's rod and staff, which were used to ward off wild animals as well as poachers. The "dark valley" can be a reference to the darkest part of the terrain or to the gloom that can overwhelm an individual. However, it also has a mythological connotation and is frequently interpreted as death. Whichever meaning is intended here, the psalmist claims to be unafraid, for the presence of the LORD is reassuring.

The image of the shepherd securing nourishment for the flock suggests another metaphor, that of the host who prepares a lavish banquet for guests. Many societies have a very strict code of hospitality. They are obliged to provide the very best provisions they have, even for their enemies. The LORD spreads out such a banquet here, which not only affords nourishment but also is a public witness to God's high regard for the psalmist, who will continue to enjoy God's favor in God's house. Whether this indicates the temple or is merely a reference to the place where God dwells, the fundamental meaning is clear. The psalmist has been under the loving guidance of the LORD and will remain there forever.

Ephesians 2:13-18

The principal theme of this reading is the union, accomplished in Christ, between two groups of people. The author declares that a change has taken place in the Ephesians. Previously they had been "far off" from faith, but now, through the blood of Christ, they have been brought near to all those who believed in Christ before they did. Christ is their peace; in Christ they are one people.

The reading does not expressly identify the people from whom the Ephesians had been divided. However, there are enough clues to suggest that the reference is to those with Israelite background. Because these other people have been joined to the Ephesians in Christ, they must be Jewish Christians rather than the Jewish people themselves. This is a very important point to make, lest we read an anti-Judaic bias here, a bias that has too long been used to justify various forms of anti-Semitism. At issue here is the division within the Christian community itself.

Christianity grew out of the religion of Israel, and initially the Jewish Christians saw no need to relinquish the traditions and practices they knew so well. It was only with the inclusion of Gentile converts that the role of the Jewish tradition was questioned. Would these new believers have to accept Jewish customs and practices? Before this question could be definitively decided, the various sectors of the Church had become divided on many topics.

The "dividing wall of enmity" might refer to the barrier that kept non-Jewish people out of designated precincts of the temple. It could be a reference to various cultic regulations that forbade association with people who did not belong to the community. Or it could be an allusion to the entire law, which set the people of Israel apart from all others. The Ephesian (Gentile) converts would be separated from those Jewish Christians who held to these restrictions.

The author of the letter insists that through the blood of the cross Christ has broken down this wall of division. He has reconciled both groups with God and thereby with each other. By his death he has put their enmity to death. More than this, he has brought them together in himself. He has not merely brought them peace, he has become their peace. Neither one of the groups has been taken up into the other. Rather, reconciled with God and with each other, they have become a new creation, a new body. Where once there were two, now there is one.

Christ Jesus is the herald of this peace. First he preached peace to the Ephesians who had been far off, just as he had preached peace to those who had come to believe earlier. Through the shedding of his blood he brought the previously separated groups together in their faith in him, thus becoming their peace. He will now serve as the one through whom all have access to

God. This is a reference to a custom observed in many ancient oriental courts. An ordinary person could not gain access to the court without some form of introduction. This was often provided by someone of influence or status. Christ Jesus is now the introduction needed to gain access to God. The passage ends with a trinitarian proclamation of faith. Jesus has died and is risen from the dead and now lives in the Spirit. Through him, in the Spirit, all believers have access to the Father.

Mark 6:30-34

The disciples of Jesus are here called apostles (the only time the word appears in this Gospel). Although disciple and apostle are often used interchangeably, strictly speaking, the words are different. Of the two Greek words that mean "to send" *(apostéllō* and *pémpō),* the first stresses the relationship between the sender and the one sent, implying a kind of commissioning. Words derived from it denote a function rather than a status. An apostle, then, is an authorized agent or representative who is appointed to a particular task rather than a permanent position and who, while performing that task, acts with the full authority of the sender. This nuance of the word can be clearly seen in the reading for today. Accountable to Jesus for their use of his authority, the apostles return to him and give a report of their words and deeds.

Either the apostles had been quite successful in their mission or the fame of Jesus had spread abroad or both, for the people were coming in such numbers that the missionaries had to get away from the crowds (cf. 4:35-41, Twelfth Sunday in Ordinary Time; 5:21-43, Thirteenth Sunday in Ordinary Time). Jesus took them to a deserted place *(erēmos),* the kind of place to which he himself withdrew for periods of prayer (cf. Mark 1:35, Fifth Sunday in Ordinary Time). The desert was not only a place of escape, it held great symbolic meaning. It reminded the people of the formative period of their past, when in the desert God entered into covenant with them. A return to the desert was often a time of recommitment.

However, their departure did not deter the crowds, who seemed to know where they were going and who arrived there before Jesus and the apostles did. Seeing them, Jesus was moved with pity *(splanchnízomai),* a word that means profound inner emotion, which is used only by or about Jesus and which has messianic significance (cf. Mark 1:42; 8:2; 9:22). The reason for Jesus' intense response is given. He was moved by the plight of the people, not by their enthusiasm, which might well have arisen from their desire for miracles rather than from religious motivation. He saw them as sheep without a shepherd, searching for someone or something they could follow. This is a bold criticism of the leadership of the time, a criticism not unfamiliar to the people of God (cf. Num 27:17; 1 Kgs 22:17; Ezek 34:5).

The shepherd image, which would have had particular significance to a people engaged in shepherding, became an important metaphor to signify the responsibility of the kings, and subsequently, those who acted in any capacity of leadership. They were to govern the people, to provide for them, and to safeguard them. Despite this characterization, Israel always maintained that God was the only true shepherd of the people (Ezek 34:11-16), and the legitimate leaders served in God's place. Jesus realized that these people followed him so eagerly because they were bereft of strong and dependable leadership. To remedy this, he began to teach them.

Themes of the Day

Our meditation on the person of Christ ends on the same note as found in last week's reflection. The one who was able to calm the storm, who had power over the forces of death, and who exercised a prophetic ministry in establishing the reign of God has commissioned ordinary people to continue his work. Last week he sent them out; this week they return and enthusiastically report the wonders they have accomplished through him. The unselfishness that characterizes their commitment, reflected in the responsorial psalm, is in sharp contrast to the picture of the shepherds presented in the first reading. Finally, criteria for distinguishing one type of leader from the other is found in the epistle.

Like the Good Shepherd

Jesus chose those who would continue his work; he instructed them and empowered them. He sent them out on a mission, and they returned. They obviously had been successful, for the crowds would not let them alone. People followed them everywhere because they wanted to hear what Jesus and his disciples had to say; they wanted to be released from the sickness and the demons that possessed them. These were clearly people on a search; they were looking for direction. And so Jesus took pity on them.

There are so many searching people in the world today, people hungering for instruction, good people who are looking for direction. They may be parents who are sick with grief over the future of a troubled child; a man stripped of his dignity due to unemployment; a woman facing a pregnancy alone; elderly people who can feel the surge of life leave their declining bodies; people who are angry and confused because they believe that the Church is no longer dependable. They are people looking for answers and for meaning. They are like sheep without a shepherd, and Jesus looks to us to shepherd them.

False Shepherds

Like the people at the time of the Exile, we live in a period of transition. Like the crowds who heard Jesus announce that the reign of God had come, we are being told to adjust our worldview, perhaps even to embrace a totally different one. To whom do we go for guidance? Where do we find the words of eternal life? There are so many voices that claim to have the answer; how do we know which ones to heed? Who accurately interprets the word of God for us? Is it the one who makes us feel good about ourselves, or the one who makes us feel guilty? Should we cling to the teachings of the past or open ourselves to creative new insights? Should we expect that God will rescue us from our plight, or should we allow it to refine and transform us? How do we know what to do? Which path should we choose? Who will lead us? There is a danger that we will listen to the voice that gives us the easiest answers, or that we will give up our search and resign ourselves to being like sheep without a shepherd.

He Is Our Peace

In the midst of our confusion, there are some clues that should help us discern which voices to heed. Reliable shepherds walk with us in the dark valleys. They are willing to share the dangers through which we pass, even at the risk of their own safety. They do not pit one segment of the community or one theological perspective against another, scattering the sheep and driving them away. Instead, they work to dismantle the walls that divide us. They speak the word that gathers us together. They reconcile us with God and with each other. They may not give us easy answers, but their primary concern is to lead us to Jesus, the one who is our peace.

Ordinary Time (Part Three)

Seventeenth Sunday 2 Kings 4:42-44 More than enough to eat	Psalm 145:10-11, 15-18 The LORD feeds us	Ephesians 4:1-6 One body, one Lord	John 6:1-15 He feeds the multitude
Eighteenth Sunday Exodus 16:2-4, 12-15 Bread from heaven	Psalm 78:3-4, 23-25, 54 Bread from heaven	Ephesians 4:17, 20-24 New self created in God	John 6:24-35 Faith satisfied hunger
Nineteenth Sunday 1 Kings 19:4-8 Food from heaven	Psalm 34:2-9 Taste and see God's goodness	Ephesians 4:30—5:2 Walk in love	John 6:41-51 I am living bread
Twentieth Sunday Proverbs 9:1-6 Eat my food, drink my wine	Psalm 34:2-7 Taste and see God's goodness	Ephesians 5:15-20 Understand God's will	John 6:51-58 My flesh is food
Twenty-First Sunday Joshua 24:1-2a, 15-17, 18b We will serve the LORD	Psalm 34:2-3, 16-21 Taste and see God's goodness	Ephesians 5:21-32 The mystery of the Church	John 6:60-69 Words of eternal life

Ordinary Time (Part Three)

Initial Reading of the Ordinary Lectionary (Part Three)

Introduction

It is clear that all of the readings of these five Sundays either expand or support the meaning of the bread of life discourse. They have been chosen precisely for that purpose. This pivotal teaching of Jesus, placed as it is within Ordinary Time, invites us to step back from the ordinariness of life to meditate on the marvels with which God has blessed us.

First Testament Readings

Of the five First Testament readings, four of them are accounts of extraordinary feedings. Both at the time of Elisha and during the wandering in the wilderness the people are fed by God in a miraculous manner. Food is mysteriously provided for Elijah, and Wisdom spreads a banquet for all to feast. The last reading invites the people to choose which god they will serve. Will it be one they may have worshiped in the past? Or will they choose the God who has so generously provided for them?

Psalms

The psalm responses are very focused and suitable to the themes of this segment of readings. The first two responses, a wisdom psalm and a historical account, describe some of the wonderful things God has done for the people. The other three responses are songs of thanksgiving for God's graciousness.

Epistles

The epistle readings, all from the letter to the Ephesians, instruct us about appropriate Christian behavior. We are called to live in the unity of one Lord, one faith, and one baptism, to lay aside our former way of life and to walk in love. We are told to make the most of our present opportunities and to reexamine the relationships we share with one another.

Gospels

All of the Gospel readings come from the bread of life discourse. In it Jesus gradually reveals his true identity and invites us into a life of union with him. He first miraculously feeds the multitude. Next he claims that those who believe in him will not hunger, because he is the bread of life. He concludes with instruction, boldly insisting that if we do not feed on his flesh and blood we will have no life. Although the claims are incredible, Jesus does not retract them. It is up to us to decide whether or not we will accept him as the one who has the words of eternal life.

Mosaic of Readings

The readings do not so much create a mosaic as a multi-dimensional view of the same reality. They allow us to witness Jesus' miraculous power, and then they provide us glimpses into his true identity.

Readings

Seventeenth Sunday in Ordinary Time

2 Kings 4:42-44

The vignette found in the first reading may be short, but it is charged with meaning. It recounts an episode in the life of the prophet Elisha. Several people play active roles in this drama. There is the man who comes from another place, the prophet also called the "man of God," a servant, and the people who are fed the bread and grain.

An unnamed man brings the first fruits of the crop, so it must be harvest time. First fruits were offered to God because they were considered the best and freshest—that portion of the produce that contained the most vibrant force of life. Since the first fruits were normally offered to God as a token of the entire harvest, we can presume that the setting is a shrine and the prophet is somehow attached to it. The village Baal-shalishah was located in the western foothills of the central hill country in the vicinity of Gilgal, which could well be the location where the incident took place.

The man comes from a place named for and probably devoted to Baal, the Canaanite god of fertility. It should be noted that he does not offer his crops to this particular deity, but he brings them to the "man of God." In the early years of Israel's history, before priests had exclusive authority over the public practice of worship, the prophets who were attached to the shrines may have acted as intermediaries between the worshipers and God. This seems to be the case here. Most likely the man brought the loaves and the grain either to be offered to God or to serve as shewbread, or "bread of the presence," which was kept at the shrine for a time and then eaten by those who served there.

Elisha directed that the bread and grain be given to the people who had gathered. This was an extraordinary directive, since the bread belonged to God or to the ones who had been set apart by God. Why would the prophet suggest such an action? Only something as serious as a severe hunger would have warranted the violation of this cultic regulation (cf. 1 Sam 21:5-6). Those who ministered at the shrine objected, but Elisha insisted, and his insistence overrode their objection. This is clear evidence of the authority the "man of God" wielded and the others recognized. Since it waived a cultic regulation, the authority of the prophet had to have come from God.

The miracle is remarkable. One hundred men were fed by a mere twenty loaves. There is no mention of women here. They were either denied access to this part of the shrine or their presence or absence was of no interest to the author of the story. Either way, the gender bias cannot be denied.

The miracle is the result of the words spoken by the LORD through the prophet (v. 43). The origin of the citation is uncertain. It cannot be a reference to the manna in the wilderness where God miraculously fed the multitude, for there the people took only what they needed and nothing was left over. This miracle reveals the bounteous generosity of God.

Psalm 145:10-11, 15-16, 17-18

The responsorial psalm is a hymn of praise of the greatness of God. In the first two sections the psalmist speaks directly to God, inviting all of God's works to give thanks and proclaiming the LORD's universal providence. In the third section the psalmist speaks about God, extolling divine righteousness.

The works of the LORD include everything God has made as well as everything God has done, everything God has fashioned as well as everything God has accomplished. There is a comprehensiveness to this call for praise (vv. 10–11). The psalmist cries out to all the wonders of the created world, whose very existence testifies to the magnificence of the Creator. More than this, the God before whom the psalmist stands in awe is also a savior who has performed marvelous deeds on behalf of the people. God has delivered them from bondage, has provided for them in their need, has established them as a people, and has promised them a secure and prosperous future. As they unfold in the sight of all, these acts of graciousness themselves celebrate the LORD.

The faithful of the LORD are those who are holy *(hāsîd),* those who are bound to God in covenant loyalty. Whether their holiness is the result of God's faithfulness to them (cf. v. 17) or their faithfulness to God is not clear. It does not seem to matter to the psalmist, who is preoccupied with the praise of God and not with extolling others. These faithful are summoned to bless the LORD, to praise or honor God in reverence and awe. God is characterized here as a monarch who rules over a kingdom. The word for glory *(kābôd)* means "heavy" or "weighty." Used here, it implies that God's kingdom is substantial, distinguished because of its magnitude, comprehensive in its splendor. The character and extent of God's rule demonstrates the essence and scope of God's power.

Next is celebrated divine providence, one of the most prominent of God's works (vv. 15–16). Everything that has been created relies on this providence. A vivid image is used to depict both the dependence of all living creatures and the generosity of God. All of life stands needy and trusting before God, in whose hands is the sustenance upon which life depends, and God is open-handed in satisfying this need. The image bespeaks the confidence that creation has in God and the tender concern that God has toward creation.

Finally, the basis of God's loving attention is proclaimed (vv. 17–18). God's covenant commitment is revealed as justice *(ṣedeq)* and lovingkindness *(ḥesed).* These constitute the firm foundation upon which the faithful ones can trust and the source of God's provident care. God has entered a solemn agreement, has made serious promises, and can be depended upon to be faithful. In order to experience the benefits of this covenant, one needs only to call upon God, who is always there to hear.

Ephesians 4:1-6

The unity within the Church is the overarching theme in this reading. It begins with a strong exhortation by Paul to live according to Christian standards. He does not merely invite the Ephesians to live this life, he urges them to do so. He then provides a catalogue of social virtues that characterize the Christian life followed by a list of seven elements that bind the Christians to God and to each other in faith.

There is an ironic dimension to the ethical exhortation in this letter. From prison Paul is admonishing the Christians to lead the kind of life that, in fact, has resulted in his own captivity. Rather than deterring them from following his example, Paul's imprisonment seems to be demonstrating the price he is willing to pay for having been invited into a life of Christian virtue. He insists that only such a life is worthy of the call they too have received from God.

They themselves have not initiated their Christian vocation. They have been called by God; their virtuous living is the appropriate response to God's choice of them. The Greek verb *(peripateō)* translated "live" really means to walk on a certain path, a theme that is prominent in the wisdom tradition (cf. Prov 4:11; Mark 1:3). It suggests that a righteous life is more than conformity to a collection of regulations. It is a commitment to set oneself on a particular path of life and to hold fast to that path even in the face of difficulty.

All the virtues cited are relational attitudes that foster community harmony. Humility and gentleness are in many ways similar. The first virtue keeps an individual from seeking to gain undue prominence over others; the second is an attitude of thoughtful consideration of others. Patience, which literally means long-tempered as opposed to short-tempered, and forbearance are really two aspects of the same attitude, constituting a single thought. They enable an individual to act courteously toward people whose behavior is truly trying and who pose difficulty for them. The Christian motivation for patience is love. According to Paul, this is the kind of conduct that engenders peace within the community and provides the members with the inner dispositions needed in order to preserve the unity that comes from the Spirit.

This unity is grounded in their belonging to the one body of Christ, their being filled with and fashioned by the one Spirit of God, and their being moved by the one hope of their call to salvation. Their life is trinitarian; they have all been called by God to salvation in Christ through the Spirit. This is the basis of their unity, which is expressed in their allegiance to one Lord, their commitment to one faith, and their celebration of one baptism. The final unifying element is their belief in the one God of Jewish monotheism, who is both transcendent ("over all") and immanent ("in all") and is actively at work in all creation ("through all").

John 6:1-15

This scene from the Gospel shows that the power of Jesus had a mesmerizing effect on the crowds. They followed him from place to place. However, they did this less out of faith than out of the hope that they might witness the performance of some marvel or even, if they were so fortunate, that they might be the beneficiaries of one. There is no indication they came to hear his teaching, and in this particular passage Jesus does not teach. The focus here is on his wondrous power. Unlike most of the miracles of Jesus, this one was not a response to an expressed need. Jesus feeds the people, but the text does not say they were hungry. There was a much deeper reason for this miracle.

Jesus took the barley loaves (note the link with the feast of the Unleavened Bread), gave thanks *(eucharistéō)*, distributed them, and then did the same with the fish. The eucharistic allusions here are obvious. Once again the crowds were overwhelmed by Jesus. They had followed him to the other side of the lake in order to witness his exceptional power. They were not disappointed. However, they now recognize him as more than a wonder-worker. He is the long-awaited prophet like Moses (cf. Deut 15:18), the one who would usher in the messianic age.

Although the words "crowd" (vv. 2, 5) and "people" (vv. 10, 14) are inclusive, only the "men" (v. 10) are told to recline. There were certainly women and children (the boy, v. 9) among the crowd, and they too would have sat in the grass. The gender bias of the writer is obvious.

Some commentators have tried to explain away the miraculous character of the incident. They have argued that this event was nothing more than an example of human sharing that was embellished by the Gospel writer. Regardless of how later readers might understand the event, the people who were present clearly saw it as an act of God. They perceived this "sign" as a sign of the end-time. However, they misunderstood its meaning, and they decided to make Jesus king, by force if necessary.

The disciples are both faithful and lacking in faith. They accompanied Jesus across the sea and sat down with him on the mountain. They were directed by Jesus to collect the fragments that were left over after the crowd had eaten its fill. Two of the disciples played significant roles in this incident. First Philip was put to the test (v. 5). Jesus asked him where they would find enough money to buy bread to feed the crowd, knowing full well that neither money nor a supply of bread would be necessary. Philip took Jesus' words literally, insisting that they did not have enough to provide for all of the people. Next Andrew offered information about some food, but he was as incredulous as Philip had been. Neither realized that Jesus' words had a meaning far deeper than they suspected.

Finally, the event took place at the time of the Passover, the feast that coincided with the feast of the Unleavened Bread. This latter festival marked the barley harvest and commemorated two important periods in the history of the people. The first is the time of the people's release from Egyptian bondage, when the urgency of escape prevented them from waiting for their bread to rise. The second is the time of the first harvest after their arrival in the land of promise, when the new grain was still fresh and uncorrupted by yeast. Passover and the Unleavened Bread were feasts of remembrance and anticipation. They celebrated the saving events of the past and they looked forward in hope to the final age of fulfillment, the age that was revealed in the miracle of the loaves.

Themes of the Day

The next five Sundays all develop some aspect of the mystery of the bread of life. Like a good teacher, Jesus reveals the meaning of this mystery little by little. This Sunday's readings invite us to reflect on the mysterious and magnanimous power of God that meets the basic need of people, which is survival. This gift is not only for the individual; it is the community that survives. Finally, being granted life, we are told how to live it.

God Meets Our Needs

Both the first reading and the Gospel passage remind us that, though we do have a responsibility to care for ourselves and for each other, it is really God who provides for us. We live in a world that feeds us and shelters us and supplies us with everything we need to grow and to thrive, and all of this comes to us from the hand of God. It is usually when we are in desperate straits that we become painfully conscious of our dependence on God, but this dependence is there all the time. God does not merely intervene when we are helpless; God's providence is operating in our lives at all times.

Both readings also underscore a second characteristic of this providence. Besides being constant, it is extravagant. God gives us more than we need. The earth is prodigal in its generosity. It yields food in abundance—food for our bodies but also food for our spirits. The skies are exquisitely painted; the meadows burst forth in sweet smells. We are warmed by the sun and cooled by breezes—all for our enjoyment and pleasure. God gives us everything we need to survive. God gives us food in due season and satisfies the desire of every living thing.

Life for the Community

Living in a society that cherishes the individual and even promotes individualism, we may sometimes undervalue the communal dimension of life. While God certainly cares passionately for each one of us (not even a sparrow falls without God knowing it), God's concern is for the whole people. In both readings the bread was distributed among the entire crowd. Narrow individualism can sometimes blind us to the fact that we are first and foremost members of a people. We would never have seen the light of day, we would not endure or develop, without others. As unique as we may be, we are a unique expression of a communal reality. God created a race; God formed a people; Jesus died for the world. By the grace of God, we belong to the community.

New Life for the Community

It is not enough that we belong; it is not enough that our needs are satisfied. As members of the people of God, we are called to a manner of living that is noble, not selfish. We are to live with each other in humility and gentleness, with patience. We are to bear with one another in love. We are one with each other not merely because we belong to the same species but because we have been born to a new life in baptism. We all live by the same Spirit of Jesus; we are all united through the bond of God's love. The bread we receive from the hand of God is more than mere barley loaves. It is the bread of full life, life in all its dimensions, life in Christ.

Eighteenth Sunday in Ordinary Time

Exodus 16:2-4, 12-15

The episode of the murmuring in the wilderness highlights more than the Israelites' discouragement in the face of hunger. Their very real need for food put their faith in God to the test. The entire Israelite community grumbled to Moses and Aaron. Although it is God's leadership that is being challenged, it is God's appointed leaders who are being blamed. Since the people are in a very vulnerable situation in the wilderness, a certain amount of complaint is understandable. It is not the complaint itself but its content that is disturbing. The people prefer their former situation of oppression in Egypt with food rather than their present freedom without food.

The deliverance from Egypt was the founding event that shaped the motley group of forced laborers into a distinctive people with a singular relationship with the liberating God. The events that surrounded the Exodus demonstrated again and again God's preference for the descendants of Jacob. Now they are suggesting that it would have been better had God not intervened on their behalf. To them, freedom with a commitment to the liberating God seems a small price to pay for the satisfaction of the meat (fleshpots) and bread of Egypt.

One would think that the phenomenal character of the Exodus events would have prompted the people to develop a faith that would be unshakable amid the obstacles they were now facing. After all, God had conquered the forces of the pharaoh, a ruler who claimed to have divine power and whose subjects revered that power. Elements within the descriptions of God's mighty acts suggest that the deliverance itself was a kind of cosmic battle and God was the victor. Now the people wished this to be undone. Such a desire is a total rejection of God.

God heard their rebellious grumbling and responded with provisions. They had longed for the meat and bread of Egypt, and God promises to send meat and bread from heaven. There is probably a natural explanation for the availability of this food. The bread (*mān hû,* meaning "what is it?") was probably a substance secreted from the tamarisk tree, which first hardened when the dew evaporated but then deteriorated during the heat of the day. The quail may have been birds that were too weary to soar after having flown in from the sea. Although they were natural phenomena, these providential occurrences were perceived as acts of God, and that is exactly how they should be understood.

Once again God demonstrates divine power and a preference for the Israelites. However, the reason for this display is that the people may know that the LORD is their God (v. 12). Their grumbling implies that they were willing to relinquish their privileged status. God's action on their part shows that God is not willing to do so.

Psalm 78:3-4, 23-24, 25, 54

The responsorial psalm provides a description of the practice of handing stories down from generation to generation (vv. 3–4), a practice that is found in every society. Its purpose is the preservation of the traditions that shape the identity and ethos of the people, giving them a sense of who they are by reminding them of the founding and formative events of their past. They in turn will transmit these traditions to their descendants. This is a very serious undertaking, for it is precisely in the handing down of traditions that the identity of the group is preserved. Although this transmission occurs in various situations, it normally happens during some kind of cultic celebration.

The essence of Israel's historical recital is the proclamation of the glorious deeds of the LORD. Chief among them are the events that surrounded the deliverance from Egypt, the sojourn in the wilderness, and the entrance into the land of promise. The verses that make up the responsorial psalm concentrate on the incident of the manna and the entrance into the land.

The psalmist adds something to the earlier manna tradition (cf. Exod 16:4), here describing God as exercising authority over the heavens. This is a significant point, since in the ancient world different deities wielded power over the respective segments of the cosmos. The God of Israel would have to enjoy supreme authority to be able to govern the heavens as well as direct the fortunes of the people themselves. This is exactly what this reference is implying. The God of Israel is sovereign.

The psalmist further embellishes the earlier tradition, which has been reinterpreted for us by contemporary translators. The manna is really called heavenly grain (*dāgān,* v. 24) and the bread of the strong (*ʿabbîr,* v. 25), two expressions that are unfamiliar to us. The first may simply refer to the cereal composition of the bread. However, it might also be a polemic against the worship of Dagon, a Philistine god of agriculture. If it means the latter, it implies that this deity is nothing before the God of Israel.

The second designation does not contain the customary word for angels or messengers *(mal*ʾ*āk).* The word used comes from the verb that means both "to fly" and "mighty" *(*ʿ*ābar).* The combination of mighty and winged is represented in the figure of the divine winged bull. Once again we have an indirect denigration of an ancient Near Eastern god. The strong ones referred to could be heavenly beings who do God's bidding or else the Israelites themselves, who are strengthened by the bread provided for them by God. The passage ends with the people established in the land. The mountain is probably Zion, the hill upon which the temple was built. The people have been brought to God's land, to God's holy mountain.

The recital of all of these wonders is meant to remind the people of who they have become because of what they have experienced. It is further intended to challenge them to live in the present as a people faithful to who they are so they can hand down their noble identity to the next generation.

Ephesians 4:17, 20-24

The admonition Paul gives to the Ephesians is in the manner of a wisdom teaching. In that tradition the contrasts are drawn in an uncompromising manner. There are only two ways of living: the way of the wise or righteous and the way of the foolish or wicked. There is no middle path. One chooses to walk one way or the other. Paul contrasts the life the Ephesians lived before their conversion to Christ with the one to which they have now committed themselves. In very strong language he testifies *(martyréō)* that they must no longer live (walk, *peripatéō)* the way non-believers do.

Much of the vocabulary Paul uses in this passage underscores this wisdom theme. He speaks of the futility or vanity of the mind, of learning Christ and being taught the truth. Paul is not really setting the Christians over against the Gentiles so as to make them think they are in some way better. He is comparing two ways of living and insisting that since they have learned Christ, Christians are bound to live a new life in Christ. The old way of living was futile; the new way of living is true.

The new life of the Christians demands a radical change. They must put away their old selves and put on new selves. Although this image suggests substituting one garment for another, it should not be understood as a superficial or merely external change. Clothing is often an index of personality. It indicates role or status in society, and it reflects culture and taste. We may not be what we wear, but what we wear reveals who we are. Here Paul uses clothing as a metaphor for identity. Conversion to Christ requires a stripping of the old identity and a clothing in the new.

The newness of which Paul speaks is not merely the freshness of youth *(néos)*. He is talking about a new *(kainós)* nature, the miraculous newness of the eschatological age of salvation. It is the newness of the new heaven and earth, of the new covenant, of the new spirit, of the new wine, of the new Jerusalem. The new age has come with Christ, and the Ephesians must be re-created as new selves if they are to be part of it. A radical transformation is required. However, it is not out of reach of the Ephesians. In accord with the admonitions of the wisdom tradition, they are called to choose the path they will follow. Will it be the way of futility, or will they be re-created in God's own righteousness and holiness?

John 6:24-35

Jesus' discourse on the bread of life follows a traditional method of rabbinic interpretation. First a passage from the Scriptures is quoted (v. 31); then a word-for-word analysis is given. The homily that is given here is actually a response to the challenge of the people who demand a sign that will verify Jesus' authority, and this after they have been filled by the bread he provided for them. The entire reading weaves together these three themes: bread, sign, work.

The idea of bread is used in three different yet connected ways. First, Jesus is well aware of the reason the crowds have followed him. He knows it is not really or basically for any religious reason. They were not looking for signs of the presence of God in their midst. They had been fed by him and they wanted more of the same. Jesus turns their desire for bread into an opportunity to teach them about a different kind of food. The bread they desired would only satisfy them temporarily, but he had food that would endure.

The crowds had been given bread without having had to work for it, but they know that normally they would have to toil very hard for it. Once again Jesus uses a idea they know well to teach a deeper truth. He reinterprets work. Manual labor produces common bread; a different kind of work is required for the bread of which Jesus speaks. When they ask him how they can accomplish the works of God (presumably the works of the law), he reinterprets work once again. *The* work of God is faith in Jesus. This is a bold claim, and the crowds demand that he give them a reason to believe in him. For example, God fed their ancestors with bread from heaven. What can he do? A startling challenge after Jesus himself has just provided them with bread.

The biblical reference (v. 31) is to the story of the manna in the wilderness (cf. Exod 16:4). Although the Jews never suggested that Moses gave the bread to their ancestors, Jesus uses a well-known debating technique to make the point very clear. Just as God gave their ancestors manna from heaven, so God gives them the true bread from heaven, the bread that gives life to the world. Through careful explanation, Jesus has led them away from a superficial search for physical satisfaction to a desire for the deeper things of God. More than that, he has prepared them for his self-proclamation: I am the bread of life.

Several comments prepare them for this astounding assertion. Jesus has already said that the food that endures will be given to them by the Son of Man (v. 27), and he has stated that both the Son of Man and he himself have a special relationship with the one whom he calls Father (vv. 27, 23), thus identifying himself with the mysterious Son of Man. The people realized that Jesus is claiming to be the one sent by God in whom they must believe (vv. 29–30). This all adds up to the conclusion that Jesus, the Son of Man, is also the bread of life that God has sent down from heaven. While the metaphor of bread requires the idea of eating, the teaching of this section has to do with faith, not Eucharist. Here bread of life is a wisdom theme, and those who believe will be satisfied (v. 35).

Themes of the Day

This Sunday continues the theme of the bread of life. The readings show again God's loving care of the people. However, this Sunday the meaning of this feeding begins to unfold. The food that is given is not just bread from the earth; it is bread from heaven. We hear this in the first reading. The Gospel tells us that Jesus is the true bread from heaven. Once again it is the epistle that instructs us as to the implications of this reality in our daily lives.

Bread from Heaven

In many ways the Exodus story of the bread from heaven is similar to last Sunday's accounts. God uses natural means to feed the people. Last week it was barley loaves; this week it is substance from the tamarisk tree and low-flying quail. However, something is different in today's story. There is not an overabundance of food. In fact, the people are forbidden to collect more than they need for that day. The point of this story is not divine prodigality but total dependence on God. The bread comes from heaven not merely because the food seems to come down from the sky but because it comes from God. The restriction about collecting it was meant to emphasize this point. Our survival is in God's hands, not ours.

The True Bread from Heaven

Jesus insists that he is the true bread from heaven; he is the real basis of our survival. The people followed him because they saw him as a source of bread; they did not realize that he is also the source of life. If we fill ourselves with all that the world provides as nourishment we will still hunger. Neither the barley loaves nor the food that God supplied in the wilderness will permanently satisfy us. We will feast on it, but we will be hungry again. The bread that Jesus is, this bread that really comes from heaven, is different. Its effects will endure for eternal life. It is faith in Jesus that will satisfy our deepest hungers, and we will not be able to survive apart from him.

Put On the New Self

Acceptance of Jesus as the source of our life and the very nourishment of our spirits effects a total transformation in us. We are no longer content to live with full bellies but empty minds. We put aside our old selves steeped in ignorance and self-interest, and we put on a new self created in his image. Having fed on the bread from heaven, we are mysteriously transformed into it. The spirit of our minds has been renewed. We have learned Christ; we are nourished by his teaching. As a result, we launch out into a way of living that witnesses to our new understanding, our new life.

Nineteenth Sunday in Ordinary Time

1 Kings 19:4-8

The prophet Elijah goes into the desert, not to pray or to recommit himself to the service of the LORD but in the hope that he will die. The scene is both tragic and comic. He has had enough. The office of prophet has become too heavy to bear. He has been no more successful in turning the people away from their sinful lives than were his ancestors before him. Suicide does not appear to have been an option, and so he prays that God will take his life. This is a tragic picture.

Having journeyed a significant distance into the desert, he sits under a broom tree. This is not a hardy tree. It does not afford much shade, but it is better than nothing. The tree is common to the wadi, a watercourse that is dry except during rainfalls. Then it can become a raging torrent. When in bloom the tree produces a delicate white flower with a maroon center. The sight of this man of God, sitting dejected under a delicate plant that is determined to survive in the face of impossible odds, creates a scene that is rather comic.

The prophet's prayer for death is not heard. His mission has not yet been completed. An angel of the LORD, a messenger from God, comes to him twice, offering him food and drink. It is not uncommon that God reveals something in a dream (cf. Jacob; Genesis 22) or that people are roused from sleep in order to accept a mission from God (cf. Samuel; 1 Sam 3:2-11). The prophet should have realized that God was at work in these events, since otherwise it would have been unlikely for him to find a baked cake and a jug of water in the wilderness. Still, it took two visits from the angel before he responded adequately. All of this is probably the author's way of emphasizing the supernatural origin of the feats that the prophet was about to accomplish.

In the strength of this mysterious food and water, Elijah walks forty days and forty nights. This is a conventional number that carries great significance. Four probably derives its importance from the number of quadrants in a circle. Ten is a cardinal number that denotes totality. Four times ten signifies completeness. The symbolism of the number forty indicates the miraculous abilities of the nourishment. It is also a number that is closely associated with the Exodus tradition, which is linked with the mountain to which Elijah walks. In this he is like Moses, who was with the Lord for forty days and forty nights, neither eating nor drinking, while he was being given the Law (Exod 34:28).

Horeb rather than Sinai is the name of the mountain of revelation, according to the biblical traditions associated with the northern tribes. Since this is a story about a northern prophet, the designation is appropriate. Elijah travels to the mountain of revelation, perhaps to have a revelation of his own. Whatever the case may be, a story that begins with desperation ends with the prophet once again actively involved in the affairs of God.

Psalm 34:2-3, 4-5, 6-7, 8-9

The psalm response is part of an acrostic, a poem whose structure follows the order of the alphabet. Although the content of such psalms may vary, the form (the entire alphabet) always signifies the same thing, completeness. This psalm is less a prayer than an instruction. Its teaching is the conventional understanding of retribution: the righteous will be blessed and the wicked will be punished. In this first part of the poem the psalmist thanks God for having been delivered from distress and invites others to join in praising God. The attitude of the psalmist gives witness to others and develops into a pedagogical technique, teaching others to act in the same way.

The psalm begins with an expression of praise of God and an acknowledgment of the appropriateness of blessing God. This praise probably takes place in some kind of liturgical setting, for it is heard by the lowly (*ʿănāwîm*), those who live in trust and dependence on the LORD. They are here invited to join with the psalmist in rejoicing and praising God's name.

Normally in psalms of thanksgiving the reasons for gratitude are recited. Without going into detail, the psalmist confesses having been in distress, having turned to the LORD, and having been rescued. This is the reason for gratitude. This is why the psalmist glorifies God and bids others to do the same.

The congregation is now given explicit directions. They are encouraged to look to the LORD so that they too may rejoice in gratitude, their faces radiant and not filled with shame. The face is the expression of one's dignity, of one's status in the community. To lose face is to lose honor, to be shamed. The companions of the psalmist are encouraged to attach themselves to God and thereby to enjoy the blessings this ensures. The fate of the psalmist is placed before them as an example to follow.

An image that might be unfamiliar is used to demonstrate this. An angel or messenger from God pitches a protective camp around those who fear the LORD, who stand in awe and reverence of God's majesty and power. Thus they are guarded by the power of God against anything that might endanger them.

The passage ends with an admonition. The congregation is encouraged to taste God's goodness, to partake of it a little, to sample it a bit. The psalmist is saying that if only they put God's goodness to the test they will see for themselves how delectable it is, how satisfying it can be. They have the psalmist's witness. It is now time for them to experience God's goodness for themselves.

Ephesians 4:30–5:2

The reading from Ephesians contains two very unusual exhortations: do not grieve the Spirit, and be imitators of God. We can get some sense of what each exhortation means, since the author gives two lists of behaviors, each of which characterizes one of these pivotal dispositions. The entire reading reflects a trinitarian theology, which, if they are faithful, should shape the behavior of the Christians.

The passage opens with a plea directed to the Christians not to grieve the Holy Spirit of God. They have been sealed by this Spirit, a seal that is a pledge of the fulfillment of their redemption. The language denotes a personal relationship; the verb suggests that the Spirit can be saddened by the unseemly behavior of the believers. There is a presumption here that the seal not only sets the Christians apart as belonging to the Spirit, it also guarantees that they have been transformed into people who live according to that Spirit.

The author warns against several weaknesses that can undermine a community. Bitterness is that disposition that cherishes resentment. It clings to former grievances, real or imaginary. Fury is anger expressed in violent outbursts of temper. Anger is the eruption of impulsive passion. Shouting refers to voices raised in face-to-face quarreling. Reviling denotes slanderous words spoken behind another's back. Malice is less a vice than a quality of evil. It includes within itself all sinful dispositions that oppose living in the Spirit. It is very clear from this list that the Spirit is saddened by anything that threatens the harmony of the Christian community.

The author urges the Christians to live in a completely different way. They should be kind *(chrēstos)* and treat others with the same grace or generosity of heart as shown to them by God. They are to be compassionate or tender-hearted with deep interior feelings toward others. Kindness and compassion forge a spirit of acceptance, tolerance, and patience. Finally, the Christians are to forgive others as God has forgiven them by accepting the sacrifice of Christ on their behalf.

The second exhortation is even more unusual than the first. The Christians are admonished to be imitators of God just as children are imitators of their parents. This leads into a further admonition to live lives governed by love. In this Christ is to be their example. As Christ, out of love, offered himself for them, so they must be willing, out of love, to live lives of self-sacrifice. The trinitarian theology is obvious. As imitators of God, and after the example of Christ, they have been called to live according to the Spirit.

John 6:41-51

The murmuring of Jesus' Jewish opponents, prompted by his claim to be the bread that came down from heaven, is reminiscent of the murmuring of the Israelites in the wilderness, to which God responded with manna from heaven. Some of the people were unwilling to accept Jesus' assertion because they were acquainted with him and with his parents. Since they knew his human origins, how could he rightfully maintain a heavenly origin?

The exchange between Jesus and his opponents was a kind of social sparring that was meant to enhance the status of one member of the exchange as it diminished the status of the other. Criticizing Jesus as they did was bound to produce a sharp response from him, and respond he did, by explaining that their rejection of him was evidence that they had not been called by God. In a clever turn of phrase, he declares that only those drawn by God will be drawn to the one who was sent by God. If one does not come to Jesus, it is probably a sign that person was never called by God. This argument ends with a declaration of Jesus' eschatological authority and power. Not only is he the one who came down from heaven, but he is the one who will raise people up from the dead.

The relationship between Jesus and God is taken up again (vv. 45–46). Quoting a passage from one of the prophets (cf. Isa 54:13), Jesus reinterprets a wisdom theme in order to demonstrate this relationship. He maintains that those who have been drawn by God will be taught by God that Jesus is indeed the one who was sent by God. When they have learned this lesson from God, they will come to Jesus. Salvation is the work of God, whom Jesus calls his Father. The argument concludes with an audacious statement. Jesus claims that he is the only one who has seen the Father, because he is the only one who has come from God. He further states that whoever believes this has eternal life.

Jesus returns to his teaching on the bread of life (vv. 48–51). In it he makes two self-revelatory proclamations: I am the bread of life; I am the living bread from heaven. The implications of these claims become clear when they are seen as proceeding from the distinctive relationship with God that he has just explained. Picking up again the familiar story of the manna in the wilderness, he compares and contrasts the former bread from heaven with himself, the living, life-giving bread. Unlike the manna that provided sustenance for a short time, Jesus is the source of life eternal. Although he is like the manna in that both he and it were sent from heaven by God, the manna was merely rained from the sky, while in the incarnation Jesus proceeded from God's very self.

The final theme of the reading is both striking and ambiguous. Jesus identifies the bread of heaven as his flesh. There is probably an allusion here to the Eucharist. However, the word "flesh" could also refer to the human way of his being in the world. To give his flesh is to surrender his own human life so that the world may have eternal life. Thus the Eucharist and the death of Jesus cannot be separated.

Themes of the Day

The significance of Jesus as the bread of life is further revealed. Today's readings lay before us two different ways of responding to the demands of God. One of them is doubt and disapproval, the other is acceptance in obedient faith. The claims that Jesus made about himself in his bread of life discourse are quite radical. People began to murmur against him. In response he defended himself by tracing his origin back to God. He concluded his teaching by making an even more radical claim.

Murmuring Against God

There are times when it seems that God is just asking too much of us. We have labored on behalf of others, but we do not see the fruits of our labor, or it does not seem to be appreciated. Our families take us for granted, and we are exploited in our work. This is particularly trying when all we have wanted was to be of service to others, to help them wherever we could. The work itself is hard enough, but when we meet such opposition we are tempted to give up. What is the point of giving of oneself when it only seems to be futile? In this we are like Elijah.

There are other times when we are challenged to change our way of thinking and to accept a new perspective that seems to make extraordinary demands on us. A new way of understanding Church may call us to be open to the cultural diversity within the community. Or it might claim that we have a responsibility toward the poor and homeless in our midst. New biblical insights make us question our familiar understanding of God or of Jesus or of ourselves. In this we might be like the Jews who murmured against Jesus. We want evidence to substantiate these radical new claims.

Jesus' Defense

Despite the fact that he was so boldly challenged, Jesus gave those who murmured against him an answer to their protest. He traced his origin back to God, thus showing that he had the right to make such claims. However, the evidence he offered could only be accepted in faith. And so it is with us. When we ask God for some kind of sign that will assure us that this new challenge is really what God wants of us, the answers we receive must themselves be accepted and understood in faith. The only assurance we are given is the promise that those who are open to God will be taught by God. The only assurance we have is rooted in faith, and those who are not open in faith will not understand. God does indeed ask a great deal from us.

Acceptance in Obedient Faith

Once again it is the epistle that furnishes us guidelines for living out this faith. It should be noted that these all pertain to life in community. They do not tame the challenge of the other readings, they open it up. We are told to put away our murmuring, our bitterness and anger. We are exhorted to be kind.

Twentieth Sunday in Ordinary Time
Proverbs 9:1-6

The account of Wisdom preparing a banquet and inviting people to it can be interpreted on several levels. First, the setting for the banquet and the food that will be served, along with the maidens who attend to Woman Wisdom and the simple people invited to the feast, are all quite average. This suggests that the account is of some ordinary social function. However, the one who is doing the planning and inviting is none other than Wisdom, a figure who is much more than merely human. This mysterious figure has been interpreted principally as either an ancient deity or a cosmic being. Most likely the reading contains aspects of the ordinary, the divine, and the cosmic perspectives.

The most striking characteristic of this account is the importance it gives to women. There is no prominent man in the report; there is no indication that men controlled the behavior of Wisdom or of her maidens. The implications of this change in gender importance are interesting, regardless of one's own basic interpretation of the identity of Wisdom.

If Wisdom is an ancient deity, then her house would be regarded as a temple with seven pillars. The banquet she prepares would be a sacrificial feast, and those she invites would be her devotees. If she is a cosmic being (cf. Prov 8:22-31), her house would be the universe, built on the foundation of seven heavenly bodies. Her banquet would consist of the life-giving forces that sustain all created things. If Wisdom is to be perceived as neither a cultic nor a cosmological being, the reference could be to a house of study where young men would be invited to come and feast on knowledge and understanding. Each perspective offers an interesting interpretation, though no one of them can make any conclusive claims.

Wisdom's banquet is lavish. Meat, always a luxury, has been carefully prepared, and wine has probably been mixed with spices in order to improve its taste and strengthen its potency. Everything is ready, and servants are sent out to call in the guests. Regardless of the interpretation preferred, the picture has been sketched in the contours of the wisdom tradition. Wisdom always invites, cajoles, persuades. She never commands, as does law. She feeds the desire for knowledge and insight; she satisfies the hunger for learning. Wisdom is interested in the simple, the innocent, the childlike, those who are eager to learn. She oversees all of the mysteries of the universe; in her hands are the secrets of life. These are the delicacies with which she spreads her table; this is the fare that she offers her guests. No one can survive without Wisdom; the way of understanding is the way to life.

Psalm 34:2-3, 4-5, 6-7

The psalm response is part of an acrostic, a poem whose structure follows the order of the alphabet. Although the content of such psalms may vary, the form (the entire alphabet) always signifies the same thing, completeness. This psalm is less a prayer than an instruction. Its teaching is the conventional understanding of retribution: the righteous will be blessed and the wicked will be punished. In the first part of the poem the psalmist thanks God for having been delivered from distress and invites others to join in praising God. The attitude of the psalmist gives witness to others and develops into a pedagogical technique, teaching others to act in the same way.

The psalm begins with an expression of praise of God and an acknowledgment of the appropriateness of blessing God. This praise probably takes place in some kind of liturgical setting, for it is heard by the lowly *(ʿănāwîm)*, those who live in trust and dependence on the LORD. They are here invited to join with the psalmist in rejoicing and in praising God's name.

Normally, in psalms of thanksgiving the reasons for gratitude are recited. Without going into detail the psalmist confesses having been in distress, having turned to the LORD, and having been rescued. This is the reason for gratitude. This is why the psalmist glorifies God and bids others to do the same.

The congregation is now given explicit directions. They are encouraged to look to the LORD so that they too may rejoice in gratitude, their faces radiant and not filled with shame. The face is the expression of one's dignity, of one's status in the community. To lose face is to lose honor, or to be shamed. The companions of the psalmist are here encouraged to attach themselves to God and thereby to enjoy the blessings that this ensures. The fate of the psalmist is placed before them as an example to follow.

Ephesians 5:15-20

Once again the author lays out a wisdom instruction. The Christians are encouraged to live (walk, *peripateō*) like the wise, not like the foolish. The wise are those who know how to make the most out of every opportunity. They can recognize the decisive point of the moment *(kairós)*, and they can seize it. This is an indispensable trait to have, especially at a time when the days are evil. The urgency in this admonition could spring from the belief that the time was short and opportunities might not come again. However, every generation goes through evil days, and from a wisdom point of view, such circumspection was always appropriate.

The ignorance against which the author warns is the inability to draw prudent conclusions in practical situations. Some people just do not seem able to learn from experience. This can be a very serious situation, since it means they have not learned from the consequences of their actions. These consequences should help them discern which is the right path of behavior to follow. When they are unable or unwilling to draw such conclusions, they live lives that have no direction. As a remedy to such disorder, the author urges the Christians to try to discover what might be God's will for them and to live in accordance with it.

The way of the foolish and the way of the wise are next distinguished by the characteristic spirit influencing each of them. The way of the foolish is frequently under the sway of the spirit of drunkenness, which deprives them of the ability to perceive clearly and to discern accurately. Debauchery probably stands for any kind of conduct that results from uninhibited freedom, such as that produced by drunkenness. In contrast to this type of behavior, the way of the wise is prompted by the Spirit of God, which can also be quite intoxicating and which manifests itself in the community in several different ways.

The nature of the manifestations of the Spirit described here suggests that the setting is probably some kind of a liturgical assembly. The service itself includes congregational participation in communal exchange, praying, and singing, as well as silent prayer to God. Giving thanks to God *(eucharistéō)* is at the heart of the community's devotion. They are exhorted to thank God always and for everything, because everything is a gift from God. The trinitarian character of their lives and of their prayer is again clearly defined. Prompted by the Spirit, in the name of the Lord Jesus Christ they are to thank God, who is called Father. Living in this manner is the true way of wisdom.

John 6:51-58

The bread of life discourse that has been the subject of the Gospel reading for the last several Sundays ends here with a eucharistic reinterpretation of the manna tradition. Today's passage begins where last Sunday's reading ended, with Jesus identifying his flesh as the bread of heaven and alluding to his death given for the life of the world. The thought of feeding on the flesh of another was repulsive to some of his hearers, as it most likely is to many today. Such an assertion demands some kind of explanation, and Jesus offers it.

In unmistakable language Jesus declares that his flesh is food and his blood is drink. Lest this claim go unnoticed, he states it four times (vv. 53–56). The phrase "flesh and blood" is rich in meaning. On a literal level, it is a common way of characterizing a human being. When applied to Jesus, it is a proclamation of faith in the incarnation. He was indeed "flesh and blood." On another level, it calls to mind the victim of sacrifice that is first slaughtered (flesh and blood) and then shared at a cultic meal (food and drink). Jesus is "flesh and blood" in this way as well, first as the sacrificial victim on the cross and then as eucharistic food and drink.

The christological interpretation of the manna has taken on new meaning here. The flesh and blood of Jesus have become the source of life for those who partake of it. In other words, eternal life comes from feeding on Jesus, not simply from believing in him, as was stated in the Gospel readings of earlier Sundays (John 6:29, Eighteenth Sunday in Ordinary Time; 6:47, Nineteenth Sunday in Ordinary Time). Jesus goes one step further in his teaching on eternal life. He implies that it is not something that believers merely hope to enjoy in the future. Instead, those who share in the Eucharist already possess eternal life. What the future holds for them is the fullness of life that will be enjoyed after the general resurrection on the last day.

The course through which eternal life passes from God to us is simply sketched. The living God whom Jesus calls Father is the source of this life; Jesus already enjoys it because of his intimate union with God; believers already enjoy it because they feed on Jesus, who is the bread of life.

Jesus develops the eating metaphor still further. He maintains that just as we and what we eat and drink become one, so Jesus and those who feed on him form an intimate union. In a mutually intimate way, they abide in him and he in them. The Greek word used here *(ménō)* means "to stay in a place," "to abide forever." This implies that Jesus does not merely visit those who feed on him, he stays with them; he dwells there permanently. Eucharistic union with Jesus is as intimate as is the act of eating, and the mutual indwelling that results from it is just as personal.

There should now be no question in the minds of his hearers. Jesus, not manna, is the bread that came, not from the sky but from the very being of God. Those who ate manna died; those who feed on Jesus live forever.

Themes of the Day

Today the significance of Jesus as the bread of life and the implications for our own lives are revealed in all their fullness. We have seen that he is not merely bread from heaven, he is also the bread of life. We have also seen that only those who believe in him have the promise of eternal life. In today's readings we are invited to sit at the banquet he has prepared for us, there to feed on his own flesh and blood.

The Banquet of Wisdom

Wisdom, this mysterious being that was with God at the time of creation, invites us to her banquet. Since she is the way to God, those who accept her invitation will feast on the things of God. This is not a paltry meal that meets only basic needs. It is a lavish banquet with delicious food and exhilarating drink. Wisdom is not only generous in what she offers, she extends her invitation to all. In fact, she goes out in search of those she wishes to feed. The banquet of Wisdom is an apt symbol of the generosity of God, open to all, enriching all.

This is in sharp contrast to the kind of feasting depicted in the epistle. Fools follow their own designs and do not heed the call of Wisdom. They succumb to the temptations of the evil days in which they live, and they feast on selfishness, ignorance, and debauchery. Two banquets are set before us. Both of them are tempting. Which one will we choose?

The Bread Is His Flesh

In many ways the banquet Jesus offers is like the banquet of Wisdom. It is lavish with choice foods and drink that gladdens the heart. It promises to enrich us in ways beyond our imagination, and it is open to all. However, the banquet to which Jesus invites us far exceeds even the table that Wisdom spreads out for her guests. At it we feast on his body and his blood. He gives himself totally to us, to enliven us, to nourish us, to strengthen us. If we feed at Wisdom's table, we will know the things of God. If we feed at the table of the Lord, we will have life because of him, and we will be raised up on the last day to live forever.

This is truly a bold claim and a hard saying. We are told that the food we eat is his body and what we drink is his blood. We are told that his body, not merely his teaching, is the true bread that came down from heaven. We are told that only if we eat and drink what he offers will we have eternal life. He makes the claim and extends the invitation. How will we hear it? How will we respond?

Twenty-First Sunday

Joshua 24:1-2a, 15-17, 18b

This short passage contains several clues that help us sketch a setting for the events that unfold. Moses must be dead, for Joshua is the undisputed leader. The people are gathered at Shechem, an ancient shrine located between Mount Ebal and Mount Gerizim in that part of the land that will one day be known as Samaria. This is a universal convocation of all of the tribes along with all those who hold a position of leadership. It is a religious assembly, for the people are standing "before God," an expression that probably refers to the ark of the covenant. The ark was a chest which contained several of Israel's sacred objects and which became the symbol of God's presence in the midst of the people. There are many indicators here of the seriousness of the gathering.

Joshua's address to the assembly is in the form of a prophetic declaration: Thus says the LORD. He places before the people a choice that will shape their own self-identity and will determine the path they—and their descendants— will travel for the rest of their lives. Whom will they serve? Three options are given. They can continue to serve their ancestral gods and thus remain true to their past identity. They can opt for the gods of the people in whose land they are now dwelling and thus hope to reap the blessings that accompany that land. Or they can worship the LORD, who is tied neither to their cultural past nor to their geographic present. They must make a choice from among all the gods to whom they can commit themselves.

Joshua's statement of choice is decisive: We will serve the LORD. The rest of the people make the same decision: We will serve the LORD. In explaining the reasons for their choice, they rehearse the high points of the saving acts that God performed in their midst and for their sake. These include the deliverance from bondage, the wonders in the wilderness, and the entrance into the land. Through all of this God was there, protecting them every step of the way. Their choice of a god was determined not by the territory within which they lived, as was the case with many of the nations of the time, but by the personal involvement of God in their lives.

The fact that this historical recital was given as the reason for choosing God, a characteristic of a covenant ritual, suggests that the event recounted was some ceremony of this type. Since the narrative leads one to believe that there are some in the community who have not yet definitively committed themselves to the LORD, it is possible that this was a covenant renewal ceremony that also incorporated new members.

Psalm 34:2-3, 16-17, 18-19, 20-21

The responsorial psalm for today is the third part of the acrostic poem that constituted the reading for the Nineteenth and Twentieth Sundays in Ordinary Time. It has already been noted that this psalm is less a prayer than an instruction. Its content teaches that the righteous will be blessed and the wicked will be punished. As was the case last week, the passage for today begins with the first two verses of the psalm, altering its alphabetical sequence but providing a fitting context for today's verses. The psalmist's praise of God and description of the benefits that flow from such devotion teach others to praise God so they might enjoy similar blessing. Mention of the lowly ones suggests a communal, probably liturgical, setting.

The contrast between the just and the wicked is clearly drawn. God looks favorably toward the righteous. Their cries for help will be heard and God will provide them with what they need. The fortunes of the wicked will be just the reverse. The face of the LORD will be set against them and they will experience God's hostility in the worst possible way. Remembrance of them will be wiped out. In a society that does not have a clear teaching about life after this life, such a fate means that no trace of the person will survive, and it will be as if that person had never even existed.

The psalmist is not naive about the vicissitudes of life, even the life of the upright. In many instances the theory of retribution is more a statement of faith in God's justice than an accurate description of the circumstances of life. Good people do indeed suffer, but they turn to God in their pain and misery. Whether they are rescued from their affliction or not, they stand under the promise of God's loving presence. Because suffering is often seen as the result of alienation from God, assurance of God's nearness can alleviate the distress that such a misperception might cause.

Not only do good people suffer, but sometimes it seems that they suffer precisely because they are good. This might be because they are more sensitive to right and wrong, or perhaps they are the victims of the sinfulness of others. Whatever the reason may be, the lives of the righteous are often fraught with trouble. The psalmist claims that God hears the cry of these upright people and draws them out of their afflictions. The response's final statement of faith characterizes God as the protector of the vulnerable, watching over them lest they be harmed in any way. The kind of teaching found in this psalm is intended to inspire virtuous living and to instill certain trust in the promises of reward for such living.

Ephesians 5:21-32

This reading addresses some of the responsibilities of husbands in traditional patriarchal marriage. The passage begins with a general statement recommending mutual subordination. However, the reading itself does not demonstrate true mutuality. Wives are told to be subordinate; husbands are not. Although the subordination of wives is stated, the reading really focuses on the obligations of husbands. The patriarchal character of the human relationship described here presents a strong challenge for contemporary believers, who have a very different understanding of the dignity of women and the mutuality that is expected in male-female relationships, especially marriage.

The argument developed is somewhat circular. First, marriage becomes a metaphor for characterizing the relationship between Christ and the Church. Then this latter relationship is employed as an analogy for understanding marriage. The analogy was intended to function in ways that would enhance the dignity of each of the human partners. However, it has often been used to reinforce the inferior status of the wives and, because the husbands are compared with Christ, to assign Christ's authority to the men. When this has been done, the primary point of the analogy, which is the self-sacrificing love required of husbands, is misrepresented.

Christ loved the Church enough to give his life for it. This is the degree of spousal commitment envisioned for husbands. If husbands were to love their wives to this degree, the patriarchal structure of domination might be undermined. Following the example of Christ, who sacrificed his divine privileges for the sake of the Church, husbands would be sacrificing their patriarchal privileges for the sake of their wives.

Another metaphor is used in the second part of the reading (vv. 28–30). The Genesis account of the physical union of the couple is reinterpreted here to describe the character of the love husbands are to have for their wives. In

Genesis the two are described as constituting one flesh (Gen 2:24). Building on this concept, the author argues that when husbands love their partners they are loving themselves. This does not mean that wives have been subsumed into their husbands. It means that the intimacy portrayed is one of identification. The husbands are identified with their wives, just as Christ is identified with the Church. The unusual marriage custom of the man leaving his home of origin in order to be joined to his wife, rather than the wife leaving hers, demonstrates the lengths to which husbands should be willing to sacrifice for their wives.

In the last statement (v. 32) the argument takes a final twist. The author seems caught in the complexity of the argument and moves away from developing the notions of spousal relationship and responsibilities. The transformed understanding of marriage is now used to characterize the mysterious union of Christ and the Church.

John 6:60-69

In so many situations Jesus' words or deeds were met with disbelief. This is the case in the episode recounted in today's Gospel. What is shocking, however, is that the disbelief comes not from the Jewish opponents of Jesus but from some of his own disciples. They were more than shocked, they were scandalized by what he said. What he had just been saying to them about himself was more than even they could take. The author was referring here to Jesus' identification of himself as the Son of Man who had come down from heaven.

Rather than soften the hardness of his message, Jesus responds to the challenge of these unbelievers with one of his own. If they were troubled by the thought of him descending from heaven, what would they think about him ascending back to where he had been originally? Both descending and ascending imply that he is a heavenly being, the very claim that scandalized his hearers in the first place. Jesus does not say they will witness his ascent, he simply asks them how they would respond if they saw it happen. It is a wonderful question, for one would think that such an extraordinary occurrence would certainly fill them with wonder and faith. However, the question implies that since they have not believed Jesus descended from heaven in the first place, they would probably remain unconvinced even if he ascended back to heaven.

Jesus continues the defense of his teaching by setting the notion of flesh over against that of spirit. He insists that the flesh, which here refers to the human way of being in the world, cannot give life. He points out that only the Spirit gives life, and then he claims that his teaching is both Spirit and life. Jesus knows that in many instances seeing is not believing. Those who have followed him as disciples have seen the wonders he has performed, yet they do not believe. Faith in Jesus is not something that comes easily or naturally. It is a grace given by God. This grace may have been available to all, but Jesus knew that some would accept him and some would not. As a result of this particular discourse, some of the disciples no longer followed him.

Jesus is not indifferent toward the departure of these disciples. He turns to the Twelve to see what they are going to do. He neither asks them to stay nor gives them permission to go. He simply poses the question: Do you want to leave too? Assuming the role of spokesperson of the Twelve, Simon Peter responds with three statements of faith. The first is quite guileless. He declares that there is no one else to whom they can go, because there is no one else quite like Jesus. With his second statement he shows that he has accepted what Jesus has just been teaching about eternal life. The final statement brings his profession of faith to an amazing conclusion. He uses a messianic title to identify Jesus. This passage indicates that while some of his followers have turned away, others have been convinced of the trustworthiness of Jesus' claims.

Themes of the Day

Our consideration of Jesus' teaching about the bread of life leads us to the threshold of decision. Will we choose Jesus, despite the incredible claims he makes? Or will we decide to stay where we are, satisfied with the lives we are living? Choosing Jesus will bring us deeper and deeper into the mystery of the Eucharist. Are we willing to go there?

Decide Today

The decisions called for in today's readings are not the kind we face everyday. They are not choices among several options, all of relatively the same value. Rather, they are life decisions, the kind that determine the fundamental direction we will take and consequently influence every other decision we will make. The people at the time of Joshua had to decide which god they would worship. This decision would determine their identity. They would be known as the people of whichever god they would choose, and they would be bound to the norms and practices set down by that god. "Decide today whom you will serve." The disciples of Jesus had to make a similar decision. Was he the one who would fulfill their messianic expectations? And if not to him, "To whom shall we go?"

We make our decisions based on our experience and our aspirations. Is the direction we will take a familiar one? And if it is not, is there reason to think it is still the one for us to take? Is there someone who knows this path and who can help us in our decision? If there is not, is there any reason for us still to decide on this course of action? It seems that the major decisions in life must be made on the basis of insufficient information. In other words, they demand faith.

The Price of Decision

The choices we make really determine the character of our union with God. It is God who has called us out of the slavery of sin and protected us throughout the journey of our lives. When we find ourselves at the point of decision, why should we choose someone else? If we have walked with Jesus through some of the challenges of life and have witnessed the wonders he can perform, why should we choose someone else? The new demands placed on us may be so great, or the commitment required of us may be so demanding, that we feel we can walk with him no longer. The Church may be changing in ways we do not appreciate, or it may not be changing in the ways we believe it should, so we may feel that we can walk with him no longer.

Union with God

If we decide to commit ourselves, we will enter into a union with God deeper than anything we have previously known. However, this union will be based on faith. We may understand no more than we did in the past, and things may be no more to our liking. But "to whom shall we go?" Jesus is God's holy one; he has the words of eternal life.

Ordinary Time (Part Four)

Twenty-Second Sunday Deuteronomy 4:1-2, 6-8 Keep the commandments	Psalm 15:2-5 The just live with God	James 1:17-18, 21b-22, 27 Be doers of the word	Mark 7:1-8, 14-15, 21-23 Cling to God's commandments
Twenty-Third Sunday Isaiah 35:4-7a God will heal, the earth will bloom	Psalm 146:7-10 Praise the LORD	James 2:1-5 The poor are heirs	Mark 7:31-37 Jesus heals
Twenty-Fourth Sunday Isaiah 50:4c-9a I gave my back to those who beat me	Psalm 116:1-6, 8-9 I walk before the LORD	James 2:14-18 Faith without works is dead	Mark 8:27-35 You are the Christ
Twenty-Fifth Sunday Wisdom 2:12, 17-20 Condemn with a shameful death	Psalm 54:3-8 The LORD upholds my life	James 3:16–4:3 The fruit of righteousness is peace	Mark 9:30-37 The Son of Man is handed over
Twenty-Sixth Sunday Numbers 11:25-29 Are you jealous for my sake?	Psalm 19:8, 10, 12-14 God's precepts give me joy	James 5:1-6 Your wealth has rotted	Mark 9:38-43, 45, 47-48 Who is not against us is for us
Twenty-Seventh Sunday Genesis 2:18-24 The two become one flesh	Psalm 128:1-6 May the LORD bless us	Hebrews 2:9-11 All have one origin	Mark 10:2-16 What God has joined together

Sunday	Psalm	Second Reading	Gospel
Twenty-Eighth Sunday Wisdom 7:7-11 Wisdom is better than riches	Psalm 90:12-17 Fill us with your love	Hebrews 4:12-13 God's word is discerning	Mark 10:17-30 Sell what you have
Twenty-Ninth Sunday Isaiah 53:10-11 He gives his life as an offering	Psalm 33:4-5, 18-20, 22 Let your mercy be on us	Hebrews 4:14-16 Let us approach God	Mark 10:35-45 He came to give his life
Thirtieth Sunday Jeremiah 31:7-9 God consoles the needy	Psalm 126:1-6 God has done great things	Hebrews 5:1-6 A priest forever	Mark 10:46-52 I want to see
Thirty-First Sunday Deuteronomy 6:2-6 Hear, O Israel	Psalm 18:2-4, 47, 51 I love you, LORD	Hebrews 7:23-28 His priesthood lasts forever	Mark 12:28b-34 Love the Lord your God
Thirty-Second Sunday 1 Kings 17:10-16 The widow made a cake	Psalm 146:7-10 Praise the LORD	Hebrews 9:24-28 Christ was offered for sin	Mark 12:38-44 The poor widow gave all
Thirty-Third Sunday Daniel 12:1-3 Your people will escape	Psalm 16:5, 8-11 You are my inheritance	Hebrews 10:11-14, 18 One offering made all perfect	Mark 13:24-32 The elect are gathered
Thirty-Fourth Sunday **(Christ the King)** Daniel 7:13-14 An everlasting dominion	Psalm 93:1-2, 5 The LORD is king	Revelation 1:5-8 A kingdom of priests	John 18:33b-37 I am a king

Ordinary Time (Part Four)

Initial Reading of the Ordinary Lectionary (Part Four)

Introduction

There is no recognizable pattern to the readings for this segment of Ordinary Time. They seem to resemble life itself, which is like a quilt made up of various pieces of cloth sewed together to create a distinctive design, or a tapestry wherein are woven threads of various colors, all contributing to a work of art. As a collection of liturgical readings they provide us with direction and inspiration as we move from Sunday to Sunday.

First Testament Readings

The readings from the First Testament are a series of vignettes that reveal what it means to be numbered among the people of God. They open with an exhortation to obey God's commandments, and they close with a view of the glorious end of time. In between we find prophetic messages of consolation, warnings of the hardships we must face, promises of blessings to come, and examples of human frailty to be avoided and heroic virtue to follow.

Psalms

The psalm responses are also varied in the sentiments they express. It is interesting that, grouped as they are in this segment, they form a kind of *inclusio*. The first psalm is a liturgical entrance prayer, and the last one is a hymn of praise that celebrates God's enthronement. The others are hymns of thanksgiving or praise, laments, or wisdom instructions, all fitting responses to some experience of life.

Epistles

With the exception of the reading from the book of Revelation assigned to the solemnity of Christ the King, the epistles are continuous readings from the letter of James and the letter to the Hebrews. The passages from the letter written by James seem to be more in the style of wisdom instruction than of moral injunction. They address the relationship between faith and good works, wealth and poverty, justice and peace.

The letter to the Hebrews is primarily concerned with the priesthood of Jesus. These readings treat his human nature and the cosmic and eternal character of his priesthood, as well as the quality and effect of his sacrifice.

Gospels

The Gospel readings continue the account of the life of Jesus as recorded by Mark. They report the wonders Jesus performed wherever he went and the opposition they frequently generated. They describe the struggles encountered by those who followed Jesus and the unfortunate departure of some. There are several accounts of their misunderstanding of him and his mission, an instruction on the centrality of love, one on the danger of hypocrisy, and a description of the trials that will accompany the end of time. The Gospel readings conclude with Jesus' acknowledgment of his kingdom.

Mosaic of Readings

The readings for this last segment of Ordinary Time seem to focus their attention on messianic fulfillment. There are some final instructions about discipleship and various exhortations about righteous living in accord with the teachings of Jesus. The central theme of that teaching, the covenant of love, which was inaugurated by God and is shared by all, is the content of our final meditation before we look at the end of time and the glorious enthronement of Christ. The Liturgical Year has come to an end. The reign of God has been established, and we share in the triumph of our glorious Savior.

Readings

Twenty-Second Sunday in Ordinary Time
Deuteronomy 4:1-2, 6-8

This address of Moses opens with the exhortation to hear *(sh^ema[>])*. It is a solemn summons used to assemble the people of God for consultation, worship, or war. It is used here to stress the significance of the proclamation of the law that is to follow. A statute *(hōq)* is something that has been chiseled into stone. It is firm and lasting. An ordinance *(mishpāt)* is a decision handed down by a judge. Because disputes were frequently decided by priests and the decisions were remembered at times of worship, laws came to be associated with shrines.

Blessings from God can be classified under two major categories: those freely given with no return required (e.g., the promise made to Abraham, Gen 12:2-3), and those given conditionally, dependent upon the fulfillment of certain requirements. The promise of blessing found in this passage belongs to the second category. Possession of the land is contingent upon obedience to God's commandments. Lest there be any mistake about the identity of the God who makes this promise and exacts its condition, the people are told that it is the same God who was worshiped by their ancestors.

The insistence on keeping the law as it has been received, with no additions or omissions, is a prohibition against tampering with this most solemn revelation from God. The law is not to be treated lightly, as if it were a mere human invention or social convention. In some ways it may have developed out of customary practices, but it now enjoys the authority of God and it must be given the respect that is its due.

Obedience to the law is not for Israel's sake alone. Israel's compliance will serve as a witness to the other nations of the extraordinary character of these statutes and decrees. The law codes of other nations were perceived as collections of requirements meant to win the favor of the god of that people. In contrast to this, Israel's laws were considered the directives that guided the nation's response to the graciousness of *the* God who initiated a relationship with the people in the first place. Obedience to this law was, then, a sign of Israel's wisdom. The nations would recognize the wisdom contained in this law and conclude that only a great people would merit a God who was so close to them and so concerned for their welfare. In other words, Israel's obedience to the law will reveal its own incomparability.

This is a bold claim, but it too is conditional. Israel will be considered wise by the nations only if it is compliant; it will be honored by the nations for its fidelity. This claim is probably meant to act as an incentive for obedience rather than as grounds for boasting. It certainly did instill a respect for the law, a respect that survives to our day.

Psalm 15:2-3, 3-4, 4-5

The psalm addresses the question of religious fitness. Although the presence of the LORD is generally a liturgical reference, it has a broader meaning as well. We have come to realize that God is present among us in various ways. However, the requirements for standing in that presence are the same regardless of how the phrase is understood. The answers given in this responsorial psalm describe moral fitness. Furthermore, the requirements are communal in nature. In other words, those who are worthy to stand before God are those who live virtuously with others.

The first list of requirements (v. 1) sets the context for the rest. "Walk" denotes a way of life rather than individual actions. The foundation of this way of life is righteousness or justice, a characteristic of God. It refers to the divinely established norm against which everything else is measured. Whatever conforms to God's norm is considered righteous. In the human sphere it takes on the meaning of justice. In this psalm it refers to those who act in ways that are faithful to God's will. Such faithfulness is not merely external conformity, it originates in their innermost being. Their thoughts are aligned with the truth of God's righteousness, and their tongues speak accordingly.

What follow (vv. 3–5) are examples of concrete ways of behavior in everyday life. "Friend" or "companion" rather than "fellow" (v. 3) is a better translation of the Hebrew *(rēʿeh)*, which includes the idea of personal closeness and is not gender specific. Frequently, the quality of one's virtue is tested in the intimacy of close relationships. Walking on the path of righteousness calls to mind the wisdom theme of choosing one of two ways. This theme appears again. The righteous person disdains the reprobate who has rejected God but honors those who fear the LORD. If one is to live in the presence of God, one must choose the way of God.

Human beings are dependent in all ways on the natural world. Economic systems are established to ensure that needs are met and prosperity is possible. In many societies lending money is done as a service to others, not as a way of increasing one's own capital. In such situations demanding interest is unacceptable, even unjust. Without feeling that we must adopt the economic practices of ancient Israel, we can still be motivated by some of the principles upon which they were based.

Those who stand in the presence of God do not take economic advantage of others. The psalm verse singles out two forms of economic vulnerability. One example is the need to borrow money in the first place. It is hard enough to suffer want; having to pay interest is an additional burden. The second example is victimization through bribery. This practice is doubly heinous when it abuses the innocent.

The psalm ends with a promise of blessing for those who live with others in this righteous manner. They will know peace and security.

James 1:17-18, 21b-22, 27

The teaching found in this reading consists of three discrete themes: various properties of God, the importance of the word in the lives of believers, and the character of religion. Despite the distinctness of the themes, they all serve as exhortation to the believers to live lives of Christian holiness.

Three characteristics of God are praised (vv. 17–18): God's goodness, God's immutability, and God's re-creative power. God is first characterized as the fountain of all giving and the source of all the gifts themselves. This reference is too broad to throw light on the specifics the author had in mind. However, the spaciousness of the allusion allows interpretations that embrace all possibilities. It could include gifts that enhance the personal lives of believers as well as blessings that are communal in nature. Peace and prosperity, a sense of security and fulfillment, knowledge of God and religious insight—these are all gifts of this gracious God.

The one who gives these good gifts is called "the Father of lights," a reference to the heavenly luminaries. God is described as living in the heavens where the sun and the moon and the stars give off their radiance, which enlightens the lives of those on earth. However, unlike the benefits from these heavenly luminaries, which are intermittent, God's goodness is constant. Divine immutability may be an abstract concept, but concrete evidence of the ever-present graciousness of God is not.

God, who is called "Father," is responsible for our birth. The birth referred to here is probably not initial creation but re-creation, or salvation that is effected through the "word of truth." Within the harvest of those who have been or will be saved, the Christians are the first fruits. This means that their regeneration will be the sign of the regeneration of others.

The word of truth that first gave the Christians a rebirth remains in them as a force of ongoing transformation (vv. 21b–22). They are encouraged to welcome this powerful word, to allow it to grow within them so it can accomplish the task God has ordained. The author is arguing from the Hebrew understanding of the notion of "word," which denoted both a linguistic concept and a concrete action. He urges the people to perform the action and not merely to hear the word. This word of truth is one of the perfect gifts God has given. It is the gift that creates the believers anew as the holy people of God.

Finally, the concreteness of true religion is outlined. Admonished to preserve themselves from those practices of the world that might militate against Christian values, believers are counseled to intervene on behalf of the community's most vulnerable, the widows and orphans who have no legal status in a patriarchal society. Doing this, the word of truth will take concrete form in their lives.

Mark 7:1-8, 14-15, 21-23

The reading recounts an incident of conflict between Jesus and some of his opponents. The issue that prompted the confrontation is ritual cleansing. The scribes and Pharisees "come from Jerusalem." This not only identifies their place of residence, it also implies that they bring with them the authority of the religious leadership that resides there. It is within this capacity of authority that they challenge the behavior of some of the disciples of Jesus.

The custom of hand washing referred to here is not a hygienic practice but a ritual washing. It probably originated as one of the regulations observed by the priests when they were offering sacrifice. It seems to have developed into a requirement obliging everyone. In other words, general hand washing was not mandated by the law itself but was a custom included in the oral law, which is here called "the tradition of the elders." The Pharisees were strong proponents of this body of unwritten law, which by the time of Jesus had developed into 613 precepts. They would have expected a truly religious person to adopt their high standards of holiness. Since Jesus does not seem to have done so, they were critical of him.

Here again we see people explicitly criticizing the behavior of the disciples but not that of Jesus. However, this was an indirect criticism of Jesus, for he would be held responsible for the behavior of those who followed him. This public criticism was also an attempt to shame Jesus so that he would be minimized before others and, having lost his reputation, would cease being a threat to those who opposed him.

Jesus' rebuttal is swift and incisive. He calls these people hypocrites and uses a passage from Isaiah against them. The prophet condemns those who were faithful to outward observance of religious practices but were remiss when it came to total commitment to God. Lest anyone miss the point of the quotation, Jesus explicitly draws a comparison between those the prophet condemns and the scribes and Pharisees who condemn the disciples. The very ones who demand strict observance of their law fail to observe God's law.

Jesus uses this encounter to teach a deeper lesson. He begins with an authoritative command so that his hearers will appreciate the seriousness of his instruction. Picking up the theme of clean/unclean, he reinterprets it using ideas from the prophetic passage he has just quoted. Uncleanness or impurity are not determined by anything external. What one eats merely passes through the body. Defilement, on the other hand, originates from the innermost recesses of the heart. It is in the human heart that evil schemes are hatched. Jesus demonstrates this by listing several sins. Although these sins are external offenses against others, they are first conceived in the heart. Therefore it is correct to say that we are defiled by what comes out of us rather than by what we put into ourselves.

Themes of the Day

The overarching theme of the readings for this Sunday is "words spoken in truth." We will consider three aspects of this theme: the words of the covenant, the truth in religious practices, and the word that has taken root in us.

Words of the Covenant

On one level, the laws are the words of the covenant. They are part of the contract that was drawn up between God and the people. They stipulate the obligations that flow from this agreement. They are words of truth because they are the reliable revelation of God; they are words of truth because they genuinely reflect righteous living. The biblical covenant laws are truly humane. Although they are explicit in their demands, they do not place impossible burdens on us. Obedience to the words of the covenant leads to life and blessings, while disobedience results in the opposite.

On a deeper level, the laws themselves do not constitute the covenant. They merely arise from the relationship that binds God to us and us to God. They are directives that point the way to righteous behavior, guides that help us live out our covenant commitment. Chronologically, many of the laws may have been in force before the covenant had been cut (for example, "Thou shalt not kill"). However, they were probably not considered revelatory until the pact was made. The prophets remind us that fidelity to the law is more than rigid conformity. It must flow from deep within us, from the core of our hearts.

The Truth of Religious Practices

Usually we are born into a group that possesses some kind of religious customs, and as a member of the group, we learn them. They always carry some profound religious meaning, but we may not know what it is, or we may not care what it is, or it may have lost its meaning for us—and yet we perform these customs. How many people know why we stand or sit or kneel during liturgy? How many people care? How many people have a "church" wedding because it is a religious event? Or how many have one because "that's the way we have always done it"? This does not mean that the people are not good. It means that the practices do not always flow from a deep religious conviction, from a profound experience of God. Once we realize our need for God, these practices, regardless of how elaborate or how uncomplicated they may be, become genuine expressions of our praise or our gratitude, of our need or our repentance.

The Word That Has Taken Root

When the word of God has taken root in us, everything becomes a religious practice. This word can come to us through the teachings of our faith, through the example of good people around us, through the wonder and mystery of creation. However it comes, when it does take hold of us our inner eye is opened, our heart is softened, and we turn instinctively to God like a flower turns to the sun. When we are brought to birth in this way, covenant law becomes sacred, religious practices are cherished, and we are filled with the power that saves.

Twenty-Third Sunday in Ordinary Time
Isaiah 35:4-7a

In this oracle of salvation the prophet depicts two ways in which the renewal promised by God is manifested: those who suffer physical maladies will be healed of their infirmities, and the barren wilderness will be filled with the promise of new life. The prophet is the messenger of this good news and is told to announce it to those who have been broken by the hardships of life, those who are weak and filled with fear.

The proclamation "fear not" is a common expression found in many accounts of divine revelation (cf. Gen 15:1; Josh 8:1; Isa 41:10). It is spoken by God or a messenger of God in an attempt to assuage the very natural trepidation one experiences in the presence of a supernatural phenomenon. Here, as part of a promise of salvation, it is meant to encourage the fainthearted. It precedes the announcement of the coming of God as vindicator. While in some situations this can be a terrifying announcement, here it is a message of salvation. God may be coming in judgment for some, but to those to whom the prophet speaks, God is coming to bring new life.

In a world that believes that God has created everything in proper order, imperfection of any kind is often perceived as a consequence of some form of transgression. This is particularly true of physical infirmity, which is often considered evidence of the presence of evil forces in the world. The person with the infirmity may be innocent of serious transgression, but someone or something is responsible for the disordered condition. In such a world healing can be seen as the restoration of the proper order of creation. In vivid language this oracle describes four healing situations, which are probably representative of all cures, whether physical or spiritual. The cures symbolize the transformative power of God, who comes to save the people.

The promised salvation will not be limited to human beings. All creation will be renewed. This renewal is characterized by images of life-giving water. Streams and rivers, pools and springs, appear. It is amazing what a little water can effect in dry and barren land. It can work miracles. Just as God's saving power can restore infirm bodies to full strength, so this same power can transform deserts into oases. The oracle announces that both people and nature will enjoy abundant life.

Just as deprivation and infirmity were considered signs of evil in the world, so this restoration was perceived as a sign of the transformation that only God can effect. It was a testimony to God's presence in the world and to God's victory over evil. Once again God had reestablished the original order of creation, and all life began again to flourish.

Psalm 146:7, 8-9, 9-10

The responsorial psalm is a hymn of praise of the LORD (*Hallelujah* in Hebrew). Such hymns have a definite pattern. The summons itself *(hallelu)* appears in a plural verb form, suggesting a communal setting, and contains an abbreviation of the divine name *(jah)*. In this psalm the word is used as a refrain, a response to a series of statements that offer examples of God's indescribable graciousness.

"God of Jacob" (v. 7) is a title that points out the patronal character of God's nature. It does not refer to an abstract quality of God but to the special protection that was given to Jacob, the ancestor after whom the entire people were named, and to all his descendants. There is an allusion here to God's deliverance of the people from the bondage of Egypt and to God's providential care of them during their sojourn in the wilderness. God has been faithful. This is reason enough to praise the LORD.

God's graciousness to the vulnerable is next extolled (vv. 8–9). There are many situations in life that can force one to be bowed down, whether a physical disability, a mental or emotional affliction, an economic or social disadvantage. Whatever it might be, God raises up the needy, enables them to stand with pride, reestablishes them in security. Strangers or aliens lack certain legal rights, and since it is not their own nation, they may not be familiar with the rights they do have. Insensitive or unscrupulous people can very easily take advantage of them. These vulnerable strangers are precisely the kinds of people the God of Israel chooses. Israel itself is the prime example of this. It was when they were aliens in Egypt that God took them and made them God's own people. This is certainly reason to praise God.

In patriarchal societies only adult free men enjoy certain privileges. As part of the household, women and children are under the jurisdiction and care of such men. Women belong to the households either of their fathers, their brothers, or their sons. Here "widows" probably refers to women who cannot return to their home of origin because they have married but whose husbands are now dead, and they have no adult son to care for them. Such women are marginal in society and need some patron to care for them. Likewise, it is presumed that the orphans referred to have no extended family within whose jurisdiction they might take refuge. These are the ones for whom God cares.

The final verse praises God as sovereign and eternal ruler in Jerusalem. All the other verses of the psalm testify to the glory of this God who reigns forever from the very hill that is at the center of the lives of the people. This is not a God who is far off. This God has entered into their history and into the very social fabric of their existence. Such a God deserves praise.

James 2:1-5

In developing his instruction, the author of this letter uses a diatribe, a very popular Greek technique of argumentation. As a wisdom teacher, he does more than transmit sayings: he develops extensive explanations with examples to demonstrate his point. This is the approach he uses in the teaching on impartiality found in this passage.

The instruction opens with a stern and succinct admonition: Show no partiality! Such an injunction could be appropriate in any number of situations. The particular concern here has to do with the proper attitude toward economic status. Whether or not the example that follows stems from an actual occurrence within the community, it convincingly demonstrates the point the author is trying to make.

The setting is the assembly of the believers *(synagōgē)*. Although we normally think of this as a meeting for prayer, following the Jewish custom it was primarily a gathering of men for the purpose of teaching and study. Each assembly also had authority to set up its own court, to pass judgment on certain community offenses, and to impose fines. Again, only the free adult men participated in this. Mention of judges (v. 4) indicates that the situation described here was juridical in character.

In broad and clear strokes the author paints a picture of unacceptable discrimination. He condemns the preference for the man dressed in fine clothing, exposing the community's bias. First, they err by judging from external appearances without taking into account the faith of the individual. Since the way one dresses is an indication of one's social status, fine clothing suggests wealth and prominence within the community. Showing preference toward such people is often a way of ingratiating oneself with them in order to benefit in some way from their reputation or resources.

In contrast, the man who appears in shabby clothing is treated contemptuously. Unlike the richly clothed one who is given a place of honor, this one is told to stand or sit at the feet of those in a position to assign places. Such discrimination is not only an example of social snobbery, it is also in direct opposition to the basis upon which the Church was founded, specifically, the gathering of all into the reign of God. Such behavior is condemned for two reasons. First, the people are reestablishing distinctions where God had eliminated them. Second, their partiality jeopardizes the justice they are called to administer.

The final admonition clearly defines God's preferential option for the poor. God is on the side of those who suffer discrimination because they do not possess what the world values. These are the ones who are chosen to be heirs of the reign of God. It is not their poverty that entitles them to this promise but their love of God. Those who love what the world values seem to prefer lives of privilege to lives of faith.

Mark 7:31-37

The route described in this episode is extraordinarily circuitous. It traces a large arc from Tyre through the district of Sidon, northeast in the direction of Damascus, then southward along the eastern shore of the Jordan River through the area known as the Decapolis. This was a league of ten Gentile cities in Transjordan that had been set free from Jewish domination but that continued to be the home of many Jews. During this entire trip Jesus is outside of the land of Israel, in Gentile territory.

The description of the healing is distinctive in that it is so typical of contemporary accounts of cures. Normally the Gospel writers portray Jesus as exercising his power in a manner unique among healers of his time. Here, however, the miracle is described with details that are quite standard. Miracle workers frequently touched the afflicted person; they often used some material such as saliva in the performance of healing; they made various sounds and uttered incantations in foreign languages. It may be that the Gentile setting influenced the details of this story. However, they also add to its dramatic character.

Despite the fact that these details depict Jesus as a miracle worker like others, each of them can be explained by some other feature of Jesus as portrayed by the Gospel writer. Jesus frequently lays his hand on afflicted people. It was a way for him to overturn the purity prohibition against touching the unclean and, by contagion, incurring the same impurity. His use of saliva reflects the belief that it contained some of the personal power of the miracle worker. He looks up to heaven and groans, which could be understood as a form of prayer. The healing may have been surrounded by these familiar elements, but the miracle itself is accomplished by Jesus' command: Be opened!

Some dimensions of the healing of the deaf man are not found in other miracle accounts. First, in an oral culture such as this one, those who cannot hear are at a great disadvantage. They are marginalized in ways that others are not. Second, the importance of hearing is reflected in Israel's preeminent prayer, the *Shᵉmaᶜ* ("Hear, O Israel!" Deut 6:4). Hearing symbolizes openness to God. Third, at the heart of Jesus' ministry is his teaching about the reign of

God. It is significant that in this episode he unstops the ears of a man who is unable to hear his words, so that now the man can hear them and be open to their message.

The command for silence regarding this wonder (v. 36) is directed toward the crowd, not toward the man who has been healed. In their astonishment the people relate the wonders Jesus can perform with the prophetic promise of regeneration, which will take place during the new age of the reign of God (cf. Isa 35:5). They proclaim that Jesus has accomplished here exactly what will be accomplished in that time of fulfillment.

Themes of the Day

The readings for this Sunday offer us a vision of eschatological fulfillment, a time when eyes will be opened and ears unstopped and hearts will leap for joy. They tell us very clearly that these marvels are brought about through the power of God and that, left to our own devices, we sometimes make distinctions that divide.

Jesus Opens Our Eyes and Our Ears

From the times of our religious ancestors God promised to save us, to open eyes that are blind and ears that are deaf, to enable us to leap with the joy of being saved, to release us from the cruel bondage of hate and oppression and suffering. God made these promises, and God is faithful because these promises have been fulfilled by Jesus. He opens our eyes to the reality of God's presence in our midst in the goodness of people and in the tenderness of life, even in its vulnerability. He opens our ears to hear the word of God spoken to us by others, revealed to us through the created world. Touched by Jesus in this way, our hearts leap with joy; our world and our lives are charged with the presence of God.

Word from the Future

There is an eschatological dimension to being open to the word of God, because we are opened to hear something from the future. The prophets always speak about this future in the present tense. They say that marvels *will* occur because they see them happening already. Isaiah proclaims, "Here is your God!"—and the world is transformed. Jesus says, "Be open"—and we begin to see with our eyes and hear with our ears and understand with our hearts. Oftentimes when we listen to the Gospel, we only hear it as if it were coming to us from the past rather than as coming to us from the future. The good news always opens us to future possibilities, to personal and communal transformation, to a new creation. With the word of God the future invades our present, and even the natural world bursts forth with new life.

A Community of the Future

Although the eschatological future is already present to us, it is only unfolding, it has not yet opened completely. We still might judge one another by appearances, according to the standards of the world. We still might not be as open to one another as God has been to us. We still might miss the presence of God in the poor and the dispossessed, in those who suffer from disease or war or loneliness. We still might shun those of another race, or those who have been shaped by another culture, or those who worship God in a different way. Although the eschatological future is already present, we have not yet put aside all of the biases of the past, we have not yet been fully transformed. But God has spoken, God has come to save us; and God is trustworthy, God keeps faith forever.

Twenty-Fourth Sunday in Ordinary Time
Isaiah 50:4c-9a

Although this passage is classified as one of the Servant Songs, in form and content it resembles a personal lament. The recounting of the abuse that is suffered (v. 6) is followed by a profession of confidence in divine providence (vv. 7–9). The opening verse of the passage sets the stage for what follows: My ears are open! As is the case with all of the senses, hearing is an ability that is most intimate. The ear catches the sound and carries it into the very core of the person. Because of its importance, openness to sound carries the symbolic meaning of openness before God. At the outset the speaker acknowledges that his ears are open to hear but that it is God who opened them. In other words, though he stands ready to accept God's will in his life, the readiness itself comes from God. The speaker takes credit for nothing; he is totally dependent on God.

This openness to God's will was tested by various torments inflicted upon him by others. In the face of it, he willingly handed himself over to be beaten and shamed. He does not say why he has become the victim of such abuse nor why he seems to have accepted it without complaint. He only says that he did not try to escape it, nor did he defend himself against it. He did not rebel, he did not turn back.

Despite all the suffering he is forced to endure, he is confident that God is on his side. This is a remarkable statement, since suffering was generally thought to be deserved recompense for some transgression. Actually, the rest of the reading seems to be a challenge to the customary understanding of suffering. There is no suggestion that God will take it away. Instead, God is present with the afflicted one, and the suffering itself is no cause for shame. In fact, suffering actually strengthens the one who laments.

The language in the last verses (vv. 8–9a) is reminiscent of the law court. God is characterized as the one who upholds the innocence of the sufferer, who challenges his accuser to bring his case to court. Most likely the issue to be argued is the innocence or guilt of the one suffering. It should be remembered that affliction was considered the consequence and sign of guilt. It is not clear whether the ones being called to court are the same as those who inflicted the abuse in the first place. Actually, it does not make much difference, since the issue is the innocence of the one suffering, and it would be beneficial if this innocence were to be demonstrated to all. The very last verse is a profession of exceptional confidence. With God on the side of the one suffering, any opponents will be unable to make a case against him.

This righteous person knows that even in suffering God is there as an advocate. The affliction may not be alleviated, but the added burden of thinking that suffering is a concrete sign of alienation from God has been removed. This testimony of faith is framed by the same declaration of confidence: God is my help.

Psalm 116:1-2, 3-4, 5-6, 8-9

This is an individual prayer of thanksgiving, which appears as Psalm 114 in the Greek and Latin Bibles. In it God is praised for having rescued the psalmist from trouble. Although the exact nature of the trouble is not identified, the imagery used in the description suggests it was a life-threatening situation.

The reason for the psalmist's love of God is given: God has heard the psalmist's cry for help. Hearing is not merely a passive exercise. It includes listening to the petitioner and granting the petition. To say that God has heard the voice of the psalmist is to say that God has rescued the psalmist.

The ancients believed that death was an elemental force that could take possession of people at any time, undermining their lives and draining them of their vitality. Whenever they were stricken with an ailment, regardless of the seriousness of its nature, they concluded that death had some kind of hold on them. Illness is not the only way that death could intrude in their lives. Serious trouble could also jeopardize their lives and hand them over to the power of death. Actually, they believed that death was present in anything that weakened life. While still alive people can wage war against death and enjoy small partial victories, but in the end death will be triumphant.

In this psalm death is placed in parallel construction with the netherworld *(sh^e'ôl)*. While this might underscore the fatal nature of the threat facing the psalmist, it can also be a metaphor characterizing the magnitude of the distress experienced. It was precisely this overwhelming distress that prompted the psalmist to cry out to the LORD.

After the psalmist's suffering is reported, the mood shifts from one of despair to one of grateful praise. God is acclaimed to be gracious and just and merciful, all qualities that characterize God's covenantal relationship with the people. These are the very qualities that inspired the psalmist's confidence and devotion. Having trusted that God would listen to the prayer of those who are suffering, the psalmist has now experienced God's saving power and illustrates this in three ways. First, the soul is freed from death. Here soul is not the indestructible component of human nature as found in ancient Greek philosophy. Instead, it is the life force *(nephesh)* that makes a person a living being. Next, the eyes are freed from tears, from the grief and sorrow that accompany suffering. Finally, the feet are freed from stumbling. The psalmist is now on sure footing, secure in the salvation that has been granted by God. It is no wonder that the psalmist breaks out in a song of thanksgiving.

James 2:14-18

The author is addressing a misunderstanding that has arisen in the church regarding the nature of true faith. It seems that some within the community were satisfied with correct belief articulated in orthodox doctrine. James insists that genuine faith must be practical, expressed in action. Furthermore it must manifest itself in more than acts of authentic worship. While the issue here is certainly ethical, it is soteriological as well: What kind of faith will save?

The passage describes a pointed dialogue in the style of a diatribe. Questions are asked, but they really do not seek answers. They are rhetorical questions that argue in favor of the position of the questioner. What good is it? —no good at all. Can such faith save?—no. Following this imaginative exchange, a very straightforward example is sketched in order to demonstrate the hollowness of faith that does not express itself in action. The example is intended to prove the point the author is making.

The people involved in the case described are referred to as brothers and sisters, indicating that this hypothetical situation has been taken from the life of the community. Brothers and sisters in faith are in dire need of food and clothing, and the dialogue recounted shows that this need was recognized by others but was not met. It is shocking how this need was callously disregarded. "Go in peace" is a standard expression of dismissal. In this example, members of the Christian community fail to live out their faith, which claims that all have been saved through the death and resurrection of Jesus and all are now part of the body of Christ.

The example does not present an unusual situation that might require an extraordinary response. It recounts circumstances that could be very common. Furthermore, as members of the community, the needy people would be well known, perhaps even neighbors. The familiarity that is a feature of this case underscores the barrenness of faith without works. If believers do not even care for those within their number, how little will they be concerned with people they might consider outsiders! This is not the lively faith called for by Jesus, who spent himself for all people even unto death. Faith that does not manifest itself in action is dead.

The imaginative dialogue continues in the last verse. Anticipating an objection that separates faith from works, James exposes the absurdity of such a prospect. How can a saving faith be demonstrated except through some kind of visible or tangible action, presumably acts of charity? James' opponents, whether real or imaginary, want to separate faith and works so they can then be ranked, believing that faith will predominate and that these opponents will be justified in their claim. James insists that such a separation is impossible. If they cannot show this through their own actions, he will show it through his.

Mark 8:27-35

Although this reading consists of two distinct episodes from the ministry of Jesus, the first one prepares for the second. Only after he is proclaimed the Christ, or anointed one of God, does Jesus predict his suffering, death, and resurrection. Also, the faith professed by Peter in the first episode is tested in the second. The conversation about the identity of Jesus (vv. 27–30) seems to have been between him and his disciples, as was the prediction of his death and resurrection (vv. 31–33). Only the exhortation to follow him in his suffering (vv. 34–35) was addressed to a broader audience.

Jesus asks the disciples what people are saying about him, who they think he is. The question is not self-serving. It seeks to discover how Jesus' words and actions are understood by the people, and it prepares the disciples for their own assessment of him. The answers given to his questions are telling. Some believe that he is John the Baptist, others that he is Elijah, still others that he is one of the other prophets. These are all religious figures who have already died. The people seem to believe that Jesus is a prophetic figure who has come back from the dead, a point that seems to be lost on Peter when he hears of Jesus' death.

It is not clear why Jesus should be associated with John the Baptist, since both their lifestyles and the central message of their respective teachings were so different. The connection may have been made simply because the memory of this exceptional man was still fresh in the minds of the people. They had set their hopes on John, and with his death they transferred them to Jesus. Elijah was the mysterious prophet whose return would herald the advent of the reign of God. Since Jesus had launched his ministry with the announcement that the long-awaited reign was now at hand, it is understandable that he would be linked with Elijah. In some way, all of the prophets had looked forward to the coming of this reign, and so the general reference was not inappropriate.

Peter speaks in the name of the others when he proclaims that Jesus is the Christ, the Messiah, the anointed one of God. Hearing this, Jesus elaborates on the character of his messiahship. He will be a Messiah as was envisioned in the tradition that grew up around the concept of the Son of Man, the enigmatic figure who will come on the clouds at the end of this age. Much to the chagrin of Peter, Jesus then adds that he will be rejected, will suffer and die, but will rise again. This perception of the Messiah does not appear to conform to the expectations of the people, and Jesus' insistence on it could jeopardize his acceptance by them. Peter's rebuke exemplifies this. Despite the opposition Jesus persists, and he even declares that those who follow him will have to do so on the same path of suffering. This is indeed a hard saying.

Themes of the Day

Today we direct our attention to the figure of the Messiah. There are several messianic traditions, each one characterizing the anointed one of the future in a unique way. The readings show us the diverse expectations of the people and how unexpected Jesus' radical self-proclamation was. Finally, the epistle is a reminder of how far we still are from recognizing the presence of the Messiah in our midst.

Messianic Expectations

Believers are all waiting for the coming of the Messiah; some are waiting for the first coming, others for the second, but they are all waiting. Just what are we expecting? Do we expect a prophetic figure who will enter our world and reform the structures of society, or a strong leader who will overturn these structures and establish a new order? Are we waiting for a teacher who will transform our minds and hearts, or a judge who will punish us for our infidelities? Are we expecting someone who will renew the face of the earth, or someone who will come in fire and brimstone to destroy it? What kind of a Messiah do we expect? For what kind of a change are we preparing ourselves?

These expectations are not merely intellectual perceptions of a Messiah who will come in the future. They are ways of thinking that influence ways of acting. They often determine the manner in which we await this future coming. Some people think that we must prepare ourselves for the inevitable; others believe that their actions can bring it about more quickly. Messianic expectations are not idle speculations; they set some of the parameters of our worldview.

The Son of Man Must Suffer

Jesus seems to overturn our expectations. We look for one who will save us from the predicaments in which we find ourselves, and he comes to us as one who seems to be a victim of his own predicament. It is no wonder that we think there must be some mistake. Even the one who cries out in faith, "You are the Christ," can insist that there must be another way. Because of this thinking, that person must be rebuked: "You are thinking not as God does, but as human beings do." How does God think? God's thinking seems to be the reverse of ours: Those who save their lives lose them; those who lose their lives save them; the seed must die before it can bear fruit; Jesus will be killed but will then be raised from the dead.

By What Kind of Faith Do We Live?

There are so many different understandings of the Messiah, many of them firmly rooted in our religious tradition. This very fact causes much of our misunderstanding. The people of Jesus' time held various views. They expected Jesus to act in a certain way, and they misunderstood him. Even the disciples were confused by what he said, and they also misunderstood him. Can we be so sure that we have the kind of insight they lacked? Can we claim to understand him? Or are we more like the people in James' community: people who profess faith in Jesus but who do not live it out; people who speak pleasant words to others, who say the right things but do not back up their words with good works? Is our faith really living? Do we recognize the Messiah in our midst?

Twenty-Fifth Sunday in Ordinary Time
Wisdom 2:12, 17-20

It is the ungodly who speak in this passage. They conspire to assault the righteous one, who has become a living reproach to them. Three things in particular plague these people. This honorable person (always referred to as "he") stands in opposition to the wrongdoings of the wicked; he denounces them for their sin; and he accuses them of not being faithful to their upbringing. This last point is probably a reference to training in the law. It implies that the wicked are members of the same community as the righteous one. If this is the case and they have strayed from the teaching of the tradition, they could be considered apostates, and then the conflict is an internal community affair.

The decision has been made among the wicked to put the righteous one to the test (vv. 17–20) to see whether God will actually intervene and save the person of virtue from the onslaughts being planned. This kind of thinking rests on the principles of retribution, namely, that the righteous will be rewarded and the wicked punished. In a certain way this is a test of God as well. It seeks to discover the truthfulness of God's promise of protection as well as God's ability to keep that promise.

The just one has boasted that he is the son of God. Although this epithet has divine connotations, they are probably not intended here. Some societies believed their monarchs were either direct descendants or human manifestations of the gods. In such cases this title would be a royal epithet. Most likely, neither connotation is meant here. Instead, the reference is probably an allusion to the intimate, even familial, relationship that the just one enjoys with God, a relationship that could very well be unique. The wicked maintain that if this boast is true, then God will defend the one who is just.

The mistreatment being planned is extreme, even fatal. The righteous one, described as gentle and patient, is now an innocent victim of the evildoers' resentment. The reading ends on a note of apprehension. Will the righteous one succumb to the persecution of the wicked? Will God in fact intervene on behalf of this just person?

Psalm 54:3-4, 5, 6-8

This prayer for deliverance begins with a cry to God for help in a time of need. It is a fine example of individual prayers of petition, containing most of the characteristics that distinguish this particular category of psalms. It is in the first person style of direct address, it contains a plea to be heard and to be helped, the trouble that precipitates the cry is described, there is a declaration of confidence in God, and a vow is made to offer some kind of sacrifice in gratitude for having been heard.

The specific formulation of the petition indicates that God's name, as part of the very essence of God, possesses divine power. The poetic construction of this petition places the word "name" in a parallel relationship with "might," thus further explaining the character of God's name. God is here called upon to act as judge. This suggests that the petitioner is a righteous person and looks to God for the protection that is thought to be the reward for righteousness. A guilty person would hardly ask God to act as judge.

The difficulty the psalmist faces is caused by enemies who are described as haughty (the Hebrew has strangers, *zārîm*) and ruthless. They not only viciously seek the life of the psalmist, they arrogantly have no regard for God. The lines are clearly drawn here. There is no question about the virtue of the petitioner and the sinfulness of the enemies, and there is also no question about the role God will play in this struggle.

Regardless of how bleak the situation appears to be, the psalmist is filled with confidence. God is already present as a helper; those who rise up against the psalmist will be subdued. God is already there as the one who sustains life; those who threaten it will be thwarted. The psalmist never questions why the presence of God did not prevent the misfortune in the first place. God's providence is not being challenged, rather, it is being trusted and summoned.

In the concluding verse the psalmist promises to offer a sacrifice to honor the name of God. This would probably be some kind of a thank-offering freely given. The initial petition, "by your name save me," is here balanced by the vow, "I will praise your name." The confidence that inspired the psalmist to turn to God in the first place, and that served to assure the psalmist that God would hear and would respond with help, is based on the truthfulness of God's name. This name is not only powerful, it is also reliable. The psalmist has sure footing if confidence is grounded in this trustworthy name.

James 3:16–4:3

One of the fundamental characteristics of wisdom teaching is the contrast drawn between the path taken by the wise or upright and that taken by the foolish or sinful. In a way that is quite distinctive though sometimes simplistic, the features of each are carefully sketched so as to encourage one to choose the path of wisdom over the path of folly. The instruction in this reading is an example of such wisdom teaching.

Two styles of behavior are described. In the first one foolishness reigns. It reveals itself in various forms of social unrest—jealousy, selfish ambition, and the like. On the other hand, a life motivated by wisdom generates harmony and peace, which give birth to all of the manifestations of love. While wisdom is generally thought to proceed from reflection on experience, it is also believed to be a gift from God. It is this latter dimension of wisdom that James addresses. This wisdom is pure, totally committed to the things of God; it is peaceable, drawing the members of the community together in unity; it is fruitful, producing good works in abundance. Most of all it brings forth the riches of peace. Wisdom seeks the right order of things; peace is the order that wisdom seeks. This is the path that believers are called to walk.

The focus of the instruction shifts from the vision of peace to the reality of conflicts within the community. The strife in which the members are engaged is an indication of their failure to travel along the path of wisdom. James wants to know the cause of these conflicts, not so that he can reprimand the members but that he can instruct them. Before they can respond to his questions he answers them himself, and he does so through the use of a rhetorical question. He is not seeking information, he is providing it.

The conflict within the community is not caused by outside forces. The Christians have no one to blame but themselves for the lack of harmony in their personal and communal lives. The evil inclinations that take hold of the individuals exert their influence over others. The jealousy and ambition that grip the heart of one spill over into the lives of many. There is no peace because they do not choose the path that leads to peace, and the path they do choose leads to frustration.

The frustration or pointlessness that they have chosen is laid bare. What they covet, they cannot possess. They ask, but they do not receive. Even the use of force cannot guarantee success, because they have chosen the wrong path. What is required of them is a complete turnabout, a change of heart, a reversal of lifestyle. In order to experience the peace they desire they must choose the path of wisdom, the course of righteousness, the way of peace.

Mark 9:30-37

There are two parts to this reading. The first (vv. 30–32) recounts Jesus' prediction of his death and resurrection; the second is a report of the disciples' quarrel over status within the community (vv. 33–37). Although the two accounts do not appear to be connected, their literary juxtaposition warrants that they be linked. In both of them Jesus instructs the disciples about matters they have not been able to grasp fully.

The first episode clearly states that Jesus and the disciples are by themselves, away from the crowds. In fact, Jesus does not want their whereabouts known. It may be that he desires privacy so he can give the disciples his full attention. Whatever the reason, the instruction is given to the disciples and to them alone.

Identifying himself as the mysterious Son of Man who comes on the clouds to announce the end of one age and the beginning of another, Jesus tells his closest associates that he will be handed over and killed but that he will rise from the dead after three days. That the disciples did not understand is not surprising. What is surprising is their reluctance to question him about it. Were they afraid to know what it all meant? Afraid to hear some of the terrifying details? Afraid of the implications that his suffering may have for their own lives? Jesus merely announces his fate. He does not describe it, nor does he explain it. The account is startling in its brevity.

The prediction happened while they were traveling through Galilee. However, this was not the only exchange that took place on the way to Capernaum. The story reports that although the disciples could not comprehend what Jesus said about his death and resurrection, they were able to engage in a heated discussion about status within the community. Jesus had just admitted his ultimate vulnerability, and they were quarreling about rank. This shows they were not only insensitive to him but they were also competitive among themselves. Without reprimanding them, Jesus seized the moment to teach an important lesson: following his own example, those who would be first must be willing to be last.

In the world of Jesus' time, neither servants nor children had any legal rights or social status. They were like women, dependent on the good will of the male head of the household. In this instruction Jesus turns the social ranking system upside down. He maintains that those who hold the highest positions within the community must be willing to take the lowest place. They must be the servants of all. He then offers himself as an example of one who empties himself for the sake of others. He does this by identifying with the subordinate status of a child. He then traces the connections he has just drawn back to God: whoever receives those who hold the lowest social positions receives Jesus, and those who receive Jesus receive the one who sent him. The disciples have much to learn.

Themes of the Day

Although we are still in Ordinary Time, we are entering into a new season of the natural cycle of the year. In the Northern Hemisphere the days are still warm, but they will soon begin to be shorter. We realize that the Liturgical Year is taking a turn. Even the readings have a slightly different hue. Today we are invited to consider some of the features of righteousness and the fate of those who are considered righteous.

Who Are the Righteous?

Who are the righteous? This is a question that holds little interest for many people. They would be more concerned with knowing who are the successful or who are the famous. In a world rife with jealousy and selfish ambition righteousness is not a quality that is highly prized. We want people to be honest, at least in their dealings with us, but we are more apt to applaud those who are clever. We commend people who know how to make a good deal, who know how to get ahead, who know how to strike it rich. We extol the beautiful, the strong, the self-assured, those who have made a name for themselves, those who entertain us. We encourage people to be ambitious, to think of themselves first. Seldom is one's popularity based on righteousness.

On the other hand, righteousness is one of the pillars upon which the reign of God is established. Those who would enter that reign must be gentle and merciful, faithful and sincere. They must be lovers of peace. The righteous must be willing to take the last place, to be the servant of all. There is a dimension of all of this that is somewhat obscure or enigmatic. Because it is so often at odds with the standards of the world, we are not always sure by what criteria the characteristics of righteousness should be judged. Therefore, we must look to Jesus for an authentic portrait of righteousness.

The Fate of the Righteous

Because righteousness itself is not highly valued in our society, those who are righteous are not often held in high regard. They may even be considered obnoxious. In fact, they are often ridiculed and even persecuted. When they are considered a reproach to the standards of society, they may even be put to death. Such treatment is difficult to bear when it comes from an outsider, but it is particularly bitter when the one who is striking out at the righteous person is someone close at hand, a colleague or a neighbor or a member of the family.

There are times when we might be inclined to envy and resentment. We do not want to feel that we are morally inferior to others, and so we relish the opportunity of putting their virtue to the test. We may say that we want to draw forth their strengths, but we may really hope that their weaknesses will be revealed and they will prove to be no better than we are. Sometimes the righteous have nowhere else to turn but to Jesus, whose life they are following and into whose death they have been plunged.

Twenty-Sixth Sunday in Ordinary Time
Numbers 11:25-29

This is a very unusual story in several ways. First, the spirit of prophecy that had been conferred on Moses was shared by others. Second, this spirit was bestowed on men who were absent from the group. Third, Joshua was upset that those who received the spirit in a way that was different from the rest would prophesy.

Contrary to some popular thinking, the primary role that Moses plays is that of prophet, spokesperson of God. In fact, Moses appears to be the fountainhead of prophecy. His importance is quite clear in this reading: the spirit of prophecy that was upon him was bestowed on the elders so that the burden of prophecy would not be so heavy on his own shoulders. This was a theophanic event, a revelation of God, for God came down in the cloud in order to grant this gift. Although some of the spirit of Moses was taken by God, this does not mean that what Moses possessed was diminished. Rather, it means that the elders now shared in Moses' prophetic ministry.

The principal site of revelation was the tent of meeting, which at this time was located outside the camp. Two men who had been designated for this conferral of the spirit but who had remained in the camp also received the spirit. The dissension this caused highlights some important issues. Despite the fact that Eldad and Medad had been preordained to receive the spirit (v. 26), according to some their absence from the group disqualified them.

Even Joshua, Moses' second in command, criticized their prophesying. As a priest, Joshua was permanently attached to the tent and may have resented anyone who might be seen as a challenge to his own exclusive authority. This narrative may demonstrate the struggle that existed between the authority exercised by leaders whose roles had been incorporated into the religious structure of the nation and those charismatic individuals who had not been institutionally appointed and who ministered outside the centers of power.

Moses, however, did not hinder the two men. It did not seem to matter to him whether or not they conformed in every detail to the ceremony of bestowal of the spirit in which the others participated. In fact, he questioned the forthrightness of Joshua's opposition. Was he concerned with probity or was he protecting the privilege that official prophesying often brought with it? Moses was concerned with the good of the entire people. If their welfare required that he and others share their privilege as leaders, so be it. The work of God took precedence over the institutional ordering of the community.

Psalm 19:8, 10, 12-13, 14

Several synonyms are used to extol the glories of the law. Although the general theme of the psalm is praise, its tone is didactic and exhortative. It describes the blessings that acceptance of the law can impart, but it does so not merely to describe the law but also to persuade the people to embrace it as the will of God and to live in accord with it. Each of the statements in this psalm identifies the law as belonging to the LORD. This is not just any religious law, it is uniquely Israel's, because in a very specific way it represents the will of the God of Israel.

When most people today talk about law, they normally mean legal enactments that have some degree of binding force. While this is certainly one dimension of the meaning of the Hebrew word, *tôrâ* might be better translated "instruction" or "teaching." As found in the Bible, the law consisted of directives for living a full and God-fearing life. Teaching the law was the special task of both the wisdom school and the priesthood. The former group collected and safeguarded the insights gleaned from various life experiences. The latter group functioned as mediator between God and the people in a society that believed that ultimate wisdom was revealed by the deity.

If the law is understood as the will of God for human beings, then the qualities enshrined in that law could legitimately be considered reflections of divine attributes. If the law is thought to be that point where an encounter with God takes place, then those who are shaped by the law will be godlike. The qualities associated with the law found in this psalm are some of the most highly prized attributes in any tradition. The law is perfect, or complete; it is trustworthy and clean; it is true and just. Fidelity to the law should lead one to the godliness that is enshrined within it.

The effects of the law enumerated here are all relational, enhancing human life itself. The psalmist maintains that the law imbues the soul with new vitality; it gives wisdom to those who would not ordinarily have it. It is constant and just. It establishes an enduring attitude of awe; it is a path to righteousness. This description of the law shows clearly that the psalmist found it life-giving and not restrictive, ennobling and not demeaning. Reverence for the law seems to promise the best that life has to offer.

Despite a sincere commitment to observance of the law, the psalmist admits the possibility, even probability, of some form of transgression. The reference is probably not to deliberate acts of defiance but to the failings that result from basic human inadequacy. Acknowledging this weakness, the psalmist prays for God's forgiveness and asks to be cleansed of any guilt.

James 5:1-6

The depiction of the plight of the wealthy does not include an admonition to change their ways so that their misfortune will be reversed. Although the reading resembles a prophetic pronouncement of doom, it is really a wisdom teaching that describes the consequences of a way of living that does not conform to the path of righteousness. The misfortune described does not appear to have been brought on by outsiders. Rather, the rich have fallen victim to the corruption of their own ways.

A lesson to be learned from this sorry situation is the precariousness of wealth. It is not lasting. There is an impermanence to everything. Clothing will be moth-eaten and precious metals will corrode. It is foolish to put one's trust in those things that do not endure, and the rich have done just that.

The wealthy have foolishly and ravenously hoarded the treasures of the earth. Preoccupied with their own comfort, they have ignored the needs of others. Clothes are moth-eaten when they are not worn. This suggests that the wealthy have not only amassed more than they need, but they have failed to share their abundance with those who suffer want. The same is true about their gold and silver. Although these metals do not really rust as the reading suggests, the description emphasizes the lack of generosity on the part of the wealthy. They have been busy accruing money rather than sharing it with the poor, and this selfish attitude will be a testimony against them. The reference is probably to the final judgment, when both their foolishness in storing up treasures and their greed in not sharing the wealth will condemn them.

The second part of the reading reveals that the rich have gained their wealth at the expense of those under their employ. They have exploited their workers, holding back their wages. Such victimization is particularly loathsome in Israel, since the very event that shaped them into a people was their deliverance from indentured slavery in Egypt. The parallel between the early Israelites and the workers in this account is undeniable. Both groups worked for ruthless overlords; both groups cried out to God; both groups were heard.

The author depicts the unscrupulous people foolishly enjoying their wealth and comfort, oblivious that they are really being fattened for the day of slaughter, the impending day of judgment. They do not know it, but their self-indulgence works to their own ruin. Once again their wickedness and their foolishness intersect.

The murder of which they are accused could be an actual killing or it might be a figurative way of describing the death-dealing consequences of the oppression they have forced upon their workers. Because these vulnerable people have no social status, they can offer no resistance.

James does not really denounce wealth as such. What he condemns is the injustice and inhumanity that so frequently accompany it.

Mark 9:38-43, 45, 47-48

This reading is a collection of pronouncements of Jesus on the topics of acceptance, hospitality, and scandal. The first saying follows a report of the intolerance of the apostle John. Like Joshua in the first reading, he challenges someone who is not a member of the close-knit group of disciples but who presumes to perform the marvels they themselves have been commissioned to perform. In this account someone who is not of their number is casting out demons in the name of Jesus. This man would have to possess some degree of faith in Jesus or he would never be using his name. Furthermore, the reading suggests that the exorcisms he has performed have been successful.

This is precisely the response Jesus gives. Unlike Moses, he does not question the motivation of his close companion. He merely authenticates the right of the other man to cast out demons. Jesus points out that this man is not an enemy, nor are the exorcisms he is performing in any way undermining Jesus' own ministry. On the contrary, they may be contributing to it. It is important that the work of the reign of God be done; it is not important who does it.

In a second and related saying, Jesus continues to justify works of mercy performed in his name. Not only are they commendable, they will be highly rewarded regardless of how insignificant they may appear. Giving a cup of water may not sound like a momentous deed, but its implications are far-reaching. In a world where water is scarce it can be the difference between life and death. For this reason the act of giving water became a symbol for any kind of good deed.

Jesus next warns against giving scandal. Some interpreters believe that "little ones" should be taken literally to mean children. Others maintain that since the entire section speaks of discipleship and the "little ones" are here qualified as those who believe in Jesus, the reference is to the disciples who followed him. However the phrase is understood, the stern warning is the same. Those who cause Christians to sin will be severely punished.

Jesus is probably addressing the disciples when he instructs them to take even drastic means if necessary as a precaution against falling into sin. As important as hands and feet and eyes may be for engaging in all of the aspects of life, one can dispense with them if they jeopardize the possibility of enjoying life in the reign of God. The alternative to this privileged enjoyment is exile in Gehenna, a valley just outside the city of Jerusalem where the early Canaanites once offered human sacrifice. The Israelites turned this sacrilegious site into a garbage heap where refuse was constantly being burned. The stench that arose from this site was a constant reminder of corruption. Gehenna became the symbol of the unquenchable punishing fires of the afterlife.

Themes of the Day

A very contemporary issue is placed before us for our consideration: Who has the right to minister in God's name? The readings offer us two very different yet related answers: those who are authorized by the community, and those who are called by the Spirit. There is also an unrelated theme today: the plight of the wealthy.

Authorized by the Community

The readings are evidence that the question they pose is not a new one. However, the dispute over legitimacy of ministry has only recently become a pressing issue for us. Not too many years ago we would have thought that the answer is obvious: The authorities of the Church are the ones who decide. They make the ultimate decisions about the needs of the Church, how these needs are to be met, and who is to meet them. That is one of the responsibilities of their office, an office that is found among the gifts of the Spirit given to the Church (cf. 1 Cor 12:28; Rom 12:9). They stand in the line of succession of the apostles, to whom was given the power to bind and to loose (cf. Matt 16:19; 18:18).

Without outrightly rejecting this authority, many today question the way it is exercised. They believe that many people who are authorized to minister do not seem competent, and many people who seem competent are not authorized. They maintain that rigid conformity to structures and practices of the past inhibit the movement of the Spirit, and they advocate reform.

Anointed by the Spirit

There is a solid biblical tradition that maintains that the movement of the Spirit of God is not confined by human structure or custom. We see this in the judges, the prophets, and even the early kings. The Pentecost story describes the coming of the Spirit upon all people—sons and daughters, young and old, slaves and free (cf. Acts 2:17). The Acts of the Apostles shows the Spirit moving uninhibited, bringing Philip to the Ethiopian (cf. 8:26-30), Peter to Cornelius (cf. 10:1-48), Paul to the Gentile world (cf. 13:2).

There seems always to have been a certain amount of tension between the institutional and the charismatic aspects of the Church. To say that one is Spirit-driven and the other is not is to misunderstand Jesus' promise to remain with the Church until the end of time. God normally calls ministers through the structures of the community, but God calls in other ways as well. And when God calls it is up to us, the Church, to recognize that call and to test its spirit. Perhaps the primary criterion we have for judging is the biblical measure: By their fruits you shall know them.

Reaping the Fruits of One's Sin

The epistle promises that those who have benefited from their exploitation of the vulnerable will reap the fruits of their sin. This warning stems from a belief in the justice of God. Just as we believe that God will not allow the righteous to go unrewarded, so we are confident that neither will the wicked escape punishment.

Twenty-Seventh Sunday in Ordinary Time
Genesis 2:18-24

The reason given for the creation of the animals was companionship for the human creature (v. 18). Despite the features they held in common (made of the same material, v. 19), no animal was found fit to serve as a suitable partner for this unique creature. The word for partner *(ᶜezer)* denotes a source of blessing after some kind of deliverance. It is not good that the human creature is alone, and the other animals are not suitable partners, so God creates the woman.

For centuries, this passage has been used against the woman. This bias stems from a misreading of the story. The woman may have been taken from the man, but he played no part in her creation, nor did he even witness it. Like the man, she is brought forth by a deliberate and unique act of God. The fact that she was built from one of his ribs has led some to consider her inferior to him. Such an argument is empty, since the man is never thought to be inferior to the ground from which he was formed.

There is an ancient myth of the creation of the goddess Ninti, whose title in Sumerian, "woman of life," has the same root as "woman of the rib." As is so often the case in oral cultures, the pun plays a significant role in this account. Although the linguistic similarity was lost in translation into Hebrew, the Israelite author retained the image of the rib, which forms the basis of this creation narrative. This "woman of the rib" is indeed the "woman of life" (cf. 3:20).

The word pair "bone and flesh" (v. 23a) is a typical way of expressing comprehensiveness, similar to "flesh and blood" or "body and soul." The words have psychological as well as physiological meanings and should be understood in this larger context. "Bone" implies strength and "flesh" suggests weakness. In this poetic form they refer to the total range of human strength and weakness. The man recognizes that the woman is the one with whom he can interact totally. He is no longer alone. He now has a suitable partner.

The author makes use of assonance, a device that catches both the ear and the imagination (v. 23b). The woman *(ᵓiššâ)* is built from the man *(ᵓiš)*. Where the first part of the passage uses the general word for man *(ᵓadam)*, this piece of poetry has a word with relational overtones often translated as husband *(ᵓiš)*. The man and the woman are indeed partners.

This poetic construction indicates that the author did not set out to provide an accurate account of the creation of the first couple but sought to focus on their relationship. This is confirmed in the last verse, which speaks of the very powerful and natural drive of the sexes to be physically united as one flesh. This drive prompts a man to disengage himself from his primary relationship and responsibility (his family of origin) and to establish a new social unit. The importance of such a shift of loyalties of a man in the ancient world cannot be underestimated. In this patriarchal society, the woman is considered the only suitable partner for the establishment of a new relationship.

Psalm 128:1-2, 3, 4-5, 6

This psalm is classified as a wisdom psalm. It is a clearly descriptive instruction that teaches rather than an address directed to God in praise or thanksgiving. The psalm contains some of the themes and vocabulary associated with the wisdom tradition. Examples include reward and punishment; happy, or blessed; ways, or path. It begins with a macarism (v. 1), which is a formal statement that designates a person or group as happy or blessed. This statement includes mention of the characteristic that is the basis of the happiness and then describes the blessings that flow from that characteristic. In this psalm, those called happy are the ones who fear the LORD, who walk in God's ways (vv. 1, 4), and the blessing that flows from this attitude of mind and heart is a life of prosperity (vv. 2–3).

In the wisdom tradition fear of the LORD is the distinguishing characteristic of the righteous person. It denotes profound awe and amazement before the tremendous marvels of God. While this may include some degree of terror, it is the kind of fear that accompanies wonder at something amazing rather than dread in the face of mistreatment. The one who fears the LORD is one who acknowledges God's sovereignty and power and lives in accord with the order established by God. If anyone is to be happy and enjoy the blessings of life, it is the one who fears the LORD.

The blessings promised here are both material good fortune and a large and extended family. Large families, like vast fields, were signs of fertility and prosperity. They not only provided companionship through life and partnership in labor, they were also assurances of protection in a hostile world. The promise of future generations (v. 6) guaranteed perpetuity for the family; its bloodline and its name would survive death and would endure into the next generation. Although the androcentric bias in the psalm is seen in its reference to the fruitful wife and numerous children (the Hebrew reads "sons"), the concern is really with the family as a cohesive and abiding unit.

The reference to children's children holds both familial and civic importance. It bespeaks a long life and the continuation of the family, but it also implies that the nation is prospering and that it will endure. The blessings come from God, but God resides at the heart of the nation in Jerusalem, the city of Zion (v. 5). The good fortune of the individual is really a share in the good fortune of the nation.

The final statement (v. 6b) is less a prayer than an exclamation: "Peace be upon Israel!" Peace, *shalom,* is fullness of life. This includes personal contentment, harmony with others and the rest of creation, adequate material resources. All of this is the result of right relationship with God. The psalm begins and ends on the same note: "Blessed are you who fear the LORD" and "Peace."

Hebrews 2:9-11

The solidarity of Jesus with the rest of the human family is precisely outlined in the few short verses that make up this reading. The author turns to a passage from one of the earlier anthropological traditions in order to underscore the dignity of the human race. In its original context (Ps 8:6) the verse extolled human creatures who had been made just a little bit lower than the heavenly beings and to whom was given the care of the rest of the natural world.

The author uses this characterization of human creation but alters it slightly in order to make a point about Jesus. While in his human nature Jesus shared the status that human beings enjoyed, for him to be made lower than the heavenly beings was a humbling experience, not an elevating one. In order to be so made, Jesus emptied himself of his divine privileges, and if this was not humbling enough, he did so in order to empty himself in death for the sake of everyone else.

The author continues with a commentary on the meaning of the phrase "by the grace of God" (v. 10). Jesus tasted disgrace and torment because it was God's will. Such a depiction suggests a cruel and malicious God and challenges the very concept of divine justice. For this reason it seemed necessary to give an explanation of God's actions. It is a question of theodicy, the vindication of the goodness of God in the face of what appears to be evil and unjust.

The explanation given affirms that Jesus' self-emptying death is consistent with God's character and purpose. God, the Creator of all things, seeks to bring all women and men to glory. However, because they have sinned, they are in need of salvation. It seems only right that the one who will lead them to this salvation will himself have been brought to perfect reconciliation with God through the kind of suffering that will reconcile the rest. Requiring this kind of solidarity is consistent with divine justice.

The salvation that Jesus accomplishes is spoken of in cultic language. He is the one who, through his death, brings others to the glory intended for them from their creation. He is the one who consecrates; they are the ones who are consecrated. One would think that this would cause a distinction that would separate Jesus from others. Such is not the case. Like all women and men, Jesus has been made a little lower than the angels, and he is not ashamed of the human nature that he shares with all the rest.

Mark 10:2-16

The reading consists of three scenes. First, the Pharisees test Jesus with a question about divorce. Later, in the privacy of the house Jesus provides his disciples with further explanation of his response to the question. Finally, Jesus is surrounded by children, whom he uses in order to speak about the reign of God.

The Pharisees were not asking about the acceptability of divorce; it was permitted by law. Jesus responds to their challenge with one of his own. He first uses his knowledge of the Mosaic Law to answer their question. He then goes beyond this tradition to the original intent of God as found in the creation account. Doing this, he does not undermine the authority of the Mosaic tradition. Instead, he points out its concession to human weakness. However, in God's design the couple become one flesh and must not be separated.

The Pharisees could be testing to see if Jesus would disagree with Moses, or they might be trying to force Jesus to take a stand on the question of appropriate grounds for divorce. Should the only reason be adultery, as some of the rabbis insisted, or should a more liberal position be held? Jesus takes neither side, but his teaching presumes the original intent of permanent marital union.

Inside the house, Jesus' explanation challenges a patriarchal understanding of divorce and remarriage. In societies where women's reproductive potential belonged first to their fathers and then to their husbands, adultery could be committed only against the man whose rights over the woman had been violated. In saying that the man who remarries is committing adultery against his first wife, Jesus is claiming that she has rights in the relationship as well. Furthermore, he envisions a situation where a woman could divorce her husband, a custom not found in Jewish law. By remarrying, the woman, not her second husband, would be violating the rights that her first husband had over her. Jesus' teaching does not make the demands of marriage easier, but it does place the marriage partners on an equal footing.

Mark does not explain why the disciples disapproved of the children who came to Jesus (vv. 13–16), but he does say that Jesus was indignant over this behavior. Jesus then makes these children the symbol and model of those who would receive and enter the reign of God. Jesus' statement about accepting the reign like a child allows for more than one interpretation. It could mean that the reign must be received with innocence and openness and trust, the way that children receive everything they need. Or it could mean that the disciples must become like children, who in the eyes of society are insignificant, weak, and dependent. The reign of God cannot be judged by the standards of this world. It must be accepted as children might accept a gift. Furthermore, it must also be entered with the unselfconsciousness of children.

Themes of the Day

We see a connection among the various themes present in today's readings when we consider them through the lens of the psalm: "Blessed are you who fear the LORD." Who are the ones who fear God, who walk in God's ways? Those who bind themselves together with Christ in marriage, those who are brothers and sisters of Christ, those who accept the reign of God in the manner of a child—these walk in God's ways.

Bound Together with Christ in Marriage

There are so many reasons why people marry. Although most do so out of love, some marry for companionship, or for money, or because a child is involved. Unfortunately, too many people fail to consider marriage from a religious point of view. This is sometimes even true of believers. There is no question in their minds about being joined to each other, but when people marry, they do not always think about being joined with Christ. It is not that Christ is a third party in the union. It is more profound than that. Christ, who is the sign or sacrament of God's presence in the world, is the ground of that union.

The couple does not merely receive a sacrament, they become one. They become an outward sign of the love of God. They are able to open themselves to each other in love because God has first loved them. When they become one in marriage, they create something new, something that is a sign of the creative power of God. This in no way minimizes the passionate love they may have or the unselfishness with which they give themselves to each other. Instead, it underscores the origin of that passion and the model of that unselfishness. Blessed are they who fear the LORD!

Brothers and Sisters of Christ

We are brothers and sisters of Christ in more than one way. First, through his incarnation he became one of us, a little lower than the angels. He shared our human existence; he knew the highs and lows of human life. Then he redefined family relationships, claiming that blood bonds were no longer the determinant for establishing kinship. Instead, those who hear the word of God and keep it, those who commit themselves to God in faithful discipleship, are his brothers and sisters. Blessed are they who fear the LORD!

In the Manner of a Child

Marriage and every other form of discipleship as well make significant religious demands on us, particularly trust and openness. Because we are taking a step into the unknown, they require a profound act of trust—trust in ourselves, trust in each other, and, most important, trust in God. They also expect openness on our part—openness to give and openness to receive. Unfortunately, we associate these characteristics with unpretentious children. While children may possess them because they are innocent, we must repossess them because we have been re-created in Christ. Blessed are they who fear the LORD!

Twenty-Eighth Sunday in Ordinary Time
Wisdom 7:7-11

This report in the first person is a reinterpretation of the account of Solomon's prayer for wisdom (1 Kgs 3:5-9). In it, Wisdom has been personified as a woman, and she is praised as a priceless treasure beyond compare. Within the tradition wisdom is understood in three ways: empirical wisdom; theological wisdom; and wisdom that is associated with the cosmos. Empirical wisdom, which is akin to prudence, is gained through thoughtful reflection on life experiences. Theological wisdom is like the first, but it presumes that the reflection has been guided by religious principles, and the insights gained are in accord with the religious tradition. The wisdom associated with the cosmos originates in a realization that the real answers to life cannot be achieved merely through reflection on experience. Only God understands the ultimate meaning of reality. However, God might bestow wisdom of this sort on those who ask for it.

In this reading the speaker is depicted as a king (v. 8) who prayed for wisdom. Presumably it was the kind of wisdom that would enable him to rule judiciously. He proclaims that he preferred her to riches, to health, to beauty, to everything that women and men normally cherish. Of all the wonders life has to offer, in his eyes wisdom is the most precious treasure. In fact, in comparison with her, other riches are of little value.

The passage ends on an interesting note. Although he spurned riches, in the end he received them along with the wisdom he sought. The traditional understanding of retribution, so fundamental to the sapiential tradition, posits this direct correlation between one's manner of living and the prosperity one enjoys. It maintains that one who follows the path of wisdom and righteousness will abound in blessings. On the other hand, a life of foolishness and sin will bring on due punishment. Actually, to choose wisdom over everything else is the wisest action one can take, and according to this theory, it will result in the greatest blessings.

The personification of Wisdom as feminine raises an interesting question. Several explanations for this have been advanced. Some scholars believe this is a remnant of ancient Near Eastern worship of a goddess of wisdom. Others maintain that it merely reflects the feminine form of the Hebrew word for wisdom (*hokmâ*). A third position holds that the answer is found in the character of the society. If wisdom is treasured beyond all riches, it is understandable that a patriarchal, male-preferred society would personify it as a desirable woman. However it is understood, Wisdom is depicted as a cherished female companion, who gives extraordinary meaning to life.

Psalm 90:12-13, 14-15, 16-17

The responsorial psalm is a collection of petitions from a community in great distress. Apparently it has been suffering for some time, for it cries out to God in prayer: "How long?" Its confidence in God's willingness to relent from chastising the community and to grace it with kindness is based in the covenant relationship that it shares with God (*ḥesed,* v. 14). God has made a promise, and even in the face of the people's infidelity God will honor that promise.

Israel's way of understanding suffering was quite complex. They seldom questioned why their enemies were burdened with misfortune. The reason for this was obvious to them: enemies of God's people were enemies of God, and so they deserved to suffer hardship. The misfortune that befell Israel was quite another matter. If it was a punishment for ungodly behavior, it was seen as necessary recompense meant to restore the harmony that had been disturbed by the sin. However, even this kind of distress was thought to be only temporary. The people expected that the guilty ones would recognize their error and reform their ways, and then good fortune would return. The pleading found in this psalm arises from a situation from which relief has been long in coming—too long, in fact.

Daybreak usually brings thoughts of hope. The gradual appearance of light dispels the darkness of despair and speaks of promise and well being. However, when it appears that relief is not on the horizon that is slowly taking shape, discouragement turns to desperation, and hope evaporates like early morning dew in the light of day. In such a situation each new day is an added burden rather than a herald of hope. The petitioners have known both kinds of day. Now they pray that they will know days of gladness rather than days of affliction. They are really pleading for a reversal of fortune.

The work of God includes many things. However, the context of this psalm suggests that the focus is on the reversal of fortune of the faithful or the transformation of their lives. Their deliverance will glorify God in the eyes of those who are set free and of those from whom they are set free. Everyone will see and acknowledge God's graciousness toward this people. God will be known as the one who hears the cry of the afflicted and who rescues them.

Hebrews 4:12-13

The word of God is here extolled for both its creative and its juridical force. It is living and effective because it is the expression of the God who is living and effective. As performative speech it accomplishes what it describes; as juridical speech it passes judgment on what it discovers.

God's word is incisive and probing, sharper than a sword that cuts both ways. It can pierce the inner recesses of a person, cutting cleanly between soul and spirit and body, penetrating the most secret thoughts of the heart. Although these four anthropological terms denote distinct components of the human personality, they are probably used here quite generally, referring to every aspect of the person. God's word has both a comprehensive and a profound effect; nothing can escape it.

The anthropological focus of the first verse is replaced with an interest in all of creation. The identification of God's word with God's very self becomes clear as the comprehensive scope of God's influence is further revealed. Nothing is concealed from God; everything is exposed. Such exposure is hazardous only if one has something to hide. Then it can work to one's detriment. The word realizes what it set off to do, and it enhances the life-giving reality it discovers and condemns whatever is unauthentic. Everything that is stands open before this great God.

Mark 10:17-30

The initial exchange between Jesus and the rich man raises an important theological question: Can one gain eternal life, or is it a gift from God? The man's question implies that he believes that he can do something to deserve eternal life. Jesus' response about obeying the law indicates that a particular way of living is indeed required of those who desire eternal life. The man is not putting Jesus to the test; he has approached him with great respect. This is an honest and upright man, one who has been observant from his youth but who realizes that there is still something missing in his life. Jesus recognizes this goodness, and he loves him *(agapáō)*.

Two details of this account require comment. Jesus does not seem to accept the man's salutation, insisting that only God is good. Yet he is certainly not denying his own goodness. This may be his way of indicating its origin and thereby affirming the divine authority with which he acts and speaks. When the man addresses him a second time, he does not use the adjective. The second point is the list of commandments. Included among them is a prohibition against defrauding. While the Decalogue does not include such a commandment, this could be a reference to covetousness, a temptation to which the wealthy might be particularly prone. The commandments themselves are not the issue here. They are included in order to point out the moral integrity of this rich man. Evidently he acquired his wealth honestly.

The detailed description of the man's goodness is important in order to show that even the righteous find it difficult to respond to the radical demands of discipleship. The man could not renounce his riches. Jesus uses this specific case to make a general statement that shocked even his disciples. He uses a graphic example to illustrate how hard it is for those who are encumbered to squeeze through a narrow opening. Nowhere in his teaching does

Jesus say that wealth is bad. In fact, riches were considered an indication of divine favor and a reward for piety. Jesus is claiming that they can be a diversion from the real goal of life, a hindrance to entrance into the reign of God. The power and security they provide can obscure the need to trust in God.

Jesus admits that this is a hard saying. His response is probably the key to understanding the entire passage. While those who wish to inherit eternal life are bound to the commandments, only divine grace can enable them to enter the reign of God. While they must live lives of moral integrity, they must rely completely on God.

Peter uses the rich man's failure to renounce his wealth and follow Jesus to point out the commitment of the disciples. They have done precisely what the other was unable to do. Jesus responds by outlining the reward they can expect. Those who have given up the security of family and property, the basis of identity in the ancient world, will receive a new kind of security, a new family and identity grounded in faith in Jesus. However, this alternative form of relationships and this new set of values not based on material goods will threaten the general social patterns and the values that are in place. Because they are a challenge, the disciples will be criticized and attacked. Thus the real cost of discipleship is personal renunciation and persecution by others.

Themes of the Day

This Sunday's readings confront us with the need to make choices in life, choices for God. They also remind us that no significant choice is without its price. However, if we make the right choices, we are assured that we will be richly rewarded.

Choose Life

We all want to be happy in life. We all want to make the kind of choices that will open doors of possibility and guarantee success. Everyone wants security and well being, and everyone wants peace. We just don't always know which doors to open and how far to enter them. We need wisdom for that. The more options that are open to us, the more difficult it is to choose, but choose we must. Do we want power or riches or beauty, or even health? These are all good, but will they really satisfy the deepest yearnings of our heart? Sometimes there is a clear choice between right and wrong. Often all the various options are somehow good, or we have to choose when no option is to our liking.

There Is a Price to Pay

To choose one option is to relinquish the others. This is not an easy thing to do, especially when all of the options before us are in some way desirable. We select one job or career and thereby close the door on the opportunities that others might offer. We take one trip and miss the excitement of another. The young man wanted eternal life. Surely there is nothing more worthy than that. However, the price he was asked to pay was more than he had expected, and he went away saddened. He was not insulted or frustrated because he could not get what he desired. He was saddened, because what he really wanted he now discovered would exact a heavy cost. To choose is to face the consequences of the word of God, and sometimes this is as sharp as a two-edged sword.

The Hundredfold

One of the mysteries of faith is the incomprehensible generosity of God. We choose wisdom instead of all of the good things of the world, and we receive these good things along with wisdom itself. We are asked to relinquish all of the things we value, and we get them back a hundredfold. We are asked to make these choices in faith. We can never be sure of the outcome until we make the choice and we see what happens. We are invited to take a step into the unknown. We are told that we will not fall. However, we are never sure of this until we take the step and discover that we have not fallen. Or if we do fall, we are not really hurt. Perhaps the faith needed to make the choice also supplies us with the ability to see everything as a hundredfold blessing. God demands so much but gives so much more.

Twenty-Ninth Sunday in Ordinary Time
Isaiah 53:10-11

This short passage contains several related themes. It provides a partial sketch of the portrait of the suffering servant of God; it offers an example of vicarious suffering; it suggests a way of breaking the vicious cycle of violence.

The reading opens on a discomforting note: the suffering of this forlorn individual was brought on by the LORD. The role that God plays in suffering has long plagued religious people. The misfortune of sinners is seen as the just punishment for their offenses, but the suffering of the righteous has always been disturbing. Quite diverse explanations for this situation have been advanced, though none has been completely satisfying. If God causes suffering or allows it to happen, God is thought to be unjust. If God cannot prevent suffering, God is considered powerless. If it is merely a test, God seems to be capricious. This passage clearly states that the servant is crushed to the point of losing his life, and God is the perpetrator of this torment.

The vicarious nature of this suffering is stated in both verses. The servant gives himself as a sin offering; he endures his agony so that others can be justified. His death will win life for others, and in this way he will accomplish God's will. It seems that the LORD delights in crushing this pitiable victim because his agony will bring about salutary benefits in the lives of others. The prophet claims that the servant too will eventually be relieved and will experience fullness of days. However, the principal consequence of his sufferings will be felt in the lives of others.

The servant is cast in the role of the scapegoat, the sacrificial animal upon whose back the sins of others are placed and whose death expiates the guilt of the very ones who killed it. This brutal death not only appeases the guilt of the blameworthy, it also puts an end to the violence that is perpetrated in the original transgressions as well as the violence inherent in the savage sacrifice itself. So often violence begets violence. Here the suffering servant offers no defensive response, no retaliation. The violence inflicted upon him is accepted, embraced, and put to rest. With the fifty-eight vicarious offerings of this innocent scapegoat, reconciliation with God is accomplished.

Psalm 33:4-5, 18-19, 20, 22

The verses of this psalm response contain a collection of themes. The passage opens with a statement that reflects the basis of ancient Israel's faith in God (vv. 4–5). This faith is rooted in the truth of God's word, the faithfulness of God's works, the justice of God's covenant, and the steadfastness of God's love. These four attributes encourage the people to place their trust in God. The attributes themselves connote the magnanimity of God's love. Each one of them describes something of God's manner of relating with others.

The fear of the LORD is the posture of respect with which one stands before the awe-inspiring God (vv. 18–19). Those who possess this kind of fear are committed to God and to the ways of God. They are wise and righteous, because they live their lives before the constant gaze of God. The virtuous attitude of fear delights God, who is then inclined to attend to the needs of those who fear. Famine and death, the evils from which the psalmist pleads to be delivered, represent all of the dangers that intrude in the lives of women and men. Those who fear the LORD turn to God for relief in their distress, and they are rescued. Those without faith look elsewhere for help, and they are confounded.

The psalm ends with a final reference to covenant commitment, or lovingkindness (*ḥesed*, v. 22). Because of this bond God will act as a protecting shield, warding off dangers and bestowing kindness and blessing.

Hebrews 4:14-16

The reading contains a double exhortation: to hold fast to faith and to approach the throne of grace with confidence. It develops the theme of Jesus the high priest who intercedes for all those who turn to him. This is a high priest who was tempted in all things and, therefore, can sympathize with human struggle.

The basis of constancy in the confession of the community is the identity of Jesus. He is the Son of God as well as the great high priest. In order to demonstrate Jesus' preeminence, the author applies to him several features of the high-priestly office. Just as the high priest passed through the curtain into the presence of God in the holy of holies, there to sprinkle sacrificial blood on the mercy seat (Heb 9:7), so Christ, exalted after shedding his own blood, passed through the heavens into the presence of God. Being the Son of God, his sacrifice far exceeds anything that the ritual performed by the high priest might have actually accomplished or hoped to accomplish.

Jesus' exalted state has not distanced him from us. On the contrary, he knows our limitations; as a man he shared many of them. He was tried to the limit, but he did not succumb to despair or blasphemy. Furthermore, it is precisely his exalted state that gives us access to the throne of God. As an authentic human being he carries all of the members of the human race with him as he approaches the heavenly throne. Unlike former high priests who approached the mercy seat alone and only on the Day of Atonement, Christ enables each one of us to approach God, and to do so continually.

This short instruction ends with the second exhortation. The confidence we have in our relationship with Christ should empower us to approach the throne of God boldly, there to receive the grace we need to be faithful. The throne of grace from which we receive mercy is in striking contrast to the mercy seat on which the blood of reconciliation was sprinkled. Where previously the mercy seat was inaccessible, now we are invited to approach God's throne with confidence. Reconciliation has been achieved through the blood of Christ. Now grace reigns.

Mark 10:35-45

The narrative is filled with misunderstandings, paradoxes, and reversals. James and John seek places of prominence in Jesus' kingdom, and Jesus informs them that real prominence is found in service, not in wielding authority over others. The other apostles were probably indignant not because the request of James and John was so audacious but because it was made before any of the others were able to make comparable requests. The instructions that follow indicate that the apostles were all ambitious and misunderstood the nature of Jesus' life and ministry.

The stated willingness of the sons of Zebedee to accept the cup that Jesus will eventually drink and to be baptized in his baptism is another example of their misunderstanding. Even if they had grasped the meaning of his words, they could hardly have imagined their implications. Since they believed that Jesus would reign in glory, they could certainly not conceive of his ignominious suffering and death. Jesus' initial query implied that they would not be able to drink of the cup or be baptized with his baptism. With only a slight shift in meaning, Jesus assures them that they will indeed face what he must face, but they will not do so as willingly as they presume they will.

Returning to the request of James and John for places of honor in the kingdom, Jesus says that it is not for him to make that assignment. With this assertion he indirectly admits that he will indeed be seated in glory. Jesus never denies that he will be prominent in the reign of God. However, whenever he discusses either the reign itself or the role he will play in it, he always indicates that it is God's reign and that he has been appointed by God to do God's work. This is a complete reversal of the reign of God that is expected by the world. Identifying himself as the mysterious Son of Man who will come in the clouds, Jesus offers himself as a model for his followers. He has come to serve others, and to ransom them.

Themes of the Day

As we move closer to the end of the Liturgical Year we look again at the question of discipleship. What reward do we hope to receive for our loyal service? The answer to this question is found in the character of the Messiah. Two images are offered to us today: the suffering servant and the suffering high priest. If we follow in the footsteps of Jesus, we must follow to the end.

The Reward of Discipleship

When we set out to follow Jesus, faithful to the promises we made at baptism to renounce sin and to live lives that are directed by the Spirit, we normally do so with generosity of heart. It is the love of God that impels us, not the thought of reward. However, after we have borne the burden of this decision for a while and we realize some of the implications of our commitment, we begin to wonder what it is all worth. How will we benefit from our dedication? What will we get out of it? We know that we will be generously blessed by God, that we will inhabit one of the mansions that Jesus has gone ahead to prepare for us. Would it be so wrong to hope for a little more, especially if we have made significant sacrifices along the way?

It seems that two of Jesus' closest disciples felt the same way. These two brothers belonged to Jesus' inner circle. They had already been set apart from the others. They had been privileged to witness his transfiguration (cf. Mark 9:2-8). Surely they were not asking for a privilege that God had not already granted them.

A Servant to All

Of those to whom much has been given, much will be required in return. The closer we are to Jesus, the more we will be expected to mirror him. James and John asked for places of honor, places reserved for those who exercise authority. Jesus did not deny that they would have such authority. He assured them that they would have places that were set apart. However, he described these places of distinction in a way the brothers had not expected. The great ones in the reign of God, the ones who exercise authority over others, must be the servants of the rest. Parents, teachers, civil authorities, managers of every kind, pastoral leaders, must all be servants, as Jesus was a servant.

A Suffering Servant—High Priest

Besides modeling our leadership after his, we will also have to model our hardship after his; we will drink from his cup of suffering and be baptized into his death. As we draw close to the one who gave his life as an offering for sin, we will find that the same self-sacrifice is being asked of us. Put another way, when we struggle with the misfortunes we encounter, misfortunes we face because of our commitment to Jesus, we will have him as an inspiration and a model to follow. He can sympathize with our weaknesses, identify with our suffering. For this reason, we can draw strength from his example, and we can hope for his kindness.

Thirtieth Sunday in Ordinary Time
Jeremiah 31:7-9

This reading is an oracle of salvation ("Thus says the LORD"), which contains a summons to praise God for the blessings of deliverance and restoration. The oracle itself is found within an *inclusio* (vv. 5, 7) which frames the picture of people returning from a forced diaspora. Although the mention of Jacob and Ephraim calls to mind the northern kingdom, the reference here is probably to the entire nation. The enthusiasm of the prophet spills out into imperative after imperative, urging the people to praise, exult, proclaim. This is a time of immense joy. The LORD has delivered the people.

Salvation is an accomplished fact; the return is an event of the future. However, this anticipated return is described in vivid detail. The procession of returnees seems to be retracing the very path that was taken when the people were exiled to the land of the north. They left their cherished homeland in tears, but they will return amid shouts of joy. Yet only a remnant will return, and this remnant will consist of the most vulnerable of the people. It includes those who are blind or lame, who are mothers or who are pregnant, all people who are utterly dependent upon God. It will be through them that the nation will be restored.

God is referred to as "father to Israel," and Ephraim is called "my first-born." Both references suggest a patriarchal household. However, the picture of the returnees is in sharp contrast to this model. From one perspective the returnees represent the people who would be ineligible for major leadership positions within a patriarchal society. Because of their gender or physical impairment, they would be the last ones to be called on for the task of rebuilding a nation.

On the other hand, the imagery used here is replete with allusions to new life. Mothers and pregnant women may be vulnerable, but they are also symbols of fecundity and hope. In their bodies they hold the promise of the future. The image of brooks of water also evokes visions of fruitfulness and refreshment. As they leave the land of their exile behind, this remnant carries within itself the possibilities of new beginnings.

Ephraim is called the first-born. He is listed along with the tribes of Israel even though he was neither a son of Jacob nor the first-born of his father Joseph. He received his inheritance through adoption by Jacob, and like Jacob himself, he was granted the privileges of the first-born in place of his older brother (cf. Gen 48:5-20). The status of this ancestor takes on an interesting dimension in this particular passage. It is fitting that the one who represents the remnant is an ancestor who has been grafted onto the family tree, one through whom a people are given a new start. Just as the returnees are evidence of God's willingness to grant a second chance, so Ephraim symbolizes kinship through God's choice. The restoration promised here is clearly a work of God. Customary human initiative plays no role in it.

Psalm 126:1-2, 2-3, 4-5, 6

Confidence in God's saving power is usually based on the remembrance of some saving act in the past. Believers trust that God will surely act on their behalf, because God has done so before. The great blessing of Israel's past was the return from exile. Zion, the mountain on which the temple was built, became a symbol with many levels of meaning. It stood for the temple itself, the city of Jerusalem, the southern kingdom, or the entire nation of Israel. Here it probably represents Jerusalem and the area surrounding it.

The response of the returnees was threefold: amazement, laughter, and joy. Their release and return was so extraordinary that it was almost beyond their comprehension. It was as if they were in a dream. This suggests that there was little in their situation leading them to believe they could come back to the land from which they had been taken. Painting the situation in such bleak shades was a technique employed by the author to help the people see how helpless they were to improve, much less reverse, their predicament. In such circumstances only God would have the authority and power to change anything.

The graciousness of God as seen in the deliverance of and blessings given to the Israelites speaks volumes to the other nations. It throws into bold relief God's saving power. It also shows that this power is not restricted by the limitations of geographic boundary or ethnic particularity. It was exercised over the Israelites, but it could be effective in a foreign country. This is a God who shows preference for those who are poor and marginalized in society, for the homeless and the foreigner, the displaced and the refugee. The portrait that Israel's history paints of such a God has clarity, depth, and nuance. Seeing this history unfold before their very eyes, the nations will marvel at the greatness of a God that can accomplish such amazing feats, and they will acclaim him LORD.

The prayer for deliverance is straightforward: Restore us now as you restored us in the past. The image used as a comparison reflects the impossible character of the present situation. The restoration will be like a flood of water in the southern desert, which is not only infrequent but even most unlikely. The image itself contains a paradox. One element of it (torrents of water) is the complete reverse of the other (arid desert). This contradiction underscores the implausibility of what is being asked. However, the petitioner boldly offers the petition because the grace requested had been granted in the past.

The reversal of fortune is further described in symbolic language: sowing in tears and reaping in joy; leaving with only the promise of harvest and returning with its abundant fruits. God will replace the tragedy that marks the circumstances of the people with good fortune. This is their prayer; it is for this that they hope. They are confident their prayer will be answered and their hope will be realized, because God has been gracious to them in the past.

Hebrews 5:1-6

In casting Jesus in the role of high priest, the author states the general qualifications a man must meet before he can assume the responsibilities of the office. Patterned after the model of Aaron, the prospective high priest must be able to empathize with the frailty of those he serves, and he must have been called by God.

Since they were expected to intercede with God on behalf of the people, it was important that Aaron and his descendants be familiar with the conditions under which the people lived. They would have to experience the challenges that faced the people, and like the others, they would have to know what it means to repent and to try again to be faithful. Acknowledgment of their commonly shared human limitations and weaknesses would prevent the high priests from assuming an arrogant air and from making demands on the people that would only add to their burdens. In order to be credible mediators, the high priests would have to be humble.

The second qualification is appointment by God. No one can take the office of high priest upon himself, not can it be granted by anyone but God. Like Aaron, who was explicitly called by God (Exod 28:1; Num 3:10), the high priest must belong to one of the divinely appointed priestly families. This selection should not be understood as an indication of the superiority of some families over others. Rather, it underscores the importance of the office. All those who assume it must have divine approval.

Jesus did not trace his ancestry to one of the priestly families, and there was no need for him to make sin offerings for himself. Therefore his right to function as high priest had to be explained. The author does this first by referring to him as Christ and then by reinterpreting two very familiar biblical passages, both of which have messianic significance. The title "Christ" is the Greek for "anointed one." Since both kings and priests were anointed, the title carries both royal and priestly connotations. To call Jesus by this title is to make a claim about his identity.

The psalm verses within this reading both point to the exceptional station to which Jesus was called. In the first he is identified as a son of God (Ps 2:7); in the second, as a priest-king like the mysterious Melchizedek of old who, because the tradition contained no information about his origin, was believed to have had no beginning (Ps 110:4). In both of these verses the individual is perceived as a royal figure, which in the ancient world was considered somehow divine. However, in both instances the special status did not belong to the person by right but was conferred by God. Applying these verses to Jesus, the author is saying that the offices Jesus held were conferred by God. Like the high priest, Jesus was made a representative before God.

Although the reading does not mention Jesus' solidarity with human weakness, as king and priest he shared in the limitations of the human condition. His profound humility is seen in his willingness to empty himself of his divine privileges and to become human. His life shows his solidarity with others.

Mark 10:46-52

This account of the healing of a blind man is in some ways also a call narrative. Although Jesus' words do not actually invite the man to follow him, the man interprets his actions as doing so. It is unusual that the name of the one healed is given. If the man were merely one of the many beggars who lined the road, there would be no way of knowing who he was. In this episode Jesus was surrounded by a large crowd, indicating that the man who was sitting on his cloak could not be easily seen or recognized. As it is, he seems to be known to the author of this narrative. The fact that he followed Jesus after being healed may indicate that he actually became a well-known disciple.

The account contains two Aramaic words. One is part of the man's name; the other is the title with which he addresses Jesus directly. The commonly used Hebrew word for son is *ben*. The Aramaic word *bar* is used here. The title *Rabboni*, which means "my master" or "teacher," is a more reverential address than the customary title *Rabbi*.

The faith of this man is both demonstrated by his actions and explicitly recognized by Jesus. When he hears that it is Jesus of Nazareth who is passing by him, he cries out to him using a title that has strong messianic connotations. "Son of David" identifies Jesus not only as a descendant of this royal figure but also as the long-awaited one who was to fulfill both the religious and the political expectations of the people. Bartimaeus knows that Jesus has the power to heal him, but he also believes that he is the anointed of God who has come to inaugurate the reign of God.

Unlike so many other healing narratives in which people bring those who are sick and afflicted to Jesus to be healed, in this instance the people around the blind man try to silence him. No reason for this is given. Might it be that they do not want him to bother Jesus? This would be curious, since they certainly would be eager to witness a miraculous cure. Or is it that they do not want Jesus to be acclaimed in this way? Whatever the case may be, Jesus hears the man's cries and has him brought to him. Beggars normally would spread out their cloaks so they would be able to collect alms. This beggar throws his cloak aside, apparently leaving behind both the alms he has already collected and his life of begging. He has left what he had in order to respond to the call of Jesus.

The man who was blind already had eyes of faith and he acted on this faith, publicly proclaiming it. As a consequence of his profession, Jesus tells him it is this faith that gave him his sight. In his eagerness to respond to Jesus' call, he had already left everything. Having been cured, he now follows Jesus.

Themes of the Day

As we come to the close of the Liturgical Year, we pause this Sunday to see how far we have come. It is a time to examine how we are maturing in the Spirit. To what degree have we followed God, who leads us out of captivity? Have our fortunes been restored? Have our eyes been opened? Has this been a good year?

The Wonderful Deeds of God

Throughout this Liturgical Year we have examined several aspects of our faith. We have pondered the history of our salvation, the merciful compassion of God shown to us after we have sinned, God's willingness to lead us out of the bondage of our addictions. We have meditated often and long on the person of Jesus, on his life and death, on the meaning of his sacrifice, on his resurrection, on his influence in our lives today. We have considered our own ongoing transformation as disciples of Jesus—baptized into his death and resurrection, commissioned to bring the news of his love to all those with whom we come into contact. We have reflected on all of these wonderful deeds of God, and now we must ask the question: what difference has it made?

Do We See?

As we come to the close of Ordinary Time and we review our consideration of the faith, can we say that we have gained new insight? Have we merely acquired some information about the biblical readings, about our religious ancestors in Israel, about the ministry of Jesus and the life of the early Church? Or have our eyes really been opened; have we been enabled to leave behind whatever prevents us from living the Christian life fully, to abandon our exile or the trappings of our former lives? Have we accepted more genuinely the Christian responsibilities that are ours as baptized followers of Christ—in our own personal lives, in our families, in our relationships with others, at the workplace? To what degree have we been transformed into Christ? How open have we become to the action of the Spirit in our lives? Have we been transformed into a new creation? And do we recognize Christ in our midst?

Christ in Our Midst

Have we come to see more deeply who this Christ is and who we are in Christ? Do we recognize him as our teacher, and have we learned from him the mysteries of God's love and how we can adequately respond to that love? Do we realize that the poor and unassuming man who walked the roads of life is the son of David, the one of royal descent who has come to establish the reign of God? Have we learned to recognize God's reign—present in the poor and the unassuming as well as in those who struggle with their prosperity, in the people who are burdened with doubt and insecurity as well as those who rejoice in the truth, in the needy and the seriously limited as well as those who minister out of strength and ability?

Do we recognize him as the healer who will open our eyes so that we can really see? Have we heard his coming in the words of today's prophets and teachers who open for us the treasures of our religious tradition, in the wisdom of those who know that life is precious and must not be squandered, in the mystics who experience God's presence in the mysteries of nature, in the leaders who take us by the hand and bring us to the feet of Jesus? We may see all of this in the readings, but do we recognize it in our own lives? Has this been a good year?

Thirty-First Sunday in Ordinary Time
Deuteronomy 6:2-6

The reading contains what many consider to be the most significant prayer of the Israelite religion. It is a profession of faith in the one God to whom belongs Israel's exclusive and undivided attention, commitment, and worship. The prayer itself contains only four words, two of which are the personal name of God. They are: LORD; our God; LORD; one. Following the prayer or profession of faith is a call to commitment.

Two creedal testimonies are made in this short prayer, each preceded by the personal name of God. This God is the patron deity of Israel, not a god attached to a shrine or identified with some natural occurrence. All of Israel's history with God is contained in the phrase "our God." This is the God who drew the people out of Egyptian bondage, led them through the perils of the wilderness, and brought them into the land of promise. This is also the God within whom all of the attributes of deity can be found, not a divided deity whose various characteristics are worshiped at various shrines.

The profession of faith is found within a summons to obedience. Twice Israel is called to hear, to listen, and to obey (vv. 3, 4). It is obedience to this one and personal God that will ensure the blessings of long life and prosperity in the land. Although there are various statutes and commandments (v. 2), they can all be summarized under the rubric "Love the LORD, your God" (v. 5). Just as the responsibility of obedience is handed down from generation to generation (v. 2), so they can be assured that the blessings promised will also endure from generation to generation.

The love that is enjoined on them must be complete. Obedience cannot be simply external conformity to law. It must be total commitment to God, and all of their interior faculties must be involved in this commitment. This would include the heart, which was thought to be the seat of mind and will; the soul, which was considered the source of vitality; and all of their strength.

Psalm 18:2-3, 3-4, 47, 51

This psalm of praise for deliverance is a composite of direct address to God and description about God addressed to someone else. Perhaps the most noteworthy aspect of the psalm is the array of metaphors employed to characterize God. They include rock, fortress, deliverer, shield, horn of salvation, stronghold. Although each has its respective meaning, all embody some aspect of deliverance.

"Rock," "fortress," and "stronghold" depict God as an impregnable bulwark against which no enemy can triumph. "Shield" and "horn of my salvation" are military accouterments that protect the soldier from harm. A "deliverer" *(miplāt)* is one who rescues someone from a calamity, such as war. All of these characterizations imply that the psalmist is protected by God from grave danger of every kind. In a world where people feel that they are always at risk and where violence is the common response to threat, the idea that a powerful God will step in and act as defender is very consoling.

The word translated "love" *(rāham)* is very unusual. It comes from the word for womb, and it denotes the kind of intimate love that a mother has for the child she is carrying or has already borne. It conveys the sense of elemental connection, a connection with something that has come forth from one's very being. This word is usually used to characterize the extraordinary, even incomprehensible love that God has for human beings. Its claim to love God with this kind of devotion is a bold claim indeed.

The victory cry "The LORD lives!" is a cultic formula that extols God's dynamic activity. Because the psalm speaks of the psalmist's need for defense and deliverance, the reference is certainly to God's saving activity in history. What began as a hymn of thanksgiving has now become a doxology, a prayer in praise of God's mighty accomplishments.

The very last verse of this response introduces a royal theme. The God who has been the defense of the psalmist has also secured victory for the king. It may be that the king is another one of the people saved by the LORD, or perhaps the king and the psalmist are one and the same. Since the point of the psalm is the secure defense that is offered by God, either interpretation would be acceptable.

Hebrews 7:23-28

Three aspects of the extraordinary high priesthood of Jesus are here celebrated, namely, its permanence, the holiness of Jesus the high priest, and the legitimacy of the high priesthood. This passage underscores the excellence of Jesus' high office by contrasting its divine character with the very human character of the Levitical priesthood.

Jesus is a priest forever, according to the order of Melchizedek (cf. Heb 5:6, Thirtieth Sunday in Ordinary Time). This identification with the enigmatic high priest of old might emphasize Jesus' mysterious origin. Here it focuses on the perpetuity of his office. The contrast between the permanence of his priesthood and the fleeting nature of the Levitical priests' term of office is meant to celebrate the priesthood of Jesus, not to negate the value of the priesthood of Israel. Because each Levitical priest was subject to death, hereditary transmission of office was necessary for the priesthood itself to endure. Because he conquered death by his own death and resurrection, Jesus' priesthood is inviolable and will not pass away.

The permanent nature of Jesus's high priesthood enables him to intercede for others, as the high priests did, but without interruption. All can now come to God through him. There is no need constantly to reaffirm the efficacy of his mediatorial authority. This has been accomplished once and for all through his exaltation by God.

The holiness of Jesus is the second characteristic that distinguishes his priesthood from the other. The four adjectives that describe him—holy, innocent, undefiled, and separated from what is sinful—recall the attributes that constitute Levitical purity. If these characteristics are understood as cultic requirements, it is clear that Jesus certainly possesses the qualifications necessary for the office of high priest. However, Jesus is further described as being "higher than the heavens." This characteristic lifts the other four attributes out of the realm of cultic purity into one of moral rectitude and heavenly transcendence.

It is because he is son that Jesus is holy, innocent, undefiled, and separated from what is sinful. This is why he has no need to offer sacrifice for his own sins, as do mere human beings. They may be members of a distinguished priesthood, but they are sinners nonetheless. Furthermore, the excellence of his own sacrificial offering has made additional sacrifices unnecessary. He has accomplished once and for all what even the continuous offerings of the Levitical priesthood could not accomplish.

Finally, because Jesus' high priesthood cannot be traced back to the religious institution established by God through Aaron, it had to be legitimated in another way. This was done by identifying Jesus with Melchizedek, whose priesthood was established by a divine oath (cf. Heb 7:20; Ps 110:4). The tradition that surrounded this enigmatic figure has here been reinterpreted in order to typify a particular aspect of the divine nature of this incomparable high priest.

Mark 12:28b-34

This pronouncement story is different from most such accounts. Frequently Jesus' answer is a response to a challenge that has been hurled at him. Such is not the case here. In fact, the integrity of the scribe who poses the question can be seen in Jesus' assurance of his proximity to the reign of God.

The 613 commandments that had grown up surrounding the official biblical law were divided into two major categories. Although all laws were considered binding because they had been delivered by God to Moses, some were regarded as "heavy" or very important and others were looked upon as "less weighty." Presumably the scribe, whose very profession included the interpretation of the law, should have understood it better than Jesus, who was not a scribe. Because of the complexity of the law, however, the professional seems unable to prioritize it. He must have recognized something in Jesus to prompt him to ask this very significant question.

Jesus' answer is faithful to his own Jewish faith. He does not single out any particular statute but rather endorses the summons that constitutes the *Shᵉmaᶜ*, the most significant prayer of the Israelite religion (cf. Deut 6:5). To the injunction to love God with all one's heart, soul, and strength, Jesus adds "with all your mind," simply to emphasize the total engagement of the person. This is his way of saying that the love of God must occupy one's entire being.

Jesus is asked to identify one commandment, and he offers two. The second is a citation from the book of Leviticus (19:18). Twice Jesus has reached into the biblical law in order to answer the scribe's question. By bringing these admonitions together as he does, he has shown that, though not identical, they are interrelated. Clearly commitment to God takes priority over everything else.

The scribe, who is schooled in the religious tradition, recognizes Jesus' response as both accurate and profound. He calls him Teacher, a title that has special significance coming from one who was himself an official interpreter of the law. His own development of Jesus' pronouncement demonstrates his skill as an interpreter.

The controlling theme in the response is the character of God. There is no other God but this God! From this flows the responsibility to love God with one's entire being and to love one's neighbor as oneself. It is the scribe who merges the two admonitions as if they were one. It is the scribe who further points out that love of God and of others far surpasses any kind of cultic obligation. He now sees through the complexity of the law and is able to discriminate between what is "heavy" and what is "light." He is on the threshold of the reign of God.

The final statement could mean that no one dared challenge Jesus again, that this answer covered all other questions. What else was there to ask? What other answer could be given?

Themes of the Day

The readings for this Sunday all cluster around one central theme: the covenant in the lives of the people. The originator of the covenant is God, the one, holy God; the mediator of the covenant is Jesus Christ, the high priest; and the essence of the covenant is love.

Hear, O Israel

The call to hear, to be attentive comes from outside the one being called. Israel is called by God; God is the initiator. To what was Israel called? To what were the crowds who followed Jesus called? To what are we called? To a covenant relationship with the LORD, who is God, the one who is LORD alone. We have been invited into an intimate personal relationship with the creator of the universe, the one who, with infinite interest, has numbered the very hairs on our head (cf. Matt 10:30).

We have heard this so often that it may have become commonplace. The marvel of it may escape our attention, because it has become just a part of our religious language. In a way it is like the sun. It is always there, holding us in our place in the vast universe, warming us and lighting our days, painting our skies with shades of color every morning and every evening, and yet we usually give it very little thought. It is well that once in a while we are shaken to our senses. "Hear, O Israel! The LORD is our God, the LORD alone!"

The Great High Priest

It is not marvel enough that this mysterious God has created us; we have also been redeemed. We who have foolishly turned away from the very Sun that holds us in our place, that warms us and enlightens us, are brought back into relationship with God. As victim-priest Jesus has offered himself on our behalf. He is the sacrifice that sealed the covenant; his blood was the expiation for our sins; he is our rock, our fortress, our deliverer, our shield, our stronghold. Multiply metaphor upon metaphor as we might, we will never be able to grasp the depth of Jesus' willingness to give of himself to us. Only one thing is asked of us in return: that we open ourselves to him and cling to the covenant, that we proclaim with all our hearts, "The Lord is our God, the Lord alone!"

Take to Heart These Words

It has been said that falling in love with God is the central act of the religious person. It certainly is the essence of the covenant. We are to love with all our heart and all our soul and all our strength; we are to love God and to love others. Love is as fundamental to human nature as the sun is to the earth, and yet it is so difficult. If only we could fall in love with God; if only we would see in each other the image that God loves so passionately. Then we too would be close to the reign of God.

Thirty-Second Sunday in Ordinary Time
1 Kings 17:10-16

Several themes have been woven together in this dramatic account. The story is based on the ancient obligation of hospitality. It also contains a prophetic pronouncement (v. 14) and a miraculous event (vv. 15–16). It can be read as a story that recounts the faith of the woman or as an episode in the extraordinary life of the prophet. Though the woman is unnamed, the prophet's name means "My God *[Eli]* is the LORD *[jah]*." This name suggests that the story is really about the efficacy of the power of God in a land that has been considered the domain of another god.

The woman is in a perilous situation. As a widow in a patriarchal society, she has very few resources to call upon. Through marriage she has left the protection of her father's house; through widowhood she has lost the security of her husband. It is ironic that the prophet himself is dependent upon one of the most vulnerable members of the society. Furthermore, the woman and her son are on the brink of starvation. Despite this she is still required by custom to provide hospitality to whoever approaches her, regardless of the cost this might exact of her. The woman does not question the prophet's initial request for water. Nor does she resist when he asks her to feed him before she attends to her own needs and those of her son. The prophet's request should not be seen as an example of selfish insensitivity. Actually, this very request becomes the avenue through which God provides for the woman and her son.

The question of the sovereignty of Elijah's God can be seen in the exchange between the woman and the prophet. In her oath, she refers to "your God." It is clear that the woman does not share Elijah's religious commitment. The prophet responds with words that are associated with a revelation of God: "Do not be afraid!" Using the formula of prophetic proclamation, "Thus says the LORD," he then tells her that it is his God, the God of Israel, who will provide for her and her son, just as she has provided for God's prophet. Furthermore, it is the God of Israel who controls the rain, the source of fertility in the land.

The reason that the woman is in such dire straits in the first place is that God has withheld the rain. Her reserve of water and flour and oil has been depleted and the land has not been able to produce anything that might replenish her supply. The oracle of salvation proclaimed by the prophet promises that God will miraculously provide for them until that time when God will send the rains enabling them to rely again on nature.

The woman followed the word of the prophet, and God's word spoken through the prophet came to pass. The text says that the woman's miraculous supply of flour and oil lasted for a year. In her oath the woman had declared that Elijah's God lives. She made this proclamation in the face of what appeared to be inevitable death. The miracle showed the woman that this God who lives can and will grant life even in the face of death.

Psalm 146:7, 8-9, 9-10

The responsorial psalm is a hymn of praise of the LORD (*Hallelujah* in Hebrew). Such hymns have a very definite pattern. The summons itself *(hallelu)* appears in a plural verb form, suggesting a communal setting, and contains an abbreviation of the divine name *(jah)*. In this psalm the word is used as a refrain, a response to a series of statements that offer examples of God's indescribable graciousness.

"God of Jacob" (v. 5) is a title that points out the patronal character of God's nature. It does not refer to an abstract quality of God but to the special protection that was given to Jacob, the ancestor after whom this entire people was named, and to all of his descendants. There is an allusion here to God's deliverance of the people from the bondage of Egypt and to God's providential care of them during their sojourn in the wilderness. God has been faithful. This is reason enough to praise the LORD.

God's graciousness to the vulnerable is next extolled (vv. 8–9). There are many situations in life that can force one to be bowed down, whether a physical disability, a mental or emotional affliction, an economic or social disadvantage. Whatever it might be, God raises up the needy, enables them to stand with pride, reestablishes them in security. Strangers or aliens lack certain legal rights, and since it is not their own nation, they may not be familiar with the rights they do have. Insensitive or unscrupulous people can easily take advantage of them. These vulnerable strangers are precisely the kinds of people that the God of Israel chooses. Israel itself is the prime example of this. It was when they were aliens in Egypt that God intervened and made them God's own people. This is certainly reason to praise God.

In patriarchal societies only adult free men enjoy certain privileges. As part of the household, women and children are under the jurisdiction and care of such men. Women belong to the households of their fathers, their brothers, or their sons. Here widows probably refers to women who cannot return to their home of origin because they have married but whose husbands are now dead and they have no adult son to care for them. Such women are marginal in society and need some patron to defend and protect them. Likewise, it is presumed that the orphans referred to here have no extended family within whose jurisdiction they might take refuge. These are the ones for whom God cares.

The final verse praises God as sovereign and eternal ruler in Jerusalem. All of the other verses of the psalm testify to the glory of this God who reigns forever from the very hill that is at the center of the lives of the people. This is not a God who is far off. This God has entered into their history and into the very social fabric of their existence. Such a God deserves praise.

Hebrews 9:24-28

The argument employed in this reading, which seeks to show the unsurpassing excellence of the sacrifice of Christ, is based on an understanding of the significance of the temple and of the ritual that was performed within it. Temples were normally constructed on sites that were already considered sacred, places that claimed to have had a manifestation of the divine, which made them qualitatively different. Such an experience was thought to create an opening that connected the three levels of reality: heaven, earth, and the underworld. The opening, called the "navel of the earth," or the *axis mundi,* made communication among these levels possible. Sanctuaries were often established on this sacred opening, and by virtue of the communication that took place there, the world was sanctified again and again.

The temple was built according to the *imago mundi,* the pattern of the universe that was itself considered the real temple of the Creator God. Its structure reflected the four celestial horizons with their respective heavenly bodies, and its interior was decorated with elements of the natural environment within which it was built (cf. Exod 25:40). In this way it demonstrated the connection between heaven and earth. The people believed that when they entered the earthly temple they were somehow entering the realm of heaven.

The argument in this reading plays on the difference between the true sanctuary and the one that is patterned after it. It claims that while the high priests performed their sacrificial duties in the earthly temple, the exalted Jesus entered the true sanctuary. It insists that the cultic system, established to enable the people to participate in cosmic events by reenacting them, was only able to actualize these events for a short period of time. This explains why the ritual of the Day of Atonement was reenacted year after year.

In contrast to this, Jesus offered himself once for all. His sacrifice, like all cosmic acts, was unrepeatable. Earthly ritual may reenact his sacrifice, but there is no need for Jesus himself to repeat it.

The notion of sacred time is intimately associated with that of sacred space. Sacred time is really cosmogonic time, the time when order was established and creation was pristine. It is *illo tempore,* the time sanctified by the activity of God, the time that has no beginning and no end. Ritual activity enables people to enter into this time for a brief moment in order to participate in the sacred events. In the Jewish understanding of eschatology, at the end of time everything will be transformed. Holding to this idea, Christians believe that the sacrifice of Christ bridged the gap between the time of human life on this earth and *illo tempore.* The transformation has already begun with the exaltation of Jesus. The final transformation will take place when Jesus returns to bring irrevocable salvation to the faithful who have died.

Mark 12:38-44

What appear to be two very distinct narratives connected only by the term "widow" are really contrasting examples of expressions of piety. Jesus' condemnation of the scribes has in succeeding generations frequently led to anti-Jewish sentiments. There is no indication that Jesus is here condemning all scribes. He may just as well be singling out those whose ostentatious piety really cloaks their exploitation of wealthy widows.

While at prayer in the synagogues, men wore long outer garments called *tallith*. Some scribes may have continued to wear these robes in public, hoping that people would consider them prayerful men and admire them for it. In addition to this outward display, they sought other ways to be treated with deference and to enjoy privilege. The congregation sat on benches facing the chest that contained the sacred scrolls. The most important seats in the synagogue were the front benches. At banquets the honored guests flanked the host, the most honored sitting at the right, the second honored at the left. These places of honor, along with reverential salutations, were sought after by scribes for whom public acclaim was vital.

The need to be so highly esteemed may be frivolous, but it is not immoral. However, Jesus' denunciation further accuses these scribes of exploiting widows. The description of their swindle suggests that they somehow appropriated the widows' property, perhaps having it deeded to them in exchange for prayers. Scribes received no set salary, so they had another occupation or relied on donations and gifts. What is described here is probably an extreme example of the latter. Severe condemnation was not called down upon them simply because they had taken possession of the women's property but because the women were exploited in the name of religion.

In the second scene Jesus is seated in the temple, in the court of the women, just opposite the treasury. Thirteen trumpet-shaped containers were set up in this area to collect the alms donated for the upkeep of the temple. The sound of the money rolling to the bottom of the container probably reverberated throughout the area, announcing the charity of the donor. Large sums and heavy money made a conspicuous noise. The poor widow offered the smallest coins in circulation at that time. The amount equaled about one sixty-fourth of a denarius, the normal daily wage of an unskilled worker.

Jesus' criticism of the scribes' behavior had been made publicly. He proclaimed it to the crowd that had gathered around him. His comparison of the generosity of the wealthy and of this woman was imparted privately to his disciples. He did not evaluate the contribution itself. Rather, he spoke of the source of the offering. The wealthy donated from their surplus; they gave what they did not need. The woman donated the little she had; she gave what she needed. Her total giving implied absolute trust in God. The passage that opened with a condemnation of the false piety of the unscrupulous closes with praise of the genuine piety of the simple.

Themes of the Day

The giving of oneself in love that was the focus of our reflection last week is found in a slightly different form in the readings for this Sunday. The willingness to give all that one has becomes the central theme. The readings offer us three models of such unselfish giving, and they suggest some of the rewards that will accrue to those who are courageous enough to attempt it.

Unselfish Giving

People usually give out of their abundance, but there are still several reasons for their giving. Many people give out of genuine generosity. They see others who are needy, and they want to help. Others give out of guilt. They may feel that sharing what they have will satisfy some kind of debt they owe. There are people who give for tax purposes. They discover that they will be better off financially if they give from their excess. Finally, we all give openhandedly to those we love, and we do this regardless of whether we have adequate resources or not.

The generosity depicted in the readings for today is a different kind of giving. It is religiously inspired, and it comes from those who have the least material possessions to give. This kind of giving requires that we reach deep into ourselves, that we almost strip ourselves of our hold on life, and that we do this for religious reasons. This giving, pictured in today's readings, is nothing less than heroic generosity.

Models of Unselfish Giving

Jesus is the ultimate example of heroic generosity. He first offered himself as expiation for our sins. Now, as the eternal high priest, he stands before God as our mediator, pleading on our behalf, bringing salvation to those who eagerly await him.

It is interesting to note that the other two models of selfless giving are widows, individuals who are doubly disadvantaged by the patriarchal societies of which they are members. We must be careful here lest we fall into the same trap as do societies with gender or class biases that expect women and slaves to give unselfishly. The narratives do not support or reinforce this bias, nor should we. Instead, they choose women as examples of heroic virtue precisely because their societies have relegated them to a status of inferiority and vulnerability. They do this not to reward them but to show that God chooses the weak of the world to confound the strong.

Rewards for Generosity

God will not be outdone in generosity. Sometimes we become the beneficiaries of obvious blessing, as was the case in the story of the woman of Zarephath, who was granted a year's supply of flour and oil. At other times we simply continue living life as usual, like the woman in the temple who was unaware of the commendation that Jesus had given her. The truly generous do not look for reward. They carry out their responsibilities and place the rest in God's hands.

Thirty-Third Sunday in Ordinary Time
Daniel 12:1-3

The apocalyptic scene described here is part of the revelation granted to the prophet Daniel. It depicts the final struggle of human beings at the end of time and their subsequent resurrection, either to a life of horror or a life of glorification. The prophetic phrase "at that time" appears three times in the very first verse and marks the future-oriented character of the event described. It seems that each nation had an advocate in the heavenly court who came to its defense, whether in battle or in a court of law. Michael, whose name means "who is like God," is the patron guardian of Israel (cf. 10:23).

The reading says that Michael rises up, but it does not explain why he does so. It may be as protector of Israel as the nation faces the distress of the end of time. Since the judgments meted out to the righteous and to the wicked are described later in the reading, one might conclude that Michael stands in order to present those under his charge (Israel) to the judgment seat of God, or to participate in some way in the judgment itself.

The distress that is to come is unparalleled. It is probably the final tribulation that will come to pass before the appearance of the eschatological reign of God. This suffering was considered by some to be the "birth pangs of the Messiah," the agony that must be endured if the reign of God is to be born. Daniel is told that those whose names appear in the book (presumably the Book of the Righteous) will be spared. They will have to endure the agony of the end-time, but they will escape ultimate destruction.

The allusion to some kind of resurrection from the dead followed by reward and punishment is clear. Since the idea of the end-time sets the context for this passage, the resurrection referred to here is the general resurrection believed to be coming at the end of time. Death is described as sleeping in the dust of the earth, and resurrection is an awakening. After they have been raised, the dead must give an account of the record of their deeds. This is the basis upon which they are separated, some rewarded with everlasting life, others punished with horror and disgrace.

Within the circle of those who are granted everlasting life, some are singled out for further distinction (v. 3). The verse is structured after the pattern of poetic parallelism, suggesting that the reference is to one group and not to two. Elements from astral religion are employed to characterize reward of the wise. Previously they had been a source of illumination in the lives of others. In the new age they will continue to shine, but then their brilliance will be seen by all. They will be like the stars in the heavens.

This vision is a message of hope and challenge for those who are undergoing great distress. The righteous are encouraged to remain steadfast in their commitment. They are promised a spectacular reward if they do. The reading also warns the reprobates of the fate that awaits them. The choice is theirs.

Psalm 16:5, 8, 9-10, 11

The psalm verses speak of covenant relationship with God and the confidence that abounds from it. Two images express this relationship. The allotted portion of land is the inheritance each tribe was given and which was handed down within the tribes generation after generation. This land provided the people with identity and membership, sustenance and prosperity. Without land they had no future, and they would not last long in the present. Here the psalmist is claiming that God the eternal deity has replaced the land in the religious consciousness of the people. The blessings and promises that are customarily associated with land are now associated with the LORD.

The second image is the cup. This might be the communal cup passed around and from which all drank. Such an action solidified the union of those who drank from the common cup. When this action took place at a cultic meal, those participating in the feast were joined not only to each other but to the deity as well. The psalmist declares that the LORD is actually this unifying cup. In other words, the psalmist is joined so closely with God as almost to defy separation. God is there, at the psalmist's right hand, standing as an advocate or a refuge.

Such protection is reason for profound rejoicing. Regardless of the terrifying, even life-threatening ordeals the psalmist must face, God is steadfast. This kind of confidence in God may appear to be foolhardy, but the psalmist's trust is unshakable. Ultimately the fullness of joys will abound in the presence of God.

Hebrews 10:11-14, 18

An understanding of the Jewish practice of sin offering is behind the explanation of the unique sacrifice of Christ. The primary purpose of both the Jewish ritual and the sacrifice of Christ is the expiation of sin.

Various circumstances came into play when one was determining the specifics of the traditional sacrifice. The status of the one officiating determined which victim was to be offered. For example, the high priest would offer a bull. Also, the station of the one whose sins were to be expiated played a role in this determination. A political dignitary would offer a he-goat, while a common citizen could offer a sheep. While the expiatory power might extend beyond spatial boundaries (an offering might be made for the entire nation), it could not be projected into the future.

As a gesture of respect for God, priests stood while offering sacrifice. Because of the pervasiveness of human sinfulness and the limited efficacy of the sacrificial system, the need for expiation is constant. Therefore, over and over again priests offered sacrifices in expiation for their own transgressions and for the transgressions of the people.

The efficacy of the sacrifice of Jesus, on the other hand, transcends both spatial and temporal limits. Through his unrepeatable sacrifice he is able to expiate all transgressions of all people of all time. The singular status of Jesus the priest and the inestimable value of Jesus the victim have set this sacrifice apart from all others. Total and complete expiation has been accomplished through him. There is no need for Jesus to stand and offer another sacrifice. Therefore, he takes his seat next to God in glory.

This reference to Jesus enthroned in heaven next to God is significant. First, he is seated at God's right hand, the recognized place of highest honor. Second, the image is a reference to Psalm 110, where the king is enthroned in this same place of honor, with his enemies vanquished under his feet. The juxtaposition of these images suggests that with his sacrifice Jesus has decisively expiated all sin and conquered all evil. He has been able to accomplish what the sacrificial system of Israel, despite its preeminence, has been unable to accomplish.

Mark 13:24-32

The character and appearance of the end of time are described by means of allusions to earlier apocalyptic traditions. Chief among them are the reference to the tribulations that precede the advent of the new age and the coming of the Son of Man in the clouds. Cosmic occurrences will accompany the distress that will take hold of the world, indicating that all of creation has been thrown into disarray. In the ancient world the rudimentary conflict was between order and chaos. God's creative power was seen in God's ability to bring primordial chaos under control. The return of chaos (cf. Gen 7:17-24) was a sign of the complete reversal of the order of creation. The ancient Israelites believed that such a reversal would occur before the birth of the new age of fulfillment. This is the scene Jesus is describing to his disciples.

The coming of the Son of Man in the clouds, an allusion to the mysterious figure found in the book of Daniel (7:13), heralds the advent of the new age. This mysterious figure comes in power and glory, not in fury and destruction; he comes to gather the elect, not to scatter them. This is the great ingathering of the elect, the time of harvesting, the "Day of the Lord." Many of the prophets described this day as one of wrath and judgment (Amos 5:18-20). However, it was originally anticipated as a joyful occasion, when God's victory over Israel's enemies would be celebrated. In one way or another, all of these features are present in Jesus' pronouncement. For some it will be a day of terror; for others it will be a time of rejoicing.

The fig is a staple fruit in the Middle East. It grows in abundance, and for this reason the fig tree was often used as a symbol of the messianic age. In this parable Jesus points to the tree's blossoming in the spring as a sign of the advent of the events he has just described. Unlike the ripening of the figs, which can be expected at a particular time of the year, the exact time of the coming of the new age is shrouded in mystery.

In this reading one saying of Jesus seems to contradict another. He first states that the events will take place sometime during the present generation (v. 30). He then claims that no one knows the exact time of their unfolding, not even the Son. Generation *(geneá)* can refer to a descent group or to a period of time. The second meaning fits this instruction better than the first one does. Jesus is saying that the things he has described will happen before this age passes away. The reliability of his words is affirmed with a bold statement. Heaven and earth, the world as it is known, will pass away, but his words will stand.

Despite this remarkable claim of authority, Jesus admits that all things are in God's hands. Just as God exercised supreme authority over chaos at the time of creation, so the new creation is the exclusive work of God. The lesson to be learned from all of this is: Be prepared! At all times, be prepared! Be prepared for the coming tribulation; be prepared for the appearance of the Son of Man. Be prepared!

Themes of the Day

Although this is not the last Sunday of the Liturgical Year, the major theme found in the readings is the end of time. The events that will usher in and will take place during this time are described in apocalyptic terms. This worldview claims that regardless of the scope and intensity of the devastation that will take place during the last days, good will ultimately triumph. For this reason, believers are admonished to trust in God.

Apocalyptic Struggle

Biblical faith holds that the struggles of life will culminate in a massive cosmic confrontation between the forces of good and the forces of evil. This last battle will be universal in scope, just like the first primordial conflict between chaos and God. God emerged from that battle victorious and subsequently created the world. Though conquered, evil was only temporarily restrained. The last battle at the end of time will be as comprehensive as was the first: the entire universe will be involved. The readings speak of a time unsurpassed in distress: days of tribulation and of cosmic disorder. However, unlike the outcome of the primordial conflict, at the end of time evil will be completely destroyed and the reign of God will endure unchallenged forever.

Good Will Triumph

All of the readings state that good will finally prevail over evil. In the last days Michael, the angelic warrior of God, will rise up. In the epistle Christ is pictured seated triumphantly at the right hand of God with his enemies under his feet, a sign of conquest. Finally, in the Gospel the Son of Man, the mysterious figure from apocalyptic literature, comes in the clouds with great power and glory. All of these images are apocalyptic; each of them is hopeful.

Apocalyptic literature usually arises out of a community whose very existence is being threatened by deadly forces. The imagery of which it consists may appear to be exaggerated, but it is probably the most suitable way of characterizing the seriousness of the situation. The fact that good always triumphs over evil serves to encourage the people to remain faithful, since according to this genre the struggle is only temporary and the outcome will be favorable.

Trust in God

We read these stories toward the end of the calendar year when, in the Northern Hemisphere, life forces have retreated deep into the recesses of the earth, there to await the invitation of spring and resurrection. We read them at the close of the Liturgical Year because we are coming to the conclusion of our yearly telling of the story of salvation. However, apocalyptic images are timely whenever we find ourselves in the throes of the battle with evil and it appears that we will succumb. These forms will remind us that good will be able to withstand evil. From this we will conclude that we need only trust in God.

Thirty-Fourth Sunday in Ordinary Time (Christ the King)
Daniel 7:13-14

Visions and dreams were traditionally thought to be avenues of divine revelation. The seer is on earth, but the vision itself takes place in heaven. Everything about this vision bespeaks revelation, yet it is symbolic with all of the ambiguous traits of symbol. It reveals only the symbol. The seer must be able to interpret it.

Four distinct Hebrew words can be translated "man." ʾadam is the most general term and can designate both a single individual and humankind collectively (cf. Gen 2:7). ʾenosh denotes a frail mortal human being. ʾish is a relational term and is frequently translated as husband (cf. Gen 2:23b). A geber is a strong man, often a warrior (cf. Job 38:3). Unlike the epithet "son of man" (ben adam) found in the prophet Ezekiel (Ezek 3:1), the phrase used here is the Aramaic bar enash. Its literal translation is "son of weak man." Of itself it denotes a limited human being. However, the figure that comes on the clouds is not really a human being; he only resembles a son of man. When one thing symbolizes another the element of likeness is either obvious or is explained. The only defining characteristic here is weakness. This seems to be the way the mysterious figure resembles a human being.

The picture painted here of the coming and arrival of the Son of Man is colored with both mythic and royal tones. The figure comes with the clouds, which are the most frequent accompaniment of a theophany, or revelation of God. He comes riding them as one would ride a chariot (cf. Ps 18:10). He is presented before God in the manner of courtly decorum, where one would not simply approach the ruler, but would be presented by an attendant. The one who sits on the throne is called the "Ancient One." This implies that God is the one who has endured and, presumably, who will continue to endure. In other words, God is everlasting.

This mysterious figure is installed by God as ruler over the entire universe. The authority and dominion that belong to other nations is handed over to him. Unlike other kingdoms that rise and eventually fall, this will be an everlasting kingdom. This dominion has been granted by God, not attained by means of conquest or political alliance. Finally, what is described is a reign that is exercised on earth. The "Son of Man" may have been in heaven when he received his commission, he may even rule from some exalted place in the heavens, but his kingdom belongs to the earth.

Psalm 93:1, 1-2, 5

The opening acclamation clearly identifies this as a hymn in praise of God's kingship. Four very important themes converge in these few verses to describe this kingship: a military theme (v. 1), a creation theme (v. 1), a legal theme (v. 5), and a cultic theme (v. 5).

The military and creation themes are closely associated with divine kingship. In several ancient myths creation followed the primordial battle between chaos and order. After chaos has been vanquished, the triumphant divine warrior established order in the universe. Of itself creation may have been an orderly process, but it occurred only after a fierce victory had been won. The creator was, then, a conquering warrior. The culminating event of this drama was the installment of the victor as king over the universe. Enthroned in heaven, he then ruled over all.

This is clearly the picture painted in the psalm response. Still girt with military strength, the LORD is acclaimed king. The order that God established after his victory is sure; the world is firmly established because the LORD is its foundation. The victory, the creation, and the enthronement of the LORD all took place in the primordial past, and so they can be trusted to endure.

Having established the trustworthiness of God as cosmic champion and creator, the psalmist moves to the praise of God's decrees or testimonies. The reference is probably to the law. The theological development that takes place here is quite interesting. The psalmist uses the stability perceived in the universe to inspire acceptance of the law. This law is perceived as having come from the very God who conquered chaos and who reigns from heaven. If one can rely on the order that this God has established in the universe, then one can surely trust the order implied in the law.

Holiness and house, which is probably a reference to the temple, introduce the cultic theme. Although the connections with the other themes are loose, they are still there. First, the temple was considered a copy of the heavenly palace constructed after the cosmic battle had been won and the universe put in order. Second, the uniqueness of God as cosmic conqueror and creator sets God and the things of God apart from all others, and this is precisely what holiness means. In other words, the primordial and cosmic feats of the LORD are celebrated in the temple, where the testimonies of God are remembered and revered.

Revelation 1:5-8

The christological statements in this reading are followed by a doxology praising Christ for the salvation he has won for others. Jesus is first identified as the anointed one (the Christ) and then described as such with themes long associated with the Messiah. He is a witness who faithfully mediates to others the message he has received from God. He is the firstborn, the one to whom belong both priority of place and sovereignty (cf. Ps 89:27a). He is the ruler of all the kings of the world (cf. Ps 89:27b). These epithets sketch a "high" christology, one that emphasizes the more-than-human aspects of Jesus.

These three titles also call to mind the death, resurrection, and ascension of Jesus. As witness *(mártys)* Jesus stands faithfully for truth, even to the point of his death. Through his resurrection he has conquered death and blazed the trail for all those who, through him, will also rise from death to life. Finally, his ascension, or exaltation, has entitled him to rule enthroned above all other rulers.

The writer speaks in the name of all believers: "[He] loves us . . . has freed us . . . made us into a kingdom, priests for his God and Father." This last statement is a reference to the promise made to Moses on the condition that the people would be faithful to the law (cf. Exod 19:6). No condition is stated here. Instead, it is the self-sacrificing love of Jesus that has made the people kings and priests. This is covenant language. Through his blood, not the blood of a sacrificial animal, the people have been made God's people. Through his death he has earned the right to be their king, and so he deserves their praise.

Two other biblical traditions stand behind the image of Jesus' appearance amid the clouds. They are the Son of Man (Dan 7:13) and an unnamed victim of violence (Zech 12:10). All people will witness Jesus' coming amid the clouds, even those responsible for his suffering. This saying points to the universal scope of the manifestation of Jesus. All the peoples of the earth will witness it, those who accepted him, those who rejected him, and even those who never heard anything about him. The affirmation of this is made in both Greek (Yes.) and Hebrew (Amen.).

The final statement reenforces the more-than-human character of Jesus. Alpha and Omega are the first and the last letters of the Greek alphabet. Together they include all letters and, by implication, connote total inclusivity. Once again there is a threefold characterization of Jesus. He comprises everything that is; he transcends the limits of time; he is the almighty *(pantokrátōr)*, the ruler of all things. The phrase "I am" *(egō eimi)* has come to be a technical way of expressing self-disclosure. Here Jesus, the one who will come amid the clouds, appropriates to himself attributes that belong to God. The last verse brings the reader back to the opening statement. Jesus has indeed accomplished all that is described; he truly is all that he claims to be.

John 18:33b-37

The kingship of Jesus is the subject of Pilate's interrogation. The title "King of the Jews" means one thing to the Jewish leaders who handed Jesus over to Pilate and another to the Roman official who tried him. It was a messianic designation that identified the bearer as that descendant of David who would inaugurate the reign of God. In the eyes of the Jewish leaders the title could indicate only messianic pretensions and was therefore blasphemous. It was also a political claim that challenged the absolute authority of Roman control.

From the perspective of the Roman occupiers such revolutionary contentions were dangerous.

Jesus is asked, "Are you the King of the Jews?" And he answers yes and no. Pilate's questions are straightforward, and so are Jesus' answers, although they appear to be ambiguous. The Roman asks about a political reality that may have a religious dimension, while Jesus speaks about a religious truth that certainly has political implications. Because he does not think that Jesus has adequately answered, Pilate questions him three times (vv. 33, 35, 37), the number required by Roman law before a defendant could be acquitted. Each time Jesus responds.

The exchange that follows Pilate's first query reveals the real charge against Jesus. Pilate's disclaimer to Jesus' question about the official's own view of Jesus' kingship shows that it is the messianic claim that is on trial. In his second answer Jesus defines his reign negatively by contrasting it to the kingdoms of this world. His kingdom is not *of* this world. This can mean both that it does not originate from this world and that it does not belong to it. It does not mean that it is not *in* the world. Unlike the kingdoms of this world, it does not need to be forcefully defended by its subjects. This is precisely what both the leaders of the Jews and Pilate are doing, defending their respective realms from Jesus.

The events that led to Jesus' trial are alluded to here. Though he stands before Pilate, Jesus was handed over to him by the religious leaders of his own people. But he had been handed over to them by some of the Jewish people themselves.

By describing his kingdom through negative contrast, Jesus has indirectly admitted that he is a king. Pilate's third query seeks a positive affirmation of this. In a certain sense Jesus' response to this last question is both a denial and an avowal. Earlier he never really said that he was a king, but he did admit that he had a kingdom. Here he makes another oblique admission. In his second response he declared that his kingdom is not *of* this world. Here he characterizes the role that he will play *in* this world. He came into the world to testify to the truth. This truth is the foundation of his kingdom. It establishes the relationship that determines membership in it.

Jesus' answers show that both the Jewish leaders and the Roman officials had reason to be concerned about his claims. Though not of this world, his kingdom would indeed challenge both messianic expectations and the powers of this world.

Themes of the Day

As with all of the major liturgical feasts, the theme of the day determines the choice of readings and then the readings themselves tell us what the feast means. This feast celebrates the kingship of Jesus. It also marks the end of the Liturgical Year. Although at first glance the themes might appear to be quite independent of each other, they are actually intimately connected.

The Enthronement of Christ

Each one of the readings depicts the enthronement of Christ, who is revealed as the Messiah-king. While on earth Jesus himself refused to be identified as a king. He knew that the royal messianic expectations that prevailed during his lifetime were predominantly political, and if they were taken up by him, his followers might instigate a rebellion against the Roman occupiers. When finally he did acknowledge his royal identity, he insisted that his rule was not like that of other kings. The readings for today tell us that the one who was unrecognized by human beings while he was on earth is clearly recognized in heaven, where he is robed in glory.

Enthroned in heaven, Christ is revealed as the faithful witness to all that God has done and will continue to do, as the firstborn from the dead whose resurrection is the promise of our own resurrection, as the king who reigns above all other kings. The dominion he has received from God is universal and exclusive and it will last forever. When he comes again on the last day, he will be revealed in all his glory. Every eye will behold him and all peoples will recognize him as the Son of Man and the only-begotten of God.

The End

The feast of Christ the King is placed at the conclusion of the Liturgical Year because it celebrates the realization of all of our theology. It is not only the goal toward which our Sunday meditations have been taking us, Christ's enthronement is the omega point toward which all of history has been moving. On a broader scale it is the climax of all of creation as contained in the major myths. There we read that after the primordial battle has been won, the triumphant warrior is enthroned above the heavens. This feast celebrates that enthronement.

Christ's kingdom is a kingdom of truth and life, of holiness and grace, of justice and love and peace. We need not stand at a distance from him, afraid to approach because of our human vulnerability. He is the one who loved us so much that he handed himself over to suffering and death so that we might live. He has already brought us to birth in this kingdom through baptism, and he has taught us how to live in it, although we live in it only by faith. Today we look to that time when his glory will be revealed, when we will all be gathered into the embrace of God, there to sing praise to that glory forever.

Solemnities

Solemnities of the Lord

The Solemnity of the Most Holy Trinity
Deuteronomy 4:32-34, 39-40

Moses admonishes the people to commit themselves to the LORD. He does this by pointing out to them the singular majesty of the God who has taken such a personal interest in their welfare. He invites the people to test the truthfulness of his claim. Ask anyone, he says. They will tell you there is no one like this God. Go as far back in time as the beginning; canvass the entire heavens. Such exaggerated suggestions are Moses' way of asserting that the mighty deeds of God that took place before their eyes were not only unprecedented in history, they are also unparalleled in the universe.

What are these deeds that Moses claims are so extraordinary? First there is the divine revelation to the people. The allusion is to the bush that kept burning but was not destroyed, which Moses came upon at Horeb (cf. Exod 3:2). The bush itself was a marvel, but even more amazing was the fact that from it God spoke directly to Moses, telling him of God's concern for the people in their plight. The mortal danger present in getting too close to God is universally known. In this instance, proximity to God did not put Moses at risk.

The second impressive deed was God's choice of Israel out of all the nations and God's deliverance of them through numerous signs and wonders, a reference to the Exodus and Sinai events. Here God's action is distinctive in two ways—first, that God should even do it; second, that no other God is able to do it for any other people. In all of this God acted as a mighty warrior. The expression "strong hand and outstretched arm" is evidence of this. It is a military image that denotes movement of strength and force in defense and attack. From a historical point of view the Exodus is an event that involved God and the people of Israel. From a theological point of view it was a victory of God over the forces of the gods of Egypt. In this exhortation, Moses is not just reminding the people of God's deliverance of them. He is proclaiming that no other god could have done what the God of Israel did.

All of this praising and calling to mind had one purpose: to encourage the people to commit themselves to this God who had been so good to them in the past; to accept God's law and to obey it so that God would be equally good to them in the future. Perhaps the most daring claim that Moses made is of monotheism: "There is no other." The God of Israel is not merely one patron god among others; the God of Israel is the only God there is. This is the final reason for committing themselves as Moses directed them to do.

The monotheism that Moses advocated was not grounded in a doctrinal statement that was the fruit of long and careful theoretical development or religious speculation about creation. It came from human experience, the events that took place in the history of one quite common nation. Since there never had been a god who was able to perform the wonders performed by the God of Israel, there could be no other god.

Psalm 33:4-5, 6, 9, 18-19, 20, 22

The verses of this psalm response contain a collection of themes. The passage opens with a statement that reflects the basis of ancient Israel's faith in God. This faith is rooted in the truth of God's word, in the faithfulness of God's works, in the justice of God's covenant, and in the steadfastness of God's love. Everything else flows from these convictions.

The first theme that is emphatically stated is the trustworthiness of God's word. It is as firm as is God's own self. The order and stability manifested through the marvels of creation not only stem from God's power and faithfulness, they are witnesses to it. If we rely on the firmness and regularity found in the natural world, surely we can trust the creator from whom it flows. All of this is grounded in God's kindness, which is more than simple benevolence or thoughtful consideration. It is the steadfastness of covenant loyalty *(ḥesed)*. The trustworthiness of God's word parallels the constancy of God's covenant.

The psalm picks up the theme of God's creative word and carries us with it back to the account in Genesis, where this word establishes the heavens. God's creation provides a welcoming and sustaining home for all living beings. They in turn are invited to stand in respectful awe (fear of the LORD) of this God. The psalmist has moved from consideration of creation to that of divine providence. For whom does God care? For all those who fear the LORD. Fear means standing in awe. Having surveyed the marvels of creation and having reflected on the trustworthy word of God that called them into being, what other attitude would be appropriate? This is wisdom language, and wisdom, like creation, spreads its influence across the entire universe. It enjoys a universal sway. These verses suggest that anyone with the requisite religious attitude will be gathered under the wings of God's providence and will be protected from famine and death.

The psalm ends with a return to the theme of covenant kindness *(ḥesed)*. The placement of these themes is significant: creation imagery is bracketed by covenant language. This literary arrangement can make two quite startling theological statements. First, it implies that the covenant God made with the people is as firm and reliable as is creation. Second, it suggests that from the very beginning creation actually serves the goals of the covenant.

Romans 8:14-17

Paul is explaining the unique privilege of being children of God. This is not a new idea for those with a Jewish background. As far back as the traditions found in the book of Deuteronomy, Israelites believed that they were children of God (cf. Deut 14:1). However, there is a difference here. In the earlier tradition, the idea of children of God was associated with following the law and obedience to its precepts. That is not the case here. Paul very clearly states that those who are children of God are so because they are led (compelled or constrained) by the Spirit.

Paul uses "spirit" in various ways. The Spirit of God or Christ is a divine reality; the spirit of slavery is a disposition or mentality; the spirit of adoption is a relationship. Paul does not merely contrast the spirit of slavery and the spirit of adoption; he also identifies children of God with those who are compelled by the Spirit. So compelled, we have been taken into the family of God. There we enjoy the status of children, and we have the right to call God "Father."

There is another way of understanding the way we become children of God: through the sonship of Christ. First and foremost, Jesus is the Son of God. When we are joined to him we are led by the same Spirit that led him. Therefore, we can say that it is with and through Christ that we become children of God. If Jesus can call God "Abba," then we who are joined to him can as well. Here Paul's trinitarian theology springs from his conviction of our transformative union with Christ.

There has been a great deal of discussion about the Aramaic epithet *Abba*, Father, which is a familial, colloquial term of intimacy. There is no reason to doubt that Jesus used it. What is remarkable here is that he, who is son by nature, is inviting us, who are children by adoption, to address God in the very way that he does. The Father is the source from whom Jesus proceeded. Following Paul's argument, we are made children of God, not by the Father but by the Spirit, or through the Son. It is the Spirit of Jesus in us that cries out.

According to law, two witnesses are required to corroborate the truth of a story. The two witnesses mentioned here are the Spirit of God and our own spirit. Together they testify to the truth of what Paul says about being the children of God. Paul is making bold claims here. That could explain why he felt it necessary to call on witnesses to confirm the truth of his claims.

If we are truly children of God then we are also heirs. But heirs to what? Although the text is not explicit here, one could conclude that we are heirs to the very inheritance to which Jesus is heir—the glory of God in the coming reign of God. Whatever that inheritance may be, it is only gained through suffering. Once again, it is our union with Jesus that entitles us to privileges.

Matthew 28:16-20

This account of the commissioning of the disciples by Jesus is replete with familiar theological themes. The disciples returned to Galilee, the place where the ministry of Jesus had begun. This was to assure those who still harbored doubts that this mysterious person was indeed the same Jesus with whom they had previously walked. We are not told the name of the mountain to which they had been directed, but the relationship between this commissioning on a mountain and Jesus' earlier sermon on the mountain could not have been lost on them.

They see him on the mountain and they worship him, but not with full understanding. This is all reminiscent of his earlier transfiguration. Jesus declared that all power in heaven and earth had been given to him, a reference to the Son of Man, who was exalted by God and granted eschatological authority (cf. Dan 7:14). Employing that power, he commissioned them. The text does not explicitly state that he conferred his power upon them. Instead, it closes with an assurance by him that he will remain with them until the end of the age. He was Emmanuel, God-with-us, while in the flesh; he will continue to be Emmanuel until the end of time.

The great missionary commission is straightforward and all-encompassing. The disciples are told to go out and make other disciples of all nations. All social or cultural boundaries are dissolved; ethnic and gender restrictions are lifted. The universality of this commission has challenged believers from the time of its utterance to our very day. Different ages confront various aspects of it. The early Church experienced tension as it moved from an exclusively Jewish context into the Gentile world. Today we struggle with the diversity that is at the heart of inculturation. The commission remains the same: make disciples of all nations.

The way to accomplish this is twofold: by baptizing and by teaching. The trinitarian formula for baptism gathers together elements already found in Jesus' teaching. Throughout his ministry he spoke of God as Father (cf. Matt 11:25-27), indicating the intimate relationship that exists between them. He also spoke of the Spirit who came upon him at his baptism (cf. Matt 3:16) and through whose power he cast out demons (cf. 12:28-32). It is in this threefold name (one name, not three) that the disciples are to baptize. True to the Jewish roots of this community, the divine name is not actually given: it is enough to refer to it. Those to be baptized are plunged into the mystery of that name and re-created as new beings. While the elements of the baptismal formula may have come from Jesus, the formula itself does not appear again except in a second-century church manual (*Didache* 7.1), leading some to question its actual dating.

The specific teaching alluded to here is moral rather than doctrinal. Those who hear the teaching are to observe what Jesus commanded. He inaugurated the reign of God, at the heart of which is a radically different way of life. This is to be the essence of the teaching of the disciples. Jesus assures them that he will be with them until the end of the age. Although the text does not say it, we can presume that, after this, all who have been baptized and have accepted this teaching will be with him.

Themes of the Day

The feast of the Holy Trinity brings us face to face with the foundation of our faith. The readings for today attempt to provide answers to the question: Who is God? They can only suggest something about the mystery of God, and they can only do this indirectly. They call to mind some of the wonders that God has accomplished for us and in us. It is through reflection on these gracious divine acts that we can get glimpses of God.

Who Is God?

From the infinitesimal atomic particles to the galactic expanses of the universe, all of creation cries out in splendor and majesty and glory. Believers and non-believers alike are captivated by the grandeur of it all. Some of those who gaze in awe move through it and beyond it and wonder about its origin and its ability to sustain itself. Surely there must be a creator, and what a creator there must be! All creation proclaims the glory of God. The harmony and interdependence that are observed suggests that there is one power beyond this, one fundamental law that governs all. All creation proclaims the glory of one God.

The history of God's people reveals a God who desires to establish an intimate relationship with people, a God who is willing to enter into their history as their protector and guide, a God who forgives disloyalty again and again. Jesus teaches us about a God who sent him into the world to save it, a God who has made us adopted children through the Holy Spirit, a God who will ultimately clothe us in divine glory.

God with Us; God for Us

The little that we know about God's own self, we know from Jesus. He has told us about the divine procession: the Son proceeding from the Father and the Spirit proceeding from the Father and the Son. He is the one who has told us that the Spirit is his Spirit. We may only know about the mystery of God from Jesus, but we know about God from our own experience. We know that God creates because we are immersed in creation. We know that God saves because we have been freed from the bondage of our addictions, from the tyranny of our demons. We know that God sustains because we are cared for by the very world within which we live.

Our experience tells us that God is with us. More than this, it tells us that God is for us. Everything we know about this phenomenal, resplendent, incomprehensible (words are empty to describe God) deity declares that God is passionately, boundlessly in love with us!

The Solemnity of the Most Holy Body and Blood of Christ (*Corpus Christi*)

Exodus 24:3-8

God's ratification of the covenant with the people is described in dramatic terms. There is first a ritual of word, then a ritual of blood. What Moses related to the people were the Ten Commandments, otherwise known as the ten words (*d^ebārîm*), and the Covenant Code (*mishpāṭîm*, cf. Exod 21:1), which consists mainly of case law. These were the laws that generally governed Israel's life. After hearing the laws read aloud, the people answered in one voice: "We will do everything." The spoken word is then made physical and permanent. This was probably done not out of fear that the people might forget them (oral cultures have techniques that enhance retention) but in order to preserve a record of the covenant for later liturgical use.

In preparation for the sacrifice that would seal the covenant Moses erected symbols that presented the partners of the covenant: an altar, which generally connoted the presence of the deity; and twelve pillars, which stood for the totality of the people. He then chose young men, not priests or Levites, to offer the sacrifices (The gender bias is obvious.). Perhaps these were youths who were on the brink of manhood who had neither taken part in war nor entered into marriage. They would be apt symbols of a nation that was about to enter into a lifelong relationship.

Two different sacrifices were offered, the holocaust and the peace offering. Holocausts were burnt offerings in which the whole animal was consumed by fire on the altar. It signified the worshiper's total self-offering to God. Peace offerings either established peace by the very offering, or they celebrated a peace that had already been made. The latter was probably the case here. Since blood is the life force, to shed blood—even in sacrifice—is to exercise control over that life force. Here the blood signifies the life that binds the covenant partners. Through it they make two pledges: to lay down life itself if need be for the sake of the other; to surrender life to the partner if one is unfaithful to the covenant.

Finally, the pouring of the blood, which is the most solemn and the most binding part of the sacrifice, seals the covenant. Since it was God who initiated the covenant, and since God is the principal partner in the relationship, the altar is splashed first. Once again the people hear the law; this time it is read to them. It is almost as if Moses wants the people to be very sure about what they are doing. They have a second opportunity to say, "We will!" With that the blood is sprinkled on them, and their relationship with God is sealed.

The last pronouncement of Moses makes clear the relationship between the words of the covenant and the blood. He maintains that the blood ritual ratifies the covenant, which the words both describe and fashion. The interplay between word and action is quite clear. Each element has its part to play in the ritual. Neither can adequately perform its role alone.

Psalm 116:12-13, 15-16, 17-18

This psalm is an example of a temple service of thanksgiving. In it someone who made an appeal to God and promised to perform some act of devotion when the request was granted now comes to the temple and, before God and the assembly of believers, gives thanks for the favor granted and fulfills the vow. Most vows were promises to offer some form of sacrifice (cf. Ps 56:13); holocaust (cf. Ps 66:13; Lev 22:18-20); peace offerings (cf. Ps 50:14; Lev 7:16; 22:21-22); or cereal offerings and libations (cf. Num 15:3, 8).

The psalm response opens with an acknowledgment that there is nothing the psalmist can do and no gift that can be offered that will even begin to compare with the favors that have been received from God. Inadequate as it is, the psalmist still renders what can be offered, expressing devotion by offering a cup of salvation. It is not clear exactly what the cup of salvation is. It might be a libation offered in thanksgiving. Or it could be a festive drink, the wine that was shared at a sacred meal, a symbol of the joy God's graciousness has produced. Whatever its identify, it serves as a cup of joy for having been saved.

Along with the offering of this wine is the proclamation of the name of God. Since God's name holds part of the divine essence, to proclaim that name is to recognize and praise God's greatness and, in this case, the graciousness of God's saving action. The cup is taken up, and God's name is proclaimed.

The psalmist insists that, contrary to any appearances, God is concerned with the fate of the righteous. The psalmist's own situation is an example of this. The psalmist may have suffered, but ultimately God did intervene. Mention of the righteous *(hāsîdîm)*, indirectly identifies the psalmist as one of this group. The psalmist could be making another point here: virtue and misfortune are not incompatible; good people do in fact suffer. Still, the point of this psalm is not the sufferings the psalmist had to endure but the deliverance that came from God and the psalmist's response to divine graciousness.

The relationship between the psalmist and God is strikingly characterized in the metaphors "servant" and its parallel, "son of your handmaid." Although the first image has taken on a profound theological connotation (servant of God), the second clearly identifies both images as classifications within a structured household. A slave born into a household had neither a justified claim to, nor any guaranteed likelihood of, emancipation. By using these legal metaphors to characterize his relationship with God, the psalmist is dramatizing his own situation. Like a slave who has no hope of release, the psalmist was bound to a life of great difficulty. However, God looked kindly upon him and loosed him from his servitude.

The last verses (vv. 17–18) clearly identify the ceremony that will take place as a public ritual. A sacrifice of thanksgiving will be offered (cf. Lev 7:11-18), the name of the LORD will be proclaimed, and vows will be paid in the presence of the people of God. The psalmist, who once faced the prospect of death, now stands in the midst of the assembly, humble and grateful to God.

Hebrews 9:11-15

Several features of the ritual performed during the Day of Atonement serve as a model for discussing the high priesthood of Christ. The author does this, however, not to show the similarities between the early Israelite ceremony and the atoning action of Christ but to show the differences. It is the author's intent to compare the heavenly with the earthly. Christ is said to have entered the holy of holies once, just as the high priest did yearly on that solemn occasion in order to sprinkle blood on the mercy seat. Both ritual acts were mediative, and both were expiatory. The fundamental similarities end there.

At the outset, the eschatological character of Christ's sacrifice is stated. The good things that had been promised in the past have now come to be. There is an eschatological finality to what Christ does; he does it once and for all. The new covenant promised by the prophet (cf. Jer 31:31) has been established, and Christ is its mediator. The inheritance of the reign of God can now unfold.

The tabernacle within which the high priest performed his duties was made by human hands and it belonged to earth; Christ passed through a greater and more perfect tabernacle, the heavenly or spiritual archetype of all other sacred tents or temples. The ritual of the Day of Atonement included the sacrifice of goats, offered for the sins of the people, and calves, offered for the sins of the priests. The atoning blood that Christ brings is his own, and his sacrifice secures eternal redemption.

The *a fortiori* argument the author uses is not meant to repudiate the sacrifices of the past. The comparison "how much more" implies that they did achieve the purposes for which they were intended; they removed ceremonial defilement. This was particularly true of the ashes of the heifer (cf. Num 19:9). However, the external cleansing they could effect cannot be compared with the cleansing of consciences that the blood of Christ brings about. His is a more valuable sacrifice; it is the sacrifice of his very self. Therefore what it accomplishes is much more significant than the effects of former ceremonies.

Although there is no trinitarian theology developed here, there are references to God and to the eternal Spirit through whom Christ offered himself. The real focus of this reading is the sacrifice of Christ and its atoning effects in our lives. Our consciences, not merely our bodies, are purified, and we are made acceptable for a manner of worship that is no longer temporary or provisional.

In the final verse of this reading, the author continues the *a fortiori* argument, insisting that as noble as the first covenant may have been, it was not able to accomplish the deliverance from sin that Christ's sacrifice achieved. The connection between sacrifice and covenant is then underscored. Since some kind of sacrifice is the foundation of any covenant, the action of Christ not only atones for sin but also inaugurates a new covenant, one that promises an eternal inheritance. Through Christ, those who have been called have been richly blessed.

Mark 14:12-16, 22-26

The passage for today consists of two parts: a description of the preparation for the Passover meal; and an account of the institution of the Eucharist, which took place during the meal itself. The first part sets the stage for the second, not only from a literary point of view but from a theological perspective as well. Reference to the sacrifice of the Passover lamb on the first day of the feast of the Unleavened Bread has raised many questions, because customarily that was not the day when the lamb was sacrificed. Various explanations of this discrepancy have been advanced. It is obvious that what is a problem for contemporary interpreters was not one for the author of the Gospel. This is probably because the details of the chronology are not pivotal to the argument but the identification of the feast is.

It is obvious at the outset that Jesus is in charge. He initiates the preparations, he directs the disciples, he gives orders to the master of the house, and he claims the guest room as his own. Jesus' words set everything in motion and bring everything to pass as he describes. We do not know why the man was carrying water in a jar, when men usually carried it in skins. Nor do we know why he unquestioningly volunteered a large furnished room. He must have been some kind of a follower, because he responded positively to the requests of Jesus, who has been identified as Teacher.

One final note of interest. Jesus tells the disciples to make preparations for him to eat the Passover. They in turn tell the man that Jesus was to eat the Passover with his disciples. The disciples probably saw this as a Passover meal like other Passover meals. On the other hand, Jesus knew he would not participate in this meal as he had previously.

The economy of the words and actions of Jesus during this memorable meal is striking. It begins as most celebratory meals begin, with the breaking of bread. He blesses it in the Jewish manner of giving thanks: "Blessed are you, O LORD our God, King of the universe, who bring forth bread from the earth." The disciples know this is a different kind of meal only when Jesus tells them to eat the bread which is now his body (*sōma*, meaning "person," rather than *sárx*, meaning "flesh"). The blessing that he speaks over the cup is also probably traditional: "Blessed are you, O LORD our God, King of the universe, who created the fruit of the vine." Though they may not have understood fully, the disciples must have realized that there was profound meaning in the words and actions of Jesus, for they did not object to what would otherwise have been offensive, even scandalous, commands. "Take it; this is my body . . . this is my blood of the covenant. . . ."

The symbolism in this ceremony both recalls the covenant of old and reinterprets it. Eating bread was a common ritual expression of companionship; the reference to the blood of the covenant recalls the ratification of the earlier covenant through the blood of the sacrifice (cf. Exod 24:6-8). When Jesus says that he will not eat again, he may be referring to his death. More likely the author is alluding to the messianic banquet of the future, the banquet which is symbolized by the body and blood of the Lord and which will be enjoyed by all when the reign of God is brought to fulfillment.

Themes of the Day

As is the case with the readings for most of the major feasts of the Liturgical Year, those assigned for today reflect some aspect of the feast being celebrated. One of the most prominent themes that emerges is the role that blood plays in the ratification of the covenant. In line with this is the peerless nature of the atoning actions of Christ. Finally, the devotional attitude of thanksgiving appears again and again.

Ratification of the Covenant

Most people in modern society would probably be repelled by the thought of some ritual use of blood. Drinking blood would be looked upon as ghoulish; being sprinkled with blood would be no less offensive. Yet birth blood is not subject to the same revulsion, nor is the thought of a blood transfusion frowned upon. Blood is recognized as a life force. There is another way in which blood is held in high regard, and that is blood relationships. They are some of the most cherished bonds we know, and they have both social and legal ramifications that are quite binding. Blood and blood bonds continue to play important roles in our lives today.

How generous of God, who is not bound to a body like ours, to bend to our needs and to relate to us in ways we can understand! God makes a binding pact with us and then seals it with blood, not God's blood and not our blood but the blood of a substitute. In a sense, this ritual makes us blood sisters and brothers of God and of each other. It seals our fate, and it entitles us to the family inheritance.

Christ's Atoning Action

This is the feast that celebrates the incomparable love Christ has for us. It provides us with two portraits of this self-sacrificing Savior. In the first we see him offering himself as the victim to be sacrificed for the expiation of our sins. Having done that, he brings his own blood into the heavenly tabernacle to give constant witness, before the face of God, to his atoning action. In the second portrait, he spreads a banquet table for us at which we are able to eat the bread of companionship and share the blood of the new covenant. This banquet, which we have been given, is really the eschatological banquet, the meal on which we will dine for all eternity. How blessed we are that we have been called to share it! How blessed we are that we can approach it so frequently! The atoning action of Christ is really a magnanimous gesture of love.

A Life of Eucharist

How shall I make a return to the Lord for all the good that I have received? The only appropriate response to God's graciousness is thanksgiving *(eucharistía)*. We have been chosen; we have been delivered; we have a witness in heaven; and now we have been given the bread of eternal life and the blood of salvation. What return can we give? A life of gratitude lived in the presence of God; a life of union with all those who eat the same bread and drink from the same cup; a life of faithful expectation, waiting for the coming of the reign of God in all its fullness.

The Presentation of the Lord (Feast)
February 2

Malachi 3:1-4

This passage describes a messenger of God. The very name Malachi *(mal'āki)* means "my messenger." It is the LORD of hosts who speaks here. Commentators are not in agreement as to the actual identity of the messenger. What seems to be of more significance to the author is the role this messenger will play. Several themes mark the passage's strong eschatological character: the future coming of the LORD, the present day of the LORD, and the idea of judgment.

Although the passage states that the LORD of hosts is coming, it really focuses on the messenger who will precede God. The first thing he will do will be to prepare the way that God will use to approach the people. It is a very common custom to prepare for the coming of a dignitary. Even today we clean and repair the streets and neighborhoods through which such prominent people will pass. Everything must be in proper order as befits the station of the visitor. Isaiah vividly described such comprehensive improvements (cf. Isa 40:3-4; 57:14). Also part of the preparation for such an event is the announcement of the actual approach of the dignitary. Isaiah depicts this aspect as well (cf. Isa 52:7).

It is very common in the Bible for the coming of God to be in some way delayed. Those who anticipate this momentous event are told to be vigilant and to wait patiently. Such is not the case here, Instead, God declares this messenger will come suddenly. There is something ominous in this statement. It is almost as if the messenger will come before the people have a chance to complete the necessary repairs. Furthermore, the messenger is coming to the Temple. His destination is a clear indication of the particular focus of the eschatological events that will unfold.

Translations may not always indicate that the word for "Lord" (whom you seek) is *'ādôn*, a common word that can refer to anyone whose status demands our respect. It is not the personal name of God, which is frequently rendered as "LORD." This is important to know because it is used to refer to the messenger described in this passage. Parallel construction illustrates this:

the Lord	whom you seek
the messenger of the covenant	whom you desire

It is this messenger, not God, who comes to the Temple. Since fidelity to the covenant is the standard by which the people are judged, it will be the character of their fidelity that determines whether they will be rewarded or punished. In the Isaian passages mentioned above, the LORD will come with salvation and blessing. Here the messenger of the covenant will come with judgment and affliction.

Judgment is passed on the priests, the sons of Levi. The punishment is among the harshest described in the Bible. Their purification will be searing. Two striking metaphors are used to describe the agents of this purging: the inferno that refines ores, and the lye used by fullers to whiten cloth (cf. Zech 13:9). The messenger will supervise the purification that will serve to transform these priests, making them worthy to offer sacrifice once more. There is no thought of their total destruction, only of their purification. There is a note of hope at the end of this passage. The sacrifice of the people, offered at the hands of the priests, will once again be pleasing to God.

Psalm 24:7, 8, 9, 10

There are few themes more central to the faith of ancient Israel than that of the kingship of God. While "king" is the prominent title accorded God in the responsorial psalm for this feast, other titles throw light on the nature of God's kingship. The idea of king is itself a metaphor that comes from a world where royalty held sway. It represents power and majesty, authority and dominion. When applied to a deity it could refer to the rule exercised over people or the sovereignty wielded over other gods. In monotheistic Israel, God's kingship functioned in both ways.

Besides being referred to as king, the LORD is also described in military terms. Since hosts ($ṣ^eḇā^ʾôt$) are army divisions, the title "LORD of hosts" would suggest that God is the commander of military forces. Such a characterization recalls the ancient Near Eastern myth of creation. In it a young and vibrant warrior god first defeats the cosmic powers of chaos and then reorders the universe. A shout of victory rings out over all creation: Such-and-such is king! As is fitting for such a demonstration of power, a palace for this victorious god is constructed in the heavens. From there the mighty warrior rules as sovereign over all. In this psalm, the God of Israel is praised as LORD of hosts and king of glory, who is strong and mighty in battle.

There is a liturgical dimension to this response. Since the psalm clearly depicts God as king, and since kings seldom travel without some kind of entourage, it is safe to conclude that the approach of the king as described in this psalm is a form of a procession. What appears to be a question-answer dialogue can be explain by a custom practiced in walled cities. Individuals were able to enter these cities through a small door in the much larger gate. This door was usually narrow enough to allow passage in and out of the city to be monitored by guards. However, military or celebrative processions had to go through the gate. Before entrance, a sentinel would require some form of identification. The sentinel on the city wall would shout out the questions; and the people on the ground would shout back the answers. The exchange in the psalm reflects this practice. The titles used here suggest that God has been victorious, and so as the people shout out their answer to the sentinel's question, they are also proclaiming God's glory.

Hebrews 2:14-18

When we think of Jesus as a high priest, we generally think of him as majestic and accomplishing our salvation with the power of God. The author of the letter to the Hebrews invites us to fasten our gaze on Jesus' humanity. He argues that Jesus is one with all women and men, because he fully entered into the human existence of flesh *(sárx)* and blood *(haíma)*. He did not merely appear to be human, as some down through the centuries have erroneously claimed. He was genuinely human. It was necessary that it be so, for if he was to conquer death, he would first have to be subject to it. Only under such circumstances would his victory have any power in the lives of others. One would expect God to be triumphant over death, but one would never expect someone subject to mortality to have such power.

The author draws lines of conflict between Jesus, who has the power of life, and the devil, who holds the power of death. In vanquishing death, Jesus has neutralized the power of the devil. According to this author, it is the devil who tempts human beings to sin, and it is their sin that leads to their death. Through his death Jesus has conquered this process of perdition. What is astounding is that he accomplished this not for himself but for us. He became human so that through the death of his human body he might deliver all human beings from the ravages of human death. It is natural to fear death, but it is also natural to die. Understanding human weakness because it is his weakness as well, Jesus' death put an end to the fear of death. No longer need human beings think of death as the enemy that lurks in the darkness. It can now be seen as the necessary passageway that leads into a new life.

The death of Jesus did nothing to benefit the angels, not because they did not need his help but because he was not one of them. He did not share physical solidarity with them as he did with human beings. The author of the letter refers to the human race as descendants of Abraham, a common boast made by the Israelite people. Perhaps the author did not trace their common ancestry back to Adam because the traditions about Adam are associated with myth, while descent from Abraham might be traced through lines of kinship.

After having examined what it means to be human, the author turns to Jesus' role as a high priest. Jesus knows all about human weakness, for he was tested like everyone else. This prompts him to be merciful. His own integrity prompts him to be faithful. As victim on the cross, he has offered himself for the salvation of all. As high priest he offers a sacrifice of expiation for the sins of all. He is truly a merciful and faithful high priest.

Luke 2:22-40

This account of the presentation of Jesus in the Temple is a celebration of piety—the piety of Mary and Joseph, of Simeon, and of Anna. It is clear that Jesus was raised in an observant family. Five times the author declares that the parents of Jesus conformed to the ritual prescriptions of the Law (vv. 22, 23, 24, 27, 39). Just as they had complied with the imperial decree to be enrolled in the census (2:1-5), so now they observe the religious requirements of purification (cf. Lev 12:1-8) and redemption of the firstborn (cf. Exod 13:2, 12).

The first ritual requirement sprang from the belief that the life-power within blood was sacred and belonged to God. Because of the mysterious nature of its power, it was to be kept separate from the secular activities of life. When separation was not possible, the people and the objects that came into contact with the blood had to be purified. It is obvious why birth and death were surrounded with many purification regulations. The second ritual requirement was a way of reclaiming the firstborn male child who, they believed, really belonged to God. Buying back the child was a way of acknowledging God's initial claim.

Simeon, like the prophets of ancient Israel, had been seized by the Spirit of God (cf. Isa 61:1). Three times the author states that it was the Holy Spirit that directed him (vv. 25, 26, 27). The consolation of Israel for which he waited probably referred to the time of messianic fulfillment. Seeing the child, he recognized him as the object of his longing, the one who was both the glory of Israel and the light for the rest of the world. He also predicted the opposition that Jesus would inspire. Some would accept him and others would not.

This latter scene must have taken place in an outer court of the Temple, where women were allowed, for Simeon explicitly addressed Mary. This was very unusual behavior, for typically men did not speak to women with whom they were unfamiliar, especially in public. His words are somewhat enigmatic. It is clear why the rejection of her son would be like a sword in Mary's heart, but what this might have to do with the thoughts of others is not as obvious.

Another woman joins the group, Anna the prophetess. She is old and a widow, constantly in the Temple praying and fasting. As with Simeon, her entire life was an advent, awaiting the fulfillment of messianic promises. She probably witnessed the meeting with Simeon and heard what he said, for she is convinced of the identity of the child, and she proclaims this to all those who cherished messianic hopes.

Though neither Simeon nor Anna belonged to the ranks of formal temple personnel, they were the ones who recognized the divine child, while the others did not. This should not be seen as an anti-Judaic bias. It points to the fact that religious insight comes from fidelity and genuine devotion rather than official status or privileged role. God and the ways of God are revealed to those who have open minds and open hearts. The piety of this man (v. 25) and this woman (v. 37) disposed them to the unexpected revelation of God.

The family returns to Nazareth to resume its unpretentious life, but it is not the same. Even though the child grows up like other children, he is merely waiting for his time to come.

Themes of the Day

Traditionally this is the fortieth day of Christmas. Even though the Christmas season closed with the feast of the Epiphany, this feast brings us back to some of the Christmas themes. However, the feast is also on the edge. This makes it a kind of hinge between the seasons of Christmas and Lent.

The Temple

The Temple is not merely a building where believers gather to worship God. It is sacred because it is the dwelling place of God on earth. It symbolizes God's presence among us. The advent of God to the Temple was always a time of great anticipation and excitement. It promised blessing and rejoicing.

Today's readings hold a Christmas and a Lenten theme in balance. In the gospel the child Jesus is brought to the Temple to fulfill the requirements of redemption. By right he belongs to God, since he opened his mother's womb. Here for the price of two turtledoves he will be redeemed and returned to his parents. His willingness to submit to the religious traditions of his people adds a dimension of legitimation to these traditions that they had not previously enjoyed. The child enters the Temple quietly, not with the fanfare proclaimed in the responsorial psalm. However, the sentiments found in the psalm are still appropriate. This child is indeed the king of glory, the strong and mighty one. Simeon recognizes this, as does the prophetess Anna. Do we recognize the Lord of the Temple in the unassuming? The poor? The vulnerable?

The scene depicted in the first reading is startling in its contrast. It announces that God will indeed come to the Temple in might and power. However, this advent will be terrifying. God will come not be to purified but to purify with fire and lye. The Temple has been violated; the sacred precincts have been desecrated. Devotion to the Temple requires that it be cleansed and reconsecrated. Only then will it be a suitable place for God to take up residence again. This picture of purification is modified by the reading from the letter to the Hebrews. There we see that the purging and refinement are accomplished in the self-sacrifice of Christ. He has expiated sin through the shedding of his blood (clearly a Lenten theme). His death was the ultimate act of purification.

A Light to the Nations

It took the eyes of an old man and the faith of an old woman to recognize that the Lord had indeed come into the Temple. These two had been waiting for his coming, as the world had waited for thousands of years (the Church marks this waiting during the season of Advent). Ritually, it was the child who was redeemed. In fact, it is the world that will be redeemed. This child will be the light that shines in the darkness of the world (clearly a Christmas theme). He will enlighten all people, Jew and Gentile alike. This feast shares the theme of universality so prominent on the feast of the Epiphany. Having come to a backwater nation, the king of glory opens the portals for the entire universe to enter.

The Nativity of St. John the Baptist (Solemnity)
June 24

Isaiah 49:1-6

The first reading for this feast is a "prophetic speech" (The LORD said to me). In it God refers to the speaker as "my servant." Hence the designation "Servant Song." The actual identity of this servant is quite mysterious. At first reading it sounds like the prophet is the servant (The LORD said to *me:* You are my servant.). But then the servant is identified as Israel. Even this causes confusion, because the servant is called to accomplish the return of Jacob, the gathering back together of Israel (vv. 1, 5). Because the speaker is said to have been formed as a servant from the womb, reminiscent of the call of the prophet Jeremiah (cf. Jer 1:5), some think the servant is Isaiah himself. Commentators are hard pressed to discover the precise identity of this mysterious individual. Most of them direct the reader to lay aside the search for the exact identity of the servant and instead to concentrate on his mission.

The passage opens with a summons to the many peoples of a vast expanse of land. This could be an instance of universalism. However, the servant's task of gathering Israelites suggests they have been scattered as a result of the deportation and exile. This summons is followed by a self-description of the servant. Beyond being called from birth, he was named while yet unborn. It is as if he had been formed in the womb precisely for this mission. His prophetic message is identified as sharp, cutting. However, he is hidden by God until the appropriate time arrives. This prophetic vocation is not a chance occurrence. God planned it and nurtured it.

The text states that Israel is the servant, and it is through this people that God will be glorified *(pā'ar)*. Since the verb suggests a kind of boasting, we can say that God boasts through Israel. But why? "Jacob" and "Israel" are two terms that refer to the entire nation. The poem states that Jacob will be brought back and Israel will be gathered together. The prediction presumes that at this time the people are at some distance from their home; they are scattered. This is probably a reference to the Exile. It will be the mission of the servant, whoever that is, to bring them back to the LORD. The accomplishment of this mission will make the servant glorious in the sight of God. This is the cause for the boasting mentioned earlier. The spectacular return of the scattered exiles and their reestablishment as a people will be seen as the work of God. The glory will shine forth not from their own accomplishments but from what God has accomplished in them through the agency of the servant.

The commission of the servant shifts dramatically (v. 6). Once again it is the LORD who speaks, so the words are authoritative. Gathering the dispersed people of Israel, as important as it may be, is a matter with too narrow a scope. Therefore, the mission of the servant will be expanded to include all the nations, that is, to the ends of the earth. A mission that originally focused on the rebirth of one nation has been broken open to include the salvation of all. It is noteworthy that a people struggling with its own survival after its defeat at the hands of a more powerful nation should envision its God as concerned with the salvation of all, presumably even the nation at whose hands it suffered. Yet this is precisely what "light to the nations" suggests.

Psalm 139:1-3, 13-14, 14-15

Regardless of the level of sophistication in a society, it frequently has a rather uncomplicated understanding of justice. It maintains that reality unfolds according to a certain pattern, and for the good of society every member of the group must conform to that basic pattern. When there is unexplained misfortune, it is necessary to discover the guilty person or persons so that a remedy can be applied. One technique of discovery is trial by ordeal. The suspected person is submitted to a test, usually one with great physical danger. The outcome of the ordeal is seen to be the judgment determining that person's innocence or guilt. This seems to be the situation that generated the sentiments of the psalmist.

The words themselves reveal confidence, first in the psalmist's own innocence and then in God's omniscience. It is God who is doing the probing, and God has intimate knowledge of the inner dispositions of the psalmist. The scope of God's investigation is described in several ways. "Sitting down and rising up" and "journeys and rest" are expressions each of which includes every aspect of waking life. They are similar to the pairs "night and day," "up and down," "north and south," all of which denote totality. In other words, there is nothing about the psalmist's life that is beyond the ken of God.

The second and third stanzas of the response explain why God possesses complete comprehension of every aspect of the psalmist's life. It is because God is the one who created the psalmist in the first place. The psalmist's attention now moves from God's comprehensive knowledge to divine ingenuity in creating. The imagery used to describe the act of creation suggests both tenderness and artistry. The "inmost being" of which the psalmist speaks is really the kidneys *(kilyâ)*, the seat of profound emotions. The psalmist's physical being was carefully knit together in the womb or belly *(beten)* of his mother. Since creation is a personal activity and takes place in secret, the knowledge God has of human beings is privileged knowledge. Only God knows how the psalmist was formed; consequently, God would know whether or not the psalmist is innocent.

To the image of being formed in the womb, the psalmist adds the idea of being formed in the lowest part of the earth. Some commentators see here an allusion to chthonic (under the earth) mythology. While Israel did not teach that human creation took place with the earth, it certainly insists that it took place from the earth (cf. Gen 2:7).

Acts 13:22-26

Paul provides a brief summary of some of the stages in the unfolding of God's plan of salvation. He does this by highlighting the importance of two biblical figures, David and John the Baptist. David was a virtual unknown, the youngest of seven sons. Even in his own family he held an unimportant role. When the prophet Samuel came to his father looking for a possible king, Jesse never considered David as a candidate (cf. 1 Sam 16:1-13). Here is another example of how God seems to prefer the insignificant things of the world to confound the prominent. Despite this, it was David who consolidated the tribes into the monarchy; it was David who expanded the territory that comprised the kingdom. Most important to the author of the Acts of the Apostles, it was David who established the royal dynasty from which came the Messiah.

As the appointed time approached God continued to ready the world for the advent of this Messiah. This was accomplished through the preaching of John the Baptist. His message was one of repentance, a sign the people had strayed from their appointed course. But then, the fact that a Messiah had been promised was a sure indication that the human situation was not as it should be. Although both John and Jesus called for repentance (cf. Mark 1:4, 15), their fundamental message was quite different. John declared that "one is coming"; Jesus announced that "the time is fulfilled" (cf. Mark 1:15). Though John attracted followers from far and near, he knew that he was only the precursor; he was not the long-awaited one. The measure of John's greatness can be seen in his willingness to draw people to himself only to step aside and point them to another. It was with prophetic insight and profound humility that John would declare that the one for whom he was preparing the way was far greater than he himself was.

Paul's purpose in reminding his hearers of the roles played by these two men was to place his own preaching squarely within this tradition. Just as God had chosen David as an instrument in the development of the messianic tradition, and just as God had called John to lead the people to Jesus, who was the fulfillment of the promises made to David, so now Paul has been appointed by God to proclaim this message of salvation. Although Paul's ministry was primarily to the Gentiles, here he is speaking to people who are either themselves Jewish or who are Godfearers, a name given to those who were sympathetic to the teachings of the Israelite religion. It was clear from the beginning that the audience was made up of Jewish people and potential converts, for only they would have appreciated his references to David, and, most likely, only they would have had some acquaintance with John the Baptist.

Luke 1:57-66, 80

In many cultures the act of naming a child is viewed as giving that child its identity. Some societies even believed an unnamed child was not fully human. In Israelite society circumcision was the boy's initiation into the community of the People of God (cf. Gen 17:9-14). The gender bias of this ritual is obvious, since it presumes that the female participates in the community only indirectly, through her father, brother, husband, or son. In this narrative the two initiatory ceremonies have been combined. There does not seem to be any general rule determining who names the child. Sometimes it is the father (cf. Gen 21:3), at other times it is the neighboring women (cf. Ruth 4:17). In this episode it is the neighbors and relatives. The communal character of this society is evident. It is clear the parents are not the only ones who have a stake in a new child.

Since the name given is somehow linked with the person's identity, the name put forward reveals what the namer expects of the child. The neighbors and relatives presume the boy will be called Zechariah after his father. They see his identity and destiny linked with his family, his kin group. The boy's parents both insist he will be called John, a name that means "God is gracious." The name could refer to God's goodness in granting this child to a couple who were advanced in years (cf. Luke 1:7), or it could be a promise of future blessings. The name was given by the angel. Since it came from heaven, it is correct to say this child's destiny would be a heavenly destiny.

There is evidence in the reading that this was truly a chosen child. At his birth the neighbors and relatives rejoiced that God had shown great mercy (*éleos*), not simply kindness (*chrēstótēs*), toward his mother Elizabeth. This suggests she was in great need and God took pity on her, making the child particularly cherished. Furthermore, his father Zechariah was given back his speech when he confirmed that the child was to be named John. He is but eight days old and already he has been a source of blessing for both his parents. While Zechariah blessed God for the marvels that had been performed, the neighbors were frightened by them. They did not know what to make of these events, but they were convinced God had great designs for this child.

The last verse of the reading shows their impressions were correct. John had indeed been set apart by God for a mission to the people of Israel. In preparation for this, he spent his days in the wilderness, the place traditionally considered a testing ground. It was there that he was strengthened in spirit for the task before him.

Themes of the Day

A Cosmic Hinge

Like the feast of the nativity of Jesus, this feast falls on one of the solstices, a hinge point in the cosmos. Some of patristic writings tell us that the birth of Jesus was placed in the calendar when, in the Northern Hemisphere, the days begin to lengthen. So this day was chosen to celebrate the birth of John precisely because the days were getting shorter. This calendric decision exemplified John's declaration: He must increase while I must decrease (John 3:30). This is the time of seasonal change, of cosmic reversal. The entire universe has been alerted. Something new is about to happen.

A nativity is always a dramatic entry into history, whether this be the birth of a child of note or of a simple laborer. Each new birth is a new beginning for the entire human race. Parents either hope the child will enjoy a life that will be richer than their own, or they believe the child will effect a change in the lives of others. Hopes are always high at new births. Some births are believed to change even the movements of the heavens. Many people believe we are influenced by the astral arrangements under which we are born. Others are convinced that the stars themselves proclaim the significance of the new birth.

The meaning of John's birth may well hinge on the meaning of the birth of Jesus, but it is significant enough to make us step out of liturgical Ordinary Time for a moment and reflect again on the entrance of God into ordinary human time. John's birth shares in the meaning of the incarnation.

An Eschatological Hinge

John the Baptist is the hinge between the old age and the new eschatological age of fulfillment. John himself was never a disciple of Jesus; he did not enter the age that he heralded (cf. Matt 11:11; Luke 7:28). He was the trumpet that sounded the coming of the king; he was the rooster that announced the dawning of the new day. He brought the people to the threshold of the new age, but he himself never stepped over into it. The idiosyncratic character of his life caught the attention of the crowds, but he did not keep this attention on himself. Instead, he used it to point to Jesus, who appears to have been so commonplace that he might have been overlooked had not John cried out. It was John's prophetic destiny to be the sharp-edged sword, the polished arrow. He was the voice that cried in the wilderness: Hear me! Listen! Behold, he is coming!

The Hand of the Lord

From the beginning the hand of the Lord was on John. His conception had been extraordinary (cf. Luke 1:7); his name had been announced by the angel (cf. Luke 1:13); like many prophetic figures, he had been chosen from his mother's womb; his father had been struck speechless and remained so until his name was proclaimed to others (cf. Luke 1:22, 64). Everything about this child pointed to a divinely determined destiny. His almost appears to be a thankless role, but it was not. His was the last prophetic voice that challenged the people to prepare; he was privileged to see the one that others did not see. John opened the door to the future and then stepped back so that the voice from the future might call us forth.

SS. Peter and Paul, Apostles (Solemnity)
June 29

Acts 12:1-11

The execution of James and the imprisonment of Peter demonstrate again how the reign of God is embroiled in the political circumstances of the day. The Herod of this episode is Herod Agrippa I, the grandson of the hated Herod the Great. He was a child when his father was executed, so his mother sent him to Rome, both for the sake of safety and to procure a Roman education. There he grew up with various members of the imperial family. This explains both the privilege he enjoyed with his Roman overlords and the disfavor in which he was held by the Jewish people. It was because of the former that he was able to expand the scope of the territory over which he ruled;

it was because of the latter that he seemed always eager to curry the favor of the leaders of the Jewish people.

Belonging to an occupied people, the Jewish leaders had only as much power and authority as was granted them by their occupiers. However, since Herod Agrippa was always trying to please them, they exercised a considerable amount of influence. Both James, who appears to have been the leader of the Christian community in Jerusalem, and Peter, the recognized leader of the apostles, become victims of the antagonism of the Jewish leaders and the pusillanimity of the king. James is put to death, and Peter faces the same fate. He is still alive only because it is the feast of Unleavened Bread and executions are unlawful during festivals. Unleavened Bread began on the fourteenth of Nisan, the evening of Passover, and it lasted a week. The similarity between Peter's imprisonment and impending execution and the circumstances surrounding the death of Jesus is striking.

The restraints Peter was forced to endure suggest that this similarity was not lost on Herod. He was probably afraid the supporters of Peter might try to release him. Most likely Peter was kept in the Tower of Antonia, the headquarters of the Roman garrison in Jerusalem, which was northwest of the temple area. Roman night guard was divided into four three-hour watches with a squadron of four soldiers assigned to each watch. Peter was chained on each side to a soldier, while the other two kept watch outside the cell. Although the Christians prayed for his release, there was little chance this would occur.

The author provides all these details so the miraculous character of Peter's release will stand out boldly. Peter himself is completely passive throughout the incident. On the eve before he is to be put to death, he is awakened from sleep, told to dress and to follow the one who is freeing him. Even as the events unfold, Peter is not fully conscious of what is transpiring. His deliverance is all God's doing, enacted by an angel of the Lord. It is clear that the future of the Church is being directed by the hand of God and not by the political maneuverings of human potentates.

Psalm 34:2-3, 4-5, 6-7, 8-9

The psalm response is part of an acrostic, a poem whose structure follows the order of the alphabet. Although the content of this type of psalm may vary, the form (the entire alphabet) always signifies the same thing, completeness. This psalm is less a prayer than an instruction. Its teaching is the conventional understanding of retribution: the righteous will be blessed and the wicked will be punished. In this first part of the poem the psalmist thanks God for having been delivered from distress, and he invites others to join in praising God. The attitude of the psalmist gives witness to others and develops into a pedagogical technique, teaching others to act in the same way.

The psalm begins with an expression of praise of God and an acknowledgment of the appropriateness of blessing God. This praise probably takes place in some kind of liturgical setting, for it is heard by the lowly (*'ănāwîm*), those who live in trust and dependence on the LORD. They are here invited to join with the psalmist in rejoicing and in praising God's name.

Normally in psalms of thanksgiving the reasons for gratitude are recited. Without going into detail, the psalmist confesses having been in distress, having turned to the LORD, and having been rescued. This is the reason for gratitude. This is why the psalmist glorifies God and bids others to do the same.

The congregation is now given explicit directions. They are encouraged to look to the LORD so they too may rejoice in gratitude, their faces radiant and not filled with shame. One's face, we should remember, is the expression of one's dignity, of one's status in the community, and to lose face is to lose honor or to be shamed. The companions of the psalmist are encouraged to attach themselves to God and thereby to enjoy the blessings this ensures. The fate of the psalmist is placed before them as an example to follow.

An image that might be unfamiliar to us is used to demonstrate this. An angel or messenger from God pitches a protective camp around those who fear the LORD, who stand in awe and reverence of God's majesty and power. Thus they are guarded by the power of God against anything that might endanger them.

The passage ends with an admonition. The congregation is encouraged to taste God's goodness, to partake of it a little, to sample it a bit. The psalmist is saying that if only they put God's goodness to the test they will see for themselves how delectable it is, how satisfying it can be. They have the psalmist's witness. It is now time for them to experience God's goodness for themselves.

2 Timothy 4:6-8, 17-18

Paul is aware that his days are numbered, that his death is imminent. He does not resent it, but neither does he run toward it eagerly. He faces it with the calm resignation that springs from deep faith. He uses moving imagery to characterize his death. The first metaphor is taken from the context of the cult. There we find the rite of pouring out wine as a kind of drink offering (cf. Num 15:5, 7, 10). This practice may have been introduced into the ritual as a substitute for blood libation. Paul states that he is being poured out like this sacrificial blood. Not only is every ounce of life being exacted of him, but his offering of it is viewed as a sacrificial act.

A second metaphor is no less poignant. Paul views his death as a departure, a kind of leave-taking (*análýō*, a compound derived from *lýō*, meaning "to loose") associated with sailors who weigh anchor or soldiers who break camp. Like them, Paul has completed a demanding tour of service and is now preparing to return home. The references suggest eager anticipation. In none of these metaphors is Paul in control. The cultic image suggests he is poured out by another. Although the sailor and the soldier perform important roles in their leave-taking, they certainly did not make the decision to leave on their own. They were merely carrying out the decisions made by another.

Finally, Paul uses imagery derived from athletic competition to evaluate the course of his ministerial commitment. He has competed well; he has finished the race. To this he adds that he has kept the faith, an idiomatic expression that means remaining loyal to one's oath. He has done what he could. Now he has only to wait for the conferral upon him of the crown promised by God. The reference is to Christ's eschatological manifestation. For a moment Paul moves away from focusing solely on his fate in order to anticipate joining with all the others who will be awarded the victorious crown. He claims no special privilege. This man, who is facing death at the hands of others, is looking forward to a time of communal fulfillment.

Paul compares the trustworthiness of God with the unreliability of human companions. It seems everyone had deserted him during one of his trials, perhaps because they would have been putting themselves in jeopardy had they stood with him. Whatever the case, Paul is not resentful, for God was there to strengthen him when all others fled. Throughout this discourse, he extols the marvelous deeds God has done on his behalf. He even maintains that the gospel benefits from his adversity. His imprisonment and trial have provided an opportunity for him to proclaim the good news to the people involved. Because of it he is able to spread the word even more broadly, despite the difficult circumstances in which he finds himself.

Paul is confident that just as God had previously rescued him from peril, so God would rescue him again. He is not speaking of being freed from prison but of being preserved from anything that might threaten his spiritual well-being and prevent him from being led safely into the kingdom of heaven.

Matthew 16:13-19

This reading consists of two distinct yet related themes. The first is christological (vv. 13-16); the second is ecclesiological (vv. 17-19). Only after Simon Peter has proclaimed Jesus to be the Christ, the anointed one of God, does Jesus announce that his own Church will be founded on Peter.

Jesus asks the disciples what people are saying about him; Who do they think he is? He applies to himself the messianic apocalyptic title "Son of Man." The question is not self-serving. Jesus seeks to discover how his words and actions are being understood by the people, and he is preparing the disciples for their own assessment of him. The answers given to his questions are telling. Some believe that he is John the Baptist; others that he is Elijah; still others that he is one of the other prophets. These religious figures have already died; the people seem to believe Jesus is a prophetic figure who has come back from the dead.

It is not clear why Jesus should be associated with John the Baptist, since in both their life-styles and their central messages they were so different. The connection may have been made simply because the memory of this exceptional man was still fresh in the minds of the people. Many had set their hopes on John, and with his death they transferred them to Jesus. Elijah had been the mysterious prophet whose return would herald the advent of the reign of God. Since Jesus launched his ministry with the announcement that the long-awaited reign was now at hand, it is understandable that people would link him with Elijah. In some way, all the prophets had looked forward to the coming of this reign, so the people's general reference was not inappropriate. Simon Peter speaks in the name of the others when he proclaims that Jesus is the Christ, the Messiah, the anointed one of God. To this he adds the divine title "Son of the living God."

Using a macarism (Blessed are you), Jesus opens his discussion of the role Peter will play in the assembly of believers. Jesus insists that the only reason Peter could make such a testimony of faith was that Jesus' identity had been revealed to him by God. With a play on Greek words, the author has Jesus declare that Peter *(Petros)* is the rock *(petra)* upon which Jesus will establish his church. Although the image of a rock suggests stability and endurance, we should not presume that these characteristics are natural to Peter. Also, "church" *(ekklēsía)* is certainly a reference to the assembly of people, not the building within which they gather.

Jesus promises that the forces of the netherworld will not be able to encircle this church. It is clear this promise is not based on any strength of Peter's. It is solely a gift from Jesus. For his part, Peter will exercise the power of the keys. Controlling the keys is a sign of authority. However, here the symbol of keys refers to a special kind of authority, one that is more judicial or disciplinary than managerial. Peter is given the authority to enforce laws and to exempt from their obligation. This does not suggest that Peter legislates. Rather he interprets the Law, determining when it should be binding and when not. In a sense, Peter is cast in the role of the chief rabbi.

Themes of the Day

This feast celebrates the two pillars on which Christianity was built. Peter is associated with the community in Jerusalem and Paul with the Gentile converts. Together they represent the universality of the Church. The red vestments worn on this day remind us of the price that the commitment of these men exacted of them. The focus here is not on the offices either of them might have held within the community but on the character of their witness of faith.

Who Do You Say I Am?

The church is rooted in the identity of Christ. His followers have come from every race and culture, every generation and social class. It is not a common culture that has drawn them together but a common faith. They do not consider Jesus the reincarnation of some great personage of the past. Rather, they profess him to be the Christ, the Son of the Living God. Today the successors of these two great apostles sometimes struggle with the appropriate response to the proclamation of the gospel. This may be due in part to the fact that there are so many cultural ways of expressing one's Christian faith. However, there is no question about the identity of Jesus. He is the same yesterday, today, and forever.

I Have Kept the Faith

Today we remember that throughout the ages the Church has been strengthened by the blood of the martyrs. This was the case in its earliest years, and it is the case even today. Both Peter and Paul are examples of how God can take those who are weak in faith and transform them into champions for the cause of the gospel. Once transformed, each of them threw himself wholeheartedly into the mission that was his. Their fate should not surprise us, for they were disciples of one who gave his last breath for the life of the world.

In so many places in the world today modern martyrs are called upon to pay the ultimate price for their faith. We see this in Latin America, in many African countries, in the Middle East, and in Asia, to name but a few areas. Although the word "martyr" usually refers to one who dies for the faith, the Greek word *(mártys)* really means witness, one who gives testimony. Like Peter and Paul, the martyr is one whose life gives witness to the faith. However, when this witness becomes too much of a challenge to the world, the witness's life is placed in jeopardy. Peter and Paul call us all to this kind of testimony to faith.

The Transfiguration of the Lord (Feast)
August 6

Daniel 7:9-10, 13-14

An apocalyptic vision unfolds before the seer. Visions and dreams were traditionally thought to be avenues of divine revelation. The seer is usually on earth, while the vision itself takes place in heaven. Everything about this vision bespeaks revelation, yet it is symbolic, with all of the ambiguous traits of symbol.

It reveals only the symbol. The seer must be able to interpret it. The reading for today comprises two scenes, both of which take place in the throne room. The two major figures are the Ancient One and the one like a Son of Man.

The description of the Ancient One is not only brilliant in itself, but its contrast with the flames of fire only exaggerates the brilliance. The name given this heavenly being is telling. "Ancient One" implies both eternity and great wisdom. Therefore it demands reverence, respect, and obedience. Enthroned in the heavens presumes that the Ancient One rules wisely over all that is. White clothing implies purity and luminosity. Since often exquisite white linen was worn by kings, here it might also be an indication of royal raiment. White hair is a symbol of the age and wisdom of this ruler. It reinforces the notion of eternity.

Only the Ancient One was seated, an honor reserved for rulers. Presumably the throngs that attend him are standing around the throne, as is the practice with all royalty. The throne itself is reminiscent of the fiery chariot in Ezekiel's apocalyptic vision (cf. Ezek 1:15-21). Flames of fire suggest a divine theophany (cf. Exod 19:18). The scene depicts the courts of heaven at the end of the ages, as is clear from the mention of the books that are now opened. At creation, according to ancient Near Eastern mythology, the destinies of the nations were written in books, which were then sealed and kept secret. Only at the end of time would these seals be broken and the fates of all revealed (cf. Revelation 5–9).

The one who comes on the clouds is described as one like the Son of man (in Aramaic *bar enash*). Its literal translation is "son of weak man." Of itself it denotes a limited human being. However, this figure is not really a human being; he only resembles a Son of man. The picture painted here is colored with both mythic and royal tones. The figure comes with the clouds, which are the most frequent accompaniment of a theophany, or revelation of God. He comes riding them as one would ride a chariot (cf. Ps 18:10). He is presented before God in the manner of courtly decorum, where one would not simply approach the ruler but would be presented by an attendant. This is no ordinary man.

The mysterious figure is installed by God as ruler over the entire universe. The authority and dominion that belong to other nations is handed over to him. Unlike other kingdoms that rise and eventually fall, his will be an everlasting kingdom, granted by God, not attained by means of conquest or political alliance. Finally, his dominion will be exercised on earth. The one like a Son of man may have been in heaven when he received his commission, he may even rule from some exalted place in the heavens, but his kingdom belongs to the earth.

Psalm 97:1-2, 5-6, 9

The psalm opens with the traditional enthronement declaration, "The LORD is king!" Behind this exclamation is the theme of divine kingship. The ancients believed the gods were always vying with each other for power and status. The god that could be victorious over this chaotic situation, if only for a time, was enthroned as king over all. There are echoes of this mythology in the responsorial psalm. The god who rules is the LORD, the God of Israel.

The exclamation is appropriately followed by an exhortation: "Let the earth rejoice!" God's victory and rule call for celebration, one that extends beyond the confines of Israel to many islands, an image denoting the furthest parts of the world. God's throne is established on a firm foundation. Unlike other regimes built on brute force or military victory, both of which might fail and result in dethronement, God's rule is constructed in the permanence of justice *(ṣedeq)* and judgment *(mishpāt)*. It is not only impregnable, it is immutable. It stands secure, enabling God to govern undisturbed by any threat and assuring reliable protection to all those under God's jurisdiction.

With three phrases the psalmist declares the sovereignty of the LORD. First, the reference to the heavens includes all the celestial beings once thought to be gods themselves, now merely luminaries or winds or forms of rain. No longer is there any vying among them. Instead, they are all intent on praising God's justice; the order that was set after the primordial battle had been won. Second, not only Israel but all people see God's glory *(kābôd)*, the splendor that shines from God's holiness and that is usually a characteristic of divine theophany or manifestation. Third, all other gods are prostrate before the LORD in an attitude of utter subservience. Actually, the verb *(bôsh)* means to put to shame or to lose face before the other. In a society where honor and shame play such important roles, this is a significant point. The universal kingship of the LORD is beyond question.

The passage from the psalm ends with a proclamation of praise addressed directly to the LORD. It captures the essence of the preceding verses. God is exalted above both heaven and earth. There is no threat of future upheaval or rebellion. God has no rivals. The divine king has been enthroned, and the rule of this God will last forever.

2 Peter 1:16-19

A defensive tone seems to surface in this reading. The authenticity of the gospel message preached by the author appears to have come under attack, and he counters with two arguments. The first one is based on personal experience, and the second one, on the revelatory nature of the Scriptures.

A myth is a creative literary form that expresses some of the mysteries of life and of the broader universe. Its very creativity enables people to enter into the depths of the mysteries it describes. Because it is an imaginative rather than a scientific or historical way of conceiving reality, the richness of a myth will be diminished if it is forced into one of these other categories. A myth must be understood on its own creative terms. Those who would understand it in a literal fashion, which is really to misunderstand it, might be tempted to say it is not true because the universe does not work in the way the myth describes it. In a similar manner, reality itself can be misunderstood. It does not fit into a neat pattern. Those who try to force it to do so might be tempted to dismiss as impossible or untrue whatever does not fit the patterns of their understanding.

This seems to be the issue with which the author is struggling. The extraordinary, even incomprehensible, character of the final coming *(parousía)* of the Lord Jesus Christ has led some to denounce it as myth. One can almost hear them exclaim: That could never happen! The author counters the denunciation: Oh yes it did, and I was an eyewitness to it. The event of which they speak is the transfiguration of Jesus. His full and solemn title is used in this report of his wondrous manifestation *(megaleiótōs)* of divine glory. This glory is probably a reference to the cloud from which the voice was heard. Those who were with him on the mountain were witness both to his glory and to God's affirmation of him. If Jesus could have been so transformed during his lifetime, surely this same Lord can return in the same glory.

The second witness to which the author appeals is the Scriptures, the prophetic message that foretold the coming of the Messiah. The Christians inherited these Scriptures from the Jewish community, and they held them in the same esteem as the inspired word of God. The prophetic words acted as beacons in the darkness, guiding the people through trial and doubt. If the detractors will not believe the testimony of the eyewitnesses, they should at least accept the reliability of these sacred words.

Two very powerful metaphors are used to describe the *parousía* of the Lord, both of which characterize it as the coming of light out of darkness. They are the dawning of the day, the eschatological day of fulfillment, and the rising of the morning star. The latter image recalls the messianic prophecy spoken by the Moabite prophet Balaam: "A star shall come out of Jacob" (cf. Num 24:17). The Christian community placed the fulfillment of this prophecy on the lips of Jesus: "I am the root and the descendant of David, the bright morning star" (cf. Rev 22:16). The Scriptures themselves bear witness to the veracity of the gospel message.

Mark 9:2-10

The account of the transfiguration of Jesus knits together traditions of Israel's past, insights into Jesus' own identity, and a glimpse into the future of eschatological fulfillment. The word for transfiguration *(metamorphóō)* literally means "to change form." Many religious traditions believe that gods can easily change into different forms. Various schools of mysticism maintain that human beings and certain animals as well can change their forms. In Jewish apocalyptic hope the righteous will take on a glorious new heavenly form. Although this account emphasizes the new brilliance of Jesus' clothing, it is he who was transfigured. The question then is not can it happen, but what does it mean?

Peter, James, and John, privileged to witness this transfiguration, seem to form an inner circle. Their presence makes this a historical event, not a celestial one. Although only Jesus was transformed and only he spoke with the apparitions, the disciples were caught up into the experience as well. They beheld the transfigured Jesus, along with Moses and Elijah. They were overshadowed by the cloud, and the voice spoke directly to them.

The account contains many details associated with Moses and Elijah. Both are associated with mountains (Sinai, Exodus 19; Horeb, 1 Kings 19); both underwent a kind of transformation (Moses' face was made radiant, Exod 34:29-35; Elijah was transported in a fiery chariot, 2 Kgs 2:11). Finally, these men are associated with two very important traditions. First, together they represent the basis of Israel's tradition, the law and the prophets respectively. Second, they both prefigure the prophetic dimension of the messianic era (cf. Deut 18:15, 18-19; Mal 3:1, 23).

Peter's plea for permission to set up three tents recalls the feast of Tabernacles, when the Jews remembered the temporary dwellings in which they lived during their sojourn in the wilderness. By the time of Jesus the feast had taken on messianic undertones (cf. Zech 14:16-19). If Peter's request springs from a desire to enjoy messianic blessings, Jesus' final directive to tell no one until after the resurrection reminds him that Jesus' debasement must precede his glorification. The transfiguration is, then, a prefigurement of that fulfillment.

The words from the cloud are both clear and cryptic. Jesus is identified as the beloved Son, reminiscent of Isaac, who was also a beloved son (cf. Gen 22:2). The voice directs the three disciples to listen to Jesus. This could be understood in a very general sense, but the words of Jesus on the way down the mountain suggest something more specific. It is clear that the disciples did not understand what he meant by "rising from the dead." The connection with Isaac and Jesus' final charge suggest that the voice is referring to Jesus' teaching about his death. It may be that the transfiguration was intended to prepare the inner circle of disciples for the unthinkable suffering and death in order to strengthen them in advance.

Themes of the Day

In the midst of Ordinary Time we are invited to join Peter, James, and John as they behold the transfiguration of Christ. By some horrible coincidence we recall Christ's brilliance on the day the world marks another cosmic event, the anniversary of its birth into the atomic age at Hiroshima. The paradox of these events should not be lost on us. The white light that shone from Christ was a mere suggestion of the divine splendor that is beyond human comprehension; the flashing light from the atomic explosion was an omen of the destructive force that is within human grasp. It is imperative that the horror of the latter be brought under the control of the glory of the former.

Transfiguration

The transfiguration of Christ was not a simple metamorphosis. Christ was not changed from a terrestrial human being to a celestial divine one. Rather, his transfiguration was a moment in time when the divine glory he had always possessed broke through his humanity and shone with a brilliance that was blinding. Nothing could prepare the apostles for this experience, and there was no way to describe it except with cosmic imagery. The brightest light flashed forth from his countenance, like the birth of a new star. His hair, his garments, everything about him shone like the sun. Moses and Elijah stood as witnesses to his glory, and the voice of God confirmed his divinity. It is no wonder the apostles fell prostrate.

Eyewitnesses

Who would believe such an explosion of power and might would have taken place? We sing of this glory time and again in the psalms. We proclaim that nothing can stand before the splendor of the Lord; even mountains melt like wax. Yet when it really appears we can hardly believe it ourselves. The readings outline three moments when this glory was revealed. The first was reported by the visionary in the book of Daniel. He was granted a glimpse of the throne room in heaven. In that scene it is the Ancient One who shines forth with indescribable radiance. The second moment was the scene of the transfiguration. The third is hidden in the testimony of the author of the letter of Peter. The pseudonymous author of the letter was probably a second-generation Christian who may or may not have shared in the actual vision of the transfigured Lord but who was a witness to faith in his divine glory. The splendor of God is manifested in each generation of believers.

We Possess the Prophetic Message

We are the ones who today possess the prophetic message; we are the present-day eyewitnesses of Christ's majesty. We too have moments when we might behold his glory and hear the voice proclaiming his identity, but we need eyes of faith and ears that are open. We really never know when God will choose to reveal a glimpse of divine glory. The disciples probably thought Jesus was merely taking them up a mountain to pray, as he had done on other occasions. Like them, all we can do is follow Jesus and open ourselves to whatever God has in store for us.

The Assumption of the Blessed Virgin Mary (Solemnity)
Revelation 11:19a; 12:1-6a, 10ab

Several mythological themes lie behind the apocalyptic vision that unfolds before us. The basic one is the primordial cosmic battle. The principal opponents in that battle are a sea monster or dragon and a young warrior god. Although the dragon is fearsomely powerful, victory goes to the warrior. A second very common tale found in the folk literature of many cultures is the story of someone who seeks to usurp the position of an unborn prince. His plan to kill the prince at his birth is thwarted by attendants who snatch the child from him and carry the baby to safety. These two myths have been superimposed in this vision. The complex interweaving of detail from both myths along with the fact that this is an apocalyptic vision should caution us not to force an allegorical interpretation on it.

The vision is not only apocalyptic, it is also eschatological. After it had been installed in the Temple, the earthly ark of the covenant was approached only by the high priest and only on the Day of Atonement. In this vision, the heavenly ark is revealed to all. The Israelites believed this revelation would take place only at the time of eschatological fulfillment. Two signs appear in the heavens: a pregnant woman and the cosmic dragon. She is no ordinary woman. Rather, she is depicted as an astral deity, superior even to the moon. The twelve stars symbolize the signs of the zodiac. The seven-headed dragon is a composite of the cosmic monster (cf. Pss 74:13-14; 89:9-10; Isa 27:1) and the evil empire drawn from the vision of Daniel (cf. Dan 7:7). The diadems on its head represent its blasphemous claims to sovereignty. While it waits for the birth of the child, the dragon engages in cosmic battle and is relatively successful. However, complete victory is not yet in sight. It fact, ultimate victory is denied.

The child is described in royal terms. He is destined to shepherd (*poimaínō*) all of the nations. Because of the responsibility they had for their subjects, kings were often thought of as shepherds. This newly born king will rule with a rod of iron, which is an image of harsh punishment. Finally, he will exercise this authority universally, over all the nations. Upon his birth he is rescued from the threat of the dragon and caught up to the throne of God. His mother is also protected by God, but she flees into the wilderness.

The passage ends with a great exclamation of praise. The accomplishments of God's anointed one are described in four phrases. He has brought salvation; he has manifested his power; he has established the kingdom of God; and his own authority has been revealed. It is not clear whether this acclamation is referring to the ultimate fulfillment in the future or to the fulfillment this anointed one has inaugurated, which is unfolding in the present.

Psalm 45:10, 11, 12, 16

The verses of this response have been taken from a royal psalm, specifically a royal wedding psalm. All attention is given to the queen. Each verse of the response treats a different aspect of her person. The change in pronouns suggests the psalmist is talking first to the king (v. 10) and then to the queen herself (vv. 11-12, 16).

We are directed first to three characteristics of her royal dignity. She is identified as a queen, an indication that she and the king are already married. She stands at the king's right hand. Although she is standing, the proper sign of respect when in the presence of the king, she holds the place of honor at his right hand. Finally, she is arrayed in gold. We may also note that although Ophir's reputation as a source of gold is referred to several times in the Bible, its exact location is not known.

The psalmist next turns directly to the woman, and gives her advice or direction as a Wisdom teacher might: Hear and see! Listen to my words and realize their value! The title "daughter" fits well with the theme of kinship. The patriarchal custom of the woman leaving the household of her father to become part of the household of her husband is clearly reflected. The psalmist encourages the woman to conform to this practice.

The king is characterized as the lord (*'ādôn*) of the woman. This probably refers to his royal role and not to his role as husband. Were the latter situation the case the word used for "lord" would probably be *ba'al,* which is also translated "husband." There is surely a sexual connotation in the reference to his desire for her beauty. Since it is the king who desires her and not merely her husband, one could conclude that he wishes to incorporate her into his harem. This idea may be repugnant to contemporary sensibilities, but in the ancient Near Eastern world it would have been considered the highest honor to which a woman might aspire.

The final verse alludes to the wedding procession that was part of most marriages. Usually the bride and her attendants walked in procession to the home of the groom. The high station of this wedding couple is seen in the fact that the wedding entourage is carried into the palace, probably on exquisitely decorated litters. Once the bride arrived, the feasting would commence. From this point on the bride would reside in the home of her husband.

1 Corinthians 15:20-27

This reading from Paul's Corinthian correspondence brings together several of his most treasured theological themes: the efficacy of Christ's resurrection; human solidarity in Adam and in Christ; the sequence of eschatological events; and the victory of Christ. The reading carries us first back through time to the primordial period of beginnings, and then forward to the end of time and the eschatological age of fulfillment. Christ is identified as the first-fruits of those who have fallen asleep. In double fashion the expression speaks of the end-time. "Fallen asleep" is a euphemism for death, and firstfruits refers to harvest. It was believed the firstfruits of a crop functioned in two ways. They contained the most forceful expression of the life of the plant, and they stood as a promise of more yield to come. As the firstfruits of the dead, the risen Christ is the most forceful expression of life after death, and his resurrection contains the promise of resurrection for all who are joined to him.

It is fair to say that, as did his contemporaries, Paul considered Adam the first human being. However, Adam also stands for the entire race. The Hebrew word itself (*'ādām*) yields both a singular and a collective meaning. Here Paul is referring to human solidarity in Adam when he declares that one man sinned and brought death into the world, and in that one man is all of humankind. In an analogous fashion, Christ is the person Jesus, and joined in faith, all believers participate in the resurrected life of Christ. This is clearly meant by the phrase: Death came through humankind (*ánthrōpos*); resurrection from the death came through humankind (*ánthrōpos*). In both instances the deed is accomplished by one *ánthrōpos* who stands for all.

Paul sketches a picture of the risen Christ with his foot on the neck of death, his vanquished enemy. This picture of victory was common in the ancient Near Eastern world. The enemy could be either dead or merely quelled. Whichever the case, the enemy was conquered.

The eschatological events Paul is describing will transcend time. Every aspect of these events is grounded in the resurrection of Christ. First he is raised; then at his final coming (*parousía*) those who are joined to Christ are raised. Only when this has taken place will the end (*télos*) come. This end is the fulfillment, the goal toward which all reality tends. Paul seems to be suggesting there is an interval between the *parousía* and the final end, when Christ will hand over everything to God. During this time all of Christ's enemies will be vanquished. This eschatological perspective corresponds to the Jewish apocalyptic worldview of his day. Paul does not indicate how long this interval will last. We can only presume it will last as long as it takes for Christ to accomplish the decisive victory. When this happens, Christ will bring the fruits of his victory to God.

Luke 1:39-56

The gospel reading falls naturally into two parts: the account of Mary's visit to Elizabeth (vv. 39-45); and Mary's prayer of praise (vv. 46-56). Mary's greeting to Elizabeth is a customary salutation *(aspázomai)*, but its effect is profound. It causes the child in Elizabeth's womb to leap with joy *(skirtáō)*. This is reminiscent of the joy that filled David as he leapt before the ark of the covenant, the symbol of God in the midst of the people (cf. 2 Sam 6:14-15). Elizabeth is filled with the Holy Spirit and proclaims her faith in the child Mary is carrying. In the cases of both David and Elizabeth's unborn child, it is their realization of being in the presence of God that cause them to rejoice. It is as if Mary is the ark and the child within her is the glory of God.

In response to this wondrous experience, Elizabeth exalts first Mary and then her child (v. 42). She recognizes the blessedness they possess and she praises it. This blessedness is derived from the dignity of the child, a dignity Elizabeth acknowledges by referring to him as her Lord *(kýrios)*. As David had wondered how the ark of God could come to him (cf. 2 Sam 6:9), so Elizabeth wonders how the mother of her Lord should come to her. Mary is here called "blessed" *(makários)* for having believed what had been spoken to her by the Lord, a reference to the annunciation (cf. Luke 1:26-38). In this case it is faith, not some work of righteousness, that is extolled. She believed she would conceive and bear a son, and it has come to pass. It is this son she carries in her womb that precipitated the events recorded in this passage. The way the good fortune will be manifested in Mary's life is not stated; she is merely called blessed.

Mary's hymn of praise has strong parallels in the victory hymns of Miriam (Exod 15:1-18), Hannah (1 Sam 2:1-10), and Judith (Jdt 16:1-17). She does not deny the greatness of the things that will be accomplished through her. On the contrary, the more magnificent the things accomplished, the clearer will God's power and might be seen, for only God could bring about such wonders. She praises God for having singled out the lowly and for having reversed their fortunes. This is the way God has acted from age to age, offering mercy to those who are open to it, to those who stand in awe of God's greatness.

While the first section of the prayer describes the great things God did to Mary, the last verses list some of the past blessings enjoyed by Israel. First is the reversal of fortune that had happened so often in the past: the hungry are filled, while the rich are sent away empty (v. 53). The choice of Mary is another example of God's preference for those who do not enjoy abundant prosperity.

The reference to the promise made to Abraham places all God's blessings within the context of the covenant associated with this prominent ancestor (Gen 15:1-21; 17:1-14). These promises included a pledge that they would be a great nation; that they would be given a land of their own; and that they would live prosperous and peaceful lives, secure from outside threats. The history of Israel is an account of the people's infidelity to their responsibilities and God's mercy in the face of their failures. Mary's hymn of praise suggests that the marvels accomplished in her are a final example of God's mercy. The salvation of the people has finally come.

Themes of the Day

In the Western Church this feast celebrates the assumption of Mary into heaven; in the East it commemorates her dormition, or falling asleep. However, the readings invite us to reflect on the role she plays in the mystery of our redemption. Whatever we honor in Mary in some way points to her Son.

The Celestial Woman

Over the centuries devotion to Mary has been expressed in forms taken from the culture out of which it developed. Sometimes she is pictured as a humble peasant girl. At other times she is depicted as a queen, robed in gold of Ophir, who rules from heaven. Probably the most familiar pose is that of a mother with her child. Just as Christian theologians have reached into various religious traditions to explain some dimension of christology, so have they appropriated various images in their development of Mariology. Perhaps the most dramatic of these themes is that of the celestial woman from the vision found in the book of Revelation. It is because of the cosmic significance of Jesus that this tradition has been applied to Mary.

Reading this passage on a Marian feast suggests a Marian interpretation. The woman, now interpreted as Mary, brings forth her child, who is destined to rule all the nations. Mythological themes from other traditions take on new meaning here. For example, the mythic enmity between the dragon and the child recalls a similar enmity between the serpent in the garden of Eden and the offspring of the primordial woman. This cosmic vision places Mary in the heavens at the outset of God's plan of redemption. This feast declares that upon the completion of her role in this plan, Mary returns to heaven triumphant.

A Prophetic Voice

The gospel reading for this feast characterizes Mary in a very different way. Here she is a simple peasant woman intent on offering service to another. However, the words placed in her mouth belie this unassuming picture. They are words of prophetic challenge. She announces the great reversals of God's good news. The structures of privilege and discrimination will be overturned. The dispossessed and the needy will experience the goodness of God. Mary did not presume that she would accomplish such great feats. Rather, they would be accomplished by the child she was carrying. Once again we see that the greatness of Mary is a reflection of the greatness of the Son of God, whom she bore. He was the firstfruits of salvation. He was the victor who won the kingdom. Her part in this victory was to bring him to birth and into maturity.

The Exaltation of the Holy Cross (Feast)

Numbers 21:4b-9

The setting of this episode is the wilderness. In the tradition of Israel the wilderness can be understood in two ways, which are diametrically opposed to each other. On the one hand, it is considered a place of love and intimacy, the site where God and the people first entered into a covenant relationship (cf. Hos 2:14). On the other hand, it is a place of testing, and for Israel, a place of failure. It is the second understanding that is operative in this passage.

There is something astonishing about the murmuring of the people. They acknowledge that God had brought them out of Egypt. They admit that they do have food (probably the manna). Still they complain. Their experience of deliverance from bondage should have grounded them in trust in God, but it did not. Besides this, they have been miraculously supplied with sustenance, and they complain about the quality of the food. It is no wonder they are punished. The text says the people grew impatient, when the only attitude appropriate for them would have been gratitude. Given all that God had done for them, it was God who should have been impatient with them.

The account of the bronze serpent brings together various themes that originally may have had little if anything to do with one another. First, there may have been actual snakes in the wilderness whose bite caused a terrible burning sensation. If this was the case, the people would certainly have looked for some kind of remedy. Second, there is evidence that either this bronze serpent or a replica of it called "Nehushtan" was set up in the Temple, and the people made offerings to it (cf. 2 Kgs 18:4). The similarity in sound between copper *(nᵉḥōšet)* and serpent *(nāḥāš)* cannot be denied, adding a level of credibility to the connection. The bronze serpent did not prevent the people in the wilderness from being bitten. Rather, it healed them from the deadly effects of the snakebite, and it only healed those who looked toward the bronze serpent in faith and repentance

This narrative brings the desert serpents together with the Nehushtan in a cause and effect relationship. Most likely the relationship really worked in the direction opposite the one described in the narrative. In other words, the wilderness tradition developed in order to explain why a monotheistic people would have installed a talisman in their Temple. If they could persuade people that the construction of this image had been directed by Moses as a means of curing people of the venom of the serpents, then perhaps its presence in the Temple might stand not as a blasphemous fetish but as a reminder, both of the punishment that they would have to face if they sinned and of the mercy of God that was always at hand if they repented.

Psalm 78:1-2, 34-35, 36-37, 38

Each phrase of the introductory verses of this psalm response contains language that clearly identifies the didactic character of the psalm. The parallel construction only serves to underscore this:

a) harken	b) my teaching (*tôrâ*)
a¹) incline your ears	b¹) saying of my mouth
a) I will open my mouth	b) parable (*mashāl*)
b) I will utter	b¹) riddles (*hîdâ*)

Tôrâ, which is usually translated "law," is more instruction than legislation; *mashāl* is the generic word for "wisdom saying," but it also refers to the particular form of proverb; *hîdâ*, or mysterious saying, is one that draws one into an intellectual adventure. In such a context it is clear to see that the sayings are to be understood as specifically Wisdom sayings.

Again, it is the vocabulary that sets the context for understanding what follows. Three words in particular should be noted: steadfast or faithful (*'ēmūn*); covenant (*berit*); and compassionate (*rahûm*). The psalm shows that God upheld the integrity of this intimate bond even when the people did not. Without naming specific incidents, the psalm sketches a bit of the history of the people. They turned to God only after they had been severely punished. Several times God allowed enemy forces to overtake the Israelites, but only one time does the text say that it was God who slew the people. That occurred when many people died from the bites of the fiery serpents God had sent, the incident referred to in the first reading. It seems the people only clung to God when their very survival was at stake. Their commitment was not sincere; their promises of fidelity were empty. Yet, despite the untrustworthiness of the people God's commitment was unfailing. Even as the text proclaims God's compassion, it recounts their guilt. They sinned, but God forgave them. God held in check the anger and wrath that were justifiably provoked by the people's disloyalty.

This is a Wisdom psalm; a very clear lesson is to be learned here. The past is offered as an example of what can happen in the present and the future. And what is that? Both judgment and salvation. Take heed! Harken! When our ancestors sinned, they were punished; when they repented, even if it was half-hearted repentance, God was merciful.

Philippians 2:6-11

This christological reflection on the nature and mission of Jesus can be divided into two parts. In the first (vv. 6-8), Jesus is the subject of the action; in the second (vv. 9-11), God is. The first part describes Jesus' humiliation, the second recounts his exaltation by God.

The first verse sets the tone for the actions of Christ Jesus. He did not cling to the dignity that was rightfully his. Two phrases identify this dignity: he is in the form of God; he is equal to God. The form of something is its basic appearance, and from this its essential character can be known. Hence, since Christ is in the form of God, he enjoys a Godlike manner of being. The parallel phrase restates this in a slightly different way: he is equal to God. The verb reports that Christ did not cling to this prerogative; he did not use his exalted status for his own ends. Christ freely gave up the right to homage that was his due.

Once again the verb plays an important role in this recital. Not only did Christ relinquish his Godlike state, he emptied himself of it. The contrasts drawn here are noteworthy. Though in the form of God, he chose the form of a servant or slave. Without losing his Godlike being, he took on the likeness of human beings. This does not mean he only resembled a human being but really was not one. Christ did take on human form, but the qualification suggested by "likeness" points to the fact that he was human like no one else was human. Although the word "Lord" (*kýrios*, a word that is also applied to God) is not found in these early verses, the contrast between "Lord" and "servant" stands conspicuously behind them.

Christ emptied himself and took on the human condition. The final verb states he then humbled himself and became obedient. Having taken on the form of a slave, he made himself vulnerable to all the particulars of that station in life. For a slave, obedience is the determining factor. The extent of his obedience is striking. Compliance with God's will in a world that is alienated from God requires that one be open to the possibility of death. In a sense,

Christ's crucifixion was inevitable. It was a common punishment for slaves, the nadir of human abasement. Such ignominy was a likely consequence of emptying himself and taking on human form.

The exaltation of Christ is as glorious as his humiliation was debasing. It is important to note that while Christ was the subject of his self-emptying, his super-exaltation is attributed directly to God. Once again there is a play on words and ideas. Just as form and appearance denote being, so name contains part of the essence of the individual. In exalting Jesus, God accords his human name a dignity that raises it above every other name. It now elicits the same reverence the title "Lord" *(kýrios)* does. Every knee shall do him homage and every tongue shall proclaim his sovereignty.

The extent to which Christ is to be revered is total. The entire created universe is brought under his lordship. This includes the spiritual beings in heaven, all living beings on earth, and even the dead under the earth. Distinctions such as spiritual or physical, living or dead, are meaningless here. All will praise Christ, whose exaltation gives glory to God.

John 3:13-17

Nicodemus was the leader of the Jewish people who was interested in the teaching of Jesus but who came to him at night, presumably out of fear of being detected. The lesson Jesus provides for him was well worth his effort.

Just as healing came to those in the wilderness who looked upon the bronze serpent Moses raised up before them (cf. Num 21:8-9), so life eternal comes to those who believe in the "Son of Humanity" (the Greek has *ánthrōpos*, which means "humankind"), who is raised up in both ignominy and exaltation. The image of something raised up suggests Jesus was tied to a pole, as was the effigy of the serpent. However, the verb used means "to be raised in exaltation." Choosing this verb with its various meanings, the evangelist is saying it was precisely in his humiliation that Jesus was glorified. This thought calls to mind the Suffering Servant in Isaiah, who also suffered for others and who, in his affliction, was "raised high and greatly exalted" (cf. Isa 52:13).

"Son of Humanity" is a Semitic idiom that refers to a symbolic figure who will inaugurate the last days (cf. Dan 7:13-14). Given the way the thought is developed here, one is led to conclude that this Son of Humanity is also the only begotten Son of God (vv. 14-16). The juxtaposition of these two titles brings together the diverse and rich theologies each represents. As different as these representations may be, there is one characteristic they hold in common: both the Son of Humanity and the Son of God are agents of eternal life for all.

The extent of God's love is drawn in bold lines in two different but very significant ways. The first is the scope of divine love; the second is the price God is willing to pay because of that love. Ancient Israel continually marveled at the love God had for this chosen people. While this love can be seen throughout the religious tradition, it is particularly evident in the writings of the prophets. Christian writers also spoke of God's love, but their main interest was with those who had committed themselves in faith to Jesus Christ. This passage is remarkable in its explicit declaration of God's love for the entire world.

The author maintains that God's love for the world is so deep and so magnanimous that for the world to be saved nothing is spared, not even God's only Son. God gave/sent this Son first in the incarnation and again in his saving death. This plan of salvation tragically and inevitably became judgment for some.

The world *(kósmos)* can be understood in three ways. It can refer to the totality of natural creation, the inhabited world generally, or the inhabited world in its sinfulness. Although the passage speaks of salvation, it is set in contrast with judgment and perishing. This indicates that here the world is understood in the third way, as subject to and guilty of sin. The world was created as good, but it often stands in opposition to God and, consequently, is in need of being saved. Such is the situation presumed here, since otherwise there would be no need for salvation. It is this sinful world that God loved (v. 16); it is into this sinful world that God's only Son was sent (v. 17).

The passage says that God both gave *(dídōmi)* and sent *(apostéllō)* God's only Son. The first verb implies that this Son was a gift from God. It underscores God's generosity to the world. The second verb indicates that the Son had a mission to perform. It includes the notion of serious responsibility on the part of the Son. In both cases, it is the world that benefits from God's actions.

Themes of the Day

This feast recalls the exaltation of the cross, which we celebrated on Good Friday. It is through feasts such as this that the major themes of our faith are woven in and out throughout the Liturgical Year. The feast itself marks the finding of relics of the true cross by the mother of the emperor Constantine. Today we concentrate on the power of the cross in our lives.

He Emptied Himself

The cross is the ultimate demonstration of the nature of God. The reading from Paul's letter to the Philippians describes the kenosis, the emptying of Christ. He gave of himself even to death on the cross. This is characteristic not only of the man Jesus but of the Godhead. Creation is the first example of divine emptying; redemption is the ultimate example. Unlike Good Friday when we stand before the stark cross and mourn the death of our innocent Messiah, today we stand before the glorious cross and praise God for God's incomprehensible goodness toward us. God's graciousness is poured out indiscriminately, prodigally, as only profound love can be given. Such is the nature of our God, and the cross is the symbol of this nature.

The Sign of Healing

The readings play with the symbolism of the pole on which the bronze serpent hung. In the wilderness it was merely a pole. Jesus compares it to the cross that becomes the source of our healing. As painful as life's crosses may be, they serve to transform us. They strip away what is superficial and they give us insight into the true meaning of life. They are the testing ground of virtue, the fire within which we are refined. The cross may at times be bitter medicine, but it can combat the human weakness that eats away our goodness. It can be our hope in the midst of pain and suffering and brokenness, because it promises to carry us into new life.

Our Access to God

It was through the cross that Jesus conquered sin and death and won for us access to God. It is through the cross that we die to sin and rise to new life in Christ. Through the goodness of God, which has been poured out for us, we have been granted eternal life. It is incomprehensible to think that death is the way to life, but that is the message of this feast. The cross, which is a sign of shame and misery, is now a symbol of glory and exaltation.

All Saints (Solemnity)
Revelation 7:2-4, 9-14

John the seer relates two extraordinary apocalyptic visions that were granted to him. Although they differ, placed together as they are here the second adds a dimension to the first. The events of the first vision seem to unfold on earth; those of the second take place in heaven. Both visions depict vast assemblies of the righteous.

The signing angel comes from the east. Because of all the symbolism associated with the rising of the sun, this is the direction from which salvation was expected. The seal was probably a kind of signet ring used to mark official documents or personal possessions. It belongs to God, signifying that those sealed are God's possession. Finally, God is the living God, not the God of the dead. Obviously the author felt it was important to state that death does not play a significant role in the drama unfolding here. In fact, this angel commands those destroying angels to desist so that the vast assembly can be sealed with the seal of God and, presumably, preserved from the suffering these angels bring to the earth. The singing is reminiscent of a similar mandate reported in the writings of the prophet Ezekiel. That narrative recounts how, at the outset of the destruction of Jerusalem, a sign was placed on the foreheads of some of the inhabitants, protecting them from the disastrous fate of the city (cf. Ezek 9:4-6). Here the sign has the identical function.

The number 144,000 is clearly symbolic. It is the number twelve squared and then multiplied by a thousand. Twelve stands for the number of the original tribes of Israel. Since the Christian community appropriated to itself the identity of the People of God, the reference here is probably to them. Both the squaring of twelve and the multiplication by a thousand are ways of indicating completeness. These also suggest that the number is impossible to count.

The second scene is the divine throne room in heaven (the throne represents the divine presence). The multitude gathered there came from every nation, every race, every people, and every tongue. The universality is complete. They are described in terms that denote victory: white robes and palms. Their exclamation acknowledges that they did not win this victory through their own merits. Rather, they are recipients of blessings received from God through the agency of the Lamb. Next the angels, the four elders (cf. Rev 4:4), and the four living creatures (cf. Rev 4:6) pay their homage to God and to the Lamb. Their exclamation of praise begins and ends with the acclamation "Amen"—So be it! It is true! The divine attributes they praise are proclaimed in traditional songs of praise (cf. Rev 5:12).

When John the seer is asked about the identity of those who constitute the multitude, he employs in his reply two themes from ancient Israel's tradition. The first is the eschatological concept of the great tribulation *(thlípsis)* that will precede the dawning of the age of fulfillment. The second is a reference to the atoning efficacy of the blood of the sacrificial lamb. There is no suggestion in the text that these people are martyrs. Rather, they are those who have survived eschatological distress because they were purified through the blood of the sacrificial Lamb. This distinction certainly entitles them to participate in the eschatological celebrations.

Psalm 24:1-2, 3-4, 5-6

The psalm response consists of a hymn of praise of God the Creator (vv. 1-2) and a section suggesting the question-response ritual associated with a liturgical pilgrimage (vv. 3-6). An interesting feature of this response is the variety of images of God that it contains: Creator, savior, patron deity.

Behind the imagery of the opening verses is ancient Near Eastern cosmology. In various myths from that tradition we find a primeval struggle between gods of chaos and deities who would establish order. Chief among the former were Yam (the Hebrew word for "sea") and Nahar (Hebrew for "river"). In the myths a vibrant, young warrior-god conquers the chaotic waters, establishes dominion over the universe, and assigns the celestial bodies their places in the heavens. The similarities, both linguistic and in content, between such a myth and the picture painted in the psalm response are obvious. However, in this psalm response the focus is the earth, which the ancients believed floated like a saucer on the cosmic waters. This earth and all those who live on it belong to or are under the protection of the LORD. Such a claim would not be made if there were any doubt about the LORD's sovereignty. This is the deity who exercises dominion, and this would only be the case if the LORD were the victorious warrior who conquered the chaotic cosmic force.

The liturgical portion of the response opens with an exchange of question and answer. In the mythological tradition the high god dwelt on the highest mountain. In Israel's liturgical tradition Jerusalem with its Temple was identified with this high mountain. Therefore, as the pilgrims approached the walls of the city, certain persons (probably priests) inquired about the suitability of those who would enter the sacred precincts. According to the strict regulations in Israel's cultic tradition, only those who conformed to the prescriptions of holiness, or cultic purity, were allowed to enter. These prescriptions generally governed external regulations. Hands that had not touched forbidden objects were considered "sinless." However, here external conformity is not enough. An appropriate inner disposition is required as well. The polarities of chaos-order have been transformed into those of unclean-clean and then unworthy-worthy.

The male bias in Israel's liturgical participation is seen in the reference to those who receive blessing. This notwithstanding, God is identified as the God of Jacob and savior of the chosen people, clear allusions to both the ancestral and exodus traditions of Israel. These epithets are not only divine titles, they are also reminders of God's special election and care of this people. Fidelity to the prescriptions of the religious tradition was the primary way of living out faithfully one's role as covenant partner of God—the covenant associated either with the ancestors (cf. Gen 17:2) or with the exodus tradition (cf. Exod 19:5). The blessing and reward flowed from such fidelity, from the people's desire to seek the face of God, to be united to God through commitment and devotion.

One very important final point must be made. The two sections of this psalm response may at first glance appear to be quite separate. However, joined together as they are, they interpret each other. In other words, the God who first called and then saved Israel is none other than the Creator who vanquished the cosmic powers of chaos; the God who exercises dominion over all creation is the one who established an intimate covenant with this people.

1 John 3:1-3

These few short verses are brimming with theological meaning. The first and more important point is the love God has for believers. A second theme is eschatological fulfillment. Although the latter is dependent upon the former, it is also a direct result of it.

The love *(agápē)* of which the author speaks is generative; it is transforming; it makes believers children of God. Everything that happens in the lives of believers is a consequence of their having been re-created as God's children. A related theme is introduced. As children of God they are a new reality, and thus they are not accepted by the world, the old reality. Certain similarities between Jesus and the believers are drawn. The world, the entire inhabited world that is subject to sin, recognizes only its own. It did not recognize the only begotten Son of God, and it does not recognize these new children of God. The implications of this are clear. Believers should not be surprised if they encounter the same kind of rejection, even persecution and death, that befell Jesus.

The reading does not identify what it is about Jesus and the believers that is so difficult for the world to comprehend. However, it is probably the manner of living that flows from their relationship with God, a manner of behavior that contradicts the life-style promoted by the sinful world and that results in the world's rejection of what it cannot claim.

The "now but not yet" of Christian eschatology is clearly stated. As a consequence of God's love believers have already been reborn as children of God. However, transformation has not yet been completed, nor has it been fully made known to them. All of this is dependent upon a future manifestation. It is not clear from the text whether this will be a manifestation of Christ or of God. Although the Greek construction is ambiguous, the theological intent is not. Actually, any manifestation of the risen Christ is a manifestation of God, and in like manner, the ultimate manifestation of God is found in the risen Christ.

Having been made children of God, the community of believers is promised an even fuller identification with God. They will see God as God is, for they will be like God. The Hellenist influence here is obvious. Widespread in the ancient world was the notion that a reality can be understood only by another reality similar to it. For their part, believers must do what they can to pattern their lives after the purity of God. The basis of their hope is the ultimate vision of God, a vision denied believers "now" but promised for "later."

Matthew 5:1-12a

The preaching and miracles of Jesus attracted crowds of people, making it necessary for him to take his disciples up a mountain. There he taught them. The instruction known as the Sermon on the Mount was directed to his close followers, not to the broader crowds. The first part of that sermon, the Beatitudes, constitutes the gospel reading for today. By form and content the Beatitudes are wisdom teaching, not Christian law, as is sometimes claimed. Most if not all the sentiments expressed are found somewhere in ancient Jewish teaching.

The beatitude, or macarism, is a literary form belonging to the Wisdom tradition. It takes its name from the Greek word *makários* (happy or blessed). It is a descriptive statement intended for purposes of teaching. Like most Wisdom literary forms, it describes a life situation that draws a connection between a particular manner of behavior and the consequences that flow from such behavior. Though it is a simple description, it is meant to encourage the behavior if the consequences are satisfying and to discourage it if they are not. The Beatitudes follow this pattern exactly: a group of people who act in a particular way are said to be happy; the blessings they will enjoy are stated.

It is important to remember that while the teachings of Jesus are all in some way directed toward the establishment of the reign of God, the type of behavior or of values he advocates is frequently the opposite of that espoused by society at large. This fact offers us a way to understand the challenges set before us in the Beatitudes. Perhaps the way to interpret them is to look first at the blessings promised. We may see that the behavior that Jesus is advocating is at odds with what society would say will guarantee the blessing we seek.

The first and third beatitudes are very similar. They treat the notion of power, which is often determined by the extent of one's material possessions. Societies are usually ruled by those with power and means. The reign of God, however, will be in the hands of the powerless (the meek) and those who have no means with which to exert power (the poor). The second and fourth beatitudes promise the alleviation of some form of inner turmoil. A strict reading of the theory of retribution insists that suffering is usually the consequence of sin or some kind of inappropriate behavior. According to that theory, those who grieve do so because of something they have brought on themselves, and those who hunger for justice need only live justly to enjoy it. On the contrary, the Beatitudes suggest that those suffering are innocent of anything that would result in their misfortune, but the situations in which they find themselves will be remedied for them.

The fifth, sixth, and seventh beatitudes treat aspects of religious piety. Mercy is the disposition God has for sinners (cf. Exod 34:6). Those who seek this attitude from God are exhorted to extend it to others. Already in Israel's' religious tradition we read that it is not ritual conformity but a simple yet open heart that gives one entrance to the presence of God (cf. Ps 24:4). Finally, peace and tranquil order have been God's desire for us from the beginning. It is sin that disrupted this order and destroyed the peace. Those who overcome evil with good in order to reestablish peace are doing God's work and will be known as God's children.

The last beatitude very clearly underscores the reversal referred to above. Commitment to Jesus and to his cause are bound to bring insult and persecution. When this happens, the disciples should rejoice, knowing that the world is persecuting them because they belong to a kingdom that is not of this world, a kingdom with values that are the reverse of those espoused by this world. It is clear that each beatitude invites us to turn the standards of our world and our way of life upside down and inside out.

Themes of the Day

Today we celebrate the memory of all the baptized who have gone before us and whose lives were virtuous. It is the memory of all these people that we keep, not merely of those who have been made models of virtue through the process of canonization. Though we do remember those officially considered saints by the Church, we celebrate the lives of all those who have been marked with the sign of faith, those we have known personally, those whose names we do not know.

The Saints of God

The saints of God are all those who have been baptized into Christ, who have washed their robes in the blood of the Lamb. Sanctity is not an accumulation of merit. It is a gift that comes with baptism to be nurtured throughout life. We are made saints when in baptism we are made children of God. We all know people whose lives were steeped in genuine holiness. We remember the unselfish love of our parents, the heroism of members of the armed forces, the piety of our colleagues, the patience of those who suffered intensely. The life of every one of us has been blessed by the holiness of others. This is a day for us to remember and to celebrate their holiness.

Children of God

As earthy and human as our saints may have been, there was a genuine mystical sense to their sanctity. They are children of God, sharing the very life of God. They were so during their lives, and they continue to be so even after death. What this means is beyond our comprehension, but Paul insists that it is truly the case. This identity carries with it a challenge for us to live life in terms of our identity as children of God. The saints who have gone before us met this challenge. Their lives revealed the family features. They lived their lives in terms of who they were as children of God.

Blessed Are You

In the Beatitudes, listed in today's gospel, we are given examples of what it means to live lives of holiness. Those who live such lives are said to be truly blessed. It is important to remember that this gospel really does not present a blueprint for holiness. Rather, it offers a series of snapshots that demonstrate the holiness that is ours by virtue of our baptism. Those who have gone before us lived such lives. Today as we remember them, we hold up their lives as examples of holiness and models for our imitation. The sentiments expressed and the commitment illustrated in the Beatitudes clearly stand in opposition to the standards of the world. Their radicality may be more than some can understand, but theirs are traits that are recognizable by those who belong to the family of God, for theirs are genuine Godly traits.

The Commemoration of the Faithful Departed (All Souls)

Daniel 12:1-3

The apocalyptic scene described in this reading is part of the revelation granted to the prophet Daniel. It depicts the final struggle of human beings at the end of time and their subsequent resurrection to a life of glorification or one of horror. The prophetic phrase "at that time" appears three times in the very first verse and marks the future-oriented character of the event described. It seems that in the ancient Near Eastern world each nation had an advocate in the heavenly court who came to its defense, whether in battle or in a court of law. Michael, whose name means "who is like God," is the patronal guardian of Israel (cf. 10:23).

The reading says that Michael rises up but does not explain why he does so. It may be as protector of Israel while the nation faces the distress of the end of time. Since the judgments meted out to the righteous and to the wicked are described later in the reading, one might conclude that Michael stands prepared to present those under his charge (Israel) to the judgment seat of God or to participate in some way in the judgement itself.

The distress that is to come is unparalleled. It is probably the final tribulation that will come to pass before the appearance of the eschatological reign of God. This suffering was considered by some to be the "birth pangs of the Messiah," the agony that must be endured if the reign of God is to be born. Daniel is told that those whose names appear in the book (presumably the Book of the Righteous) will be spared. They will have to endure the agony of the end-time, but they will escape ultimate destruction.

The allusion to some kind of resurrection from the dead followed by reward and punishment is clear. Since the idea of the end-time sets the context for this passage, the resurrection referred to here is the general resurrection believed to be coming at the end of time. Death is described as sleeping in the dust of the earth, and resurrection is an awakening. After they have been raised the dead must give an account of the record of their deeds. This is the basis upon which the separation takes place: some are rewarded with everlasting life, others are punished with horror and disgrace.

Within the circle of those granted everlasting life, some are singled out for further distinction (v. 3). The verse is structured after the pattern of poetic parallelism, suggesting the reference is to one group and not two. Elements from astral religion are employed to characterize the reward of the wise. Previously they had been a source of illumination in the lives of others. In the new age they will continue to shine, but then their brilliance will be seen by all. They will be like the stars in the heavens.

This vision is a message of hope and challenge for those who are undergoing great distress. The righteous are encouraged to remain steadfast in their commitment. They are promised a spectacular reward if they do. The reading also warns the reprobates of the fate that awaits them. The choice is theirs.

Psalm 23:1-3a, 3b-4, 5, 6

This responsorial psalm is one of the most familiar and best loved psalms of the entire Psalter. It paints vivid pictures of a carefree existence, peaceful rest, and abundant fruitfulness. Although "shepherd" suggests a flock rather than merely one sheep, here the focus is on the individual. In addition to this image God is characterized as a host, one who supervises a banquet and within whose house the psalmist ultimately dwells.

The psalm opens with a metaphor that sets the tone of the entire song. It is the responsibility of the shepherd to find pastures that will provide enough grazing and abundant water for the entire flock, to lead them there without allowing any of the sheep to stray and be lost, to guard them from predators or dangers of any kind, and to attend to their every need. To characterize the LORD as a shepherd is to trust that God will discharge all of these responsibilities. The personal dimension of the psalm shifts from the care given the entire flock to concern for one individual, making God's care a very intimate matter. Not only are the physical needs of the psalmist satisfied, but the soul, the very life force *(nepesh)* of the person, is renewed.

The guidance of the shepherd is more than provident, it is moral as well. The psalmist is led in the paths of righteousness (v. 3), and this is done for the sake of the LORD's name. Since one's name is a part of the very essence of the person, this indicates that the way of the LORD is the way of righteousness. Following this, we can say that the magnanimous care shown by the shepherd flows from enduring righteousness rather than some passing sentiment of the heart. This is confirmed by the reference to the covenant kindness *(ḥesed)* that surrounds the psalmist (v. 6). In other words, the divine shepherd's tender commitment to the flock, and to each individual within it, is as lasting as is God's covenant commitment.

The psalmist is confident of the LORD's protection, as demonstrated in his mention of the shepherd's rod and staff, which were used to ward off wild animals as well as poachers. The valley of "deep darkness," can be a reference to the darkest part of the terrain or to the gloom that can overwhelm an individual. However, it also has a mythological connotation and is frequently interpreted as death. Whichever meaning is intended here, the psalmist claims to be unafraid, for the presence of the LORD is reassuring.

The image of the shepherd securing nourishment for the flock suggests another metaphor, that of the host who prepares a lavish banquet for guests. Many societies have a very strict code of hospitality. The people are obliged to provide the best provisions they have, even for their enemies. The LORD spreads out such a banquet here, which not only affords nourishment but also is a public witness to God's high regard for the psalmist, who will continue to enjoy God's favor in God's house. Whether this means the Temple or is merely a reference to the place where God dwells, the fundamental meaning is clear. The psalmist has been under the loving guidance of the LORD and will remain there forever.

Romans 6:3-9

Paul explains how baptism has enabled the Christians to participate in the death and resurrection of Jesus. The ritual is itself the reenactment of this death and resurrection. As the Christians were engulfed in the water, they were buried with Christ in death; as they emerged from the water, they rose with him into new life. In drawing these lines of comparison between the death and resurrection of Jesus and the baptism and new life of the Christians, Paul's real intent is ethical exhortation. He seeks to encourage them to set aside their old manner of living and take on the new life of holiness.

While the descent into baptismal waters can symbolize Christ's descent into death, there is another dimension of the water imagery that strengthens Paul's argument. According to a long tradition cosmic waters were chaotic, therefore, death-dealing (cf. Genesis 6–9; Job 22:11; Ps 73:13-14; Isa 27:1). To be engulfed by water is to be swallowed up by chaos and death. This symbolism lends itself to describing both the death of Christ and the baptism of Christians. Christ was plunged into the chaos of death; the Christians are plunged into the death of chaos. By the power of God, Christ conquered death and rose to a new life of glory; by the power of God, the Christians participate in Christ's victory and are raised to the glory of a new life.

Paul characterizes their former lives as slavery to sin. Through baptism this old enslaved self has been crucified. Just as death had no power over the resurrected Christ, so sin now has no power over the baptized Christians. They now have the power of the resurrected Lord to withstand the assaults of sin. However, Paul is not naive about the struggles of life. He knows that these call for constant vigilance and self-denial. Crucifixion is a fitting image for both Christian conversion and ongoing fidelity, not only because of the role it played in Christ's death but because the torment it entails exemplifies the suffering that a change of life will exact on the Christians. However, as is evident in the case of Christ's death and resurrection, the cross is the only way to new life. So it is also for the Christians who are united with Christ.

John 6:37-40

In this discourse, Jesus assures his audience that those who are joined to him will never be separated from him. This assurance is grounded in the mission God gave to Jesus and the faithfulness with which Jesus intends to carry out his responsibilities. The fulfillment of this divinely appointed mission was the reason Jesus came down from heaven and assumed human flesh in the first place. If any of these disciples were lost, it would be seen as failure on Jesus' part. This was unthinkable, because the incarnation occurred so God's plan of salvation would be realized. Jesus repeats this teaching in various ways throughout this short reading.

God's plan of salvation has two related purposes. The first is that those to whom Jesus was sent might believe in him. The second is that their faith might grow deeper and deeper until the last day, when they will be blessed by him with the gift of eternal life. This twofold purpose reflects the Christian paradoxical teaching on eschatology. The age of fulfillment has dawned already in faith, but it has not yet unfolded completely. However, the first depends upon the second: eternal life comes with faith already dynamic during this life, not merely at the end-time. Since faith is the passage from condemnation to acceptance, we can see how it is also a passage from the death of sin to the new life that will not end. It is because of their faith that believers in Jesus will not be driven away. It is because of their faith that they will be raised up with Jesus on the last day.

Themes of the Day

This particular feast has no specific readings assigned to it. Pastoral judgment allows us to choose any readings for the Masses for the Dead. The readings that appear here are those that have been recommended for use in the United States. The following themes come from the readings analyzed. The readings themselves do not speak of the doctrine of purgatory. However, they invite us to think of all those who, through the mercy of God, continue the journey of purification en route to the face of God.

Remnants of Sin

By virtue of our baptism we are given a rich inheritance. We have died with Christ to sin and we have risen with him to new life. However, if we are honest we will have to admit we do not always live out of that gift. Though baptized into Christ's death, we do not fully die to sin. In fact, there are many times in our lives when we live in sin, when we actually cling to sin. We do not follow the example of the saints, which we celebrated yesterday. Instead we capitulate; we give in to our baser nature; we live lives of selfishness and greed, hatred and immorality. We lose the battle against the forces of evil in the world and we settle for the easier road.

What happens to those who die in that state? They may not have turned completely away from the goodness of God, but they have not been faithful either. The remnants of sin cling to them, making them somewhat unfit to stand before the face of God. Are they lost? Or are they saved?

Divine Mercy

Even though we may not always live in the strength of our baptism, there is still a burning desire on the part of God to save us. In God there is mercy in abundance. It seems that Jesus is not willing to lose anyone. Therefore, the power of Jesus and the strength of his promises give us hope that even after death there is the possibility of purification and pardon. We have no idea of when this might happen or how it will happen. All we know is that the lovingkindness of God far surpasses any infidelity of which we might be guilty. We do not deserve this mercy, but then we have never deserved God's mercy. It is a gift freely given. Even to the end we believe God will not abandon us to ourselves.

The Good Shepherd

The image of Jesus the Good Shepherd is a very comforting image. It assures us that he not only feeds us and gives us drink, but he also protects us as we travel through the dark valley into the fullness of life. He is there at our side as we continue the journey of purification to the face of God. Though we are weak and vulnerable, we can rely on his rod and his staff.

The feast of All Souls is not a feast of sadness but one of great hope and confidence. It invites us to entrust our dead to God, because we know they are really God's dead. We know that if we have loved them, God has loved them more. They are in God's care, and God will lead them to peace.

The Dedication of the Lateran Basilica (Feast)

Ezekiel 47:1-2, 8-9, 12

Ezekiel recounts a vision of the temple that was granted to him. He is brought to the door of the temple, and from there he is able to observe a stream of water flowing from the threshold of the temple and growing in force until it is a mighty river. Temples were constructed in such a way as to face the east, the direction from which, according to ancient tradition, salvation comes because it is the horizon above which the new dawn of promise rises. The course the water takes is quite complicated. More important for this reading are the meaning of its source and the effects it is able to achieve.

The waters flow from the east to the Arabah *('ărābâ)*, a desert plain that stretches south into the Rift Valley, where it becomes the southern depression of the Dead Sea. It is into this sea that the waters flow. The Dead Sea, the lowest point on the surface of the earth, is thirteen hundred feet below sea level. Seven million tons of water flow into it daily. Because it has no outlet, the constant evaporation of water results in a high concentration of salt, chlorides, and bromides. In this vision, the waters that flow from the temple miraculously purify these stagnant waters, allowing living creatures to live within them and to thrive. Plants too are able to grow on the banks of the sea and to produce fruits. What was once a place of death is now a place of burgeoning life and productivity. This picture recalls the primordial river that flowed out of Eden. It too divided into four branches, and it watered all the surrounding land, making it fertile (cf. Gen 2:10-14).

The last verse of the reading makes an ever greater claim. Not only is the water that flows from the temple itself transformative, but the fruits it produces share in its transformative power. The fruits themselves serve as food; the leaves of the trees that produced the fruit possess curative powers. The saving power of God goes out from the temple in a series of concentric circles: first the water from the sanctuary itself; then whatever the water touches; and finally the fruits produced by that which the water touched. The power of the presence of God radiates throughout creation.

Psalm 46:2, 3, 5-6, 8, 9

This psalmist employs various metaphors to encourage the people to trust in God. The metaphors can all be understood on both an experiential level and a mythological level. The psalmist appears to be describing a natural disaster (vv. 1-3) and extolling the glories of the city of Jerusalem (vv. 5-6, 8-9). However, mythological themes lie beneath these metaphors. It should be noted that each stanza of this response contains a distinct title for God, each one suggesting a distinct characterization.

Mountains are symbols of strength and stability. However, if they are subject to an earthquake, they can break into pieces and tumble into the sea. God is a different kind of refuge and strength, one that will never fail, one that is not subject to stronger forces. Behind this metaphor is the mythological story of primordial creation. There we see that the victorious God has conquered the sea (v. 3) and firmly established the mountains (cf. Ps 65:6-7). With God as our help in distress, we have nothing to fear.

We discover many documents of ancient mythology stating that the gods live on the mountain tops. This stands to reason, for such places would be the closest spots to the heavens. The theme of mountain calls to mind Zion, the mountain upon which the city of Jerusalem was built and within which the Temple was erected (vv. 5-6). We know this is Zion because the title for God is Most High *('elyôn)*, the name of the god who was worshiped in the Jebusite city Jerusalem (cf. Gen 14:18-19). After David captured that city the Israelites appropriated much of the religious culture of the city and incorporated it into their own tradition. They insisted that their God was the Most High. They also believed this mountain was not only sacred but also secure, because God dwelt on it in a very special way. Dawn, the time when darkness was finally conquered, would reveal that it was this God who had been their protector.

"LORD of Hosts" is a military title. It is found in the accounts of Israel's military conflicts (cf. 1 Sam 1:3; 15:2; Ps 24:10). It is also a reference to the primordial conflict between the mighty warrior God and the evil waters of chaos. Whether we see the title as referring to ancient Israel's military encounters with its enemies or to the cosmic battle between the forces of good and the forces of evil, it is still the God of Israel/Jacob who is victorious. The astonishing feats this God has accomplished can be either the victories that God has won or the works of creation that God has wrought.

The psalmist calls all those who can hear to behold the marvels of God. Their magnificence should instill both gratitude and confidence in the hearts of all.

1 Corinthians 3:9c-11, 16-17

Paul characterizes the community at Corinth as the temple of God. He first describes the preliminary steps that are taken in constructing the building, and he then extolls the excellence of this temple, which is the community of believers. Speaking without pride but from the humble acknowledgment of God's goodness, Paul declares that by the grace of God he was chosen to be the wise architect *(sophós architékton)* responsible for the temple. It cannot be denied that every step in the building process is important. None is more pivotal that the laying of the foundation. The entire structure is dependent on it. Paul boldly claims this is precisely what he did through his preaching of the gospel.

He laid the foundation, and the foundation is Christ. Every other minister builds on Paul's initial work.

Paul next extols the excellence of this building. In doing so he uses a method of argumentation that resembles the Greek rhetorical style of diatribe. He addresses his audience, referring to assumptions they share but do not seem to be living out. These assumptions have to do with the holiness of the temple of God. It is clear that Paul is not thinking of a material building. He is, rather, referring to the collection of people who gather in God's name. Paul declares that the Corinthians are this temple. This notion was not original with Paul, for it is found in the literature of the Qumran community as well. There we find the members referred to as a "holy house" (*bêt qôdeš*, cf. 1 QS 5:5; 8:4). However, at Qumran the general community was only the "holy house," while the priestly members were considered the "holy of holies," the inner sanctum where the presence of God resides. The word Paul uses for "temple" *(naós)* refers to the sanctuary rather than to the broader temple precincts. Thus, in his thinking the entire assembly is the "holy of holies" of this temple. Just as the presence of God made the Temple in Jerusalem holy, so it is the presence of the Spirit of God that makes this new temple holy, and the Spirit dwells in all of the members.

Those who defiled the Temple in Jerusalem were liable to death. Outside the inner court of the Temple a sign was posted that excluded Gentiles from entering and warned of severe consequences for violation of this prohibition. Why such a harsh penalty? Because the Temple of God is holy, and only those people and things that have been set aside as holy can enter it. With this regulation in mind Paul plays with the meaning of the Greek word *phtheírō,* which can be translated both "to corrupt" and "to destroy." Those who corrupt or defile God's temple will be destroyed. It is up to the Corinthians to determine whether the temple of God, which they are, will continue to be holy or whether it might be defiled.

John 2:13-22

The reading revolves around the theme of temple. Jesus' actions there are acted-out prophecy, and his play on words constitutes prophetic forthtelling. The episode takes place at the time of the observance of the Jewish feast of Passover in the city of Jerusalem. Themes from each of these important details are woven together and used by Jesus.

At first glance it seems that Jesus' intensity was aroused by the erosion of temple decorum and the diminishment of religious fervor this represented. Roman coins, the currency of the day, were stamped with the head of Caesar, who was considered a deity, and sometimes with the images of other pagan gods. This made them unfit for temple use, and so money-changing became indispensable. The Jews, who came from around the world for major feasts, probably did not bring along animals for sacrifice. Thus, the sellers provided a second necessary service. All of this took place in the temple precincts, a vast area that included the outer court and the Court of the Gentiles, but not the sanctuary or Temple proper. Why was Jesus so irate? He accused the merchants of making the Temple a marketplace. But a part of it really was a marketplace. The transactions were legitimate; they were conducted in the appropriate temple area; and they were essential supports of the temple service. The explanation of his behavior is found both in an allusion to a passage from the prophet Zechariah (14:21), who said that at the end-time there would be no need for merchants in the house of the LORD, and in a psalm text remembered by the disciples. This latter passage states that zeal for the house of God makes the psalmist vulnerable to the scorn and abuse of others (cf. Ps 69:9).

Jesus makes a double claim. First, by driving the merchants out of the temple precincts, he announces that the time of fulfillment has come. Second, identifying God as his Father affirms his right to make such a claim and to act in accord with it. The Jews, most likely the temple authorities, demand that Jesus justify his actions. His words here, translated into Greek, convey this by means of a clever use of language. Two words for temple are used in this passage. Only *hierón* appears when the entire temple area is intended (vv. 14, 15), and Jesus uses *naós* when he is referring to his body (vv. 19, 21). The Jewish authorities mistakenly use *naós* in a general sense, though in Jesus' words, it is used here very specifically.

Since Jesus is portrayed as using *naós,* the word for temple proper or sanctuary, in referring to his body, he is actually predicting his death and resurrection. This corresponds to the earlier allusion to Zechariah and the replacement of the temple sacrifice by his own suffering. His challengers take his words literally and believe he is speaking about the Temple within which they stand and which is still under construction. This encounter ends with a second statement about the disciples remembering. It would require their experience of the risen Lord for them to be able to gain insight into this last saying.

Themes of the Day

The basilica of St. John erected on the Lateran Hill is the cathedral of Rome, the mother church of all Roman Catholic churches. When we celebrate the dedication of this church, we celebrate all other churches as well.

The Temple

The Temple was important because it was believed to be the place on earth where God dwelt in the midst of the people. It was God's presence, not the worship performed by human beings, that made this a sacred site. There is something incarnational about the presence of God. It is not merely an abstract reality. It allows itself to be manifested in the concrete, in something that has shape and character. This presence reveals itself in the various cultural forms of the people, and the people respond to God's presence in their own cultural ways.

We Are the Temple of God

As important as the temple building may be, it is only a building. Paul insists that we are the temple of God; we are the manifestation of God in the world today. The Spirit of God dwells in us, making the believing community the living temple of God. This is an indescribable privilege as well as an exacting challenge. If we do not obscure this reality, the glory of God will shine out from us. The community, not the building, will be the place where prayer and sacrifice are offered to God. It will be within the community that others will experience God's saving presence. They will come to the community to be sanctified, to be made holy.

A Den of Thieves or Life-Giving Water?

Today's readings provide us with two pictures of the temple of God, two characterizations of the community of believers. The picture in the gospel is a sobering one. The Temple has become a marketplace; the community has become so preoccupied with the business of the world that it has forgotten its identity. In a fury, Jesus upsets the worldly order that had been established and drives it out of the house of God. The vision from Ezekiel offers a very different picture. There we see water from the temple transforming everything in its path. As water flowed from the temple in Ezekiel's vision, so grace flows from the temple that is the People of God.

Which image more closely characterizes the community of which we are a part? Are we able to refresh what was once brackish? Can we transform the wilderness into a place teeming with life? Can we make all things productive and fruitful? Can we heal what has been threatened with death? Is the community truly the presence of God in the world today? Or is it a simply a site where ritual is performed but the concerns of God take second place to the affairs of the world? Will the zeal of Jesus be unleashed on us? Do we need to be overturned in order to be reformed? As we celebrate the dedication of this sacred place, we are reminded that we are the temple of God, that we have been dedicated, that the Spirit of God has made us a living temple.

Index of Scripture Readings